Pro ASP.NET Core Identity

Under the Hood with Authentication
and Authorization in ASP.NET Core 5 and 6
Applications

Adam Freeman

Apress®

Pro ASP.NET Core Identity: Under the Hood with Authentication and Authorization in ASP.NET Core 5 and 6 Applications

Adam Freeman
London, UK

ISBN-13 (pbk): 978-1-4842-6857-5   ISBN-13 (electronic): 978-1-4842-6858-2
https://doi.org/10.1007/978-1-4842-6858-2

Managing Director, Apress Media LLC: Welmoed Spahr
Acquisitions Editor: Joan Murray
Development Editor: Laura Berendson
Editorial Operations Manager: Mark Powers

Cover designed by eStudioCalamar

Cover image designed by Freepik (www.freepik.com)

Distributed to the book trade worldwide by Apress Media, LLC, 1 New York Plaza, New York, NY 10004, U.S.A. Phone 1-800-SPRINGER, fax (201) 348-4505, e-mail orders-ny@springer-sbm.com, or visit www.springeronline.com. Apress Media, LLC is a California LLC and the sole member (owner) is Springer Science + Business Media Finance Inc (SSBM Finance Inc). SSBM Finance Inc is a Delaware corporation.

For information on translations, please e-mail booktranslations@springernature.com; for reprint, paperback, or audio rights, please e-mail bookpermissions@springernature.com.

Apress titles may be purchased in bulk for academic, corporate, or promotional use. eBook versions and licenses are also available for most titles. For more information, reference our Print and eBook Bulk Sales web page at www.apress.com/bulk-sales.

Any source code or other supplementary material referenced by the author in this book is available to readers on GitHub via the book's product page, located at www.apress.com/9781484268575. For more detailed information, please visit www.apress.com/source-code.

Printed on acid-free paper

Dedicated to my lovely wife, Jacqui Griffyth.

(And also to Peanut.)

Table of Contents

About the Author

Adam Freeman is an experienced IT professional who has held senior positions in a range of companies, most recently serving as chief technology officer and chief operating officer of a global bank. Now retired, he spends his time writing and long-distance running.

About the Technical Reviewer

Fabio Claudio Ferracchiati is a senior consultant and a senior analyst/developer using Microsoft technologies. He works for BluArancio (`www.bluarancio.com`). He is a Microsoft Certified Solution Developer for .NET, a Microsoft Certified Application Developer for .NET, a Microsoft Certified Professional, and a prolific author and technical reviewer. Over the past ten years, he's written articles for Italian and international magazines and coauthored more than ten books on a variety of computer topics.

PART I

Using ASP.NET Core Identity

CHAPTER 1

Getting Ready

ASP.NET Core Identity is the user management system for ASP.NET Core applications. It provides an API for managing users and roles and for signing users into and out of applications. Users can sign in with simple passwords, use two-factor authentication, or sign in using third-party platforms provided by Google, Facebook, and Twitter.

In this book, I explain how ASP.NET Core Identity is used and how it works behind the scenes. I describe the built-in features, from those that can be used for simple applications through to deep customizations for advanced projects.

What Do You Need to Know?

This is an advanced book written for experienced developers. You should not attempt to read this book unless you are familiar with web development using ASP.NET Core. You must understand HTML and how it is produced using Razor Pages and the MVC Framework. You must have at least a basic understanding of application security, although I introduce key concepts as I explain how they are implemented by ASP.NET Core Identity.

What Is the Structure of This Book?

This book is split into two parts, each of which covers a set of related topics.

Part 1: Using ASP.NET Core Identity

In Part 1 of this book, I show you how to apply ASP.NET Core Identity to an ASP.NET Core project. I show you how to set up and configure Identity, how to use the built-in Identity UI package to manage user accounts, and how to use the API to create custom workflows. By the end of this part of the book, you will be ready to use ASP.NET Core Identity in your projects.

Part 2: Understanding ASP.NET Core

In Part 2 of this book, I dig deep into the detail and explain how the features used in Part 1 are implemented, how they can be customized, and how they relate to the features provided by the ASP.NET Core platform. By the end of this part of the book, you will be ready to create custom implementations of the interfaces that shape ASP.NET Core Identity to suit the needs of the most advanced ASP.NET Core projects.

© Adam Freeman 2021
A. Freeman, *Pro ASP.NET Core Identity*, https://doi.org/10.1007/978-1-4842-6858-2_1

What Doesn't This Book Cover?

As noted, this book is for experienced ASP.NET Core developers who want to understand ASP.NET Core Identity and apply it in their ASP.NET Core project. It doesn't explain the basics of web applications or programming. It doesn't describe the ASP.NET Core platform, other than as it relates to how Identity works.

I cover the authentication scenarios that are used by the majority of Internet-facing ASP.NET Core projects. I don't describe the ASP.NET Core authentication features that are not related directly to ASP.NET Core Identity, such as integration with Active Directory or with third-party products, such as IdentityServer (which, despite its name, is not directly related to ASP.NET Core Identity and is more of an alternative).

What Software Do I Need for the Examples?

You need the same set of tools you use for ASP.NET Core development, including the .NET SDK and Visual Studio or Visual Studio Code. I describe the setup required for this book in Chapter 2.

How Do I Set Up the Development Environment?

Chapter 2 introduces ASP.NET Core Identity by creating a simple application, and, as part of that process, I tell you how to create a development environment for following the examples in this book.

What If I Have Problems Following the Examples?

The first thing to do is to go back to the start of the chapter and begin over. Most problems are caused by accidentally skipping a step or not fully applying the changes shown in a listing. Pay close attention to the emphasis in code listings, which highlights the changes that are required.

Next, check the errata/corrections list, which is included in the book's GitHub repository. Technical books are complex, and mistakes are inevitable, despite my best efforts and those of my editors. Check the errata list for the list of known errors and instructions to resolve them.

If you still have problems, then download the project for the chapter you are reading from the book's GitHub repository, `https://github.com/Apress/pro-asp.net-core-identity`, and compare it to your project. I create the code for the GitHub repository by working through each chapter, so you should have the same files with the same contents in your project.

If you still can't get the examples working, then you can contact me at `adam@adam-freeman.com` for help. Please make it clear in your email which book you are reading and which chapter/example is causing the problem. A page number or code listing is always helpful. Please remember that I get a lot of emails and that I may not respond immediately.

There are examples in Chapters 11, 22, and 23 that rely on third-party services from Google, Facebook, and Twitter. I am unable to provide support for these examples because problems can only be diagnosed using your private account credentials. Even if you are willing to share your credentials, I am not willing to use them. If you have problems with these examples, you should raise a support query with the authentication service provider.

What If I Find an Error in the Book?

You can report errors to me by email at `adam@adam-freeman.com`, although I ask that you first check the errata/corrections list for this book, which you can find in the book's GitHub repository at `https://github.com/Apress/pro-asp.net-core-identity`, in case it has already been reported.

I list errors that are likely to confuse readers, especially problems with example code, in the errata/ corrections file on the GitHub repository, with a grateful acknowledgment to the first reader who reported it. I keep a list of less serious issues, which usually means errors in the text surrounding examples, and I correct them when I write a new edition.

Are There Lots of Examples?

There are *loads* of examples. The best way to learn is by example, and I have packed as many of them as I can into this book. To help make the examples easier to follow, I have adopted a simple convention, which I follow whenever possible. When I create a new file, I list the complete contents, as shown in Listing 1-1. All code listings include the name of the file in the listing's header, along with the folder in which it can be found.

Listing 1-1. The Contents of the Delete.cshtml File in the Pages/Identity/Admin Folder

```
@page "{id?}"
@model IdentityApp.Pages.Identity.Admin.DeleteModel
@{
    ViewBag.Workflow = "Delete";
}

<div asp-validation-summary="All" class="text-danger m-2"></div>

<form method="post">

    <h3 class="bg-danger text-white text-center p-2">Caution</h3>

    <h5 class="text-center m-2">
        Delete @Model.IdentityUser.Email?
    </h5>
    <input type="hidden" name="id" value="@Model.IdentityUser.Id" />
    <div class="text-center p-2">
        <button type="submit" class="btn btn-danger">Delete</button>
        <a asp-page="Dashboard" class="btn btn-secondary">Cancel</a>
    </div>
</form>
```

This listing is taken from Chapter 9. Don't worry about what it does; just be aware that this is a complete listing, which shows the entire contents of the file, and the header tells you what the file is called and its location in the project.

When I make changes to the code, I show the altered statements in bold, as shown in Listing 1-2.

Listing 1-2. Disabling a Button in the Delete.cshtml File in the Pages/Identity/Admin Folder

```
@page "{id?}"
@model IdentityApp.Pages.Identity.Admin.DeleteModel
@inject Microsoft.Extensions.Configuration.IConfiguration Configuration
@{
    ViewBag.Workflow = "Delete";
    string dashboardUser = Configuration["Dashboard:User"] ?? "admin@example.com";
}
```

```
<div asp-validation-summary="All" class="text-danger m-2"></div>

<form method="post">
    <h3 class="bg-danger text-white text-center p-2">Caution</h3>
    <h5 class="text-center m-2">
        Delete @Model.IdentityUser.Email?
    </h5>
    <input type="hidden" name="id" value="@Model.IdentityUser.Id" />
    <div class="text-center p-2">
        <button type="submit" class="btn btn-danger"
            disabled="@(Model.IdentityUser.Email == dashboardUser)">
                Delete
        </button>
        <a asp-page="Dashboard" class="btn btn-secondary">Cancel</a>
    </div>
</form>
```

This listing is taken from a later example, which requires changes to the file created in Listing 1-1. To help you make follow the example, the changes are marked in bold.

Some examples require a small change to a large file. So that I don't waste space listing the unchanged parts of the file, I just show the region that changes, as shown in Listing 1-3. You can tell this listing shows only part of a file because it starts and ends with an ellipsis (...).

Listing 1-3. Counting Users in the Dashboard.cshtml.cs File in the Pages/Identity/Admin Folder

```
...
public void OnGet() {
    UsersCount = UserManager.Users.Count();
    UsersUnconfirmed = UserManager.Users
        .Where(u => !u.EmailConfirmed).Count();
    UsersLockedout = UserManager.Users
        .Where(u => u.LockoutEnabled && u.LockoutEnd > System.DateTimeOffset.Now)
        .Count();
    UsersTwoFactor = UserManager.Users.Where(u => u.TwoFactorEnabled).Count();
}
...
```

In some cases, I need to make changes to different parts of the same file, in which case I omit some elements or statements for brevity, as shown in Listing 1-4. This listing adds new using statements and defines additional methods to an existing file, much of which is unchanged, and which has been omitted from the listing.

Listing 1-4. Supporting External Services in the SignIn.cshtml.cs File in the Pages/Identity Folder

```
using System.ComponentModel.DataAnnotations;
using System.Threading.Tasks;
using Microsoft.AspNetCore.Identity;
using Microsoft.AspNetCore.Mvc;
using SignInResult = Microsoft.AspNetCore.Identity.SignInResult;
using Microsoft.AspNetCore.Authorization;
using Microsoft.AspNetCore.Authentication;
using System.Net;
```

```
namespace IdentityApp.Pages.Identity {

    [AllowAnonymous]
    public class SignInModel : UserPageModel {

        // ...methods and properties omitted for brevity...

        public IActionResult OnPostExternalAsync(string provider) {
            string callbackUrl = Url.Page("SignIn", "Callback", new { ReturnUrl });
            AuthenticationProperties props =
                SignInManager.ConfigureExternalAuthenticationProperties(
                    provider, callbackUrl);
            return new ChallengeResult(provider, props);
        }

        public async Task<IActionResult> OnGetCallbackAsync() {
            ExternalLoginInfo info = await SignInManager.GetExternalLoginInfoAsync();
            SignInResult result = await SignInManager.ExternalLoginSignInAsync(
                info.LoginProvider, info.ProviderKey, true);
            if (result.Succeeded) {
                return Redirect(WebUtility.UrlDecode(ReturnUrl ?? "/"));
            } else if (result.IsLockedOut) {
                TempData["message"] = "Account Locked";
            } else if (result.IsNotAllowed) {
                TempData["message"] = "Sign In Not Allowed";
            } else {
                TempData["message"] = "Sign In Failed";
            }
            return RedirectToPage();
        }
    }
}
```

This convention lets me pack in more examples, but it does mean it can be hard to locate a specific technique. To this end, the chapters in this book begin with a summary table that describes the techniques it contains, and many of the chapters in Part 1 contain quick reference tables that list the methods used to implement a specific feature.

Where Can You Get the Example Code?

You can download the example projects for all the chapters in this book from https://github.com/Apress/pro-asp.net-core-identity.

How Do I Contact the Author?

You can email me at adam@adam-freeman.com. It has been a few years since I first published an email address in my books. I wasn't entirely sure it was a good idea, but I am glad I did it. I have received emails from around the world, from readers working or studying in every industry, and—for the most part, anyway—the emails are positive, polite, and a pleasure to receive.

I try to reply promptly, but I get many emails, and sometimes I get a backlog, especially when I have my head down trying to finish writing a book. I always try to help readers who are stuck with an example in the book, although I ask that you follow the steps described earlier in this chapter before contacting me.

While I welcome reader emails, there are some common questions for which the answers will always be "no." I am afraid that I won't write the code for your new startup, help you with your college assignment, get involved in your development team's design dispute, or teach you how to program.

What If I Really Enjoyed This Book?

Please email me at adam@adam-freeman.com and let me know. It is always a delight to hear from a happy reader, and I appreciate the time it takes to send those emails. Writing these books can be difficult, and those emails provide essential motivation to persist at an activity that can sometimes feel impossible.

What If This Book Has Made Me Angry and I Want to Complain?

You can still email me at adam@adam-freeman.com, and I will still try to help you. Bear in mind that I can only help if you explain what the problem is and what you would like me to do about it. You should understand that sometimes the only outcome is to accept I am not the writer for you and that we will have closure only when you return this book and select another. I'll give careful thought to whatever has upset you, but after 25 years of writing books, I have come to accept that not everyone enjoys reading the books I like to write.

Summary

In this chapter, I outlined the content and structure of this book. The best way to learn ASP.NET Core Identity is by example, so in the next chapter, I jump right in and show you how to set up your development environment and use it to create your first ASP.NET Core Identity project.

CHAPTER 2

■ ■ ■

Your First Identity Application

The best way to appreciate a software development framework is to jump right in and use it. In this chapter, I explain how to prepare for ASP.NET Core development and how to create and run an ASP.NET Core application that uses ASP.NET Core Identity.

UPDATES TO THIS BOOK

Microsoft has an active development schedule for .NET and ASP.NET Core, which means that there may be new releases available by the time you read this book. It doesn't seem fair to expect readers to buy a new book every few months, especially since most changes are relatively minor. Instead, I will post free updates to the GitHub repository for this book (`https://github.com/Apress/pro-asp.net-core-identity`) for breaking changes.

This kind of update is an ongoing experiment for me (and for Apress), and it continues to evolve—not least because I don't know what the future major releases of ASP.NET Core will contain—but the goal is to extend the life of this book by supplementing the examples it contains.

I am not making any promises about what the updates will be like, what form they will take, or how long I will produce them before folding them into a new edition of this book. Please keep an open mind and check the repository for this book when new ASP.NET Core versions are released. If you have ideas about how the updates could be improved, then email me at `adam@adam-freeman.com` and let me know.

Setting Up the Development Environment

Identity is used in ASP.NET Core projects, so you should already have everything you need to follow the examples, although you must install the specific version of the .NET SDK I used in this book and the Node. js package that is used in Chapter 12. In this section, I recap the basic setup process that will prepare a development environment suitable for following the examples in this book.

© Adam Freeman 2021
A. Freeman, *Pro ASP.NET Core Identity*, https://doi.org/10.1007/978-1-4842-6858-2_2

■ **Note**   This book describes ASP.NET Core Identity development for Windows. It is possible to develop and run ASP.NET Core applications on Linux and macOS, but most readers use Windows, and that is what I have chosen to focus on. Many of the examples in this book rely on LocalDB, which is a Windows-only feature provided by SQL Server that is not available on other platforms. If you want to follow this book on another platform, then you can contact me using the email address in Chapter 1, and I will try to help you get started.

Installing the .NET SDK

You must install the same version of the SDK that I used to follow the examples. You are free to use any SDK version for your projects, but to get the expected results, version 5.0.100 is required. Go to https://dotnet. microsoft.com/download/dotnet/5.0 and download version 5.0.100, which is the SDK version for .NET 5.0.0. Run the installer; once the installation is complete, open a new PowerShell command prompt from the Windows Start menu and run the command shown in Listing 2-1, which displays a list of the installed .NET Core SDKs.

Listing 2-1. Listing the Installed SDKs

```
dotnet --list-sdks
```

Here is the output from a fresh installation on a Windows machine that has not previously been used for .NET development:

```
5.0.100 [C:\Program Files\dotnet\sdk]
```

Installing Node.js

Node.js is a server-side JavaScript runtime that I use in Chapter 12 to explain how to provide authentication to API clients. You must download the same version of Node.js that I use in this book. Although Node.js is relatively stable, there are still breaking API changes from time to time.

The version I have used is 14.15.4, which is the Long-Term Support release at the time of writing. There may be a later version available by the time you read this, but you should stick to the 14.15.4 release for the examples in this book. A complete set of 14.15.4 installers for Windows is available at https://nodejs.org/dist/v14.15.4. Run the installer and ensure that the "npm package manager" option and the two Add to PATH options are selected, as shown in Figure 2-1.

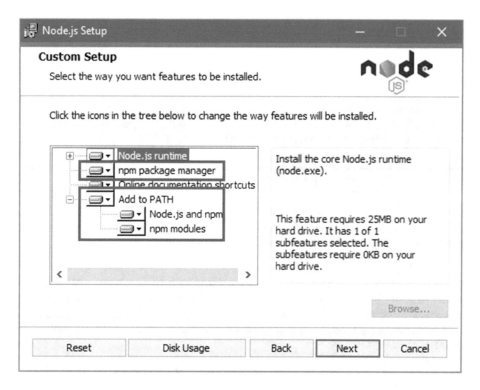

Figure 2-1. *Configuring the Node installation*

When the installation is complete, run the command shown in Listing 2-2.

Listing 2-2. Running Node.js

```
node -v
```

If the installation has gone as it should, then you will see the following version number displayed:

```
v14.15.4
```

The Node.js installer includes the Node Package Manager (NPM), which is used to manage the packages in a project. Run the command shown in Listing 2-3 to ensure that NPM is working.

Listing 2-3. Running NPM

```
npm -v
```

If everything is working as it should, then you will see the following version number:

```
6.14.10
```

Installing a Code Editor

You can use any code editor to follow the examples for this book. The most popular choices are Visual Studio and Visual Studio Code, for which I provide installation instructions in the sections that follow. Visual Studio has better support for C# development, but Visual Studio Code is lighter and quicker. It doesn't matter which one you pick—or whether you use a different editor entirely—because all the commands for building and running projects are run from the command line.

But, regardless of your editor, you will require the exact version of the .NET SDK, and you must ensure that LocalDB is installed (see the following instructions for details).

MUDDLING THROUGH THE MICROSOFT NAMING SCHEME

Microsoft doesn't seem able to settle on a naming convention. The .NET Framework evolved into .NET Core, which has now become .NET (just .NET, without *Framework* or *Core*). To make things more confusing, ASP.NET became ASP.NET Core but hasn't been renamed to follow the change from .NET Core to .NET.

The name changes have been one part of a years-long period of disruptive change, U-turns, confusion, and a general lack of leadership and direction, all of which have trickled down to developers. I am sure that there is someone at Microsoft who thinks this has all been worthwhile, but I have yet to meet them. This is a shame because I have a wide-ranging and expletive-filled rant on this topic that I have been saving for that occasion.

ASP.NET Core and ASP.NET Core Identity have remained relatively stable through the transition from .NET Core to .NET, and the main impact for this book is that I may have used the wrong name of .NET in places. So, if you see a reference to .NET Core, please just take a pencil and cross out the Core part.

Installing Visual Studio

Before installing Visual Studio, make sure you have installed the .NET SDK as described in the previous section. ASP.NET Core 5 requires Visual Studio 2019. I use the free Visual Studio 2019 Community Edition, which can be downloaded from www.visualstudio.com. Run the installer, and you will see the prompt shown in Figure 2-2.

Figure 2-2. *Starting the Visual Studio installer*

Click the Continue button, and the installer will download the installation files, as shown in Figure 2-3.

Figure 2-3. *Downloading the Visual Studio installer files*

When the installer files have been downloaded, you will be presented with a set of installation options, grouped into workloads. Ensure that the "ASP.NET and web development" workload is checked, as shown in Figure 2-4.

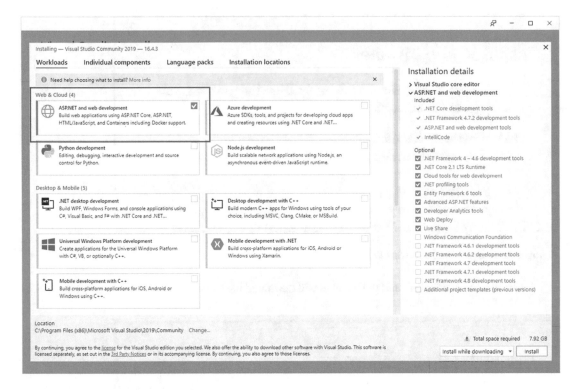

Figure 2-4. *Selecting the workload*

Select the "Individual components" section at the top of the window and ensure the SQL Server Express 2016 LocalDB option is checked, as shown in Figure 2-5. This is the database component that I will be using to store data.

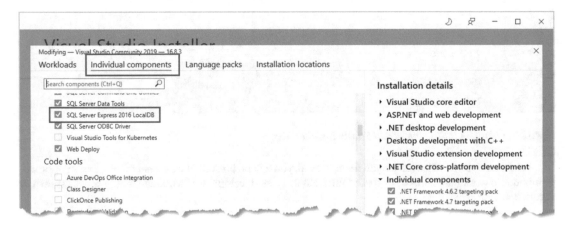

Figure 2-5. *Ensuring LocalDB is installed*

Click the Install button, and the files required for the selected workload will be downloaded and installed. To complete the installation, a reboot is required, as shown in Figure 2-6.

Reboot required

Success! One more step to go. Please restart your computer before you start Visual Studio
Community 2019.

Get troubleshooting tips   Restart   Not now

Figure 2-6. *Completing the installation*

Installing Visual Studio Code

If you have chosen to use Visual Studio Code, download the installer from `https://code.visualstudio.com`.
No specific version is required, and you should select the current stable build. Run the installer and ensure you
select the Add to PATH option, as shown in Figure 2-7.

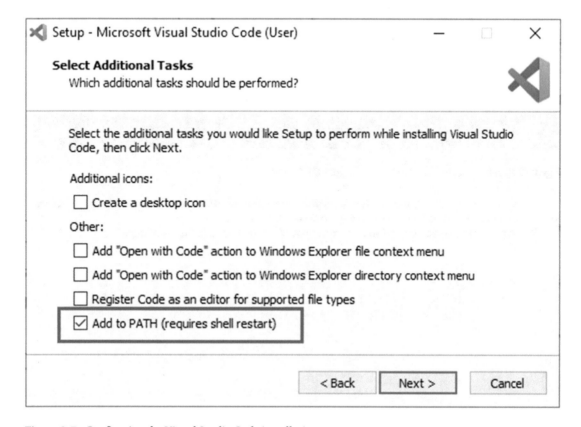

Figure 2-7. *Configuring the Visual Studio Code installation*

Installing SQL Server LocalDB

Many of the examples in this book require LocalDB, which is a zero-configuration version of SQL Server that can be installed as part of the SQL Server Express edition, which is available for use without charge from `https://www.microsoft.com/en-in/sql-server/sql-server-downloads`. Download and run the Express edition installer and select the Custom option, as shown in Figure 2-8.

Figure 2-8. *Selecting the installation option for SQL Server*

Once you have selected the Custom option, you will be prompted to select a download location for the installation files. Click the Install button, and the download will begin.

When prompted, select the option to create a new SQL Server installation, as shown in Figure 2-9.

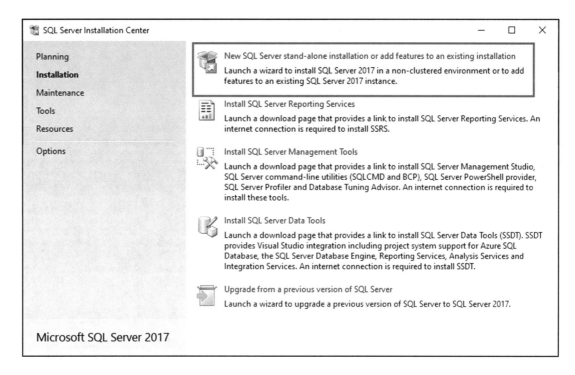

Figure 2-9. *Selecting an installation option*

Work through the installation process, selecting the default options as they are presented. When you reach the Feature Selection page, ensure that the LocalDB option is selected, as shown in Figure 2-10. (You may want to deselect the options for R and Python, which are not used in this book and take a long time to download and install.)

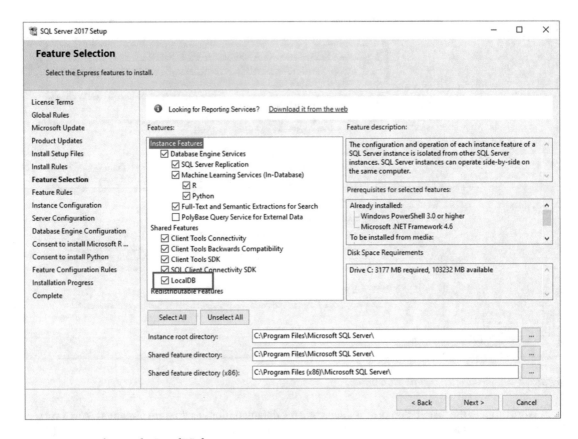

Figure 2-10. *Selecting the LocalDB feature*

On the Instance Configuration page, select the "Default instance" option, as shown in Figure 2-11.

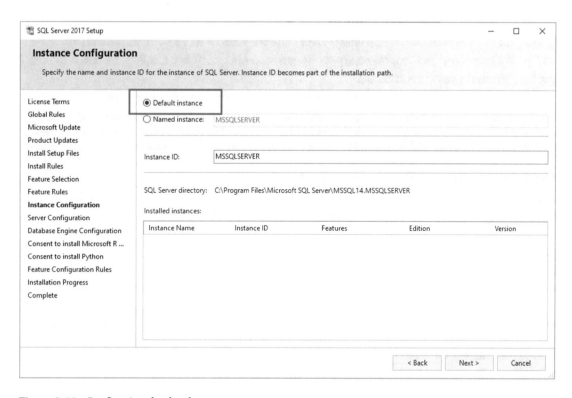

Figure 2-11. *Configuring the database*

Continue to work through the installation process, selecting the default values. Once the installation is complete, install the latest cumulative update for SQL Server. At the time of writing, the latest update is available at https://support.microsoft.com/en-us/help/4577467/kb4577467-cumulative-update-22-for-sql-server-2017, although newer updates may have been released by the time you read this chapter.

■ **Caution**   It can be tempting to skip the update stage, but it is important to perform this step to get the expected results from the examples in this book. As an example, the base installation of SQL Server has a bug that prevents LocalDB from creating database files, which will cause problems when you create a project later in this chapter.

Creating an Application with Identity

In this section, I am going to create an ASP.NET Core project that uses ASP.NET Core Identity. This isn't a complex process because I have chosen a project that fits neatly with the default Identity, which is an application where users can register themselves and that requires no administration tools. The application is a to-do list, with support for multiple users, and the result is a simple demonstration of how Identity can be used with minimum configuration or interference with the normal ASP.NET Core development practices.

■ **Tip** You can download the example project for this chapter—and for all the other chapters in this book—from https://github.com/Apress/pro-asp.net-core-identity. See Chapter 1 for how to get help if you have problems running the examples.

Open a new PowerShell command prompt, navigate to a convenient location, and run the commands shown in Listing 2-4 to create a new project named IdentityTodo. The second command contains a trailing backtick so that both lines will be treated as part of the same command by PowerShell.

Listing 2-4. Creating a New Project

```
dotnet new globaljson --sdk-version 5.0.100 --output IdentityTodo
dotnet new webapp --auth Individual --use-local-db true `
  --output IdentityTodo --framework net5.0
dotnet new sln -o IdentityTodo
dotnet sln IdentityTodo add IdentityTodo
```

These commands create a basic project that includes ASP.NET Core Identity. Once you have created the project, run the commands shown in Listing 2-5 to navigate to the project folder and build the project.

Listing 2-5. Building the Project

```
cd IdentityTodo
dotnet build
```

If the build is successful, there will be no output from the dotnet build command. You may receive this error instead:

```
Could not execute because the application was not found or a compatible .NET SDK is not
installed.
```

This means you have not installed the correct version of the .NET SDK. Return to the instructions at the start of this chapter and install the SDK, which is required even when you are using Visual Studio.

Preparing the Project

I use the command-line tools to build and run the ASP.NET Core projects throughout this book. Open the project (by opening the IdentityTodo.sln file with Visual Studio or the IdentityTodo folder in Visual Studio Code) and change the contents of the launchSettings.json file in the Properties folder, as shown in Listing 2-6, to set the ports that will be used to listen for HTTP requests.

Listing 2-6. Setting Ports in the launchSettings.json File in the Properties Folder

```
{
  "iisSettings": {
    "windowsAuthentication": false,
    "anonymousAuthentication": true,
```

```
  "iisExpress": {
    "applicationUrl": "http://localhost:5000",
    "sslPort": 44350
  }
},
"profiles": {
  "IIS Express": {
    "commandName": "IISExpress",
    "launchBrowser": true,
    "environmentVariables": {
      "ASPNETCORE_ENVIRONMENT": "Development"
    }
  },
  "IdentityTodo": {
    "commandName": "Project",
    "dotnetRunMessages": "true",
    "launchBrowser": true,
    "applicationUrl": "https://localhost:44350;http://localhost:5000",
    "environmentVariables": {
      "ASPNETCORE_ENVIRONMENT": "Development"
    }
  }
}
}
```

I use port 5000 for HTTP requests and port 44350 for HTTPS throughout this book, and these changes apply the ports for both the command line and when the project is started with Visual Studio.

Creating the Data Model

Add a class file named TodoItem.cs to the Data folder with the code shown in Listing 2-7. I use a folder named Models in later chapters, which has been the ASP.NET Core convention, but for this chapter, I am going to use the folder structure provided by the template.

Listing 2-7. The Contents of the TodoItem.cs File in the Data Folder

```
namespace IdentityTodo.Data {

    public class TodoItem {

        public long Id { get; set; }

        public string Task { get; set; }

        public bool Complete { get; set; }

        public string Owner { get; set; }
    }
}
```

This class will be used to represent to-do items, which will be stored in a database using Entity Framework Core. Entity Framework Core is also used to store Identity data, and the project template has created a database context class.

I usually recommend keeping the Identity data in a separate database, but for this chapter, I am going to focus on simplicity and use the same database for all the data. Add the property shown in Listing 2-8 to the ApplicationDbContext.cs file in the Data folder.

Listing 2-8. Adding a Property in the ApplicationDbContext.cs File in the Data Folder

```
using System;
using System.Collections.Generic;
using System.Text;
using Microsoft.AspNetCore.Identity.EntityFrameworkCore;
using Microsoft.EntityFrameworkCore;

namespace IdentityTodo.Data {

    public class ApplicationDbContext : IdentityDbContext {

        public ApplicationDbContext(DbContextOptions<ApplicationDbContext> options)
            : base(options) {}

        public DbSet<TodoItem> TodoItems { get; set; }
    }
}
```

Creating and Applying the Database Migrations

The example application requires two databases: one to store the to-do items and one for the Identity user accounts. To install the command-line tool package that will be used to manage the databases, use a PowerShell command prompt to run the command shown in Listing 2-9.

Listing 2-9. Installing the Entity Framework Core Tools Package

```
dotnet tool uninstall --global dotnet-ef
dotnet tool install --global dotnet-ef --version 5.0.0
```

The first command removes any existing version of the Entity Framework Core tools package, and you may see an error if no version of this package is installed. The second command installs the version of the tools package required for the examples in this book.

Use a PowerShell prompt to run the commands shown in Listing 2-10 in the IdentityTodo folder to create a database migration that will add support for storing to-do items.

Listing 2-10. Creating the Database Migrations

```
dotnet ef migrations add AddTodos
```

Run the commands shown in Listing 2-11 in the `IdentityTodo` folder to remove any existing database, which may have been previously created if you are re-reading this chapter, and create a new database using the migration created in Listing 2-11.

Listing 2-11. Creating the Database

```
dotnet ef database drop --force
dotnet ef database update
```

Configuring ASP.NET Core Identity

A configuration change is required to prepare ASP.NET Core Identity, as shown in Listing 2-12.

Listing 2-12. Configuring the Application in the Startup.cs File in the IdentityTodo Folder

```
using System;
using System.Collections.Generic;
using System.Linq;
using System.Threading.Tasks;
using Microsoft.AspNetCore.Builder;
using Microsoft.AspNetCore.Identity;
using Microsoft.AspNetCore.Identity.UI;
using Microsoft.AspNetCore.Hosting;
using Microsoft.AspNetCore.HttpsPolicy;
using Microsoft.EntityFrameworkCore;
using IdentityTodo.Data;
using Microsoft.Extensions.Configuration;
using Microsoft.Extensions.DependencyInjection;
using Microsoft.Extensions.Hosting;

namespace IdentityTodo {
    public class Startup {
        public Startup(IConfiguration configuration) {
            Configuration = configuration;
        }

        public IConfiguration Configuration { get; }

        public void ConfigureServices(IServiceCollection services) {
            services.AddDbContext<ApplicationDbContext>(options =>
                options.UseSqlServer(
                    Configuration.GetConnectionString("DefaultConnection")));
            services.AddDatabaseDeveloperPageExceptionFilter();

            services.AddDefaultIdentity<IdentityUser>(options =>
                    options.SignIn.RequireConfirmedAccount = false)
                .AddEntityFrameworkStores<ApplicationDbContext>();
            services.AddRazorPages();
        }
```

```
        public void Configure(IApplicationBuilder app, IWebHostEnvironment env) {
            if (env.IsDevelopment()) {
                app.UseDeveloperExceptionPage();
                app.UseMigrationsEndPoint();
            } else {
                app.UseExceptionHandler("/Error");
                app.UseHsts();
            }

            app.UseHttpsRedirection();
            app.UseStaticFiles();

            app.UseRouting();

            app.UseAuthentication();
            app.UseAuthorization();

            app.UseEndpoints(endpoints => {
                endpoints.MapRazorPages();
            });
        }
    }
}
```

Identity is added to the application using the AddDefaultIdentity extension method, and the default configuration created by the project template sets the configuration so that user accounts cannot be used until they are confirmed, which requires the user to click a link they are emailed. I explain the confirmation process in Chapters 8 and 9 and describe it in detail in Chapter 17, but I don't want to use it in this chapter, so I have set the RequireConfirmedAccount configuration option to false. (All the Identity configuration options are described in Chapter 5.)

Creating the Application Content

To present the user with their list of to-do items, replace the contents of the Index.cshtml file in the Pages folder with those shown in Listing 2-13.

Listing 2-13. Replacing the Contents of the Index.cshtml File in the Pages Folder

```
@page
@model IndexModel
@{
    ViewData["Title"] = "To Do List";
}

<h2 class="text-center">To Do List</h2>
<h4 class="text-center">(@User.Identity.Name)</h4>

<form method="post" asp-page-handler="ShowComplete" class="m-2">
    <div class="form-check">
        <input type="checkbox" class="form-check-input" asp-for="ShowComplete"
            onchange="this.form.submit()"/>
```

```html
            <label class="form-check-label">Show Completed Items</label>
    </div>
</form>

<table class="table table-sm table-striped table-bordered m-2">
    <thead><tr><th>Task</th><th/></tr></thead>
    <tbody>
        @if (Model.TodoItems.Count() == 0) {
            <tr>
                <td colspan="2" class="text-center py-4">
                    You have done everything!
                </td>
            </tr>
        } else {
            @foreach (TodoItem item in Model.TodoItems) {
                <tr>
                    <td class="p-2">@item.Task</td>
                    <td class="text-center py-2">
                        <form method="post" asp-page-handler="MarkItem">
                            <input type="hidden" name="id" value="@item.Id" />
                            <input type="hidden" asp-for="ShowComplete" />
                            <button type="submit" class="btn btn-sm btn-secondary">
                                @(item.Complete ? "Mark Not Done" : "Done")
                            </button>
                        </form>
                    </td>
                </tr>
            }
        }
    </tbody>
    <tfoot>
        <tr>
            <td class="pt-4">
                <form method="post" asp-page-handler="AddItem" id="addItem">
                    <input type="hidden" asp-for="ShowComplete" />
                    <input name="task" placeholder="Enter new to do"
                        class="form-control" />
                </form>
            </td>
            <td class="text-center pt-4">
                <button type="submit" form="addItem"
                        class="btn btn-sm btn-secondary">
                    Add
                </button>
            </td>
        </tr>
    </tfoot>
</table>
```

This content presents the user with a table containing their to-do list, along with the ability to add items to the list, mark items as done, and include completed items in the table. To define the features that support the content in Listing 2-13, replace the contents of the Index.cshtml.cs file in the Pages folder with the code shown in Listing 2-14.

Listing 2-14. Replacing the Contents of the Index.cshtml.cs File in the Pages Folder

```
using IdentityTodo.Data;
using Microsoft.AspNetCore.Authorization;
using Microsoft.AspNetCore.Mvc;
using Microsoft.AspNetCore.Mvc.RazorPages;
using System.Collections.Generic;
using System.Linq;
using System.Threading.Tasks;

namespace IdentityTodo.Pages {

    [Authorize]
    public class IndexModel : PageModel {
        private ApplicationDbContext Context;

        public IndexModel(ApplicationDbContext ctx) {
            Context = ctx;
        }

        [BindProperty(SupportsGet = true)]
        public bool ShowComplete { get; set; }

        public IEnumerable<TodoItem> TodoItems { get; set; }

        public void OnGet() {
            TodoItems = Context.TodoItems
                .Where(t => t.Owner == User.Identity.Name).OrderBy(t => t.Task);
            if (!ShowComplete) {
                TodoItems = TodoItems.Where(t => !t.Complete);
            }
            TodoItems = TodoItems.ToList();
        }

        public IActionResult OnPostShowComplete() {
            return RedirectToPage(new { ShowComplete });
        }

        public async Task<IActionResult> OnPostAddItemAsync(string task) {
            if (!string.IsNullOrEmpty(task)) {
                TodoItem item = new TodoItem {
                    Task = task,
                    Owner = User.Identity.Name,
                    Complete = false
                };
```

```
            await Context.AddAsync(item);
            await Context.SaveChangesAsync();
        }
        return RedirectToPage(new { ShowComplete });
    }

    public async Task<IActionResult> OnPostMarkItemAsync(long id) {
        TodoItem item = Context.TodoItems.Find(id);
        if (item != null) {
            item.Complete = !item.Complete;
            await Context.SaveChangesAsync();
        }
        return RedirectToPage(new { ShowComplete });
    }
  }
}
```

There is no direct use of Identity in the code in Listing 2-14 or the Razor content in Listing 2-13. That's because Identity fits neatly into the features provided by the ASP.NET Core platform. The Authorize attribute that decorates the page model class in Listing 2-14 tells ASP.NET Core that only authenticated users should be able to access this Razor Page, and the configuration in the Startup class, shown in Listing 2-12, has set up Identity as the means by which user accounts are created and used.

Running the Example Application

Start ASP.NET Core by running the command shown in Listing 2-15 in the IdentityTodo folder.

Listing 2-15. Running the Example Application

```
dotnet run
```

The project will be compiled and started. After a few seconds, you will see messages that ASP.NET Core is listening for requests on the configured ports, like this:

```
...
Building...
info: Microsoft.Hosting.Lifetime[0]
      Now listening on: https://localhost:44350
info: Microsoft.Hosting.Lifetime[0]
      Now listening on: http://localhost:5000
info: Microsoft.Hosting.Lifetime[0]
      Application started. Press Ctrl+C to shut down.
info: Microsoft.Hosting.Lifetime[0]
      Hosting environment: Development
info: Microsoft.Hosting.Lifetime[0]
      Content root path: C:\IdentityTodo
...
```

Open a new browser window and request `https://localhost:44350`. This request targets the `Index.cshtml` Razor Page, but since that page has been decorated with the `Authorize` attribute, you will be redirected to a page that prompts you to sign in or create an account, as shown in Figure 2-12. This content is provided by the Identity UI package, which provides a standard set of Razor Pages for managing accounts. There are some placeholder items, such as a message about setting up external providers, which I explain in Chapter 11.

Figure 2-12. *The Identity UI sign-in screen*

Click the Register link in the top right of the browser window to navigate to the Razor Page used to register a new account. Enter **alice@example.com** as the email address, and enter the password **MySecret1$** in the Password and Confirm Password fields. (Identity has a punitive default password policy, which I explain how to change in Chapter 8.) Click the Register button, and a new user account will be created and used to sign into the application. Enter a task in the text field, such as **Walk the dog**, and click the Add button. A new item will be stored in the database.

Click the `alice@example.com` email address shown at the top of the browser window, and you will be presented with an account self-management portal, as shown in Figure 2-13. This is another feature provided by the Identity UI package and can be adapted to suit the needs of different projects, as I explain in Chapter 6. If the Identity UI package doesn't suit your project, Identity also provides a complete API for creating custom workflows, which I describe in Chapters 7 to 11.

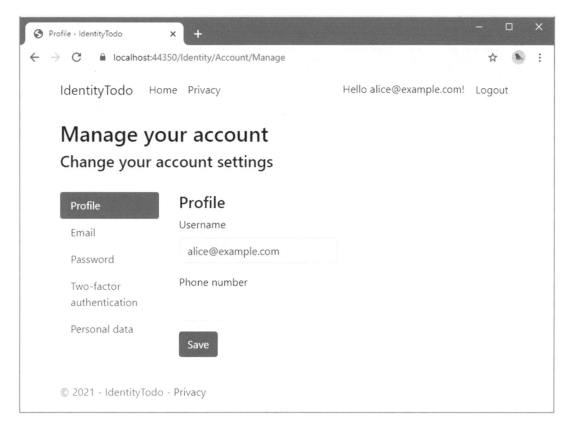

Figure 2-13. *The IdentityUI self-management portal*

Summary

In this chapter, I described the tools required for ASP.NET Core and ASP.NET Core Identity development. I created an application using a project template that includes Identity and demonstrated the features that Identity can offer with minimal configuration. In the next chapter, I create a more complex project and use it to start exploring the ASP.NET Core Identity features in detail.

CHAPTER 3

Creating the Example Project

In the previous chapter, I created an ASP.NET Core application that used Identity in the simplest way possible, which is to include Identity when the project is created and accept the default configuration.

But to explain how Identity works—and make it much more useful—I need a project that doesn't contain Identity at first and doesn't fit as neatly into the pattern that the default Identity configuration expects.

This application isn't complex. I need three types of application feature: features that can be accessed by anyone, features that can be accessed only once a user signs in, and features that can be accessed only by administrators.

Creating the Project

Open a new PowerShell command prompt from the Windows Start menu and run the commands shown in Listing 3-1.

■ Tip You can download the example project for this chapter—and for all the other chapters in this book—from `https://github.com/Apress/pro-asp.net-core-identity`. See Chapter 1 for how to get help if you have problems running the examples.

Listing 3-1. Creating the Project

```
dotnet new globaljson --sdk-version 5.0.100 --output IdentityApp
dotnet new web --no-https --output IdentityApp --framework net5.0
dotnet new sln -o IdentityApp
dotnet sln IdentityApp add IdentityApp
```

Open the project for editing and make the changes shown in Listing 3-2 to the `launchSettings.json` file in the `Properties` folder to set the port that will be used to handle HTTP and requests.

Listing 3-2. Configuring HTTP Ports in the launchSettings.json File in the Properties Folder

```
{
  "iisSettings": {
    "windowsAuthentication": false,
    "anonymousAuthentication": true,
    "iisExpress": {
      "applicationUrl": "http://localhost:5000",
```

© Adam Freeman 2021
A. Freeman, *Pro ASP.NET Core Identity*, https://doi.org/10.1007/978-1-4842-6858-2_3

```
      "sslPort": 0
    }
  },
  "profiles": {
    "IIS Express": {
      "commandName": "IISExpress",
      "launchBrowser": true,
      "environmentVariables": {
        "ASPNETCORE_ENVIRONMENT": "Development"
      }
    },
    "IdentityApp": {
      "commandName": "Project",
      "dotnetRunMessages": "true",
      "launchBrowser": true,
      "applicationUrl": "http://localhost:5000",
      "environmentVariables": {
        "ASPNETCORE_ENVIRONMENT": "Development"
      }
    }
  }
}
```

Installing the Bootstrap CSS Framework

Use a command prompt to run the commands shown in Listing 3-3 in the IdentityApp folder to initialize the Library Manager tool and install the Bootstrap CSS package, which I use to style HTML content.

Listing 3-3. Installing the Client-Side CSS Package

```
dotnet tool uninstall --global Microsoft.Web.LibraryManager.Cli
dotnet tool install --global Microsoft.Web.LibraryManager.Cli --version 2.1.113
libman init -p cdnjs
libman install twitter-bootstrap@4.5.0 -d wwwroot/lib/twitter-bootstrap
```

Install Entity Framework Core

Open a new PowerShell command prompt and run the commands shown in Listing 3-4 in the IdentityApp folder.

Listing 3-4. Installing the Entity Framework Core Packages

```
dotnet add package Microsoft.EntityFrameworkCore.Design --version 5.0.0
dotnet add package Microsoft.EntityFrameworkCore.SqlServer --version 5.0.0
```

Entity Framework Core relies on a global tool package to manage databases and schemas. Run the commands shown in Listing 3-5 to remove any existing version of the tool package and to install the version required for the examples in this book.

Listing 3-5. Installing the Entity Framework Core Tools Package

```
dotnet tool uninstall --global dotnet-ef
dotnet tool install --global dotnet-ef --version 5.0.0
```

Defining a Connection String

Add the configuration setting shown in Listing 3-6 to the appsettings.json file in the IdentityApp folder. This setting defines a connection string that identifies the database that Entity Framework Core will use to store Product data.

■ **Tip** Connection strings must be expressed as a single unbroken line, which is fine in the code editor but doesn't fit on the printed page and is the cause of the awkward formatting in Listing 3-6. When you define the connection string in your projects, make sure the value of the AppDataConnection item is on a single line.

Listing 3-6. Defining a Connection String in the appsettings.json File in the IdentityApp Folder

```
{
  "Logging": {
    "LogLevel": {
      "Default": "Information",
      "Microsoft": "Warning",
      "Microsoft.Hosting.Lifetime": "Information"
    }
  },
  "AllowedHosts": "*",
  "ConnectionStrings": {
    "AppDataConnection": "Server=(localdb)\\MSSQLLocalDB;Database=IdentityAppData;
    MultipleActiveResultSets=true"
  }
}
```

Creating the Data Model

Create the IdentityApp/Models folder and add to it a class file named Product.cs with the code shown in Listing 3-7.

Listing 3-7. The Contents of the Product.cs File in the Models Folder

```
using System.ComponentModel.DataAnnotations.Schema;
namespace IdentityApp.Models {
```

```
public class Product {
    public long Id { get; set; }

    public string Name { get; set; }

    [Column(TypeName = "decimal(8, 2)")]
    public decimal Price { get; set; }

    public string Category { get; set; }
    }
}
```

The Product class has an Id property, which will be used as the primary database key, along with Name, Price, and Category properties. I applied the Column attribute to the Price property so that Entity Framework Core will know which numeric type to use when creating the database schema for storing Product objects.

To create the Entity Framework Core context class, add a file named ProductDbContext.cs to the Models folder with the code shown in Listing 3-8. This class provides access to the Product objects that Entity Framework Core stores in the database and seeds the database with sample data.

Listing 3-8. The Contents of the ProductDbContext.cs File in the Models Folder

```
using Microsoft.EntityFrameworkCore;

namespace IdentityApp.Models {
    public class ProductDbContext: DbContext {

        public ProductDbContext(DbContextOptions<ProductDbContext> options)
            : base(options) { }

        public DbSet<Product> Products { get; set; }

        protected override void OnModelCreating(ModelBuilder builder) {
            builder.Entity<Product>().HasData(
                new Product { Id = 1, Name = "Kayak",
                    Category = "Watersports", Price = 275 },
                new Product { Id = 2, Name = "Lifejacket",
                    Category = "Watersports", Price = 48.95m },
                new Product { Id = 3, Name = "Soccer Ball",
                    Category = "Soccer", Price = 19.50m },
                new Product { Id = 4, Name = "Corner Flags",
                    Category = "Soccer", Price = 34.95m },
                new Product { Id = 5, Name = "Stadium",
                    Category = "Soccer", Price = 79500 },
                new Product { Id = 6, Name = "Thinking Cap",
                    Category = "Chess", Price = 16 },
                new Product { Id = 7, Name = "Unsteady Chair",
                    Category = "Chess", Price = 29.95m },
                new Product { Id = 8, Name = "Human Chess Board",
                    Category = "Chess", Price = 75 },
```

```
                new Product { Id = 9, Name = "Bling-Bling King",
                    Category = "Chess", Price = 1200});
        }
    }
}
```

Creating MVC Controllers and Views

Create the IdentityApp/Controllers folder and add to it a class file named HomeController.cs with the content in Listing 3-9.

Listing 3-9. The Contents of the HomeController.cs File in the Controllers Folder

```
using IdentityApp.Models;
using Microsoft.AspNetCore.Mvc;

namespace IdentityApp.Controllers {

    public class HomeController : Controller {
        private ProductDbContext DbContext;

        public HomeController(ProductDbContext ctx) => DbContext = ctx;

        public IActionResult Index() => View(DbContext.Products);
    }
}
```

This controller will present the first level of access, which will be available to anyone. To create the corresponding view, create the IdentityApp/Views/Home folder and add to it a Razor View named Index.cshtml file with the content shown in Listing 3-10.

Listing 3-10. The Contents of the Index.cshtml File in the Views/Home Folder

```
@model IQueryable<Product>

<h4 class="bg-primary text-white text-center p-2">MVC - Level 1 - Anyone</h4>

<div class="text-center">
    <h6 class="p-2">
        The store contains @Model.Count() products.
    </h6>
</div>
```

Add a class file named StoreController.cs in the Controllers folder with the content shown in Listing 3-11. This controller will present the second level of access, which is available to users who are signed into the application.

Listing 3-11. The Contents of the StoreController.cs File in the Controllers Folder

```
using IdentityApp.Models;
using Microsoft.AspNetCore.Mvc;

namespace IdentityApp.Controllers {

    public class StoreController : Controller {
        private ProductDbContext DbContext;

        public StoreController(ProductDbContext ctx) => DbContext = ctx;

        public IActionResult Index() => View(DbContext.Products);
    }
}
```

To provide the view for the Store controller's action method, create the IdentityApp/Views/Store folder and add a Razor View named Index.cshtml with the content shown in Listing 3-12. This view presents a table containing details of the Product objects in the database but does not provide any means to edit them.

Listing 3-12. The Contents of the Index.cshtml File in the Views/Store Folder

```
@model IQueryable<Product>

<h4 class="bg-primary text-white text-center p-2">MVC - Level 2 - Signed In Users</h4>

<div class="p-2">
    <table class="table table-sm table-striped table-bordered">
        <thead>
            <tr>
                <th>ID</th><th>Name</th><th>Category</th>
                <th class="text-right">Price</th>
            </tr>
        </thead>
        <tbody>
            @foreach (Product p in Model.OrderBy(p => p.Id)) {
                <tr>
                    <td>@p.Id</td>
                    <td>@p.Name</td>
                    <td>@p.Category</td>
                    <td class="text-right">$@p.Price.ToString("F2")</td>
                </tr>
            }
        </tbody>
    </table>
</div>
```

Add a class file named AdminController.cs to the Controllers folder and use it to define the controller shown in Listing 3-13. This controller will present the third level of content, which will be available only to administrators.

Listing 3-13. The Contents of the AdminController.cs File in the Controllers Folder

```
using IdentityApp.Models;
using Microsoft.AspNetCore.Mvc;

namespace IdentityApp.Controllers {

    public class AdminController : Controller {
        private ProductDbContext DbContext;

        public AdminController(ProductDbContext ctx) => DbContext = ctx;

        public IActionResult Index() => View(DbContext.Products);

        [HttpGet]
        public IActionResult Create() => View("Edit", new Product());

        [HttpGet]
        public IActionResult Edit(long id) {
            Product p = DbContext.Find<Product>(id);
            if (p != null) {
                return View("Edit", p);
            }
            return RedirectToAction(nameof(Index));
        }

        [HttpPost]
        public IActionResult Save(Product p) {
            DbContext.Update(p);
            DbContext.SaveChanges();
            return RedirectToAction(nameof(Index));
        }

        [HttpPost]
        public IActionResult Delete(long id) {
            Product p = DbContext.Find<Product>(id);
            if (p != null) {
                DbContext.Remove(p);
                DbContext.SaveChanges();
            }
            return RedirectToAction(nameof(Index));
        }
    }
}
```

Create the IdentityApp/Views/Admin folder and add to it a Razor View named Index.cshtml with the content shown in Listing 3-14.

Listing 3-14. The Contents of the Index.cshtml File in the Views/Admin Folder

```
@model IQueryable<Product>

<h4 class="bg-primary text-white text-center p-2">MVC Level 3 - Administrators</h4>

<div class="p-2">
    <table class="table table-sm table-striped table-bordered">
        <thead>
            <tr>
                <th>ID</th><th>Name</th><th>Category</th>
                <th class="text-right">Price</th><th></th>
            </tr>
        </thead>
        <tbody>
            @foreach (Product p in Model.OrderBy(p => p.Id)) {
                <tr>
                    <td>@p.Id</td>
                    <td>@p.Name</td>
                    <td>@p.Category</td>
                    <td class="text-right">$@p.Price.ToString("F2")</td>
                    <td class="text-center">
                        <form method="post">
                            <a class="btn btn-sm btn-warning" asp-action="edit"
                                asp-route-id="@p.Id">Edit</a>
                            <button class="btn btn-sm btn-danger"
                                asp-action="delete" asp-route-id="@p.Id">
                                    Delete
                            </button>
                        </form>
                    </td>
                </tr>
            }
        </tbody>
    </table>
</div>
<a class="btn btn-primary mx-2" asp-action="Create">Create</a>
```

This view presents a table that shows the `Product` details, along with buttons for creating, editing, and deleting data. To create the HTML that will be used to create and edit data, add a Razor View named `Edit.cshtml` to the `Views/Admin` folder with the contents shown in Listing 3-15.

Listing 3-15. The Contents of the Edit.cshtml File in the Views/Admin Folder

```
@model Product

<h4 class="bg-primary text-white text-center p-2">MVC Level 3 - Administrators</h4>

<form method="post" asp-action="save" class="p-2">
    <div class="form-group">
        <label>ID</label>
        <input class="form-control" readonly asp-for="Id" />
```

```
        </div>
        <div class="form-group">
            <label>Name</label>
            <input class="form-control" asp-for="Name" />
        </div>
        <div class="form-group">
            <label>Category</label>
            <input class="form-control" asp-for="Category" />
        </div>
        <div class="form-group">
            <label>Price</label>
            <input class="form-control" type="number" asp-for="Price" />
        </div>
        <div class="text-center">
            <button type="submit" class="btn btn-primary">Save</button>
            <a class="btn btn-secondary" asp-action="Index">Cancel</a>
        </div>
</form>
```

To enable tag helpers and import the data model namespace and some useful ASP.NET Core Identity namespaces, add a Razor View Imports file named _ViewImports.cshtml file in the Views folder with the content shown in Listing 3-16.

Listing 3-16. The Contents of the _ViewImports.cshtml File in the Views Folder

```
@addTagHelper *, Microsoft.AspNetCore.Mvc.TagHelpers
@using IdentityApp.Models
@using Microsoft.AspNetCore.Identity
@using System.Security.Claims
```

To automatically specify a layout for the views in the application, add a Razor View Start file named _ViewStart.cshtml to the Views folder with the content shown in Listing 3-17.

Listing 3-17. The Contents of the _ViewStart.cshtml File in the Views Folder

```
@{
    Layout = "_Layout";
}
```

Create the IdentityApp/Views/Shared folder and add to it a Razor Layout named _Layout.cshtml with the content shown in Listing 3-18. This file provides the HTML structure into which views (and Razor Pages) will render their content, including a link for the CSS stylesheet from the Bootstrap package.

Listing 3-18. The Contents of the _Layout.cshtml File in the Views/Shared Folder

```
<!DOCTYPE html>
<html>
<head>
    <meta name="viewport" content="width=device-width" />
    <title>Identity App</title>
    <link href="/lib/twitter-bootstrap/css/bootstrap.min.css" rel="stylesheet" />
</head>
```

```
<body>
    <partial name="_NavigationPartial" />
    @RenderBody()
</body>
</html>
```

The layout relies on a partial view to display content that will allow easy navigation between the different levels of content. Add a Razor View named _NavigationPartial.cshtml to the Views/Shared folder with the content shown in Listing 3-19.

Listing 3-19. The Contents of the _NavigationPartial.cshtml File in the Views/Shared Folder

```
<div class="text-center m-2">
    <a class="btn btn-secondary btn-sm" asp-controller="Home">Level 1</a>
    <a class="btn btn-secondary btn-sm" asp-controller="Store">Level 2</a>
    <a class="btn btn-secondary btn-sm" asp-controller="Admin">Level 3</a>
</div>
```

Creating Razor Pages

Create the IdentityApp/Pages folder and add to it a Razor Page named Landing.cshtml with the content shown in Listing 3-20. This page will present the first level of access, which is available to anyone.

Listing 3-20. The Contents of the Landing.cshtml File in the Pages Folder

```
@page "/pages"
@model IdentityApp.Pages.LandingModel

<h4 class="bg-info text-white text-center p-2">Pages - Level 1 - Anyone</h4>

<div class="text-center">
    <h6 class="p-2">
        The store contains @Model.DbContext.Products.Count() products.
    </h6>
</div>
```

To define the page model class, add the code shown in Listing 3-21 to the Landing.cshtml.cs file in the Pages folder. (You will have to create this file if you are using Visual Studio Code. I repeat this note throughout this book because even experienced readers become used to the way that Visual Studio creates files and don't understand why they are missing in Visual Studio Code.)

Listing 3-21. The Contents of the Landing.cshtml.cs File in the Pages Folder

```
using IdentityApp.Models;
using Microsoft.AspNetCore.Mvc.RazorPages;

namespace IdentityApp.Pages {
    public class LandingModel : PageModel {

        public LandingModel(ProductDbContext ctx) => DbContext = ctx;
```

```
        public ProductDbContext DbContext { get; set; }

    }
}
```

Add a Razor Page named Store.cshtml to the Pages folder with the content shown in Listing 3-22. This page will be available to signed-in users.

Listing 3-22. The Contents of the Store.cshtml File in the Pages Folder

```
@page "/pages/store"
@model IdentityApp.Pages.StoreModel

<h4 class="bg-info text-white text-center p-2">Pages - Level 2 - Signed In Users</h4>

<div class="p-2">
    <table class="table table-sm table-striped table-bordered">
        <thead>
            <tr>
                <th>ID</th><th>Name</th><th>Category</th>
                <th class="text-right">Price</th>
            </tr>
        </thead>
        <tbody>
            @foreach (Product p in Model.DbContext.Products.OrderBy(p => p.Id)) {
                <tr>
                    <td>@p.Id</td>
                    <td>@p.Name</td>
                    <td>@p.Category</td>
                    <td class="text-right">$@p.Price.ToString("F2")</td>
                </tr>
            }
        </tbody>
    </table>
</div>
```

To define the page model, add the code shown in Listing 3-23 to the Store.cshtml.cs file. (You will have to create this file if you are using Visual Studio Code.)

Listing 3-23. The Contents of the Store.cshtml.cs File in the Pages Folder

```
using IdentityApp.Models;
using Microsoft.AspNetCore.Mvc.RazorPages;

namespace IdentityApp.Pages {
    public class StoreModel : PageModel {
        public StoreModel(ProductDbContext ctx) => DbContext = ctx;

        public ProductDbContext DbContext { get; set; }
    }
}
```

Next, add a Razor Page named `Admin.cshtml` to the `IdentityApp/Pages` folder with the content shown in Listing 3-24. This page will be available only to administrators.

Listing 3-24. The Contents of the Admin.cshtml File in the Pages Folder

```
@page "/pages/admin"
@model IdentityApp.Pages.AdminModel

<h4 class="bg-info text-white text-center p-2">Pages Level 3 - Administrators</h4>

<div class="p-2">
    <table class="table table-sm table-striped table-bordered">
        <thead>
            <tr>
                <th>ID</th><th>Name</th><th>Category</th>
                <th class="text-right">Price</th><th></th>
            </tr>
        </thead>
        <tbody>
            @foreach (Product p in Model.DbContext.Products.OrderBy(p => p.Id)) {
                <tr>
                    <td>@p.Id</td>
                    <td>@p.Name</td>
                    <td>@p.Category</td>
                    <td class="text-right">$@p.Price.ToString("F2")</td>
                    <td class="text-center">
                        <form method="post">
                            <button class="btn btn-sm btn-danger"
                                asp-route-id="@p.Id">
                                    Delete
                            </button>
                            <a class="btn btn-sm btn-warning" asp-page="Edit"
                                asp-route-id="@p.Id">Edit</a>
                        </form>
                    </td>
                </tr>
            }
        </tbody>
    </table>
</div>
<a class="btn btn-info mx-2" asp-page="Edit">Create</a>
```

To create the page model class for the `Admin` page, add the code shown in Listing 3-25 to the `Admin.cshtml.cs` file. (You will have to create this file if you are using Visual Studio Code.)

Listing 3-25. The Contents of the Admin.cshtml.cs File in the Pages Folder

```
using IdentityApp.Models;
using Microsoft.AspNetCore.Mvc;
using Microsoft.AspNetCore.Mvc.RazorPages;

namespace IdentityApp.Pages {
```

```
    public class AdminModel : PageModel {

        public AdminModel(ProductDbContext ctx) => DbContext = ctx;

        public ProductDbContext DbContext { get; set; }

        public IActionResult OnPost(long id) {
            Product p = DbContext.Find<Product>(id);
            if (p != null) {
                DbContext.Remove(p);
                DbContext.SaveChanges();
            }
            return Page();
        }
    }
}
```

Add a Razor Page named Edit.cshtml to the Pages folder with the content shown in Listing 3-26. This page will display the HTML form that will be used to create and edit Product objects.

Listing 3-26. The Contents of the Edit.cshtml File in the Pages Folder

```
@page "/pages/edit/{id:long?}"
@model IdentityApp.Pages.EditModel

<h4 class="bg-info text-white text-center p-2">Product Page</h4>

<form method="post" class="p-2">
    <div class="form-group">
        <label>ID</label>
        <input class="form-control" readonly asp-for="@Model.Product.Id" />
    </div>
    <div class="form-group">
        <label>Name</label>
        <input class="form-control" asp-for="@Model.Product.Name" />
    </div>
    <div class="form-group">
        <label>Category</label>
        <input class="form-control" asp-for="@Model.Product.Category" />
    </div>
    <div class="form-group">
        <label>Price</label>
        <input class="form-control" type="number" asp-for="@Model.Product.Price" />
    </div>
    <div class="text-center">
        <button type="submit" class="btn btn-secondary">Save</button>
        <a class="btn btn-secondary" asp-page="Admin">Cancel</a>
    </div>
</form>
```

Add the code shown in Listing 3-27 to the Edit.cshtml.cs file to define the page model class for the editor. (You will have to create this file if you are using Visual Studio Code.)

Listing 3-27. The Contents of the Edit.cshtml.cs File in the Pages Folder

```
using IdentityApp.Models;
using Microsoft.AspNetCore.Mvc;
using Microsoft.AspNetCore.Mvc.RazorPages;

namespace IdentityApp.Pages {

    public class EditModel : PageModel {

        public EditModel(ProductDbContext ctx) => DbContext = ctx;

        public ProductDbContext DbContext { get; set; }
        public Product Product { get; set; }

        public void OnGet(long id) {
            Product = DbContext.Find<Product>(id) ?? new Product();
        }

        public IActionResult OnPost([Bind(Prefix = "Product")] Product p) {
            DbContext.Update(p);
            DbContext.SaveChanges();
            return RedirectToPage("Admin");
        }
    }
}
```

Add a Razor View Imports file named _ViewImports.cshtml to the Pages folder and add the content shown in Listing 3-28, which will enable tag helpers in Razor Pages and import some namespaces used in the views (and some that are useful for working with ASP.NET Core Identity).

Listing 3-28. The Contents of the _ViewImports.cshtml File in the Pages Folder

```
@addTagHelper *, Microsoft.AspNetCore.Mvc.TagHelpers
@using Microsoft.AspNetCore.Mvc.RazorPages
@using Microsoft.AspNetCore.Identity
@using System.Security.Claims
@using IdentityApp.Pages
@using IdentityApp.Models
```

Add a Razor View Start file named _ViewStart.cshtml to the Pages folder with the content shown in Listing 3-29.

Listing 3-29. The Contents of the _ViewStart.cshtml in the Pages Folder

```
@{
    Layout = "_Layout";
}
```

Add a Razor Layout named _NavigationPartial.cshtml to the Pages folder with the content shown in Listing 3-30.

Listing 3-30. The Contents of the _NavigationPartial.cshtml File in the Pages Folder

```
<div class="text-center m-2">
    <a class="btn btn-secondary btn-sm" asp-page="Landing">Level 1</a>
    <a class="btn btn-secondary btn-sm" asp-page="Store">Level 2</a>
    <a class="btn btn-secondary btn-sm" asp-page="Admin">Level 3</a>
</div>
```

The Razor Pages share a layout with the MVC controllers, and only the contents of the partial view will be different, allowing easy navigation between pages.

Configure the Application

Listing 3-31 shows the changes required to the Startup class to set up Entity Framework Core, the MVC Framework, and Razor Pages.

Listing 3-31. Configuring the Application in the Startup.cs File in the IdentityApp Folder

```
using Microsoft.AspNetCore.Builder;
using Microsoft.AspNetCore.Hosting;
using Microsoft.AspNetCore.Http;
using Microsoft.Extensions.DependencyInjection;
using Microsoft.Extensions.Hosting;
using Microsoft.Extensions.Configuration;
using Microsoft.EntityFrameworkCore;
using IdentityApp.Models;

namespace IdentityApp {

    public class Startup {

        public Startup(IConfiguration config) => Configuration = config;

        private IConfiguration Configuration { get; set; }

        public void ConfigureServices(IServiceCollection services) {
            services.AddControllersWithViews();
            services.AddRazorPages();
            services.AddDbContext<ProductDbContext>(opts => {
                opts.UseSqlServer(
                    Configuration["ConnectionStrings:AppDataConnection"]);
            });
        }

        public void Configure(IApplicationBuilder app, IWebHostEnvironment env) {
            if (env.IsDevelopment()) {
                app.UseDeveloperExceptionPage();
            }
            app.UseStaticFiles();
            app.UseRouting();
```

```
        app.UseEndpoints(endpoints => {
            endpoints.MapDefaultControllerRoute();
            endpoints.MapRazorPages();
        });
    }
  }
}
```

You should already be familiar with the methods used in Listing 3-31, which provide access to the configuration data in the appsettings.json file and configure the services and middleware required for static content, Razor Pages, and the MVC Framework.

Creating the Database

To create Entity Framework Core migration for the product database, use a PowerShell command prompt to run the command shown in Listing 3-32 in the IdentityApp folder.

Listing 3-32. Creating the Migration and Database

```
dotnet ef migrations add Initial
```

Once the migration has been created, run the commands shown in Listing 3-33, which will remove the IdentityAppData database if it exists and then re-create it.

Listing 3-33. Deleting and Creating the Database

```
dotnet ef database drop --force
dotnet ef database update
```

Running the Example Application

Using a PowerShell command prompt, run the command shown in Listing 3-34 to start the example application.

Listing 3-34. Running the Example Application

```
dotnet run
```

One ASP.NET Core has started, request http://localhost:5000. This request will be handled by the Index action of the Home controller, which presents the first level of content, available to anyone. The layouts defined earlier included buttons that allow easy movement between the controllers and the different levels of content they present. There are no access restrictions in place at the moment, which means that all the content is accessible to anyone, as shown in Figure 3-1.

Figure 3-1. *The content produced by the MVC Framework*

Request `http://localhost:5000/pages` to see the same functionality implemented using Razor Pages. I have used a different color scheme and clear labels to make it obvious that Razor Pages have produced the content, as shown in Figure 3-2.

Figure 3-2. *The content produced by Razor Pages*

Enabling HTTPS Connections

There is one more set of changes required to prepare the example application. ASP.NET Core relies on cookies and HTTP request headers to authenticate requests, which presents the risk that an eavesdropper might intercept an HTTP request and use the cookie or header it contains to send a request that will appear as though it has been sent by the user.

When using an ASP.NET Core application that requires authentication, it is important to ensure that all requests are sent using HTTPS, which encrypts the messages between the browser and ASP.NET Core to guard against eavesdropping.

HTTPS VS. SSL VS. TLS

HTTPS is the combination of HTTP and the transport layer security (TLS) or secure sockets layer (SSL). TLS has replaced the obsolete SSL protocol, but the term SSL has become synonymous with secure networking and is often used even when TLS is responsible for securing a connection. If you are interested in security and cryptography, then the details of HTTPS are worth exploring, and `https://en.wikipedia.org/wiki/HTTPS` is a good place to start.

Generating a Test Certificate

An important HTTPS feature is the use of a certificate that allows web browsers to confirm they are communicating with the right web server and not an impersonator. To make application development simpler, the .NET SDK includes a test certificate that can be used for HTTPS. Use a PowerShell command prompt to run the commands shown in Listing 3-35 in the `IdentityApp` folder to generate a new test certificate and add it to the set of certificates that Windows will trust.

Listing 3-35. Generating and Trusting a New Certificate

```
dotnet dev-certs https --clean
dotnet dev-certs https --trust
```

Click Yes to the prompts to delete the existing certificate it has already been trusted, and click Yes to trust the new certificate, as shown in Figure 3-3.

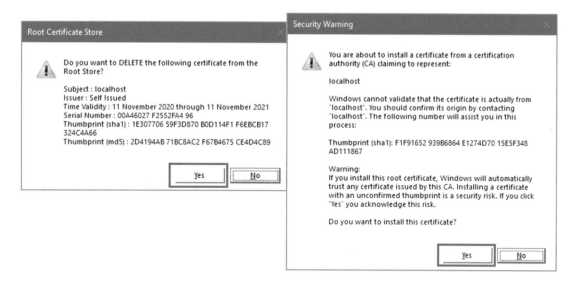

Figure 3-3. *Generating and trusting a test certificate for HTTPS*

USING A CERTIFICATE FOR DEPLOYMENT

The .NET test certificate can be used only during development, and you will need to use a real certificate when you are ready to deploy a project. If you don't have a certificate, I recommend `https://letsencrypt.org/`, which is a nonprofit organization that issues certificates for free. As part of the registration process, you will need to prove you control the domain for which you require a certificate, but Let's Encrypt provides tools for this process.

Once you have a certificate—regardless of how you obtain one—you can find instructions for configuring ASP.NET Core at `https://docs.microsoft.com/en-us/aspnet/core/security/authentication/certauth?view=aspnetcore-5.0`.

Enabling HTTPS

To enable HTTPS, make the changes shown in Listing 3-36 to the `launchSettings.json` file in the Properties folder.

Listing 3-36. Enabling HTTPS in the launchSettings.json File in the Properties Folder

```
{
  "iisSettings": {
    "windowsAuthentication": false,
    "anonymousAuthentication": true,
    "iisExpress": {
      "applicationUrl": "http://localhost:5000",
      "sslPort": 44350
    }
  },
  "profiles": {
```

```
    "IIS Express": {
      "commandName": "IISExpress",
      "launchBrowser": true,
      "environmentVariables": {
        "ASPNETCORE_ENVIRONMENT": "Development"
      }
    },
    "IdentityApp": {
      "commandName": "Project",
      "dotnetRunMessages": "true",
      "launchBrowser": true,
      "applicationUrl": "http://localhost:5000;https://localhost:44350",
      "environmentVariables": {
        "ASPNETCORE_ENVIRONMENT": "Development"
      }
    }
  }
}
```

I have chosen port 44350 for the example application, largely because IIS supports HTTPS only between ports 44300 and 44399.

I use ports 5000 (for HTTP) and 44350 (for HTTPS) during development because it avoids operating system restrictions on using low-numbered ports. Deployed applications will typically use port 80 for HTTP and 443 for HTTPS, but this will depend on your hosting environment. You may need to use different ports or find that HTTPS is handled for you as part of a shared infrastructure, which is often the case when deploying to a corporate data center. If you are unsure, check with your administrators or consult the documentation for your chosen deployment platform.

Enabling HTTPS Redirection

ASP.NET Core provides a feature that will redirect HTTP requests to the HTTPS port supported by the application. To enable HTTPS redirection, add the statement shown in Listing 3-37 to the Startup class.

Listing 3-37. Enabling HTTPS Redirection in the Startup.cs File in the IdentityApp Folder

```
using Microsoft.AspNetCore.Builder;
using Microsoft.AspNetCore.Hosting;
using Microsoft.AspNetCore.Http;
using Microsoft.Extensions.DependencyInjection;
using Microsoft.Extensions.Hosting;
using Microsoft.Extensions.Configuration;
using Microsoft.EntityFrameworkCore;
using IdentityApp.Models;

namespace IdentityApp {

    public class Startup {

        public Startup(IConfiguration config) => Configuration = config;

        private IConfiguration Configuration { get; set; }
```

```
public void ConfigureServices(IServiceCollection services) {
    services.AddControllersWithViews();
    services.AddRazorPages();
    services.AddDbContext<ProductDbContext>(opts => {
        opts.UseSqlServer(
            Configuration["ConnectionStrings:AppDataConnection"]);
    });

    services.AddHttpsRedirection(opts => {
        opts.HttpsPort = 44350;
    });
}

public void Configure(IApplicationBuilder app, IWebHostEnvironment env) {
    if (env.IsDevelopment()) {
        app.UseDeveloperExceptionPage();
    }

    app.UseHttpsRedirection();
    app.UseStaticFiles();
    app.UseRouting();

    app.UseEndpoints(endpoints => {
        endpoints.MapDefaultControllerRoute();
        endpoints.MapRazorPages();
    });
}
}
}
```

The AddHttpsRedirection method is used to configure the HTTPS redirection. For the example application, I need to specify that the redirection will be to port 44350, overriding the default port 443. The UseHttpRedirection method applies an ASP.NET Core middleware component that responds with a redirection when HTTP requests are received, using the settings specified by the AddHttpsRedirection method.

Restart ASP.NET Core and request http://localhost:5000. The example application will respond with a redirection, causing the browser to request https://localhost:44350, as shown in Figure 3-4.

Figure 3-4. *Enabling HTTPS in the example application*

Restricting Access with an Authorization Policy

The final step in this chapter is to apply access restrictions so that ASP.NET Core will only allow users who meet the authorization policy access to protected actions or pages. The changes in this section break the application. ASP.NET Core provides a complete set of features for enforcing authentication and authorization, which I describe in Part 2. The following changes tell ASP.NET Core to restrict access but do not provide the features required to allow requests to be authenticated or to allow users to sign into the application. I address this in later chapters by installing and configuring ASP.NET Core Identity, but, until then, the result is that requests for restricted content will produce an exception.

Applying the Level 2 Authorization Policy

The Authorize attribute is used to restrict access, and Listing 3-38 applies the attribute to the Store controller.

Listing 3-38. Restricting Access in the StoreController.cs File in the Controllers Folder

```
using IdentityApp.Models;
using Microsoft.AspNetCore.Mvc;
using Microsoft.AspNetCore.Authorization;

namespace IdentityApp.Controllers {

    [Authorize]
    public class StoreController : Controller {
        private ProductDbContext DbContext;

        public StoreController(ProductDbContext ctx) => DbContext = ctx;

        public IActionResult Index() => View(DbContext.Products);
    }
}
```

When the attribute is applied without any arguments, the effect is to restrict access to any signed-in user. I applied the attribute to the class, which applies this authorization policy to all of the action methods defined by the controller. In Listing 3-39, I have applied the attribute to the page model class of the Store Razor Page, which is the counterpart to the Store controller.

Listing 3-39. Restricting Access in the Store.cshtml.cs File in the Pages Folder

```
using IdentityApp.Models;
using Microsoft.AspNetCore.Mvc.RazorPages;
using Microsoft.AspNetCore.Authorization;

namespace IdentityApp.Pages {

    [Authorize]
    public class StoreModel : PageModel {
        public StoreModel(ProductDbContext ctx) => DbContext = ctx;

        public ProductDbContext DbContext { get; set; }
    }
}
```

The attribute can also be applied to Razor Pages with the @attribute expression, which I use for convenience in later examples, although the effect is the same.

Applying the Level 3 Authorization Policy

The Authorize attribute can be used to define more specific access restrictions. The most common approach is to restrict access to users who have been assigned to a specific *role*. In Listing 3-40, I have applied the Authorize attribute to the Admin controller using the Roles argument.

Listing 3-40. Restricting Access in the AdminController.cs File in the Controllers Folder

```
using IdentityApp.Models;
using Microsoft.AspNetCore.Mvc;
using Microsoft.AspNetCore.Authorization;

namespace IdentityApp.Controllers {

    [Authorize(Roles = "Admin")]
    public class AdminController : Controller {
        private ProductDbContext DbContext;

        public AdminController(ProductDbContext ctx) => DbContext = ctx;

        public IActionResult Index() => View(DbContext.Products);

        [HttpGet]
        public IActionResult Create() => View("Edit", new Product());

        [HttpGet]
        public IActionResult Edit(long id) {
            Product p = DbContext.Find<Product>(id);
            if (p != null) {
                return View("Edit", p);
            }
            return RedirectToAction(nameof(Index));
        }

        [HttpPost]
        public IActionResult Save(Product p) {
            DbContext.Update(p);
            DbContext.SaveChanges();
            return RedirectToAction(nameof(Index));
        }

        [HttpPost]
        public IActionResult Delete(long id) {
            Product p = DbContext.Find<Product>(id);
            if (p != null) {
                DbContext.Remove(p);
                DbContext.SaveChanges();
            }
```

```
            return RedirectToAction(nameof(Index));
        }
    }
}
```

Listing 3-41 applies the same policy to the Admin page model class, which is the Level 3 Razor Page and the counterpart to the controller in Listing 3-40.

Listing 3-41. Restricting Access in the Admin.cshtml.cs File in the Pages Folder

```
using IdentityApp.Models;
using Microsoft.AspNetCore.Mvc;
using Microsoft.AspNetCore.Mvc.RazorPages;
using Microsoft.AspNetCore.Authorization;

namespace IdentityApp.Pages {

    [Authorize(Roles = "Admin")]
    public class AdminModel : PageModel {

        public AdminModel(ProductDbContext ctx) => DbContext = ctx;

        public ProductDbContext DbContext { get; set; }

        public IActionResult OnPost(long id) {
            Product p = DbContext.Find<Product>(id);
            if (p != null) {
                DbContext.Remove(p);
                DbContext.SaveChanges();
            }
            return Page();
        }
    }
}
```

I need to apply the same restriction to the page model class for the Edit page, as shown in Listing 3-42, which handles editing on behalf of the Admin page.

Listing 3-42. Restricting Access in the Edit.cshtml.cs File in the Pages Folder

```
using IdentityApp.Models;
using Microsoft.AspNetCore.Mvc;
using Microsoft.AspNetCore.Mvc.RazorPages;
using Microsoft.AspNetCore.Authorization;

namespace IdentityApp.Pages {

    [Authorize(Roles = "Admin")]
    public class EditModel : PageModel {

        public EditModel(ProductDbContext ctx) => DbContext = ctx;

        public ProductDbContext DbContext { get; set; }
```

```
        public Product Product { get; set; }

        public void OnGet(long id) {
            Product = DbContext.Find<Product>(id) ?? new Product();
        }

        public IActionResult OnPost([Bind(Prefix = "Product")] Product p) {
            DbContext.Update(p);
            DbContext.SaveChanges();
            return RedirectToPage("Admin");
        }
    }
}
```

Configuring the Application

The remaining step is to enable the ASP.NET Core features that handle authorization and authentication, as shown in Listing 3-43. As I explain in Part 2, these are the features with which ASP.NET Core Identity integrates but are provided by ASP.NET Core.

Listing 3-43. Enabling Features in the Startup.cs File in the IdentityApp Folder

```
using Microsoft.AspNetCore.Builder;
using Microsoft.AspNetCore.Hosting;
using Microsoft.AspNetCore.Http;
using Microsoft.Extensions.DependencyInjection;
using Microsoft.Extensions.Hosting;
using Microsoft.Extensions.Configuration;
using Microsoft.EntityFrameworkCore;
using IdentityApp.Models;

namespace IdentityApp {

    public class Startup {

        public Startup(IConfiguration config) => Configuration = config;

        private IConfiguration Configuration { get; set; }

        public void ConfigureServices(IServiceCollection services) {
            services.AddControllersWithViews();
            services.AddRazorPages();
            services.AddDbContext<ProductDbContext>(opts => {
                opts.UseSqlServer(
                    Configuration["ConnectionStrings:AppDataConnection"]);
            });

            services.AddHttpsRedirection(opts => {
                opts.HttpsPort = 44350;
            });
        }
```

```
public void Configure(IApplicationBuilder app, IWebHostEnvironment env) {
    if (env.IsDevelopment()) {
        app.UseDeveloperExceptionPage();
    }

    app.UseHttpsRedirection();
    app.UseStaticFiles();
    app.UseRouting();

    app.UseAuthentication();
    app.UseAuthorization();

    app.UseEndpoints(endpoints => {
        endpoints.MapDefaultControllerRoute();
        endpoints.MapRazorPages();
    });
}
```

The UseAuthentication and UseAuthorization methods set up, as their names suggest, the ASP.NET Core authentication and authorization features. You don't need to understand how these features work to use ASP.NET Core Identity, but you will find full details in Part 2.

Restart ASP.NET Core and request https://localhost:44350. This request will be handled by the Home controller, to which no authorization restrictions have been applied and which will return a normal response, as shown in Figure 3-5. Request https://localhost:44350/store, and you will receive an error, also shown in Figure 3-5. This request is handled by the Store controller, to which the Authorize attribute has been applied. ASP.NET Core tries to establish the identity of the user who has sent the request but cannot do so because the required services are missing, causing an exception.

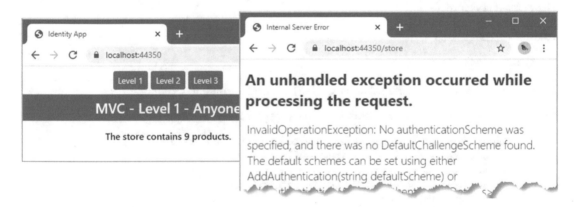

Figure 3-5. *The effect of applying authorization restrictions*

Summary

In this chapter, I created the example application that I will use throughout this part of the book. The application is simple but defines three levels of access control, which I use to explain how ASP.NET Core Identity works and how it integrates into the ASP.NET Core platform. In the next chapter, I show you how to install Identity and use the built-in Identity UI package.

CHAPTER 4

■ ■ ■

Using the Identity UI Package

Microsoft provides a build user interface for Identity, known as *Identity UI*, which makes it possible to get up and running quickly. In this chapter, I add Identity to the example project created in Chapter 3 and explain the features that the Identity UI package provides. In Chapter 6, I explain how to adapt those features to suit different project types.

Even with the adaptations that I describe in Chapter 6, the Identity UI package is only suitable for applications with a specific set of characteristics. I describe the restrictions those characteristics lead to and, starting in Chapter 7, explain how to create entirely custom workflows as an alternative to using the Identity UI package.

But, as this chapter will demonstrate, if your application does meet the requirements, you can get a lot of benefit from the Identity UI package with little effort. Table 4-1 puts the Identity UI package in context.

Table 4-1. *Putting the Identity UI Package in Context*

Question	Answer
What is it?	The Identity UI package is a set of Razor Pages and supporting classes provided by Microsoft to jump-start the use of ASP.NET Core Identity in ASP.NET Core projects.
Why is it useful?	The Identity UI package provides all the workflows required for basic user management, including creating accounts and signing in with passwords, authenticators, and third-party services.
How is it used?	The Identity UI package is added to projects as a NuGet package and enabled with the AddDefaultIdentity extension method.
Are there any pitfalls or limitations?	The approach that Identity UI takes doesn't suit all projects. This can be remedied either by adapting the features it provides or by working directly with the Identity API to create custom alternatives.
Are there any alternatives?	Identity provides an API that can be used to create custom alternatives to the Identity UI package, which I describe in Chapters 7 to 11.

© Adam Freeman 2021
A. Freeman, *Pro ASP.NET Core Identity*, https://doi.org/10.1007/978-1-4842-6858-2_4

Table 4-2 summarizes the chapter.

Table 4-2. *Chapter Summary*

Problem	Solution	Listing
Add Identity and the Identity UI package to a project	Add the NuGet packages to the project and configure them using the AddDefaultIdentity method in the Startup class. Create a database migration and use it to prepare a database for storing user data.	1–7
Present the user with the registration or sign-in links	Create a shared partial view named _LoginPartial.cshtml.	8, 9
Create a consistent layout for the application and the Identity UI package	Define a Razor Layout and refer to it in a Razor View Start created in the Areas/Identity/Pages folder.	10–12
Add support for confirmations	Create an implementation of the IEmailSender interface and register it as a service in the Startup class.	13, 14
Display QR codes for configuring authenticator applications	Add the qrcodejs JavaScript package to the project and create a script element that applies it to the URL produced by the Identity UI package.	15, 16

Preparing for This Chapter

This chapter uses the IdentityApp project created in Chapter 3. No changes are required to prepare for this chapter. Open a PowerShell command prompt, navigate to the IdentityApp folder, and run the commands shown in Listing 4-1 to delete and then re-create the database the application uses.

■ **Tip** You can download the example project for this chapter—and for all the other chapters in this book—from https://github.com/Apress/pro-asp.net-core-identity. See Chapter 1 for how to get help if you have problems running the examples.

Listing 4-1. Resetting the Application Database

```
dotnet ef database drop --force
dotnet ef database update
```

Use the PowerShell prompt to run the command shown in Listing 4-2 in the IdentityApp folder to start the application.

Listing 4-2. Running the Example Application

```
dotnet run
```

Open a web browser and request `https://localhost:44350`, which will show the output from the Home controller, and `https://localhost:44350/pages`, which will show the output from the Landing Razor Page, as shown in Figure 4-1. Clicking the Level 2 or Level 3 button produces an exception because ASP.NET Core hasn't been provided with the services it needs to authenticate requests and enforce the restrictions applied with the `Authorize` attribute.

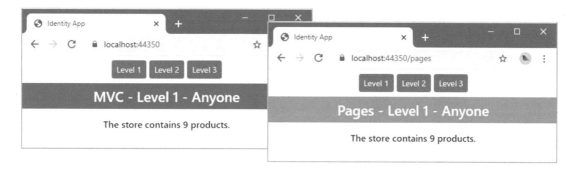

Figure 4-1. *Running the example application*

Adding ASP.NET Core Identity to the Project

Use a PowerShell command prompt to run the commands shown in Listing 4-3 in the IdentityApp folder to add the ASP.NET Core Identity packages to the project.

Listing 4-3. Adding the ASP.NET Core Identity Packages

```
dotnet add package Microsoft.Extensions.Identity.Core --version 5.0.0
dotnet add package Microsoft.AspNetCore.Identity.EntityFrameworkCore --version 5.0.0
```

The first package contains the core Identity features. The second package contains the features required to store data in a database using Entity Framework Core.

Adding the Identity UI Package to the Project

Use PowerShell to run the command shown in Listing 4-4 in the IdentityApp folder to install the Identity UI package.

Listing 4-4. Installing the Identity UI Package

```
dotnet add package Microsoft.AspNetCore.Identity.UI --version 5.0.0
```

Defining the Database Connection String

The easiest way to store Identity data is in a database, and Microsoft provides built-in support for doing this with Entity Framework Core. Although you can use a single database for the application's domain data and the Identity data, I recommend you keep everything separate so that you can manage the schemas independently.

   To define the connection string that Entity Framework Core will use for the Identity database, add the configuration item shown in Listing 4-5 to the appsettings.json file, which specifies a LocalDB database named IdentityAppUserData using a connection string named IdentityConnection. (Connection strings should be on a single unbroken line but are too long to show this way on the printed page.)

Listing 4-5. Adding a Connection String in the appsettings.json File in the IdentityApp Folder

```
{
  "Logging": {
    "LogLevel": {
      "Default": "Information",
      "Microsoft": "Warning",
      "Microsoft.Hosting.Lifetime": "Information"
    }
  },
  "AllowedHosts": "*",
  "ConnectionStrings": {
    "AppDataConnection": "Server=(localdb)\\MSSQLLocalDB;Database=IdentityAppData;
    MultipleActiveResultSets=true",
    "IdentityConnection": "Server=(localdb)\\MSSQLLocalDB;Database=IdentityAppUserData;
    MultipleActiveResultSets=true"
  }
}
```

Configuring the Application

The next step is to configure the application to set up the database that will be used to store user data and to configure ASP.NET Core Identity. Add the statements shown in Listing 4-6 to the Startup class.

Listing 4-6. Configuring the Application in the Startup.cs File in the IdentityApp Folder

```
using Microsoft.AspNetCore.Builder;
using Microsoft.AspNetCore.Hosting;
using Microsoft.AspNetCore.Http;
using Microsoft.Extensions.DependencyInjection;
using Microsoft.Extensions.Hosting;
using Microsoft.Extensions.Configuration;
using Microsoft.EntityFrameworkCore;
using IdentityApp.Models;
using Microsoft.AspNetCore.Identity;
using Microsoft.AspNetCore.Identity.EntityFrameworkCore;
```

```
namespace IdentityApp {

    public class Startup {

        public Startup(IConfiguration config) => Configuration = config;

        private IConfiguration Configuration { get; set; }

        public void ConfigureServices(IServiceCollection services) {
            services.AddControllersWithViews();
            services.AddRazorPages();
            services.AddDbContext<ProductDbContext>(opts => {
                opts.UseSqlServer(
                    Configuration["ConnectionStrings:AppDataConnection"]);
            });

            services.AddHttpsRedirection(opts => {
                opts.HttpsPort = 44350;
            });

            services.AddDbContext<IdentityDbContext>(opts => {
                opts.UseSqlServer(
                    Configuration["ConnectionStrings:IdentityConnection"],
                    opts => opts.MigrationsAssembly("IdentityApp")
                );
            });
            services.AddDefaultIdentity<IdentityUser>()
                .AddEntityFrameworkStores<IdentityDbContext>();
        }

        public void Configure(IApplicationBuilder app, IWebHostEnvironment env) {
            if (env.IsDevelopment()) {
                app.UseDeveloperExceptionPage();
            }

            app.UseHttpsRedirection();
            app.UseStaticFiles();
            app.UseRouting();

            app.UseAuthentication();
            app.UseAuthorization();

            app.UseEndpoints(endpoints => {
                endpoints.MapDefaultControllerRoute();
                endpoints.MapRazorPages();
            });
        }
    }
}
```

The AddDbContext method is used to set up an Entity Framework Core database context for Identity. The database context class is `IdentityDbContext`, which is included in the Identity packages and includes details of the schema that will be used to store identity data. You can create a custom database context class if you prefer—and this is the approach taken by the project template I used in Chapter 2—but there is no good reason to do so, and it is just another class to add to the project. (And, as you will see by the end of this part of the book, using Identity can add a lot of files to a project.)

Because the `IdentityDbContext` class is defined in a different assembly, I have to tell Entity Framework Core to create database migrations in the `IdentityApp` project, like this:

```
...
services.AddDbContext<IdentityDbContext>(opts => {
    opts.UseSqlServer(
        Configuration["ConnectionStrings:IdentityConnection"],
        opts => opts.MigrationsAssembly("IdentityApp")
    );
});
...
```

The other new statement in Listing 4-6 sets up ASP.NET Core Identity. The first part calls the AddDefaultIdentity method, like this:

```
...
services.AddDefaultIdentity<IdentityUser>()
    .AddEntityFrameworkStores<IdentityDbContext>();
...
```

The reason that ASP.NET Core threw exceptions for requests to restricted URLs in Chapter 3 was that no services had been registered to authentication requests. The AddDefaultIdentity method sets up those services using sensible default values. The generic type argument specifies the class Identity will use to represent users. The default class is `IdentityUser`, which is included in the Identity package.

`IdentityUser` is known as the *user class* and is used by Identity to represent users. `IdentityUser` is the default user class provided by Microsoft. In Part 2, I create a custom user class, but `IdentityUser` is suitable for almost every project. The second part of this statement sets up the Identity datastore:

```
...
services.AddDefaultIdentity<IdentityUser>()
    .AddEntityFrameworkStores<IdentityDbContext>();
...
```

The AddEntityFrameworkStores method sets up data storage using Entity Framework Core, and the generic type argument specifies the database context that will be used. Identity uses two kinds of datastore: the *user store* and the *role store*. The user store is the heart of Identity and is used to store all of the user data, including email addresses, passwords, and so on. Confusingly, membership of roles is kept in the user store. The role store contains additional information about roles that are used only in complex applications. I explain every aspect of the user store and role store in Part 2, but you don't typically need to get into the detail of either store when using Identity, other than to know that they exist and to check they support all of the features you require, which I demonstrate in Chapter 7.

Creating the Database

Entity Framework Core requires a database migration, which will be used to create the database for Identity data. Run the commands shown in Listing 4-7 to create and then apply a migration for Identity. These commands require the --context argument because there are two database context classes set up in the Startup class: one for Identity and one for the application data.

Listing 4-7. Creating and Applying a Migration for ASP.NET Core Identity

```
dotnet ef migrations add IdentityInitial --context IdentityDbContext
dotnet ef database drop --force --context IdentityDbContext
dotnet ef database update --context IdentityDbContext
```

The result of these commands is that a new migration will be added to the IdentityApp folder, which is then used to create a new database. The database drop command ensures that any existing database named IdentityAppUserData is deleted.

Preparing the Login Partial View

The Identity UI package requires a partial view named _LoginPartial, which is displayed at the top of every page. This approach means the same partial view can be used by the rest of the application, presenting the user with a consistent user interface. Add a Razor View named _LoginPartial.cshtml to the Views/Shared folder with the content shown in Listing 4-8.

Listing 4-8. The Contents of the _LoginPartial.cshtml File in the Views/Shared Folder

```
<div>Placeholder Content</div>
```

I return to this listing later to make it more useful. For now, it is enough to know that you can't use the Identity UI package without creating this partial view.

Testing the Application with Identity

Restart ASP.NET Core and request https://localhost:44350 or https://localhost:44350/pages, which will present the content that is always accessible. Click the Level 2 button, and you will see the content shown in Figure 4-2.

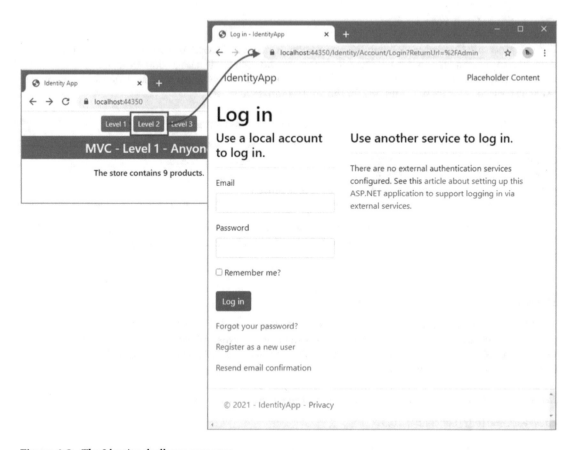

Figure 4-2. *The Identity challenge response*

Clicking the Level 2 button sends a request to ASP.NET Core that requires authorization. The request doesn't provide ASP.NET Core with any information about the user, which triggers the response shown in the figure, called the *challenge response*. The term *challenge* is used because the user is challenged to identify themselves in a modern-day equivalent of asking "who goes there?"

The challenge response is a redirection to the `Identity/Account/Login` URL. The Identity UI package contains a set of Razor Pages in a separate area, named `Identity`, which keeps them isolated from the rest of the application.

SIGNING IN OR LOGGING IN?

I have tried to be consistent throughout this book and use the term *sign in* to refer to the process of a user identifying themselves to an application. You will, however, see references to *logging in*, including in the default content provided by the Identity UI package, as shown in Figure 4-2.

Sign in and *log in* mean the same thing. Some studies show users find the terms *sign up* and *sign in* easier to understand, but I am skeptical and suspect there is little difference in practice. I have chosen *sign in* for consistency and because that is the term that has been adopted by the Identity API, even though it isn't used by the Identity UI package, which uses the Identity API behind the scenes.

It doesn't matter, and you should use whichever terms suit your projects and are likely to be understood by your target users.

Creating a New User Account

In a self-service application, it is the responsibility of the user to create an account. Identity supports using third-party services, such as Google and Facebook, to create accounts, which I demonstrate in Chapter 11. By default, no external services are configured, and users can only create local accounts, which means that users must authenticate themselves with a password, which is compared to data stored in the Identity database.

Click the Register link at the top right of the page, and you will be presented with a registration page. Use the form fields to enter the data values shown in Table 4-3. (Identity has a password policy that requires a mix of different types, which I describe in Chapter 5.)

Table 4-3. *Account Registration Details*

Field	Value
Email	alice@example.com
Password	MySecret1$
ConfirmPassword	MySecret1$

Click the Register button, and a new user account will be created. You will be signed into the application and redirected to the URL you requested that triggered the challenge response, as shown in Figure 4-3.

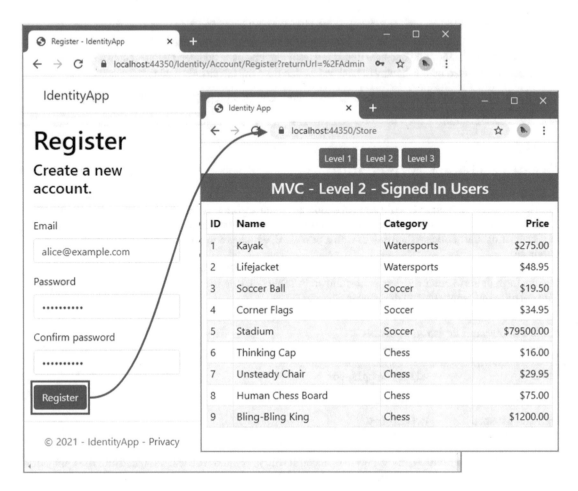

Figure 4-3. *Creating a new account*

Managing an Account

Request `https://localhost:44350/identity/account/manage`, and you will be presented with the account self-management features provided by the Identity UI package, as shown in Figure 4-4.

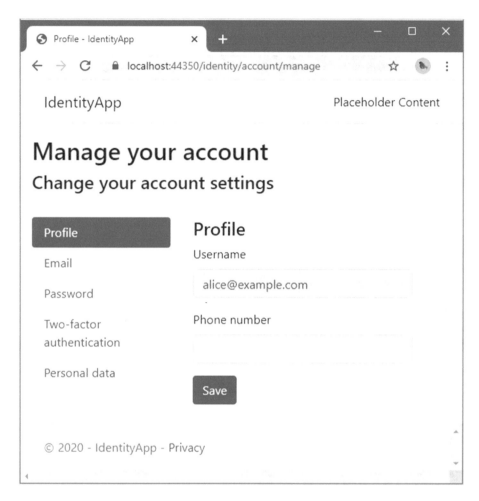

Figure 4-4. *The Identity UI account self-management features*

Additional work is required to build out the example project, as explained in the next section, so not all of the features work fully. But the basics are in place, and users can update their details, change their password, and increase the security of their account by adding a second factor. I revisit each of these features later in the chapter and explain how they work in detail.

Completing the Application Setup

The basic configuration is complete, but several features require additional work before they function correctly. In the sections that follow, I will go through the process of completing the setup process for the self-service UI.

Displaying Login Information

Earlier in the chapter, I created a partial view named _LoginPartial.cshtml, which the Identity UI requires. The purpose of this partial view is to present the user with links to Identity UI pages, making it easy to navigate to the sign-in page or the account self-management management features. Replace the placeholder content in the partial view with the content in Listing 4-9.

Listing 4-9. Replacing the Contents of the _LoginPartial.cshtml File in the Pages/Shared Folder

```
<nav class="nav">
    @if (User.Identity.IsAuthenticated) {
        <a asp-area="Identity" asp-page="/Account/Manage/Index"
            class="nav-link bg-secondary text-white">
                @User.Identity.Name
        </a>
        <a asp-area="Identity" asp-page="/Account/Logout"
            class="nav-link bg-secondary text-white">
                Logout
        </a>
    } else {
        <a asp-area="Identity" asp-page="/Account/Login"
                class="nav-link bg-secondary text-white">
            Login/Register
        </a>
    }
</nav>
```

The @if expression in the partial view determines whether there is a signed-in user by reading the User.Identity.IsAuthenticated property. ASP.NET Core represents users with the ClaimsPrincipal class and a ClaimsPrincipal object for the current user is available through the User property defined by the Controller and RazorPageBase classes, which means the same features are available for the MVC Framework and Razor Pages. (The nav elements and the classes to which the elements are assigned apply styles from the Bootstrap CSS framework and are not related to Identity.)

If there is a signed-in user, the partial view displays two anchor (a) elements, which will navigate to the Identity UI pages for managing an account or logging out. The anchor elements are configured using tag helpers and specify the Identity area that contains the Identity UI Razor Pages.

```
...
  <a asp-area="Identity" asp-page="/Account/Manage/Index"
        class="nav-link bg-secondary text-white">
     @User.Identity.Name
</a>
...
```

The asp-area and asp-page tags work together to create a link for the Index Razor Page in the Account/ Manage folder of the Identity UI package.

One drawback of Identity UI is you need to know the names of the pages that provide key features, such as signing in, signing out, and managing an account. I detail the URLs for each feature in the "Using the Identity UI Workflows" section, later in the chapter.

Restart ASP.NET Core, and request `https://localhost:44350/identity/account/login`. If you are still logged in from the previous section, you will see a link to manage the account and a logout button. If you have logged out—or your session has expired—you will see a prompt to sign in or register, as shown in Figure 4-5.

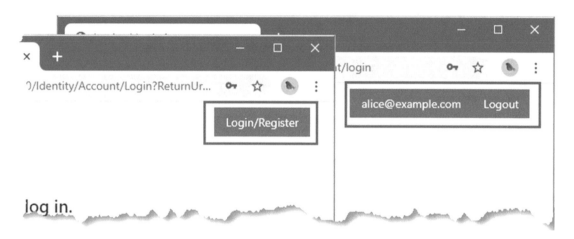

Figure 4-5. *Displaying login information*

Creating a Consistent Layout

The Identity UI package is a collection of Razor Pages set up in a separate ASP.NET Core area. This means a project can override individual files from the Identity UI package by creating Razor Pages with the same names. I show you how this can be used to adapt the Identity UI functionality in later examples, but the simplest use of this feature is to provide a consistent layout that will be used for both the application's content and the Identity UI package.

Add a Razor Layout named `_CustomIdentityLayout.cshtml` to the Pages/Shared folder with the contents shown in Listing 4-10.

Listing 4-10. The Contents of the _CustomIdentityLayout.cshtml File in the Pages/Shared Folder

```
<!DOCTYPE html>

<html>
<head>
    <meta name="viewport" content="width=device-width" />
    <title>Identity App</title>
    <link rel="stylesheet" href="/Identity/lib/bootstrap/dist/css/bootstrap.css" />
    <link rel="stylesheet" href="/Identity/css/site.css" />
    <script src="/Identity/lib/jquery/dist/jquery.js"></script>
    <script src="/Identity/lib/bootstrap/dist/js/bootstrap.bundle.js"></script>
    <script src="/Identity/js/site.js" asp-append-version="true"></script>
</head>
```

```
<body>
    <nav class="navbar navbar-dark bg-secondary">
        <a class="navbar-brand text-white">IdentityApp</a>
        <div class="text-white"><partial name="_LoginPartial" /></div>
    </nav>
    <div class="m-2">
        @RenderBody()
        @await RenderSectionAsync("Scripts", required: false)
    </div>
</body>
</html>
```

This layout contains includes content rendered by the _LoginPartial view, as part of a larger navigation bar.

■ **Tip**　I looked at the layout in the Identity UI package to determine the link and script elements required in Listing 4-10. You can see the contents of the package at https://github.com/dotnet/aspnetcore/tree/master/src/Identity/UI/src/Areas/Identity/Pages/V4.

To use the new view, create the Areas/Identity/Pages folder and add to it a Razor View Start file named _ViewStart.cshtml with the content shown in Listing 4-11. The location of this file overrides the Razor View Start file in the Identity UI package.

Listing 4-11. The Contents of the _ViewStart.cshtml File in the Areas/Identity/Pages Folder

```
@{
    Layout = "_CustomIdentityLayout";
}
```

The final step is to update the layout used by the rest of the application to display the same header, as shown in Listing 4-12.

Listing 4-12. Adding a Header in the _Layout.cshtml File in the Views/Shared Folder

```
<!DOCTYPE html>
<html>
<head>
    <meta name="viewport" content="width=device-width" />
    <title>Identity App</title>
    <link href="/lib/twitter-bootstrap/css/bootstrap.min.css" rel="stylesheet" />
</head>
<body>
    <nav class="navbar navbar-dark bg-secondary">
        <a class="navbar-brand text-white">IdentityApp</a>
        <div class="text-white"><partial name="_LoginPartial" /></div>
    </nav>
    <partial name="_NavigationPartial" />
    @RenderBody()
</body>
</html>
```

Restart ASP.NET Core, and request `https://localhost:44350`. You will see the new header at the top of the page, which is also shown if you click one of the links presented by the login partial view, as shown in Figure 4-6.

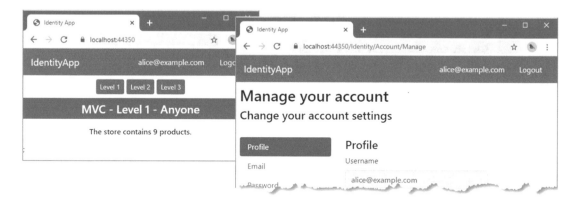

Figure 4-6. *Creating a consistent layout*

Configuring Confirmations

A confirmation is an email message that asks the user to click a link to confirm an action, such as creating an account or changing a password. The Identity support for confirmations is described in detail in Part 2, but the Identity UI package provides a simplified confirmation process that requires an implementation of the IEmailSender interface, which is defined in the `Microsoft.AspNetCore.Identity.UI.Services` namespace. The IEmailSender interface defines one method, which is described in Table 4-4.

Table 4-4. *The Method Defined by the IEmailSender Interface*

Name	Description
SendEmailAsync(emailAddress, subject, htmlMessage)	This method sends an email using the specified address, subject, and HTML message body.

The Identity UI package includes an implementation of the interface whose SendEmailAsync method does nothing. I am going to create a dummy email service in this chapter because the process of setting up and integrating with a real service is beyond the scope of the book. In Chapter 17, where I describe the confirmation process in depth, I provide suggestions for commercial messaging platforms, but, in this book, I demonstrate the Identity support for confirmations by writing messages to the .NET console. Create the IdentityApp/Services folder and add to it a class file named ConsoleEmailSender.cs with the code shown in Listing 4-13.

Listing 4-13. *The Contents of the ConsoleEmailSender.cs File in the Services Folder*

```
using Microsoft.AspNetCore.Identity.UI.Services;
using System.Threading.Tasks;
using System.Web;
```

```
namespace IdentityApp.Services {
    public class ConsoleEmailSender : IEmailSender {

        public Task SendEmailAsync(string emailAddress,
                string subject, string htmlMessage) {
            System.Console.WriteLine("---New Email----");
            System.Console.WriteLine($"To: {emailAddress}");
            System.Console.WriteLine($"Subject: {subject}");
            System.Console.WriteLine(HttpUtility.HtmlDecode(htmlMessage));
            System.Console.WriteLine("-------");
            return Task.CompletedTask;
        }
    }
}
```

In Listing 4-14, I have registered the ConsoleEmailSender class as the implementation of the
IEmailSender that will be used for dependency injection.

Listing 4-14. Registering the Email Sender Service in the Startup.cs File in the IdentityApp Folder

```
using Microsoft.AspNetCore.Builder;
using Microsoft.AspNetCore.Hosting;
using Microsoft.AspNetCore.Http;
using Microsoft.Extensions.DependencyInjection;
using Microsoft.Extensions.Hosting;
using Microsoft.Extensions.Configuration;
using Microsoft.EntityFrameworkCore;
using IdentityApp.Models;
using Microsoft.AspNetCore.Identity;
using Microsoft.AspNetCore.Identity.EntityFrameworkCore;
using Microsoft.AspNetCore.Identity.UI.Services;
using IdentityApp.Services;

namespace IdentityApp {

    public class Startup {

        public Startup(IConfiguration config) => Configuration = config;

        private IConfiguration Configuration { get; set; }

        public void ConfigureServices(IServiceCollection services) {
            services.AddControllersWithViews();
            services.AddRazorPages();
            services.AddDbContext<ProductDbContext>(opts => {
                opts.UseSqlServer(
                    Configuration["ConnectionStrings:AppDataConnection"]);
            });

            services.AddHttpsRedirection(opts => {
                opts.HttpsPort = 44350;
            });
```

```
        services.AddDbContext<IdentityDbContext>(opts => {
            opts.UseSqlServer(
                Configuration["ConnectionStrings:IdentityConnection"],
                opts => opts.MigrationsAssembly("IdentityApp")
            );
        });

        services.AddScoped<IEmailSender, ConsoleEmailSender>();

        services.AddDefaultIdentity<IdentityUser>()
            .AddEntityFrameworkStores<IdentityDbContext>();
    }

    public void Configure(IApplicationBuilder app, IWebHostEnvironment env) {
        if (env.IsDevelopment()) {
            app.UseDeveloperExceptionPage();
        }

        app.UseHttpsRedirection();
        app.UseStaticFiles();
        app.UseRouting();

        app.UseAuthentication();
        app.UseAuthorization();

        app.UseEndpoints(endpoints => {
            endpoints.MapDefaultControllerRoute();
            endpoints.MapRazorPages();
        });
    }
  }
}
```

Notice that I have registered the email service before the call to the AddDefaultIdentity method so that my custom service takes precedence over the placeholder implementation in the Identity UI package.

To test the confirmation process, restart ASP.NET Core. If you are not already signed to the application from earlier examples, request https://localhost:44350/identity/account/login and sign into the application as alice@example.com, with the password MySecret1$. Click the alice@example.com email address in the header to request the self-management features and click the Email link.

Enter alice@acme.com into the New Email field and click the Change Email button. Examine the console output from ASP.NET Core, and you will see the email message that the Identity UI has sent to the user, which will look like this:

```
---New Email----
To: alice@acme.com
Subject: Confirm your email
Please confirm your account by <a href='https://localhost:44350/Identity/
Account/ConfirmEmailChange?userId=cb55600e-9e03-43b8-a7b4-4e347c9d3943&email=alice@acme.com&
code=Q2ZESjhBMVB3bFFBQ3g'>clicking here</a>.
-------
```

The message contains a link for the user to click to confirm their new address. I have shortened the URL, but the query string contains a long security token used to validate the request securely. I explain how these tokens are created and validated in detail in Part 2, but you don't need to know how they work to use them.

Use your browser to navigate to the URL specified in the email message, and you will receive a response confirming the change of email address, as shown in Figure 4-7.

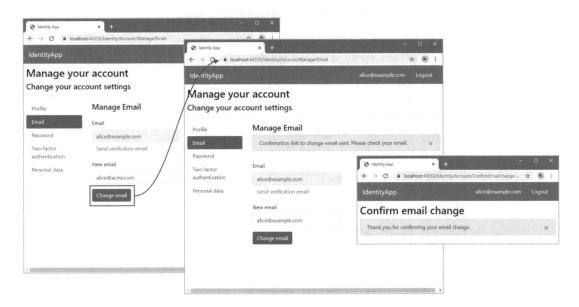

Figure 4-7. *Changing an email address*

Displaying QR Codes

Identity provides support for two-factor authentication, where the user has to present additional credentials to sign into the application. The Identity UI package supports a specific type of additional credential, which is a code generated by an authenticator application. An authenticator application is set up once and then generates authentication codes that can be validated by the application. To complete the setup for authenticators with Identity UI, a third-party JavaScript library named qrcodejs is required to generate QR codes that can be scanned by mobile devices to simplify the initial setup process.

Use a PowerShell command prompt and run the command shown in Listing 4-15 in the IdentityApp folder to install the package that Microsoft recommends for generating QR codes.

Listing 4-15. Adding a JavaScript Package

```
libman install qrcodejs@1.0.0 -d wwwroot/lib/qrcode
```

I explain how to customize the Identity UI package in Chapter 6, so for this chapter I am going to take a shortcut to display QR codes without needing to use the customization features. Add the script elements shown in Listing 4-16 to the _CustomIdentityLayout.cshtml file in the Views/Shared folder.

Listing 4-16. Adding Script Elements in the _CustomIdentityLayout.cshtml File in the Views/Shared Folder

```
<!DOCTYPE html>

<html>
<head>
    <meta name="viewport" content="width=device-width" />
    <title>Identity App</title>
    <link rel="stylesheet" href="/Identity/lib/bootstrap/dist/css/bootstrap.css" />
    <link rel="stylesheet" href="/Identity/css/site.css" />
    <script src="/Identity/lib/jquery/dist/jquery.js"></script>
    <script src="/Identity/lib/bootstrap/dist/js/bootstrap.bundle.js"></script>
    <script src="/Identity/js/site.js" asp-append-version="true"></script>
    <script type="text/javascript" src="/lib/qrcode/qrcode.min.js"></script>
</head>
<body>
    <nav class="navbar navbar-dark bg-secondary">
        <a class="navbar-brand text-white">IdentityApp</a>
        <div class="text-white"><partial name="_LoginPartial" /></div>
    </nav>
    <div class="m-2">
        @RenderBody()
        @await RenderSectionAsync("Scripts", required: false)
    </div>
    <script type="text/javascript">
        var element = document.getElementById("qrCode");
        if (element !== null) {
            new QRCode(element, {
                text: document.getElementById("qrCodeData").getAttribute("data-url"),
                width: 150, height: 150
            });
            element.previousElementSibling?.remove();
        }
    </script>
</body>
</html>
```

The first script element includes the JavaScript file from the qrcodejs package in the layout used for the Identity UI Razor Pages. The second script element looks for an HTML element with an ID of qrcode. If such an element exists, it is used to create a QR code image using the qrcodejs package, with the data used to generate the QR code obtained from the data-url attribute of an HTML element with an ID of qrCodeData. Finally, the element that occurs before the qrcode element is removed. This may seem like an oddly specific sequence of actions until you learn that the HTML produced by the Razor Page used to set up authenticators contains these elements:

```
...
<div class="alert alert-info">Learn how to
    <a href="https://go.microsoft.com/fwlink/?Linkid=852423">
        enable QR code generation
    </a>.
</div>
```

```
<div id="qrCode"></div>
<div id="qrCodeData" data-url="@Model.AuthenticatorUri"></div>
...
```

I explain how I knew the Razor Page contained these elements in Chapter 6, where I explain how to customize the Identity UI package.

Restart ASP.NET Core, ensure you are signed in using alice@acme.com with MySecret1$ as the password. Click the email address on the right of the header and click Two-Factor Authentication. Click the Add Authenticator App button, and you will be presented with instructions for configuring an authenticator, as shown in Figure 4-8, including a QR code that can be scanned by devices with a camera.

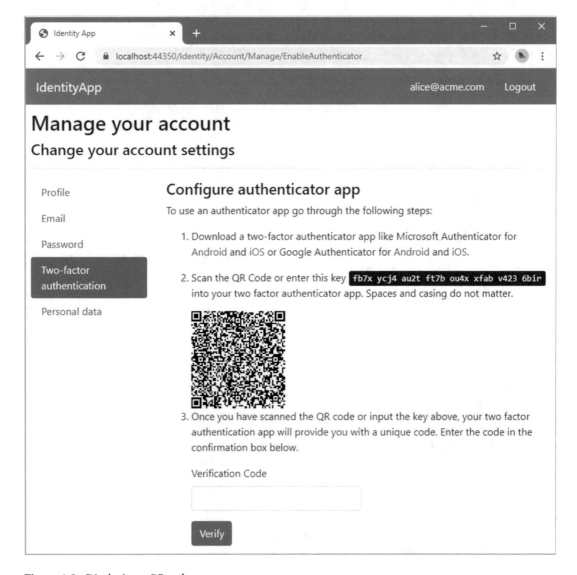

Figure 4-8. *Displaying a QR code*

Using the Identity UI Workflows

The basic configuration of the Identity UI package is complete. In Chapter 6, I explain how to customize the Identity UI package, but before doing that, I describe the features the Identity UI package provides by default and detail the Razor Pages that each relies on, which is useful when it comes to customization.

I use the term *workflow* in this book to refer to the processes that can be performed using Identity. Each workflow combines multiple features to support a task, such as creating a new user account or changing a password.

Registration

The Identity UI package supports self-registration, which means that anyone can create a new account and then use it to sign into the application. There is one additional feature enabled by the configuration changes in the previous section, which is that a confirmation email is sent when a new account is created. Restart ASP.NET Core, request `https://localhost:44350/Identity/Account/Register`, and use the values in Table 4-5 to create a new account.

Table 4-5. *Account Registration Details*

Field	Value
Email	bob@example.com
Password	MySecret1$
ConfirmPassword	MySecret1$

Click the Register button, and you will see an email like this one displayed in the console output:

```
---New Email----
To: bob@example.com
Subject: Confirm your email
Please confirm your account by <a href='https://localhost:44350/Identity/Account/
ConfirmEmail?userId=9e8c0aed-3990-4806-9d8d-19b9b543d7c2&code=Q2ZESjhBMVB9&returnUrl=%2FStore'>
clicking here</a>.
-------
```

Identity can be configured to require the user to click the confirmation link before signing into the application, as I explain in Chapter 9. Table 4-6 lists the Identity UI Razor Pages used in the registration process.

Table 4-6. *The Identity UI Pages for Registration*

Page	Description
Account/Register	This page prompts the user to create a new account.
Account/RegisterConfirmation	This is the page that handles the URLs sent in confirmation emails.
Account/ResendEmailConfirmation	This page allows the user to request another confirmation email.
Account/ConfirmEmail	This is the page that handles the URLs sent in the emails when the user requests a confirmation be reset.

Signing In and Out of the Application

One of the most important features provided by the Identity UI package is to sign users in and out of the application, establishing their identity with which authorization policies can be evaluated.

You didn't need to explicitly sign into the application earlier in the chapter because the Identity UI package signs in new accounts automatically. To explicitly sign in, request `https://localhost:44350/Identity/Account/Login` and sign in using `alice@acme.com` as the email address and `MySecret1$` as the password, as shown in Figure 4-9.

You can log out of the application by requesting `https://localhost:44350/Identity/Account/Logout` and clicking the link to log out, also shown in Figure 4-9.

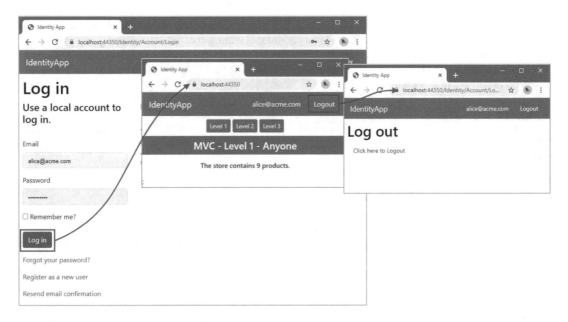

Figure 4-9. *The basic login sequence*

Table 4-7 lists the Identity UI Razor Pages for signing in and out of an application.

Table 4-7. *The Identity UI Pages for Signing In and Signing Out*

Page	Description
Account/Login	This page asks the user for their credentials or, if configured, to choose an external authentication service (which I describe in Chapter 11).
Account/ExternalLogin	This page is displayed after the user has signed into the application using an external authentication service, as described in Chapter 11.
Account/SetPassword	This page is used when an account has been created with an external authentication provider but the user wants to be able to sign in with a local password.
Account/Logout	This page allows the user to sign out of the application.
Account/Lockout	This page is displayed when the account is locked out following a series of failed sign-ins. I explain how to configure the lockout feature in Chapter 9.

Using Two-Factor Authentication

As noted earlier, Identity supports a range of two-factor authentication options, one of which—authenticators—is available through the Identity UI package. To explore this workflow, you will need an authenticator application. I use the Authy app (authy.com) for the examples in this book because there is a Windows client, but there are popular options from Google and Microsoft that run on mobile devices.

Request https://localhost:44350/Identity/Account/Login and sign in using alice@acme.com as the email address and MySecret1$ as the password. Navigate to the self-management feature by clicking the email address in the header, click Two-Factor Authentication, and then the Set Up Authenticator App button. You will be presented with a setup key and a QR code that can be used to set up an authenticator app. Scan the QR code or type in the setup key, and the authenticator will start generating codes every 30 seconds. Enter the current code into the Verification Code text field to complete the two-factor authentication setup, as shown in Figure 4-10.

Figure 4-10. *Setting up two-factor authentication*

Once you have set up an authenticator, you will be redirected to the TwoFactorAuthentication page, which presents buttons for different management tasks. The Reset Recovery Codes button is used to generate single-use codes that can be used to sign in if the authenticator app is unavailable (such as when a mobile device has been lost or stolen).

Click the button, and you will be presented with a set of recovery codes, as shown in Figure 4-11. It is not obvious, but each line shows two recovery codes, separated by a space. Each code can be used only once, after which it is invalidated. The Identity UI package doesn't allow the remaining codes to be inspected by the user, although this is possible when using Identity directly, as I demonstrate in Part 2. Make a note of the first code you generated, which will be different from the ones shown in the figure.

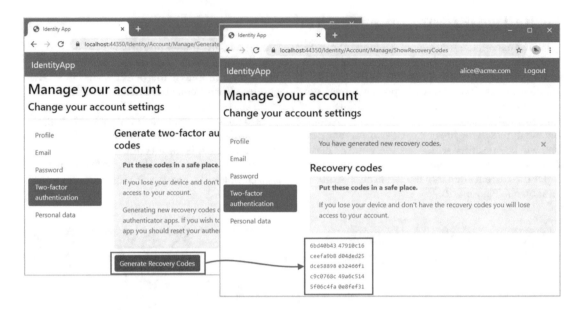

Figure 4-11. *Generating recovery codes*

Table 4-8 describes the Identity UI Razor Pages used to configure an authenticator and generate recovery codes.

Table 4-8. *The Identity UI Pages for Managing an Authenticator*

Page	Description
Account/Manage/TwoFactorAuthentication	This is the page displayed when the user clicks the Two-Factor Authentication link in the self-management feature. It links to other pages that handle individual authenticator tasks.
Account/Manage/EnableAuthenticator	This page displays the QR code and setup key required to configure an authenticator.
Account/Manage/ResetAuthenticator	This page allows the user to generate a new authenticator setup code, which will invalidate the existing authenticator and allow a new one to be set up, which is done by the EnableAuthenticator page.
Account/Manage/GenerateRecoveryCodes	This page generates a new set of recovery codes and then redirects to the ShowRecoveryCodes page to display them.
Account/Manage/ShowRecoveryCodes	This page displays a newly generated set of recovery codes.
Account/Manage/Disable2fa	This page allows the user to disable the authenticator and return to signing into the application with just a password.

Click Logout in the header and sign into the application again, using alice@acme.com as the email address and MySecret1$ as the password. Once the password has been checked, you will be prompted to enter the current code displayed by the authenticator app. Enter the code and click the Log In button, as shown in Figure 4-12. (You can also select the "Remember this machine" option, which creates a cookie that allows sign-in without needing the authenticator, as explained in Chapter 11.)

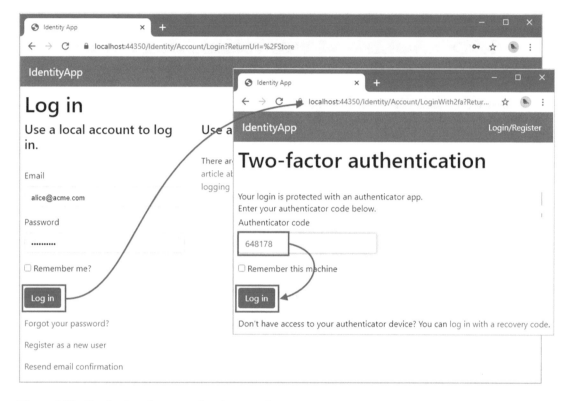

Figure 4-12. *Signing in using an authenticator code*

Repeat the process, but click the Log In with a Recovery Code link instead of entering the authenticator code. You will be prompted to enter one of the recovery codes you generated earlier, as shown in Figure 4-13.

Figure 4-13. *Signing in with a recovery code*

Table 4-9 describes the Razor Pages used when signing into the application using an authenticator or with a recovery code.

Table 4-9. *The Identity UI Pages for Two-Factor Authentication*

Name	Description
Account/LoginWith2fa	This page prompts the user to enter an authenticator code.
Account/LoginWithRecoveryCode	This page prompts the user to enter a recovery code.

Recovering a Password

If a user has forgotten their password, they can go through a recovery process to generate a new one. Password recovery works only if a user confirmed their email address following registration—the Identity UI package won't send the recovery password email if a user hasn't confirmed their email address. To see the recovery workflow, request https://localhost:44350/Identity/Account/Login and click the Forgotten Your Password? link. Enter bob@example.com into the text field and click the Reset Password button, as shown in Figure 4-14.

■ **Note** The bob@example.com account was created after email configurations were configured earlier in the chapter. If you want to test recovery for the alice@acme.com account, then click the Resend Email Confirmation link displayed by the Account/Login page and paste the link from the confirmation email into a browser window.

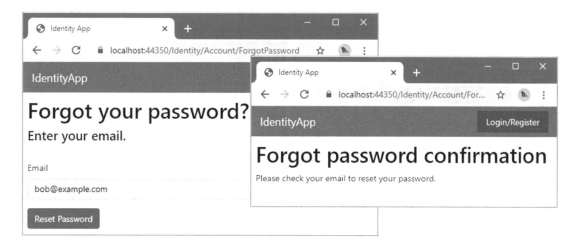

Figure 4-14. *Requesting password recovery*

Examine the console output from ASP.NET Core, and you will see a password recovery email, like this (although I have shortened the security code for brevity):

```
---New Email----
To: bob@example.com
Subject: Reset Password
Please reset your password by
<a href='https://localhost:44350/Identity/Account/ResetPassword?code=Q2ZESjhBM'>
    clicking here
</a>.
-------
```

Copy the link from the email into a browser window, and you will be prompted to reenter the email address and choose a new password, as shown in Figure 4-15. Enter bob@example.com into the email field and enter MySecret2$ as the new password.

Figure 4-15. *Choosing a new password*

When you click the Reset button, the password stored in the Identity user store will be updated, and you can sign into the application using the new password. Table 4-10 describes the Identity UI Razor Pages that support the password recovery process.

Table 4-10. *The Identity UI Pages for Password Recovery*

Name	Description
Account/ForgotPassword	This page prompts the user for their email address and sends the confirmation email.
Account/ForgotPasswordConfirmation	This page is displayed once the confirmation email has been sent.
Account/ResetPassword	This page is targeted by the URL sent in the confirmation email. It prompts the user for their email address and a new password.
Account/ResetPasswordConfirmation	This page is displayed once the password has been changed and provides the user with confirmation that the process has been completed.

Changing Account Details

The self-management features include support for changing the user's details, including the phone number, email address, and password. Request `https://localhost:44350/Identity/Account/Login` and sign in using `bob@example.com` as the email address and `MySecret2$` as the password. Click the email address in the header, and you will be presented with the default self-management page, which allows the user's phone number to be set or changed.

Click the Email link, and you will be presented with the page that allows a new email address to be specified. Click the Password link, and you will be prompted for the existing password and a new password. Figure 4-16 shows the phone number and password pages.

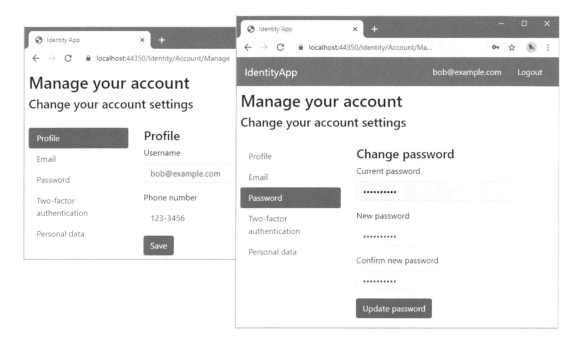

Figure 4-16. *The phone and password change pages*

Table 4-11 describes the Identity UI Razor Pages that support changing account details.

Table 4-11. *The Identity UI Pages for Changing Account Details*

Name	Description
`Account/Manage/Index`	This page allows the user to set a phone number
`Account/Manage/ChangePassword`	This page allows a new password to be chosen.
`Account/Manage/Email`	This page allows a new email address to be chosen and sends a confirmation email to the user.
`Account/ConfirmEmailChange`	This page is targeted by the URL in the confirmation email and updates the user store with the new email address.

Managing Personal Data

In some regions, users have a right to personal data and to request that their data is deleted. The Identity UI package provides a generic personal data feature that provides access to the data in the user store and allows the user to delete their account.

■ **Caution**   Don't assume that the features provided by the Identity UI package are sufficient to comply with any specific data access and retention regulation. You must ensure your application complies with the regulations in every region in which you have users.

Request `https://localhost:44350/Identity/Account/Login` and sign in using `bob@example.com` as the email address and `MySecret2$` as the password. Click the email address in the header to navigate to the self-management page and then click the Personal Data link. Clicking the Download button generates a JSON document containing the data from the user store. Clicking the Delete button prompts the user for their password before deleting their account, as shown in Figure 4-17.

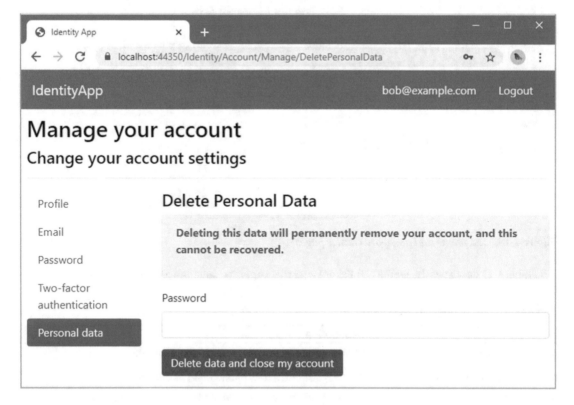

Figure 4-17. *Managing personal data*

Table 4-12 describes the Identity UI Razor Pages that support the personal data features.

Table 4-12. *The Identity UI Pages for Managing Personal Data*

Name	Description
Account/Manage/PersonalData	This is the page that presents the user with the buttons for downloading or deleting data.
Account/Manage/DownloadPersonalData	This is the page that generates the JDON document containing the user's data.
Account/Manage/DeletePersonalData	This is the page that prompts the user for their password and deletes the account.

Denying Access

The final workflow is used when the user is denied access to an action or Razor Page. This is known as the *forbidden response*, and it is the counterpart to the challenge response that prompts for user credentials. (The difference is that the challenge response is used when authorization is required but no user is signed in. The forbidden response is used when authorization is required but the signed-in user is not allowed access.)

One limitation of the Identity UI package is that it doesn't cater for users being assigned to roles, which is the authorization requirement I specified for the most restricted part of the example application. This means that no user account created using the Identity UI package will be granted access, which you can confirm by signing in and clicking the Level 3 button. The application sends the Identity UI package's forbidden response, as shown in Figure 4-18.

■ **Tip**   I explain how to use the Identity API to add users to roles in Chapter 10.

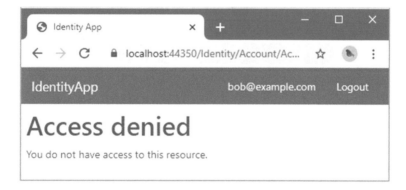

Figure 4-18. *The forbidden response*

For completeness, Table 4-13 describes the Identity UI Razor Page used for the forbidden response.

Table 4-13. *The Identity UI Page for the Forbidden Response*

Name	Description
Account/AccessDenied	This page displays a warning to the user.

Summary

In this chapter, I explained how to add Identity and the Identity UI package to a project. I showed you how to prepare the Identity database, I explained how to override individual files to create a consistent layout, and I described the default workflows that the Identity UI package provides. In the next chapter, I show you how to configure ASP.NET Core Identity.

CHAPTER 5

Configuring Identity

In this chapter, I explain how to configure Identity, including how to support third-party services from Google, Facebook, and Twitter. Some of these configuration options are part of the ASP.NET Core platform, but since they are so closely related to ASP.NET Core Identity, I have included them anyway. Table 5-1 puts the configuration options in context.

Table 5-1. *Putting Identity Configuration Options in Context*

Question	Answer
What are they?	The Identity configuration options are a set of properties whose values are used by the classes that implement the Identity API, which can be used directly or consumed through the Identity UI package.
Why are they useful?	These configuration options let you change the way that Identity behaves, which can make your application easier to use or allow you to meet the type of security standard that is commonly found in large corporations.
How are they used?	Identity is configured using the standard ASP.NET Core options pattern. The configuration for external authentication services is done using extension methods provided in the package that Microsoft provides for each provider.
Are there any pitfalls or limitations?	It is important to ensure that configuration changes do not cause problems for existing user accounts by enforcing a restriction that prevents the user from signing in.
Are there any alternatives?	The configuration options are used by the classes that provide the Identity API, which means the only way to avoid them is to create custom implementations, which I explain in Part 2.

© Adam Freeman 2021
A. Freeman, *Pro ASP.NET Core Identity*, https://doi.org/10.1007/978-1-4842-6858-2_5

Table 5-2 summarizes the chapter.

Table 5-2. *Chapter Summary*

Problem	Solution	Listing
Specify policies for usernames, email addresses, passwords, account confirmations, and lockouts	Set the properties defined by the `IdentityOptions` class.	1–4
Configure Facebook authentication	Install the package Microsoft provides for Facebook and use the `AddFacebook` method to configure the application ID and secret.	5–7
Configure Google authentication	Install the package Microsoft provides for Google and use the `AddGoogle` method to configure the application ID and secret.	8–10
Configure Twitter authentication	Install the package Microsoft provides for Twitter and use the `AddTwitter` method to configure the application ID and secret.	11–13

Preparing for This Chapter

This chapter uses the IdentityApp project from Chapter 4. No changes are required to prepare for this chapter. Open a PowerShell command prompt, navigate to the `IdentityApp` folder, and run the commands shown in Listing 5-1 to delete and then re-create the application and Identity databases.

■ **Tip**   You can download the example project for this chapter—and for all the other chapters in this book—from `https://github.com/Apress/pro-asp.net-core-identity`. See Chapter 1 for how to get help if you have problems running the examples.

Listing 5-1. Resetting the Databases

```
dotnet ef database drop --force --context ProductDbContext
dotnet ef database drop --force --context IdentityDbContext
dotnet ef database update --context ProductDbContext
dotnet ef database update --context IdentityDbContext
```

Use the PowerShell prompt to run the command shown in Listing 5-2 in the `IdentityApp` folder to start the application.

Listing 5-2. Running the Example Application

```
dotnet run
```

Open a web browser and request `https://localhost:44350`, which will show the output from the Home controller, and `https://localhost:44350/pages`, which will show the output from the Landing Razor Page, as shown in Figure 5-1.

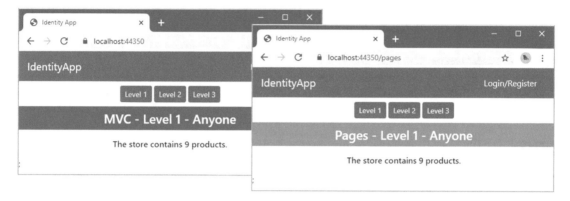

Figure 5-1. *Running the example application*

Click the Login/Register link, click Register as a New User, and create a new account using the values shown in Table 5-3.

Table 5-3. *Values for Creating a New Account*

Field	Value
Email	alice@example.com
Password	MySecret1$

Click the Register button; the new account will be created, and you will be signed into the application, as shown in Figure 5-2.

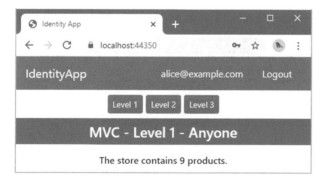

Figure 5-2. *Creating a new account*

91

Configuring Identity

Identity is configured using the standard ASP.NET Core options pattern, using the settings defined by the IdentityOptions class defined in the Microsoft.AspNetCore.Identity namespace. Table 5-4 describes the most useful properties defined by the IdentityOptions class, each of which leads to its own set of options, described in the sections that follow.

Table 5-4. *Useful IdentityOptions Properties*

Name	Description
User	This property is used to configure the username and email options for user accounts using the UserOptions class, as described in the "Configuring User Options" section.
Password	This property is used to define the password policy using the PasswordOptions class, as described in the "Configuring Password Options" section.
SignIn	This property is used to specify the confirmation requirements for accounts using the SignInOptions class, as described in the "Configuring Sign IN Confirmation Requirements" section.
Lockout	This property uses the LockoutOptions class to define the policy for locking out accounts after a number of failed attempts to sign in, as described in the "Configuring Lockout Options" section.

Configuring User Options

The IdentityOptions.User property is assigned a UserOptions object, which is used to configure the properties described in Table 5-5.

Table 5-5. *The UserOptions Properties*

Name	Description
AllowedUserNameCharacters	This property specifies the characters allowed in usernames. The default value is the set of upper and lowercase A–Z characters, the digits 0–9, and the symbols -._@+ (hyphen, period, underscore, at character, and plus symbol).
RequireUniqueEmail	This property determines whether email addresses must be unique. The default value is false.

The Identity UI package isn't affected by either property because it uses email addresses as usernames. One consequence of this decision is that email addresses are effectively unique because Identity requires usernames to be unique.

Request https://localhost:44350/Identity/Account/Register and try to create an account using the email address alice@example.com with the password MySecret1$. Even though the default value of the UserOptions.RequireUniqueEmail property is false, you will receive an error message, as shown in Figure 5-3, because the Identity UI package uses the email address as the username when creating an account.

Figure 5-3. *Creating an account with an existing email address*

Configuring Password Options

The IdentityOptions.Password property is assigned a PasswordOptions object, which is used to configure the properties described in Table 5-6.

Table 5-6. *The PasswordOptions Properties*

Name	Description
RequiredLength	This property specifies a minimum number of characters for passwords. The default value is 6.
RequiredUniqueChars	This property specifies the minimum number of unique characters that a password must contain. The default value is 1.
RequireNonAlphanumeric	This property specifies whether passwords must contain nonalphanumeric characters, such as punctuation characters. The default value is true.
RequireLowercase	This property specifies whether passwords must contain lowercase characters. The default value is true.
RequireUppercase	This property specifies whether passwords must contain uppercase characters. The default value is true.
RequireDigit	This property specifies whether passwords must contain number characters. The default value is true.

The IdentityUI package only uses email addresses to identify users, to which the UserOptions. AllowedUserNameCharacters does not apply. Listing 5-3 uses the other user property and changes the password properties to change the Identity configuration.

Listing 5-3. Configuring Password Settings in the Startup.cs File in the IdentityApp Folder

```
...
services.AddDefaultIdentity<IdentityUser>(opts => {
    opts.Password.RequiredLength = 8;
    opts.Password.RequireDigit = false;
    opts.Password.RequireLowercase = false;
    opts.Password.RequireUppercase = false;
    opts.Password.RequireNonAlphanumeric = false;
}).AddEntityFrameworkStores<IdentityDbContext>();
...
```

Restrictive password policies are falling out of use, with simple minimum length requirements combined with the use of two-factor authentication. The settings in Listing 5-3 increase the length requirement to eight characters and disable the other restrictions.

Restart ASP.NET Core, make sure you are signed in as alice@example.com with password MySecret1$, click the email address in the header, and click the Password link. Use MySecret1$ as the current password, which complies with the default password policy, and use secret as the new password, which does not meet the length requirement of the new policy. The new password will be rejected, as shown in Figure 5-4. Change the password again using mysecret as the new password, which does meet the length requirement specified in Listing 5-3. As shown in Figure 5-4, the longer password is accepted.

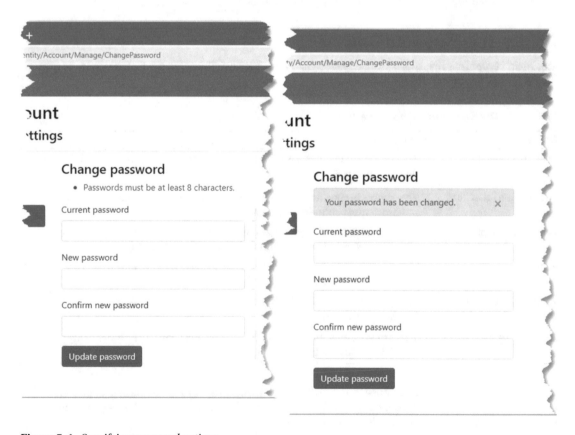

Figure 5-4. *Specifying password options*

Configuring Sign-in Confirmation Requirements

The IdentityOptions.SignIn property is assigned a SignInOptions object, which is used to configure the confirmation requirements for accounts using the properties described in Table 5-7.

Table 5-7. *The SignInOptions Properties*

Name	Description
RequireConfirmedEmail	When this property is set to true, only accounts with confirmed email addresses can sign in. The default value is false.
RequireConfirmedPhoneNumber	When this property is set to true, only accounts with confirmed phone numbers can sign in. The default value is false.
RequireConfirmedAccount	When set to true, only accounts that pass verification by the IUserConfirmation<T> interface can sign in. I describe this interface in detail in Chapter 9, and the default implementation checks that the email address has been confirmed. This default value for this property is false.

The Identity UI package doesn't support phone number confirmations, so the RequireConfirmedPhoneNumber property must not be set to true because it will lock all users out of the application.

It is a good idea to set the RequireConfirmedAccount property to true, as shown in Listing 5-4, if the application uses email for tasks such as password recovery.

Listing 5-4. Requiring Email Confirmations in the Startup.cs File in the IdentityApp Folder

```
...
services.AddDefaultIdentity<IdentityUser>(opts => {
    opts.Password.RequiredLength = 8;
    opts.Password.RequireDigit = false;
    opts.Password.RequireLowercase = false;
    opts.Password.RequireUppercase = false;
    opts.Password.RequireNonAlphanumeric = false;
    opts.SignIn.RequireConfirmedAccount = true;

}).AddEntityFrameworkStores<IdentityDbContext>();
...
```

The Identity UI features that send emails to users, such as password recovery, will silently fail if the user hasn't confirmed their email address. Enabling the RequireConfirmedAccount setting displays the Account/RegisterConfirmation page at the end of the sign-in process, which instructs the user to check for the confirmation email. To see this behavior, restart ASP.NET Core and navigate to https://localhost:44350/Identity/Account/Register. Create a new account using the values shown in Table 5-8.

■ **Tip**   I show you how to provide the user with more helpful feedback by customizing the Identity UI package in Chapter 6.

95

Table 5-8. *Values for Creating a New Account*

Field	Value
Email	bob@example.com
Password	mysecret

Click the Register button, and you will be presented with the confirmation page, as shown in Figure 5-5.

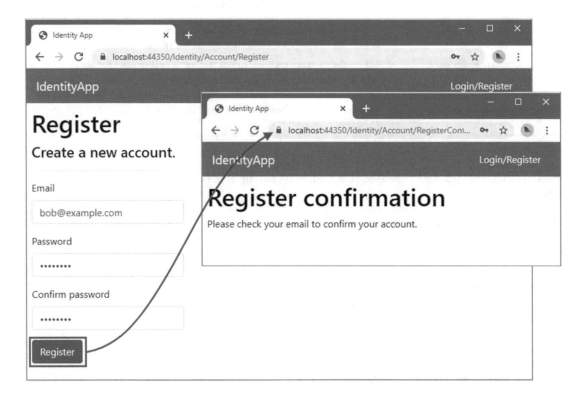

Figure 5-5. *The Identity UI confirmation behavior*

If you attempt to sign in using the new account without using the confirmation link, then you will be presented with a generic Invalid Login Attempt error.

Click the Resend Email Confirmation link displayed by the Login page to generate a new confirmation email, and you will see the confirmation link displayed in the console output from ASP.NET Core. Copy the URL into a browser, and you will be able to sign into the application, as shown in Figure 5-6.

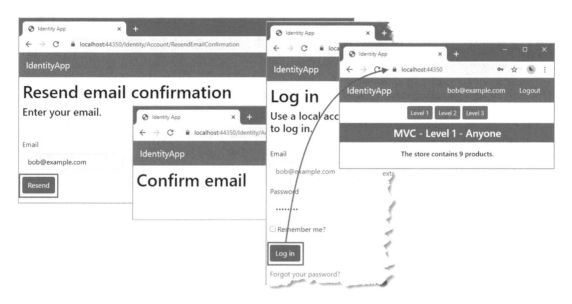

Figure 5-6. *Confirming an email address and signing into the application*

Configuring Lockout Options

The IdentityOptions.Lockout property is assigned a LockoutOptions object, which is used to configure lockouts that prevent sign-ins, even if the correct password is used, after a number of failed attempts. Table 5-9 describes the properties defined by the LockoutOptions class. The Identity UI package signs users into the application in such a way that the lockout feature is not triggered. I demonstrate how to change this behavior in Chapter 9.

Table 5-9. *The LockoutOptions Properties*

Name	Description
MaxFailedAccessAttempts	This property specifies the number of failed attempts allowed before an account is locked out. The default value is 5.
DefaultLockoutTimeSpan	This property specifies the duration for lockouts. The default value is 5 minutes.
AllowedForNewUsers	This property determines whether the lockout feature is enabled for new accounts. The default value is true.

Configuring External Authentication

External authentication delegate the process of authenticating users to a third-party service. In a corporate environment, the third-party service can be a company-wide user directory, which allows multiple applications to authenticate users from the same set of accounts.

For most Internet-facing applications, the external services are provided by the big technology/social media companies, such as Google, Facebook, and Twitter, taking advantage of the huge userbases these companies enjoy and the wider range of two-factor authentication schemes these services support and that are not available in Identity.

External authentication generally uses the OAuth protocol, which I describe in detail in Chapter 22. A registration process is required for each external service, during which the application is described and the level of access to user data, known as the *scope*, is declared.

During registration, you will usually have to specify a *redirection URL*. During the authentication process, the external service will send the user's browser an HTTP redirection to this URL, which triggers a request to ASP.NET Core, providing the application with data required to complete the sign-in. During development, this URL will be to localhost, such as https://localhost:44350/signin-google, for example, so that you can easily test external authentication on your development machine.

■ **Note** When you are ready to deploy your application, you will need to update your application's registration with each external service to use a publicly accessible URL that contains a hostname that appears in the DNS.

The registration process produces two data items: the client ID and the client secret. The client ID identifies the application to the external authentication service and can be shared publicly. The client secret is secret, as the name suggests, and should be protected.

GETTING HELP WITH EXTERNAL AUTHENTICATION

The setup procedures I describe in the following sections are correct at the time of writing but may change by the time you read this chapter. Microsoft publishes instructions for the most popular external authentication services, which you can find at https://docs.microsoft.com/en-us/aspnet/core/security/authentication/social. Each authentication service also provides documentation, for which there are links in the sections that follow.

Please do not email me to ask for help setting up external authentication. I try to help readers with most problems, but figuring out external authentication issues would require signing into a reader's Google/Facebook/Twitter accounts, which is something that I will not do.

Configuring Facebook Authentication

To register the application with Facebook, go to https://developers.facebook.com/apps and sign in with your Facebook account. Click the Create App button, select Build Connected Experiences from the list, and click the Continue button. Enter IdentityApp into the App Display Name field and click the Create App button. This sequence is shown in Figure 5-7.

Figure 5-7. *Creating a new application*

Once you have created a Facebook application, you will be returned to the developer dashboard and presented with a list of optional products to use. Locate Facebook Login and click the Setup button. You will see a set of quick-start options, but these can be ignored because the important configuration options are shown under the Facebook Login ➤ Settings section that appears on the left side of the dashboard display, as shown in Figure 5-8.

Figure 5-8. *The Facebook Login settings*

You don't need to specify a redirection URL because Facebook allows redirection to `localhost` URLs during development. When you are ready to deploy the application, you will need to return to this page and finalize your configuration, including providing the public-facing redirection URL. Details of the configuration options are included in the Facebook Login documentation, which can be found at `https://developers.facebook.com/docs/facebook-login`.

Navigate to the Basic section in the Settings area to get the App ID and App Secret, as shown in Figure 5-9, which are the terms that Facebook uses for the client ID and secret. (The App Secret is hidden until you click the Show button.) Make a note of these values, which will be required to configure the application in the next section.

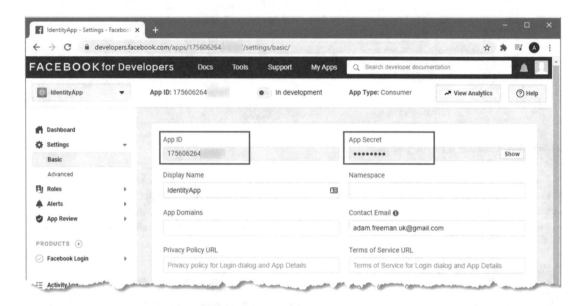

Figure 5-9. *The application credentials for external authentication*

Configuring ASP.NET Core for Facebook Authentication

Run the commands shown in Listing 5-5 to store the App ID and secret using the .NET secrets feature, which ensures that these values won't be included when the source code is committed into a repository.

Listing 5-5. Storing the Facebook ID and Secret

```
dotnet user-secrets init
dotnet user-secrets set "Facebook:AppId" "<app-id>"

dotnet user-secrets set "Facebook:AppSecret" "<app-secret>"
```

The first command initializes the secret store. The other commands store the data values so they can be accessed in the application using the ASP.NET Core configuration system. Next, run the command shown in Listing 5-6 in the IdentityApp folder to add the package containing Facebook authentication to the project.

Listing 5-6. Adding the Facebook Package

```
dotnet add package Microsoft.AspNetCore.Authentication.Facebook --version 5.0.0
```

To configure the application, add the statements shown in Listing 5-7 to the Startup class.

Listing 5-7. Configuring Facebook Authentication in the Startup.cs File in the IdentityApp Folder

```
...
public void ConfigureServices(IServiceCollection services) {
    services.AddControllersWithViews();
    services.AddRazorPages();
    services.AddDbContext<ProductDbContext>(opts => {
        opts.UseSqlServer(
            Configuration["ConnectionStrings:AppDataConnection"]);
    });

    services.AddHttpsRedirection(opts => {
        opts.HttpsPort = 44350;
    });

    services.AddDbContext<IdentityDbContext>(opts => {
        opts.UseSqlServer(
            Configuration["ConnectionStrings:IdentityConnection"],
            opts => opts.MigrationsAssembly("IdentityApp")
        );
    });

    services.AddScoped<IEmailSender, ConsoleEmailSender>();

    services.AddDefaultIdentity<IdentityUser>(opts => {
        opts.Password.RequiredLength = 8;
        opts.Password.RequireDigit = false;
        opts.Password.RequireLowercase = false;
        opts.Password.RequireUppercase = false;
        opts.Password.RequireNonAlphanumeric = false;

        opts.SignIn.RequireConfirmedEmail = true;
    })
    .AddEntityFrameworkStores<IdentityDbContext>();

    services.AddAuthentication()
        .AddFacebook(opts => {
            opts.AppId = Configuration["Facebook:AppId"];
            opts.AppSecret = Configuration["Facebook:AppSecret"];
        });
}
...
```

The AddAuthentication method sets up the ASP.NET Core authentication features, which I describe in detail in Part 2. This method is called automatically by the AddDefaultIdentity method, which is why it has not been needed until now. The AddFacebook method sets up the Facebook authentication support provided by Microsoft, which is configured using the options pattern with the FacebookOptions class. Table 5-10 describes the most important configuration properties.

Table 5-10. *Selected FacebookOptions Properties*

Name	Description
AppId	This property is used to configure the App ID, which is the term Facebook uses for the client ID. In the example, I read the value from the secret created in Listing 5-5.
AppSecret	This property is used to configure the App Secret, which is the term Facebook uses for the client secret. In the example, I read the value from the secret created in Listing 5-5.
Fields	This property specifies the data values that are requested from Facebook during authentication. The default values are name, email, first_name, and last_name. See https://developers.facebook.com/docs/graph-api/reference/user for a full list of fields, but bear in mind that some fields require applications to go through an additional validation process.

Restart ASP.NET Core and make sure you are signed out of the application by clicking the Logout link in the header and then again in the page that is displayed. Next, click the Level 2 button to trigger a challenge response, and you will see that the Identity UI package has automatically detected the Facebook configuration. Click the Facebook button, and you will be redirected to the Facebook authentication service. Once authenticated, you will be asked to approve the example application's accessing your data and then redirected to the application to complete the registration process, as shown in Figure 5-10.

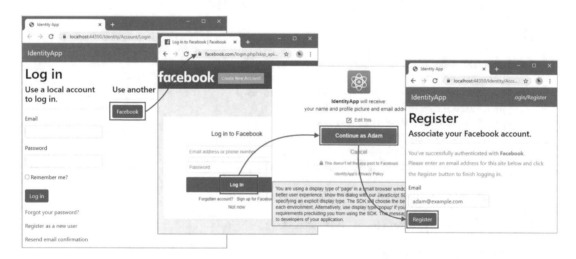

Figure 5-10. *Signing in with Facebook*

The default external authentication registration workflow provided by the Identity UI package allows the user to create an account with an email address that is different from the one associated with the Facebook account. This means that a confirmation message has to be sent to ensure the user has control of the specified email address. If you examine the ASP.NET Core console output, you will see a message similar to this one (I have shortened the confirmation code for brevity):

```
---New Email----
To: adam@example.com
Subject: Confirm your email
Please confirm your account by <a href='https://localhost:44350/Identity/Account/
ConfirmEmail?userId=8917d84d'>
```

```
    clicking here
</a>.
-------
```

As a consequence, the user must click the link in the email before they can sign in again. I show you how to customize the Identity UI package to change this behavior in Chapter 6.

Configuring Google Authentication

To register the example application, navigate to `https://console.developers.google.com` and sign in with a Google account. Click the OAuth Consent Screen option and select External for User Type, which will allow any Google account to authenticate for your application.

■ **Tip**   You may see a message telling you that no APIs are available to use yet. This is not important when you only need to authenticate users.

Click Create, and you will be presented with a form. Enter IdentityApp into the App Name field and enter your email address in the User Support Email and Developer Contact Information sections of the form. The rest of the form can be left empty for the example application.

Click Save and Continue, and you will be presented with the scope selection screen, which is used to specify the scopes that your application requires.

Click the Add or Remove Scopes button, and you be presented with the list of scopes that your application can request. Check three scopes: `openid`, `auth/userinfo.email`, and `auth/userinfo.profile`. Click the Update button to save your selection.

Click Save and Continue to return to the OAuth consent screen and then click Back to Dashboard. Figure 5-11 shows the sequence for configuring the consent screen.

Figure 5-11. *Configuring the Google OAuth consent screen*

Click the Publish App button and click Confirm, as shown in Figure 5-12, which will allow any Google account to be authenticated.

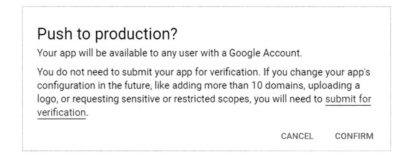

Figure 5-12. *Publishing the application*

Click the Credentials link, click the Create Credentials button at the top of the page, and select OAuth Client ID from the list of options.

Select Web Application from the Application Type list and enter IdentityApp in the Name field. Click Add URI in the Authorized Redirect URIs section and enter `https://localhost:44350/signin-google` into the text field. Click the Create button, and you will be presented with the client ID and client secret for your application, as shown in Figure 5-13 (although I have blurred the details, since these are for my account). Make a note of the ID and secret, which will be used to configure the application.

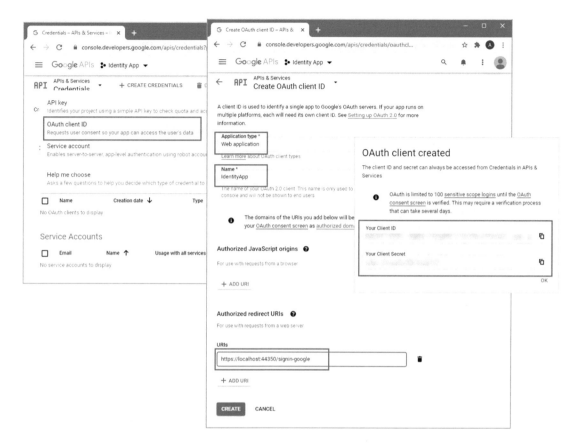

Figure 5-13. *Configuring application credentials*

Configuring ASP.NET Core for Google Authentication

Run the commands shown in Listing 5-8 to store the client ID and secret using the .NET secrets feature, which ensures that these values won't be included when the source code is committed into a repository.

Listing 5-8. Storing the Google Client ID and Secret

```
dotnet user-secrets init
dotnet user-secrets set "Google:ClientId" "<client-id>"

dotnet user-secrets set "Google:ClientSecret" "<client-secret>"
```

The first command initializes the secret store. The other commands store the data values so they can be accessed in the application using the ASP.NET Core configuration system. Next, run the command shown in Listing 5-9 in the IdentityApp folder to add the package containing Google authentication to the project.

Listing 5-9. Adding the Google Package

```
dotnet add package Microsoft.AspNetCore.Authentication.Google --version 5.0.0
```

To configure the application, add the statements shown in Listing 5-10 to the Startup class.

Listing 5-10. Configuring Google Authentication in the Startup.cs File in the IdentityApp Folder

```
...
services.AddAuthentication()
    .AddFacebook(opts => {
        opts.AppId = Configuration["Facebook:AppId"];
        opts.AppSecret = Configuration["Facebook:AppSecret"];
    })
    .AddGoogle(opts => {
        opts.ClientId = Configuration["Google:ClientId"];
        opts.ClientSecret = Configuration["Google:ClientSecret"];
    });
...
```

The AddGoogle method sets up the Google authentication handler and is configured using the options pattern with the GoogleOptions class. Table 5-11 describes the most important GoogleOptions properties.

Table 5-11. *Selected GoogleOptions Properties*

Name	Description
ClientId	This property is used to specify the client ID for the application. In the example, I use the value stored in Listing 5-8.
ClientSecret	This property is used to specify the application's client secret. In the listing, I use the value stored in Listing 5-8.
Scope	This property is used to set the scopes that are requested from the authentication service. The default value requests the scopes specified during the setup process, but additional scopes are available. See https://developers.google.com/identity/protocols/oauth2/web-server.

Restart ASP.NET Core and make sure you are signed out of the application by clicking the Logout link in the header and again in the page that is displayed. Next, click the Level 2 button to trigger a challenge response, and you will see that the Identity UI package has automatically detected the Google configuration. Click the Google button, and you will be redirected to the Google authentication service. Once authenticated, you will be redirected to the application to complete the registration process, as shown in Figure 5-14.

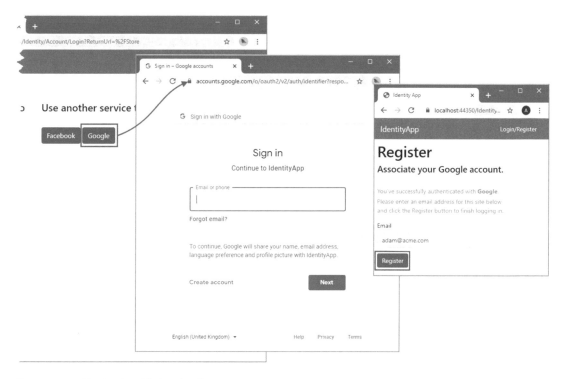

Figure 5-14. *Signing in with Facebook*

As with the previous example, users can enter a different email address from the one associated with the Google account, which means the user has to follow the link in a confirmation email before they can sign into the application again. If you examine the ASP.NET Core console output, you will see a message similar to this one (I have shortened the confirmation code for brevity):

```
---New Email----
To: adam@acme.com
Subject: Confirm your email
Please confirm your account by <a href='https://localhost:44350/Identity/Account/
ConfirmEmail?userId=65e6b14e'>
    clicking here
</a>.
-------
```

Once the email address has been confirmed, the user can sign in again using the Google account.

Configuring Twitter Authentication

To register the application with Twitter, go to `https://developer.twitter.com/en/portal/dashboard` and sign in with a Twitter account. Click the Create Project button, set the project name to Identity Project, and click the Next button. Select a description from the list and click the Next button. Enter a name and click the Complete button to finish the first part of the setup, as shown in Figure 5-15. The name must be unique, so it can take a while to find an available name, but it doesn't matter what it is for this example.

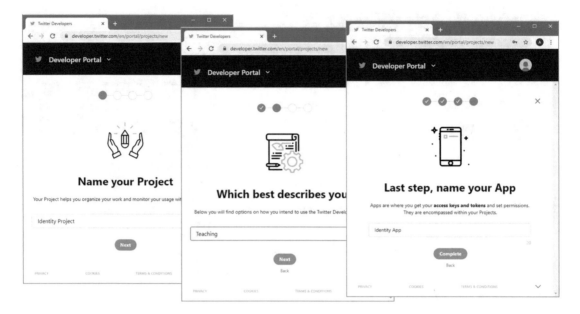

Figure 5-15. *Creating a Twitter application configuration*

When you create the Twitter app, you will be presented with a set of keys, as shown in Figure 5-16. It is important to make a note of the API key and the API key secret (which are how Twitter refers to the client ID and the client secret) because you won't be able to see them again.

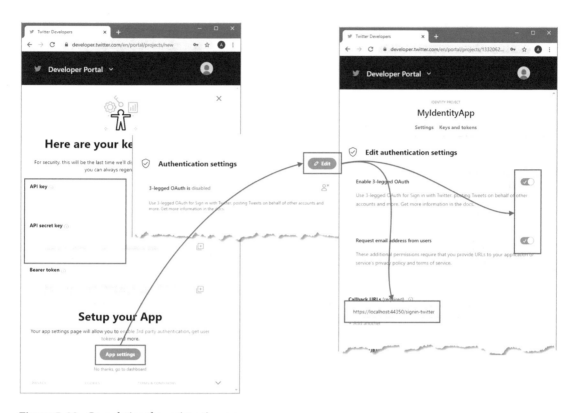

Figure 5-16. *Completing the registration process*

Click the App Settings button and click the Edit button for the Authentication Settings category. Select the Enable 3-Legged OAuth and Request Email Address from Users options and enter `https:// localhost:44350/signin-twitter` into the Callback URLs field. You will also have to enter URLs for the website, terms of service, and privacy policy fields. It doesn't matter what URLs you use for this chapter, but you will require URLs with suitable content when you register a real project.

Configuring ASP.NET Core for Twitter Authentication

Run the commands shown in Listing 5-11 to store the client ID and secret using the .NET secrets feature, which ensures that these values won't be included when the source code is committed into a repository.

Listing 5-11. Storing the Twitter Client ID and Secret

```
dotnet user-secrets init
dotnet user-secrets set "Twitter:ApiKey" "<client-id>"

dotnet user-secrets set "Twitter:ApiSecret" "<client-secret>"
```

The first command initializes the secret store. The other commands store the data values so they can be accessed in the application using the ASP.NET Core configuration system. Next, run the command shown in Listing 5-12 in the `IdentityApp` folder to add the package containing Twitter authentication to the project.

Listing 5-12. Adding the Twitter Package

```
dotnet add package Microsoft.AspNetCore.Authentication.Twitter --version 5.0.0
```

To configure the application, add the statements shown in Listing 5-13 to the Startup class.

Listing 5-13. Configuring Twitter Authentication in the Startup.cs File in the IdentityApp Folder

```
...
services.AddAuthentication()
    .AddFacebook(opts => {
        opts.AppId = Configuration["Facebook:AppId"];
        opts.AppSecret = Configuration["Facebook:AppSecret"];
    })
    .AddGoogle(opts => {
        opts.ClientId = Configuration["Google:ClientId"];
        opts.ClientSecret = Configuration["Google:ClientSecret"];
    })
    .AddTwitter(opts => {
        opts.ConsumerKey = Configuration["Twitter:ApiKey"];
        opts.ConsumerSecret = Configuration["Twitter:ApiSecret"];
    });
...
```

The Twitter method sets up the Twitter authentication handler and is configured using the options pattern with the TwitterOptions class. Table 5-12 describes the most important TwitterOptions properties.

Table 5-12. *Selected TwitterOptions Properties*

Name	Description
ConsumerKey	This property is used to specify the client ID for the application. In the example, I use the value stored in Listing 5-11.
ConsumerSecret	This property is used to specify the application's client secret. In the listing, I use the value stored in Listing 5-11.
RetrieveUserDetails	When set to true, this property requests user data, including the email address, as part of the authentication process. This property isn't required when using the Identity UI package, which allows users to enter an email address.

Restart ASP.NET Core and make sure you are signed out of the application by clicking the Logout link in the header and again in the page that is displayed. Next, click the Level 2 button to trigger a challenge response, and you will see that the Identity UI package has automatically detected the Twitter configuration. Click the Twitter button, and you will be redirected to the Twitter authentication service. Once authenticated, you will be redirected to the application to complete the registration process, as shown in Figure 5-17.

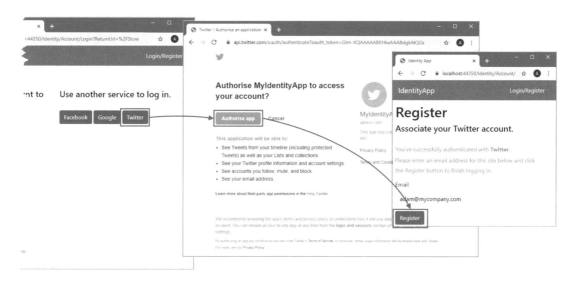

Figure 5-17. *Signing in with Twitter*

As with the previous example, users can enter a different email address from the one associated with the Twitter account, which means the user has to follow the link in a confirmation email before they sign into the application again. If you examine the ASP.NET Core console output, you will see a message similar to this one (I have shortened the confirmation code for brevity):

```
---New Email----
To: adam@mycompany.com
Subject: Confirm your email
Please confirm your account by <a href='https://localhost:44350/Identity/Account/
ConfirmEmail?userId=fa1b86c2'>
    clicking here
</a>.
-------
```

Once the email address has been confirmed, the user can sign in again using the Twitter account.

Summary

In this chapter, I described the Identity configuration options, which determine the validation requirements for accounts, passwords, and control-related features such as lockouts. I also described the process for configuring ASP.NET Core and the Identity UI package to support external authentication services from Google, Facebook, and Twitter. In the next chapter, I show you how to adapt the workflows the Identity UI package provides.

CHAPTER 6

■ ■ ■

Adapting Identity UI

The Identity UI package has been designed for self-service applications that support authenticators for two-factor authentication and external authentication with third-party services. There is some flexibility within that design so that individual features can be altered or disabled, and new features can be introduced. In this chapter, I explain the process for adapting the Identity UI package, showing the different ways it can be customized.

There are limits to the extent of the changes, however, and in Chapters 7 to 12, I show you how to work directly with the API that Identity provides to create completely custom workflows that replace the Identity UI package. Table 6-1 puts adapting Identity UI in context.

Table 6-1. *Putting Identity UI Adaptations in Context*

Question	Answer
What are they?	Adaptations allow the files in the Identity UI package to be added to the project so they can be modified, allowing features to be created, customized, or disabled.
Why are they useful?	If your project almost fits into the general model expected by the Identity UI package, adaptations can customize Identity UI to make it fit your needs exactly.
How are they used?	Razor Pages, views, and other files are added to the project using a process known as *scaffolding*. Scaffolded files are given precedence over those in the Identity UI package, which means that changes made to the scaffolded files become part of the content presented to the user.
Are there any pitfalls or limitations?	Although you can customize individual features, you cannot adjust the underlying approach taken by the Identity UI package, which means there are limits to extent of the changes you can make. Some scaffolding operations overwrite files even if they have been changed, requiring an awkward shuffling of files to protected customizations.
Are there any alternatives?	Identity provides an API that can be used to create custom workflows, as described in Chapters 7 to 12.

© Adam Freeman 2021
A. Freeman, *Pro ASP.NET Core Identity*, https://doi.org/10.1007/978-1-4842-6858-2_6

Table 6-2 summarizes the chapter.

Table 6-2. *Chapter Summary*

Problem	Solution	Listing
Scaffold an Identity UI file	Install the code generator global tool package, add the Identity UI scaffolding package to the project, and use the dotnet `aspnet-codegenerator` command to scaffold the files you require.	1–13
Scaffold the account management features or appearance	Use the scaffolding command to select files whose name starts with `Account.Manage`, which corresponds to the `Areas/Identity/Pages/Account/Manage` folder.	14–16, 20, 21
Add a new feature the Identity UI	Scaffold the navigation class and Razor Page and add links to a Razor Page in which you implement the new feature.	17–19
Scaffold new files after changing shared views or classes	Move the modified files into a safe location and scaffold additional files without causing the project to be compiled.	22–26
Disable an Identity UI feature	Scaffold the file that defines the feature and replace the handler methods in the page model class. Scaffold the files that contain navigation links to the disabled feature and remove them.	27–29

Preparing for This Chapter

This chapter uses the IdentityApp project from Chapter 5. Open a new PowerShell command prompt and run the commands shown in Listing 6-1 to reset the application and Identity databases.

■ **Tip** You can download the example project for this chapter—and for all the other chapters in this book—from `https://github.com/Apress/pro-asp.net-core-identity`. See Chapter 1 for how to get help if you have problems running the examples.

Listing 6-1. Resetting the Databases

```
dotnet ef database drop --force --context ProductDbContext
dotnet ef database drop --force --context IdentityDbContext
dotnet ef database update --context ProductDbContext
dotnet ef database update --context IdentityDbContext
```

Use the PowerShell prompt to run the command shown in Listing 6-2 in the `IdentityApp` folder to start the application.

Listing 6-2. Running the Example Application

```
dotnet run
```

Open a web browser and request `https://localhost:44350`, which will show the output from the Home controller, and `https://localhost:44350/pages`, which will show the output from the Landing Razor Page, as shown in Figure 6-1.

Figure 6-1. *Running the example application*

Click the Login/Register link, click Register as a New User, and create a user account with the details shown in Table 6-3.

Table 6-3. *Account Details*

Field	Value
Email	alice@example.com
Password	mysecret

Click the Register button to create the account. Check the ASP.NET Core console output, and you will see a confirmation email, similar to this one:

```
---New Email----
To: alice@example.com
Subject: Confirm your email
Please confirm your account by <a href='https://localhost:44350
/Identity/Account/ConfirmEmail?userId=395a955f &returnUrl=%2F'>
    clicking here
</a>.
-------
```

Copy the URL into a browser to confirm the account so that you can sign in again, as shown in Figure 6-2.

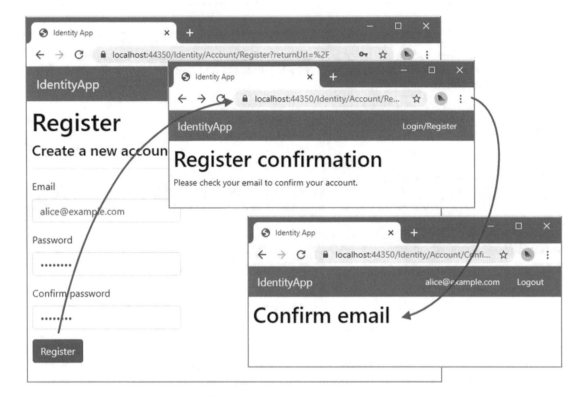

Figure 6-2. *Creating and confirming an account*

Understanding Identity UI Scaffolding

The Identity UI package uses the ASP.NET Core areas feature, which allows Razor Pages defined in the project to override those in the UI package, just as long as they are in a specific folder, which is Areas/ Identity/Pages. This folder already exists in the project, and it contains the Razor View Start file I created to enforce a consistent layout.

You can simply create Razor Pages whose names match those described in the workflows in Chapter 4, and they will override the pages in the Identity UI package, but this means you are responsible for re-creating the HTML content and C# code that provides the features of the original page. To make it easy to build on the existing features, the Identity UI package will create replacement Razor Pages in your project, so you can modify features rather than re-creating them completely. This process is known as *scaffolding*.

Preparing for Identity UI Scaffolding

The scaffolding process relies on a global .NET tool package. Use a PowerShell command prompt to run the commands shown in Listing 6-3 to remove any existing version of the package and install the version required for this chapter. (You may receive an error from the first command if you have not previously installed this package.)

Listing 6-3. Installing the Scaffolding Tool Package

```
dotnet tool uninstall --global dotnet-aspnet-codegenerator
dotnet tool install --global dotnet-aspnet-codegenerator --version 5.0.0
```

An additional package must be added to the project to provide the global tool with the templates it needs to create new items. Use the PowerShell prompt to run the command shown in Listing 6-4 in the IdentityApp folder.

Listing 6-4. Adding the Scaffolding Package

```
dotnet add package Microsoft.VisualStudio.Web.CodeGeneration.Design --version 5.0.0
```

Listing the Identity UI Pages for Scaffolding

The command-line scaffolding tool allows individual pages to be scaffolded. You can see a complete list of the Razor Pages available for scaffolding by running the command shown in Listing 6-5 in the IdentityApp folder.

OTHER USES FOR THE IDENTITY SCAFFOLDING TOOL

The scaffolding tool can also be used to add Identity to a project, including generating database context classes and adding statements to the Startup class. I do not describe these features because it is important to understand how Identity is configured to ensure you get the features you expect, even when using the Identity UI package to provide a user experience. You can see the list of options by running the dotnet aspnet-codegenerator identity command in a project that has been configured for use with the Identity scaffold tool, but my advice is to examine the results carefully to make sure you produced the effect you expected.

Listing 6-5. Listing the Pages Available for Scaffolding

```
dotnet aspnet-codegenerator identity --listFiles
```

Here is the first part of the output, which corresponds to the Razor Pages described in Chapter 5:

```
...
Account._StatusMessage
Account.AccessDenied
Account.ConfirmEmail
Account.ConfirmEmailChange
Account.ExternalLogin
Account.ForgotPassword
```

```
Account.ForgotPasswordConfirmation
Account.Lockout
Account.Login
Account.LoginWith2fa
...
```

To use the scaffolding feature, determine which pages relate to the features that interest you from the workflows described in Chapter 5 and use one of the techniques described in the following sections to disable, change, or add features.

Using the Identity UI Scaffolding

In the sections that follow, I show you how to use the scaffolding feature to change the Razor Pages that Identity UI uses.

Using Scaffolding to Change HTML

The simplest way to use the scaffolding feature is to change only the HTML produced by a Razor UI page. In this section, I will use this technique to improve the appearance of the buttons that allow signing in with external services, such as Google and Facebook. To prepare, run the command shown in Listing 6-6 in the IdentityApp folder to install the Font Awesome package, which includes company logos for the main platforms.

Listing 6-6. Installing the Font Awesome Package

```
libman install font-awesome@5.15.1 -d wwwroot/lib/font-awesome
```

Add the element shown in Listing 6-7 to the layout used by the Identity UI package to incorporate the Font Awesome styles into the HTML sent to the browser.

Listing 6-7. Adding an Element in the _CustomIdentityLayout.cshtml File in the Views/Shared Folder

```
<!DOCTYPE html>

<html>
<head>
    <meta name="viewport" content="width=device-width" />
    <title>Identity App</title>
    <link rel="stylesheet" href="/Identity/lib/bootstrap/dist/css/bootstrap.css" />
    <link rel="stylesheet" href="/Identity/css/site.css" />
    <script src="/Identity/lib/jquery/dist/jquery.js"></script>
    <script src="/Identity/lib/bootstrap/dist/js/bootstrap.bundle.js"></script>
    <script src="/Identity/js/site.js" asp-append-version="true"></script>
    <script type="text/javascript" src="/lib/qrcode/qrcode.min.js"></script>
    <link href="/lib/font-awesome/css/all.min.css" rel="stylesheet" />
</head>
```

```
<body>
    <nav class="navbar navbar-dark bg-secondary">
        <a class="navbar-brand text-white">IdentityApp</a>
        <div class="text-white"><partial name="_LoginPartial" /></div>
    </nav>
    <div class="m-2">
        @RenderBody()
        @await RenderSectionAsync("Scripts", required: false)
    </div>
    <script type="text/javascript">
        var element = document.getElementById("qrCode");
        if (element !== null) {
            new QRCode(element, {
                text: document.getElementById("qrCodeData").getAttribute("data-url"),
                width: 150, height: 150
            });
            element.previousElementSibling?.remove();
        }
    </script>
</body>
</html>
```

Add a Razor View named _ExternalButtonPartial.cshtml to the Views/Shared folder and use it to define the partial view shown in Listing 6-8.

Listing 6-8. The Contents of the _ExternalButtonPartial.cshtml File in the Views/Shared Folder

```
@model Microsoft.AspNetCore.Authentication.AuthenticationScheme

<button type="submit"
        class="btn btn-primary" name="provider" value="@Model.Name">
    <i class="@($"fab fa-{Model.Name.ToLower()}")"></i>
    @Model.DisplayName
</button>
```

The model for the partial view is an AuthenticationScheme object, which is how ASP.NET Core describes an authentication option, with Name and DisplayName properties. (The AuthenticationScheme class—and many, many other classes—are described in Part 2.)

The partial view renders an HTML button that has an icon from the Font Awesome package, which is added with the i element.

Now scaffold the page that displays the login buttons to the user by running the command shown in Listing 6-9 in the IdentityApp folder.

Listing 6-9. Scaffolding an Identity UI Razor Page

```
dotnet aspnet-codegenerator identity --dbContext Microsoft.AspNetCore.Identity.
EntityFrameworkCore.IdentityDbContext --files Account.Login
```

The dotnet aspnet-codegenerator identity selects the Identity UI scaffolding tool. The --dbContext argument is used to specify the Entity Framework Core database context class. This argument must specify the complete name, including the namespace, of the context class used by the application. If the name does not match exactly, the scaffolding tool will create a new database context class, which will lead to inconsistent results later. The `--files` argument specifies the files that should be scaffolded, using one or more names from the list produced in the previous section, separated by semicolons. I have selected the `Account.Login` page, which is responsible for presenting users with the external authentication buttons.

The command in Listing 6-9 adds several files to the project. The `Areas/Identity/IdentityHostingStartup.cs` file is used to set up features that are specific to the Identity UI package but that should contain only an empty `ConfigureServices` method for this chapter, like this:

```
using Microsoft.AspNetCore.Hosting;

[assembly: HostingStartup(typeof(IdentityApp.Areas.Identity.IdentityHostingStartup))]

namespace IdentityApp.Areas.Identity {

    public class IdentityHostingStartup : IHostingStartup {

        public void Configure(IWebHostBuilder builder) {
            builder.ConfigureServices((context, services) => {
            });
        }
    }
}
```

If you did not correctly specify the context class when running the command in Listing 6-9, you will see statements in this class that register a newly created context. If that happens, the simplest approach is to delete the entire `Areas` folder, re-create it with the Razor View Start file, and run the command in Listing 6-9 again.

The command also creates view import files, a partial view containing validation script references, and, of course, the specified Razor Page and its page model class. Edit the contents of the `Login.cshtml` file in the `Areas/Identity/Pages/Account` folder to replace the `button` element with a `partial` element that applies the partial view, as shown in Listing 6-10.

Listing 6-10. Applying a Partial in the Login.cshtml File in the Areas/Identity/Pages/Account Folder

```
...
<section>
    <h4>Use another service to log in.</h4>
    <hr />
    @{
        if ((Model.ExternalLogins?.Count ?? 0) == 0) {
            <div>
                <p>There are no external authentication services configured. See
                <a href="https://go.microsoft.com/fwlink/?LinkID=532715">
                    this article</a>
                for details on setting up this ASP.NET application to support
                logging in via external services.
                </p>
            </div>
        } else {
            <form id="external-account" asp-page="./ExternalLogin"
                asp-route-returnUrl="@Model.ReturnUrl" method="post"
                class="form-horizontal">
```

```
        <div>
            <p>
                @foreach (var provider in Model.ExternalLogins) {
                    <partial name="_ExternalButtonPartial"
                        model="provider" />
                }
            </p>
        </div>
    </form>
}
}
</section>
...
```

The content in the Login Razor Page is verbose, so I have shown only the part that should be changed. It can take a little effort to figure out which section of HTML relates to a specific feature, but just as long as you are careful to preserve the attributes and tag helpers on elements, changes are generally easy to make.

Some changes have to be applied in multiple places. In the case of the external authentication buttons, I also need to change the Account/Register page, which also presents buttons for the configured services. Run the command shown in Listing 6-11 in the IdentityApp to scaffold the page.

Listing 6-11. Scaffolding an Identity UI Razor Page

```
dotnet aspnet-codegenerator identity --dbContext Microsoft.AspNetCore.Identity.
EntityFrameworkCore.IdentityDbContext --files Account.Register
```

Edit the contents of the Register.cshtml file in the Areas/Identity/Pages/Account folder to replace the button element with a partial element that applies the partial view, as shown in Listing 6-12. This is the same change I applied to the Login page because the Identity UI package duplicates the markup instead of using a partial view.

Listing 6-12. Applying a Partial View in the Register.cshtml File in the Areas/Identity/Pages/Account Folder

```
...
<section>
    <h4>Use another service to register.</h4>
    <hr />
    @{
        if ((Model.ExternalLogins?.Count ?? 0) == 0) {
            <div>
                <p>
                    There are no external authentication services configured.
                    See <a href="https://go.microsoft.com/fwlink/?LinkID=532715">
                    this article</a>
                    for details on setting up this ASP.NET application to support
                    logging in via external services.
                </p>
            </div>
```

```
        } else {
            <form id="external-account" asp-page="./ExternalLogin"
                asp-route-returnUrl="@Model.ReturnUrl" method="post"
                class="form-horizontal">
                <div>
                    <p>
                        @foreach (var provider in Model.ExternalLogins) {
                            <partial name="_ExternalButtonPartial"
                                model="provider" />
                        }
                    </p>
                </div>
            </form>
        }
    }
</section>
...
```

Restart ASP.NET Core and https://localhost:44350/Identity/Account/Login. The scaffolded page takes precedence over the one in the Identity UI package, and the external authentication buttons are displayed with appropriate icons. The same icons are displayed if you click the Register As a New User link, as shown in Figure 6-3.

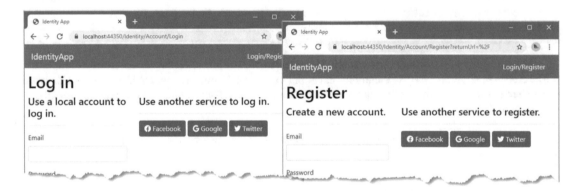

Figure 6-3. *Using scaffolding to change HTML*

Using Scaffolding to Modify C# Code

Scaffolding doesn't just override the view part of a Razor Page. It also creates a page model class containing the C# code that implements the features presented by the page. The command that scaffolded the Login page created a Login.cshtml.cs file in the Areas/Identity/Pages/Account folder, and changing the code in this file will alter how users are signed into the application.

Making changes to the page model class often requires knowledge of the Identity API, and care must be taken to understand the impact of the changes you intend to make. I describe the Identity API features in Chapters 7–12 and describe almost every aspect of the API in detail in Part 2, but for now, there is one change that can be made without needing to get into details. Locate the OnPostAsync method in the Login.cshtml.cs file and change the final argument to the PasswordSignInAsync method, as shown in Listing 6-13.

Listing 6-13. Changing an Argument in the Login.cshtml.cs File in the Areas/Identity/Pages/Account Folder

```
...
public async Task<IActionResult> OnPostAsync(string returnUrl = null) {
    returnUrl ??= Url.Content("~/");

    ExternalLogins = (await _signInManager.GetExternalAuthenticationSchemesAsync())
                        .ToList();

    if (ModelState.IsValid) {
        // This doesn't count login failures towards account lockout
        // To enable password failures to trigger account lockout,
        // set lockoutOnFailure: true
        var result = await _signInManager.PasswordSignInAsync(Input.Email,
            Input.Password, Input.RememberMe, lockoutOnFailure: true);
        if (result.Succeeded) {
            _logger.LogInformation("User logged in.");
            return LocalRedirect(returnUrl);
        }
        if (result.RequiresTwoFactor) {
            return RedirectToPage("./LoginWith2fa", new { ReturnUrl = returnUrl,
                RememberMe = Input.RememberMe });
        }
        if (result.IsLockedOut) {
            _logger.LogWarning("User account locked out.");
            return RedirectToPage("./Lockout");
        } else {
            ModelState.AddModelError(string.Empty, "Invalid login attempt.");
            return Page();
        }
    }

    // If we got this far, something failed, redisplay form
    return Page();
}
...
```

By default, the Login page signs users into the application so that failed attempts do not lead to lockouts. The change in Listing 6-13 alters this behavior so that failed attempts count toward a lockout, based on the configuration options described in Chapter 5.

Restart ASP.NET Core and request https://localhost:44350/Identity/Account/Login. Enter alice@example.com into the email field and notmypassword into the password field. Click the Log In button, and you will receive an error message telling you that the login has failed. Repeat this process, attempting to sign in using notmypassword each time.

After five failed attempts, the account will be locked out, and the browser is redirected to the Lockout page, as shown in Figure 6-4. Further attempts to sign in, even with the correct password, will fail until the lockout expires.

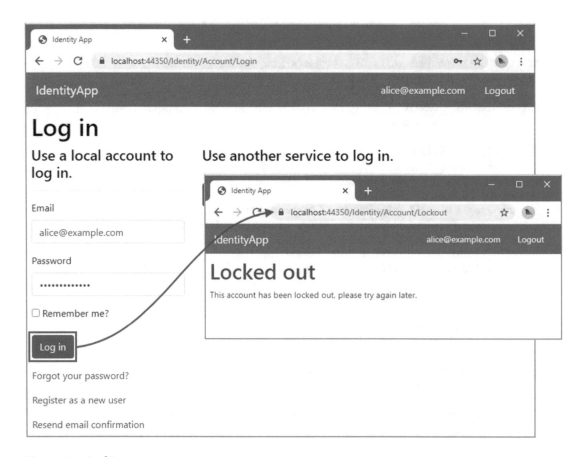

Figure 6-4. *Locking out an account*

Configuring the Account Management Pages

The Identity UI package uses a layout and partial view to present the navigation links for the self-management features. To see the default layout, shown in Figure 6-5, sign in to the application using alice@example.com as the email address and mysecret as the password and click the email address shown in the header. (You may have to wait until the lockout from the previous section has expired. The lockout lasts for 5 minutes.)

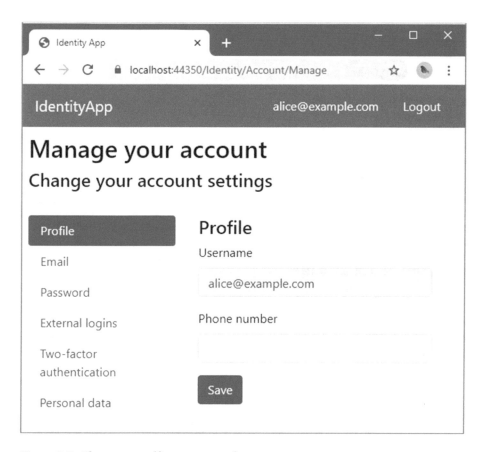

Figure 6-5. *The account self-management features*

The Identity UI Razor Pages for account management are defined in the Areas/Identity/Pages/ Account/Manage folder and have the Account.Manage prefix when listed with the scaffolding tool. Use a PowerShell command prompt to run the command shown in Listing 6-14 in the IdentityApp folder to display only the management pages.

Listing 6-14. Listing the Management Pages

```
dotnet aspnet-codegenerator identity --listFiles | Where-Object {$_ -like '*Manage*'}
```

This command produces the following output:

```
Account.Manage._Layout
Account.Manage._ManageNav
Account.Manage._StatusMessage
Account.Manage.ChangePassword
Account.Manage.DeletePersonalData
Account.Manage.Disable2fa
Account.Manage.DownloadPersonalData
```

```
Account.Manage.Email
Account.Manage.EnableAuthenticator
Account.Manage.ExternalLogins
Account.Manage.GenerateRecoveryCodes
Account.Manage.Index
Account.Manage.PersonalData
Account.Manage.ResetAuthenticator
Account.Manage.SetPassword
Account.Manage.ShowRecoveryCodes
Account.Manage.TwoFactorAuthentication
```

In addition to the Razor Pages for specific features, the list contains two files that are useful in their own right: Account.Manage._Layout and Account.Manage._ManageNav. The _Layout file is the Razor Layout used by the management Razor Pages. The _ManageNav file is a partial view that generates the links on the left of the layout shown in Figure 6-6.

Run the command shown in Listing 6-15 to scaffold these two files. As with previous examples, take particular care with the name of the database context class.

Listing 6-15. Scaffolding the Management Layout Files

```
dotnet aspnet-codegenerator identity --dbContext
Microsoft.AspNetCore.Identity.EntityFrameworkCore.IdentityDbContext --files
"Account.Manage._Layout;Account.Manage._ManageNav"
```

This command creates the Areas/Identity/Pages/Account/Manage folder and populates it with the _Layout.cshtml, _ManageNav.cshtml, and ManageNavPages.cs files. There is also a Razor View Imports file, which is used to import the classes used by the Razor Pages in the Manage folder, but which isn't needed for this chapter.

Changing the Management Layout

The _Layout.cshtml file created by the command in Listing 6-15 is used to present a consistent layout for all the account management Razor Pages. Listing 6-16 replaces the header text, just to make an easily discernible change.

Listing 6-16. Changing Text in the _Layout.cshtml File in the Areas/Identity/Pages/Account/Manage Folder

```
@{
    if (ViewData.TryGetValue("ParentLayout", out var parentLayout)) {
        Layout = (string)parentLayout;
    } else {
        Layout = "/Areas/Identity/Pages/_Layout.cshtml";
    }
}
<h2>Account Self-Management</h2>
<div>
    <h4>Change your account settings</h4>
    <hr />
    <div class="row">
```

```
        <div class="col-md-3"><partial name="_ManageNav" /></div>
        <div class="col-md-9">@RenderBody()</div>
    </div>
</div>
@section Scripts {
    @RenderSection("Scripts", required: false)
}
```

This layout displays the contents of the _ManageNav.cshtml partial view, which I describe in the next section, and uses the RenderBody method to display the content generated by the Razor Page. The code block at the top of the layout allows the base layout to be selected dynamically using view data, also described in the next section. Restart ASP.NET Core, sign into the application as alice@example.com with the password mysecret, and click the email address displayed in the header to see the modified content, as shown in Figure 6-6.

Figure 6-6. *Modifying the self-management layout*

Adding an Account Management Page

In this section, I am going to demonstrate the process of adding a new management Razor Page, which requires a little additional effort to integrate it into the rest of the management layout.

Preparing the Navigation Link

To add a new page to the management interface, the first step is to modify the ManageNavPages class, which is used to keep track of the selected page so that the appropriate link is highlighted in the layout. Make the changes shown in Listing 6-17 to prepare for a new page that will be called StoreData.

Listing 6-17. Preparing for a New Page in the ManageNavPages.cs File in the Areas/Identity/Pages/Account/Manage Folder

```
using Microsoft.AspNetCore.Mvc.Rendering;
using System;

namespace IdentityApp.Areas.Identity.Pages.Account.Manage {

    public static class ManageNavPages {
        public static string Index => "Index";

        public static string Email => "Email";

        public static string ChangePassword => "ChangePassword";

        public static string DownloadPersonalData => "DownloadPersonalData";

        public static string DeletePersonalData => "DeletePersonalData";

        public static string ExternalLogins => "ExternalLogins";

        public static string PersonalData => "PersonalData";

        public static string TwoFactorAuthentication => "TwoFactorAuthentication";

        public static string StoreData => "StoreData";

        public static string IndexNavClass(ViewContext viewContext)
            => PageNavClass(viewContext, Index);

        public static string EmailNavClass(ViewContext viewContext)
            => PageNavClass(viewContext, Email);

        public static string ChangePasswordNavClass(ViewContext viewContext)
            => PageNavClass(viewContext, ChangePassword);

        public static string DownloadPersonalDataNavClass(ViewContext viewContext)
            => PageNavClass(viewContext, DownloadPersonalData);

        public static string DeletePersonalDataNavClass(ViewContext viewContext)
            => PageNavClass(viewContext, DeletePersonalData);

        public static string ExternalLoginsNavClass(ViewContext viewContext)
            => PageNavClass(viewContext, ExternalLogins);

        public static string PersonalDataNavClass(ViewContext viewContext)
            => PageNavClass(viewContext, PersonalData);

        public static string TwoFactorAuthenticationNavClass(ViewContext viewContext)
            => PageNavClass(viewContext, TwoFactorAuthentication);
```

```
public static string StoreDataNavClass(ViewContext viewContext)
    => PageNavClass(viewContext, StoreData);

private static string PageNavClass(ViewContext viewContext, string page) {
    var activePage = viewContext.ViewData["ActivePage"] as string
        ?? System.IO.Path.GetFileNameWithoutExtension(
                viewContext.ActionDescriptor.DisplayName);
    return string.Equals(activePage, page,
        StringComparison.OrdinalIgnoreCase) ? "active" : null;
    }
  }
}
```

The first part of the ManageNavPages class is a set of read-only string properties for each of the Razor Pages for which links are displayed. These properties make it easy to replace the default pages without breaking the way the links are displayed.

The next section is a set of methods used by the _ManageNav partial to set the classes for the link elements for each page. These methods used the private PageNavClass method to return the string active if the page they represent has been selected, which is determined by reading a view data property named ActivePage.

Adding the Navigation Link

The _ManageNav partial view that was scaffolded by the command in Listing 6-17 presents the navigation links for the individual management Razor Pages. The Index page in the Areas/Identity/Pages/Account/Manage folder is presented by default, and there are links for changing email address, changing password, managing external authentication, configuring two-factor authentication, and managing personal data. The next step is to add a link to the _ManageNav.cshtml partial view for the new Razor Page, as shown in Listing 6-18.

■ **Note** The _ManageNav partial uses the GetExternalAuthenticationSchemesAsync method defined by the SignInManager<IdentityUser> class to determine whether the current user has logged in using an external authentication service. I describe this method in Chapter 11.

Listing 6-18. Adding a Link in the _ManageNav.cshtml File in the Areas/Identity/Pages/Account/Manage Folder

```
@inject SignInManager<IdentityUser> SignInManager
@{
    var hasExternalLogins = (await SignInManager
        .GetExternalAuthenticationSchemesAsync()).Any();
}
<ul class="nav nav-pills flex-column">
    <li class="nav-item">
        <a class="nav-link @ManageNavPages.IndexNavClass(ViewContext)"
            id="profile" asp-page="./Index">Profile</a>
    </li>
```

```
<li class="nav-item">
    <a class="nav-link @ManageNavPages.StoreDataNavClass(ViewContext)"
        id="personal-data" asp-page="./StoreData">Store Data</a>
</li>
<li class="nav-item">
    <a class="nav-link @ManageNavPages.EmailNavClass(ViewContext)"
        id="email" asp-page="./Email">Email</a>
</li>
<li class="nav-item">
    <a class="nav-link @ManageNavPages.ChangePasswordNavClass(ViewContext)"
        id="change-password" asp-page="./ChangePassword">Password</a>
</li>
@if (hasExternalLogins) {
    <li id="external-logins" class="nav-item">
        <a id="external-login" class="nav-link
            @ManageNavPages.ExternalLoginsNavClass(ViewContext)"
            asp-page="./ExternalLogins">External logins</a>
    </li>
}
<li class="nav-item">
    <a class="nav-link
        @ManageNavPages.TwoFactorAuthenticationNavClass(ViewContext)"
        id="two-factor" asp-page="./TwoFactorAuthentication">
            Two-factor authentication</a>
</li>
<li class="nav-item">
    <a class="nav-link @ManageNavPages.PersonalDataNavClass(ViewContext)"
        id="personal-data" asp-page="./PersonalData">Personal data</a>
</li>
</ul>
```

The anchor element provides a link to the StoreData page, and its class attribute is set using the StoreDataNavClass method added to the ManageNavPages class earlier. This method returns active if the StoreData page has been selected, which is the Bootstrap CSS class for active links.

Defining the New Razor Page

Add a Razor Page named StoreData.cshtml to the Areas/Identity/Pages/Account/Manage folder with the content shown in Listing 6-19.

Listing 6-19. The Contents of the StoreData.cshtml File in the Areas/Identity/Pages/Account/Manage Folder

```
@page
@inject UserManager<IdentityUser> UserManager
@{
    ViewData["ActivePage"] = ManageNavPages.StoreData;
    IdentityUser user = await UserManager.GetUserAsync(User);
}

<h4>Store Data</h4>
```

130

```
<table class="table table-sm table-bordered table-striped">
    <thead>
        <tr><th>Property</th><th>Value</th></tr>
    </thead>
    <tbody>
        <tr>
            <td>Id</td><td>@user.Id</td>
        </tr>
        @foreach (var prop in typeof(IdentityUser).GetProperties()) {
            if (prop.Name != "Id") {
                <tr>
                    <td>@prop.Name</td>
                    <td class="text-truncate" style="max-width:250px">
                        @prop.GetValue(user)
                    </td>
                </tr>
            }
        }
    </tbody>
</table>
```

This Razor Page uses the `UserManager<IdentityUser>` class, which provides access to the data in the Identity user store. I describe this class in more detail in Chapter 7 to 12, but this statement in the code block at the start of the page gets an object that describes the signed-in user:

```
...
IdentityUser user = await UserManager.GetUserAsync(User);
...
```

The user is represented by a `IdentityUser` object, and I use the standard .NET reflection features to generate an HTML table containing each property defined by the `IdentityUser` class. Restart ASP.NET Core, sign in as `alice@example.com` with the password `mysecret`, and click the Store Data link in the self-management section of the application, which produces the output shown in Figure 6-7. (You will see different values for some property values, which are generated dynamically.)

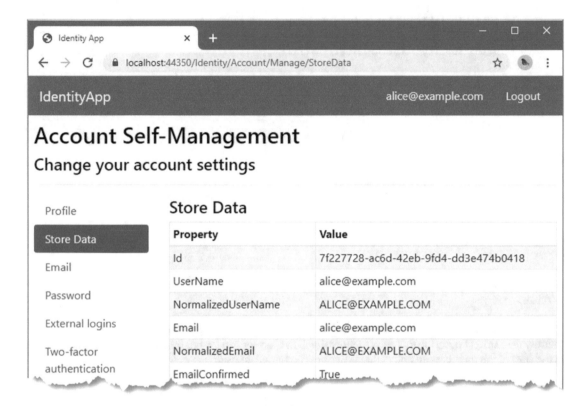

Figure 6-7. *Adding an account management page*

Notice the first statement in the code block defined by the StoreData page:

```
...
ViewData["ActivePage"] = ManageNavPages.StoreData;
...
```

This statement sets the ActivePage view data property that the ManageNavPages.PageNavClass method uses to determine which page has been selected. This works with the preparations made at the start of this section to highlight the link for the StoreData page, as shown in the figure.

Overriding the Default Layout in an Account Management Page

The Razor layout that is scaffolded for the account management pages allows Razor Pages to override the default layout by setting a view data property named ParentLayout. Add a Razor Layout named _ InfoLayout.cshtml to the Views/Shared folder and add the content shown in Listing 6-20.

Listing 6-20. The Contents of the _InfoLayout.cshtml File in the Views/Shared Folder

```
<!DOCTYPE html>
<html>
<head>
    <meta name="viewport" content="width=device-width" />
```

```
    <title>Identity App</title>
    <link href="/lib/twitter-bootstrap/css/bootstrap.min.css" rel="stylesheet" />
</head>
<body>
    <nav class="navbar navbar-dark bg-info">
        <a class="navbar-brand text-white">IdentityApp</a>
        <div class="text-white"><partial name="_LoginPartial" /></div>
    </nav>
    <partial name="_NavigationPartial" />
    <div class="m-2">
        @RenderBody()
    </div>
    @RenderSection("Scripts", false)
</body>
</html>
```

To select the view, add the statement shown in Listing 6-21 to the code block defined by the StoreData page.

Listing 6-21. Selecting a Top-Level View in the StoreData.cshtml File in the Areas/Identity/Pages/Account/ Manage Folder

```
@page
@inject UserManager<IdentityUser> UserManager
@{
    ViewData["ActivePage"] = ManageNavPages.StoreData;
    ViewData["ParentLayout"] = "_InfoLayout";
    IdentityUser user = await UserManager.GetUserAsync(User);
}

<h4>Store Data</h4>

<table class="table table-sm table-bordered table-striped">
    <thead>
        <tr><th>Property</th><th>Value</th></tr>
    </thead>
    <tbody>
        <tr>
            <td>Id</td><td>@user.Id</td>
        </tr>
        @foreach (var prop in typeof(IdentityUser).GetProperties()) {
            if (prop.Name != "Id") {
                <tr>
                    <td>@prop.Name</td>
                    <td class="text-truncate" style="max-width:250px">
                        @prop.GetValue(user)
                    </td>
                </tr>
            }
        }
    </tbody>
</table>
```

To see the effect, restart ASP.NET Core, navigate to the account management features, and click the Store Data link. The top-level view selected in Listing 6-21 is used, presenting the header in a different color, as shown in Figure 6-8.

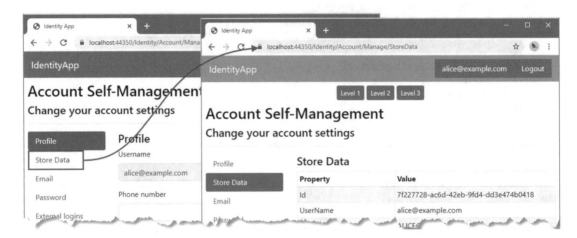

Figure 6-8. *Overriding the top-level header*

Tidying Up the QR Code Support

In Chapter 4, I added support for displaying QR codes for authenticators by using JavaScript in the layout used for the Identity UI Razor Pages and by using the DOM API to inspect the HTML document and change it if it contained specific elements. This worked, but it requires the JavaScript code to be included in every page that uses the layout, even though all but one of them doesn't display a QR code. In this section, I am going to scaffold the Razor Page that displays the QR code and modify it to remove the placeholder content and include the JavaScript files that are required.

Doing the Scaffold File Shuffle

When you scaffold the account management files, the scaffolding tool tries to create the `ManageNavPages.cs` and `_ManageNav.cshtml` files, even though these files already exist. The result is an awkward file shuffle, which is most easily accomplished using two PowerShell command prompts.

Open the first command prompt, navigate to the `IdentityApp\Areas\Identity\Pages\Account\Manage` folder, and run the command shown in Listing 6-22. These commands move the files that the scaffolding tool will try to create.

Listing 6-22. Moving Files Before Scaffolding

```
Move-Item -Path ManageNavPages.cs -Destination ManageNavPages.cs.safe
Move-Item -Path _ManageNav.cshtml -Destination _ManageNav.cshtml.safe
```

Open the second command prompt and run the command shown in Listing 6-23 in the `IdentityApp` folder. This command scaffolds the Razor Page that displays the authenticator setup details. Pay close attention to the name of the Entity Framework Core database context class, which must match exactly to prevent the scaffolding tool from generating a new class.

Listing 6-23. Scaffolding the Identity UI Page for Authenticator Setup

```
dotnet aspnet-codegenerator identity --dbContext
Microsoft.AspNetCore.Identity.EntityFrameworkCore.IdentityDbContext --files
Account.Manage.EnableAuthenticator --no-build
```

The .NET command-line tools build the project before they run, which is usually helpful because it ensures the latest code changes are used. But this causes a problem in this situation because the ManageNavPages class that was moved in Listing 6-22 is referred to in other files, which breaks the build process. To avoid this issue, the command in Listing 6-23 includes the --no-build argument, which prevents the project from being built before the file is scaffolded.

Return to the first command prompt and run the commands shown in Listing 6-24 in the IdentityApp\ Areas\Identity\Pages\Account\Manage folder to copy the modified ManageNavPages.cs and _ManageNav. cshtml back into place and overwrite the files created by the scaffolding process.

Listing 6-24. Moving Files After Scaffolding

```
Move-Item -Path ManageNavPages.cs.safe -Destination ManageNavPages.cs -Force
Move-Item -Path _ManageNav.cshtml.safe -Destination _ManageNav.cshtml -Force
```

The result of the file shuffle is that the EnableAuthenticator Razor Page has been scaffolded, and the changes made to the ManageNavPages class and the _ManageNav partial view have been preserved.

Modifying the Razor Page

Replace the contents of the EnableAuthenticator.cshtml file with those shown in Listing 6-25 to incorporate the QR code directly in the content produced by the page. This is a simplification of the HTML in the original page, with additional script elements to generate the QR code.

Listing 6-25. Replacing the Contents of the EnableAuthenticator.cshtml File in the Areas/Identity/Pages/ Account/Manage Folder

```
@page
@model EnableAuthenticatorModel
@{
    ViewData["Title"] = "Configure authenticator app";
    ViewData["ActivePage"] = ManageNavPages.TwoFactorAuthentication;
}

<partial name="_StatusMessage" for="StatusMessage" />
<h4>@ViewData["Title"]</h4>
<div>
    <p>To use an authenticator app go through the following steps:</p>
    <ol class="list">
```

```
        <li>
            <p>
                Download a two-factor authenticator app like
                Microsoft Authenticator or Google Authenticator.
            </p>
        </li>
        <li>
            <p>Scan the QR Code or enter this key <kbd>@Model.SharedKey</kbd>
                into your two factor authenticator app. Spaces
                and casing do not matter.
            </p>
            <div id="qrCode"></div>
            <div id="qrCodeData" data-url="@Html.Raw(@Model.AuthenticatorUri)"></div>
        </li>
        <li>
            <p>
                Once you have scanned the QR code or input the key above,
                your two factor authentication app will provide you
                with a unique code. Enter the code in the confirmation box below.
            </p>
            <div class="row">
                <div class="col-md-6">
                    <form id="send-code" method="post">
                        <div class="form-group">
                            <label asp-for="Input.Code" class="control-label">
                                Verification Code
                            </label>
                            <input asp-for="Input.Code" class="form-control"
                                autocomplete="off" />
                            <span asp-validation-for="Input.Code"
                                class="text-danger"></span>
                        </div>
                        <button type="submit" class="btn btn-primary">Verify</button>
                        <div asp-validation-summary="ModelOnly" class="text-danger">
                        </div>
                    </form>
                </div>
            </div>
        </li>
    </ol>
</div>

@section Scripts {
    <partial name="_ValidationScriptsPartial" />
    <script type="text/javascript" src="/lib/qrcode/qrcode.min.js"></script>
    <script type="text/javascript">
        new QRCode(document.getElementById("qrCode"), {
            text: document.getElementById("qrCodeData").getAttribute("data-url"),
            width: 150, height: 150
        });
    </script>
}
```

Moving the JavaScript code into the Razor Page means that it can be removed from the shared layout, as shown in Listing 6-26.

Listing 6-26. Removing JavaScript Code from the _CustomIdentityLayout.cshtml File in the Views/Shared Folder

```
<!DOCTYPE html>

<html>
<head>
    <meta name="viewport" content="width=device-width" />
    <title>Identity App</title>
    <link rel="stylesheet" href="/Identity/lib/bootstrap/dist/css/bootstrap.css" />
    <link rel="stylesheet" href="/Identity/css/site.css" />
    <script src="/Identity/lib/jquery/dist/jquery.js"></script>
    <script src="/Identity/lib/bootstrap/dist/js/bootstrap.bundle.js"></script>
    <script src="/Identity/js/site.js" asp-append-version="true"></script>
    @*<script type="text/javascript" src="/lib/qrcode/qrcode.min.js"></script>*@
    <link href="/lib/font-awesome/css/all.min.css" rel="stylesheet" />
</head>
<body>
    <nav class="navbar navbar-dark bg-secondary">
        <a class="navbar-brand text-white">IdentityApp</a>
        <div class="text-white"><partial name="_LoginPartial" /></div>
    </nav>
    <div class="m-2">
        @RenderBody()
        @await RenderSectionAsync("Scripts", required: false)
    </div>
    @*<script type="text/javascript">
        var element = document.getElementById("qrCode");
        if (element !== null) {
            new QRCode(element, {
                text: document.getElementById("qrCodeData").getAttribute("data-url"),
                width: 150, height: 150
            });
            element.previousElementSibling?.remove();
        }
    </script>*@
</body>
</html>
```

Restart ASP.NET Core, request https://localhost:44350/Identity/Account/Login, and sign in to the application using the email address alice@example.com and the password mysecret. Request https://localhost:44350/Identity/Account/Manage/TwoFactorAuthentication and click Set up Authenticator App to see the modified content, which is shown in Figure 6-9.

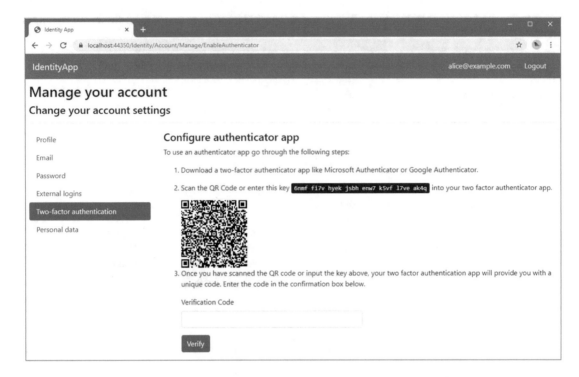

Figure 6-9. *Tidying up QR code generation*

Using Scaffolding to Disable Features

Scaffolding can also be used to disable features, which can be a useful way to benefit from the useful parts of the Identity UI package without offering workflows that don't suit your project. In this section, I demonstrate the process of disabling the password recovery feature, which may not be required in corporate environments where credentials are managed centrally, for example.

In Listing 6-27, I have changed the link for password recovery in the Login page.

Listing 6-27. Removing a Link in the Login.cshtml File in the Areas/Identity/Pages/Account Folder

```
...
<div class="form-group">
    @*<p>
        <a id="forgot-password" asp-page="./ForgotPassword">Forgot your password?</a>
    </p>*@
    <p>
        <a asp-page="./Register" asp-route-returnUrl="@Model.ReturnUrl">
            Register as a new user
        </a>
    </p>
```

```
<p>
    <a id="resend-confirmation" asp-page="./ResendEmailConfirmation">
        Resend email confirmation
    </a>
</p>
</div>
...
```

It isn't enough to just disable a link because the user can navigate directly to the URL for the password recovery pages. It isn't possible to delete pages from the Identity UI package, so the next best approach is to scaffold the files and redefine the page model class handler methods, which has the effect of safety disabling the page.

Use a PowerShell command prompt to run the command shown in Listing 6-28 in the IdentityApp folder. As with earlier commands, you must take care to specify the name of the database context class correctly to prevent a new class from being generated.

Listing 6-28. Scaffolding the Password Recovery Pages

```
dotnet aspnet-codegenerator identity --dbContext
Microsoft.AspNetCore.Identity.EntityFrameworkCore.IdentityDbContext --files
Account.ForgotPassword
```

Once you have scaffolded the page, modify the page model class to remove the OnPostAsync method and add GET and POST handler methods that redirect the browser to the Login page, as shown in Listing 6-29.

Listing 6-29. Redefining Methods in the ForgotPassword.cshtml.cs File in the Areas/Identity/Pages/ Account Folder

```
using System;
using System.Collections.Generic;
using System.ComponentModel.DataAnnotations;
using System.Text.Encodings.Web;
using System.Text;
using System.Threading.Tasks;
using Microsoft.AspNetCore.Authorization;
using Microsoft.AspNetCore.Identity;
using Microsoft.AspNetCore.Identity.UI.Services;
using Microsoft.AspNetCore.Mvc;
using Microsoft.AspNetCore.Mvc.RazorPages;
using Microsoft.AspNetCore.WebUtilities;

namespace IdentityApp.Areas.Identity.Pages.Account {
    [AllowAnonymous]
    public class ForgotPasswordModel : PageModel {
        private readonly UserManager<IdentityUser> _userManager;
        private readonly IEmailSender _emailSender;
```

```
        public ForgotPasswordModel(UserManager<IdentityUser> userManager,
                IEmailSender emailSender) {
            _userManager = userManager;
            _emailSender = emailSender;
        }

        [BindProperty]
        public InputModel Input { get; set; }

        public class InputModel {
            [Required]
            [EmailAddress]
            public string Email { get; set; }
        }

        //public async Task<IActionResult> OnPostAsync() {
        //    if (ModelState.IsValid) {
        //        var user = await _userManager.FindByEmailAsync(Input.Email);
        //        if (user == null || !(await _userManager.
        //                IsEmailConfirmedAsync(user))) {
        //            return RedirectToPage("./ForgotPasswordConfirmation");
        //        }
        //
        //        var code = await _userManager.
        //            GeneratePasswordResetTokenAsync(user);
        //        code = WebEncoders.Base64UrlEncode(Encoding.UTF8.GetBytes(code));
        //        var callbackUrl = Url.Page(
        //            "/Account/ResetPassword",
        //            pageHandler: null,
        //            values: new { area = "Identity", code },
        //            protocol: Request.Scheme);
        //        await _emailSender.SendEmailAsync(
        //            Input.Email,
        //            "Reset Password",
        //            $"Please reset your password by <a href='{HtmlEncoder.
        //                Default.Encode(callbackUrl)}'>clicking here</a>.");
        //        return RedirectToPage("./ForgotPasswordConfirmation");
        //    }
        //    return Page();
        //}

        public IActionResult OnGet() => RedirectToPage("./Login");
        public IActionResult OnPost() => RedirectToPage("./Login");
    }
}
```

The GET handler prevents the page from rendering content. I like to add a POST handler as well so that attempts to submit a POST request also result in a redirection. Restart ASP.NET Core and request https://localhost:44350/Identity/Account/Login. You will see no link for password recovery, as shown in Figure 6-10. If you attempt to navigate to https://localhost:44350/Identity/Account/ForgotPassword, you will be redirected back to the Login page.

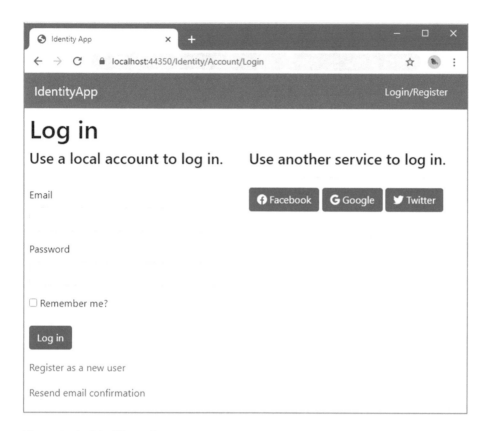

Figure 6-10. *Disabling a feature*

Summary

In this chapter, I explained the different ways in which the Identity UI package can be adapted to suit the needs of a project. I demonstrated how the scaffolding process can be used to bring Razor Pages into the application where they take precedence over the default pages in the Identity UI package. This feature can be used to modify the features that the Identity UI package provides, create new features, or remove features entirely. Although the adaptations provide flexibility, there are limits to the customizations that can be made. In the next chapter, I start to describe the API that Identity provides for creating custom workflows that can replace the Identity UI package.

CHAPTER 7

■ ■ ■

Using the Identity API

As I explained in Chapter 6, there are limits to the customizations that can be made to the Identity UI package. Minor changes can be achieved using scaffolding, but if your application doesn't fit into the self-service model that Identity UI expects, then you won't be able to adapt its features to suit your project.

In this chapter—and for the rest of this part of the book—I describe the API that ASP.NET Core Identity provides, which can be used to create completely custom workflows. This is the same API that Identity UI uses, but using it directly means you can create any combination of features you require and implement them exactly as needed. In this chapter, I describe the basic features that the API provides. In later chapters, I explain more advanced features and create administrator and self-service workflows for every major Identity feature. Table 7-1 puts the Identity API in context.

Table 7-1. *Putting the Identity API in Context*

Question	Answer
What is it?	The Identity API provides access to all of the Identity features.
Why is it useful?	The API allows custom workflows to be created that perfectly match the requirements of a project, which may not be what the Identity UI package provides.
How is it used?	Key classes are provided as services that are available through the standard ASP.NET Core dependency injection feature.
Are there any pitfalls or limitations?	The API can be complex, and creating custom workflows requires a commitment of time and effort. It is also important to think through the workflows you create to ensure that you are creating a secure application.
Are there any alternatives?	You can use and adapt the Identity UI package if your project fits into the model it is designed for.

Table 7-2 summarizes the chapter.

© Adam Freeman 2021
A. Freeman, *Pro ASP.NET Core Identity*, https://doi.org/10.1007/978-1-4842-6858-2_7

Table 7-2. *Chapter Summary*

Problem	Solution	Listing
Create a user account	Create a new instance of the IdentityUser class and pass it to the user manager's CreateAsync method.	1–15
Determine the outcome from a user manager operation	Read the properties defined by the IdentityResult class, which indicate the outcome and describe any errors.	16–18
Query the user store	Formulate a LINQ query with the user manager's Users property.	19–22
Display user details	Enumerate the properties of an IdentityUser object or call the corresponding user manager methods.	23–26
Update user details	Set new IdentityUser property values or call the corresponding user manager methods and then call the UpdateAsync method to store the changes.	27–30
Determine the features supported by the user store	Access the user store through the user manager's Store property and read the properties that are defined for each feature.	31–33
Enable support for roles in the default user store	Use the AddIdentity method to set up Identity, with generic type arguments to specify the user and role classes.	34

Preparing for This Chapter

This chapter uses the IdentityApp project from Chapter 6. Open a new PowerShell command prompt and run the commands shown in Listing 7-1 to reset the application and Identity databases.

■ **Tip** You can download the example project for this chapter—and for all the other chapters in this book—from https://github.com/Apress/pro-asp.net-core-identity. See Chapter 1 for how to get help if you have problems running the examples.

Listing 7-1. Resetting the Databases

```
dotnet ef database drop --force --context ProductDbContext
dotnet ef database drop --force --context IdentityDbContext
dotnet ef database update --context ProductDbContext
dotnet ef database update --context IdentityDbContext
```

Use the PowerShell prompt to run the command shown in Listing 7-2 in the IdentityApp folder to start the application.

Listing 7-2. Running the Example Application

```
dotnet run
```

Open a web browser and request `https://localhost:44350`, which will show the output from the Home controller, and `https://localhost:44350/pages`, which will show the output from the Landing Razor Page, as shown in Figure 7-1.

Figure 7-1. *Running the example application*

Creating the User and Administrator Dashboards

For this part of the book, I am going to create custom workflows for the operations commonly required by most applications, in versions that can be used by administrators and, where appropriate, by self-service users.

I am going to create two "dashboard"-style layouts, one for administrator functions and one for self-service. As I develop individual workflows, I will add navigation elements to the dashboards so that the new features can be easily accessed.

These layouts will be color-coded so that it is obvious when an example is intended for an administrator or a user. It will also give the custom workflows an appearance that is distinct from the Identity UI examples shown in earlier examples. Initially, the new workflows will exist alongside Identity UI, but at the end of this chapter, once I have some basic features established, I change the Identity configuration to disable Identity UI.

Create the `IdentityApp/Pages/Identity` folder and add to it a Razor Layout named `_Layout.cshtml`, with the contents shown in Listing 7-3.

USING RAZOR PAGES OR THE MVC FRAMEWORK

I use Razor Pages throughout this book for the examples where I consume the Identity API, following the same basic pattern as the Identity UI package from Microsoft. The development style of Razor Pages fits nicely with the nature of Identity, where features are generally self-contained. You don't have to use Razor Pages in your projects, and every service, method, and property that I use in a Razor Page can be accessed in the same way using the MVC Framework.

Listing 7-3. The Contents of the _Layout.cshtml File in the Pages/Identity Folder

```
@{
    string theme = ViewData["theme"] as string ?? "primary";
    bool showNav = ViewData["showNav"] as bool? ?? true;
    string navPartial = ViewData["navPartial"] as string ?? "_Workflows";
    string workflow = ViewData["workflow"] as string;
    string banner =  ViewData["banner"] as string ?? "User Dashboard";
    bool showHeader = ViewData["showHeader"] as bool? ?? true;
}

<!DOCTYPE html>
<html>
<head>
    <meta name="viewport" content="width=device-width" />
    <title>Identity App</title>
    <link href="/lib/twitter-bootstrap/css/bootstrap.min.css" rel="stylesheet" />
</head>
<body>
    @if (showHeader) {
        <nav class="navbar navbar-dark bg-@theme">
            <a class="navbar-brand text-white">IdentityApp</a>
            <div class="text-white"><partial name="_LoginPartial" /></div>
        </nav>
    }
    <h4 class="bg-@theme text-center text-white p-2">@banner</h4>
    <div class="my-2">
        <div class="container-fluid">
            <div class="row">
                @if (showNav) {
                    <div class="col-auto">
                        <partial name="@navPartial" model="@((workflow, theme))" />
                    </div>
                }
                <div class="col">
                    @RenderBody()
                </div>
            </div>
        </div>
    </div>
</body>
</html>
```

I use ViewData values to select the Bootstrap theme to determine whether to display navigation content and to display a banner.

Next, add a Razor View named _Workflows.cshtml to the Pages/Identity folder with the content shown in Listing 7-4. This partial view will display navigation buttons that will lead to different workflows.

Listing 7-4. The Contents of the _Workflows.cshtml File in the Pages/Identity Folder

```
@model (string workflow, string theme)

@{
    Func<string, string> getClass = (string feature) =>
        feature != null && feature.Equals(Model.workflow) ? "active" : "";
}

<a class="btn btn-@Model.theme btn-block @getClass("Overview")" asp-page="Index">
    Overview
</a>
```

Next, create the `IdentityApp/Pages/Identity/Admin` folder and add to it a Razor Layout, called `_AdminLayout.cshtml`, with the content shown in Listing 7-5. This layout builds on the one in Listing 7-4 and will denote the administration workflows.

Listing 7-5. The Contents of the _AdminLayout.cshtml File in the Pages/Identity/Admin Folder

```
@{
    Layout = "../_Layout";
    ViewData["theme"] = "success";
    ViewData["banner"] = "Administration Dashboard";
    ViewData["navPartial"] = "_AdminWorkflows";
}

@RenderBody()
```

This may seem odd for a layout, but I only need to set the view data properties to differentiate the administration view from the user view, as you will see once the parts start to come together. Add a Razor View named `_AdminWorkflows.cshtml` to the `Pages/Identity/Admin` folder with the content shown in Listing 7-6. This partial view will contain the navigation elements for the administration workflows.

Listing 7-6. The Contents of the _AdminWorkflows.cshtml File in the Pages/Identity/Admin Folder

```
@model (string workflow, string theme)

@{
    Func<string, string> getClass = (string feature) =>
        feature != null && feature.Equals(Model.workflow) ? "active" : "";
}

<a class="btn btn-@Model.theme btn-block @getClass("Dashboard")"
        asp-page="Dashboard">
    Dashboard
</a>
```

Add a Razor View Start file named `_ViewStart.cshtml` to the `Pages/Identity/Admin` folder with the content shown in Listing 7-7. I have kept the names of the user and administration files distinct to make it easier to follow the examples, and the Razor View Start file ensures that the `_AdminLayout.cshtml` file will be used as the default layout for pages in the `Admin` folder.

Listing 7-7. The Contents of the _ViewStart.cshtml File in the Pages/Identity/Admin folder

```
@{
    Layout = "_AdminLayout";
}
```

Creating the Custom Base Classes

As I start to define workflows, they will be publicly accessible to make development easier. Once I get enough functionality in place, I will use the ASP.NET Core authorization features to restrict access so that user features are only available for signed-in users and administration features are only available to designated administrators. Applying the authorization policy is simpler when all the related Razor Pages share a common page model base class. To define the base class for user features, add a class file named `UserPageModel.cs` to the `Pages/Identity` folder with the content shown in Listing 7-8.

Listing 7-8. The Contents of the UserPageModel.cs File in the Pages/Identity Folder

```
using Microsoft.AspNetCore.Mvc.RazorPages;

namespace IdentityApp.Pages.Identity {

    public class UserPageModel : PageModel {

        // no methods or properties required
    }
}
```

To create the common base class for the administration features, add a class file named `AdminPageModel.cs` to the `Pages/Identity/Admin` folder with the content shown in Listing 7-9.

Listing 7-9. The Contents of the AdminPageModel.cs File in the Pages/Identity/Admin Folder

```
namespace IdentityApp.Pages.Identity.Admin {

    public class AdminPageModel: UserPageModel {

        // no methods or properties required
    }
}
```

I return to these classes when I apply the authorization policy that will restrict access to the custom Identity workflows.

Creating the Overview and Dashboard Pages

Add a Razor Page named `Index.cshtml` to the `Pages/Identity` folder with the content shown in Listing 7-10.

Listing 7-10. The Contents of the Index.cshtml File in the Pages/Identity Folder

```
@page
@model IdentityApp.Pages.Identity.IndexModel
@{
    ViewBag.Workflow = "Overview";
}

<table class="table table-sm table-striped table-bordered">
    <tbody>
        <tr><th>Email</th><td>@Model.Email</td></tr>
        <tr><th>Phone</th><td>@Model.Phone</td></tr>
    </tbody>
</table>
```

The view part of the page displays the user's email address and phone number. To define the page model class, add the code shown in Listing 7-11 to the `Index.cshtml.cs` file in the `Pages/Identity` folder. (You will have to create this file if you are using Visual Studio Code.)

Listing 7-11. The Contents of the Index.cshtml.cs File in the Pages/Identity Folder

```
namespace IdentityApp.Pages.Identity {

    public class IndexModel : UserPageModel {

        public string Email { get; set; }
        public string Phone { get; set; }
    }
}
```

The page model class defines the properties required by its view. I'll add the code to retrieve the data from the store later in this chapter.

Next, add a Razor Page named `Dashboard.cshtml` to the `Pages/Identity/Admin` folder with the content shown in Listing 7-12.

Listing 7-12. The Contents of the Dashboard.cshtml File in the Pages/Identity/Admin Folder

```
@page "/identity/admin"
@model IdentityApp.Pages.Identity.Admin.DashboardModel
@{
    ViewBag.Workflow = "Dashboard";
}

<table class="table table-sm table-striped table-bordered">
    <tbody>
        <tr><th>Users in store:</th><td>@Model.UsersCount</td></tr>
        <tr><th>Unconfirmed accounts:</th><td>@Model.UsersUnconfirmed</td></tr>
        <tr><th>Locked out users:</th><td>@Model.UsersLockedout</td></tr>
        <tr>
            <th>Users with two-factor enabled:</th>
            <td>@Model.UsersTwoFactor</td>
        </tr>
    </tbody>
</table>
```

The view part of this page displays a table with some useful overview data that will be useful in later chapters. To define the page model class, add the code shown in Listing 7-13 to the Dashboard.cshtml.cs file. (You will have to create this file if you are using Visual Studio Code.)

Listing 7-13. The Contents of the Dashboard.cshtml.cs File in the Pages/Identity/Admin Folder

```
using Microsoft.AspNetCore.Mvc.RazorPages;

namespace IdentityApp.Pages.Identity.Admin {

    public class DashboardModel : AdminPageModel {

        public int UsersCount { get; set; } = 0;
        public int UsersUnconfirmed { get; set; } = 0;
        public int UsersLockedout { get; set; } = 0;
        public int UsersTwoFactor { get; set; } = 0;
    }
}
```

The final change is to update the link that allows users to manage their accounts, as shown in Listing 7-14.

Listing 7-14. Changing URLs in the _LoginPartial.cshtml File in the Views/Shared Folder

```
@inject SignInManager<IdentityUser> SignInManager

<nav class="nav">
    @if (User.Identity.IsAuthenticated) {
        <a asp-page="/Identity/Index" class="nav-link bg-secondary text-white">
            @User.Identity.Name
        </a>
        <a asp-area="Identity" asp-page="/Account/Logout"
            class="nav-link bg-secondary text-white">
                Logout
        </a>
    } else {
        <a asp-area="Identity" asp-page="/Account/Login"
                class="nav-link bg-secondary text-white">
            Login/Register
        </a>
    }
</nav>
```

To check the preparations for the administration workflows, restart ASP.NET Core and request https://localhost:44350/identity, which will show the overview that will be provided to the user. Next, request https://localhost:44350/identity/admin, which will show the dashboard for administrators. Both are shown in Figure 7-2.

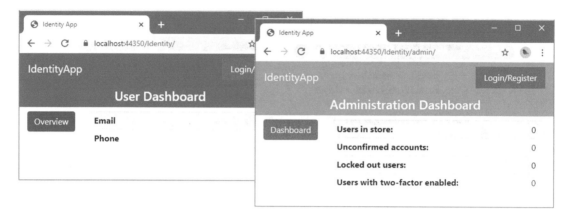

***Figure 7-2.** Preparing the user and administration dashboards*

Using the Identity API

Two of the most important parts of the Identity API are the user manager and the user class. The user manager provides access to the data that Identity manages, and the user class describes the data that Identity manages for a single user account.

The best approach is to jump in and write some code that uses the API. I am going to start with a Razor Page that will create instances of the user class and ask the user manager to store them in the database. Add the code shown in Listing 7-15 to the Dashboard.cshtml.cs file.

***Listing 7-15.** Using the Identity API in the Dashboard.cshtml.cs File in the Pages/Identity/Admin Folder*

```
using Microsoft.AspNetCore.Mvc.RazorPages;
using Microsoft.AspNetCore.Identity;
using Microsoft.AspNetCore.Mvc;
using System.Threading.Tasks;

namespace IdentityApp.Pages.Identity.Admin {

    public class DashboardModel : AdminPageModel {

        public DashboardModel(UserManager<IdentityUser> userMgr)
            => UserManager = userMgr;

        public UserManager<IdentityUser> UserManager { get; set; }

        public int UsersCount { get; set; } = 0;
        public int UsersUnconfirmed { get; set; } = 0;
        public int UsersLockedout { get; set; } = 0;
        public int UsersTwoFactor { get; set; } = 0;

        private readonly string[] emails = {
            "alice@example.com", "bob@example.com", "charlie@example.com"
        };
```

```
    public async Task<IActionResult> OnPostAsync() {
        foreach (string email in emails) {
            IdentityUser userObject = new IdentityUser {
                UserName = email,
                Email = email,
                EmailConfirmed = true
            };
            await UserManager.CreateAsync(userObject);
        }
        return RedirectToPage();
    }
  }
}
```

There are only a few statements, but there is a lot to understand because this is the first code that deals directly with the Identity API. Let's start with the user class. Identity is agnostic about the user class, and you can create a custom user class, which I demonstrate in Part 2. There is a default class, named IdentityUser, which is the class I have used in the example application and which should be used unless you are creating a custom user store.

The user class is declared when configuring Identity in the Startup class. Here is the statement that sets up Identity in the example application:

```
...
services.AddDefaultIdentity<IdentityUser>(opts => {
    opts.Password.RequiredLength = 8;
    opts.Password.RequireDigit = false;
    opts.Password.RequireLowercase = false;
    opts.Password.RequireUppercase = false;
    opts.Password.RequireNonAlphanumeric = false;
    opts.SignIn.RequireConfirmedAccount = true;
}).AddEntityFrameworkStores<IdentityDbContext>();
...
```

The type of the user class is specified using the generic type argument to the AddDefaultIdentity method. The user class defines a set of properties that describe the user account and provide the data values that Identity needs to implement its features. To create a new user object, I create a new instance of the IdentityUser class and set three of these properties, like this:

```
...
IdentityUser userObject = new IdentityUser {
    UserName = email,
    Email = email,
    EmailConfirmed = true
};
...
```

I describe all the properties defined by the IdentityUser class later in this chapter, but these properties are enough to get started. As the property names suggest, the UserName and Email properties store the user's account name and email address. The EmailConfirmed is used to indicate if the user's control of the email address has been confirmed. I describe the process for confirmation in Chapter 9, but I have set this property to true for the test accounts.

I am going to follow the policy used by the Identity UI package and use the user's email address for both the username and email address. (You can see examples that handle them separately in Part 2.)

The second key class is the user manager, which is UserManager<T>. The generic type argument, T, is used to specify the user class. Since the example application uses the built-in user class, the user manager will be UserManager<IdentityUser>.

REFERRING TO A SPECIFIC USER CLASS

Identity can work with just about any user class, but most projects end up using the default IdentityUser class because there are few good reasons to use anything else, especially if you are using Entity Framework Core to store the Identity data. For this reason, I am going to refer to UserManage<IdentityUser> instead of "UserManager<T>, where T is the user class." You will encounter "where T is the user class" a lot in in Part 2, and it is probably the phrase I repeat most often. For the rest of this part of the book, however, I am going to assume that the user class is IdentityUser for the sake of simplicity and brevity.

The user manager is configured as a service through the ASP.NET Core dependency injection feature. To access the user manager in the Razor Page model class, I added a constructor with a UserManager<IdentityUser> parameter, like this:

```
...
public DashboardModel(UserManager<IdentityUser> userMgr) => UserManager = userMgr;
...
```

When the page model class is instantiated, the constructor receives a UserManager<IdentityUser> object, which I assign to a property named UserManager so that it can be used by the page handler methods or accessed from the view part of the page.

The user manager class has a lot of methods, but there are three that are used to manage the stored data, as described in Table 7-3. These methods are all asynchronous, as are many of the methods defined by the Identity API.

Table 7-3. *The UserManager<IdentityUser> Methods for Managing Stored Data*

Name	Description
CreateAsync(user)	This method stores a new instance of the user class.
UpdateAsync(user)	This method updates a stored instance of the user class.
DeleteAsync(user)	This method removes a stored instance of the user class.

To store the test IdentityUser objects, I call the user manager's CreateAsync method.

```
...
foreach (string email in emails) {
    IdentityUser userObject = new IdentityUser {
        UserName = email,
        Email = email,
        EmailConfirmed = true
    };
```

```
    await UserManager.CreateAsync(userObject);
}
...
```

The CreateAsync method stores the IdentityUser objects I create, seeding the database with accounts.

Processing Identity Results

My use of the CreateAsync method in Listing 7-15 assumes that everything works as expected, which is a level of optimism that is rarely warranted in software development. The methods in Table 7-3 return IdentityResult objects that describe the outcome of operations using the properties described in Table 7-4.

Table 7-4. *The IdentityResult Properties*

Name	Description
Succeeded	This property returns true if the operation is successful and false otherwise.
Errors	This property returns an IEnumerable<IdentityError> object containing an IdentityError object for each error that has occurred. The IdentityError class defines Code and Description properties.

If the Succeeded property is true, then an operation has worked. If it is false, then the Errors property can be enumerated to understand the problems that have arisen. When writing custom Identity workflows, a common requirement is to handle errors from the IdentityResult object by adding validation errors to the ASP.NET Core model state. Add a class file named IdentityExtensions.cs to the IdentityApp/Pages/Identity folder and use it to define the extension method shown in Listing 7-16.

Listing 7-16. The Contents of the IdentityExtensions.cs File in the IdentityApp/Pages/Identity Folder

```
using Microsoft.AspNetCore.Identity;
using Microsoft.AspNetCore.Mvc.ModelBinding;
using System.Linq;

namespace IdentityApp.Pages.Identity {
    public static class IdentityExtensions {

        public static bool Process(this IdentityResult result,
                ModelStateDictionary modelState) {
            foreach (IdentityError err in result.Errors
                    ?? Enumerable.Empty<IdentityError>()) {
                modelState.AddModelError(string.Empty, err.Description);
            }
            return result.Succeeded;
        }
    }
}
```

Each IdentityError object in the sequence returned by the IdentityResult.Errors property defines a Code property and a Description property. The Code property is used to unambiguously identify the error and is intended to be consumed by the application. I am interested in the Description property, which describes an error that can be presented to the user. I use the foreach keyword to add the value from each IdentityError.Description property and add it to the set of validation errors that ASP.NET Core will handle.

```
...
modelState.AddModelError(string.Empty, err.Description);
...
```

In Listing 7-17, I have used the new extension method to process the results from the CreateAsync method.

Listing 7-17. Handling Results in the Dashboard.cshtml.cs File in the Pages/Identity/Admin Folder

```
using Microsoft.AspNetCore.Mvc.RazorPages;
using Microsoft.AspNetCore.Identity;
using Microsoft.AspNetCore.Mvc;
using System.Threading.Tasks;

namespace IdentityApp.Pages.Identity.Admin {

    public class DashboardModel : AdminPageModel {

        public DashboardModel(UserManager<IdentityUser> userMgr)
            => UserManager = userMgr;

        public UserManager<IdentityUser> UserManager { get; set; }

        public int UsersCount { get; set; } = 0;
        public int UsersUnconfirmed { get; set; } = 0;
        public int UsersLockedout { get; set; } = 0;
        public int UsersTwoFactor { get; set; } = 0;

        private readonly string[] emails = {
            "alice@example.com", "bob@example.com", "charlie@example.com"
        };

        public async Task<IActionResult> OnPostAsync() {
            foreach (string email in emails) {
                IdentityUser userObject = new IdentityUser {
                    UserName = email,
                    Email = email,
                    EmailConfirmed = true
                };
                IdentityResult result = await UserManager.CreateAsync(userObject);
                result.Process(ModelState);
            }
            if (ModelState.IsValid) {
                return RedirectToPage();
            }
```

155

```
        return Page();
        }
    }
}
```

This is not the most elegant code because it forces together two different error handling approaches, while also signaling whether there are any errors to handle at all. But it is a helpful approach to ensure that errors are surfaced from the Identity API to the user.

The final step to get the basic features working is to add HTML elements to the view part of the Dashboard page, as shown in Listing 7-18.

Listing 7-18. Adding HTML Elements to the Dashboard.cshtml File in the Pages/Identity/Admin Folder

```
@page "/identity/admin"
@model IdentityApp.Pages.Identity.Admin.DashboardModel
@{
    ViewBag.Workflow = "Dashboard";
}

<div asp-validation-summary="All" class="text-danger m-2"></div>

<table class="table table-sm table-striped table-bordered">
    <tbody>
        <tr><th>Users in store:</th><td>@Model.UsersCount</td></tr>
        <tr><th>Unconfirmed accounts:</th><td>@Model.UsersUnconfirmed</td></tr>
        <tr><th>Locked out users:</th><td>@Model.UsersLockedout</td></tr>
        <tr>
            <th>Users with two-factor enabled:</th>
            <td>@Model.UsersTwoFactor</td>
        </tr>
    </tbody>
</table>

<form method="post">
    <button class="btn btn-secondary" type="submit">Seed Database</button>
</form>
```

The new elements display validation errors and define a form that is submitted to seed the database.

There is still work to do, but there is enough functionality for a simple test. Restart ASP.NET Core and request https://localhost:44350/identity/admin. Click the Seed Database button to create the test accounts. Nothing will happen because the Dashboard page isn't yet reading data from the database, but if you click the button again, you can confirm that the error handling features are working, as shown in Figure 7-3.

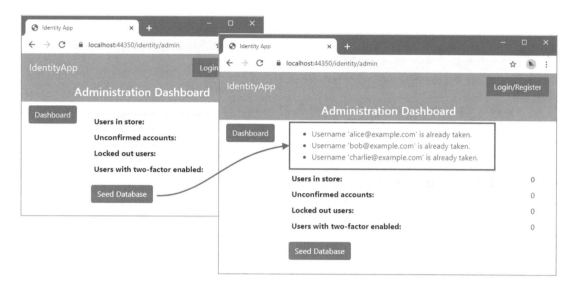

Figure 7-3. *Testing the error handling code*

On the second attempt to seed the database, the calls to the CreateAsync method produce errors because the first seeding stored IdentityUser objects with the same UserName values. Identity requires unique usernames and produces error that are displayed using the ASP.NET Core model validation features.

Querying the User Data

The problem with the code in Listing 7-17 is that it doesn't clear out existing data before storing the new IdentityUser objects. To provide access to the existing data, the user manager class defines a property named Users, which can be used to enumerate the stored IdentityUser objects and which can be used with LINQ to perform queries. Table 7-5 describes this property for future quick reference.

Table 7-5. *The UserManager<T> Property for Reading Data*

Name	Description
Users	This property returns an IQueryable<IdentityUser> object that can be used to enumerate the stored IdentityUser objects and can be used with LINQ to perform queries.

In Listing 7-19, I have added to statements the Dashboard page model's POST handler method to enumerate the stored IdentityUser objects and pass them to the DeleteAsync method, which will remove them from the database. I have also added a GET handler method that sets one of the properties displayed by the view part of the page.

Listing 7-19. Reading/Deleting Data in the Dashboard.cshtml.cs File in the Identity/Pages/Admin Folder

```
using Microsoft.AspNetCore.Mvc.RazorPages;
using Microsoft.AspNetCore.Identity;
using Microsoft.AspNetCore.Mvc;
using System.Threading.Tasks;
```

```
using System.Linq;

namespace IdentityApp.Pages.Identity.Admin {

    public class DashboardModel : AdminPageModel {

        public DashboardModel(UserManager<IdentityUser> userMgr)
            => UserManager = userMgr;

        public UserManager<IdentityUser> UserManager { get; set; }

        public int UsersCount { get; set; } = 0;
        public int UsersUnconfirmed { get; set; } = 0;
        public int UsersLockedout { get; set; } = 0;
        public int UsersTwoFactor { get; set; } = 0;

        private readonly string[] emails = {
            "alice@example.com", "bob@example.com", "charlie@example.com"
        };

        public void OnGet() {
            UsersCount = UserManager.Users.Count();
        }

        public async Task<IActionResult> OnPostAsync() {
            foreach (IdentityUser existingUser in UserManager.Users.ToList()) {
                IdentityResult result = await UserManager.DeleteAsync(existingUser);
                result.Process(ModelState);
            }
            foreach (string email in emails) {
                IdentityUser userObject = new IdentityUser {
                    UserName = email,
                    Email = email,
                    EmailConfirmed = true
                };
                IdentityResult result = await UserManager.CreateAsync(userObject);
                result.Process(ModelState);
            }
            if (ModelState.IsValid) {
                return RedirectToPage();
            }
            return Page();
        }
    }
}
```

The Users property returns an IQueryable<IdentityUser> object that can be enumerated or used in a LINQ query. In the GET handler, I use the LINQ Count method to determine how many IdentityUser objects have been stored. In the POST handler, I use the foreach keyword to enumerate the stored IdentityUser objects so I can delete them. (Notice that I use the ToList method to force evaluation in the foreach loop. This ensures I don't cause an error by deleting objects from the sequence that I am enumerating.)

Restart ASP.NET Core and request `https://localhost:44350/identity/admin`. The changes in Listing 7-19 display the number of stored `IdentityUser` objects, as shown in Figure 7-4, and clicking the Seed Database button no longer generates errors.

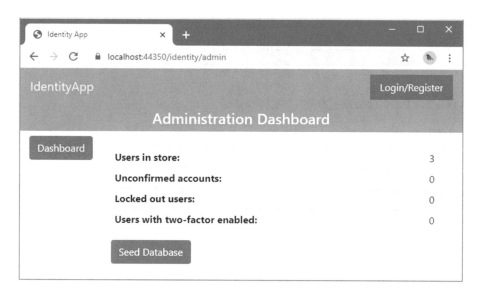

Figure 7-4. *Reading (and deleting) stored data*

Displaying a List of Users

There is now some insight into the stored data, but not enough to be useful. It would be helpful to see a list of user accounts, which can be obtained through the user manager's `Users` property. And, since the `Users` property returns an `IQueryable<IdentityUser>` object, it is easy to create a list that can be filtered. Selecting a user account is the first step in many custom Identity workflows, and this is a feature that I will reuse throughout this part of the book. Add a Razor Page named `SelectUser.cshtml` to the `Pages/Identity/Admin` folder with the content shown in Listing 7-20.

Listing 7-20. The Contents of the SelectUser.cshtml File in the Pages/Identity/Admin Folder

```
@page "{label?}/{callback?}"
@model IdentityApp.Pages.Identity.Admin.SelectUserModel
@{
    ViewBag.Workflow = Model.Callback ?? Model.Label ?? "List";
}

<form method="post" class="my-2">
    <div class="form-row">
        <div class="col">
            <div class="input-group">
                <input asp-for="Filter" class="form-control" />
            </div>
        </div>
    </div>
```

```
        <div class="col-auto">
            <button class="btn btn-secondary">Filter</button>
        </div>
    </div>
</form>

<table class="table table-sm table-striped table-bordered">
    <thead>
        <tr>
            <th>User</th>
            @if (!string.IsNullOrEmpty(Model.Callback)) {
                <th/>
            }
        </tr>
    </thead>
    <tbody>
        @if (Model.Users.Count() == 0) {
            <tr><td colspan="2">No matches</td></tr>
        } else {
            @foreach (IdentityUser user in Model.Users) {
                <tr>
                    <td>@user.Email</td>
                    @if (!string.IsNullOrEmpty(Model.Callback)) {
                        <td class="text-center">
                            <a asp-page="@Model.Callback"
                                asp-route-id="@user.Id"
                                class="btn btn-sm btn-secondary">
                                @Model.Callback
                            </a>
                        </td>
                    }
                </tr>
            }
        }
    </tbody>
</table>

@if (!string.IsNullOrEmpty(Model.Callback)) {
    <a asp-page="Dashboard" class="btn btn-secondary">Cancel</a>
}
```

The view part of the page displays a table with a text box that can be used to filter the user store by searching email addresses. When I start using this page as part of a custom workflow, each user will be displayed with a button that requests the page that is specified in the URL, including the Id value of the selected user. This will allow users to be selected and trigger a redirection back to the page that handles the workflow.

To define the page model class, add the code shown in Listing 7-21 to the SelectUser.cshtml.cs file. (You will have to create this file if you are using Visual Studio Code.)

Listing 7-21. The Contents of the SelectUser.cshtml.cs File in the Pages/Identity/Admin Folder

```
using Microsoft.AspNetCore.Identity;
using Microsoft.AspNetCore.Mvc;
using System.Collections.Generic;
using System.Linq;

namespace IdentityApp.Pages.Identity.Admin {

    public class SelectUserModel : AdminPageModel {

        public SelectUserModel(UserManager<IdentityUser> mgr)
            => UserManager = mgr;

        public UserManager<IdentityUser> UserManager { get; set; }
        public IEnumerable<IdentityUser> Users { get; set; }

        [BindProperty(SupportsGet = true)]
        public string Label { get; set; }

        [BindProperty(SupportsGet = true)]
        public string Callback { get; set; }

        [BindProperty(SupportsGet = true)]
        public string Filter { get; set; }

        public void OnGet() {
            Users = UserManager.Users
                .Where(u => Filter == null || u.Email.Contains(Filter))
                .OrderBy(u => u.Email).ToList();
        }

        public IActionResult OnPost() => RedirectToPage(new { Filter, Callback });
    }
}
```

The page model uses the UserManager<IdentityUser> object it receives via dependency injection to query the user store with LINQ. I use the ToList method to force the evaluation of the query so that I can operate on the results without triggering repeated user store searches.

The final step is to add a navigation button for the new Razor Page, as shown in Listing 7-22.

Listing 7-22. Adding Navigation in the _AdminWorkflows.cshtml File in the Pages/Identity/Admin Folder

```
@model (string workflow, string theme)

@{
    Func<string, string> getClass = (string feature) =>
        feature != null && feature.Equals(Model.workflow) ? "active" : "";
}
```

```
<a class="btn btn-@Model.theme btn-block @getClass("Dashboard")"
        asp-page="Dashboard">
    Dashboard
</a>
<a class="btn btn-success btn-block @getClass("List")" asp-page="SelectUser">
    List Users
</a>
```

To see the list of users, restart ASP.NET Core, request https://localhost:44350/Identity/Admin, and click the List Users button, which will produce the results shown in Figure 7-5. You can enter text into the field and filter the list of users, but the only stored data is the account created by the seeding process.

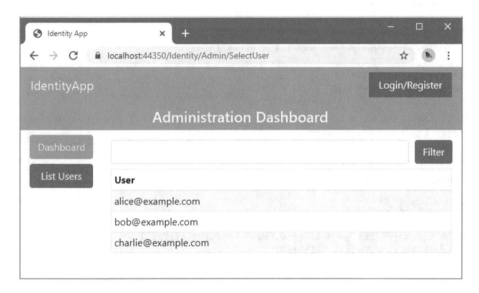

Figure 7-5. *Displaying a list of stored user accounts*

Viewing and Editing User Details

The IdentityUser class defines a set of properties that provide access to the stored data values for a user account. For example, there is an Email property that provides access to the user's email address. Some properties can be accessed through methods defined by the UserManager<IdentityUser> class so that the GetEmailAsync and SetEmailAsync methods get and set the value of the Email property.

Some properties are read-only, so the user manager class only provides methods that read the property value. For example, the IdentityUser.Id property provides access to the unique ID for an IdentityUser object that cannot be changed, so there is a UserManager<IdentityUser>.GetUserIdAsync method to read the value but no corresponding method to change the value.

Some IdentityUser properties do not have corresponding user manager methods at all. The NormalizedUserName method, for example, is automatically updated when a new UserName value is stored and there are no user manager methods for this property.

Some user manager methods do more than directly update a user object property. The UserManager<IdentityUser>.SetEmailAsync method updates the Identity.Email property but also sets the IdentityUser.EmailConfirmed property to false, which indicates that the new email address has not been confirmed.

162

Working directly with user object properties is the simplest approach and feels natural in C# development, especially when combined with the ASP.NET Core model binding features, which make it easy to receive form data. But the additional work that the user manager methods perform can be useful in ensuring that the data in the user store is consistent. In Part 2 of this book, I describe every UserManager<T> method in detail so you can understand when additional work is performed.

For quick reference, Table 7-6 describes the properties defined by the IdentityUser class, along with the most important UserManager<IdentityUser> methods that relate to them, and provides a reference to the detailed descriptions later in this book. Some of the properties in the table are part of complex features that require additional user manager methods, as noted in the table. You may find the properties and methods approach confusing at first, but it is simpler than it appears and quickly becomes second nature.

Table 7-6. *User Class Properties and User Manager Class Methods*

Property Name	Description	User Manager Methods
Id	This property stores the unique ID for the user and cannot be changed.	GetUserIdAsync
UserName	This property stores the user's username.	GetUserNameAsync SetUserNameAsync
NormalizedUserName	This property stores a normalized representation of the username that is used when searching for users.	This property is updated automatically when the object is stored.
Email	This property stores the user's email address.	GetEmailAsync SetEmailAsync
NormalizedEmail	This property stores a normalized representation of the email address that is used when searching for users.	This property is updated automatically when the object is stored.
EmailConfirmed	This property indicates whether the user's email address has been confirmed.	IsEmailConfirmedAsync, with additional methods described in Chapter 17.
PasswordHash	This property stores a hashed representation of the user's password.	HasPasswordAsync, with additional methods described in Chapter 18.
PhoneNumber	This property stores the user's phone number.	GetPhoneNumberAsync SetPhoneNumberAsync
PhoneNumberConfirmed	This property indicates whether the user's phone number has been confirmed.	IsPhoneNumberConfirmedAsync, with additional methods described in Chapter 17.
TwoFactorEnabled	This property indicates whether the user has configured two-factor access.	GetTwoFactorEnabledAsync, SetTwoFactorEnabledAsync, with additional methods described in Chapter 20.
LockoutEnabled	This property indicates whether the user account can be locked out following failed sign-ins.	GetLockoutEnabledAsync SetLockoutEnabledAsync IsLockedOutAsync
AccessFailedCount	This property is used to keep track of the number of failed sign-ins.	This property is not used directly. See Chapter 20 for details.

(continued)

Table 7-6. (*continued*)

Property Name	Description	User Manager Methods
LockoutEnd	This property is used to store the time when the account will be permitted to sign in again.	This property is not used directly.
SecurityStamp	This property stores a random value that is changed when the user's credentials are updated.	This property is not used directly and is updated automatically.
ConcurrencyStamp	This property stores a random value that is updated whenever the user data is stored.	This property is not used directly.

Add a Razor Page named `View.cshtml` to the `Pages/Identity/Admin` folder with the content shown in Listing 7-23.

Listing 7-23. The Contents of the View.cshtml File in the Pages/Identity/Admin Folder

```
@page "{Id?}"
@model IdentityApp.Pages.Identity.Admin.ViewModel
@{
        ViewBag.Workflow = "List";
}

<table class="table table-sm table-striped table-bordered">
    <thead>
        <tr><th>Property</th><th>Value</th></tr>
    </thead>
    <tbody>
        @foreach (string name in Model.PropertyNames) {
            <tr>
                <td>@name</td>
                <td class="text-truncate" style="max-width:250px">
                    @Model.GetValue(name)
                </td>
            </tr>
        }
    </tbody>
</table>

<a asp-page="Edit" asp-route-id="@Model.Id" class="btn btn-secondary">
    Edit
</a>
<a asp-page="View" asp-route-id="" class="btn btn-secondary">Back</a>
```

The view part of the page displays a table containing the properties defined by the `IdentityUser` class and the values for the selected object. To implement the page model class, add the code shown in Listing 7-24 to the `View.cshtml.cs` file. (You will have to create this file if you are using Visual Studio Code.)

Listing 7-24. The Contents of the View.cshtml.cs File in the Pages/Identity/Admin Folder

```
using Microsoft.AspNetCore.Identity;
using Microsoft.AspNetCore.Mvc;
using System.Collections.Generic;
using System.Linq;
using System.Threading.Tasks;

namespace IdentityApp.Pages.Identity.Admin {

    public class ViewModel : AdminPageModel {

        public ViewModel(UserManager<IdentityUser> mgr) => UserManager = mgr;

        public UserManager<IdentityUser> UserManager { get; set; }

        public IdentityUser IdentityUser { get; set; }

        [BindProperty(SupportsGet = true)]
        public string Id { get; set; }

        public IEnumerable<string> PropertyNames
            => typeof(IdentityUser).GetProperties()
                .Select(prop => prop.Name);

        public string GetValue(string name) =>
            typeof(IdentityUser).GetProperty(name)
                .GetValue(IdentityUser)?.ToString();

        public async Task<IActionResult> OnGetAsync() {
            if (string.IsNullOrEmpty(Id)) {
                return RedirectToPage("Selectuser",
                    new { Label = "View User", Callback = "View" });
            }
            IdentityUser = await UserManager.FindByIdAsync(Id);
            return Page();
        }
    }
}
```

To identify the user account to be edited, the GET handler page will perform a redirection to the SelectUser page if the request URL doesn't include an Id value. If there is an Id, then it is used to search the user store, using one of the methods that the UserManager<IdentityUser> class provides, as described in Table 7-7.

Table 7-7. *The UserManager<T> Members for Searching the Store*

Name	Description
FindByIdAsync(id)	This method returns an IdentityUser object representing the user with the specified unique ID.
FindByNameAsync(name)	This method returns an IdentityUser object representing the user with the specified name.
FindByEmailAsync(email)	This method returns an IdentityUser object representing the user with the specified email address.

These methods locate a single IdentityUser object using an ID, username, or email address or return null if there is no match.

If the GET handler method in Listing 7-24 is invoked by a URL that contains an ID value, then the FindByIdAsync method is used to search the user store and assign the result to a property named IdentityUser that can be accessed in the view.

```
...
IdentityUser = await UserManager.FindByIdAsync(Id);
...
```

The list of properties is obtained from the IdentityUser type using the .NET reflection feature. In Listing 7-25, I have changed the page selected by the List Users button so that the View page is requested.

Listing 7-25. Changing Navigation in the _AdminWorkflows.cshtml File in the Pages/Identity/Admin Folder

```
@model (string workflow, string theme)

@{
    Func<string, string> getClass = (string feature) =>
        feature != null && feature.Equals(Model.workflow) ? "active" : "";
}

<a class="btn btn-@Model.theme btn-block @getClass("Dashboard")"
        asp-page="Dashboard">
    Dashboard
</a>
<a class="btn btn-success btn-block @getClass("List")" asp-page="View"
        asp-route-id="">
    List Users
</a>
```

Restart ASP.NET Core, request https://localhost:44350/identity/admin, and click the List Users button. Click the View button for the alice@example.com account, and you will be presented with a table containing the IdentityUser properties and values, as shown in Figure 7-6. Some properties are assigned values automatically, while others are not assigned until the feature to which they relate is used.

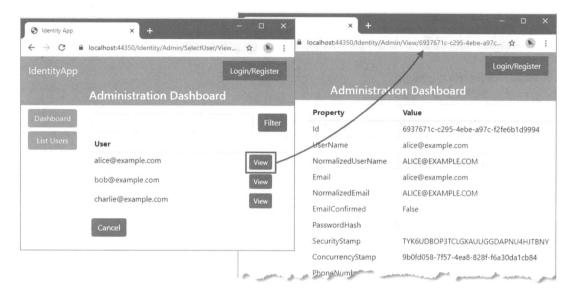

Figure 7-6. *Displaying IdentityUser properties*

Editing User Details

The previous examples demonstrated the basic operations for creating, reading, and deleting IdentityUser objects, which are three of the four classic data operations. I demonstrate how these features can be used to create custom workflows in later chapters, but there is one additional operation that creates the classic set: performing an update.

Add a Razor Page named Edit.cshtml to the Pages/Identity/Admin folder with the content shown in Listing 7-26.

Listing 7-26. The Contents of the Edit.cshtml File in the Pages/Identity/Admin Folder

```
@page "{Id?}"
@model IdentityApp.Pages.Identity.Admin.EditModel
@{
    ViewBag.Workflow = "Edit";
}

<div asp-validation-summary="All" class="text-danger m-2"></div>

<form method="post">
    <input type="hidden" asp-for="Id" />
    <div class="form-group">
        <label>Username</label>
        <input class="form-control" asp-for="IdentityUser.UserName" />
    </div>
    <div class="form-group">
        <label>Normalized Username</label>
        <input class="form-control" asp-for="IdentityUser.NormalizedUserName"
            readonly />
    </div>
```

```
<div class="form-group">
    <label>Email</label>
    <input class="form-control" asp-for="IdentityUser.Email" />
</div>
<div class="form-group">
    <label>Normalized Email</label>
    <input class="form-control"
        asp-for="IdentityUser.NormalizedEmail" readonly />
</div>
<div class="form-group">
    <label>Phone Number</label>
    <input class="form-control" asp-for="IdentityUser.PhoneNumber" />
</div>
<div>
    <button type="submit" class="btn btn-success">Save</button>
    <a asp-page="Dashboard" class="btn btn-secondary">Cancel</a>
</div>
</form>
```

The view part of the page displays an HTML form with fields for editing the UserName, Email, and PhoneNumber properties of an IdentityUser object. There is also a hidden value for the Id property, so that the user object to be modified can be identified, and read-only fields for the NormalizedUserName and NormalizedEmail properties, which I have included to demonstrate how some properties are updated automatically.

To create the page model, add the code shown in Listing 7-27 to the Edit.cshtml.cs file. (You will have to create this file if you are using Visual Studio Code.)

Listing 7-27. The Contents of the Edit.cshtml.cs File in the Pages/Identity/Admin Folder

```
using Microsoft.AspNetCore.Identity;
using Microsoft.AspNetCore.Mvc;
using System.ComponentModel.DataAnnotations;
using System.Threading.Tasks;

namespace IdentityApp.Pages.Identity.Admin {

    public class EditBindingTarget {
        [Required]
        public string Username { get; set; }
        [Required]
        [EmailAddress]
        public string Email { get; set; }
        [Phone]
        public string PhoneNumber { get; set; }
    }

    public class EditModel : AdminPageModel {

        public EditModel(UserManager<IdentityUser> mgr) => UserManager = mgr;

        public UserManager<IdentityUser> UserManager { get; set; }
```

```
        public IdentityUser IdentityUser { get; set; }

        [BindProperty(SupportsGet = true)]
        public string Id { get; set; }

        public async Task<IActionResult> OnGetAsync() {
            if (string.IsNullOrEmpty(Id)) {
                return RedirectToPage("Selectuser",
                    new { Label = "Edit User", Callback = "Edit" });
            }
            IdentityUser = await UserManager.FindByIdAsync(Id);
            return Page();
        }

        public async Task<IActionResult> OnPostAsync(
                [FromForm(Name = "IdentityUser")] EditBindingTarget userData) {
            if (!string.IsNullOrEmpty(Id) && ModelState.IsValid) {
                IdentityUser user = await UserManager.FindByIdAsync(Id);
                if (user != null) {
                    user.UserName = userData.Username;
                    user.Email = userData.Email;
                    user.EmailConfirmed = true;
                    if (!string.IsNullOrEmpty(userData.PhoneNumber)) {
                        user.PhoneNumber = userData.PhoneNumber;
                    }
                }
                IdentityResult result = await UserManager.UpdateAsync(user);
                if (result.Process(ModelState)) {
                    return RedirectToPage();
                }
            }
            IdentityUser = await UserManager.FindByIdAsync(Id);
            return Page();
        }
    }
}
```

When the user submits the form, the ASP.NET Core model binding feature assigns the form values to the properties to an instance of the EditBindingTarget class, which is defined as follows:

```
...
public class EditBindingTarget {
    [Required]
    public string Username { get; set; }
    [Required]
    [EmailAddress]
    public string Email { get; set; }
    [Phone]
    public string PhoneNumber { get; set; }
}
...
```

As I demonstrate in Part 2, you can use model binding directly with an instance of the user class, but this approach allows me to be selective about the fields that I am interested in and apply validation attributes without needing to subclass IdentityUser or declare and decorate individual handler method parameters.

The POST handler method uses the Id property, which is set using model binding, to search the user store with the FindByIdAsync and update the properties of the resulting IdentityUser object with the form data values, like this:

```
...
IdentityUser user = await UserManager.FindByIdAsync(Id);
if (user != null) {
    user.UserName = userData.Username;
    user.Email = userData.Email;
    user.EmailConfirmed = true;
    if (!string.IsNullOrEmpty(userData.PhoneNumber)) {
        user.PhoneNumber = userData.PhoneNumber;
    }
}
...
```

I could have used the methods provided by the UserManager<IdentityUser> class, but, as I explained earlier, I generally prefer to update IdentityUser properties directly.

Notice that I set the EmailConfirmed property to true in Listing 7-28. As a general rule, email addresses set by administrators should not require the user to go through the confirmation process, so I explicitly set the EmailConfirmed property. I create a workflow that does require user confirmation for email addresses in Chapter 9.

Changes to an IdentityUser object are not added to the store until the user manager's UpdateAsync method is called, like this:

```
...
IdentityResult result = await UserManager.UpdateAsync(user);
...
```

This method updates the user store and returns an IdentityResult object. To integrate the new workflow, add the element shown in Listing 7-28 to the navigation partial view.

Listing 7-28. Adding Navigation in the _AdminWorkflows.cshtml File in the Pages/Identity/Admin Folder

```
@model (string workflow, string theme)

@{
    Func<string, string> getClass = (string feature) =>
        feature != null && feature.Equals(Model.workflow) ? "active" : "";
}

<a class="btn btn-@Model.theme btn-block @getClass("Dashboard")"
        asp-page="Dashboard">
    Dashboard
</a>
```

```
<a class="btn btn-success btn-block @getClass("List")" asp-page="View"
        asp-route-id="">
    List Users
</a>
<a class="btn btn-success btn-block @getClass("Edit")" asp-page="Edit"
        asp-route-id="">
    Edit Users
</a>
```

Restart ASP.NET Core, request https://localhost:44350/Identity/Admin, click Edit Users, and click the Edit button for the alice@example.com account. Change the username to alice.smith@example.com and click the Save button. The user store will be updated, as shown in Figure 7-7.

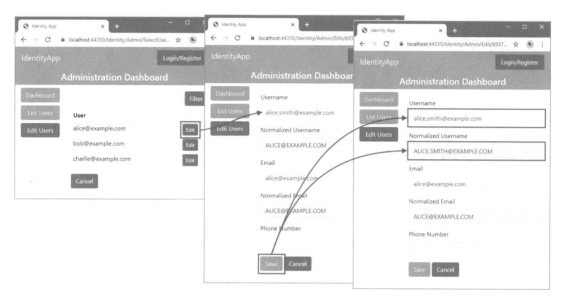

Figure 7-7. *Editing User Details*

Notice that the normalized username property is automatically updated. This is done by the user manager's UpdateAsync method, and it helps ensure consistency in the user store.

The normalization process is described in detail in Part 2, but what's important for this chapter is that it is updated automatically when data is stored.

The UpdateAsyc method also performs validation, which you can see by editing the Alice account and entering **bob@example.com** into the Username field. When you click the Save button, you will see the error message shown in Figure 7-8, which was included in the IdentityResult object returned by the UpdateAsync method. The validation process is described in Part 2.

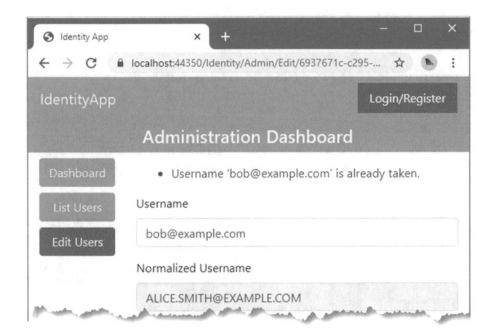

Figure 7-8. *Validating user details*

Fixing the Username and Email Problem

Identity supports different values for a user's username and email address, which are stored using the
IdentityUser class UserName and Email properties. This means a user can sign in with a username that is
not their email address, which is a common approach taken in corporate environments, especially in larger
companies where email is ring-fenced from other services.

For other applications, it makes more sense to use the email address as the username and keep both
IdentityUser fields synchronized, which is also the approach taken by the Identity UI package.

In Listing 7-29, I have updated the view part of the Edit page so that the Username text field to readonly.
There is no need to display both UserName and Email fields when they are being updated with the same
values, but I like to see the change happen.

Listing 7-29. Making a Field Read-Only in the Edit.cshtml File in the Pages/Identity/Admin Folder

```
@page "{Id?}"
@model IdentityApp.Pages.Identity.Admin.EditModel
@{
    ViewBag.Workflow = "Edit";
}

<div asp-validation-summary="All" class="text-danger m-2"></div>

<form method="post">
    <input type="hidden" asp-for="Id" />
    <div class="form-group">
        <label>Username</label>
        <input class="form-control" asp-for="IdentityUser.UserName" readonly />
    </div>
```

```
    <div class="form-group">
        <label>Normalized Username</label>
        <input class="form-control" asp-for="IdentityUser.NormalizedUserName"
            readonly />
    </div>
    <div class="form-group">
        <label>Email</label>
        <input class="form-control" asp-for="IdentityUser.Email" />
    </div>
    <div class="form-group">
        <label>Normalized Email</label>
        <input class="form-control"
            asp-for="IdentityUser.NormalizedEmail" readonly />
    </div>
    <div class="form-group">
        <label>Phone Number</label>
        <input class="form-control" asp-for="IdentityUser.PhoneNumber" />
    </div>
    <div>
        <button type="submit" class="btn btn-success">Save</button>
        <a asp-page="Dashboard" class="btn btn-secondary">Cancel</a>
    </div>
</form>
```

In Listing 7-30, I have modified the statements that apply the form data to the IdentityUser object so that the Email value is used for the Username property.

Listing 7-30. Setting Properties in the Edit.cshtml.cs File in the Pages/Identity/Admin Folder

```
...
public async Task<IActionResult> OnPostAsync(
        [FromForm(Name = "IdentityUser")] EditBindingTarget userData) {
    if (!string.IsNullOrEmpty(Id) && ModelState.IsValid) {
        IdentityUser user = await UserManager.FindByIdAsync(Id);
        if (user != null) {
            user.UserName = userData.Email;
            user.Email = userData.Email;
            user.EmailConfirmed = true;
            if (!string.IsNullOrEmpty(userData.PhoneNumber)) {
                user.PhoneNumber = userData.PhoneNumber;
            }
        }
        IdentityResult result = await UserManager.UpdateAsync(user);
        if (result.Process(ModelState)) {
            return RedirectToPage();
        }
    }
    IdentityUser = await UserManager.FindByIdAsync(Id);
    return Page();
}
...
```

Restart ASP.NET Core, request `https://localhost:44350/Identity/Admin`, click Edit Users, and click the Edit button for the Alice account. Click the Save button, and the username and email address will be updated to the same value, as shown in Figure 7-9. Notice that the normalized username is also updated.

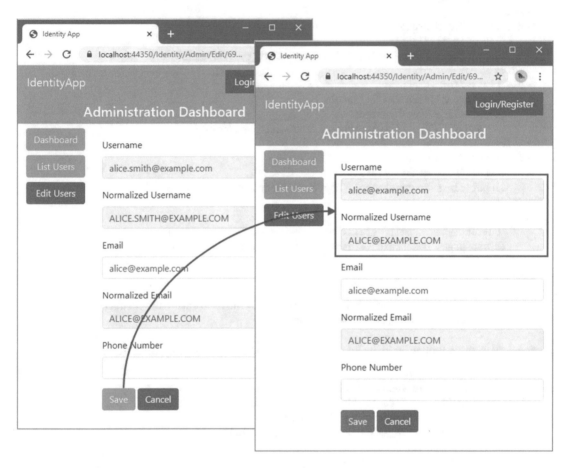

Figure 7-9. *Updating the username and email address consistently*

Understanding the User Store

The `UserManager<IdentityUser>` class doesn't store data itself. Instead, it depends on dependency injection to obtain an implementation of the `IUserStore<IdentityUser>` interface. The interface defines the operations required to store and retrieve `IdentityUser` data, and there are additional interfaces that can be implemented by user stores that support additional features. In Part 2, I create a custom user store and explain how each method and optional interface is implemented, but that is a level of detail that is rarely required in most projects.

Instead, you just have to know how to set up the user store to understand which features it implements. The user store in the example application is the one that Microsoft provides for storing data in a SQL database using Entity Framework Core.

```
...
services.AddDefaultIdentity<IdentityUser>(opts => {
    opts.Password.RequiredLength = 8;
    opts.Password.RequireDigit = false;
    opts.Password.RequireLowercase = false;
    opts.Password.RequireUppercase = false;
    opts.Password.RequireNonAlphanumeric = false;
    opts.SignIn.RequireConfirmedAccount = true;
}).AddEntityFrameworkStores<IdentityDbContext>();
...
```

The AddEntityFrameworkStores method sets up the user store, and the generic type argument specifies the Entity Framework Core context that will be used to access the database.

Separating the user manager from the user store means it is relatively simple to change the user store if the needs of the project change. As long as the new user store can work with your chosen user class, there should be little difficulty in moving from one user store to another.

Caution is required because not all user stores support all of the Identity features, which is indicated by the set of optional interfaces that the user store has implemented. It is important to check that all the features you require are supported when you start a new project and when you change user store.

You don't have to inspect the user store directly because the user manager class defines a set of properties you can read to check feature support, as described in Table 7-8. You will see these features used in the workflows created in this part of the book and described in detail in Part 2.

Table 7-8. *The User Manager Properties for Checking User Store Capabilities*

Name	Description
SupportsQueryableUsers	This property returns true if the user store supports queries via LINQ. The query feature is demonstrated in the querying the user data section and described in depth in Part 2.
SupportsUserEmail	This property returns true if the user store supports email addresses, allows searching the store using an email address, and can keep track of whether an email address has been confirmed. (The actual confirmation process is handled largely by the user manager class, as described in Part 2.)
SupportsUserPhoneNumber	This property returns true if the user store supports phone numbers and keeps track of whether a phone number has been confirmed. (The actual confirmation process is handled largely by the user manager class, as described in Part 2.)
SupportsUserPassword	This property returns true if the user store supports hashed passwords for a user. The management of passwords is demonstrated in Chapter 8 and described in depth in Part 2.
SupportsUserRole	This property returns true if the user store supports roles. The roles feature is demonstrated in Chapter 10 and described in depth in Part 2.
SupportsUserClaim	This property returns true if the user store supports claims. The claims feature is demonstrated in Chapter 10 and described in depth in Part 2.

(continued)

Table 7-8. (*continued*)

Name	Description
SupportsUserLockout	This property returns true if the user store supports user lockouts. This feature is demonstrated in Chapter 8 and described in depth in Part 2.
SupportsUserTwoFactor	This property returns true if the user store can keep track of whether a user requires two-factor authentication. This feature is demonstrated in Chapter 11 and described in depth in Part 2.
SupportsUserTwoFactorRecoveryCodes	This property returns true if the store can manage recovery codes, which allow two-factor authentication to be bypassed. This feature is described in depth in Part 2.
SupportsUserLogin	This property returns true if the store can manage details of signing in with external authentication services. This feature is demonstrated in Chapter 11 and described in depth in Part 2.
SupportsUserAuthenticatorKey	This property returns true if the store can manage keys for signing in with an authenticator app. This feature is demonstrated in Chapter 11 and described in depth in Part 2.
SupportsUserAuthenticationTokens	This property returns true if the store can manage tokens used to access APIs provided by third parties, as described in Part 2.
SupportsUserSecurityStamp	This property returns true if the store can manage security stamps, which are random values that change when the user's credentials are altered. Security stamps are used indirectly by many Identity workflows and are described in detail in Part 2.

This is a long list of features, but you will understand all of them in detail by the end of this book, and not all of them are required by every application. It is always a good idea to confirm you have access to the features you expect because the user manager class will throw exceptions if you try to perform an operation that relies on a feature that your user store does not support.

Add a Razor Page named Features.cshtml to the Pages/Identity/Admin folder with the content shown in Listing 7-31.

Listing 7-31. The Contents of the Features.cshtml File in the Pages/Identity/Admin Folder

```
@page
@model IdentityApp.Pages.Identity.Admin.FeaturesModel
@inject UserManager<IdentityUser> UserManager
@{
    ViewBag.Workflow = "Features";
}

<table class="table table-sm table-striped table-bordered">
    <thead><tr><th>Property</th><th>Supported</th></tr></thead>
    <tbody>
        @foreach ((string prop, string val) in Model.Features) {
            <tr>
                <td>@prop</td>
                <td class="@(val == "True" ? "bg-success" : "bg-danger") text-white">
```

```
                    @val
                </td>
            </tr>
        }
    </tbody>
</table>
```

The view section of the page displays a table that is populated with a set of tuples that contain each feature property and its value. To implement the page model class, add the code shown in Listing 7-32 to the Features.cshtml.cs file. (You will have to create this file if you are using Visual Studio Code.)

Listing 7-32. The Contents of the Features.cshtml.cs File in the Pages/Identity/Admin Folder

```
using Microsoft.AspNetCore.Identity;
using System.Collections.Generic;
using System.Linq;

namespace IdentityApp.Pages.Identity.Admin {
    public class FeaturesModel : AdminPageModel {

        public FeaturesModel(UserManager<IdentityUser> mgr)
            => UserManager = mgr;

        public UserManager<IdentityUser> UserManager { get; set; }

        public IEnumerable<(string, string)> Features { get; set; }

        public void OnGet() {
            Features = UserManager.GetType().GetProperties()
                .Where(prop => prop.Name.StartsWith("Supports"))
                .OrderBy(p => p.Name)
                .Select(prop => (prop.Name, prop.GetValue(UserManager)
                .ToString()));
        }
    }
}
```

The page model declares a dependency on the UserManager<IdentityUser> class by defining a constructor parameter, which is resolved by the ASP.NET Core dependency injection feature. This allows me to use .NET reflection and LINQ to get the set of properties whose names start with Supports and create a sequence of tuples containing their names and values. The final step is to add a navigation button for the new page, as shown in Listing 7-33.

Listing 7-33. Adding a Button in the _AdminWorkflows.cshtml File in the Pages/Identity/Admin Folder

```
@model (string workflow, string theme)

@{
    Func<string, string> getClass = (string feature) =>
        feature != null && feature.Equals(Model.workflow) ? "active" : "";
}
```

```
<a class="btn btn-@Model.theme btn-block @getClass("Dashboard")"
        asp-page="Dashboard">
    Dashboard
</a>
<a class="btn btn-@Model.theme btn-block @getClass("Features")" asp-page="Features">
    Store Features
</a>
<a class="btn btn-success btn-block @getClass("List")" asp-page="View"
        asp-route-id="">
    List Users
</a>
<a class="btn btn-success btn-block @getClass("Edit")" asp-page="Edit"
        asp-route-id="">
    Edit Users
</a>
```

Restart ASP.NET Core, request https://localhost:44350/Identity/Admin, and click the Store Features button, which will produce the output shown in Figure 7-10.

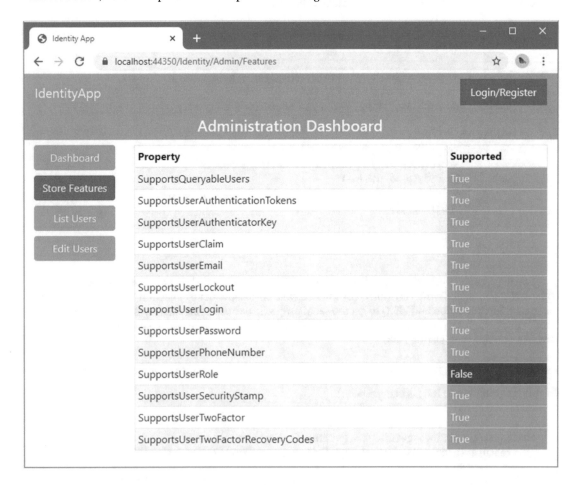

Figure 7-10. Checking the features supported by the user store

Changing the Identity Configuration

You will notice that the user store doesn't support roles. This is because the Identity UI package doesn't support roles, and the method used to set up Identity and Identity UI doesn't include the configuration information for role support.

I am going to need the role feature in Chapter 10, so I have changed the method used to set up Identity in the Startup class, as shown in Listing 7-34, which also has the effect of disabling the Identity UI package.

Listing 7-34. Changing the Identity Configuration in the Startup.cs File in the IdentityApp Folder

```
...
services.AddIdentity<IdentityUser, IdentityRole>(opts => {
    opts.Password.RequiredLength = 8;
    opts.Password.RequireDigit = false;
    opts.Password.RequireLowercase = false;
    opts.Password.RequireUppercase = false;
    opts.Password.RequireNonAlphanumeric = false;
    opts.SignIn.RequireConfirmedAccount = true;
}).AddEntityFrameworkStores<IdentityDbContext>();
...
```

The user store set up by the AddEntityFrameworkStores method does support roles but only when a role class has been selected, which isn't possible with the AddDefaultIdentity method used previously.

I have replaced the AddDefaultIdentity method the AddIdentity method. The AddIdentity method defines an additional generic type parameter that is used to specify the role class, which enables role support in the user store.

Restart ASP.NET Core, request https://localhost:44350/Identity/Admin, and click the Store Features button, and you will see that the user store now supports all of the Identity features, as shown in Figure 7-11.

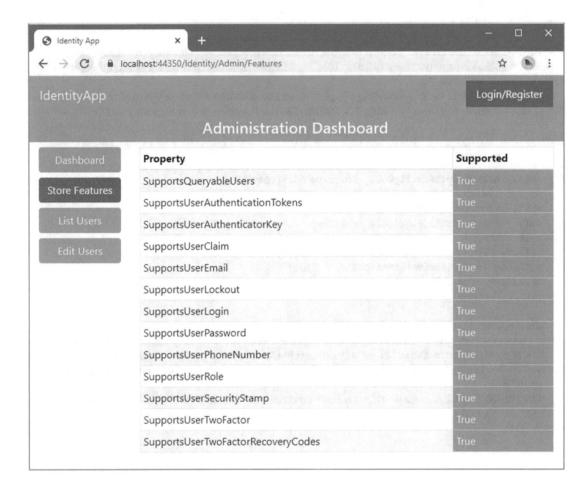

Figure 7-11. *Enabling user store features*

Summary

In this chapter, I started to describe the Identity API and used its basic features to lay the foundation for future chapters by creating administrator and self-service dashboards. In the next chapter, I create workflows for signing into the application and managing passwords.

CHAPTER 8

■ ■ ■

Signing In and Out and Managing Passwords

In this chapter, I describe the Identity API features for signing in and out of applications. Identity supports different ways of signing in, and I start with passwords in this chapter, including creating the workflows for managing passwords. In later chapters, I describe the other ways in which users can authenticate themselves. Table 8-1 puts the features for signing in and out and managing passwords in context.

Table 8-1. *Putting the Features for Signing In and Out and Managing Passwords in Context*

Question	Answer
What are they?	These API features are used to create workflows for signing the user into the application with a password and signing them out again when they have finished their session. These features are also used to manage passwords, both to set passwords administratively and to perform self-service password changes and password recovery.
Why are they useful?	Passwords are not the only way to authenticate with an Identity application, but they are the most widely used and are required by most projects.
How are they used?	Passwords are managed using methods provided by the `UserManager<IdentityUser>` class, which allows passwords to be added and removed from a user account. Users sign into and out of the application using methods defined by the sign-in manager class, `SignInManager<T>`.
Are there any pitfalls or limitations?	The sign-in process can be complex, especially if the project supports two-factor authentication and external authentication.
Are there any alternatives?	These features are built on the underlying ASP.NET Core platform, which you could use directly to achieve the same results. However, doing so would undermine the purpose of using Identity to manage users.

© Adam Freeman 2021
A. Freeman, *Pro ASP.NET Core Identity*, https://doi.org/10.1007/978-1-4842-6858-2_8

Table 8-2 summarizes the chapter.

Table 8-2. *Chapter Summary*

Problem	Solution	Listing
Manage passwords for a user account	Use the `HasPasswordAsync`, `RemovePasswordAsync`, and `HasPasswordAsync` methods defined by the user manager class.	1–3
Sign a user into the application with a password	Use the `PasswordSignInAsync` method defined by the sign-in manager class.	4, 5
Sign a user out of the application	Use the `SignOutAsync` method defined by the sign-in manager class.	6, 7
Configure ASP.NET Core to use the custom workflows for signing users in and out	Use the `ConfigureApplicationCookie` method to configure the `LoginPath`, `LogoutPath`, and `AccessDeniedPath` properties.	8–10
Get the `IdentityUser` object for the signed in user	Call the user manager's `GetUserAsync` method.	11
Support self-service password change	Call the user manager's `ChangePasswordAsync` method.	15–17
Support self-service passwords recovery	Call the user manager's `GeneratePasswordResetTokenAsync` to get a token is sent to the user. Validate the token and change the password with the `ResetPasswordAsync` method.	12–14, 18–23
Support administrator password changes	Use the `HasPasswordAsync`, `RemovePasswordAsync`, and `HasPasswordAsync` methosd defined by the user manager class or use the `GeneratePasswordResetTokenAsync` and `ResetPasswordAsync` methods to allow the user to select a new password.	24–26
Restrict access to resources to signed-in users	Apply the `Authorize` attribute, creating exceptions with the `AllowAnonymous` attribute.	27–32

Preparing for This Chapter

This chapter uses the `IdentityApp` project from Chapter 7. No changes are required for this chapter. Open a new PowerShell command prompt and run the commands shown in Listing 8-1 to reset the application and Identity databases.

■ **Tip** You can download the example project for this chapter—and for all the other chapters in this book—from `https://github.com/Apress/pro-asp.net-core-identity`. See Chapter 1 for how to get help if you have problems running the examples.

Listing 8-1. Resetting the Databases

```
dotnet ef database drop --force --context ProductDbContext
dotnet ef database drop --force --context IdentityDbContext
dotnet ef database update --context ProductDbContext
dotnet ef database update --context IdentityDbContext
```

Use the PowerShell prompt to run the command shown in Listing 8-2 in the IdentityApp folder to start the application.

Listing 8-2. Running the Example Application

```
dotnet run
```

Open a web browser and request https://localhost:44350/Identity/Admin, which will show the administration dashboard, as shown in Figure 8-1.

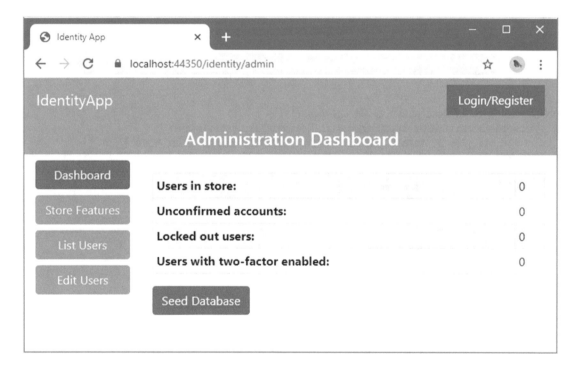

Figure 8-1. *Running the example application*

Adding Passwords to the Seed Data

The user accounts used to seed the user store won't be able to sign into the application because they have no credentials. Identity supports a range of authentication mechanisms and doesn't require IdentityUser objects to be created with any specific authentication data. The basic authentication model uses a password, and that is where I will start in this chapter before introducing other options in later chapters. Passwords are assigned using methods defined by the user class, as described in Table 8-3.

Table 8-3. *The UserManager<IdentityUser> Methods for Managing Passwords*

Name	Description
HasPasswordAsync(user)	This method returns true if the specific IdentityUser object has been assigned a password.
AddPasswordAsync(user, password)	This method adds a password to the store for the specified IdentityUser.
RemovePasswordAsync(user)	This method removes the password stored for the specified IdentityUser object.

In Listing 8-3, I have used the AddPasswordAsync method to set the same password for all the accounts used to seed the user store.

Listing 8-3. Setting Passwords in the Dashboard.cshtml.cs File in the Pages/Identity/Admin Folder

```
...
public async Task<IActionResult> OnPostAsync() {
    foreach (IdentityUser existingUser in UserManager.Users.ToList()) {
        IdentityResult result = await UserManager.DeleteAsync(existingUser);
        result.Process(ModelState);
    }
    foreach (string email in emails) {
        IdentityUser userObject = new IdentityUser {
            UserName = email,
            Email = email,
            EmailConfirmed = true
        };
        IdentityResult result = await UserManager.CreateAsync(userObject);
        if (result.Process(ModelState)) {
            result = await UserManager.AddPasswordAsync(userObject, "mysecret");
            result.Process(ModelState);
        }
    }
    if (ModelState.IsValid) {
        return RedirectToPage();
    }
    return Page();
}
...
```

I use the AddPasswordAsync method to give all of the test accounts the same password: mysecret. Later in this chapter, I create workflows for changing passwords, but this is enough to get started.

Restart ASP.NET Core and request https://localhost:44350/identity/admin. Click the Seed Database button, and the test accounts will be added to the user store, including a password.

Passwords are stored as hash codes, which means that having access to the database doesn't reveal a user's password. I describe the process by which passwords are converted into hash codes in detail in Part 2, but you can see the result by clicking the List Users button and clicking the View button for the alice@example.com account. The PasswordHash property has been assigned a value, as shown in Figure 8-2.

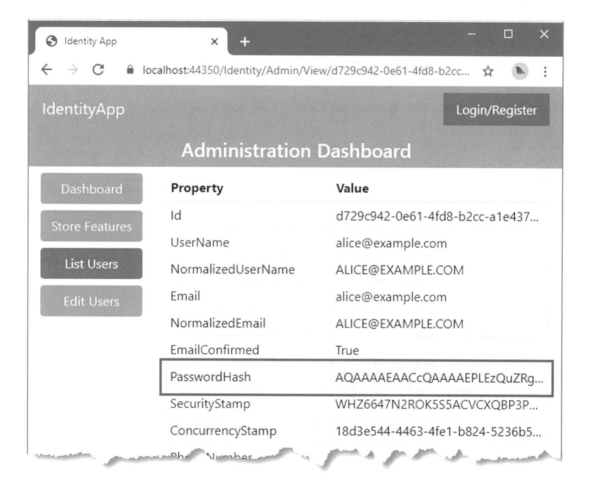

Figure 8-2. *Storing passwords*

Signing In, Signing Out, and Denying Access

The three most fundamental user-facing features are the ability to sign in to the application, the ability to sign out again, and the ability to display an error message when the user requests content for which they are not authorized. In the sections that follow, I create these essential workflows and configure the application to make use of them.

Signing into the Application

When signing into the application, the user provides credentials that are compared to the data in the user store. If the credentials match the stored data, then a cookie is added to the response that securely identifies the user in subsequent requests.

ASP.NET Core uses the `ClaimsPrincipal` class to represent the signed-in user. I describe this class in more detail in later chapters, but for now, it is enough to know that the sign-in process obtains an `IdentityUser` object from the store and uses the data that it contains to create a `ClaimsPrincipal` object that can be used by ASP.NET Core.

Evaluating the user's credentials and creating the `ClaimsPrincipal` object are the responsibilities of the sign-in manager class, `SignInManager<IdentityUser>`, which is configured as a service when Identity is configured.

Add a Razor Page named `SignIn.cshtml` to the `Pages/Identity` folder with the content shown in Listing 8-4.

Listing 8-4. The Contents of the SignIn.cshtml File in the Pages/Identity Folder

```
@page "{returnUrl?}"
@model IdentityApp.Pages.Identity.SignInModel
@{
    ViewData["showNav"] = false;
    ViewData["banner"] = "Sign In";
}

<div asp-validation-summary="All" class="text-danger m-2"></div>

@if (TempData.ContainsKey("message")) {
    <div class="alert alert-danger">@TempData["message"]</div>
}

<form method="post">
    <div class="form-group">
        <label>Email</label>
        <input class="form-control" name="email" />
    </div>
    <div class="form-group">
        <label>Password</label>
        <input class="form-control" type="password" name="password" />
    </div>
    <button type="submit" class="btn btn-primary">
        Sign In
    </button>
</form>
```

The user is prompted to enter their email address and password into a form that sends a POST request. There are elements to display model validation errors, and I have added a `div` element styled as an alert so I can display messages using the ASP.NET Core temp data feature.

As you have seen in earlier chapters, when an unauthenticated user requests content that is protected, ASP.NET Core sends a challenge response, which leads to the user being prompted to sign in. As part of this process, the URL that the user requested is provided as a query string parameter named `returnUrl`, which allows the browser to be redirected back to the content after a successful sign-in. The page directive in Listing 8-4 defines a route parameter named `returnUrl` to capture this URL.

To define the page model class, add the code shown in Listing 8-5 to the `SignIn.cshtml.cs` file. (You will have to create this file if you are using Visual Studio Code.)

Listing 8-5. The Contents of the SignIn.cshtml.cs File in the Pages/Identity Folder

```
using System.ComponentModel.DataAnnotations;
using System.Threading.Tasks;
using Microsoft.AspNetCore.Identity;
using Microsoft.AspNetCore.Mvc;
using SignInResult = Microsoft.AspNetCore.Identity.SignInResult;

namespace IdentityApp.Pages.Identity {

    public class SignInModel : UserPageModel {

        public SignInModel(SignInManager<IdentityUser> signMgr)
            => SignInManager = signMgr;

        public SignInManager<IdentityUser> SignInManager { get; set; }

        [Required]
        [EmailAddress]
        [BindProperty]
        public string Email { get; set; }

        [Required]
        [BindProperty]
        public string Password { get; set; }

        [BindProperty(SupportsGet = true)]
        public string ReturnUrl { get; set; }

        public async Task<IActionResult> OnPostAsync() {
            if (ModelState.IsValid) {
                SignInResult result = await SignInManager.PasswordSignInAsync(Email,
                    Password, true, true);
                if (result.Succeeded) {
                    return Redirect(ReturnUrl ?? "/");
                } else if (result.IsLockedOut) {
                    TempData["message"] = "Account Locked";
                } else if (result.IsNotAllowed) {
                    TempData["message"] = "Sign In Not Allowed";
                } else if (result.RequiresTwoFactor) {
                    return RedirectToPage("SignInTwoFactor", new { ReturnUrl });
                } else {
                    TempData["message"] = "Sign In Failed";
                }
            }
            return Page();
        }
    }
}
```

The page model receives a SignInManager<IdentityUser> object through its constructor and uses the PasswordSignInAsync method to sign the user into the application. For quick reference, Table 8-4 describes this method.

Table 8-4. *The SignInManager<IdentityUser> Method for Password SignIns*

Name	Description
PasswordSignInAsync(username, password, persist, lockout)	This method signs the user into the application with the specified username and password. The persist argument specifies whether the authentication cookie persists after the browser is closed. The lockout argument specifies whether a failed sign-in attempt counts toward a lockout, as described in Chapter 9. There is also a version of this method that accepts an IdentityUser object instead of a username.

The result from the PasswordSignInAsync is an instance of the SignInResult class defined in the Microsoft.AspNetCore.Identity namespace. There is also a SignInResult class defined in the Microsoft.AspNetCore.Mvc namespace, so disambiguation is required, like this:

```
...
using SignInResult = Microsoft.AspNetCore.Identity.SignInResult;
...
```

The SignInResult describes the sign attempt using the properties described in Table 8-5.

Table 8-5. *The SignInResult Properties*

Name	Description
Succeeded	This property returns true if the user has been successfully signed into the application.
IsLockedOut	This property returns true if the user is currently locked out. See Chapter 9 for details of how lockouts work.
RequiresTwoFactor	This property returns true if two-factor authentication is required. See Chapter 11 for details of creating workflows for two-factor authentication.
IsNotAllowed	This property returns true if the user is not allowed to sign in. This is most commonly the case when the email address has not been confirmed. I create a workflow that supports confirmations in Chapter 9.

If the Succeeded property is false, you can check the other properties to see if any follow-up action is required, such as prompting the user for two-factor authentication. If all the SignInResult properties are false, then the user hasn't provided a valid email address or password.

If the Succeeded property is true, then the user has been signed into the application and can be redirected back to the URL that triggered the challenge response, like this:

```
...
if (result.Succeeded) {
    return RedirectToPage(ReturnUrl ?? "/");
} else if (result.IsLockedOut) {
...
```

The other outcomes are handled by displaying an error message to the user, except when the user requires two-factor authentication. For this outcome, I perform a redirection to a Razor Page named SignInTwoFactor that I will create in Chapter 11.

Signing Out of the Application

Signing out of the application allows the user to explicitly terminate their session. Add a Razor Page named SignOut.cshtml to the Pages/Identity folder with the content shown in Listing 8-6.

Listing 8-6. The Contents of the SignOut.cshtml File in the Pages/Identity Folder

```
@page
@model IdentityApp.Pages.Identity.SignOutModel
@{
    ViewData["showNav"] = false;
    ViewData["banner"] = "Sign Out";
}

@if (User.Identity.IsAuthenticated) {
    <form method="post">
        <div class="text-center">
            <h6>Click the button to sign out of the application</h6>
            <button type="submit" class="btn btn-secondary">
                Sign Out
            </button>
        </div>
    </form>
} else {
    <div class="text-center">
        <h6>You are signed out of the application</h6>
        <a asp-page="SignIn" asp-route-returnUrl="" class="btn btn-secondary">
            OK
        </a>
    </div>
}
```

The view part of the page checks to see if there is an authenticated user by reading the User.Identity. IsAuthenticated property. I explain how this property works in Part 2, but for now, it is enough to know that it returns true if the current request is authenticated.

If there is an authenticated user, then the view presents a page that contains a form, allowing the user to sign out. If there is no authenticated user, then a message indicating the user is signed out is displayed. This is important because the browser should be redirected during the sign-out process to ensure that the cookie that authenticates the user is removed.

To define the page model class, add the code shown in Listing 8-7 to the SignOut.cshtml.cs file. (You will have to create this file if you are using Visual Studio Code.)

Listing 8-7. The Contents of the SignOut.cshtml.cs File in the Pages/Identity Folder

```
using Microsoft.AspNetCore.Identity;
using Microsoft.AspNetCore.Mvc;
using System.Threading.Tasks;

namespace IdentityApp.Pages.Identity {

    public class SignOutModel : UserPageModel    {

        public SignOutModel(SignInManager<IdentityUser> signMgr)
            => SignInManager = signMgr;

        public SignInManager<IdentityUser> SignInManager { get; set; }

        public async Task<IActionResult> OnPostAsync() {
            await SignInManager.SignOutAsync();
            return RedirectToPage();
        }
    }
}
```

Signing out of the application is done using the sign-in manager's SignOutAsync method. Once the user is signed out, I call the RedirectToPage method that will cause the browser to send a GET request to the SignOut page and to display the message confirming the user is signed out. This is the redirection that ensures the authentication cookie is deleted. For quick reference, Table 8-6 describes the method used to sign users out of the application.

Table 8-6. The SignInManager<IdentityUser> Method for Signing Out

Name	Description
SignOutAsync()	This method signs the current user out of the application.

Creating the Forbidden Page

Add a page named Forbidden.cshtml to the Pages/Identity folder with the content shown in Listing 8-8. This is the page that will be displayed when the user requests a URL for which they are not authorized.

Listing 8-8. The Contents of the Forbidden.cshtml File in the Pages/Identity Folder

```
@page
@model IdentityApp.Pages.Identity.ForbiddenModel
@{
    ViewData["showNav"] = false;
    ViewData["banner"] = "Access Denied";
}

<h6 class="text-center">You do not have access to this content</h6>
```

No page model code is required for this page, which just displays the message to the user.

Configuring the Application

Now that I have custom pages for signing in and out, I need to make some configuration changes to integrate them into the application. Listing 8-9 updates the navigation links displayed in the layout header to use the new pages. (When updating this file, take care to remove the `asp-area` attributes, which were used to select pages from the ASP.NET Core area created by the Identity UI package.)

Listing 8-9. Updating Links in the _LoginPartial.cshtml File in the Views/Shared Folder

```
<nav class="nav">
    @if (User.Identity.IsAuthenticated) {
        <a asp-page="/Identity/Index" class="nav-link bg-secondary text-white">
            @User.Identity.Name
        </a>
        <a asp-page="/Identity/SignOut" class="nav-link bg-secondary text-white">
            Sign Out
        </a>
    } else {
        <a asp-page="/Identity/SignIn" class="nav-link bg-secondary text-white">
            Sign In/Register
        </a>
    }
</nav>
```

I also need to update the ASP.NET Core configuration. By default, ASP.NET Core will use the /Account/Login and /Account/Logout URLs for signing in and out of the application. I could have used the routing system to ensure that my new Razor Pages will receive requests to these URLs, but I have chosen to change the URLs that ASP.NET Core uses instead, as shown in Listing 8-10.

Listing 8-10. Configuring URLs in the Startup.cs File in the ExampleApp Folder

```
...
public void ConfigureServices(IServiceCollection services) {
    services.AddControllersWithViews();
    services.AddRazorPages();
    services.AddDbContext<ProductDbContext>(opts => {
        opts.UseSqlServer(
            Configuration["ConnectionStrings:AppDataConnection"]);
    });

    services.AddHttpsRedirection(opts => {
        opts.HttpsPort = 44350;
    });

    services.AddDbContext<IdentityDbContext>(opts => {
        opts.UseSqlServer(
            Configuration["ConnectionStrings:IdentityConnection"],
            opts => opts.MigrationsAssembly("IdentityApp")
        );
    });
```

```
    services.AddScoped<IEmailSender, ConsoleEmailSender>();

    services.AddIdentity<IdentityUser, IdentityRole>(opts => {
        opts.Password.RequiredLength = 8;
        opts.Password.RequireDigit = false;
        opts.Password.RequireLowercase = false;
        opts.Password.RequireUppercase = false;
        opts.Password.RequireNonAlphanumeric = false;
        opts.SignIn.RequireConfirmedAccount = true;
    }).AddEntityFrameworkStores<IdentityDbContext>();

    services.AddAuthentication()
        .AddFacebook(opts => {
            opts.AppId = Configuration["Facebook:AppId"];
            opts.AppSecret = Configuration["Facebook:AppSecret"];
        })
        .AddGoogle(opts => {
            opts.ClientId = Configuration["Google:ClientId"];
            opts.ClientSecret = Configuration["Google:ClientSecret"];
        })
        .AddTwitter(opts => {
            opts.ConsumerKey = Configuration["Twitter:ApiKey"];
            opts.ConsumerSecret = Configuration["Twitter:ApiSecret"];
        });

    services.ConfigureApplicationCookie(opts => {
        opts.LoginPath = "/Identity/SignIn";
        opts.LogoutPath = "/Identity/SignOut";
        opts.AccessDeniedPath = "/Identity/Forbidden";
    });
}
...
```

The ConfigureApplicationCookie extension method is provided by Identity and can be used to override the default settings by assigning new values to the properties defined by the CookieAuthenticationOptions class. The properties used in Listing 8-10 are described in Table 8-7, and I explain the role of the CookieAuthenticationOptions class in Chapter 14.

Table 8-7. *The CookieAuthenticationOptions Used to Select URLs*

Name	Description
LoginPath	This property is used to specify the URL to which the browser is directed following a challenge response so the user can sign into the application.
LogoutPath	This property is used to specify the URL to which the browser is directed so the user can sign into the application.
AccessDeniedPath	This property is used to specify the URL to which the browser is directed following a forbidden response, indicating that the user does not have access to the requested content.

Restart ASP.NET Core and request `https://localhost:44350`. Click the Level 2 button to request content that is available only for authenticated users. This produces a challenge response that leads to the sign-in page, as shown in Figure 8-3. Sign in to the application using `alice@example.com` as the email address and `mysecret` as the password.

Click the Sign In button, and you will be signed into the application and redirected to the protected content. Click the Level 3 button to request content that is only available to users who have been assigned to a specific role. This type of request will lead to a forbidden response until I add support for roles in Chapter 10, producing the access denied message, as shown in Figure 8-3.

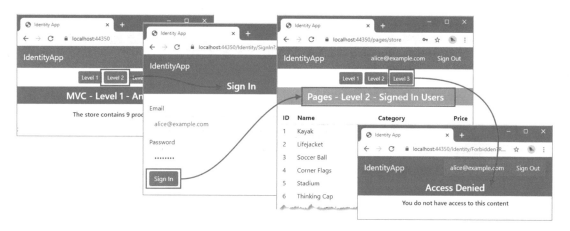

Figure 8-3. *Signing into the application with a password and triggering a forbidden response*

Click the Sign Out link in the header, click the Sign Out button, and you will be signed out of the application. Click the OK button, and you will navigate back to the sign-in page, as shown in Figure 8-4.

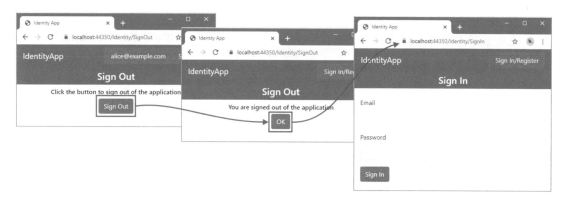

Figure 8-4. *Signing out of the application*

Completing the User Dashboard

Now that users can sign into the application, I can return to the user dashboard and complete the initial features. Listing 8-11 shows the changes required to the Index page model class to display data for the current user.

Listing 8-11. Displaying Data in the Index.cshtml File in the Pages/Identity Folder

```
using Microsoft.AspNetCore.Identity;
using System.Threading.Tasks;

namespace IdentityApp.Pages.Identity {

    public class IndexModel : UserPageModel {

        public IndexModel(UserManager<IdentityUser> userMgr)
            => UserManager = userMgr;

        public UserManager<IdentityUser> UserManager { get; set; }

        public string Email { get; set; }
        public string Phone { get; set; }

        public async Task OnGetAsync() {
            IdentityUser CurrentUser = await UserManager.GetUserAsync(User);
            Email = CurrentUser?.Email ?? "(No Value)";
            Phone = CurrentUser?.PhoneNumber ?? "(No Value)";
        }
    }
}
```

As noted earlier, ASP.NET Core uses a ClaimsPrincipal object to represent the currently authenticated user, which is accessed through the User property provided by the base classes for page models and controllers. The user manager class provides the GetUserAsync method, which obtains the IdentityUser object from the user store that represents the signed-in user, like this:

```
...
IdentityUser CurrentUser = await UserManager.GetUserAsync(User);
...
```

This provides a helpful bridge between the objects that the ASP.NET Core platform and ASP.NET Core Identity use to represent users and is useful for self-service workflows. Table 8-8 summarizes the user manager method used in Listing 8-11 for quick reference.

Table 8-8. The UserManager<IdentityUser> Method for Obtaining the Current User Object

Name	Description
GetUserAsync(principal)	This method returns the IdentityUser object that has been stored for the specified ClaimsPrincipal object, which is most often obtained through the User property defined by the base classes for page models and controllers.

Restart ASP.NET Core, and make sure you are signed in as alice@example.com. Click the email address displayed in the header, and you will see the user dashboard, which has been populated with the data for the signed-in user, as shown in Figure 8-5.

Figure 8-5. *Displaying data for the currently signed-in user*

Managing Passwords

If an application supports signing in with passwords, then workflows are required to manage them. In the sections that follow, I show you how to support the administrator setting a password, the administrator forcing the user to choose a new password, and the user changing their password.

Preparing the Email Confirmation Service

Some workflows require the user to click a link they receive in an email, either to confirm they control the email address during registration or to confirm they initiated an operation, such as password changes. Dealing with these confirmation emails is easier if they are created using a service because it means that confirmations can be sent from any Razor Page or controller and that all of the emails will be consistent.

The emails sent to the user contain confirmation tokens, and these tokens must be encoded so they can be safely sent as part of a URL and decoded again when the user clicks the link in the email. Add a file named TokenUrlEncoderService.cs to the Services folder and add the code shown in Listing 8-12.

Listing 8-12. The Contents of the TokenUrlEncoderService.cs File in the Services Folder

```
using Microsoft.AspNetCore.WebUtilities;
using System.Text;

namespace IdentityApp.Services {

    public class TokenUrlEncoderService {

        public virtual string EncodeToken(string token)
            => WebEncoders.Base64UrlEncode(Encoding.UTF8.GetBytes(token));

        public virtual string DecodeToken(string urlToken)
            => Encoding.UTF8.GetString(WebEncoders.Base64UrlDecode(urlToken));
    }
}
```

I have used Base64 encoding, which ensures that tokens can be encoded so they contain only characters that are allowed in URLs. Next, add a file named IdentityEmailService.cs to the Services folder and add the code shown in Listing 8-13.

Listing 8-13. The Contents of the IdentityEmailService.cs File in the Services Folder

```
using Microsoft.AspNetCore.Http;
using Microsoft.AspNetCore.Identity;
using Microsoft.AspNetCore.Identity.UI.Services;
using Microsoft.AspNetCore.Routing;

namespace IdentityApp.Services {

    public class IdentityEmailService {

        public IdentityEmailService(IEmailSender sender,
                UserManager<IdentityUser> userMgr,
                IHttpContextAccessor contextAccessor,
                LinkGenerator generator,
                TokenUrlEncoderService encoder) {
            EmailSender = sender;
            UserManager = userMgr;
            ContextAccessor = contextAccessor;
            LinkGenerator = generator;
            TokenEncoder = encoder;
        }

        public IEmailSender EmailSender { get; set; }
        public UserManager<IdentityUser> UserManager { get; set;}
        public IHttpContextAccessor ContextAccessor { get; set; }
        public LinkGenerator LinkGenerator { get; set; }
        public TokenUrlEncoderService TokenEncoder { get; set; }

        private string GetUrl(string emailAddress, string token, string page) {
            string safeToken = TokenEncoder.EncodeToken(token);
            return LinkGenerator.GetUriByPage(ContextAccessor.HttpContext, page,
                null, new { email = emailAddress, token = safeToken});
        }
    }
}
```

The IdentityEmailService class declares dependencies on the services it requires: the TokenUrlEncoderService defined in Listing 8-13, the user manager class, the IHttpContextAccessor service (which is used to access the HttpContext object outside of a Razor Page or controller), and the IEmailSender service, which is used to send emails.

The GetUrl method accepts an email address, a confirmation token, and a page, and it returns a URL that the user can click. I will add methods to the IdentityEmailService class to send specific emails as I create workflows that require confirmations. Add the statements shown in Listing 8-14 to the Startup class to set up the classes defined in Listing 8-12 and Listing 8-13 as services.

Listing 8-14. Configuring Services in the Startup.cs File in the IdentityApp Folder

```
...
public void ConfigureServices(IServiceCollection services) {
    services.AddControllersWithViews();
    services.AddRazorPages();
    services.AddDbContext<ProductDbContext>(opts => {
        opts.UseSqlServer(
            Configuration["ConnectionStrings:AppDataConnection"]);
    });

    services.AddHttpsRedirection(opts => {
        opts.HttpsPort = 44350;
    });

    services.AddDbContext<IdentityDbContext>(opts => {
        opts.UseSqlServer(
            Configuration["ConnectionStrings:IdentityConnection"],
            opts => opts.MigrationsAssembly("IdentityApp")
        );
    });

    services.AddScoped<IEmailSender, ConsoleEmailSender>();

    services.AddIdentity<IdentityUser, IdentityRole>(opts => {
        opts.Password.RequiredLength = 8;
        opts.Password.RequireDigit = false;
        opts.Password.RequireLowercase = false;
        opts.Password.RequireUppercase = false;
        opts.Password.RequireNonAlphanumeric = false;
        opts.SignIn.RequireConfirmedAccount = true;
    }).AddEntityFrameworkStores<IdentityDbContext>()
        .AddDefaultTokenProviders();

    services.AddScoped<TokenUrlEncoderService>();
    services.AddScoped<IdentityEmailService>();

    // ...statements omitted for brevity...
}
...
```

Listing 8-14 also adds the AddDefaultTokenProviders method to the chain of calls that set up Identity. This method sets up the services that are used to generate the confirmation tokens sent to users, which I describe in detail in Part 2.

Performing Self-Service Password Changes

The simplest password workflow is a self-service change, where the user provides their current password and a new password. Add a Razor Page named UserPasswordChange.cshtml to the Pages/Identity folder with the content shown in Listing 8-15.

Listing 8-15. The Contents of the UserPasswordChange.cshtml File in the Pages/Identity Folder

```
@page
@model IdentityApp.Pages.Identity.UserPasswordChangeModel
@{
    ViewBag.Workflow = "PasswordChange";
}

<div asp-validation-summary="All" class="text-danger m-2"></div>

@if (TempData.ContainsKey("message")) {
    <div class="alert alert-success">@TempData["message"]</div>
}

<form method="post">
    <div class="form-group">
        <label>Current Password</label>
        <input class="form-control" name="current" type="password" />
    </div>
    <div class="form-group">
        <label>New Password</label>
        <input class="form-control" name="newpassword" type="password" />
    </div>
        <div class="form-group">
        <label>Confirm New Password</label>
        <input class="form-control" name="confirmpassword" type="password" />
    </div>
    <button class="btn btn-primary">Change Password</button>
    <a asp-page="Index" class="btn btn-secondary">Cancel</a>
</form>
```

The view part of the page displays a form into which the user enters their current and new passwords. There is an @if expression that will display a div element if there is a temp data property named message, which I will use to indicate the password has been successfully changed. To define the page model class, add the code shown in Listing 8-16 to the UserPasswordChange.cshtml.cs file. (You will have to create this file if you are using Visual Studio Code.)

Listing 8-16. The Contents of the UserPasswordChange.cshtml.cs File in the Pages/Identity Folder

```
using Microsoft.AspNetCore.Identity;
using Microsoft.AspNetCore.Mvc;
using System.ComponentModel.DataAnnotations;
using System.Threading.Tasks;

namespace IdentityApp.Pages.Identity {

    public class PasswordChangeBindingTarget {
        [Required]
        public string Current { get; set; }

        [Required]
        public string NewPassword{ get; set; }
```

```
        [Required]
        [Compare(nameof(NewPassword))]
        public string ConfirmPassword{ get; set; }
    }

    public class UserPasswordChangeModel : UserPageModel {

        public UserPasswordChangeModel(UserManager<IdentityUser> usrMgr)
            => UserManager = usrMgr;

        public UserManager<IdentityUser> UserManager { get; set; }

        public async Task<IActionResult> OnPostAsync(
                PasswordChangeBindingTarget data) {
            if (ModelState.IsValid) {
                IdentityUser user = await UserManager.GetUserAsync(User);
                IdentityResult result = await UserManager.ChangePasswordAsync(user,
                    data.Current, data.NewPassword);
                if (result.Process(ModelState)) {
                    TempData["message"] = "Password changed";
                    return RedirectToPage();
                }
            }
            return Page();
        }
    }
}
```

Password changes are done using the user manager's ChangePasswordAsync method, which accepts an IdentityUser object, the current password, and the new password. The new password is validated against the password options described in Chapter 5, and if they match, the new password is stored. Since this is a self-service feature, I get the IdentityUser object using the GetUserAsync. The outcome of the password change is described using an IdentityResult object, which is processed to add errors to the model validation dictionary. If the password is successfully changed, a message is added to the temp data dictionary so it can be displayed to the user.

Listing 8-17 shows the changes required to integrate the new feature into the user dashboard.

Listing 8-17. Adding Navigation in the _Workflows.cshtml File in the Pages/Identity Folder

```
@model (string workflow, string theme)
@inject UserManager<IdentityUser> UserManager
@{
    Func<string, string> getClass = (string feature) =>
        feature != null && feature.Equals(Model.workflow) ? "active" : "";

    IdentityUser identityUser
        = await UserManager.GetUserAsync(User) ?? new IdentityUser();
}

<a class="btn btn-@Model.theme btn-block @getClass("Overview")" asp-page="Index">
    Overview
</a>
```

```
@if (await UserManager.HasPasswordAsync(identityUser)) {
    <a class="btn btn-@Model.theme btn-block @getClass("PasswordChange")"
            asp-page="UserPasswordChange">
        Change Password
    </a>
}
```

Not all users sign into the application using a password, so I use dependency injection to obtain a user manager object so that I can use the HasPasswordAsync method to determine if a navigation button for the password change page should be shown.

For quick reference, Table 8-9 describes the user manager methods used to implement self-service password changes.

Table 8-9. *The UserManager<IdentityUser> Methods for Self-Service Password Changes*

Name	Description
ChangePasswordAsync(user, current, new)	This method changes the password for the specified IdentityUser object. This method requires the existing password. If the user cannot provide the password, then password recovery is required, as described in the next section.
GetUserAsync(principal)	This method returns the IdentityUser object that has been stored for the specified ClaimsPrincipal object, which is most often obtained through the User property defined by the base classes for page models and controllers.
HasPasswordAsync(user)	This method returns true if the user store contains a password for the specified IdentityUser object and is used to ensure that only users with passwords are provided with the tools to change them.

Restart ASP.NET Core and make sure you are signed in to the application as alice@example.com using the password mysecret. Request https://localhost:44350/Identity and click the Change Password button. Enter mysecret into the password field and mysecret2 into the New Password and Confirm New Password fields. Click the Change Password button; the user store will be updated, and a confirmation message will be displayed, as shown in Figure 8-6.

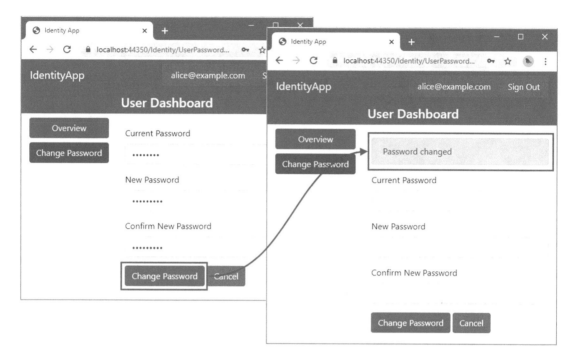

Figure 8-6. *Performing a self-service password change*

Performing Self-Service Password Recovery

Password recovery is used when the user has forgotten their password. This workflow requires the user to click a link that is emailed to them to confirm they are the owner of the account. To define the email that the user will receive, add the method shown in Listing 8-18 to the IdentityEmailService class.

Listing 8-18. Adding a Method in the IdentityEmailService.cs File in the Services Folder

```
using Microsoft.AspNetCore.Http;
using Microsoft.AspNetCore.Identity;
using Microsoft.AspNetCore.Identity.UI.Services;
using Microsoft.AspNetCore.Routing;
using System.Threading.Tasks;

namespace IdentityApp.Services {

    public class IdentityEmailService {

        // ...statements omitted for brevity...

        private string GetUrl(string emailAddress, string token, string page) {
            string safeToken = TokenEncoder.EncodeToken(token);
            return LinkGenerator.GetUriByPage(ContextAccessor.HttpContext, page,
                null, new { email = emailAddress, token = safeToken});
        }
```

```
        public async Task SendPasswordRecoveryEmail(IdentityUser user,
                string confirmationPage) {
            string token = await UserManager.GeneratePasswordResetTokenAsync(user);
            string url = GetUrl(user.Email, token, confirmationPage);
            await EmailSender.SendEmailAsync(user.Email, "Set Your Password",
                $"Please set your password by <a href={url}>clicking here</a>.");
        }
    }
}
```

The link sent to the user contains a confirmation token, which is used by Identity to prevent other users from recovering an account password. Confirmation tokens are generated by methods defined by the user manager class, and the GeneratePasswordResetTokenAsync method generates a token that can be used in password recovery workflows. I describe how tokens are generated and validated in Part 2, but for now, it is enough to know that tokens are generated for a specific purpose, such as password recovery, to prevent them from being misused.

Add a Razor Page named UserPasswordRecovery.cshtml to the Pages/Identity folder with the content shown in Listing 8-19.

Listing 8-19. The Contents of the UserPasswordRecovery.cshtml File in the Pages/Identity Folder

```
@page
@model IdentityApp.Pages.Identity.UserPasswordRecoveryModel
@{
    ViewData["showNav"] = false;
    ViewData["banner"] = "Password Recovery";
}

<div asp-validation-summary="All" class="text-danger m-2"></div>

@if (TempData.ContainsKey("message")) {
    <div class="alert alert-success">@TempData["message"]</div>
}

<form method="post">
    <div class="form-group">
        <label>Email Address</label>
        <input class="form-control" name="email" />
    </div>
    <button class="btn btn-primary">Send Recovery Email</button>
    <a asp-page="SignIn" class="btn btn-secondary">Cancel</a>
</form>
```

The user is presented with a form into which they are able to enter their email address so that a confirmation email can be sent. To create the page model class, add the code shown in Listing 8-20 to the UserPasswordRecovery.cshtml.cs file. (You will have to create this file if you are using Visual Studio Code.)

Listing 8-20. The Contents of the UserPasswordRecovery.cshtml.cs File in the Pages/Identity Folder

```
using IdentityApp.Services;
using Microsoft.AspNetCore.Identity;
using Microsoft.AspNetCore.Mvc;
using System.ComponentModel.DataAnnotations;
using System.Threading.Tasks;

namespace IdentityApp.Pages.Identity {

    public class UserPasswordRecoveryModel : UserPageModel {

        public UserPasswordRecoveryModel(UserManager<IdentityUser> usrMgr,
                IdentityEmailService emailService) {
            UserManager = usrMgr;
            EmailService = emailService;
        }

        public UserManager<IdentityUser> UserManager { get; set; }
        public IdentityEmailService EmailService { get; set; }

        public async Task<IActionResult> OnPostAsync([Required]string email) {
            if (ModelState.IsValid) {
                IdentityUser user = await UserManager.FindByEmailAsync(email);
                if (user != null) {
                    await EmailService.SendPasswordRecoveryEmail(user,
                        "UserPasswordRecoveryConfirm");
                }
                TempData["message"] = "We have sent you an email. "
                    + " Click the link it contains to choose a new password.";
                return RedirectToPage();
            }
            return Page();
        }
    }
}
```

The POST handler method receives the user's email address and retrieves the IdentityUser object from the user store, which is then passed to the IdentityEmailService object received through the constructor so that an email can be sent.

To define the page that will receive the request when the user clicks the email link, add a Razor Page named UserPasswordRecoveryConfirm.cshtml to the Pages/Identity folder with the content shown in Listing 8-21.

Listing 8-21. The Contents of the UserPasswordRecoveryConfirm.cshtml File in the Pages/Identity Folder

```
@page "{email?}/{token?}"
@model IdentityApp.Pages.Identity.UserPasswordRecoveryConfirmModel
@{
    ViewData["showNav"] = false;
    ViewData["banner"] = "Password Recovery";
}
```

```
@if (string.IsNullOrEmpty(Model.Token) || string.IsNullOrEmpty(Model.Email)) {
    <div class="h6 text-center">
        <div class="p-2">
            Check your inbox for a confirmation email and click the link it contains.
        </div>
        <a asp-page="UserPasswordRecovery" class="btn btn-primary">Resend Email</a>
    </div>
} else {
    <div asp-validation-summary="All" class="text-danger m-2"></div>
    @if (TempData.ContainsKey("message")) {
        <div class="alert alert-success">@TempData["message"]</div>
    }

    <form method="post">
        <input type="hidden" asp-for="Token" />
        <div class="form-group">
            <label>Email</label>
            <input class="form-control" asp-for="Email" />
        </div>
        <div class="form-group">
            <label>New Password</label>
            <input class="form-control" type="password" name="password" />
        </div>
        <div class="form-group">
            <label>Confirm Password</label>
            <input class="form-control" type="password" name="confirmpassword" />
        </div>
        <button class="btn btn-primary" type="submit">Set Password</button>
    </form>
}
```

The view part of the page displays a form that allows the user to select a new password. The URL contained in the email will contain email and token routing parameters, and there is a message that tells the user to check their email that is displayed if either parameter is missing, which will be the case if the user requests the page directly rather than clicking the email link. To define the page model class, add the code shown in Listing 8-22 to the UserPasswordRecoveryConfirm.cshtml.cs file. (You will have to create this file if you are using Visual Studio Code.)

Listing 8-22. The Contents of the UserPasswordRecoveryConfirm.cshtml.cs File in the Pages/Identity Folder

```
using IdentityApp.Services;
using Microsoft.AspNetCore.Identity;
using Microsoft.AspNetCore.Mvc;
using System.ComponentModel.DataAnnotations;
using System.Threading.Tasks;

namespace IdentityApp.Pages.Identity {

    public class UserPasswordRecoveryConfirmModel : UserPageModel {

        public UserPasswordRecoveryConfirmModel(UserManager<IdentityUser> usrMgr,
```

```
            TokenUrlEncoderService tokenUrlEncoder) {
        UserManager = usrMgr;
        TokenUrlEncoder = tokenUrlEncoder;
    }

    public UserManager<IdentityUser> UserManager { get; set; }
    public TokenUrlEncoderService TokenUrlEncoder { get; set; }

    [BindProperty(SupportsGet = true)]
    public string Email { get; set; }

    [BindProperty(SupportsGet = true)]
    public string Token { get; set; }

    [BindProperty]
    [Required]
    public string Password { get; set; }

    [BindProperty]
    [Required]
    [Compare(nameof(Password))]
    public string ConfirmPassword { get; set; }

    public async Task<IActionResult> OnPostAsync() {
        if (ModelState.IsValid) {
            IdentityUser user = await UserManager.FindByEmailAsync(Email);
            string decodedToken = TokenUrlEncoder.DecodeToken(Token);
            IdentityResult result = await UserManager.ResetPasswordAsync(user,
                decodedToken, Password);
            if (result.Process(ModelState)) {
                TempData["message"] = "Password changed";
                return RedirectToPage();
            }
        }
        return Page();
    }
}
}
```

The email and token included in the confirmation email link are assigned to the Email and Token properties with the BindProperty attribute. When the POST handler method is invoked, it decodes the token from its URL-safe form and passes it to the user manager's ResetPasswordAsync method, along with the IdentityUser object that represents the user and the user's new choice of password. The outcome of this method is described with an IdentityResult object, and a message is displayed to the user if the password recovery operation worked. Table 8-10 describes the user manager methods used in password recovery.

Table 8-10. *The UserManager<IdentityUser> Methods for Password Recovery*

Name	Description
GeneratePasswordResetTokenAsync(user)	This method generates a token that can be validated by the ResetPasswordAsync method. The token is securely sent to the user so that possession of the token establishes the identity of the user.
ResetPasswordAsync(user, token, password)	This method validates the token provided by the user and changes the stored password if it matches the one generated by the GeneratePasswordResetTokenAsync method.

Add the link shown in Listing 8-23 to the SignIn page to present the password recovery feature to the user.

Listing 8-23. Adding Navigation in the SignIn.cshtml File in the Pages/Identity Folder

```
@page "{returnUrl?}"
@model IdentityApp.Pages.Identity.SignInModel
@{
    ViewData["showNav"] = false;
    ViewData["banner"] = "Sign In";
}

<div asp-validation-summary="All" class="text-danger m-2"></div>

@if (TempData.ContainsKey("message")) {
    <div class="alert alert-danger">@TempData["message"]</div>
}

<form method="post">
    <div class="form-group">
        <label>Email</label>
        <input class="form-control" name="email" />
    </div>
    <div class="form-group">
        <label>Password</label>
        <input class="form-control" type="password" name="password" />
    </div>
    <button type="submit" class="btn btn-primary">
        Sign In
    </button>
    <a asp-page="UserPasswordRecovery" class="btn btn-secondary">Forgot Password?</a>
</form>
```

Restart ASP.NET Core and request https://localhost:44350/Identity/SignIn. Click the Forgot Password? button, enter bob@example.com into the text field, and click the Send Recovery Email button. You will receive a message confirming that a recovery email has been sent, as shown in Figure 8-7.

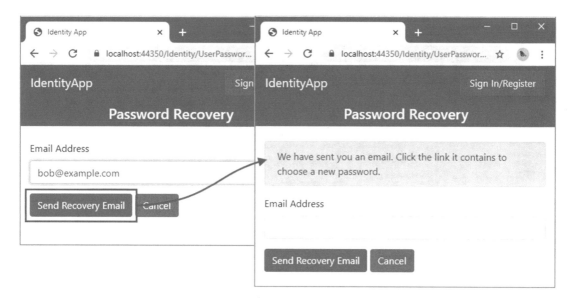

Figure 8-7. *Starting the password recovery process*

The application is configured to use the implementation of the IEmailSender interface I created for the Identity UI package, which simulates sending emails by writing messages to the console. Examine the ASP. NET Core output, and you will see a message similar to this one:

```
---New Email----
To: bob@example.com
Subject: Set Your Password
Please set your password by <a href=https://localhost:44350/Identity/UserPasswordRecovery
Confirm/bob@example.com/Q2ZESjhBMVB3bFFBQ3gxRmhXTERPQzZ1UTVOTVQvWEFJZHMxbOhpS1N3RlA1ZmpX
YXZvd3k3QUO3UENrS3dSbDMyU2ZQem41NWRJbOV5d3FWWHRqQ2YrR2dzWHBkaW81a3NsOXdlWnJnRko5ZO
d3OWE5ZTBYYlZOSzZtTEowYTc3UFNZTVI1VFN4WkhLdWYOOTRCQ2ooS2ROY2hrRWFMdU1BTXRBSDUxZ3lxcjFH
dXZaNSsrTFFOZ1NFREtIQTlwZ1hxcHFIMWO4L3VObGYxSzg3TnBabmhocExSM1NhOTNJao5IODVSbWtscEYyRTl
4>clicking here</a>.
-------
```

Copy the URL from the message (which will have a different token to the one shown here), and you will be prompted to select a new password. Enter mynewpassword into both text fields and click the Set Password button. A message will be displayed confirming the password change, as shown in Figure 8-8. Click the SignIn/Register link at the top of the page, and you will be able to sign in to the application with the new password.

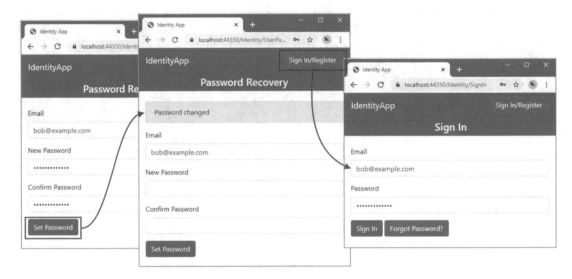

Figure 8-8. *Completing password recovery*

Performing Administrator Password Changes

The features used for self-service password management can also be used to provide administrator workflows. Add a Razor Page Passwords.cshtml to the Pages/Identity/Admin folder with the content shown in Listing 8-24.

Listing 8-24. The Contents of the Passwords.cshtml File in the Pages/Identity/Admin Folder

```
@page "{Id?}"
@model IdentityApp.Pages.Identity.Admin.PasswordsModel
@{
    ViewBag.Workflow = "Passwords";
}

<div asp-validation-summary="All" class="text-danger m-2"></div>

@if (TempData.ContainsKey("message")) {
    <div class="alert alert-success">@TempData["message"]</div>
}

<div class="container-fluid">
    <div class="row">
        <div class="col p-1">
            <div asp-validation-summary="All" class="text-danger m-2"></div>
            <form method="post" asp-page-handler="setPassword" class="pb-2">
                <input type="hidden" asp-for="Id" />
                <div class="form-group">
                    <label>New Password</label>
                    <input class="form-control" name="password" type="password" />
                </div>
```

```
            <div class="form-group">
                <label>Confirm Password</label>
                <input class="form-control" name="confirmation"
                        type="password" />
            </div>
            <button class="btn btn-secondary">Set Password</button>
        </form>
        @if (await Model.UserManager.IsEmailConfirmedAsync(Model.IdentityUser)) {
            <form method="post" asp-page-handler="userChange">
                <input type="hidden" asp-for="Id" />
                <button class="btn btn-secondary mt-2">
                    Send User Reset Email
                </button>
            </form>
        }
    </div>
</div>
</div>
```

The view part of the page displays two forms. The first allows a new password to be specified directly, which is the conventional approach for setting passwords, but which requires the administrator to communicate the new password to the user. The second form is used to send a password reset email to the user, which will allow them to choose their password, but this can be done only if the user has a confirmed email address. All the test accounts used to seed the user store have confirmed email addresses, but I create a workflow for confirming email addresses in Chapter 9.

To create the page model class, add the code shown in Listing 8-25 to the Passwords.cshtml.cs file. (You will have to create this file if you are using Visual Studio Code.)

Listing 8-25. The Contents of the Passwords.cshtml.cs File in the Pages/Identity/Admin Folder

```
using IdentityApp.Services;
using Microsoft.AspNetCore.Identity;
using Microsoft.AspNetCore.Mvc;
using Microsoft.AspNetCore.Mvc.RazorPages;
using System.ComponentModel.DataAnnotations;
using System.Threading.Tasks;

namespace IdentityApp.Pages.Identity.Admin {

    public class PasswordsModel : AdminPageModel {

        public PasswordsModel(UserManager<IdentityUser> usrMgr,
                IdentityEmailService emailService) {
            UserManager = usrMgr;
            EmailService = emailService;
        }

        public UserManager<IdentityUser> UserManager { get; set; }
        public IdentityEmailService EmailService { get; set; }

        public IdentityUser IdentityUser { get; set; }
```

```
        [BindProperty(SupportsGet = true)]
        public string Id { get; set; }

        [BindProperty]
        [Required]
        public string Password { get; set; }

        [BindProperty]
        [Compare(nameof(Password))]
        public string Confirmation { get; set; }

        public async Task<IActionResult> OnGetAsync() {
            if (string.IsNullOrEmpty(Id)) {
                return RedirectToPage("Selectuser",
                    new { Label = "Password", Callback = "Passwords" });
            }
            IdentityUser = await UserManager.FindByIdAsync(Id);
            return Page();
        }

        public async Task<IActionResult> OnPostSetPasswordAsync() {
            if (ModelState.IsValid) {
                IdentityUser = await UserManager.FindByIdAsync(Id);
                if (await UserManager.HasPasswordAsync(IdentityUser)) {
                    await UserManager.RemovePasswordAsync(IdentityUser);
                }
                IdentityResult result =
                    await UserManager.AddPasswordAsync(IdentityUser, Password);
                if (result.Process(ModelState)) {
                    TempData["message"] = "Password Changed";
                    return RedirectToPage();
                }
            }
            return Page();
        }

        public async Task<IActionResult> OnPostUserChangeAsync() {
            IdentityUser = await UserManager.FindByIdAsync(Id);
            await UserManager.RemovePasswordAsync(IdentityUser);
            await EmailService.SendPasswordRecoveryEmail(IdentityUser,
                "/Identity/UserPasswordRecoveryConfirm");
            TempData["message"] = "Email Sent to User";
            return RedirectToPage();
        }
    }
}
```

There is no user manager method to change a password in a single step that doesn't require the existing password or a confirmation token. Instead, the HasPasswordAsync method is used to determine if there is a password in the user store and, if there is, the RemovePasswordAsync method is used to remove it. The new password is stored with the AddPasswordAsync method.

The recovery email is sent to the user using the same approach as for self-service password recovery. Before sending the email, I call the RemovePasswordAsync method to remove the existing password to prevent the user from signing in until a new password is chosen. For quick reference, Table 8-11 describes the user manager methods used for administrator password changes.

Table 8-11. *The UserManager<IdentityUser> Methods for Administrator Password Changes*

Name	Description
HasPasswordAsync(user)	This method returns true if there is a stored password for the user.
RemovePasswordAsync(user)	This method removes the stored password for the specified user.
AddPasswordAsync(user, password)	This method stores a password for the specified user.
GeneratePasswordResetTokenAsync(user)	This method generates a token that can be validated by the ResetPasswordAsync method. The token is securely sent to the user so that possession of the token establishes the identity of the user.
ResetPasswordAsync(user, token, password)	This method validates the token provided by the user and changes the stored password if it matches the one generated by the GeneratePasswordResetTokenAsync method.
IsEmailConfirmedAsync(user)	This method returns true if the user has a confirmed email address. This method is used to determine if the user can receive a password reset email.

To integrate the password functionality into the administrator dashboard, add the element shown in Listing 8-26 to the _AdminWorkflows partial view.

Listing 8-26. Adding Navigation in the _AdminWorkflows.cshtml File in the Pages/Identity/Admin Folder

```
@model (string workflow, string theme)

@{
    Func<string, string> getClass = (string feature) =>
        feature != null && feature.Equals(Model.workflow) ? "active" : "";
}

<a class="btn btn-@Model.theme btn-block @getClass("Dashboard")"
        asp-page="Dashboard">
    Dashboard
</a>
<a class="btn btn-@Model.theme btn-block @getClass("Features")" asp-page="Features">
    Store Features
</a>
<a class="btn btn-success btn-block @getClass("List")" asp-page="View"
        asp-route-id="">
    List Users
</a>
```

```
<a class="btn btn-success btn-block @getClass("Edit")" asp-page="Edit"
        asp-route-id="">
    Edit Users
</a>
<a class="btn btn-success btn-block @getClass("Passwords")" asp-page="Passwords"
        asp-route-id="">
    Passwords
</a>
```

Restart ASP.NET Core, request `https://localhost:44350/identity/admin`, and click the Passwords button in the navigation panel to display a list of users. Click the Passwords button for any of the accounts, and you will be presented with the features that allow passwords to be changed, as shown in Figure 8-9.

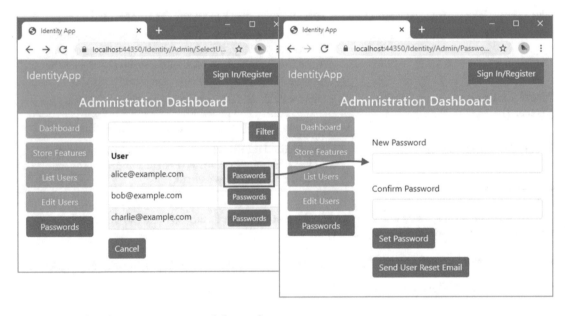

Figure 8-9. *The administrator password change feature*

Restricting Access to the Custom Workflow Razor Pages

There is enough functionality in place to restrict access to the Razor Pages that provide the custom workflows. Add the attribute shown in Listing 8-27 to the `UserPageModel` class, which is the base for the page model classes.

Listing 8-27. Restricting Access in the UserPageModel.cs File in the Pages/Identity Folder

```
using Microsoft.AspNetCore.Mvc.RazorPages;
using Microsoft.AspNetCore.Authorization;

namespace IdentityApp.Pages.Identity {
```

```
[Authorize]
public class UserPageModel : PageModel {

    // no methods or properties required
}
}
```

The `Authorize` attribute restricts access to any authenticated user, which is ideal for the features provided by the self-management dashboard. An exception has to be made for the `SignIn` page, as shown in Listing 8-28.

Listing 8-28. Granting Access in the SignIn.cshtml.cs File in the Pages/Identity Folder

```
using System.ComponentModel.DataAnnotations;
using System.Threading.Tasks;
using Microsoft.AspNetCore.Identity;
using Microsoft.AspNetCore.Mvc;
using SignInResult = Microsoft.AspNetCore.Identity.SignInResult;
using Microsoft.AspNetCore.Authorization;

namespace IdentityApp.Pages.Identity {

    [AllowAnonymous]
    public class SignInModel : UserPageModel {

        // ...statements omitted for brevity...
    }
}
```

The `AllowAnonymous` attribute allows anyone to access a page. At this point in the project, more pages require the `AllowAnonymous` attribute than not, and you may be tempted to simply use the standard page model base class instead of applying attributes individually. My preference is to make authorization the default requirement and then explicitly grant the exceptions so that the intention for each page is obvious and consistent.

The `AllowAnonymous` attribute must also be applied to the `SignOut` page model class, as shown in Listing 8-29, since it displays content to users after they have signed out.

Listing 8-29. Granting Access in the SignOut.cshtml.cs File in the Pages/Identity Folder

```
using Microsoft.AspNetCore.Identity;
using Microsoft.AspNetCore.Mvc;
using System.Threading.Tasks;
using Microsoft.AspNetCore.Authorization;

namespace IdentityApp.Pages.Identity {

    [AllowAnonymous]
    public class SignOutModel : UserPageModel {

        public SignOutModel(SignInManager<IdentityUser> signMgr)
            => SignInManager = signMgr;
```

```
        public SignInManager<IdentityUser> SignInManager { get; set; }

        public async Task<IActionResult> OnPostAsync() {
            await SignInManager.SignOutAsync();
            return RedirectToPage();
        }
    }
}
```

Finally, the same attribute must be added to the pages that deal with password recovery. Listing 8-30 applies AllowAnonymous to the page model for the UserPasswordRecovery page.

Listing 8-30. Granting Access in the UserPasswordRecovery.cshtml.cs File in the Pages/Identity Folder

```
using IdentityApp.Services;
using Microsoft.AspNetCore.Identity;
using Microsoft.AspNetCore.Mvc;
using System.ComponentModel.DataAnnotations;
using System.Threading.Tasks;
using Microsoft.AspNetCore.Authorization;

namespace IdentityApp.Pages.Identity {

    [AllowAnonymous]
    public class UserPasswordRecoveryModel : UserPageModel {

        // ...statements omitted for brevity...
    }
}
```

Listing 8-31 applies the attribute to the page model class for the UserPasswordRecoveryConfirm page.

Listing 8-31. Granting Access in the UserPasswordRecoveryConfirm.cshtml.cs File in the Pages/Identity Folder

```
using IdentityApp.Services;
using Microsoft.AspNetCore.Identity;
using Microsoft.AspNetCore.Mvc;
using System.ComponentModel.DataAnnotations;
using System.Threading.Tasks;
using Microsoft.AspNetCore.Authorization;

namespace IdentityApp.Pages.Identity {

    [AllowAnonymous]
    public class UserPasswordRecoveryConfirmModel : UserPageModel {

        public UserPasswordRecoveryConfirmModel(UserManager<IdentityUser> usrMgr,
                TokenUrlEncoderService tokenUrlEncoder) {
            UserManager = usrMgr;
            TokenUrlEncoder = tokenUrlEncoder;
        }
```

```
        public UserManager<IdentityUser> UserManager { get; set; }
        public TokenUrlEncoderService TokenUrlEncoder { get; set; }

        [BindProperty(SupportsGet = true)]
        public string Email { get; set; }

        [BindProperty(SupportsGet = true)]
        public string Token { get; set; }

        [BindProperty]
        [Required]
        public string Password { get; set; }

        [BindProperty]
        [Required]
        [Compare(nameof(Password))]
        public string ConfirmPassword { get; set; }

        public async Task<IActionResult> OnPostAsync() {
            if (ModelState.IsValid) {
                IdentityUser user = await UserManager.FindByEmailAsync(Email);
                string decodedToken = TokenUrlEncoder.DecodeToken(Token);
                IdentityResult result = await UserManager.ResetPasswordAsync(user,
                    decodedToken, Password);
                if (result.Process(ModelState)) {
                    TempData["message"] = "Password changed";
                    return RedirectToPage();
                }
            }
            return Page();
        }
    }
}
```

The default policy of restricting access to signed-in users also applies to the administration dashboard, which will be a problem the next time the database is reset: the button that seeds the user store will be accessible only to signed-in users, but no sign ins are possible because the user store will be empty.

I'll resolve this properly in Chapter 10 when I create workflows for managing roles. Until then I am going to allow anyone to access the administration features, even if there is no signed-in user. Add the attribute shown in Listing 8-32 to the AdminUserPage class.

Listing 8-32. Disabling Authorization in the AdminPageModel.cs File in the Pages/Identity/Admin Folder

```
using Microsoft.AspNetCore.Authorization;

namespace IdentityApp.Pages.Identity.Admin {

    [AllowAnonymous]
    public class AdminPageModel : UserPageModel {

        // no methods or properties required
    }
}
```

Restart ASP.NET Core, make sure you are signed out of the application, and then request `https://localhost:44350/Identity`. Now that the user dashboard is restricted to signed-in users, you will be prompted for credentials and then redirected once you have signed in, as shown in Figure 8-10.

Figure 8-10. *Restricting access to the user dashboard*

Summary

In this chapter, I introduced the Identity features for signing users into an application with a password and signing them out again. I also created the workflows required to manage passwords, both for self-service applications and those that require an administrator. I finished the chapter by using the ASP.NET Core authorization features to restrict access to the user and dashboard so that it is available only to signed-in users. In the next chapter, I create workflows for creating and deleting user accounts.

CHAPTER 9

Creating, Deleting, and Locking Accounts

In this chapter, I create workflows for creating accounts, deleting accounts, and managing account lockouts. As part of the account creation process, I explain how confirmation tokens are used to create workflows that allow the user to confirm their account. Table 9-1 puts the features described in this chapter in context.

Table 9-1. *Putting the API Features for Creating, Deleting and Locking Accounts in Context*

Question	Answer
What are they?	These features are used to create and delete accounts from the user store and to temporarily prevent a user from signing in.
Why are they useful?	Account creation is required to enable users to sign into the application. Account deletion is useful when a user no longer wants or is no longer allowed to use the application. Lockouts prevent a user from signing in following multiple failed attempts or at the action of the administrator.
How are they used?	These features are provided through a combination of user manager and sign-in manager methods and the properties of the user class.
Are there any pitfalls or limitations?	Because the Identity user store is consulted only when the user signs in, the user can continue to use the application even after they have been locked out or their account has been deleted because the authentication cookie issues to their browser remains valid. This can be minimized by enabling validation for the cookie, but this requires additional user store queries.
Are there any alternatives?	No.

Table 9-2 summarizes the chapter.

© Adam Freeman 2021
A. Freeman, *Pro ASP.NET Core Identity*, https://doi.org/10.1007/978-1-4842-6858-2_9

Table 9-2. *Chapter Summary*

Problem	Solution	Listing
Create a new account	Create a new `IdentityUser` object and pass it to the user manager's `CreateAsync` method. Generate a token that can be validated to let the user select a password.	1–9
Confirm new accounts	Generate a token using the `GenerateEmailConfirmationTokenAsync` method and send it to the user. Validate the token and confirm the account with the `ConfirmEmailAsync` method.	10–16
Determine if an account has been confirmed	Read the `IdentityUser.EmailConfirmed` property or call the user manager's `IsEmailConfirmedAsync` method.	17
Locking accounts	Call the user manager's `SetLockoutEnabledAsync` and `SetLockoutEndDateAsync` methods to enable lockouts for an account and to specify the end date for a lockout.	18–20
Force immediate sign-outs	Enable authentication cookie validation.	21–23
Deleting an account	Call the user manager's `DeleteAsync` method.	24–29

Preparing for This Chapter

This chapter uses the `IdentityApp` project from Chapter 8. Open a new PowerShell command prompt and run the commands shown in Listing 9-1 to reset the application and Identity databases.

■ **Tip**   You can download the example project for this chapter—and for all the other chapters in this book—from `https://github.com/Apress/pro-asp.net-core-identity`. See Chapter 1 for how to get help if you have problems running the examples.

Listing 9-1. Resetting the Databases

```
dotnet ef database drop --force --context ProductDbContext
dotnet ef database drop --force --context IdentityDbContext
dotnet ef database update --context ProductDbContext
dotnet ef database update --context IdentityDbContext
```

Use the PowerShell prompt to run the command shown in Listing 9-2 in the `IdentityApp` folder to start the application.

Listing 9-2. Running the Example Application

```
dotnet run
```

Open a web browser and request `https://localhost:44350/Identity/Admin`, which will show the administration dashboard. Click the Seed Database button to add the test accounts to the user store, as shown in Figure 9-1.

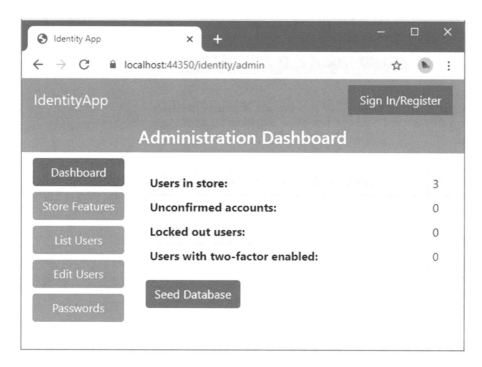

Figure 9-1. *Running the example application*

Creating User Accounts

In applications that don't support self-registration, creating accounts is one of the most important workflows. For this chapter, I am going to create a workflow that allows the administrator to create an account but that will require the user to choose their password. See Part 2 for an example of a more conventional approach where the administrator provides all the data for the new account, including the password.

Add a Razor Page named `Create.cshtml` to the `Pages/Identity/Admin` folder with the content shown in Listing 9-3.

Listing 9-3. The Contents of the Create.cshtml File in the Pages/Identity/Admin Folder

```
@page
@model IdentityApp.Pages.Identity.Admin.CreateModel
@{
    ViewBag.Workflow = "Create";
}

<div asp-validation-summary="All" class="text-danger m-2"></div>
```

```
@if (TempData.ContainsKey("message")) {
    <div class="alert alert-success">@TempData["message"]</div>
}

<form method="post">
    <div class="form-group">
        <label>Email</label>
        <input class="form-control" name="email" />
    </div>
    <div>
        <button type="submit" class="btn btn-success">Create</button>
        <a asp-page="Dashboard" class="btn btn-secondary">Cancel</a>
    </div>
</form>
```

The view part of the page is a simple form that captures the email address for the new account. To implement the page model, add the code shown in Listing 9-4 to the Create.cshtml.cs file. (You will have to create this file if you are using Visual Studio Code.)

Listing 9-4. The Contents of the Create.cshtml.cs File in the Pages/Identity/Admin Folder

```
using IdentityApp.Services;
using Microsoft.AspNetCore.Identity;
using Microsoft.AspNetCore.Mvc;
using System.ComponentModel.DataAnnotations;
using System.Threading.Tasks;

namespace IdentityApp.Pages.Identity.Admin {

    public class CreateModel : AdminPageModel {

        public CreateModel(UserManager<IdentityUser> mgr,
            IdentityEmailService emailService) {
            UserManager = mgr;
            EmailService = emailService;
        }

        public UserManager<IdentityUser> UserManager { get; set; }
        public IdentityEmailService EmailService { get; set; }

        [BindProperty(SupportsGet = true)]
        [EmailAddress]
        public string Email { get; set; }

        public async Task<IActionResult> OnPostAsync() {
            if (ModelState.IsValid) {
                IdentityUser user = new IdentityUser {
                    UserName = Email,
                    Email = Email,
                    EmailConfirmed = true
                };
                IdentityResult result = await UserManager.CreateAsync(user);
```

```
                if (result.Process(ModelState)) {
                    await EmailService.SendPasswordRecoveryEmail(user,
                        "/Identity/UserAccountComplete");
                    TempData["message"] = "Account Created";
                    return RedirectToPage();
                }
            }
            return Page();
        }
    }
}
```

The page model constructor declares dependencies on the UserManager<IdentityUser> class, which is used to add an IdentityUser object to the user store through the CreateAsync method.

```
...
IdentityUser user = new IdentityUser {
    UserName = email,
    Email = email,
    EmailConfirmed = true
};
IdentityResult result = await UserManager.CreateAsync(user);
...
```

I set the UserName, Email, and EmailConfirmed properties of a newly created IdentityUser object and use it as the argument to the CreateAsync method. As part of the storage process, other values for other properties will be generated, such as the Id, NormalizedUserName, and NormalizedEmail properties.

The CreateAsync method returns an IdentityAsync object, which indicates the outcome of the operation. If the new object was successfully added to the store, I use the IdentityEmailService to send the user an email to the user containing a link. I have used the same method defined in Chapter 8 for password recovery.

```
...
await EmailService.SendPasswordRecoveryEmail(user, "/Identity/UserAccountComplete");
...
```

The email sent to the user will contain a link with a confirmation token. To allow the user to validate the token and complete their account setup, add a Razor Page named UserAccountComplete.cshtml to the Pages/Identity folder with the content shown in Listing 9-5.

Listing 9-5. The Contents of the UserAccountComplete.cshtml File in the Pages/Identity Folder

```
@page "{email?}/{token?}"
@model IdentityApp.Pages.Identity.UserAccountCompleteModel
@{
    ViewData["showNav"] = false;
    ViewData["banner"] = "Complete Account";
}
```

```
@if (string.IsNullOrEmpty(Model.Token) || string.IsNullOrEmpty(Model.Email)) {
    <div class="h6 text-center">
        <div class="p-2">
            Check your inbox for a confirmation email and click the link it contains.
        </div>
    </div>
} else {
    <div asp-validation-summary="All" class="text-danger m-2"></div>
    <form method="post">
        <input type="hidden" asp-for="Token" />
        <div class="form-group">
            <label>Email</label>
            <input class="form-control" asp-for="Email" readonly />
        </div>
        <div class="form-group">
            <label>Password</label>
            <input class="form-control" type="password" name="password" />
        </div>
        <div class="form-group">
            <label>Confirm Password</label>
            <input class="form-control" type="password" name="confirmpassword" />
        </div>
        <button class="btn btn-primary" type="submit">Finish and Sign In</button>
    </form>
}
```

The view part of the page follows the approach I took for password recovery, although I have defined a separate Razor Page so that the account completion process can be easily customized. The user is prompted to enter a password and is presented with a Finish and Sign In button that will update the user store and redirect the browser to the sign-in page.

To define the page model class, add the code shown in Listing 9-6 to the UserAccountComplete. cshtml.cs file. (You will have to create this file if you are using Visual Studio Code.)

Listing 9-6. The Contents of the UserAccountComplete.cshtml.cs File in the Pages/Identity Folder

```
using IdentityApp.Services;
using Microsoft.AspNetCore.Authorization;
using Microsoft.AspNetCore.Identity;
using Microsoft.AspNetCore.Mvc;
using System.ComponentModel.DataAnnotations;
using System.Threading.Tasks;

namespace IdentityApp.Pages.Identity {

    [AllowAnonymous]
    public class UserAccountCompleteModel : UserPageModel {

        public UserAccountCompleteModel(UserManager<IdentityUser> usrMgr,
                TokenUrlEncoderService tokenUrlEncoder) {
            UserManager = usrMgr;
            TokenUrlEncoder = tokenUrlEncoder;
        }
```

```
    public UserManager<IdentityUser> UserManager { get; set; }
    public TokenUrlEncoderService TokenUrlEncoder { get; set; }

    [BindProperty(SupportsGet = true)]
    public string Email { get; set; }

    [BindProperty(SupportsGet = true)]
    public string Token { get; set; }

    [BindProperty]
    [Required]
    public string Password { get; set; }

    [BindProperty]
    [Required]
    [Compare(nameof(Password))]
    public string ConfirmPassword { get; set; }

    public async Task<IActionResult> OnPostAsync() {
        if (ModelState.IsValid) {
            IdentityUser user = await UserManager.FindByEmailAsync(Email);
            string decodedToken = TokenUrlEncoder.DecodeToken(Token);
            IdentityResult result = await UserManager.ResetPasswordAsync(user,
                decodedToken, Password);
            if (result.Process(ModelState)) {
                return RedirectToPage("SignIn", new { });
            }
        }
        return Page();
    }
}
}
}
```

The POST handler method decodes the token and uses it with the user manager's ResetPasswordAsync method to set the password, after which the user is redirected to the SignIn page so they can sign into the application. For quick reference, Table 9-3 describes the user manager methods used to create and complete an account in this workflow.

Table 9-3. *The UserManager<IdentityUser> Methods Used to Create a New Account*

Name	Description
CreateAsync(user)	This method adds an IdentityUser object to the store.
GeneratePasswordResetTokenAsync(user)	This method generates a token that can be validated by the ResetPasswordAsync method. The token is securely sent to the user so that possession of the token establishes the identity of the user.
ResetPasswordAsync(user, token, password)	This method validates the token provided by the user and changes the stored password if it matches the one generated by the GeneratePasswordResetTokenAsync method.

To complete the workflow, add the element shown in Listing 9-7 to create a button in the administration navigation view.

Listing 9-7. Adding Navigation in the _AdminWorkflows.cshtml File in the Pages/Identity/Admin Folder

```
@model (string workflow, string theme)

@{
    Func<string, string> getClass = (string feature) =>
        feature != null && feature.Equals(Model.workflow) ? "active" : "";
}

<a class="btn btn-@Model.theme btn-block @getClass("Dashboard")"
        asp-page="Dashboard">
    Dashboard
</a>
<a class="btn btn-@Model.theme btn-block @getClass("Features")" asp-page="Features">
    Store Features
</a>
<a class="btn btn-success btn-block @getClass("List")" asp-page="View"
        asp-route-id="">
    List Users
</a>
<a class="btn btn-success btn-block @getClass("Create")" asp-page="Create">
    Create Account
</a>
<a class="btn btn-success btn-block @getClass("Edit")" asp-page="Edit"
        asp-route-id="">
    Edit Users
</a>
<a class="btn btn-success btn-block @getClass("Passwords")" asp-page="Passwords"
        asp-route-id="">
    Passwords
</a>
```

Restart ASP.NET Core, request `https://localhost:44350/Identity/Admin` and click the Create Account button. Enter dora@example.com into the text field and click the Create button, as shown in Figure 9-2.

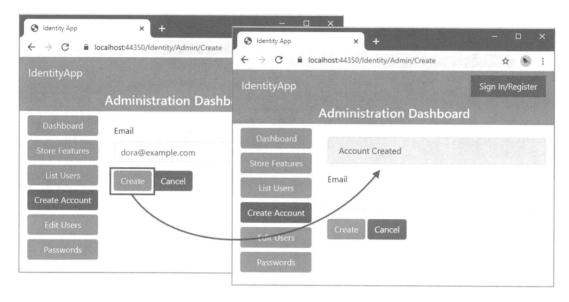

***Figure 9-2.** Creating a new account*

Look at the ASP.NET Core console output, and you will see a message like this one, albeit with a different validation token:

```
---New Email----
To: dora@example.com
Subject: Set Your Password
Please set your password by <a href=https://localhost:44350/Identity/UserAccountComplete/
dora@example.com/Q2ZESjh>
    clicking here
</a>.
-------
```

This simulated email is produced by the IEmailSender service, which I created for the Identity UI package. The encoded token is a long string, which I have shorted here for brevity.

Copy the URL from the message displayed by your application (and not the one shown earlier), and you will be prompted to select a password. Enter mysecret into the Password and Confirm Password fields and click the Finish and Sign In button. The user store will be updated, and you will be redirected to the sign-in page. Use dora@example.com with the password mysecret to sign into the application, as shown in Figure 9-3.

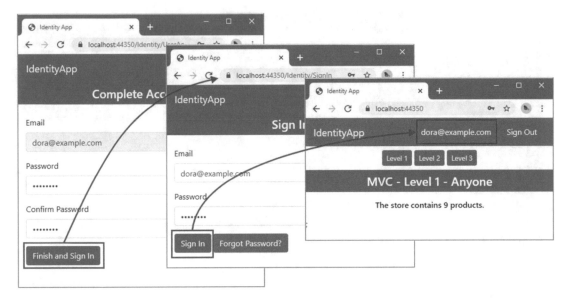

Figure 9-3. *Choosing a password and signing into the application*

Performing Self-Service Registration

Self-registration uses the basic approach as the previous example, with the exception that the email address provided by the user should not be trusted until it is confirmed until the user provides a confirmation token that has been sent securely to them. Listing 9-8 adds a method to the IdentityEmailService class that will send the user an email that contains a token for confirming their email address.

Listing 9-8. Adding a Method in the IdentityEmailService.cs File in the Services Folder

```
using Microsoft.AspNetCore.Http;
using Microsoft.AspNetCore.Identity;
using Microsoft.AspNetCore.Identity.UI.Services;
using Microsoft.AspNetCore.Routing;
using System.Threading.Tasks;

namespace IdentityApp.Services {

    public class IdentityEmailService {

        // ...methods omitted for brevity...

        public async Task SendAccountConfirmEmail(IdentityUser user,
                string confirmationPage) {
            string token =
                await UserManager.GenerateEmailConfirmationTokenAsync(user);
            string url = GetUrl(user.Email, token, confirmationPage);
```

```
        await EmailSender.SendEmailAsync(user.Email,
            "Complete Your Account Setup",
            $"Please set up your account by <a href={url}>clicking here</a>.");
    }
    }
}
```

The new email will include a token created with the user manager's GenerateEmailConfirmationTokenAsync method, which generates a token that can be used to confirm email addresses.

Add a Razor Page named SignUp.cshtml to the Pages/Identity folder with the content shown in Listing 9-9.

Listing 9-9. The Contents of the SignUp.cshtml File in the Pages/Identity Folder

```
@page
@model IdentityApp.Pages.Identity.SignUpModel
@{
    ViewData["showNav"] = false;
    ViewData["banner"] = "Sign Up";
}

<div asp-validation-summary="All" class="text-danger m-2"></div>

<form method="post" class="m-4">
    <div class="form-group">
        <label>Email</label>
        <input class="form-control" asp-for="Email" />
    </div>
    <div class="form-group">
        <label>Password</label>
        <input class="form-control" type="password" asp-for="Password" />
    </div>
    <button class="btn btn-primary">Sign Up</button>
</form>
```

The view part of the page displays a form that asks the user for their email address and password. For the page model class, add the code shown in Listing 9-10 to the SignUp.cshtml.cs file. (You will have to create this file if you are using Visual Studio Code.)

Listing 9-10. The Contents of the SignUp.cshtml.cs File in the Pages/Identity Folder

```
using IdentityApp.Services;
using Microsoft.AspNetCore.Authorization;
using Microsoft.AspNetCore.Identity;
using Microsoft.AspNetCore.Mvc;
using System.ComponentModel.DataAnnotations;
using System.Threading.Tasks;

namespace IdentityApp.Pages.Identity {

    [AllowAnonymous]
    public class SignUpModel : UserPageModel {
```

227

```
    public SignUpModel(UserManager<IdentityUser> usrMgr,
            IdentityEmailService emailService) {
        UserManager = usrMgr;
        EmailService = emailService;
    }

    public UserManager<IdentityUser> UserManager { get; set; }
    public IdentityEmailService EmailService { get; set; }

    [BindProperty]
    [Required]
    [EmailAddress]
    public string Email { get; set; }

    [BindProperty]
    [Required]
    public string Password { get; set; }

    public async Task<IActionResult> OnPostAsync() {
        if (ModelState.IsValid) {
            IdentityUser user = await UserManager.FindByEmailAsync(Email);
            if (user != null && !await UserManager.IsEmailConfirmedAsync(user)) {
                return RedirectToPage("SignUpConfirm");
            }
            user = new IdentityUser {
                UserName = Email,
                Email = Email
            };
            IdentityResult result = await UserManager.CreateAsync(user);
            if (result.Process(ModelState)) {
                result = await UserManager.AddPasswordAsync(user, Password);
                if (result.Process(ModelState)) {
                    await EmailService.SendAccountConfirmEmail(user,
                        "SignUpConfirm");
                    return RedirectToPage("SignUpConfirm");
                } else {
                    await UserManager.DeleteAsync(user);
                }
            }
        }
        return Page();
    }
}
}
```

The page model class defines a POST handler that receives the email address and password provided by the user. The email address is used to create an IdentityUser object that is added to the user store with the CreateAsync method. The password is set using the AddPasswordAsyc method, which presents a potential problem because passwords are validated before they are stored, to ensure they conform to the policy settings I described in Chapter 5. If a password doesn't pass validation, an error will be reported after the

`IdentityUser` has been stored, which will produce an account that cannot be used but which is associated with the user's email address. The simplest way to solve this problem is to use the `DeleteAsync` method to remove the `IdentityUser` object from the store if there is a problem with the password.

If the `IdentityUser` object is stored successfully, a confirmation email is sent. Once the email has been sent, the browser is redirected to a Razor Page named `SignUpConfirm`, which I create in the next section. This is also the Razor Page that will receive the request when the user clicks the link in the email they receive.

A common problem arises when the user forgets to confirm the account and subsequently repeats the signup process using the same email address. This will cause an error because the unconfirmed account is already in the user store, essentially trapping the user. To avoid this problem, I check the user store to see if it contains an unconfirmed account and perform a redirection if it does.

```
...
IdentityUser user = await UserManager.FindByEmailAsync(Email);
if (user != null && !await UserManager.IsEmailConfirmedAsync(user)) {
    return RedirectToPage("SignUpConfirm");
}
...
```

The redirection allows the user to complete the sign-up process, resending the account confirmation email if required.

Confirming Self-Registered Accounts

To allow the user to confirm their account, add a Razor Page named `SignUpConfirm.cshtml` to the `Pages/Identity` folder with the content shown in Listing 9-11.

Listing 9-11. The Contents of the SignUpConfirm.cshtml File in the Pages/Identity Folder

```
@page "{email?}/{token?}"
@model IdentityApp.Pages.Identity.SignUpConfirmModel
@{
    ViewData["showNav"] = false;
    ViewData["banner"] = "Account Confirmation";
}

@if (Model.ShowConfirmedMessage) {
    <div class="text-center">
        <h6 class="p-2">Account confirmed</h6>
        <a asp-page="SignIn" class="btn btn-primary">Sign In</a>
    </div>
} else {
    <div class="text-center">
        <h6 class="p-2">
            Check your inbox for a confirmation email and
            click the link it contains.
        </h6>
        <a asp-page="SignUpResend" class="btn btn-primary">Resend Email</a>
    </div>
}
```

This Razor Page will be shown when the user has been sent an email and will receive the request when they click the link in the email. The view section of the page alters the message it displays to suit these situations. Add the code shown in Listing 9-12 to the `SignUpConfirm.cshtml.cs` file to define the page model class. (You will have to create this file if you are using Visual Studio Code.)

Listing 9-12. The Contents of the SignUpConfirm.cshtml.cs File in the Pages/Identity Folder

```
using Microsoft.AspNetCore.Authorization;
using Microsoft.AspNetCore.Identity;
using Microsoft.AspNetCore.Mvc;
using Microsoft.AspNetCore.WebUtilities;
using System.Text;
using System.Threading.Tasks;

namespace IdentityApp.Pages.Identity {

    [AllowAnonymous]
    public class SignUpConfirmModel : UserPageModel {

        public SignUpConfirmModel(UserManager<IdentityUser> usrMgr)
            => UserManager = usrMgr;

        public UserManager<IdentityUser> UserManager { get; set; }

        [BindProperty(SupportsGet = true)]
        public string Email { get; set; }

        [BindProperty(SupportsGet = true)]
        public string Token { get; set; }

        public bool ShowConfirmedMessage { get; set; } = false;

        public async Task<IActionResult> OnGetAsync() {
            if (!string.IsNullOrEmpty(Email) && !string.IsNullOrEmpty(Token)) {
                IdentityUser user = await UserManager.FindByEmailAsync(Email);
                if (user != null) {
                    string decodedToken = Encoding.UTF8.GetString(
                        WebEncoders.Base64UrlDecode(Token));
                    IdentityResult result =
                        await UserManager.ConfirmEmailAsync(user, decodedToken);
                    if (result.Process(ModelState)) {
                        ShowConfirmedMessage = true;
                    }
                }
            }
            return Page();
        }
    }
}
```

Confirming an account is done by retrieving the IdentityUser object from the store and passing it to the ConfirmEmailAsync method, along with the token that was provided by the user. If the confirmation is successful, then the confirmation message is shown.

Resending Confirmation Emails

For self-service applications, it is important to allow the user to request the confirmation emails are sent again if the original isn't delivered. Add a Razor Page named SignUpResend.cshtml to the Pages/Identity folder with the content shown in Listing 9-13.

Listing 9-13. The Contents of the SignUpResend.cshtml File in the Pages/Identity Folder

```
@page
@model IdentityApp.Pages.Identity.SignUpResendModel
@{
    ViewData["showNav"] = false;
    ViewData["banner"] = "Account Confirmation";
}

<div asp-validation-summary="All" class="text-danger m-2"></div>

@if (TempData.ContainsKey("message")) {
    <div class="alert alert-success">@TempData["message"]</div>
}

<form method="post">
    <div class="form-group">
        <label>Your email address</label>
        <input class="form-control" asp-for="Email" />
    </div>
    <button type="submit" class="btn btn-primary">Resend Email</button>
</form>
```

The view part of the page contains a form that the user can submit to request that the confirmation email be reset. To create the page model class, add the code shown in Listing 9-14 to the SignUpResend.cshtml.cs file. (You will have to create this file if you are using Visual Studio Code.)

Listing 9-14. The Contents of the SignUpResend.cshtml.cs File in the Pages/Identity Folder

```
using IdentityApp.Services;
using Microsoft.AspNetCore.Authorization;
using Microsoft.AspNetCore.Identity;
using Microsoft.AspNetCore.Mvc;
using System.ComponentModel.DataAnnotations;
using System.Threading.Tasks;

namespace IdentityApp.Pages.Identity {

    [AllowAnonymous]
    public class SignUpResendModel : UserPageModel {
```

```
        public SignUpResendModel(UserManager<IdentityUser> usrMgr,
            IdentityEmailService emailService) {
            UserManager = usrMgr;
            EmailService = emailService;
        }

        public UserManager<IdentityUser> UserManager { get; set; }
        public IdentityEmailService EmailService { get; set; }

        [EmailAddress]
        [BindProperty(SupportsGet = true)]
        public string Email { get; set; }

        public async Task<IActionResult> OnPostAsync() {
            if (ModelState.IsValid) {
                IdentityUser user = await UserManager.FindByEmailAsync(Email);
                if (user != null && !await UserManager.IsEmailConfirmedAsync(user)) {
                    await EmailService.SendAccountConfirmEmail(user,
                        "SignUpConfirm");
                }
                TempData["message"] = "Confirmation email sent. Check your inbox.";
                return RedirectToPage(new { Email });
            }
            return Page();
        }
    }
}
```

The POST handler method receives the email address provided by the user and retrieves the
IdentityUser object from the store. If there is an IdentityUser object and the user manager's
IsEmailConfirmedAsync method reports that the email address is unconfirmed, then a new email is sent
using the IdentityEmailService.SendAccountConfirmEmail method.

A temp data value is set that will display a message to the user. This is displayed regardless of whether
the email is sent to prevent this page from being used to determine which accounts exist and if they are
awaiting confirmation.

Handling Unconfirmed Sign-ins

The user may attempt to sign in to the application after creating an account but before clicking the email
link. To avoid confusion, add the code shown in Listing 9-15 to the page model class for the SignIn page that
will notify the user that account confirmation is required.

■ **Note**   Accounts with unconfirmed email addresses are prevented from signing in only if the SignIn.
RequireConfirmedAccount configuration option is true, as described in Chapter 5.

Listing 9-15. Handling Unconfirmed Accounts in the SignIn.cshtml.cs File in the Pages/Identity Folder

```
using System.ComponentModel.DataAnnotations;
using System.Threading.Tasks;
using Microsoft.AspNetCore.Identity;
using Microsoft.AspNetCore.Mvc;
using SignInResult = Microsoft.AspNetCore.Identity.SignInResult;
using Microsoft.AspNetCore.Authorization;

namespace IdentityApp.Pages.Identity {

    [AllowAnonymous]
    public class SignInModel : UserPageModel {

        public SignInModel(SignInManager<IdentityUser> signMgr,
                UserManager<IdentityUser> usrMgr) {
            SignInManager = signMgr;
            UserManager = usrMgr;
        }

        public SignInManager<IdentityUser> SignInManager { get; set; }
        public UserManager<IdentityUser> UserManager { get; set; }

        [Required]
        [EmailAddress]
        [BindProperty]
        public string Email { get; set; }

        [Required]
        [BindProperty]
        public string Password { get; set; }

        [BindProperty(SupportsGet = true)]
        public string ReturnUrl { get; set; }

        public async Task<IActionResult> OnPostAsync() {
            if (ModelState.IsValid) {
                SignInResult result = await SignInManager.PasswordSignInAsync(Email,
                    Password, true, true);
                if (result.Succeeded) {
                    return Redirect(ReturnUrl ?? "/");
                } else if (result.IsLockedOut) {
                    TempData["message"] = "Account Locked";
                } else if (result.IsNotAllowed) {
                    IdentityUser user = await UserManager.FindByEmailAsync(Email);
                    if (user != null &&
                            !await UserManager.IsEmailConfirmedAsync(user)) {
                        return RedirectToPage("SignUpConfirm");
                    }
                    TempData["message"] = "Sign In Not Allowed";
                } else if (result.RequiresTwoFactor) {
                    return RedirectToPage("SignInTwoFactor", new { ReturnUrl });
```

```
                } else {
                    TempData["message"] = "Sign In Failed";
                }
            }
            return Page();
        }
    }
}
```

When a user signs in with the correct password but has an unconfirmed account, the sign-in manager will return a `SignInResult` whose `IsNotAllowed` property is `true`. The new code in Listing 9-15 retrieves the `IdentityUser` object for the user's email address, determines if the account has a confirmed email address with the `IsEmailConfirmedAsync` method, and performs a redirection to the `SignUpConfirm` page. For quick reference, Table 9-4 describes the user manager methods used for self-service registration.

Table 9-4. *The UserManager<IdentityUser> Methods for Self-Registration*

Name	Description
CreateAsync(user)	This method adds an `IdentityUser` object to the store.
AddPasswordAsync(user, password)	This method sets a password for the specified `IdentityUser` object.
GenerateEmailConfirmation TokenAsync(user)	This method generates a token that can be sent to the user to confirm their email address.
ConfirmEmailAsync(user, token)	This method validates a token generated by the `GenerateEmailConfirmationTokenAsync` method to confirm an email address.
IsEmailConfirmedAsync(user)	This method returns `true` if the email address for the specified `IdentityUser` object has been confirmed.

Integrating Self-Service Registration

To integrate the self-service feature into the rest of the application, add the element shown in Listing 9-16 to the `SignIn.cshtml` file.

Listing 9-16. Adding an Element in the SignIn.cshtml File in the Pages/Identity Folder

```
@page "{returnUrl?}"
@model IdentityApp.Pages.Identity.SignInModel
@{
    ViewData["showNav"] = false;
    ViewData["banner"] = "Sign In";
}

<div asp-validation-summary="All" class="text-danger m-2"></div>

@if (TempData.ContainsKey("message")) {
    <div class="alert alert-danger">@TempData["message"]</div>
}
```

```
<form method="post">
    <div class="form-group">
        <label>Email</label>
        <input class="form-control" name="email" />
    </div>
    <div class="form-group">
        <label>Password</label>
        <input class="form-control" type="password" name="password" />
    </div>
    <button type="submit" class="btn btn-primary">
        Sign In
    </button>
    <a asp-page="SignUp" class="btn btn-primary">Register</a>
    <a asp-page="UserPasswordRecovery" class="btn btn-secondary">Forgot Password?</a>
</form>
```

The final change is to display the number of unconfirmed accounts in the administrator dashboard, as shown in Listing 9-17.

Listing 9-17. Displaying Accounts in the Dashboard.cshtml.cs File in the Pages/Identity/Admin Folder

```
using Microsoft.AspNetCore.Mvc.RazorPages;
using Microsoft.AspNetCore.Identity;
using Microsoft.AspNetCore.Mvc;
using System.Threading.Tasks;
using System.Linq;

namespace IdentityApp.Pages.Identity.Admin {

    public class DashboardModel : AdminPageModel {

        public DashboardModel(UserManager<IdentityUser> userMgr)
            => UserManager = userMgr;

        public UserManager<IdentityUser> UserManager { get; set; }

        public int UsersCount { get; set; } = 0;
        public int UsersUnconfirmed { get; set; } = 0;
        public int UsersLockedout { get; set; } = 0;
        public int UsersTwoFactor { get; set; } = 0;

        private readonly string[] emails = {
            "alice@example.com", "bob@example.com", "charlie@example.com"
        };

        public void OnGet() {
            UsersCount = UserManager.Users.Count();
            UsersUnconfirmed = UserManager.Users
                .Where(u => !u.EmailConfirmed).Count();
        }
```

```
        public async Task<IActionResult> OnPostAsync() {
            // ...statements omitted for brevity...
        }
    }
}
```

■ **Tip**   Although I have been relying on the user manager's `IsEmailConfirmedAsync` method in earlier listings, the LINQ query in Listing 9-17 operates directly on the properties defined by the `IdentityUser` class. This ensures that the query can be executed by the database server, which isn't possible with the `IsEmailConfirmedAsync` method, which cannot be easily transformed into a SQL query and which requires client execution.

Restart ASP.NET Core and request `https://localhost:44350/Identity/SignUp`. Enter ezra@example. com into the Email field and mysecret into the Password field. Click the Sign Up button, and you will be prompted to check your inbox, as shown in Figure 9-4.

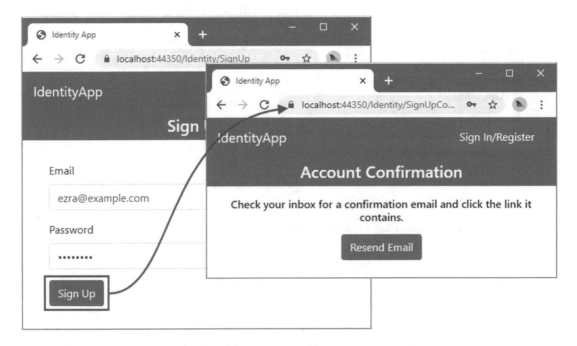

Figure 9-4. *Self-registration*

The account is created but not yet confirmed, which you can see by requesting `https://localhost:44350/Identity/admin`. The dashboard overview shows that there are now five accounts in the user store, one of which is unconfirmed, as shown in Figure 9-5.

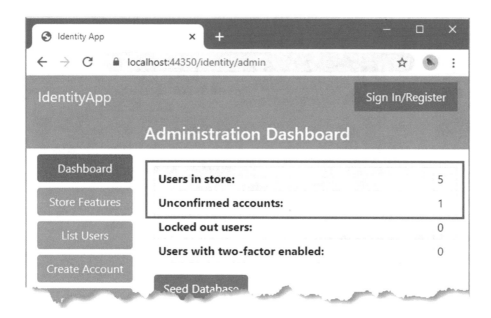

Figure 9-5. The unconfirmed account shown in the administration dashboard

Examine the ASP.NET Core console output, and you will see a message similar to this one:

```
---New Email----
To: ezra@example.com
Subject: Complete Your Account Setup
Please set up your account by <a href=https://localhost:44350/Identity/SignUpConfirm/ezra@
example.com/Q2ZESj>
    clicking here
</a>.
-------
```

I have shortened the confirmation token for brevity. Copy the URL from the email generated by your application (which will be different to the one I received because each confirmation token is unique) and paste it into a browser window to confirm the account.

Click the Sign In button, and you will be presented with the sign in page. Use ezra@example.com as the email address and mysecret as the password to sign into the application, as shown in Figure 9-6.

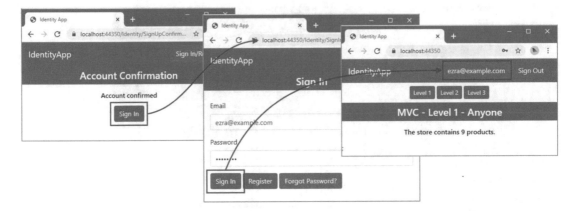

Figure 9-6. *Completing the self-registration process*

Locking Out Accounts

ASP.NET Core Identity can be configured to lock out accounts after a specified number of failed sign-ins. When an application supports lockouts, it is a good idea to create workflows that let administrators lock and unlock accounts. Locking an account is useful as a temporary measure, such as when suspicious behavior is observed. Unlocking an account is useful when a senior executive forgets their password, demands that it be changed, and won't wait for the lockout to expire. Add a Razor Page named Lockouts.cshtml to the Pages/Identity/Admin folder with the content shown in Listing 9-18.

UNDERSTANDING LOCKOUTS

For an account to be locked out, the IdentityUser.LockoutEnabled property must be true, and the final argument to the SignInManager<IdentityUser>.PasswordSignInAsync must be true when the user's credentials are checked. See Chapter 6 for the configuration options that control LockoutEnabled, and see Chapter 8 for a description of the PasswordSignInAsync method. Lockouts are described in detail in Chapter 20, including an explanation of how they are implemented in the user store.

Listing 9-18. The Contents of the Lockouts.cshtml File in the Pages/Identity/Admin Folder

```
@page
@model IdentityApp.Pages.Identity.Admin.LockoutsModel
@{
    ViewBag.Workflow = "Lockouts";
}

<table class="table table-sm table-striped table-bordered">
    <thead>
        <tr><th class="text-center py-2" colspan="3">Locked Out Users</th></tr>
    </thead>
```

```html
<tbody>
    @if (Model.LockedOutUsers.Count() == 0) {
        <tr>
            <td colspan="3" class="py-2 text-center">
                No locked out users
            </td>
        </tr>
    } else {
        <tr><th>Email</th><th>Lockout Remaining</th><th/></tr>
        @foreach (IdentityUser user in Model.LockedOutUsers) {
            TimeSpan timeLeft = await Model.TimeLeft(user);
            <tr>
                <td>@user.Email</td>
                <td>
                    @timeLeft.Days days, @timeLeft.Hours hours,
                    @timeLeft.Minutes min, @timeLeft.Seconds secs
                </td>
                <td>
                    <form method="post" asp-page-handler="unlock">
                        <input type="hidden" name="id" value="@user.Id" />
                        <button type="submit" class="btn btn-sm btn-success">
                            Unlock Now
                        </button>
                    </form>
                </td>
            </tr>
        }
    }
</tbody>
</table>

<table class="table table-sm table-striped table-bordered">
    <thead>
        <tr><th class="text-center py-2" colspan="2">Other Users</th></tr>
    </thead>
    <tbody>
        @if (Model.OtherUsers.Count() == 0) {
            <tr>
                <th colspan="2" class="py-2 text-center">
                    All users locked out
                </th>
            </tr>
        } else {
            <tr><th>Email</th><th/></tr>
            @foreach (IdentityUser user in Model.OtherUsers) {
                <tr>
                    <td>@user.Email</td>
                    <td>
                        <form method="post" asp-page-handler="lock">
                            <input type="hidden" name="id" value="@user.Id" />
                            <button type="submit" class="btn btn-sm btn-success">
```

```
                                    Lock Out
                          </button>
                      </form>
                  </td>
              </tr>
          }
      }
    </tbody>
</table>
```

The view part of the page displays two tables. The first table lists the locked-out users, showing when the lockout expires, and provides buttons to unlock accounts immediately. The second table lists the remaining users, with buttons to start lockouts. To define the page model class, add the code shown in Listing 9-19 to the Lockouts.cshtml.cs file. (You will have to create this file if you are using Visual Studio Code.)

Listing 9-19. The Contents of the Lockouts.cshtml.cs File in the Pages/Identity/Admin Folder

```csharp
using Microsoft.AspNetCore.Identity;
using Microsoft.AspNetCore.Mvc;
using System;
using System.Collections.Generic;
using System.Linq;
using System.Threading.Tasks;

namespace IdentityApp.Pages.Identity.Admin {

    public class LockoutsModel : AdminPageModel {

        public LockoutsModel(UserManager<IdentityUser> usrMgr)
            => UserManager = usrMgr;

        public UserManager<IdentityUser> UserManager { get; set; }

        public IEnumerable<IdentityUser> LockedOutUsers { get; set; }
        public IEnumerable<IdentityUser> OtherUsers { get; set; }

        public async Task<TimeSpan> TimeLeft(IdentityUser user)
            => (await UserManager.GetLockoutEndDateAsync(user))
                .GetValueOrDefault().Subtract(DateTimeOffset.Now);

        public void OnGet() {
            LockedOutUsers = UserManager.Users.Where(user => user.LockoutEnd.HasValue
                    && user.LockoutEnd.Value > DateTimeOffset.Now)
                .OrderBy(user => user.Email).ToList();
            OtherUsers = UserManager.Users.Where(user => !user.LockoutEnd.HasValue
                    || user.LockoutEnd.Value <= DateTimeOffset.Now)
                .OrderBy(user => user.Email).ToList();
        }

        public async Task<IActionResult> OnPostLockAsync(string id) {
            IdentityUser user = await UserManager.FindByIdAsync(id);
            await UserManager.SetLockoutEnabledAsync(user, true);
```

```
        await UserManager.SetLockoutEndDateAsync(user,
            DateTimeOffset.Now.AddDays(5));
        return RedirectToPage();
    }

    public async Task<IActionResult> OnPostUnlockAsync(string id) {
        IdentityUser user = await UserManager.FindByIdAsync(id);
        await UserManager.SetLockoutEndDateAsync(user, null);
        return RedirectToPage();
    }
  }
}
```

To determine if a user is locked out, the user manager's GetLockoutEndDateAsync method is called. If the result has a value and that value specifies a time in the future, then the user is locked out. If there is no value or the time has passed, then the user is not locked out.

To lock and unlock the user account, the SetLockoutEnabledAsync method is used to enable lockouts, and a time is specified using the SetLockoutEndDateAsync method. The user won't be allowed to sign in until the specified time has passed. Lockouts can be disabled by calling the SetLockoutEndDateAsync with a null argument.

This is an awkwardly implemented feature, which is made worse by the need to work directly with the LockoutEnd property defined by the IdentityUser class, which is used by the GetLockoutEndDateAsync and SetLockoutEndDateAsync methods. Using this property directly makes it possible to query the database effectively using LINQ. This isn't a huge concern for the example application but becomes an issue to watch out for in projects with large numbers of users.

I have set the lockout period to five days, which effectively suspends an account. I generally use multiday intervals for lockouts applied by an administrator so that an account that has attracted attention doesn't become active again while investigations are ongoing. By contrast, the default lockout period applied by Identity for repeated failed sign-ins is five minutes.

To display the number of lockouts in the administrator dashboard, add the statement shown in Listing 9-20 to the Dashboard.cshtml.cs file.

Listing 9-20. Displaying Lockouts in the Dashboard.cshtml.cs File in the Pages/Identity/Admin Folder

```
...
public void OnGet() {
    UsersCount = UserManager.Users.Count();
    UsersUnconfirmed = UserManager.Users
        .Where(u => !u.EmailConfirmed).Count();
    UsersLockedout = UserManager.Users
        .Where(u => u.LockoutEnabled && u.LockoutEnd > System.DateTimeOffset.Now)
        .Count();
}
...
```

This statement uses LINQ to count the number of locked-out users by checking the LockoutEnabled and LockoutEnd properties. For quick reference, Table 9-5 describes the user manager methods for managing lockouts.

Table 9-5. *The UserManager<IdentityUser> Methods for Managing Lockouts*

Name	Description
GetLockoutEndDateAsync(user)	This method returns a DateTimeOffet? object. If this object has a value and represents a time in the future, then the account is locked out.
SetLockoutEnabledAsync(user, enabled)	This method sets whether lockouts are enabled for the user account. A lockout cannot be set unless lockouts are enabled.
SetLockoutEndDateAsync(user, time)	This method sets a lockout that will prevent the user from signing into the application until the specified time, which is expressed as a DateTimeOffset? value. Using a null value for the time unlocks the account.

Forcing Immediate Sign-Outs

When a user signs into the application, a cookie is added to the response. The cookie is included in subsequent HTTP requests and is used to authenticate the user without requiring them to provide their credentials again.

When an account is logged out, the user is unable to sign in to the application, but any cookies that have already been created remain valid, which means the user won't be affected by the lockout if they were already signed into the application.

A common requirement is to terminate any existing sessions when an account is logged out, which will prevent the user from using the application even if they had signed in before the lock started. The key to implementing this feature is the security stamp, which is a random string that is changed every time an alternation to the user's security data is made. The first step is to configure Identity so that it periodically validates the cookies presented by the user to see if the security stamp has changed, as shown in Listing 9-21.

Listing 9-21. Configuring the Application in the Startup.cs File in the IdentityApp Folder

```
...
services.AddIdentity<IdentityUser, IdentityRole>(opts => {
    opts.Password.RequiredLength = 8;
    opts.Password.RequireDigit = false;
    opts.Password.RequireLowercase = false;
    opts.Password.RequireUppercase = false;
    opts.Password.RequireNonAlphanumeric = false;
    opts.SignIn.RequireConfirmedAccount = true;
}).AddEntityFrameworkStores<IdentityDbContext>()
    .AddDefaultTokenProviders();

services.Configure<SecurityStampValidatorOptions>(opts => {
    opts.ValidationInterval = System.TimeSpan.FromMinutes(1);
});

services.AddScoped<TokenUrlEncoderService>();
services.AddScoped<IdentityEmailService>();
...
```

The validation feature is enabled by using the options pattern to assign an interval to the ValidationInterval property defined by the SecurityStampValidatorOptions class. I have chosen one minute for this example, but it is important to select an appropriate value for each project. Validation requires data to be retrieved from the user store, and if you set the interval too short, you will generate a large number of additional database queries, especially in applications with substantial concurrent users. On the other hand, setting the interval too long will extend the period a signed-in user will be able to continue using the application after their account is locked out.

UNDERSTANDING THE IMMEDIATE SIGN-OUT PITFALLS

There are two potential pitfalls when enabling the cookie validation feature for immediate sign-outs. First, the term *immediate* is used from the perspective of the ASP.NET Core application. From the user's perspective, they won't know they have been signed out until the next time their browser sends a request to the application, which may occur some time after the account has been locked. This isn't an issue for most projects, but if you use short lockout periods, the lockout may expire before the user next sends a request, which means the user is signed out of the application without understanding why.

The second pitfall is that any operation that changes the user's security stamp will cause validation to fail the next time the user sends an HTTP request, signing the user out of the application. Many of the methods provided by the user manager class update the security stamp, as described in Part 2, which will trigger unexpected user sign out. For self-service operations, you can prevent this issue by signing the user into the application again, as I demonstrate in Chapter 11, when I set up two-factor authentication. There is no such solution available for operations performed by an administrator, and you should bear in mind that the user may be signed out when you update their account.

The second step is to change the security stamp when locking out an account, as shown in Listing 9-22.

Listing 9-22. Changing a Security Stamp in the Lockouts.cshtml.cs File in the Pages/Identity/Admin Folder

```
...
public async Task<IActionResult> OnPostLockAsync(string id) {
    IdentityUser user = await UserManager.FindByIdAsync(id);
    await UserManager.SetLockoutEnabledAsync(user, true);
    await UserManager.SetLockoutEndDateAsync(user,
        DateTimeOffset.Now.AddDays(5));
    await UserManager.UpdateSecurityStampAsync(user);
    return RedirectToPage();
}
...
```

The UpdateSecurityStampAsync method creates a new security stamp for the specified user account, which will cause the user to be signed out the next time a cookie is validated. For quick reference, Table 9-6 describes the user manager method I used to set the security stamp.

Table 9-6. *The UserManager<IdentityUser> Method for Changing Security Stamps*

Name	Description
UpdateSecurityStampAsync(user)	This method generates a new security stamp for the specified identityUser.

Add the element shown in Listing 9-23 to the navigation partial view to integrate the new Razor Page into the administration layout.

Listing 9-23. Adding Navigation in the _AdminWorkflows.cshtml File in the Pages/Identity/Admin Folder

```
@model (string workflow, string theme)

@{
    Func<string, string> getClass = (string feature) =>
        feature != null && feature.Equals(Model.workflow) ? "active" : "";
}

<a class="btn btn-@Model.theme btn-block @getClass("Dashboard")"
        asp-page="Dashboard">
    Dashboard
</a>
<a class="btn btn-@Model.theme btn-block @getClass("Features")" asp-page="Features">
    Store Features
</a>
<a class="btn btn-success btn-block @getClass("List")" asp-page="View"
        asp-route-id="">
    List Users
</a>
<a class="btn btn-success btn-block @getClass("Create")" asp-page="Create">
    Create Account
</a>
<a class="btn btn-success btn-block @getClass("Edit")" asp-page="Edit"
        asp-route-id="">
    Edit Users
</a>
<a class="btn btn-success btn-block @getClass("Passwords")" asp-page="Passwords"
        asp-route-id="">
    Passwords
</a>
<a class="btn btn-success btn-block @getClass("Lockouts")" asp-page="Lockouts" >
    Lockouts
</a>
```

Restart ASP.NET Core, request https://localhost:44350/Identity/Admin, and click the Lockouts button. You will be presented with a list of users. Click the Lockout button for the alice@example.com account, and the account will be locked, as shown in Figure 9-7.

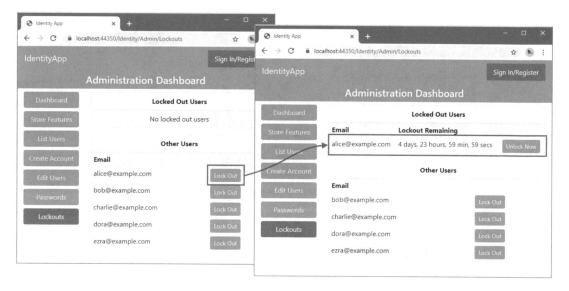

Figure 9-7. *Locking out an account*

Click the Dashboard button, and the overview will show that one account is locked out, as shown in Figure 9-8.

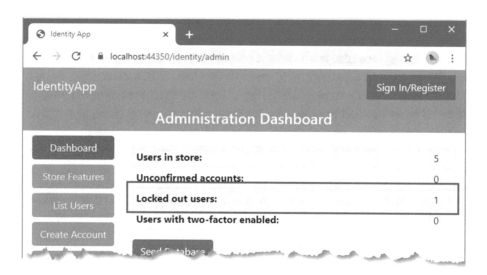

Figure 9-8. *Locked accounts in the dashboard*

Click the Sign In/Register link at the top of the page and sign in using alice@example.com as the email address and mysecret as the password. Even though these are the correct credentials, you won't be able to sign in to the application, as shown in Figure 9-9.

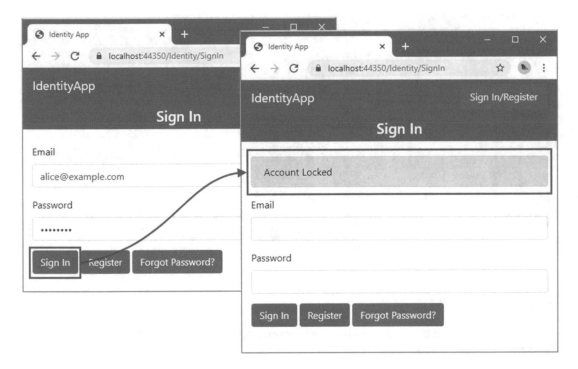

Figure 9-9. *Attempting to sign in with a locked account*

■ **Tip**   Browsers share cookies between tabs, which makes it difficult to test the forced sign-out process. The best approach is to use the guest browsing features to open a window that has its own cookies and sign into the application. Use the main browser window to lock out the account. You can then continue using the application in the guest window until the next time the cookie is validated, at which point you will be signed out of the application.

Sign in to the application using bob@example.com as the email address and mysecret as the password. Use your browser's private/guest browsing feature to request https://localhost:44350/Identity/Admin, click the Lockouts button, and lock out bob@example.com. Wait for a couple of minutes and then reload the original browser window. You will see that you have been signed out of the application, as shown in Figure 9-10.

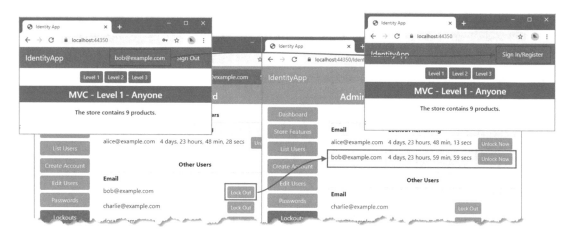

Figure 9-10. *Signing out users when locking an account*

Deleting Accounts

Accounts can be deleted for a range of reasons. For corporate applications, the most common reason is that an employee has left the organization and should no longer be able to access the application. For self-service applications, accounts are deleted because the user no longer wants to use the application.

To support administrator account deletion, add a Razor Page named Delete.cshtml to the Pages/ Identity/Admin folder with the content shown in Listing 9-24.

Listing 9-24. The Contents of the Delete.cshtml File in the Pages/Identity/Admin Folder

```
@page "{id?}"
@model IdentityApp.Pages.Identity.Admin.DeleteModel
@{
    ViewBag.Workflow = "Delete";
}

<div asp-validation-summary="All" class="text-danger m-2"></div>

<form method="post">

    <h3 class="bg-danger text-white text-center p-2">Caution</h3>

    <h5 class="text-center m-2">
        Delete @Model.IdentityUser.Email?
    </h5>
    <input type="hidden" name="id" value="@Model.IdentityUser.Id" />
    <div class="text-center p-2">
        <button type="submit" class="btn btn-danger">Delete</button>
        <a asp-page="Dashboard" class="btn btn-secondary">Cancel</a>
    </div>
</form>
```

The view part of the page contains a simple form that will delete a selected account when submitted. To define the page model class, add the code shown in Listing 9-25 to the Delete.cshtml.cs file. (You will have to create this file if you are using Visual Studio Code.)

Listing 9-25. The Contents of the Delete.cshtml.cs File in the Pages/Identity/Admin Folder

```
using System;
using System.Collections.Generic;
using System.Linq;
using System.Threading.Tasks;
using Microsoft.AspNetCore.Identity;
using Microsoft.AspNetCore.Mvc;
using Microsoft.AspNetCore.Mvc.RazorPages;

namespace IdentityApp.Pages.Identity.Admin {

    public class DeleteModel : AdminPageModel {

        public DeleteModel(UserManager<IdentityUser> mgr) => UserManager = mgr;

        public UserManager<IdentityUser> UserManager { get; set; }

        public IdentityUser IdentityUser { get; set; }

        [BindProperty(SupportsGet = true)]
        public string Id { get; set; }

        public async Task<IActionResult> OnGetAsync() {
            if (string.IsNullOrEmpty(Id)) {
                return RedirectToPage("Selectuser",
                    new { Label = "Delete", Callback = "Delete" });
            }
            IdentityUser = await UserManager.FindByIdAsync(Id);
            return Page();
        }

        public async Task<IActionResult> OnPostAsync() {
            IdentityUser = await UserManager.FindByIdAsync(Id);
            IdentityResult result = await UserManager.DeleteAsync(IdentityUser);
            if (result.Process(ModelState)) {
                return RedirectToPage("Dashboard");
            }
            return Page();
        }
    }
}
```

The user manager defines the DeleteAsync method, which removes an IdentityUser object from the store. The FindByIdAsync method is used to locate the selected account, and there is a redirection to the SelectUser page if no selection has been made. For quick reference, Table 9-7 describes the method used to delete objects from the user store.

■ **Tip**   Notice that I don't need to update the security stamp to force an immediate sign-out in Listing 9-25 because the IdentityUser data—including the security stamp—is removed from the user store. If cookie validation is enabled, as shown in Listing 9-21, the user will be automatically signed out the next time validation is performed.

Table 9-7. *The UserManager<IdentityUser> Method for Deleting Objects*

Name	Description
DeleteAsync(user)	This method removes the specified IdentityUser object from the user store.

Add the element shown in Listing 9-26 to enable navigation to the new Razor Page.

Listing 9-26. Adding Navigation in the _AdminWorkflows.cshtml File in the Pages/Identity/Admin Folder

```
@model (string workflow, string theme)

@{
    Func<string, string> getClass = (string feature) =>
        feature != null && feature.Equals(Model.workflow) ? "active" : "";
}

<a class="btn btn-@Model.theme btn-block @getClass("Dashboard")"
        asp-page="Dashboard">
    Dashboard
</a>
<a class="btn btn-@Model.theme btn-block @getClass("Features")" asp-page="Features">
    Store Features
</a>
<a class="btn btn-success btn-block @getClass("List")" asp-page="View"
        asp-route-id="">
    List Users
</a>
<a class="btn btn-success btn-block @getClass("Create")" asp-page="Create">
    Create Account
</a>
<a class="btn btn-success btn-block @getClass("Delete")" asp-page="Delete">
    Delete Account
</a>
<a class="btn btn-success btn-block @getClass("Edit")" asp-page="Edit"
        asp-route-id="">
    Edit Users
</a>
<a class="btn btn-success btn-block @getClass("Passwords")" asp-page="Passwords"
        asp-route-id="">
    Passwords
</a>
<a class="btn btn-success btn-block @getClass("Lockouts")" asp-page="Lockouts" >
    Lockouts
</a>
```

249

Restart ASP.NET Core and request `https://localhost:44350/identity/admin`. Click the Delete Account button and click the Delete button for the `bob@example.com` account. You will be prompted to confirm the deletion. Click Delete, and the account will be removed from the user store, as shown in Figure 9-11.

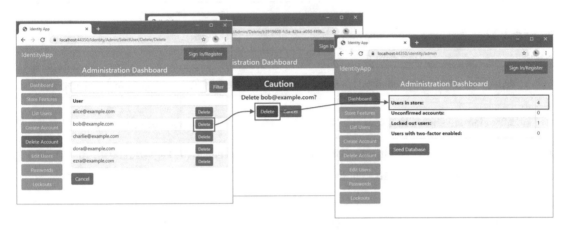

Figure 9-11. *Deleting an account*

Performing Self-Service Account Deletion

Self-service account deletion uses the same methods, and the only difference from the administrator workflow is that the `IdentityUser` object is obtained using the current `ClaimsPrincipal`, rather than querying the user store. Add a Razor Page named `UserDelete.cshtml` to the `Pages/Identity` folder, with the content shown in Listing 9-27.

Listing 9-27. The Contents of the UserDelete.cshtml File in the Pages/Identity Folder

```
@page
@model IdentityApp.Pages.Identity.UserDeleteModel
@{
    ViewBag.Workflow = "Delete";
}

<div asp-validation-summary="All" class="text-danger m-2"></div>

<form method="post">

    <h3 class="bg-danger text-white text-center p-2">Caution</h3>

    <h5 class="text-center m-2">
        Do you want to delete your account?
    </h5>
    <div class="text-center p-2">
        <button type="submit" class="btn btn-danger">Delete</button>
        <a asp-page="Dashboard" class="btn btn-secondary">Cancel</a>
    </div>
</form>
```

The view part of the page displays a simple warning and contains a form that sends a POST request. To define the page model class, add the code shown in Listing 9-28 to the UserDelete.cshtml.cs file. (You will have to create this file if you are using Visual Studio Code.)

Listing 9-28. The Contents of the UserDelete.cshtml.cs File in the Pages/Identity Folder

```
using Microsoft.AspNetCore.Identity;
using Microsoft.AspNetCore.Mvc;
using Microsoft.AspNetCore.Mvc.RazorPages;
using System.Threading.Tasks;

namespace IdentityApp.Pages.Identity {

    public class UserDeleteModel : UserPageModel {

        public UserDeleteModel(UserManager<IdentityUser> usrMgr,
                SignInManager<IdentityUser> signMgr) {
            UserManager = usrMgr;
            SignInManager = signMgr;
        }

        public UserManager<IdentityUser> UserManager { get; set; }
        public SignInManager<IdentityUser> SignInManager{ get; set; }

        public async Task<IActionResult> OnPostAsync() {
            IdentityUser idUser = await UserManager.GetUserAsync(User);
            IdentityResult result = await UserManager.DeleteAsync(idUser);
            if (result.Process(ModelState)) {
                await SignInManager.SignOutAsync();
                return Challenge();
            }
            return Page();
        }
    }
}
```

The account is deleted using the DeleteAsync method, just as in the administrator workflow with the addition that I use the SignOutAsync method defined by the SignInManager<IdentityUser> class to sign the user out of the application. This method can't be used to sign out other users in administration workflows, but it can be used for self-service workflows because it removes the authentication cookie from the response sent to the user.

Add the element shown in Listing 9-29 to create navigation for the new workflow.

Listing 9-29. Adding Navigation in the _Workflows.cshtml File in the Pages/Identity Folder

```
@model (string workflow, string theme)
@inject UserManager<IdentityUser> UserManager
@{
    Func<string, string> getClass = (string feature) =>
        feature != null && feature.Equals(Model.workflow) ? "active" : "";
```

```
    IdentityUser identityUser
        = await UserManager.GetUserAsync(User) ?? new IdentityUser();
}

<a class="btn btn-@Model.theme btn-block @getClass("Overview")" asp-page="Index">
    Overview
</a>

@if (await UserManager.HasPasswordAsync(identityUser)) {
    <a class="btn btn-@Model.theme btn-block @getClass("PasswordChange")"
            asp-page="UserPasswordChange">
        Change Password
    </a>
}
<a class="btn btn-@Model.theme btn-block @getClass("UserDelete")"
        asp-page="UserDelete">
    Delete Account
</a>
```

Restart ASP.NET Core, request https://localhost:44350/Identity/Account/Login, and sign in using the email dora@example.com and the password mysecret.

Click the email address shown in the header to navigate to the user dashboard and then click the Delete Account button. Click the Delete button, and the account will be removed from the user store, as shown in Figure 9-12. You can confirm the result by examining the administrator dashboard, which will show one fewer account in the user store.

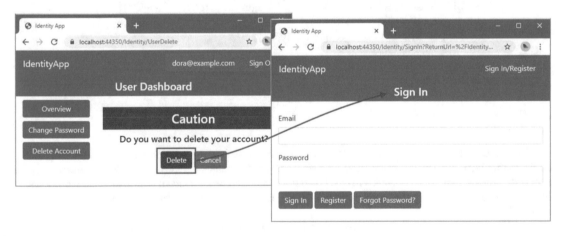

Figure 9-12. *Self-service account deletion*

Summary

In this chapter, I demonstrated administrator and self-service workflows for creating and deleting accounts. I also explained how lockouts work and how to force immediate sign-out by revalidating the cookie used to authenticate requests. In the next chapter, I describe the Identity API features for roles and claims.

CHAPTER 10

■ ■ ■

Using Roles and Claims

In this chapter, I describe the Identity API features that support roles and claims. Roles are commonly used to create fine-grained authorization policies that differentiate between different signed-in users. Claims are a general-purpose approach to describing any data that is known about a user and allow custom data to be added to the Identity user store. Table 10-1 puts these features in context.

Table 10-1. *Putting Roles and Claims in Context*

Question	Answer
What are they?	Roles differentiate groups of users to create authorization policies. Claims are used to represent any data known about a user.
Why are they useful?	Both features are used to provide the ASP.NET Core platform with data when a user signs in. Claims are not widely used, which is a shame because they make it easy to extend the data stored by Identity.
How are they used?	Users are assigned to roles, which are validated against a master list in an additional data repository, known as the *role store*. Claims are used to arbitrary data items, which are included in the data provided to the ASP.NET Core when a user signs in.
Are there any pitfalls or limitations?	It is important to prevent administrators from locking themselves out of the management tools by removing the role that grants them access.
Are there any alternatives?	Roles and claims are optional features. Roles are not required if you only need to identify signed-in users. Claims are not required if you do not need to store additional data.

Table 10-2 summarizes the chapter.

Table 10-2. *Chapter Summary*

Problem	Solution	Listing
Assign users to roles	Use the role manager to create a role. Use the user manager to assign the user to the role or to obtain the list of roles to which the user has already been assigned.	1–12
Restrict access using a role	Use the `Roles` argument of the `Authorize` attribute.	13
Assign claims to users	Use the user manager methods to create, delete, or replace claims, or to obtain a list of claims that have already been created.	14–17

(continued)

© Adam Freeman 2021
A. Freeman, *Pro ASP.NET Core Identity*, https://doi.org/10.1007/978-1-4842-6858-2_10

Table 10-2. (*continued*)

Problem	Solution	Listing
Inspect the way the data in the user store will be provided to the ASP.NET Core platform	Use the sign-in manager to create a `ClaimsPrincipal` object.	18–19
Use claims in an ASP.NET Core application	Use the claims convenience methods provided by the `ClaimsPrincipal` class.	20

Preparing for This Chapter

This chapter uses the IdentityApp project from Chapter 9. Open a new PowerShell command prompt and run the commands shown in Listing 10-1 to reset the application and Identity databases.

■ **Tip**   You can download the example project for this chapter—and for all the other chapters in this book—from `https://github.com/Apress/pro-asp.net-core-identity`. See Chapter 1 for how to get help if you have problems running the examples.

Listing 10-1. Resetting the Databases

```
dotnet ef database drop --force --context ProductDbContext
dotnet ef database drop --force --context IdentityDbContext
dotnet ef database update --context ProductDbContext
dotnet ef database update --context IdentityDbContext
```

Use the PowerShell prompt to run the command shown in Listing 10-2 in the IdentityApp folder to start the application.

Listing 10-2. Running the Example Application

```
dotnet run
```

Open a web browser and request `https://localhost:44350/Identity/Admin`, which will show the dashboard. Click the Seed Database button to add the test accounts to the user store, as shown in Figure 10-1.

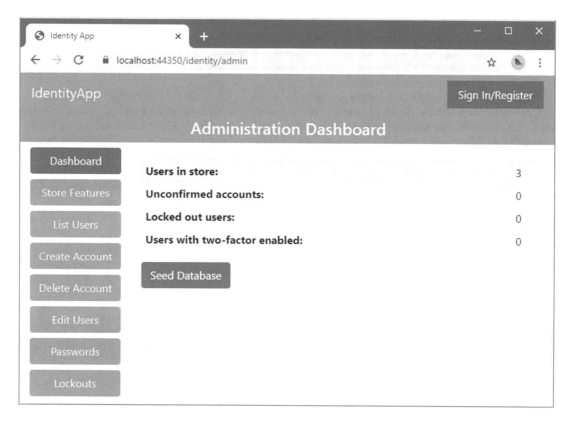

Figure 10-1. *Running the example application*

Using Roles

Roles are the most commonly used way to control access in applications. An authorization policy is defined that restricts access to one or more roles, such as the attribute I added to the most protected view and Razor Page in Chapter 3.

```
...
[Authorize(Roles = "Admin")]
public class AdminController : Controller {
...
```

Access is restricted to users that have been assigned the Admin role. The application isn't configured to support roles at present, and the Identity UI package doesn't support them at all, since they are not suitable for self-managed accounts, so there is no way to satisfy the authorization policy defined by the Authorize attribute. In the sections that follow, I set up support for roles and create the workflows for managing them.

Managing Roles

When you assign a user to a role, the user manager class asks the user store to add the role by providing it with a string to associate with the IdentityUser object but doesn't specify how this data is stored, which means that the implementation of roles can vary based on the user store you are working with.

255

In Part 2, I create a user store that keeps track of a user's roles using a collection so that the roles assigned to a user are stored independently of all other user roles. This approach is simple, but it is easy to introduce a typo so that Alice is assigned to the admin role, for example, but Bob is assigned to the amdin role. Mistakes like this can be hard to spot, and they prevent users' requests from being authorized correctly because roles names must match exactly.

One approach to avoiding this problem is to define a master list of roles and only allow users to be assigned to roles on that list. Identity has an advanced feature called the *role store*, which is used to associate extra data with roles. The role store doesn't change the way that a user's role assignments are stored, but it does provide a convenient master list to help ensure that roles are assigned consistently. (I describe the role store in detail, including its use as a master list of roles in Chapter 19.)

The master list is managed using the role manager class, RoleManager<T> where T is the role class used by the application. In Chapter 7, I enabled support for roles by selecting the default role class, IdentityRole, like this:

```
...
services.AddIdentity<IdentityUser, IdentityRole>(opts => {
    opts.Password.RequiredLength = 8;
    opts.Password.RequireDigit = false;
    opts.Password.RequireLowercase = false;
    opts.Password.RequireUppercase = false;
    opts.Password.RequireNonAlphanumeric = false;
    opts.SignIn.RequireConfirmedAccount = true;
}).AddEntityFrameworkStores<IdentityDbContext>()
    .AddDefaultTokenProviders();
...
```

This means that the role manager class for the example application is RoleManager<IdentityRole>. The role manager class provides additional features, described in Chapter 19, that are not required by most projects, but members shown in Table 10-3 are the ones that are important for this chapter.

Table 10-3. *Important RoleManager<IdentityRole> Members*

Name	Description
Roles	This property returns an IQueryable<IdentityRole> that allows the roles in the role store to be enumerated or queried with LINQ.
FindByNameAsync(name)	This method locates the IdentityRole object with the specified name in the role store.
CreateAsync(identRole)	This method adds the specified IdentityRole object to the role store and returns an IdentityResult object that describes the outcome.
DeleteAsync(identRole)	This method removes the specified IdentityRole object from the role store and returns an IdentityResult object that describes the outcome.

These methods allow the master list of roles to be managed. Since we are using the IdentityRole class only as an entry on the master role list, only the property described in Table 10-4 is important for this chapter.

Table 10-4. *The IdentityRole Property*

Name	Description
Name	This property returns the name of the role.

The RoleManager<IdentityRole> class is used only for creating the master list of roles. The UserManager<IdentityRole> class defines the methods described in Table 10-5 to manage the assignment of users to roles from the master list.

Table 10-5. *The UserManager<IdentityRole> Methods for Managing Roles*

Name	Description
GetRolesAsync(user)	This method returns an IList<string> containing the names of all the roles to which the user has been assigned.
IsInRoleAsync(user, name)	This method returns true if the user has been assigned to the role with the specified name and false otherwise.
AddToRoleAsync(user, name)	This method assigns the user to the role with the specified name and returns an IdentityResult object that describes the outcome. There is also an AddToRolesAsync method that assigns the user to multiple roles at once.
RemoveFromRoleAsync(user, name)	This method removes the user from the role with the specified name and returns an IdentityResult object that describes the outcome. There is also a RemoveFromRolesAsync method that removes the user from multiple roles at once.

Add a Razor Page named Roles.cshtml to the Pages/Identity/Admin folder with the content shown in Listing 10-3.

Listing 10-3. The Contents of the Roles.cshtml File in the Pages/Identity/Admin Folder

```
@page "{id?}"
@model IdentityApp.Pages.Identity.Admin.RolesModel
@{
    ViewBag.Workflow = "Roles";
}

<div asp-validation-summary="All" class="text-danger m-2"></div>

<table class="table table-sm table-striped table-bordered">
    <thead><tr><th colspan="2" class="text-center">Master Role List</th></tr></thead>
    <tbody>
        @foreach (IdentityRole role in Model.RoleManager.Roles) {
            int userCount =
                (await Model.UserManager.GetUsersInRoleAsync(role.Name)).Count;
            <tr>
                <td>@role.Name</td>
                <td>
                    @if (userCount == 0) {
```

257

```
                        <form method="post" asp-page-handler="deleteFromList">
                            <input type="hidden" name="role" value="@role.Name" />
                            <button type="submit" class="btn btn-sm btn-danger">
                                Delete
                            </button>
                        </form>
                    } else {
                        @: @userCount users in role
                    }
                </td>
            </tr>
        }
        <tr>
            <td>
                <form method="post" asp-page-handler="addToList" id="addToListForm">
                    <input class="form-control" name="role" />
                </form>
            </td>
            <td>
                <button type="submit" class="btn btn-sm btn-success"
                        form="addToListForm">
                    Add
                </button>
            </td>
        </tr>
    </tbody>
</table>

<table class="table table-sm table-striped table-bordered">
    <thead><tr><th colspan="2" class="text-center">User's Roles</th></tr></thead>
    <tbody>
        @if (Model.RoleManager.Roles.Count() == 0) {
            <tr>
                <td colspan="2" class="text-center py-2">
                    No roles have been defined
                </td>
            </tr>
        } else {
            @if(Model.CurrentRoles.Count() == 0) {
                <tr>
                    <td colspan="2" class="text-center py-2">
                        User has no roles
                    </td>
                </tr>
            } else {
                @foreach (string role in Model.CurrentRoles) {
                    <tr>
                        <td>@role</td>
                        <td>
                            <form method="post" asp-page-handler="delete">
                                <input type="hidden" asp-for="Id" />
```

```
                                <input type="hidden" name="role" value="@role" />
                                <button type="submit" class="btn btn-sm btn-danger">
                                    Delete
                                </button>
                            </form>
                        </td>
                    </tr>
                }
            }
            @if (Model.AvailableRoles.Count == 0) {
                <tr>
                    <td colspan="2" class="text-center py-2">
                        User is in all roles
                    </td>
                </tr>
            } else {
                <tr>
                    <td>
                        <select class="form-control" name="role" form="addForm">
                            <option selected disabled>Choose Role</option>
                            @foreach (string role in Model.AvailableRoles) {
                                <option>@role</option>
                            }
                        </select>
                    </td>
                    <td>
                        <form method="post" asp-page-handler="add" id="addForm">
                            <input type="hidden" asp-for="Id" />
                            <button type="submit" class="btn btn-sm btn-success">
                                Add
                            </button>
                        </form>
                    </td>
                </tr>
            }
        }
    </tbody>
</table>
```

The view part of this page is more complex than most other workflows because I am managing the master list and the role assignments for a user on a single page. The view presents a table containing a list of the available roles, along with a Delete button to remove the role from the store if no users have been assigned to it. There is also an input element and an Add button for adding new roles to the master list.

To assign the user to a role, a select element is populated with option elements for all the roles to which the user has not been assigned, along with a list of roles to which they have been assigned.

To define the page model class, add the code shown in Listing 10-4 to the Roles.cshtml.cs file. (You will have to create this file if you are using Visual Studio Code.)

Listing 10-4. The Contents of the Roles.cshtml.cs File in the Pages/Identity/Admin Folder

```
using Microsoft.AspNetCore.Identity;
using Microsoft.AspNetCore.Mvc;
using System.Collections.Generic;
using System.ComponentModel.DataAnnotations;
using System.Linq;
using System.Threading.Tasks;

namespace IdentityApp.Pages.Identity.Admin {

    public class RolesModel : AdminPageModel {

        public RolesModel(UserManager<IdentityUser> userMgr,
                RoleManager<IdentityRole> roleMgr) {
            UserManager = userMgr;
            RoleManager = roleMgr;
        }

        [BindProperty(SupportsGet = true)]
        public string Id { get; set; }

        public UserManager<IdentityUser> UserManager { get; set; }
        public RoleManager<IdentityRole> RoleManager { get; set; }

        public IList<string> CurrentRoles { get; set; } = new List<string>();
        public IList<string> AvailableRoles { get; set; } = new List<string>();

        private async Task SetProperties() {
            IdentityUser user = await UserManager.FindByIdAsync(Id);
            CurrentRoles = await UserManager.GetRolesAsync(user);
            AvailableRoles = RoleManager.Roles.Select(r => r.Name)
                .Where(r => !CurrentRoles.Contains(r)).ToList();
        }

        public async Task<IActionResult> OnGetAsync() {
            if (string.IsNullOrEmpty(Id)) {
                return RedirectToPage("Selectuser",
                    new { Label = "Edit Roles", Callback = "Roles" });
            }
            await SetProperties();
            return Page();
        }

        public async Task<IActionResult> OnPostAddToList(string role) {
            IdentityResult result =
                await RoleManager.CreateAsync(new IdentityRole(role));
            if (result.Process(ModelState)) {
                return RedirectToPage();
            }
```

```
            await SetProperties();
            return Page();
        }

        public async Task<IActionResult> OnPostDeleteFromList(string role) {
            IdentityRole idRole = await RoleManager.FindByNameAsync(role);
            IdentityResult result = await RoleManager.DeleteAsync(idRole);
            if (result.Process(ModelState)) {
                return RedirectToPage();
            }
            await SetProperties();
            return Page();
        }

        public async Task<IActionResult> OnPostAdd([Required] string role) {
            if (ModelState.IsValid) {
                IdentityResult result = IdentityResult.Success;
                if (result.Process(ModelState)) {
                    IdentityUser user = await UserManager.FindByIdAsync(Id);
                    if (!await UserManager.IsInRoleAsync(user, role)) {
                        result = await UserManager.AddToRoleAsync(user, role);
                    }
                    if (result.Process(ModelState)) {
                        return RedirectToPage();
                    }
                }
            }
            await SetProperties();
            return Page();
        }

        public async Task<IActionResult> OnPostDelete(string role) {
            IdentityUser user = await UserManager.FindByIdAsync(Id);
            if (await UserManager.IsInRoleAsync(user, role)) {
                await UserManager.RemoveFromRoleAsync(user, role);
            }
            return RedirectToPage();
        }
    }
}
```

The page model receives user manager and role manager objects through its constructor and uses them to populate the properties used to present the content in the view. The GET handler method locates the user object and using LINQ to work out which of the roles in the master list have already been assigned and which are still available. The other handlers add and remove roles to the role store and to add or remove a user from a role.

To integrate the new Razor Page, add the element shown in Listing 10-5 to the _AdminWorkflows.cshtml partial view.

Listing 10-5. Adding Navigation the _AdminWorkflows.cshtml File in the Pages/Identity/Admin Folder

```
@model (string workflow, string theme)

@{
    Func<string, string> getClass = (string feature) =>
        feature != null && feature.Equals(Model.workflow) ? "active" : "";
}

<a class="btn btn-@Model.theme btn-block @getClass("Dashboard")"
        asp-page="Dashboard">
    Dashboard
</a>
<a class="btn btn-@Model.theme btn-block @getClass("Features")" asp-page="Features">
    Store Features
</a>
<a class="btn btn-success btn-block @getClass("List")" asp-page="View"
        asp-route-id="">
    List Users
</a>
<a class="btn btn-success btn-block @getClass("Create")" asp-page="Create">
    Create Account
</a>
<a class="btn btn-success btn-block @getClass("Delete")" asp-page="Delete">
    Delete Account
</a>
<a class="btn btn-success btn-block @getClass("Edit")" asp-page="Edit"
        asp-route-id="">
    Edit Users
</a>
<a class="btn btn-success btn-block @getClass("Passwords")" asp-page="Passwords"
        asp-route-id="">
    Passwords
</a>
<a class="btn btn-success btn-block @getClass("Lockouts")" asp-page="Lockouts" >
    Lockouts
</a>
<a class="btn btn-success btn-block @getClass("Roles")"
        asp-page="Roles" asp-route-id="">
    Edit Roles
</a>
```

Restart ASP.NET Core and request https://localhost:44350/Identity/Admin. Click the Edit Roles button and click the Roles button for the alice@example.com account. You will be presented with the content from the new Razor Page, which will be largely empty because there are no roles in the master list and the user has not been assigned any roles.

Enter Admin into the text field and click Add to add a new role to the master list. Now select Admin from the Choose Role select element and click the Add button to assign the selected user to the role. Notice that the Delete button for the role is removed once a user has been assigned to a role, as shown in Figure 10-2, because the role store won't allow a role to be deleted while it is in use. (This is a consequence of a foreign key relationship in the database used to store user and role data.)

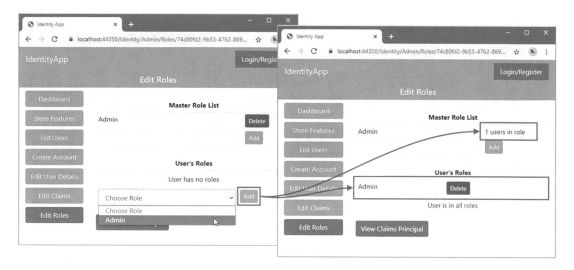

Figure 10-2. *Assigning a user to a role*

Testing the Role Membership

Until now, the application hasn't included support for assigning users to roles, which has meant that the most restricted level of content created in Chapter 3 has remained inaccessible. But now, the `alice@ example.com` account has been assigned the `Admin` role, which means the user can access all of the content from Chapter 3.

Ensure you are signed out of the application and request `https://localhost:44350/admin`, which is one of the resources to which access is restricted by role. The request will generate a challenge response, and you will be redirected to the sign-in page. Sign in to the application using `alice@example.com` as the email address and `mysecret` as the password. Click the Sign In button, and you will be signed into the application and redirected to the restricted content, as shown in Figure 10-3.

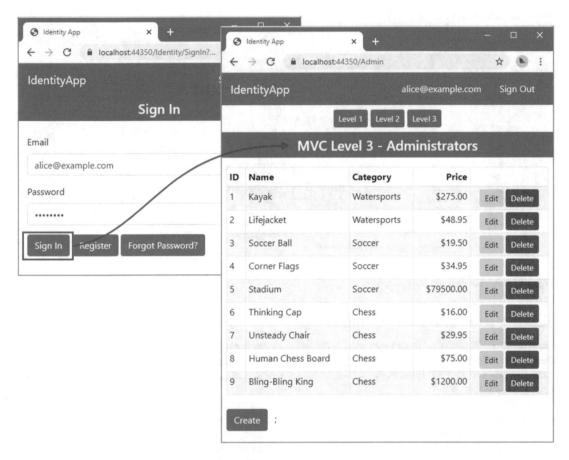

Figure 10-3. Accessing content protected by a role-based authorization policy

---

■ **Caution**   Changes to a user's roles do not take effect until the next time the user signs in.

Restricting Access to the Identity Administrator Dashboard

Now that the application has support for assigning roles, it is time to restrict access to the administrator dashboard. But, before doing that, some preparation is required to ensure that the administrator can sign in even after the database is reset and can't lock themselves out of the application once it is started.

Populating the User and Role Store During Startup

The first step is to ensure that the role that will grant access to the dashboard exists when the application starts and that there is a user account that has been assigned to that role. Add a class file named `DashboardSeed.cs` to the `IdentityApp` folder with the code shown in Listing 10-6.

Listing 10-6. The Contents of the DashboardSeed.cs File in the IdentityApp Folder

```
using Microsoft.AspNetCore.Builder;
using Microsoft.AspNetCore.Identity;
using Microsoft.Extensions.Configuration;
using Microsoft.Extensions.DependencyInjection;
using System.Threading.Tasks;

namespace IdentityApp {
    public static class DashBoardSeed {

        public static void SeedUserStoreForDashboard(this IApplicationBuilder app) {
            SeedStore(app).GetAwaiter().GetResult();
        }

        private async static Task SeedStore(IApplicationBuilder app) {
            using (var scope = app.ApplicationServices.CreateScope()) {
                IConfiguration config =
                    scope.ServiceProvider.GetService<IConfiguration>();
                UserManager<IdentityUser> userManager =
                    scope.ServiceProvider.GetService<UserManager<IdentityUser>>();
                RoleManager<IdentityRole> roleManager =
                    scope.ServiceProvider.GetService<RoleManager<IdentityRole>>();

                string roleName = config["Dashboard:Role"] ?? "Dashboard";
                string userName = config["Dashboard:User"] ?? "admin@example.com";
                string password = config["Dashboard:Password"] ?? "mysecret";

                if (!await roleManager.RoleExistsAsync(roleName)) {
                    await roleManager.CreateAsync(new IdentityRole(roleName));
                }
                IdentityUser dashboardUser =
                    await userManager.FindByEmailAsync(userName);
                if (dashboardUser == null) {
                    dashboardUser = new IdentityUser {
                        UserName = userName,
                        Email = userName,
                        EmailConfirmed = true
                    };
                    await userManager.CreateAsync(dashboardUser);
                    dashboardUser = await userManager.FindByEmailAsync(userName);
                    await userManager.AddPasswordAsync(dashboardUser, password);
                }
                if (!await userManager.IsInRoleAsync(dashboardUser, roleName)) {
                    await userManager.AddToRoleAsync(dashboardUser, roleName);
                }
            }
        }
    }
}
```

265

The class defines an extension method that makes it easy to prepare the user store from the Startup class. A new dependency injection scope is created, and the role and user managers are used to ensure the required role and user exist. The name of the role, the name of the user, and the user's initial password are obtained from the ASP.NET Core configuration system so that the default values are easily overridden.

■ **Caution** There is a balance between making sure you don't lock yourself out of the application and creating a backdoor through which malicious access can be obtained. When you deploy a project, make sure you change the default passwords and consider requiring two-factor authentication for special accounts. The workflows for two-factor authentication are described in Chapter 11 and explained in detail in Chapter 22.

Listing 10-7 invokes the extension method to prepare the user store in the Startup class.

Listing 10-7. Preparing the User Store in the Startup.cs File in the IdentityApp Folder

```
...
public void Configure(IApplicationBuilder app, IWebHostEnvironment env) {
    if (env.IsDevelopment()) {
        app.UseDeveloperExceptionPage();
    }

    app.UseHttpsRedirection();
    app.UseStaticFiles();
    app.UseRouting();

    app.UseAuthentication();
    app.UseAuthorization();

    app.UseEndpoints(endpoints => {
        endpoints.MapDefaultControllerRoute();
        endpoints.MapRazorPages();
    });

    app.SeedUserStoreForDashboard();
}
...
```

Protecting the Dashboard Role

The next step is to make sure that there is at least one user assigned to the role that will grant access to the dashboard. The changes shown in Listing 10-8 obtain the name of the role from the configuration service and prevent the last user from being removed from the role.

Listing 10-8. Protecting the Role in the Roles.cshtml.cs File in the Pages/Identity/Admin Folder

```
using Microsoft.AspNetCore.Identity;
using Microsoft.AspNetCore.Mvc;
using System.Collections.Generic;
using System.ComponentModel.DataAnnotations;
using System.Linq;
```

```
using System.Threading.Tasks;
using Microsoft.Extensions.Configuration;

namespace IdentityApp.Pages.Identity.Admin {

    public class RolesModel : AdminPageModel {

        public RolesModel(UserManager<IdentityUser> userMgr,
                RoleManager<IdentityRole> roleMgr,
                IConfiguration config) {
            UserManager = userMgr;
            RoleManager = roleMgr;
            DashboardRole = config["Dashboard:Role"] ?? "Dashboard";
        }

        [BindProperty(SupportsGet = true)]
        public string Id { get; set; }

        public UserManager<IdentityUser> UserManager { get; set; }
        public RoleManager<IdentityRole> RoleManager { get; set; }

        public IList<string> CurrentRoles { get; set; } = new List<string>();
        public IList<string> AvailableRoles { get; set; } = new List<string>();

        public string DashboardRole { get; }

        // ...methods omitted for brevity...
    }
}
```

The changes use the configuration service to get the name of the dashboard role. To prevent the role from being removed, locate the delete button in the page's view and add the attribute shown in Listing 10-9.

Listing 10-9. Disabling a Button in the Roles.cshtml File in the Pages/Identity/Admin Folder

```
...
@foreach (string role in Model.CurrentRoles) {
    <tr>
        <td>@role</td>
        <td>
            <form method="post" asp-page-handler="delete">
                <input type="hidden" asp-for="Id" />
                <input type="hidden" name="role" value="@role" />
                <button type="submit" disabled="@(role== Model.DashboardRole)"
                        class="btn btn-sm btn-danger">
                    Delete
                </button>
            </form>
        </td>
    </tr>
}
...
```

267

The effect is to disable the delete button when the user is a member of the dashboard role.

■ **Note** Disabling the HTML element doesn't prevent someone from crafting an HTTP request that will delete the role. This would require appropriate authorization in the request, and the goal with these changes is just to prevent the administrator from accidentally locking themselves out of the application.

Protecting the Dashboard User

I need to make a corresponding change to prevent the dashboard account from being deleted. Listing 10-10 shows the changes to the Delete.cshtml file. For variety, I have used Razor expressions to disable the delete button without modifying the page model class.

Listing 10-10. Disabling a Button in the Delete.cshtml File in the Pages/Identity/Admin Folder

```
@page "{id?}"
@model IdentityApp.Pages.Identity.Admin.DeleteModel
@inject Microsoft.Extensions.Configuration.IConfiguration Configuration
@{
    ViewBag.Workflow = "Delete";
    string dashboardUser = Configuration["Dashboard:User"] ?? "admin@example.com";
}

<div asp-validation-summary="All" class="text-danger m-2"></div>

<form method="post">
    <h3 class="bg-danger text-white text-center p-2">Caution</h3>
    <h5 class="text-center m-2">
        Delete @Model.IdentityUser.Email?
    </h5>
    <input type="hidden" name="id" value="@Model.IdentityUser.Id" />
    <div class="text-center p-2">
        <button type="submit" class="btn btn-danger"
            disabled="@(Model.IdentityUser.Email == dashboardUser)">
                Delete
        </button>
        <a asp-page="Dashboard" class="btn btn-secondary">Cancel</a>
    </div>
</form>
```

Updating the Test Account Seed Code

In Chapter 7, I added a handler method to the Dashboard page that deletes all the users in the store and replaces them with test accounts. In Listing 10-11, I have updated this method so that it does not remove users assigned to the role required to access the dashboard unless they are one of the test accounts.

Listing 10-11. Selecting Accounts in the Dashboard.cshtml.cs File in the Pages/Identity/Admin Folder

```
using Microsoft.AspNetCore.Mvc.RazorPages;
using Microsoft.AspNetCore.Identity;
using Microsoft.AspNetCore.Mvc;
using System.Threading.Tasks;
using System.Linq;
using Microsoft.Extensions.Configuration;

namespace IdentityApp.Pages.Identity.Admin {

    public class DashboardModel : AdminPageModel {

        public DashboardModel(UserManager<IdentityUser> userMgr,
                IConfiguration configuration) {
            UserManager = userMgr;
            DashboardRole = configuration["Dashboard:Role"] ?? "Dashboard";
        }

        public UserManager<IdentityUser> UserManager { get; set; }

        public string DashboardRole { get; set; }

        public int UsersCount { get; set; } = 0;
        public int UsersUnconfirmed { get; set; } = 0;
        public int UsersLockedout { get; set; } = 0;
        public int UsersTwoFactor { get; set; } = 0;

        private readonly string[] emails = {
            "alice@example.com", "bob@example.com", "charlie@example.com"
        };

        public void OnGet() {
            UsersCount = UserManager.Users.Count();
            UsersUnconfirmed = UserManager.Users
                .Where(u => !u.EmailConfirmed).Count();
            UsersLockedout = UserManager.Users
                .Where(u => u.LockoutEnabled
                    && u.LockoutEnd > System.DateTimeOffset.Now).Count();
        }

        public async Task<IActionResult> OnPostAsync() {
            foreach (IdentityUser existingUser in UserManager.Users.ToList()) {
                if (emails.Contains(existingUser.Email) ||
                        !await UserManager.IsInRoleAsync(existingUser, DashboardRole)) {
                    IdentityResult result
                        = await UserManager.DeleteAsync(existingUser);
                    result.Process(ModelState);
                }
            }
            foreach (string email in emails) {
```

269

```
                IdentityUser userObject = new IdentityUser {
                    UserName = email,
                    Email = email,
                    EmailConfirmed = true
                };
                IdentityResult result = await UserManager.CreateAsync(userObject);
                if (result.Process(ModelState)) {
                    result = await UserManager.AddPasswordAsync(userObject,
                        "mysecret");
                    result.Process(ModelState);
                }
                result.Process(ModelState);
            }
            if (ModelState.IsValid) {
                return RedirectToPage();
            }
            return Page();
        }
    }
}
```

Navigating Directly to the Administration Dashboard

The final preparatory change just makes it easier to reach the administrator dashboard by altering the link displayed in the page header, as shown in Listing 10-12.

Listing 10-12. Altering Navigation in the _LoginPartial.cshtml File in the Views/Shared Folder

```
@inject Microsoft.Extensions.Configuration.IConfiguration Configuration
@{
    string dashboardRole = Configuration["Dashboard:Role"] ?? "Dashboard";
}
<nav class="nav">
    @if (User.Identity.IsAuthenticated) {
        @if (User.IsInRole(dashboardRole)) {
            <a asp-page="/Identity/Admin/Dashboard"
                class="nav-link bg-secondary text-white">
                    @User.Identity.Name
            </a>
        } else {
            <a asp-page="/Identity/Index" class="nav-link bg-secondary text-white">
                    @User.Identity.Name
            </a>
        }
        <a asp-page="/Identity/SignOut" class="nav-link bg-secondary text-white">
            Sign Out
        </a>
```

```
    } else {
        <a asp-page="/Identity/SignIn" class="nav-link bg-secondary text-white">
            Sign In/Register
        </a>
    }
</nav>
```

Applying the Authorization Policy

All of the preparations are in place, and all that remains is to apply the `Authorize` attribute to the common base class used by all the administrator dashboard pages, as shown in Listing 10-13.

■ **Tip** The roles feature of the `Authorize` attribute requires a literal string, which makes it difficult to read the role name from the configuration service. In Part 2, I explain how to create code-based authorization policies, which address this limitation.

Listing 10-13. Adding an Attribute in the AdminPageModel.cs File in the Pages/Identity/Admin Folder

```
using Microsoft.AspNetCore.Authorization;

namespace IdentityApp.Pages.Identity.Admin {

    //[AllowAnonymous]
    [Authorize(Roles = "Dashboard")]
    public class AdminPageModel : UserPageModel {

        // no methods or properties required
    }
}
```

Restart ASP.NET Core and make sure you are signed out of the application. Sign in as `admin@example.com` using the password `mysecret`. Once you are signed in, click the email address at the top of the layout, and you will be presented with the administration dashboard, as shown in Figure 10-4.

Figure 10-4. *Accessing the administrator dashboard*

Click the Roles button and select the admin@example.com account; you will see that the Delete button for the membership of the Dashboard role is disabled, as shown in Figure 10-5. Click the Delete Account button and select the admin@example.com account; you will see the Delete button for the account is disabled, also shown in Figure 10-5.

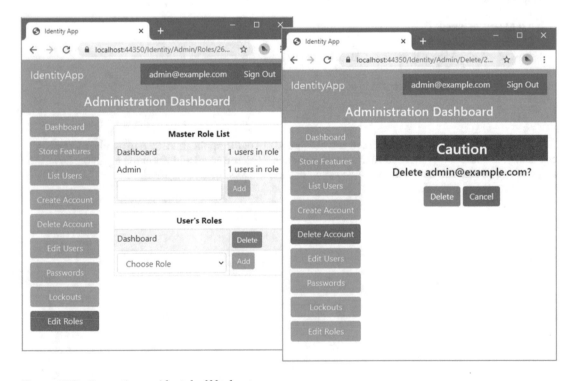

Figure 10-5. *Preventing accidental self-lockout*

Managing Claims

A claim is a piece of data that is known about the user. This is a vague description because there are no limits placed on what a claim can describe or where it comes from. Claims are represented using the Claim class defined in the System.Security.Claims namespace. Table 10-6 describes the most important properties defined by the Claim class.

Table 10-6. *Important Claim Properties*

Name	Description
Type	This property returns the claim type.
Value	This property returns the claim value.
Issuer	This property returns the source of the claim.

An application can collect claims about a user from multiple sources and act on what the claims assert about the user and how much the source of the claim is trusted. For example, when determining if I should be granted access to confidential company data, an application may obtain claims from the HR system, the payroll system, and a social media platform. The HR system and the payroll system may claim that I am a junior programmer, but the social media platform may claim that I am the CEO. The application can give more weight to the claims from the systems that it trusts, discount the claims from sources it doesn't trust, and conclude that I am, in fact, a junior programmer with an ambitious public profile.

An application can also collect multiple identities for a single user. Different systems may use account names, for example, and so there may be different sets of claims for each identity.

In practice, many applications don't use claims directly at all, relying on roles to manage a user's access to restricted resources. Even when claims are used, applications tend not to have a nuanced understanding of a user's claims and identities because building and maintaining that understanding is complex. But, even so, understanding how claims are used is important because they underpin important Identity features, such as roles, and because they are the way that Identity expresses the data in the user store to the rest of the ASP.NET Core platform.

Making Claims Easier to Use

The type and value of a claim can be anything an application requires, which is great for flexibility but can be difficult to keep track of. To help keep claims consistent, Microsoft provides the ClaimTypes class, which defines commonly required claim types. These can be supplemented by custom types as needed.

Dealing with claims is made easier if you explicitly define the selection of claim types that you require. Add a class named ApplicationClaimTypes.cs to the IdentityApp/Models folder and add the code shown in Listing 10-14.

Listing 10-14. The Contents of the ApplicationClaimTypes.cs File in the Models Folder

```
using System.Collections.Generic;
using System.Linq;
using System.Security.Claims;

namespace IdentityApp.Models {

    public static class ApplicationClaimTypes {
        public const string Country = ClaimTypes.Country;
```

```
        public const string SecurityClearance = "SecurityClearance";

        public static string GetDisplayName(this Claim claim)
            => GetDisplayName(claim.Type);

        public static string GetDisplayName(string claimType)
            => typeof(ClaimTypes).GetFields().Where(field =>
                    field.GetRawConstantValue().ToString() == claimType)
                    .Select(field => field.Name)
                    .FirstOrDefault() ?? claimType;

        public static IEnumerable<(string type, string display)> AppClaimTypes
            = new[] { Country, SecurityClearance }.Select(c =>
                (c, GetDisplayName(c)));
    }
}
```

I am going to add two types of claims to the user store, and I will refer to those types using the constants defined by the ApplicationClaimTypes class. The Country constant refers to the ClaimTypes.Country type, which is one of the types described by the ClaimTypes class provided by Microsoft. The SecurityClearance constant is a custom claim type, which I have defined with a standard .NET string.

The ApplicationClaimTypes class also defines an extension method for the Claim class, which will give me a value I can display to the user for a claim type. This is helpful because the claim types defined by the ClaimTypes class are expressed as URIs, which I don't want to display directly.

To manage the claims in the user store, add a Razor Page named Claims.cshtml to the Pages/Identity/Admin folder with the content shown in Listing 10-15.

Listing 10-15. The Contents of the Claims.cshtml File in the Pages/Identity/Admin Folder

```
@page "{id?}"
@model IdentityApp.Pages.Identity.Admin.ClaimsModel
@{
    ViewBag.Workflow = "Claims";
    int FormCounter = 0;
}

<div asp-validation-summary="All" class="text-danger m-2"></div>

<table class="table table-sm table-bordered table-striped">
    <thead><tr><th>Type</th><th>Value</th><th>Issuer</th><th/></tr></thead>
    <tbody>
        @if (Model.Claims?.Count() > 0) {
            @foreach (Claim c in Model.Claims) {
                <tr>
                    <td>@c.GetDisplayName()</td>
                    <td>
                        <form method="post" id="@(++FormCounter)">
                            <input type="hidden" asp-for="Id" />
                            <input type="hidden" name="type" value="@c.Type" />
                            <input type="hidden" name="oldValue" value="@c.Value" />
                            <input class="form-control" name="value"
```

```
                                  value="@c.Value" />
                        </form>
                    </td>
                    <td>@c.Issuer</td>
                    <td>
                        <button class="btn btn-sm btn-warning" form="@(FormCounter)"
                                asp-route-task="change">Change</button>
                        <button class="btn btn-sm btn-danger" form="@(FormCounter)"
                                asp-route-task="delete">Delete</button>
                    </td>
                </tr>
            }
        } else {
            <tr><th colspan="4" class="text-center py-3">User has no claims</th></tr>
        }
        </tbody>
        <tfoot>
            <tr><th colspan="4" class="text-center pt-3">Add New Claim</th></tr>
            <tr>
                <td>
                    <form method="post" id="addClaim" asp-route-task="add">
                        <select class="form-control" name="type">
                            @foreach (var claimType in
                                    ApplicationClaimTypes.AppClaimTypes) {
                                <option value="@claimType.type">
                                    @claimType.display
                                </option>
                            }
                        </select>
                    </form>
                </td>
                <td colspan="2">
                    <input class="form-control" form="addClaim" name="value" />
                </td>
                <td>
                    <button type="submit" form="addClaim"
                        class="btn btn-sm btn-success">Add</button>
                </td>
            </tr>
        </tfoot>
</table>

<a asp-page="ViewClaimsPrincipal" class="btn btn-secondary"
        asp-route-id="@Model.Id" asp-route-callback="Claims">
    View Claims Principal
</a>
```

The view section of the page presents a table that contains the user's claims. Each row contains the claim type, value, and issuer, along with buttons that will save changes to the claim's value or remove the claim from the store. There is also a form that allows a new claim to be created and a View Claims Principal button that targets a page that I create in the next section. To define the page model class, add the code shown in Listing 10-16 to the Claims.cshtml.cs. (You will have to create this file if you are using Visual Studio Code.)

Listing 10-16. The Contents of the Claims.cshtml.cs File in the Pages/Identity/Admin Folder

```
using System.Collections.Generic;
using System.Security.Claims;
using System.Threading.Tasks;
using Microsoft.AspNetCore.Mvc;
using Microsoft.AspNetCore.Identity;
using System.ComponentModel.DataAnnotations;

namespace IdentityApp.Pages.Identity.Admin {

    public class ClaimsModel : AdminPageModel {

        public ClaimsModel(UserManager<IdentityUser> mgr)
            => UserManager = mgr;

        public UserManager<IdentityUser> UserManager { get; set; }

        [BindProperty(SupportsGet = true)]
        public string Id { get; set; }

        public IEnumerable<Claim> Claims { get; set; }

        public async Task<IActionResult> OnGetAsync() {
            if (string.IsNullOrEmpty(Id)) {
                return RedirectToPage("Selectuser",
                    new { Label = "Manage Claims", Callback = "Claims" });
            }
            IdentityUser user = await UserManager.FindByIdAsync(Id);
            Claims = await UserManager.GetClaimsAsync(user);
            return Page();
        }

        public async Task<IActionResult> OnPostAsync([Required] string task,
                [Required] string type, [Required] string value, string oldValue) {
            IdentityUser user = await UserManager.FindByIdAsync(Id);
            Claims = await UserManager.GetClaimsAsync(user);
            if (ModelState.IsValid) {
                Claim claim = new Claim(type, value);
                IdentityResult result = IdentityResult.Success;
                switch (task) {
                    case "add":
                        result = await UserManager.AddClaimAsync(user, claim);
                        break;
                    case "change":
                        result = await UserManager.ReplaceClaimAsync(user,
                            new Claim(type, oldValue), claim);
                        break;
                    case "delete":
                        result = await UserManager.RemoveClaimAsync(user, claim);
                        break;
                };
```

```
            if (result.Process(ModelState)) {
                return RedirectToPage();
            }
        }
        return Page();
    }
    }
}
```

The GetClaimsAsync method is used to obtain the existing claims, and the AddClaimAsync, ReplaceClaimAsync, and RemoveClaimAsync methods are used to make changes. These methods automatically update the user store. For quick reference, Table 10-7 describes the methods used in the claim workflow. (See Chapter 17 for a detailed explanation of the user store support for claims.)

Table 10-7. *The UserManager<IdentityUser> Methods for Working with Claims*

Name	Description
GetClaimsAsync(user)	This method returns an IList<Claim> containing the claims in the user store for the specified user.
AddClaimAsync(user, claim)	This method adds a claim to the user store for the specified user.
ReplaceClaimAsync(user, old, new)	This method replaces one claim with another for the specified user.
RemoveClaimAsync(user, claim)	This method removes a claim from the user store for the specified user.

Add the element shown in Listing 10-17 to integrate the new page into the navigation partial view.

Listing 10-17. Adding an Element in the _AdminWorkflows.cshtml File in the Pages/Identity/Admin Folder

```
@model (string workflow, string theme)

@{
    Func<string, string> getClass = (string feature) =>
        feature != null && feature.Equals(Model.workflow) ? "active" : "";
}

<a class="btn btn-@Model.theme btn-block @getClass("Dashboard")"
        asp-page="Dashboard">
    Dashboard
</a>
<a class="btn btn-@Model.theme btn-block @getClass("Features")" asp-page="Features">
    Store Features
</a>
<a class="btn btn-success btn-block @getClass("List")" asp-page="View"
        asp-route-id="">
    List Users
</a>
<a class="btn btn-success btn-block @getClass("Create")" asp-page="Create">
    Create Account
</a>
```

```
<a class="btn btn-success btn-block @getClass("Delete")" asp-page="Delete">
    Delete Account
</a>
<a class="btn btn-success btn-block @getClass("Edit")" asp-page="Edit"
        asp-route-id="">
    Edit Users
</a>
<a class="btn btn-success btn-block @getClass("Passwords")" asp-page="Passwords"
        asp-route-id="">
    Passwords
</a>
<a class="btn btn-success btn-block @getClass("Lockouts")" asp-page="Lockouts" >
    Lockouts
</a>
<a class="btn btn-success btn-block @getClass("Roles")"
        asp-page="Roles" asp-route-id="">
    Edit Roles
</a>
<a class="btn btn-success btn-block @getClass("Claims")"
        asp-page="Claims" asp-route-id="">
    Claims
</a>
```

Restart ASP.NET Core, make sure you are signed in as admin@example.com using the password mysecret, and request https://localhost:44350/Identity/Admin.

Click the Claims button and select the alice@example.com account. The output from the Claims page shows there are no claims stored for this account.

Select Country from the select element in the Type column and enter USA into the Value field. Click the Add button to submit the form, and a new claim will be added to the store, as shown in Figure 10-6. Notice that when you create a claim, the Issuer property is set to LOCAL_AUTHORITY, which is the default value and denotes a claim originating within the application.

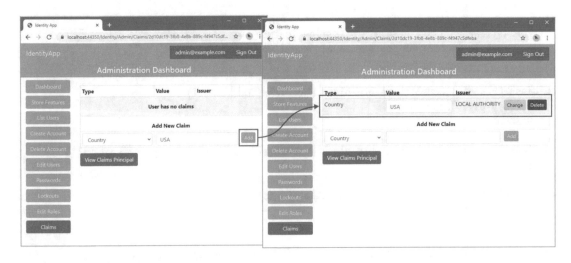

Figure 10-6. *Creating a claim*

The user store can contain multiple claims with the same type for the same user. Select the SecurityClearance claim type from the select element, enter Secret into the text field, and click Add. Repeat the process, entering VerySecret into the text field. When you click Add, a second SecurityClearance claim is added to the user store, as shown in Figure 10-7.

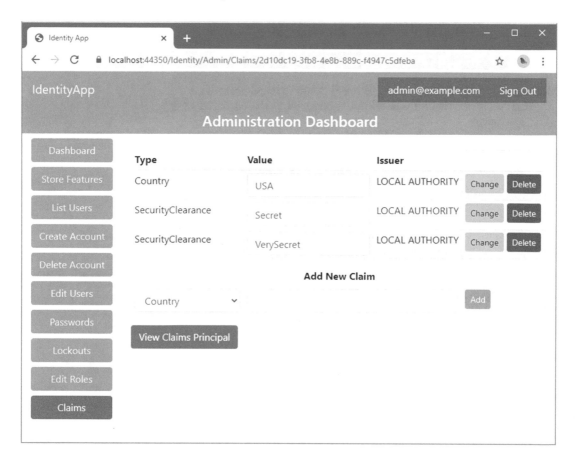

Figure 10-7. *Creating multiple claims with the same type*

Providing ASP.NET Core with Claims Data

Adding claims to the user store is helpful only if they can be used in the rest of the application. The key to this is the ClaimsPrincipal object that is created when a user signs into the application to represent the current user and that can be accessed in Razor Pages and MVC controllers.

The ClaimsPrincipal object is usually created by the SignInManager<IdentityUser> class during the sign-in workflow, but you can create one directly using the CreateUserPrincipalAsync method. In Part 2, I explain the process by which ClaimsPrincipal objects are created and show you how to customize it.

Add a Razor Page named ViewClaimsPrincipal.cshtml to the Pages/Identity/Admin folder with the content shown in Listing 10-18.

Listing 10-18. The Contents of the ViewClaimsPrincipal.cshtml File in the Pages/Identity/Admin Folder

```
@page "{id?}/{callback?}"
@model IdentityApp.Pages.Identity.Admin.ViewClaimsPrincipalModel
@{
    ViewBag.Workflow = "ClaimsPrincipal";
    ViewBag.WorkflowLabel = "View ClaimsPrincipal";
    int counter = 0;
}

@foreach (ClaimsIdentity ident in Model.Principal.Identities) {
    <table class="table table-sm table-striped table-bordered pt-3">
        <thead>
            <tr><th colspan="3" class="text-center">Identity #@(++counter)</th></tr>
        </thead>
        <tbody>
            <tr><th>Type</th><th>Value</th><th>Issuer</th></tr>
            @foreach (Claim c in ident.Claims) {
                <tr>
                    <td>@c.GetDisplayName()</td>
                    <td class="text-truncate" style="max-width:250px">@c.Value</td>
                    <td>@c.Issuer</td>
                </tr>
            }
        </tbody>
    </table>
}

@if (!string.IsNullOrEmpty(Model.Callback)) {
    <a asp-page="@Model.Callback" class="btn btn-secondary" asp-route-id="@Model.Id">
        Back
    </a>
}
```

The view part of the page obtains a ClaimsPrincipal object from the page model and enumerates each user identity it represents. For each user identity, it displays all of the claim types, values, and issuers. (I am afraid there is no avoiding the multiple uses of the term *identity* in this section, reflecting a group of related claims for a user as well as the framework that is the subject of this book.)

The ClaimsPrincipal class defines the Identities property, which returns a sequence of ClaimsIdentity objects, representing the user's identities. The ClaimsIdentity class defines the Claims property, which returns a sequence of Claim objects. I describe additional features in later examples and in Part 2, but this basic set of properties is enough to display the set of claims that will be generated by ASP.NET Core Identity when the user signs into the application.

To define the page model class, add the code shown in Listing 10-19 to the ViewClaimsPrincipal. cshtml.cs file. (You will have to create this file if you are using Visual Studio Code.)

Listing 10-19. The Contents of the ViewClaimsPrincipal.cshtml.cs File in the Pages/Identity/Admin Folder

```
using Microsoft.AspNetCore.Identity;
using Microsoft.AspNetCore.Mvc;
using System.Security.Claims;
using System.Threading.Tasks;
```

```
namespace IdentityApp.Pages.Identity.Admin {

    public class ViewClaimsPrincipalModel : AdminPageModel {

        public ViewClaimsPrincipalModel(UserManager<IdentityUser> usrMgr,
                SignInManager<IdentityUser> signMgr) {
            UserManager = usrMgr;
            SignInManager = signMgr;
        }

        [BindProperty(SupportsGet = true)]
        public string Id { get; set; }

        [BindProperty(SupportsGet = true)]
        public string Callback { get; set; }

        public UserManager<IdentityUser> UserManager { get; set; }
        public SignInManager<IdentityUser> SignInManager { get; set; }

        public ClaimsPrincipal Principal { get; set; }

        public async Task<IActionResult> OnGetAsync() {
            if (string.IsNullOrEmpty(Id)) {
                return RedirectToPage("Selectuser",
                    new {
                        Label = "View ClaimsPrincipal",
                        Callback = "ClaimsPrincipal"
                    });
            }
            IdentityUser user = await UserManager.FindByIdAsync(Id);
            Principal = await SignInManager.CreateUserPrincipalAsync(user);
            return Page();
        }
    }
}
```

The page model class obtains an IdentityUser class from the user store and uses the Create method defined by the CreateUserPrincipalAsync method defined by the sign-in manager class to produce the ClaimsPrincipal object required by the view.

Restart ASP.NET Core, request https://localhost:44350/Identity/Admin, and click the Edit Claims button. Click the Claims button to select the alice@example.com account and then click the View Claims Principal button, which will show how the data in the user store will be presented to the rest of the ASP.NET Core platform, as shown in Figure 10-8.

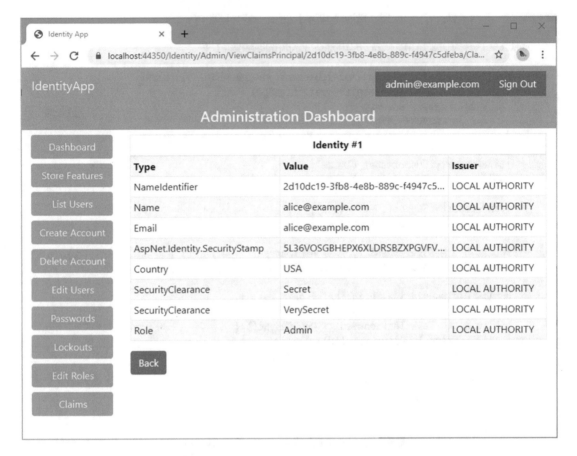

Figure 10-8. *Viewing the ClaimsPrincipal data*

There are three groups of claims for this user. The first group is created using selected properties defined by the IdentityUser class, including the Id, UserName, and Email properties, which are expressed with the NameIdentifier, Name, and Email claim types from the ClaimTypes class. This group also contains a claim for the user's SecurityStamp, but there is no ClaimTypes value for this type of claim and so the type AspNet.Identity.SecurityStamp is used.

The second group contains the Country and SecurityClearance claims added to the store in the previous section. The user's stored claims are added to the ClaimsPrincipal object without any modification.

The final group of claims describes the roles to which the user has been assigned. Each role is described with a claim whose type is set using the ClaimTypes.Role value and whose value is the name of the role.

These groups of claims describe all the data Identity has stored about a user in a way that the rest of the ASP.NET Core platform can use. However, since the data in the user store is presented to ASP.NET Core during the sign-in process, changes that you make to the user store—such as new role assignments and claims—won't take effect until the next time the user signs in.

Using Claims Data

Claims can be used in the rest of the application. In Part 2, for example, I explain how to use claims to create an authorization policy, although this is something that is usually done using roles, as demonstrated earlier in this chapter.

Add a Razor Page named Clearance.cshtml to the IdentityApp/Pages folder with the content shown in Listing 10-20.

Listing 10-20. The Contents of the Clearance.cshtml File in the Pages Folder

```
@page

@{
    Func<string, bool> HasClearance = (string level)
        => User.HasClaim(ApplicationClaimTypes.SecurityClearance, level);
}

<table class="table table-sm table-striped table-bordered">
    <thead><tr><th>Clearance Level</th><th>Granted</th></tr></thead>
    <tbody>
        <tr><td>Secret</td><td>@HasClearance("Secret")</td></tr>
        <tr><td>Very Secret</td><td>@HasClearance("VerySecret")</td></tr>
        <tr><td>Super Secret</td><td>@HasClearance("SuperSecret")</td></tr>
    </tbody>
</table>
```

Razor Pages and the MVC Framework provide access to the ClaimsPrincipal object for the current request with a User property that is available in views and the base classes used for page model and controller classes.

In Listing 10-20, I defined a function named HasClearance that reads the value of the User property to get the ClaimsPrincipal object and uses the HasClaim method to check to see if the user has a claim with a specific type and value. The HasClaim method checks all of the identities associated with the ClaimsPrincipal and is one of a set of convenience members for working with claims, as described in Table 10-8.

Table 10-8. The ClaimsPrincipal Convenience Members for Claims

Name	Description
Claims	This property returns an IEnumerable<Claim> containing the claims from all the ClaimIdentity objects associated with the ClaimsPrincipal.
FindAll(type) FindFirst(type)	This method returns all of the claims, or the first claim, with the specified type from all the ClaimIdentity objects associated with the ClaimsPrincipal.
FindAll(filter) FindFirst(filter)	This method returns the claims, or the first claim, that matches the specified filter predicate from all the ClaimIdentity objects associated with the ClaimsPrincipal.
HasClaim(type, value) HasClaim(filter)	This method returns true if any of the ClaimIdentity objects associated with the ClaimsPrincipal has a claim with the specified type and value or that matches the specified predicate.

The members in Table 10-8 are convenient because they operate across all of the claims associated with the `ClaimsPrincipal`, regardless of how many `ClaimsIdentity` objects have been created. In Listing 10-20, I used the `HasClaim` method to determine if the user has `SecurityClearance` claims with specific values. Restart ASP.NET Core, make sure you are signed out of the application, and request `https://localhost:44350/clearance`. ASP.NET Core always associated a `ClaimsPrincipal` object with requests, even when there is no user signed into the application. When you signed out of the application, there will be no claims, and you will see the response shown on the left of Figure 10-9.

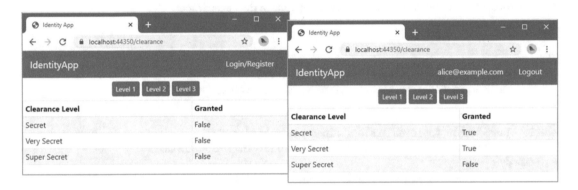

Figure 10-9. *Using claims*

Sign in to the application as `alice@example.com` and request `https://localhost:44350/clearance` again. This time the response will reflect the claims added to the store earlier, as shown on the right of Figure 10-9. (If you don't see the expected claims, then you may need to sign out of the application and sign in again. As I explained earlier, changes to the user store won't take effect until the next time the user signs in.)

Summary

In this chapter, I described the Identity support for roles and claims. Roles are the most common way of creating fine-grained authorization policies, but care has to be taken not to lock everyone out of the application or to create unexpected results with a typo. Claims are a general-purpose mechanism for describing data known about a user, and I explained how they are handled by Identity and how the data in the user store is expressed as a series of claims to the rest of the ASP.NET Core platform. In the next chapter, I describe the Identity support for two-factor authentication and external authentication services.

CHAPTER 11

Two-Factor and External Authentication

Identity supports two-factor authentication, where the user provides additional information alongside their password. In Chapter 17, I demonstrate how to create an SMS two-factor workflow, but for this chapter, I am going to focus on support for an authenticator, which is a more secure approach but requires users to have access to an app. I also create workflows for signing in with third-party services from Facebook, Google, and Twitter, using the same configuration settings created in Chapter 5. Table 11-1 puts the features described in this chapter in context.

Table 11-1. Putting Two-Factor Authentication and External Services in Context

Question	Answer
What are they?	Two-factor authentication requires the user to provide an additional credential to sign in to the application. External authentication services allow a user to authenticate themselves with a third party, such as Google or Facebook.
Why are they useful?	Two-factor authentication increases the security of a user's account. External authentication allows a user to sign in with credentials they have already established, which means they don't have to manage another account and allows ASP.NET Core applications to benefit from more advanced security options that are not directly supported by ASP.NET Core Identity.
How are they used?	An authenticator app is configured to generate codes every 30 seconds. The user provides the current code, in addition to their password, when they sign in. For external authentication, the ASP.NET Core application redirects the user to the third-party service, where they are authenticated, before being redirected back to the ASP.NET Core application, where they are signed in.
Are there any pitfalls or limitations?	The default mechanism for two-factor authentication is an authenticator application, which requires the user to go through an initial configuration process and have access to a device—typically a smartphone—when they sign in. Users won't lose or forget devices, and some users don't have them. External authentication is effective but complex and can be frustrating to configure.
Are there any alternatives?	These are optional features and are not required, although they do increase the security of a user account.

© Adam Freeman 2021
A. Freeman, *Pro ASP.NET Core Identity*, https://doi.org/10.1007/978-1-4842-6858-2_11

Table 11-2 summarizes the chapter.

Table 11-2. *Chapter Summary*

Problem	Solution	Listing
Determine if a user has two-factor authentication enabled	Call the user manager's `GetTwoFactorEnabledAsync` method or read the `IdentityUser.TwoFactorEnabled` property	3–4, 9, 10
Generate a token that can be used to set up an authenticator	Call the user manager's `GetAuthenticatorKeyAsync` or `ResetAuthenticatorKeyAsync` methods.	5, 6
Validate a token provided by the user during setup	Call the user manager's `VerifyTwoFactorTokenAsync` method.	5, 6
Use two-factor authentication to sign into the application	If the sign-in manager's `PasswordSignInAsync` returns a `SignInResult` whose `RequiresTwoFactor` property is `true`, then validate a token and sign the user into the application using the `TwoFactorAuthenticatorSignInAsync` method.	11, 12
Generate a set of recovery codes	Call the user manager's `GenerateNewTwoFactorRecoveryCodesAsync` method.	6–8, 13–14
Use a recovery code to sign a user into the application	Call the sign-in manager's `TwoFactorRecoveryCodeSignInAsync` method.	12
Determine the external authentication services that have been configured	Call the sign-in manager's `GetExternalAuthenticationSchemesAsync` method.	16, 17
Sign in or register with an external provider	Call the `ConfigureExternalAuthenticationProperties` method to select the provider and return a challenge response. Receive the callback and get the external authentication details using the `GetExternalLoginInfoAsync` method. Sign the user into the application with the `ExternalLoginSignInAsync` method.	18–24

Preparing for This Chapter

This chapter uses the `IdentityApp` project from Chapter 10. Open a new PowerShell command prompt and run the commands shown in Listing 11-1 to reset the application and Identity databases.

■ **Tip** You can download the example project for this chapter—and for all the other chapters in this book—from `https://github.com/Apress/pro-asp.net-core-identity`. See Chapter 1 for how to get help if you have problems running the examples.

Listing 11-1. Resetting the Databases

```
dotnet ef database drop --force --context ProductDbContext
dotnet ef database drop --force --context IdentityDbContext
dotnet ef database update --context ProductDbContext
dotnet ef database update --context IdentityDbContext
```

Use the PowerShell prompt to run the command shown in Listing 11-2 in the `IdentityApp` folder to start the application.

Listing 11-2. Running the Example Application

```
dotnet run
```

Open a web browser, request `https://localhost:44350/Identity/Admin`, and sign in as `admin@example.com` using `mysecret` at the password. When you sign in, you will be redirected to the administration dashboard. Click Seed Database, which will update the dashboard to indicate there are four users in the store, as shown in Figure 11-1.

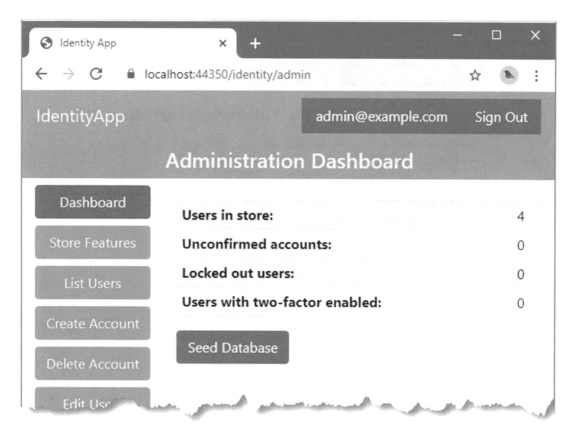

Figure 11-1. *Running the example application*

287

Supporting Two-Factor Authentication

Two-factor authentication requires the user to prove their identity with two pieces of information, typically a password and a token that is given to them securely. In Part 2, I explain how two-factor authentication works in detail and demonstrate how to use SMS messages to send the user a token. In this chapter, I am going to add support for an authenticator app, which is the same approach taken by the Identity UI package. Setting up an authenticator is a self-service operation because it requires the user to configure an app, typically on a smartphone.

Create the Two-Factor Overview Page

The first step is to create a Razor Page that will display the current account status and allow the user to enable or disable an authenticator. Add a Razor Page named UserTwoFactorManage.cshtml to the Pages/Identity folder with the content shown in Listing 11-3.

Listing 11-3. The Contents of the UserTwoFactorManage.cshtml File in the Pages/Identity Folder

```
@page
@model IdentityApp.Pages.Identity.UserTwoFactorManageModel
@{
    ViewBag.Workflow = "TwoFactor";
}

<div asp-validation-summary="All" class="text-danger m-2"></div>

@if (await Model.IsTwoFactorEnabled()) {
    <div class="text-center">
        <div class="h6 m-2">Your account is configured to use an authenticator</div>
        <div>
            <form method="post">
                <button type="submit" class="btn btn-primary m-1"
                        asp-page-handler="GenerateCodes">
                    Generate New Recovery Codes
                </button>
                <button type="submit" class="btn btn-warning m-1"
                        asp-page-handler="Disable">
                    Disable Authenticator and Sign Out
                </button>
            </form>
        </div>
    </div>
} else {
    <h6>Your account is not configured to use an authenticator.</h6>
    <a asp-page="UserTwoFactorSetup" class="btn btn-primary">Enable Authenticator</a>
}
```

The content produced by the view part of the page presents a button that allows the user to set up an authenticator by navigating to a page named UserTwoFactorSetup, which I will create shortly. If there is an authenticator, then the user is presented with a form that allows the authenticator to be disabled or a new set of recovery codes to be generated. Recovery codes are one-time passwords that can be used when the authenticator isn't available. Applications don't have to support recovery codes, but users forget or lose phones and won't always have the authenticator to hand.

To create the page model class, add the code shown in Listing 11-4 to the UserTwoFactorManage. cshtml.cs file. (You will have to create this file if you are using Visual Studio Code.)

Listing 11-4. The Contents of the UserTwoFactorManage.cshtml.cs File in the Pages/Identity Folder

```
using Microsoft.AspNetCore.Identity;
using Microsoft.AspNetCore.Mvc;
using System.Threading.Tasks;

namespace IdentityApp.Pages.Identity {

    public class UserTwoFactorManageModel : UserPageModel {

        public UserTwoFactorManageModel(UserManager<IdentityUser> usrMgr,
                SignInManager<IdentityUser> signMgr) {
            UserManager = usrMgr;
            SignInManager = signMgr;
        }

        public UserManager<IdentityUser> UserManager { get; set; }
        public SignInManager<IdentityUser> SignInManager { get; set; }

        public IdentityUser IdentityUser { get; set; }

        public async Task<bool> IsTwoFactorEnabled()
            => await UserManager.GetTwoFactorEnabledAsync(IdentityUser);

        public async Task OnGetAsync() {
            IdentityUser = await UserManager.GetUserAsync(User);
        }

        public async Task<IActionResult> OnPostDisable() {
            IdentityUser = await UserManager.GetUserAsync(User);
            IdentityResult result = await
                UserManager.SetTwoFactorEnabledAsync(IdentityUser, false);
            if (result.Process(ModelState)) {
                await SignInManager.SignOutAsync();
                return RedirectToPage("Index", new { });
            }
            return Page();
        }

        public async Task<IActionResult> OnPostGenerateCodes() {
            IdentityUser = await UserManager.GetUserAsync(User);
            TempData["RecoveryCodes"] =
                await UserManager.GenerateNewTwoFactorRecoveryCodesAsync(
                    IdentityUser, 10);
            return RedirectToPage("UserRecoveryCodes");
        }
    }
}
```

289

The user manager's `GetTwoFactorEnabledAsync` method is used to determine if the user has configured an authenticator. Applications can support multiple forms of two-factor authentication, as I demonstrate in Part 2, but this example uses only authenticators, so I can assume that an account with two-factor authentication enabled has been configured with an authenticator.

The `SetTwoFactorEnabledAsync` method is used to enable and disable two-factor authentication. In this class, I only need to disable two-factor authentication in the `Disable` POST handler method.

The `GenerateCodes` POST handler method generates a new set of recovery codes. These codes are shown to the user only once and are consumed when they are used, so it is important to ensure that the user can create a new set, either when they use up the codes or forget them. (I am not a fan of security codes that cannot be viewed, and I show you how to change this behavior in Part 2 so the user can see their unused codes.)

Creating the Authenticator Setup Page

As part of the setup process, the user must enter a secret key generated by Identity into their authenticator. To present the user with the key, add a Razor Page named `UserTwoFactorSetup.cshtml` to the Pages/ Identity folder with the content shown in Listing 11-5.

Listing 11-5. The Contents of the UserTwoFactorSetup.cshtml File in the Pages/Identity Folder

```
@page
@model IdentityApp.Pages.Identity.UserTwoFactorSetupModel
@{
    ViewBag.Workflow = "TwoFactor";
}

<div class="container-fluid">
    <div class="row">
        <div class="col">
            <h6>Step 1:</h6>
            Scan the QR Code or enter the following key into your authenticator:
            <div><kbd>@Model.AuthenticatorKey</kbd> </div>
        </div>
        <div class="col-auto p-2">
            <div id="qrCode"></div>
            <div id="qrCodeData" data-url="@Html.Raw(@Model.QrCodeUrl)"></div>
        </div>
    </div>
    <div>
        <div class="row">
            <div class="col">
                <div asp-validation-summary="All" class="text-danger m-2"></div>
                <form method="post" asp-page-handler="confirm">
                    <h6>Step 2:</h6>
                    Enter the code shown by your authenticator into the
                    text field and click the Confirm button
                    <input name="confirm" placeholder="Enter code"
                        class="form-control my-2" />
                    <button class="btn btn-primary" type="submit">Confirm</button>
                </form>
            </div>
```

```
            </div>
        </div>
</div>

<script type="text/javascript" src="/lib/qrcode/qrcode.min.js"></script>
    <script type="text/javascript">
        new QRCode(document.getElementById("qrCode"), {
            text: document.getElementById("qrCodeData").getAttribute("data-url"),
            width: 150, height: 150
        });
</script>
```

The view displays the key to the user. Most authenticators are apps on smartphones, and displaying a QR code provides the user with an easier configuration path. The view displays a QR code using the same JavaScript package added to the example project to support the Identity UI package. See Chapter 4 for the Library Manager (libman) command required to install the JavaScript package for generating QR codes.

The view prompts the user to enter a code generated by the authenticator app. A new code will be displayed every 30 seconds, and asking the user for the current code is a sensible way of ensuring that the authenticator is working before updating the account to require two-factor authentication. To define the page model class, add the code shown in Listing 11-6 to the UserTwoFactorSetup.cshtml.cs file. (You will have to create this file if you are using Visual Studio Code.)

Listing 11-6. The Contents of the UserTwoFactorSetup.cshtml.cs File in the Pages/Identity Folder

```
using Microsoft.AspNetCore.Identity;
using Microsoft.AspNetCore.Mvc;
using System.ComponentModel.DataAnnotations;
using System.Threading.Tasks;
using System.Linq;
using System.Text.RegularExpressions;

namespace IdentityApp.Pages.Identity {

    public class UserTwoFactorSetupModel : UserPageModel {

        public UserTwoFactorSetupModel(UserManager<IdentityUser> usrMgr,
            SignInManager<IdentityUser> signMgr) {
            UserManager = usrMgr;
            SignInManager = signMgr;
        }

        public UserManager<IdentityUser> UserManager { get; set; }
        public SignInManager<IdentityUser> SignInManager { get; set; }

        public IdentityUser IdentityUser { get; set; }

        public string AuthenticatorKey { get; set; }

        public string QrCodeUrl { get; set; }

        public async Task<IActionResult> OnGet() {
            await LoadAuthenticatorKeys();
```

```
            if (await UserManager.GetTwoFactorEnabledAsync(IdentityUser)) {
                return RedirectToPage("UserTwoFactorManage");
            }
            return Page();
        }

        public async Task<IActionResult> OnPostConfirm([Required] string confirm) {
            await LoadAuthenticatorKeys();
            if (ModelState.IsValid) {
                string token = Regex.Replace(confirm, @"\s", "");
                bool codeValid = await
                        UserManager.VerifyTwoFactorTokenAsync(IdentityUser,
                    UserManager.Options.Tokens.AuthenticatorTokenProvider, token);
                if (codeValid) {
                    TempData["RecoveryCodes"] = await UserManager
                        .GenerateNewTwoFactorRecoveryCodesAsync(IdentityUser, 10);
                    await UserManager.SetTwoFactorEnabledAsync(IdentityUser, true);
                    await SignInManager.RefreshSignInAsync(IdentityUser);
                    return RedirectToPage("UserRecoveryCodes");
                } else {
                    ModelState.AddModelError(string.Empty,
                        "Confirmation code invalid");
                }
            }
            return Page();
        }

        private async Task LoadAuthenticatorKeys() {
            IdentityUser = await UserManager.GetUserAsync(User);
            AuthenticatorKey =
                await UserManager.GetAuthenticatorKeyAsync(IdentityUser);
            if (AuthenticatorKey == null) {
                await UserManager.ResetAuthenticatorKeyAsync(IdentityUser);
                AuthenticatorKey =
                    await UserManager.GetAuthenticatorKeyAsync(IdentityUser);
                await SignInManager.RefreshSignInAsync(IdentityUser);
            }
            QrCodeUrl = $"otpauth://totp/ExampleApp:{IdentityUser.Email}"
                        + $"?secret={AuthenticatorKey}";
        }
    }
}
```

When the user requests the page, the GET handler uses the GetTwoFactorEnabledAsync method to see if the user is already configured for two-factor authentication. If the response is true, then a redirection to the UserTwoFactorManage page is performed.

For users without two-factor authentication enabled, the GET handler method is responsible for presenting the secret key to the user. Authenticator keys are persistent and are used to validate the codes generated by the authenticator every 60 seconds. If the stored key doesn't match the one used by the authenticator, the user won't be able to sign in.

The user manager's GetAuthenticatorKeyAsync method retrieves the secret key from the user store. If the method returns null, then no key has been stored. A new key is created and stored using the ResetAuthenticatorKeyAsync method, and the GetAuthenticatorKeyAsync method is called again to retrieve the key from the store. The key is presented to the user directly and formatted in a URL that can be displayed as a QR code. (The format of these URLs is described in Chapter 21.)

The POST handler receives the code displayed by the user's authenticator app, which is processed to remove whitespace. Some authenticators, such as the Authy app I use in this book, display tokens in groups of digits separated by a space. These must be removed before the token can be validated, which I do with a regular expression.

```
...
string token = Regex.Replace(confirm, @"\s", "");
...
```

The token is validated using the VerifyTwoFactorTokenAsync method, like this:

```
...
UserManager.VerifyTwoFactorTokenAsync(IdentityUser,
    UserManager.Options.Tokens.AuthenticatorTokenProvider, token);
...
```

The arguments are the user object, the name of the token provider class, and the code to validate. In Listing 11-6, I read the user manager's Options property to get the value of the AuthenticatorTokenProvider property, which specifies the name of the provider. The provider is configured by the AddDefaultTokenProviders extension method added to the Identity configuration in Chapter 8. This method sets up token generators that are suitable for most applications, but I describe how tokens are generated in detail in Part 2 if your application has specific requirements.

If the code provided by the user is valid, I generate a new set of recovery codes using the GenerateNewTwoFactorRecoveryCodesAsync method, like this:

```
...
TempData["RecoveryCodes"] =
    await UserManager.GenerateNewTwoFactorRecoveryCodesAsync(IdentityUser, 10);
...
```

I specified that I require 10 codes, which I store as temp data before redirecting the browser to the UserRecoveryCodes page so that I can display them to the user.

In Chapter 9, I enabled authentication cookie validation to effectively sign the user out of the application when their security stamp changes. As I explained in that chapter, this can cause the user to be signed out when other changes are performed, and this includes setting up an authenticator. The ResetAuthenticatorKeyAsync and SetTwoFactorEnabledAsync methods both update the security stamp. To prevent signing the user out of the application, I use the SignInManager<IdentityUser>. RefreshSignInAsync method to refresh the authentication cookie after these methods are called:

```
...
await UserManager.SetTwoFactorEnabledAsync(IdentityUser, true);
await SignInManager.RefreshSignInAsync(IdentityUser);
...
```

The effect of the ResetAuthenticatorKeyAsync method can be especially problematic because this method is called during the authenticator setup state, which means the user can be signed out of the application as they are configuring their authenticator, which can be confusing.

To display the recovery codes, add a Razor Page named UserRecoveryCodes.cshtml to the Pages/Identity folder with the content shown in Listing 11-7.

Listing 11-7. The Contents of the UserRecoveryCodes.cshtml File in the Pages/Identity Folder

```
@page
@model IdentityApp.Pages.Identity.UserRecoveryCodesModel
@{
    ViewBag.Workflow = "TwoFactor";
}

<h4 class="text-center">Recovery Codes</h4>

<h6>
    These recovery codes can be used to sign in if you don't have your authenticator.
    Store these codes in a safe place. You won't be able to view them again.
    Each code can only be used once.
</h6>

<table class="table table-sm table-striped">
    <tbody>
        @for (int i = 0; i < Model.RecoveryCodes.Length; i +=2 ) {
            <tr>
                <td><code>@Model.RecoveryCodes[i]</code></td>
                <td><code>@Model.RecoveryCodes[i + 1]</code></td>
            </tr>
        }
    </tbody>
</table>
<a asp-page="UserTwoFactorManage" class="btn btn-primary">OK</a>
```

The recovery codes are displayed in a table, along with a message explaining to the user that the codes cannot be viewed again and must be stored safely. To define the page model class, add the code shown in Listing 11-8 to the UserRecoveryCodes.cshtml.cs file. (You will have to create this file if you are using Visual Studio Code.)

Listing 11-8. The Contents of the UserRecoveryCodes.cshtml.cs File in the Pages/Identity Folder

```
using Microsoft.AspNetCore.Mvc;

namespace IdentityApp.Pages.Identity {

    public class UserRecoveryCodesModel : UserPageModel {

        [TempData]
        public string[] RecoveryCodes { get; set; }

        public IActionResult OnGet() {
            if (RecoveryCodes == null || RecoveryCodes.Length == 0) {
```

```
                return RedirectToPage("UserTwoFactorManage");
            }
            return Page();
        }
    }
}
```

The `TempData` attribute is used to set the value of the `RecoveryCodes` property, and the GET handler will perform a redirection to the management page if there are no recovery codes.

Updating the User and Administrator Dashboards

Add the element shown in Listing 11-9 to provide the user with navigation to the two-factor feature.

Listing 11-9. Adding Navigation in the _Workflows.cshtml File in the Pages/Identity Folder

```
@model (string workflow, string theme)
@inject UserManager<IdentityUser> UserManager
@{
    Func<string, string> getClass = (string feature) =>
        feature != null && feature.Equals(Model.workflow) ? "active" : "";

    IdentityUser identityUser
        = await UserManager.GetUserAsync(User) ?? new IdentityUser();
}

<a class="btn btn-@Model.theme btn-block @getClass("Overview")" asp-page="Index">
    Overview
</a>

@if (await UserManager.HasPasswordAsync(identityUser)) {
    <a class="btn btn-@Model.theme btn-block @getClass("PasswordChange")"
            asp-page="UserPasswordChange">
        Change Password
    </a>
    <a class="btn btn-@Model.theme btn-block @getClass("UserTwoFactor")"
            asp-page="UserTwoFactorManage">
        Authenticator
    </a>
}
<a class="btn btn-@Model.theme btn-block @getClass("UserDelete")"
        asp-page="UserDelete">
    Delete Account
</a>
```

The navigation element will be shown only to users who have password, which will prevent users who sign in with external services from using an authenticator.

The administrator dashboard overview displays the number of users with two-factor authentication. To set the value, add the statement shown in Listing 11-10 to the `Dashboard.cshtml.cs` file in the Pages/Identity/Admin folder.

Listing 11-10. Counting Users in the Dashboard.cshtml.cs File in the Pages/Identity/Admin Folder

```
...
public void OnGet() {
    UsersCount = UserManager.Users.Count();
    UsersUnconfirmed = UserManager.Users
        .Where(u => !u.EmailConfirmed).Count();
    UsersLockedout = UserManager.Users
        .Where(u => u.LockoutEnabled && u.LockoutEnd > System.DateTimeOffset.Now)
        .Count();
    UsersTwoFactor = UserManager.Users.Where(u => u.TwoFactorEnabled).Count();
}
...
```

The user manager's GetTwoFactorEnabledAsync method can't be evaluated by the database server, which means that counting users with this method would require retrieving all of the stored IdentityUser objects, calling the method on each of them, and counting the results. Instead, I have chosen to use the TwoFactorEnabled property defined by the IdentityUser class.

Restart ASP.NET Core, sign into the application as alice@example.com with password mysecret, and request https://localhost:44350/Identity. Click the Authenticator button, and you will see the message shown in the first screenshot in Figure 11-2.

Click the Enable Authenticator button, and you will be shown a secret key used to set up the authenticator and the QR code, as shown in the second screenshot in Figure 11-2.

■ **Note** If you do not see the QR code, then you may not have installed the required JavaScript package. See Chapter 4 for instructions.

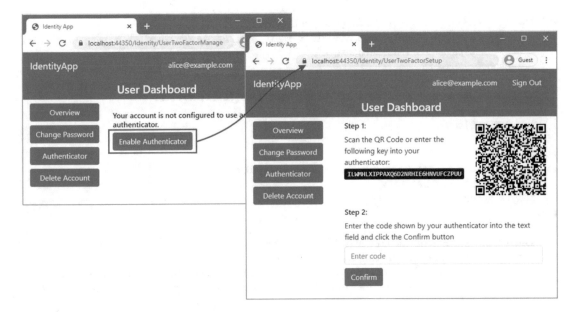

Figure 11-2. *Setting up two-factor authentication*

Enter the key into your authenticator or scan the QR code. I use the Authy app (authy.com) for the examples in this book because there is a Windows client, but there are alternatives from Google and Microsoft that run on mobile devices available in the iOS and Android app stores. (There is also a good tool at https://totp.danhersam.com that I use during development, into which you can paste a key and start receiving codes without any additional configuration, which is helpful if you are repeatedly testing a workflow.) The authenticator will start generating tokens once it has been set up, as shown in Figure 11-3.

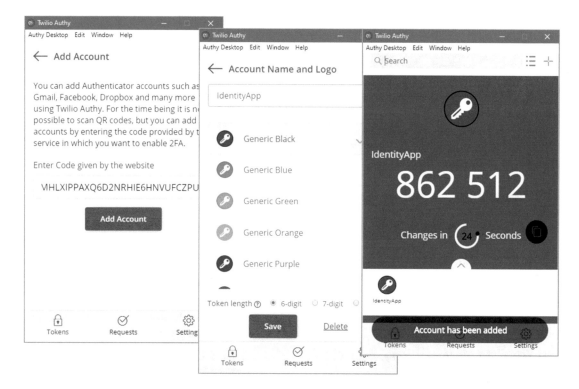

Figure 11-3. *Setting up the authenticator*

Enter the current token into the text field displayed in the browser, and click the Confirm button. You will be presented with a set of recovery codes, as shown in Figure 11-4. Click the OK button to return to the UserTwoFactorManage page, where you will be presented with buttons that generate a new set of recovery codes and disable the authenticator.

Figure 11-4. *Completing the authenticator setup*

As Figure 11-4 also shows, the administrator dashboard shows that there is now one user set up for two-factor authentication. For quick reference, Table 11-3 describes the user manager methods used to manage two-factor authentication with an authenticator.

Table 11-3. *The UserManager<IdentityUser> Methods for Two-Factor Authenticator Authentication*

Name	Description
GetTwoFactorEnabledAsync(user)	This method returns true if the user account has been configured for two-factor authentication.
SetTwoFactorEnabledAsync(user, enabled)	This method is used to enable or disable two-factor authentication. Care must be taken to configure the authenticator before calling this method.
GetAuthenticatorKeyAsync(user)	This method returns the user's authenticator secret key from the user store or null if no key has been stored.
ResetAuthenticatorKeyAsync(user)	This method is used to generate a new authenticator secret key and add it to the store.
VerifyTwoFactorTokenAsync(user, code)	This method verifies an authenticator code using the secret key in the user store. Verifying the code does not sign the user into the application.
GenerateNewTwoFactorRecoveryCodesAsync(user, count)	This method generates a new set of recovery codes.

Table 11-4 describes the SignInManager<IdentityUser> method I use to prevent the user from being signed out of the application while setting up an authenticator.

Table 11-4. *The SignInManager<IdentityUser> Method for Preventing Sign Out*

Name	Description
RefreshSignInAsync(user)	This method signs the user into the application using the existing authentication settings, refreshing the authentication cookie using the current security stamp.

Signing In with an Authenticator

When I created the SignIn page, I examined the properties of the SignInResult object to determine the outcome of the sign in, like this:

```
...
public async Task<IActionResult> OnPostAsync() {
    if (ModelState.IsValid) {
        SignInResult result = await SignInManager.PasswordSignInAsync(Email,
            Password, true, true);
        if (result.Succeeded) {
            return Redirect(ReturnUrl ?? "/");
        } else if (result.IsLockedOut) {
            TempData["message"] = "Account Locked";
        } else if (result.IsNotAllowed) {
            IdentityUser user = await UserManager.FindByEmailAsync(Email);
            if (user != null &&
                    !await UserManager.IsEmailConfirmedAsync(user)) {
                return RedirectToPage("SignUpConfirm");
            }
            TempData["message"] = "Sign In Not Allowed";
        } else if (result.RequiresTwoFactor) {
            return RedirectToPage("SignInTwoFactor", new { ReturnUrl });
        } else {
            TempData["message"] = "Sign In Failed";
        }
    }
    return Page();
}
...
```

When a user has set up an authenticator, the result of the PasswordSignInAsync method is a SignInResult object whose RequiresTwoFactor property is true (assuming that they have provided the correct password, of course). For this outcome, I send a redirection to a page named SignInTwoFactor so the user can complete the sign-in process. Add a Razor Page named SignInTwoFactor.cshtml to the Pages/ Identity folder with the content shown in Listing 11-11.

Listing 11-11. The Contents of the SignInTwoFactor.cshtml File in the Pages/Identity Folder

```
@page "{returnUrl?}"
@model IdentityApp.Pages.Identity.SignInTwoFactorModel
@{
    ViewData["showNav"] = false;
    ViewData["banner"] = "Sign In";
}
```

```html
<div asp-validation-summary="All" class="text-danger m-2"></div>

<form method="post">
    <div class="form-group">
        <label>Authenticator Token or Recovery Code:</label>
        <input class="form-control" asp-for="Token" />
    </div>
    <div class="form-check">
        <input class="form-check-input" type="checkbox" asp-for="RememberMe" />
        <label class="form-check-label" >Remember Me</label>
    </div>
    <button type="submit" class="btn btn-primary mt-2">Sign In</button>
</form>
```

The view part of the page presents the user with an input element into which an authenticator token or a recovery code can be entered. There is also a checkbox that will be used to set a cookie so the user can sign in using the same browser with just a password.

Add the code shown in Listing 11-12 to the SignInTwoFactor.cshtml.cs file to define the page model class. (You will have to create this file if you are using Visual Studio Code.)

Listing 11-12. The Contents of the SignInTwoFactor.cshtml.cs File in the Pages/Identity Folder

```csharp
using Microsoft.AspNetCore.Authorization;
using Microsoft.AspNetCore.Identity;
using Microsoft.AspNetCore.Mvc;
using System.ComponentModel.DataAnnotations;
using System.Text.RegularExpressions;
using System.Threading.Tasks;
using SignInResult = Microsoft.AspNetCore.Identity.SignInResult;

namespace IdentityApp.Pages.Identity {

    [AllowAnonymous]
    public class SignInTwoFactorModel : UserPageModel {

        public SignInTwoFactorModel(UserManager<IdentityUser> usrMgr,
                SignInManager<IdentityUser> signMgr) {
            UserManager = usrMgr;
            SignInManager = signMgr;
        }

        public UserManager<IdentityUser> UserManager { get; set; }
        public SignInManager<IdentityUser> SignInManager { get; set; }

        [BindProperty]
        public string ReturnUrl { get; set; }

        [BindProperty]
        [Required]
        public string Token { get; set; }

        [BindProperty]
```

```
    public bool RememberMe { get; set; }

    public async Task<IActionResult> OnPostAsync() {
        if (ModelState.IsValid) {
            IdentityUser user = await
                SignInManager.GetTwoFactorAuthenticationUserAsync();
            if (user != null) {
                string token = Regex.Replace(Token, @"\s", "");
                SignInResult result = await
                    SignInManager.TwoFactorAuthenticatorSignInAsync(token, true,
                        RememberMe);
                if (!result.Succeeded) {
                    result = await
                        SignInManager.TwoFactorRecoveryCodeSignInAsync(token);
                }
                if (result.Succeeded) {
                    if (await UserManager.CountRecoveryCodesAsync(user) <= 3) {
                        return RedirectToPage("SignInCodesWarning");
                    }
                    return Redirect(ReturnUrl ?? "/");
                }
            }
            ModelState.AddModelError("", "Invalid token or recovery code");
        }
        return Page();
    }
}
```

The first step is to make sure the user has provided a valid password in the first stage of the sign-in process, like this:

```
...
IdentityUser user = await SignInManager.GetTwoFactorAuthenticationUserAsync();
...
```

The sign-in manager's GetTwoFactorAuthenticationUserAsync method retrieves the IdentityUser object associated with the email address and password provided in the previous step. If this method returns null, then the user has not provided a password, and the signing-in process should be stopped.

In Part 2, I handle authenticator tokens and recovery codes separately, but, for this chapter, I first try the string provided by the user as an authenticator token and then fall back to using it as a recovery code.

The sign-in manager's TwoFactorAuthenticatorSignInAsync method is used to sign in with an authenticator token. The arguments are the token, a bool indicating whether the authentication cookie should be persistent, and a bool indicating whether a cookie should be created that will allow the user to sign in without the authenticator from the same browser.

```
...
await SignInManager.TwoFactorAuthenticatorSignInAsync(token, true, RememberMe);
...
```

If the user has provided a valid token, they are signed into the application. If the token is not valid, then I try and use it as a recovery code, like this:

```
...
result = await SignInManager.TwoFactorRecoveryCodeSignInAsync(token);
...
```

The user is signed in if the recovery code is valid. Codes can be used only once, and it is important to warn the user if they are running out of codes. I use the user manager's CountRecoveryCodesAsync method to check how many are remaining and redirect the user to a warning page if there three or fewer codes left.

```
...
if (await UserManager.CountRecoveryCodesAsync(user) <= 3) {
...
```

To define the warning page, add a Razor Page named SignInCodesWarning.cshtml to the Pages/Identity folder with the content shown in Listing 11-13.

Listing 11-13. The Contents of the SignInCodesWarning.cshtml File in the Pages/Identity Folder

```
@page "{returnUrl?}"
@model IdentityApp.Pages.Identity.SignInCodesWarningModel
@{
    ViewData["showNav"] = false;
    ViewData["banner"] = "Sign In";
}

<div class="h6">
    You are running out of recovery codes.
    Generate new codes using the user dashboard.
</div>
<a href="@Model.ReturnUrl" class="btn btn-primary my-2">Continue to application</a>
<a asp-page="UserTwoFactorManage" class="btn btn-primary m-2">Go to dashboard</a>
```

To define the page model class, add the code shown in Listing 11-14 to the SignInCodesWarning.cshtml.cs file. (You will have to create this file if you are using Visual Studio Code.)

Listing 11-14. The Contents of the SignInCodesWarning.cshtml.cs File in the Pages/Identity Folder

```
using Microsoft.AspNetCore.Mvc;

namespace IdentityApp.Pages.Identity {

    public class SignInCodesWarningModel : UserPageModel {

        [BindProperty(SupportsGet = true)]
        public string ReturnUrl { get; set; } = "/";
    }
}
```

For quick reference, Table 11-5 shows the sign-in manager methods used for two-factor sign-in with an authenticator.

Table 11-5. *The SignInManager<IdentityUser> Methods for Authenticator Two-Factor Sign-Ins*

Name	Description
GetTwoFactorAuthenticationUserAsync()	This method returns the IdentityUser object associated with the username/email address provided at the password stage. You should stop the sign-in process if this method returns null.
TwoFactorAuthenticatorSignInAsync(token, persist, remember)	This method validates an authenticator token and signs the user into the application.
TwoFactorRecoveryCodeSignInAsync(code)	This method validates a recovery code and signs the user into the application. The code is removed from the store so that it cannot be reused.

Table 11-6 describes the user manager method I used to count the unused recovery codes.

Table 11-6. *The UserManager<IdentityUser> Method for Counting Recovery Codes*

Name	Description
CountRecoveryCodesAsync(user)	This method returns the number of unused recovery codes for the specific IdentityUser object.

Restart ASP.NET Core, make sure you are signed out of the application, and request https://localhost:44350/Identity/SignIn. Enter alice@example.com into the email field and use mysecret as the password. Click the Sign In button, enter the current token displayed by your authenticator, and click the Sign In button to complete the sign-in process, as shown in Figure 11-5.

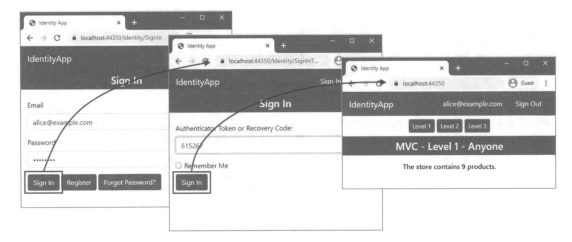

Figure 11-5. *Signing in with an authenticator*

If you select the Remember Me option when signing in, then you won't be prompted for an authenticator token the next time you sign in as the same user with the same browser. You will need to delete the browser's cookies—or wait until the cookie expires—to be prompted for a token once again. If you are close to exhausting the set of recovery codes when you sign into the application, you will see the warning shown in Figure 11-6.

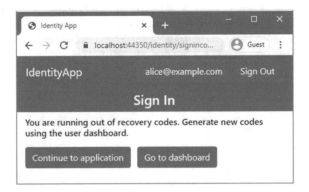

Figure 11-6. *Warning the user about recovery codes*

Supporting External Authentication Services

In Chapter 5, I explained how to configure ASP.NET Core for authentication with third-party services, such as Google and Facebook. There are several ways in which you can support external authentication services. The IdentityUI package, for example, allows users to have a local password and external authentication and move freely between them. The idea is that the user can still sign in, even when the external service is down. My preference is to have the user choose one or the other, on the basis that the external services provided by Google or Facebook are generally reliable and that presenting users with unnecessary options will lead to additional support requests.

Configuring the Application

I configured Identity to use the built-in providers for Google, Facebook, and Twitter in Chapter 5. One change is required for this chapter, to adjust the configuration of the Twitter provider so that it requests user details from the external service, as shown in Listing 11-15. These details include the user's email address, which I will use to create accounts in the user store.

Listing 11-15. Changing the Provider Configuration in the Startup.cs File in the IdentityApp Folder

```
...
services.AddAuthentication()
    .AddFacebook(opts => {
        opts.AppId = Configuration["Facebook:AppId"];
        opts.AppSecret = Configuration["Facebook:AppSecret"];
    })
    .AddGoogle(opts => {
        opts.ClientId = Configuration["Google:ClientId"];
        opts.ClientSecret = Configuration["Google:ClientSecret"];
    })
    .AddTwitter(opts => {
        opts.ConsumerKey = Configuration["Twitter:ApiKey"];
        opts.ConsumerSecret = Configuration["Twitter:ApiSecret"];
        opts.RetrieveUserDetails = true;
    });
...
```

Supporting Self-Service Registration an External Service

The first step is to display the option to create an account alongside the local authentication option that is already supported. Add the content shown in Listing 11-16 to the SignUp.cshtml file in the Pages/Identity folder.

Listing 11-16. Displaying External Services in the SignUp.cshtml File in the Pages/Identity Folder

```
@page
@model IdentityApp.Pages.Identity.SignUpModel
@{
    ViewData["showNav"] = false;
    ViewData["banner"] = "Sign Up";
}

<link href="/lib/font-awesome/css/all.min.css" rel="stylesheet" />

<div asp-validation-summary="All" class="text-danger m-2"></div>

<div class="container-fluid">
    <div class="row">
        <div class="col-6">
            <form method="post" class="m-4">
                <div class="form-group">
                    <label>Email</label>
```

```
                    <input class="form-control" asp-for="Email" />
                </div>
                <div class="form-group">
                    <label>Password</label>
                    <input class="form-control" type="password" asp-for="Password" />
                </div>
                <button class="btn btn-primary">Sign Up</button>
            </form>
        </div>
        <div class="col-auto text-center">
            <h6>Sign Up with a Social Media Account</h6>
            <form method="post" asp-page="SignUpExternal">
                @foreach (var scheme in Model.ExternalSchemes) {
                    <partial name="_ExternalButtonPartial" model="scheme" />
                }
            </form>
        </div>
    </div>
</div>
```

The link element includes the CSS stylesheet for the Font Awesome package I added to the project in Chapter 5 to display icons for the external services. The remaining additions create a grid layout that will display buttons for each of the configured external services in the application, alongside the traditional email/password sign-up option. The button for each service is displayed using the _ExternalButtonPartial partial view created for the Identity UI package. When the user clicks one of the buttons, they will submit a form to a page named SignUpExternal, which I will create shortly.

Listing 11-17 shows the corresponding changes to the page model class to provide the view with the list of external services.

Listing 11-17. Supporting External Services in the SignUp.cshtml.cs File in the Pages/Identity Folder

```
using IdentityApp.Services;
using Microsoft.AspNetCore.Authorization;
using Microsoft.AspNetCore.Identity;
using Microsoft.AspNetCore.Mvc;
using System.ComponentModel.DataAnnotations;
using System.Threading.Tasks;
using System.Collections.Generic;
using Microsoft.AspNetCore.Authentication;

namespace IdentityApp.Pages.Identity {

    [AllowAnonymous]
    public class SignUpModel : UserPageModel {

        public SignUpModel(UserManager<IdentityUser> usrMgr,
                IdentityEmailService emailService,
                SignInManager<IdentityUser> signMgr) {
            UserManager = usrMgr;
            EmailService = emailService;
            SignInManager = signMgr;
        }
```

```
    public UserManager<IdentityUser> UserManager { get; set; }
    public IdentityEmailService EmailService { get; set; }
    public SignInManager<IdentityUser> SignInManager { get; set; }

    [BindProperty]
    [Required]
    [EmailAddress]
    public string Email { get; set; }

    [BindProperty]
    [Required]
    public string Password { get; set; }

    public IEnumerable<AuthenticationScheme> ExternalSchemes { get; set; }

    public async Task OnGetAsync() {
        ExternalSchemes = await
            SignInManager.GetExternalAuthenticationSchemesAsync();
    }

    public async Task<IActionResult> OnPostAsync() {
        // ...statements omitted for brevity...
    }
    }
}
```

The sign-in manager's GetExternalAuthenticationSchemesAsync method returns a sequence of AuthenticationScheme objects, each of which describes one of the external services configured in the application. Add a Razor Page named SignUpExternal.cshtml to the Pages/Identity folder with the content shown in Listing 11-18.

Listing 11-18. The Contents of the SignUpExternal.cshtml File in the Pages/Identity Folder

```
@page "{id?}"
@model IdentityApp.Pages.Identity.SignUpExternalModel
@{
    ViewData["showNav"] = false;
    ViewData["banner"] = "Sign Up";
}

@if (TempData["errorMessage"] != null) {
        <div class="alert alert-danger">@TempData["errorMessage"]</div>
        <a asp-page="SignUp" class="btn btn-danger">Cancel Sign Up</a>
} else {
    <div class="text-center">
        <h6>
            An account for <code>@Model.IdentityUser.Email</code> has been created.
        </h6>
        <h6>Click the OK button and sign in using the
            @(await Model.ExternalProvider()) button.
        </h6>
```

```
        <a asp-page="SignIn" class="btn btn-primary">OK</a>
    </div>
}
```

The view part of this page only has to display a confirmation message when an account is set up or an error message if something goes wrong. The complexity of the process is in the page model class, which is responsible for dealing with the external service and creating an account. Add the code shown in Listing 11-19 to the SignUpExternal.cshtml.cs file. (You will have to create this file if you are using Visual Studio Code.)

Listing 11-19. The Contents of the SignUpExternal.cshtml.cs File in the Pages/Identity Folder

```
using Microsoft.AspNetCore.Authentication;
using Microsoft.AspNetCore.Authorization;
using Microsoft.AspNetCore.Identity;
using Microsoft.AspNetCore.Mvc;
using System.Linq;
using System.Security.Claims;
using System.Threading.Tasks;

namespace IdentityApp.Pages.Identity {

    [AllowAnonymous]
    public class SignUpExternalModel : UserPageModel {

        public SignUpExternalModel(UserManager<IdentityUser> usrMgr,
                SignInManager<IdentityUser> signMgr) {
            UserManager = usrMgr;
            SignInManager = signMgr;
        }

        public UserManager<IdentityUser> UserManager { get; set; }
        public SignInManager<IdentityUser> SignInManager { get; set; }

        public IdentityUser IdentityUser { get; set; }

        public async Task<string> ExternalProvider() =>
            (await UserManager.GetLoginsAsync(IdentityUser))
            .FirstOrDefault()?.ProviderDisplayName;

        public IActionResult OnPost(string provider) {
            string callbackUrl = Url.Page("SignUpExternal", "Callback");
            AuthenticationProperties props =
                SignInManager.ConfigureExternalAuthenticationProperties(
                    provider, callbackUrl);
            return new ChallengeResult(provider, props);
        }

        public async Task<IActionResult> OnGetCallbackAsync() {
            ExternalLoginInfo info = await SignInManager.GetExternalLoginInfoAsync();

            string email = info?.Principal?.FindFirst(ClaimTypes.Email)?.Value;
```

```
        if (string.IsNullOrEmpty(email)) {
            return Error("External service has not provided an email address.");
        } else if ((await UserManager.FindByEmailAsync(email)) != null ) {
            return Error("An account already exists with your email address.");
        }

        IdentityUser identUser = new IdentityUser {
            UserName = email,
            Email = email,
            EmailConfirmed = true
        };
        IdentityResult result = await UserManager.CreateAsync(identUser);
        if (result.Succeeded) {
            identUser = await UserManager.FindByEmailAsync(email);
            result = await UserManager.AddLoginAsync(identUser, info);
            return RedirectToPage(new { id = identUser.Id });
        }
        return Error("An account could not be created.");
    }

    public async Task<IActionResult> OnGetAsync(string id) {
        if (id == null) {
            return RedirectToPage("SignUp");
        } else {
            IdentityUser = await UserManager.FindByIdAsync(id);
            if (IdentityUser == null) {
                return RedirectToPage("SignUp");
            }
        }
        return Page();
    }

    private IActionResult Error(string err) {
        TempData["errorMessage"] = err;
        return RedirectToPage();
    }
    }
}
}
```

I have defined the handler methods in the order they will be used to try to help simplify a complex process. The OnPost handler method will be called when the user clicks one of the external authentication buttons shown by the SignUp page.

The sign-in manager's ConfigureExternalAuthenticationProperties method is called to create an AuthenticationProperties object that will authenticate the user with the selected external provider. These properties are configured with a callback URL, which will be called when the user has authenticated themselves with their chosen service. The AuthenticationProperties object is used to create a challenge response, which will start the authentication process and redirect the user to the selected service.

When the user has been authenticated, the OnGetCallbackAsync method will be invoked. The user's external information is obtained using the sign-in manager's GetExternalLoginInfoAsync method, which returns an ExternalLoginInfo object. The ExternalLoginInfo.Principal property returns a ClaimsPrincipal object that contains the user's account information, expressed as a series of claims. The user's email address is obtained by finding the first claim with the ClaimType.Email type, like this:

```
...
ExternalLoginInfo info = await SignInManager.GetExternalLoginInfoAsync();
string email = info?.Principal?.FindFirst(ClaimTypes.Email)?.Value;
...
```

Once I have an email address, I use it to create a new IdentityUser object and add it to the user store. I then use the FindByEmailAsync method so that I am working with the stored version of the object, including the properties that are generated automatically during the storage process. I call the user manager's AddLoginAsync method to store details of the external login in the store, so they can be used to sign into the application.

A redirection is performed that invokes the OnGetAsync method, which sets the property required to display the confirmation message to the user. For quick reference, Table 11-7 describes the sign-in methods used to create an account with an external login.

Table 11-7. The SignInManager<IdentityUser> Methods for Registration with an External Login

Name	Description
ConfigureExternalAuthenticationProperties (provider, url)	This method creates an AuthenticationProperties object for the specified provider and callback URL, which can then be used to create a challenge response.
GetExternalLoginInfoAsync()	This method returns a ExternalLoginInfo object that represents the user data provided by the external authentication service.

Table 11-8 describes the user manager method used to store the external login.

Table 11-8. The UserManager<IdentityUser> Method for Storing an External Login

Name	Description
AddLoginAsync(user, info)	This method stores an ExternalLoginInfo object for the specified IdentityUser.

Restart ASP.NET Core and request https://localhost:44350/Identity/SignUp; you will be presented with buttons for creating an account using Facebook, Google, and Twitter. Creating an account requires a real account with one of these providers, so click the button for a provider for which you have an account, and you will be redirected to a login page. Go through the sign-in process, and you will be redirected back to the example application, which will display a confirmation message. Figure 11-7 shows a basic sequence for a Google account, although you will see additional steps for passwords, authenticator tokens, SMS messages, or other factors based on your account.

Figure 11-7. *Creating an account using an external authentication service*

Supporting Administrator Registration with an External Service

An external authentication service can be chosen by the user instead of a password when an account is
created by an administrator. To start, make the changes shown in Listing 11-20 to the UserAccountComplete
page to offer the user a choice between a password and an external authentication service. Just for variety, I
have made all the changes in the view part of the page, rather than updating the page model class as well.

Listing 11-20. External Options in the UserAccountComplete.cshtml File in the Pages/Identity Folder

```
@page "{email?}/{token?}"
@model IdentityApp.Pages.Identity.UserAccountCompleteModel
@inject SignInManager<IdentityUser> SignInManager
@{
    ViewData["showNav"] = false;
    ViewData["banner"] = "Complete Account";
}

@if (string.IsNullOrEmpty(Model.Token) || string.IsNullOrEmpty(Model.Email)) {
    <div class="h6 text-center">
        <div class="p-2">
            Check your inbox for a confirmation email and click the link it contains.
        </div>
    </div>
} else {
    <div asp-validation-summary="All" class="text-danger m-2"></div>
    <div class="container-fluid">
        <div class="row">
            <div class="col mb-3">
                <div class="form-group">
                    <label>Email</label>
```

```
                <input class="form-control" asp-for="Email" readonly />
            </div>
        </div>
    </div>
    <div class="row">
        <div class="col-6">
            <h6>Sign In with a Password</h6>
            <form method="post">
                <input type="hidden" asp-for="Token" />
                <input type="hidden" asp-for="Email" />
                <div class="form-group">
                    <label>Password</label>
                    <input class="form-control" type="password"
                        name="password" />
                </div>
                <div class="form-group">
                    <label>Confirm Password</label>
                    <input class="form-control" type="password"
                        name="confirmpassword" />
                </div>
                <button class="btn btn-primary" type="submit">
                    Finish and Sign In
                </button>
            </form>
        </div>
        <div class="col-auto">
            <h6>Sign In with a Social Media Account</h6>
            <form method="post" asp-page="UserAccountCompleteExternal">
                <input type="hidden" asp-for="Email" />
                <input type="hidden" asp-for="Token" />
                @foreach (var scheme in await
                        SignInManager.GetExternalAuthenticationSchemesAsync()) {
                    <partial name="_ExternalButtonPartial" model="scheme" />
                }
            </form>
        </div>
    </div>
</div>
}
```

To handle using an external service to complete account setup, add a Razor Page named UserAccountCompleteExternal.cshtml to the Pages/Identity folder with the content shown in Listing 11-21.

Listing 11-21. The Contents of the UserAccountCompleteExternal.cshtml File in the Pages/Identity Folder

```
@page "{id?}"
@model IdentityApp.Pages.Identity.UserAccountCompleteExternalModel
@{
    ViewData["showNav"] = false;
    ViewData["banner"] = "Complete Account";
}
```

```
@if (TempData["errorMessage"] != null) {
        <div class="alert alert-danger">@TempData["errorMessage"]</div>
        <a asp-page="SignUp" class="btn btn-danger">Cancel Sign Up</a>
} else {
    <div class="text-center">
        <h6>
            Your account has been completed.
        </h6>
        <h6>Click the OK button and sign in using the
            @(await Model.ExternalProvider()) button.
        </h6>
        <a asp-page="SignIn" class="btn btn-primary">OK</a>
    </div>
}
```

This page is similar to the one defined in the previous section, but I have not attempted to reduce the duplication because most applications will require only one approach and it is easier to incorporate a workflow into a real project if it is self-contained. To define the page model class, add the code shown in Listing 11-22 to the UserAccountCompleteExternal.cshtml.cs file. (You will have to create this file if you are using Visual Studio Code.)

Listing 11-22. The Contents of the UserAccountCompleteExternal.cshtml.cs File in the Pages/Identity Folder

```
using IdentityApp.Services;
using Microsoft.AspNetCore.Authentication;
using Microsoft.AspNetCore.Authorization;
using Microsoft.AspNetCore.Identity;
using Microsoft.AspNetCore.Mvc;
using System.Linq;
using System.Security.Claims;
using System.Threading.Tasks;

namespace IdentityApp.Pages.Identity {

    [AllowAnonymous]
    public class UserAccountCompleteExternalModel : UserPageModel {

        public UserAccountCompleteExternalModel(
                UserManager<IdentityUser> usrMgr,
                SignInManager<IdentityUser> signMgr,
                TokenUrlEncoderService encoder) {
            UserManager = usrMgr;
            SignInManager = signMgr;
            TokenUrlEncoder = encoder;
        }

        public UserManager<IdentityUser> UserManager { get; set; }
        public SignInManager<IdentityUser> SignInManager { get; set; }
        public TokenUrlEncoderService TokenUrlEncoder { get; set; }

        [BindProperty(SupportsGet = true)]
```

```
    public string Email { get; set; }

    [BindProperty(SupportsGet = true)]
    public string Token { get; set; }

    public IdentityUser IdentityUser { get; set; }

    public async Task<string> ExternalProvider() =>
        (await UserManager.GetLoginsAsync(IdentityUser))
            .FirstOrDefault()?.ProviderDisplayName;

    public async Task<IActionResult> OnPostAsync(string provider) {
        IdentityUser = await UserManager.FindByEmailAsync(Email);
        string decodedToken = TokenUrlEncoder.DecodeToken(Token);
        bool valid = await UserManager.VerifyUserTokenAsync(IdentityUser,
            UserManager.Options.Tokens.PasswordResetTokenProvider,
            UserManager<IdentityUser>.ResetPasswordTokenPurpose, decodedToken);
        if (!valid) {
            return Error("Invalid token");
        }
        string callbackUrl = Url.Page("UserAccountCompleteExternal",
            "Callback", new { Email, Token });
        AuthenticationProperties props =
          SignInManager.ConfigureExternalAuthenticationProperties(
                provider, callbackUrl);
        return new ChallengeResult(provider, props);
    }

    public async Task<IActionResult> OnGetCallbackAsync() {
        ExternalLoginInfo info = await SignInManager.GetExternalLoginInfoAsync();
        string email = info?.Principal?.FindFirst(ClaimTypes.Email)?.Value;
        if (string.IsNullOrEmpty(email)) {
            return Error("External service has not provided an email address.");
        } else if ((IdentityUser =
                await UserManager.FindByEmailAsync(email)) == null) {
            return Error("Your email address doesn't match.");
        }
        IdentityResult result
            = await UserManager.AddLoginAsync(IdentityUser, info);
        if (!result.Succeeded) {
            return Error("Cannot store external login.");
        }
        return RedirectToPage(new { id = IdentityUser.Id });
    }

    public async Task<IActionResult> OnGetAsync(string id) {
        if ((id == null
            || (IdentityUser = await UserManager.FindByIdAsync(id)) == null)
            && !TempData.ContainsKey("errorMessage")) {
            return RedirectToPage("SignIn");
        }
```

```
            return Page();
        }

        private IActionResult Error(string err) {
            TempData["errorMessage"] = err;
            return RedirectToPage();
        }
    }
}
```

The basic approach is the same as for self-registration, but some changes are required to fit into the administrator-led model. First, this page has to validate the token that was sent to the user when the account was created. The token is intended for use with the method that resets a password but can be validated on its own, albeit awkwardly, with the user manager's VerifyUserTokenAsync method.

```
...
bool valid = await UserManager.VerifyUserTokenAsync(IdentityUser,
    UserManager.Options.Tokens.PasswordResetTokenProvider,
    UserManager<IdentityUser>.ResetPasswordTokenPurpose, decodedToken);
...
```

The arguments are the user object, the name of the token generator, the purpose for which the token was created, and, finally, the token. The name of the generator is obtained through the UserManager.Options.Tokens.PasswordResetTokenProvider property, and the UserManager<IdentityUser> class defines a set of constant values that describe the different reasons for which tokens are created. The result is that the token is validated without setting a password, which would undermine the purpose of the workflow.

The remaining differences arise because the external login is being added to an IdentityUser object that has already been stored by the administrator. The email address provided by the external service is checked to ensure it matches the one used by the administrator. For quick reference, Table 11-9 describes the method I used to validate the token without resetting the password.

Table 11-9. *The UserManager<IdentityUser> Method for Validating Tokens*

Name	Description
VerifyUserTokenAsync(user, provider, purpose, token)	This method returns true if the specified token is valid for the specified user and purpose and was created using the specified generator.

Restart ASP.NET Core and request https://localhost:44350/Identity/Admin. Unless you have a second external account available, click the Seed Database button to remove the account you created in the last section. Click the Create Account button, enter your external email address into the text field, and click the Create button. Examine the ASP.NET Core console output, and you will see a message similar to this one, but with your email address and a unique validation code:

```
---New Email----
To: user@domain
Subject: Set Your Password
Please set your password by
```

```
<a href=https://localhost:44350/Identity/UserAccountComplete/user@domain/Q2ZESjhBM>
    clicking here
</a>.
-------
```

Copy and paste the link from your message into a browser, and you will be prompted to either choose a password or use an external provider. After you have been authenticated by the external service, you will receive a confirmation message, as shown in Figure 11-8. You may go through an abbreviated authentication process if your browser stored cookies from the previous example. You may need to clear the cookies before you can authenticate as a different user.

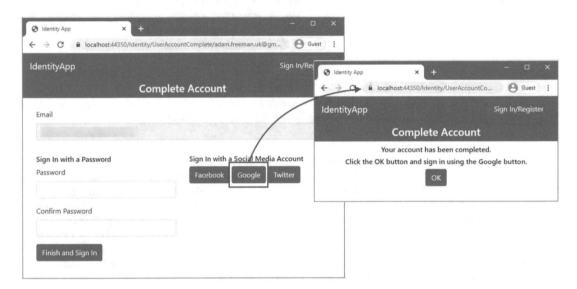

Figure 11-8. Using an external service to complete an account created by an administrator

Supporting Signing In with an External Service

To allow users to sign in with an external account, start by making the changes shown in Listing 11-23 to present the user with the set of configured external services.

Listing 11-23. Displaying External Services in the SignIn.cshtml File in the Pages/Identity Folder

```
@page "{returnUrl?}"
@model IdentityApp.Pages.Identity.SignInModel
@{
    ViewData["showNav"] = false;
    ViewData["banner"] = "Sign In";
}

<div asp-validation-summary="All" class="text-danger m-2"></div>

@if (TempData.ContainsKey("message")) {
    <div class="alert alert-danger">@TempData["message"]</div>
}
```

```html
<div class="container-fluid">
    <div class="row">
        <div class="col-6">
            <h6>Sign In with a Password</h6>
            <form method="post">
                <div class="form-group">
                    <label>Email</label>
                    <input class="form-control" name="email" />
                </div>
                <div class="form-group">
                    <label>Password</label>
                    <input class="form-control" type="password" name="password" />
                </div>
                <button type="submit" class="btn btn-primary">
                    Sign In
                </button>
                <a asp-page="SignUp" class="btn btn-primary">Register</a>
                <a asp-page="UserPasswordRecovery" class="btn btn-secondary">
                    Forgot Password?
                </a>
            </form>
        </div>
        <div class="col-auto">
            <h6>Sign In with a Social Media Account</h6>
            <form method="post" asp-page="SignIn" asp-page-handler="External">
                @foreach (var scheme in await
                    Model.SignInManager.GetExternalAuthenticationSchemesAsync()) {
                    <partial name="_ExternalButtonPartial" model="scheme" />
                }
            </form>
        </div>
    </div>
</div>
```

To allow the user to sign in, make the changes shown in Listing 11-24 to the SignIn.cshtml.cs file.

Listing 11-24. Supporting External Services in the SignIn.cshtml.cs File in the Pages/Identity Folder

```csharp
using System.ComponentModel.DataAnnotations;
using System.Threading.Tasks;
using Microsoft.AspNetCore.Identity;
using Microsoft.AspNetCore.Mvc;
using SignInResult = Microsoft.AspNetCore.Identity.SignInResult;
using Microsoft.AspNetCore.Authorization;
using Microsoft.AspNetCore.Authentication;
using System.Net;

namespace IdentityApp.Pages.Identity {

    [AllowAnonymous]
    public class SignInModel : UserPageModel {
```

```
// ...methods and properties omitted for brevity...

public IActionResult OnPostExternalAsync(string provider) {
    string callbackUrl = Url.Page("SignIn", "Callback", new { ReturnUrl });
    AuthenticationProperties props =
        SignInManager.ConfigureExternalAuthenticationProperties(
            provider, callbackUrl);
    return new ChallengeResult(provider, props);
}

public async Task<IActionResult> OnGetCallbackAsync() {
    ExternalLoginInfo info = await SignInManager.GetExternalLoginInfoAsync();
    SignInResult result = await SignInManager.ExternalLoginSignInAsync(
        info.LoginProvider, info.ProviderKey, true);
    if (result.Succeeded) {
        return Redirect(WebUtility.UrlDecode(ReturnUrl ?? "/"));
    } else if (result.IsLockedOut) {
        TempData["message"] = "Account Locked";
    } else if (result.IsNotAllowed) {
        TempData["message"] = "Sign In Not Allowed";
    } else {
        TempData["message"] = "Sign In Failed";
    }
    return RedirectToPage();
}
    }
}
```

The OnPostExternalAsync handler is called when the user clicks one of the external service buttons and produces the same type of challenge result shown in earlier examples. The OnGetCallbackAsync method is called once the user has been authenticated. The user's details from the external service are obtained using the GetExternalLoginInfoAsync method, which was also used in earlier examples. The sign-in manager's ExternalLoginSignInAsync method is used to sign the user into the application using the stored external login. For quick reference, Table 11-10 describes these methods.

Table 11-10. *The SignInManager<IdentityUser> Methods for External Signing In*

Name	Description
GetExternalLoginInfoAsync()	This method returns a ExternalLoginInfo object that represents the user data provided by the external authentication service.
ExternalLoginSignInAsync(provider, key, persist)	This method signs the user into the application using a previously stored external login. The arguments are taken from the ExternalLoginInfo object returned by the GetExternalLoginInfoAsync method.

Restart ASP.NET Core, request `https://localhost:44350/Identity/SignIn`, and click the external service button you used to create an account in one of the previous sections. Once you are authenticated, you will be signed into the application, as shown in Figure 11-9. You may not be prompted to enter any credentials if your browser has previously received cookies from the external service.

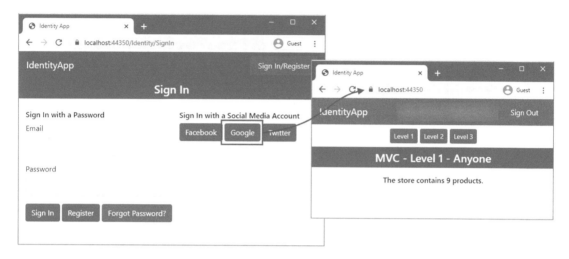

Figure 11-9. Signing into the application with an external service

Summary

In this chapter, I created custom workflows that support two-factor authentication with an authenticator and for registering and signing in with a third-party authentication. In the next chapter, I explain how to provide authentication services for API clients.

CHAPTER 12

■ ■ ■

Authenticating API Clients

In this chapter, I explain how ASP.NET Core Identity can be used to authenticate API clients using a simple JavaScript application. Some projects can rely on standard ASP.NET Core user authentication for their clients, and I demonstrate how this works. For other projects, I explain how to provide authentication using cookies and using bearer tokens, which are useful for clients that don't support cookies. Table 12-1 puts API authentication in context.

Table 12-1. *Putting API Authentication in Context*

Question	Answer
What is it?	API authentication restricts access to the controllers that provide direct access to data, rather than via HTML content. These controllers typically support RESTful web services.
Why is it useful?	Many web services provide data or support operations that should not be publicly accessible. Restricting access by requiring API requests to be authenticated allows an effective authorization policy to be defined.
How is it used?	Access to the API controller is restricted using the `Authorize` attribute. How requests are authenticated varies based on the clients that the applications support.
Are there any pitfalls or limitations?	There are no well-defined standards to describe how web services should be designed or authorized, which can be a problem when you need to support a range of third-party clients.
Are there any alternatives?	Not all applications support APIs, but when they are supported, some kind of authentication is required.

Table 12-2 summarizes the chapter.

Table 12-2. *Chapter Summary*

Problem	Solution	Listing
Authenticate JavaScript API clients that are delivered by the ASP.NET Core server	Rely on the standard authentication cookie that is created when the user signs into the application.	1–8
Return status code responses to API clients	Define a handler that overrides the default behavior for challenge and forbidden responses.	9–13
Authenticate API clients with a cookie	Create an authentication controller and use the sign-in manager's methods to sign the user into the application and return a JSON response. Ensure the JavaScript client includes the cookie in subsequent requests.	14–19
Authenticate API clients without a cookie	Use a bearer token, which the client can present in subsequent requests.	20–25

© Adam Freeman 2021
A. Freeman, *Pro ASP.NET Core Identity*, https://doi.org/10.1007/978-1-4842-6858-2_12

Preparing for This Chapter

This chapter uses the IdentityApp project from Chapter 11. To demonstrate API client authentication, I need to set up an API controller. Add a class file named ValuesController.cs to the Controllers folder with the code shown in Listing 12-1.

■ **Tip**   You can download the example project for this chapter—and for all the other chapters in this book—from https://github.com/Apress/pro-asp.net-core-identity. See Chapter 1 for how to get help if you have problems running the examples.

Listing 12-1. The ValuesController.cs File in the Controllers Folder

```
using IdentityApp.Models;
using Microsoft.AspNetCore.Mvc;
using System.Collections.Generic;
using System.ComponentModel.DataAnnotations;
using System.Threading.Tasks;

namespace IdentityApp.Controllers {

    [ApiController]
    [Route("/api/data")]
    public class ValuesController : ControllerBase {
        private ProductDbContext DbContext;

        public ValuesController(ProductDbContext dbContext) {
            DbContext = dbContext;
        }

        [HttpGet]
        public IAsyncEnumerable<Product> GetProducts() => DbContext.Products;

        [HttpPost]
        public async Task<IActionResult> CreateProduct([FromBody]
                ProductBindingTarget target) {
            if (ModelState.IsValid) {
                Product product = new Product {
                    Name = target.Name, Price = target.Price,
                        Category = target.Category
                };
                await DbContext.AddAsync(product);
                await DbContext.SaveChangesAsync();
                return Ok(product);
            }
            return BadRequest(ModelState);
        }

        [HttpDelete("{id}")]
```

```
        public Task DeleteProduct(long id) {
            DbContext.Products.Remove(new Product { Id = id });
            return DbContext.SaveChangesAsync();
        }
    }

    public class ProductBindingTarget {
        [Required]
        public string Name { get; set; }

        [Required]
        public decimal Price { get; set; }

        [Required]
        public string Category { get; set; }
    }
}
```

This is a basic API controller that provides access to the data in the product database, which has only been used to generate content in MVC views and Razor Pages until now. I don't need a full set of API functions for this chapter because the focus is on authentication. There are actions to retrieve all the products in the database, delete a product from the database, and add a product to the database. The ProductBindingTarget class is used to ensure that only selected properties defined by the Product class will be used by the model binding process.

Creating the JavaScript API Client

For this chapter, I use a pure JavaScript client, which will allow me to focus on the authentication process without the distraction of a large framework getting in the way. Create the wwwroot/js folder and add to it a JavaScript file named network.js with the content shown in Listing 12-2.

■ **Note**   I describe how to handle bearer tokens in Angular and React in my books for those frameworks, *Pro Angular* and *Pro React*.

Listing 12-2. The Contents of the network.js File in the wwwroot/js Folder

```
const baseUrl = "https://localhost:44350/api/data";

export const loadData = async function (callback, errorHandler) {
    const response = await fetch(baseUrl, {
        redirect: "manual"
    });
    processResponse(response, async () => callback(await response.json()),
        errorHandler);
}

export const createProduct = async function (product, callback, errorHandler) {
    const response = await fetch(baseUrl, {
```

```
        method: "POST",
        body: JSON.stringify(product),
        headers: {
            "Content-Type": "application/json"
        }
    });
    processResponse(response, callback, errorHandler);
}

export const deleteProduct = async function (id, callback, errorHandler) {
    const response = await fetch(`${baseUrl}/${id}`, {
        method: "DELETE"
    });
    processResponse(response, callback, errorHandler);
}

function processResponse(response, callback, errorHandler) {
    if (response.ok) {
        callback();
    } else {
        errorHandler(response.status);
    }
}
```

The functions defined in this file are responsible for sending HTTP requests to the API controller. I have used the Fetch API, which is supported by modern browsers and provides a more usable alternative to the traditional XmlHttpRequest object.

Add a JavaScript file named client.js to the wwwroot/js folder with the code shown in Listing 12-3.

Listing 12-3. The Contents of the client.js File in the wwwroot/js Folder

```
import * as network from "./network.js";

const columns = ["ID", "Name", "Category", "Price"];
let tableBody;
let errorElem;

HTMLElement.prototype.make = function (...types) {
    return types.reduce((lastElem, elemType) =>
        lastElem.appendChild(document.createElement(elemType)), this);
}

function showError(err) {
    errorElem.innerText = `Error: ${err}`;
    errorElem.classList.add("m-2", "p-2");
}

function clearError(err) {
    errorElem.innerText = "";
    errorElem.classList.remove("m-2", "p-2");
}
```

```javascript
function createStructure() {
    const targetElement = document.getElementById("target");
    targetElement.innerHTML = "";
    errorElem = targetElement.make("div");
    errorElem.classList.add("h6", "bg-danger", "text-center", "text-white");
    return targetElement;
}

function createContent() {
    const targetElement = createStructure();
    const table = targetElement.make("table");
    table.classList.add("table", "table-sm", "table-striped", "table-bordered");
    const headerRow = table.make("thead", "tr");
    columns.concat([""]).forEach(col => {
        const th = headerRow.make("th");
        th.innerText = col;
    });
    tableBody = table.make("tbody");
    const footerRow = table.make("tfoot", "tr");
    footerRow.make("td");
    columns.filter(col => col != "ID").forEach(col => {
        const input = footerRow.make("td", "input");
        input.name = input.id = col;
        input.placeholder = `Enter ${col.toLowerCase()}`;
    });
    const button = footerRow.make("td", "button");
    button.classList = "btn btn-sm btn-success";
    button.innerText = "Add";
    button.addEventListener("click", async () => {
        const product = {};
        columns.forEach(col => product[col] = document.getElementById(col)?.value);
        await network.createProduct(product, populateTable, showError);
    });
}

function createTableContents(products) {
    tableBody.innerHTML = "";
    products.forEach(p => {
        const row = tableBody.appendChild(document.createElement("tr"));
        columns.forEach(col => {
            const cell = row.appendChild(document.createElement("td"));
            cell.innerText = p[col.toLowerCase()];
        });
        const button = row.appendChild(document.createElement("td")
            .appendChild(document.createElement("button")));
        button.classList.add("btn", "btn-sm", "btn-danger");
        button.textContent = "Delete";
        button.addEventListener("click", async () =>
            await network.deleteProduct(p.id, populateTable, showError));
    });
}
```

```
async function populateTable(products) {
    clearError();
    await network.loadData(createTableContents, showError);
}

document.addEventListener("DOMContentLoaded", () => {
    createContent();
    populateTable();
})
```

Usually, I write code so that it is easy to understand, but that is not the case for this JavaScript code, which uses the browser's Domain Object Model (DOM) API to create a simple table, which is populated with data from the API controller. This is not a book about JavaScript, and I don't describe how it works because the parts that are important for this chapter are all contained in the network.js file.

To deliver the JavaScript code to the browser, add a Razor Page named JSClient.cshtml to the Pages folder with the content shown in Listing 12-4.

Listing 12-4. The Contents of the JSClient.cshtml File in the Pages Folder

```
@page

<div id="target" class="m-3">
    Loading JavaScript client...
</div>
<script type="module" src="/js/client.js"></script>
```

The div element will be used to display the content generated by the JavaScript code, which is specified by the script element.

Open a new PowerShell command prompt and run the commands shown in Listing 12-5 to reset the application and Identity databases.

Listing 12-5. Resetting the Databases

```
dotnet ef database drop --force --context ProductDbContext
dotnet ef database drop --force --context IdentityDbContext
dotnet ef database update --context ProductDbContext
dotnet ef database update --context IdentityDbContext
```

Use the PowerShell prompt to run the command shown in Listing 12-6 in the IdentityApp folder to start the application.

Listing 12-6. Running the Example Application

```
dotnet run
```

Open a web browser, request `https://localhost:44350/Identity/Admin`, and sign in as `admin@ example.com` using `mysecret` as the password. When you sign in, you will be redirected o the administration dashboard. Click the Seed Database, which will update the dashboard to indicate there are four users in the store, as shown in Figure 12-1.

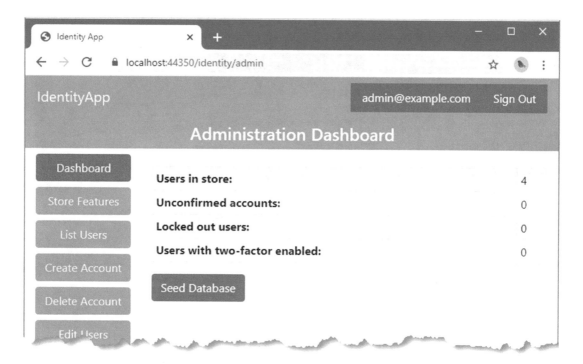

Figure 12-1. *Running the example application*

Request `https://localhost:44350/jsclient` and you will see the output from the JavaScript client, as shown in Figure 12-2.

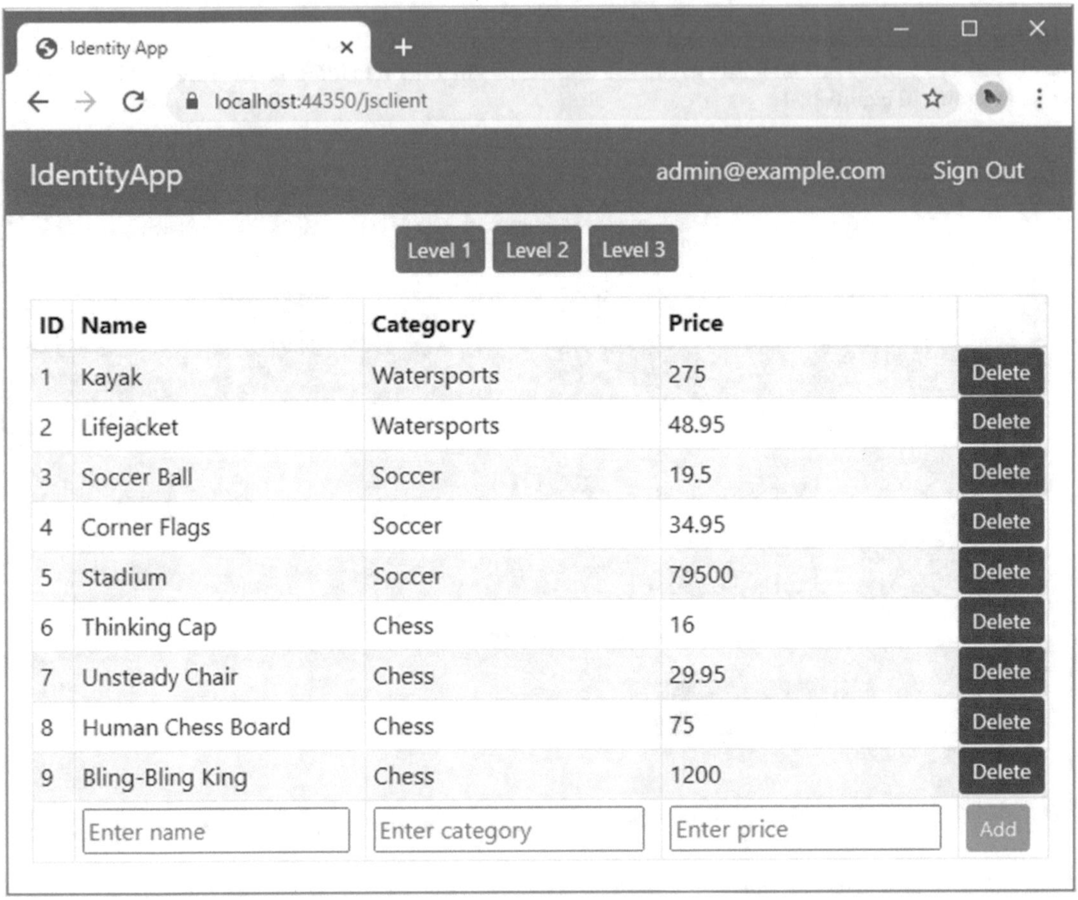

Figure 12-2. *The JavaScript API client*

Using Simple Authentication for JavaScript Clients

The easiest way to restrict access to API controllers is to rely on the standard ASP.NET Core and Identity features used in earlier chapters. This approach has some drawbacks, which I explain shortly, but it has the advantage of allowing JavaScript clients to benefit from authentication and authorization without needing to handle any of the details directly.

To demonstrate, Listing 12-7 decorates the API controller with the Authorize attribute, which will allow only signed-in users to access the actions defined by the web service controller.

Listing 12-7. Restricting Access in the ValuesController.cs File in the Controllers Folder

```
using IdentityApp.Models;
using Microsoft.AspNetCore.Mvc;
using System.Collections.Generic;
using System.ComponentModel.DataAnnotations;
using System.Threading.Tasks;
using Microsoft.AspNetCore.Authorization;
```

```
namespace IdentityApp.Controllers {

    [Authorize]
    [ApiController]
    [Route("/api/data")]
    public class ValuesController : ControllerBase {
        private ProductDbContext DbContext;

        // ...methods omitted for brevity...
    }

    public class ProductBindingTarget {
        [Required]
        public string Name { get; set; }

        [Required]
        public decimal Price { get; set; }

        [Required]
        public string Category { get; set; }
    }
}
```

This technique requires the same restriction to be applied to the Razor Page or action method that contains the `script` element for the JavaScript code, as shown in Listing 12-8.

Listing 12-8. Restricting Access in the JSClient.cshtml File in the Pages Folder

```
@page
@model IdentityApp.Pages.JSClientModel
@attribute [Microsoft.AspNetCore.Authorization.Authorize]

<div id="target" class="m-3">
    Loading JavaScript client...
</div>

<script type="module" src="/js/client.js"></script>
```

Restart ASP.NET Core and request `https://localhost:44350/jsclient`. Sign in as `alice@example.com` with the password `mysecret` and you will be redirected to the page that contains the JavaScript code, which will request the data from the API controller, as shown in Figure 12-3.

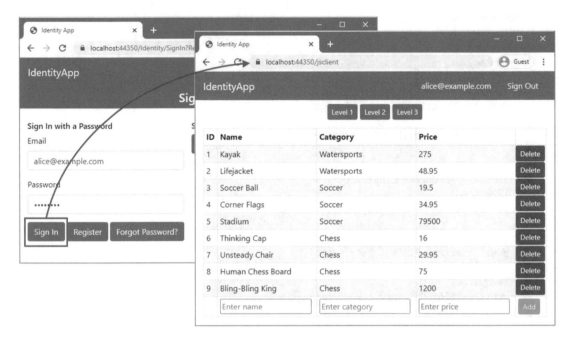

Figure 12-3. *Using the standard authentication cookie for API authorization*

When the user signs in, ASP.NET Core adds a cookie to the response that is included in future requests, including those made by the JavaScript code. ASP.NET Core doesn't differentiate between requests initiated directly by the user and requests initiated by JavaScript code and authenticates and authorizes them in the same way.

This approach works with almost no effort, but it can only be used for JavaScript applications that are delivered using ASP.NET Core and expect authentication to be handled for them. This approach doesn't work for JavaScript clients that expect to handle authentication directly, because the only way to sign in to the application is by submitting a form that is rendered by a Razor Page. You could write a JavaScript client that submits form data, but it is easier to create an authentication API as I demonstrate later in this chapter.

Using standard authentication and authorization for API clients isn't as terrible as it may seem. It is suitable for projects where the JavaScript and ASP.NET Core parts of the application are developed side by side and you know that the JavaScript client will always be able to rely on an ASP.NET Core cookie. Despite its limitations, this scenario covers a lot of projects, and you shouldn't dismiss it out of hand. Any situation in which you can deliver your project requirements without any additional effort counts as a win.

Returning Status Code Responses for API Clients

API clients typically expect web services to follow the broad principles of Representational State Transfer (REST) and use HTTP status codes to indicate the outcome of operations. That isn't what ASP.NET Core does by default because it wants to present meaningful HTML content to the user, even—or especially—when there is a problem.

To see the problem this causes, open a PowerShell command prompt, and run the command shown in Listing 12-9 to send an HTTP request to the web service.

Listing 12-9. Sending an HTTP request

```
Invoke-WebRequest -Uri https://localhost:44350/api/data
```

This command sends an HTTP GET request to the API controller, using the same URL as the JavaScript client. The request sent by the command doesn't include an authentication cookie and so ASP.NET Core generates a challenge response. However, because ASP.NET Core is expecting to present content to a user, the challenge response is intercepted and replaced with a redirection that instructs the browser to request the sign-in page, which can be seen in the output from the command.

```
...
StatusCode      : 200
StatusDescription : OK
Content         :
                  <!DOCTYPE html>
                  <html>
                  <head>
                      <meta name="viewport" content="width=device-width" />
                      <title>Identity App</title>
                      <link href="/lib/twitter-bootstrap/css/bootstrap.min.css"
...
```

The results are inconsistent and depend on the client that made the request. Some clients follow the redirection and end up with a 200 OK response that contains the HTML for the sign-in pace—this is what happens with the command in Listing 12-9. Clients that expect an HTTP status code response will believe the request succeeded because they received a 200 status code. This type of client will often attempt to parse the HTML response as JSON data and encounter an error.

Other clients won't follow the redirection but are equally stuck because they have no way to get the data they require, and the redirection response doesn't provide any information about what to do to resolve the issue.

To make matters worse, some requests will receive a status code response. Use the PowerShell command prompt to run the command shown in Listing 12-10. Make sure the entire command is on a single line.

Listing 12-10. Sending an HTTP Request with a Header

```
Invoke-WebRequest -Uri https://localhost:44350/api/data -Headers @{"X-Requested-
With"="XMLHttpRequest"}
```

This command sends a GET request to the same URL but with the addition of a header named X-Requested-With with a value of XMLHttpRequest. The response from ASP.NET Core is a 401 status code response, like this:

```
...
Invoke-WebRequest : The remote server returned an error: (401) Unauthorized.
...
```

The XMLHttpRequest header value refers to the JavaScript object with the same name, which is the traditional way to make HTTP requests in client-side applications. Some browsers and JavaScript frameworks set the X-Requested-With header to XMLHttpRequest to help servers identify HTTP requests made with JavaScript code. Unfortunately, you can't rely on this header being set because the Fetch API has been introduced as a modern alternative to the XmlHttpRequest object (Fetch is the API I used in the example JavaScript client) and because not all browsers and frameworks set the header even when XmlHttpRequest is being used.

To change how API clients are handled by the example application, add the statement shown in Listing 12-11 to the Startup class. (The method called by this statement has not yet been defined, so you will see an error in the code editor.)

Listing 12-11. Handling API Clients in the Startup.cs File in the IdentityApp Folder

```
...
services.ConfigureApplicationCookie(opts => {
    opts.LoginPath = "/Identity/SignIn";
    opts.LogoutPath = "/Identity/SignOut";
    opts.AccessDeniedPath = "/Identity/Forbidden";
    opts.Events.DisableRedirectionForApiClients();
});
...
```

The CookieAuthenticationOptions class defines an Events property, which returns an CookieAuthenticationEvents object that allows handlers to be defined for key events during authentication and authorization. There are four properties for dealing with API clients, as described in Table 12-3.

Table 12-3. *The CookieAuthenticationEvents Event Handler Properties for API Clients*

Name	Description
OnRedirectToLogin	This property is assigned a handler that is called when the user should be redirected to the sign-in URL. The default handler sends a status code response for requests with the X-Requested-With header and performs the redirection for all other requests.
OnRedirectToAccessDenied	This property is assigned a handler that is called when the user should be redirected to the access denied URL. The default handler sends a status code response for requests with the X-Requested-With header and performs the redirection for all other requests.
OnRedirectToLogout	This property is assigned a handler that is called when the user should be redirected to the sign-out URL. The default handler sends a 200 OK response with a Location header set to the sign-out URL and performs the redirection for all other requests.
OnRedirectToReturnUrl	This property is assigned a handler that is called when the user should be redirected to the URL that triggered a challenge response. The default handler sends a 200 OK response with a Location header set to the sign-out URL and performs the redirection for all other requests.

The handler functions assigned to the properties described in Table 12-3 receive an instance of the RedirectContext<CookieAuthenticationOptions> class, whose most useful properties are described in Table 12-4.

Table 12-4. *Useful RedirectContext<CookieAuthenticationOptions> Properties*

Name	Description
HttpContext	This property returns the HttpContext object for the current request.
Request	This property returns the HttpRequest object that describes the request.
Response	This property returns the HttpRequest object that describes the response.
RedirectUri	This property returns the URL to which the user should be directed.

To define the extension method that I invoked in Listing 12-11, add a class file named CookieAuthEventsExtensions.cs to the IdentityApp folder and add the code shown in Listing 12-12.

Listing 12-12. The Contents of the CookieAuthEventsExtensions.cs File in the IdentityApp Folder

```
using Microsoft.AspNetCore.Authentication;
using Microsoft.AspNetCore.Authentication.Cookies;
using Microsoft.AspNetCore.Http;
using System.Threading.Tasks;

namespace IdentityApp {

    public static class CookieAuthEventsExtensions {

        public static void DisableRedirectionForApiClients(this
                CookieAuthenticationEvents events) {
            events.OnRedirectToLogin = ctx =>
                SelectiveRedirect(ctx, StatusCodes.Status401Unauthorized);
            events.OnRedirectToAccessDenied = ctx =>
                SelectiveRedirect(ctx, StatusCodes.Status403Forbidden);
            events.OnRedirectToLogout = ctx =>
                SelectiveRedirect(ctx, StatusCodes.Status200OK);
            events.OnRedirectToReturnUrl= ctx =>
                SelectiveRedirect(ctx, StatusCodes.Status200OK);
        }

        private static Task SelectiveRedirect(
                RedirectContext<CookieAuthenticationOptions> context, int code) {
            if (IsApiRequest(context.Request)) {
                context.Response.StatusCode = code;
                context.Response.Headers["Location"] = context.RedirectUri;
            } else {
                context.Response.Redirect(context.RedirectUri);
            }
            return Task.CompletedTask;
        }

        private static bool IsApiRequest(HttpRequest request) {
            return request.Path.StartsWithSegments("/api");
        }
    }
}
```

The `DisableRedirectionForApiClients` method assigns new handler functions to the four properties defined in Table 12-3. The outcome of each handler is the same, such that API clients are sent a status code response with a `Location` header, while other clients receive the redirection. The `Location` header provides the API client with the redirection URL without forcing them to request its contents.

The difference is the way that API clients are identified, which is done by the `IsApiRequest` method. Instead of looking for the `X-Requested-With` header, the request path is examined, and if it begins with `/api`, then the client will get status code responses. This is a shift in approach from trying to determine how the request originated to determining what the request is for: if a request is for an `/api` URL, then the client is assumed to want status code responses.

Restart ASP.NET Core and use a PowerShell prompt to run the command shown in Listing 12-13.

Listing 12-13. Sending a Request

```
Invoke-WebRequest -Uri https://localhost:44350/api/data
```

The request won't be authorized because it doesn't contain an ASP.NET Core cookie, but the code in Listing 12-12 detects the request for a URL that starts with `/api` and sends a 401 response.

```
...
Invoke-WebRequest : The remote server returned an error: (401) Unauthorized.
...
```

Authenticating API Clients Directly

Not all API clients can be delivered via an authenticated Razor Page or view and must take responsibility for handling authentication directly.

Preparing ASP.NET Core for Direct API Client Authentication

Add a class file named `ApiAuthController.cs` to the `Controllers` folder and use it to create the controller shown in Listing 12-14.

Listing 12-14. The Contents of the ApiAuthController.cs File in the Controllers Folder

```
using Microsoft.AspNetCore.Identity;
using Microsoft.AspNetCore.Mvc;
using System.ComponentModel.DataAnnotations;
using System.Threading.Tasks;
using SignInResult = Microsoft.AspNetCore.Identity.SignInResult;

namespace IdentityApp.Controllers {

    [ApiController]
    [Route("/api/auth")]
    public class ApiAuthController: ControllerBase {
        private SignInManager<IdentityUser> SignInManager;

        public ApiAuthController(SignInManager<IdentityUser> signMgr) {
            SignInManager = signMgr;
        }
```

```
[HttpPost("signin")]
public async Task<object> ApiSignIn(
        [FromBody] SignInCredentials creds) {
    SignInResult result = await SignInManager.PasswordSignInAsync(
        creds.Email, creds.Password, true, true);
    return new { success = result.Succeeded  };
}

[HttpPost("signout")]
public async Task<IActionResult> ApiSignOut() {
    await SignInManager.SignOutAsync();
    return Ok();
}
}

public class SignInCredentials {
    [Required]
    public string Email { get; set; }
    [Required]
    public string Password { get; set; }
}
}
```

There are two action methods, ApiSignIn and ApiSignOut, both of which handle POST requests. The ApiSignIn method receives an object with Email and Password properties, which are used to sign the user into the application with the sign-in manager's PasswordSignInAsync method. The ApiSignOut method signs the user out of the application using the password manager's SignOutAsync method.

These are the same methods for signing in and out that I used when creating custom HTML-based workflows, and the difference is in the responses. When signing in, the API client receives an object with a success property, which indicates whether the sign in was successful, like this:

```
...
{ "success": true }
...
```

There is no standard way to deal with API client authentication, but the advantage of this approach is that the success or failure of a sign-in attempt is defining in an object that can contain additional data, which I'll use later in this chapter when I introduce bearer token authentication.

Enabling CORS

Cross-Origin Resource Sharing (CORS) is a security mechanism to restrict JavaScript code from making requests to a domain other than the one that served the HTML page that contains it. This wasn't an issue in earlier examples because the JavaScript client was delivered by the ASP.NET Core server, so the requests to the API controller were to the same domain. For this example, I am going to use a web server running on a different port, which is sufficiently different for CORS to block the request. Add the statements shown in Listing 12-15 to configure CORS so that the requests in this section will be allowed.

Listing 12-15. Adding a CORS Policy in the Startup.cs File in the IdentityApp Folder

```
using Microsoft.AspNetCore.Builder;
using Microsoft.AspNetCore.Hosting;
using Microsoft.AspNetCore.Http;
using Microsoft.Extensions.DependencyInjection;
using Microsoft.Extensions.Hosting;
using Microsoft.Extensions.Configuration;
using Microsoft.EntityFrameworkCore;
using IdentityApp.Models;
using Microsoft.AspNetCore.Identity;
using Microsoft.AspNetCore.Identity.EntityFrameworkCore;
using Microsoft.AspNetCore.Identity.UI.Services;
using IdentityApp.Services;

namespace IdentityApp {

    public class Startup {

        public Startup(IConfiguration config) => Configuration = config;

        private IConfiguration Configuration { get; set; }

        public void ConfigureServices(IServiceCollection services) {

            // ...statements omitted for brevity...

            services.ConfigureApplicationCookie(opts => {
                opts.LoginPath = "/Identity/SignIn";
                opts.LogoutPath = "/Identity/SignOut";
                opts.AccessDeniedPath = "/Identity/Forbidden";
                opts.Events.DisableRedirectionForApiClients();
            });

            services.AddCors(opts => {
                opts.AddDefaultPolicy(builder => {
                    builder.WithOrigins("http://localhost:5100")
                        .AllowAnyHeader()
                        .AllowAnyMethod()
                        .AllowCredentials();
                });
            });
        }

        public void Configure(IApplicationBuilder app, IWebHostEnvironment env) {
            if (env.IsDevelopment()) {
                app.UseDeveloperExceptionPage();
            }

            app.UseHttpsRedirection();
            app.UseStaticFiles();
            app.UseRouting();
```

```
        app.UseCors();
        app.UseAuthentication();
        app.UseAuthorization();

        app.UseEndpoints(endpoints => {
            endpoints.MapDefaultControllerRoute();
            endpoints.MapRazorPages();
        });

        app.SeedUserStoreForDashboard();
    }
  }
}
```

The AddCors method defines the CORS policy for the application. The policy is defined using the options pattern, and I use the AddDefaultPolicy method to change the default policy to allow requests that originate from JavaScript code loaded from port 5100 on the local host, with any request header, method, and credentials. The UseCors method adds middleware to the request pipeline to apply the CORS policy.

Adding Authentication to the JavaScript Client

To sign in and out of the application, the JavaScript client has to send POST requests to the action methods defined by the API controller. Add the code shown in Listing 12-16 to the network.js file to define functions that send the required requests.

Listing 12-16. Adding Functions in the network.js File in the wwwroot/js Folder

```javascript
const baseUrl = "https://localhost:44350/api/data";
const authUrl = "https://localhost:44350/api/auth";

const baseRequestConfig = {
    credentials: "include"
}

export const signIn = async function (email, password, callback, errorHandler) {
    const response = await fetch(`${authUrl}/signin`, {
        ...baseRequestConfig,
        method: "POST",
        body: JSON.stringify({ email, password }),
        headers: { "Content-Type": "application/json" }
    });
    processResponse(response, async () =>
        callback(await response.json()), errorHandler);
}

export const signOut = async function (callback) {
    const response = await fetch(`${authUrl}/signout`, {
        ...baseRequestConfig,
        method: "POST"
    });
    processResponse(response, callback, callback);
}
```

337

```
export const loadData = async function (callback, errorHandler) {
    const response = await fetch(baseUrl, {
        ...baseRequestConfig,
        redirect: "manual"
    });
    processResponse(response, async () =>
        callback(await response.json()), errorHandler);
}

export const createProduct = async function (product, callback, errorHandler) {
    const response = await fetch(baseUrl, {
        ...baseRequestConfig,
        method: "POST",
        body: JSON.stringify(product),
        headers: {
            "Content-Type": "application/json"
        }
    });
    processResponse(response, callback, errorHandler);
}

export const deleteProduct = async function (id, callback, errorHandler) {
    const response = await fetch(`${baseUrl}/${id}`, {
        ...baseRequestConfig,
        method: "DELETE"
    });
    processResponse(response, callback, errorHandler);
}

function processResponse(response, callback, errorHandler) {
    if (response.ok) {
        callback();
    } else {
        errorHandler(response.status);
    }
}
```

The Fetch API that I am using to make JavaScript HTTP requests won't process cookies unless the request is configured with the credentials property set to include. This property must be set on all requests, so I have defined an object with the required setting and assigned it to a constant named baseRequestConfig, which I have incorporated into the other requests using the JavaScript destructuring feature. I have also defined two new functions: signIn is called to sign into the application, and as you might expect, the signOut function signs out of the application.

In Listing 12-17, I have added some new content to the HTML generated by the JavaScript client that signs a user in and out of the application. The user's credentials are hard-coded into the application, which should not be done for real projects but is sufficient for this example.

Listing 12-17. Adding Authentication Support in the client.js File in the wwwroot/js Folder

```
import * as network from "./network.js";

const columns = ["ID", "Name", "Category", "Price"];
let tableBody;
let errorElem;

// ...functions omitted for brevity...

function createContent() {
    const targetElement = createStructure();
    createAuthPrompt(targetElement);
    const table = targetElement.make("table");
    table.classList.add("table", "table-sm", "table-striped", "table-bordered");
    const headerRow = table.make("thead", "tr");
    columns.concat([""]).forEach(col => {
        const th = headerRow.make("th");
        th.innerText = col;
    });
    tableBody = table.make("tbody");
    const footerRow = table.make("tfoot", "tr");
    footerRow.make("td");
    columns.filter(col => col != "ID").forEach(col => {
        const input = footerRow.make("td", "input");
        input.name = input.id = col;
        input.placeholder = `Enter ${col.toLowerCase()}`;
    });
    const button = footerRow.make("td", "button");
    button.classList = "btn btn-sm btn-success";
    button.innerText = "Add";
    button.addEventListener("click", async () => {
        const product = {};
        columns.forEach(col => product[col] = document.getElementById(col)?.value);
        await network.createProduct(product, populateTable, showError);
    });
}

function createAuthPrompt(targetElement) {
    let signedIn = false;
    const container = targetElement.make("div");
    container.classList.add("m-2", "p-2", "text-center");
    const status = container.make("span");
    status.innerText = "Not signed in";
    const button = container.make("button");
    button.classList.add("btn", "btn-sm", "btn-secondary", "m-2");
    button.innerText = "Sign In";
    button.addEventListener("click", async () => {
        if (!signedIn) {
            await network.signIn("alice@example.com", "mysecret",
                response => {
                    if (response.success == true) {
```

```
                        signedIn = true;
                        status.innerText = "Signed in";
                        button.innerText = "Sign Out";
                        populateTable();
                    }
                }, showError);
        } else {
            await network.signOut(() => {
                signedIn = false;
                status.innerText = "Signed out";
                button.innerText = "Sign In";
                createTableContents([]);
                populateTable();
            });
        }

    });
}

// ...functions omitted for brevity...

document.addEventListener("DOMContentLoaded", () => {
    createContent();
    populateTable();
})
```

The new function displays an indicator for the sign-in status and a button that calls the signIn and signOut functions when clicked. As with the existing code in this file, the emphasis is on conciseness, and the important parts of this example are the network requests made by the JavaScript client.

This example relies on delivering the JavaScript code to the browser without using a Razor Page or view. To that end, add an HTML filename index.html to the wwwroot folder with the content shown in Listing 12-18.

Listing 12-18. The Contents of the index.html File in the wwwroot Folder

```
<!DOCTYPE html>
<html>
<head>
    <title>Identity App</title>
    <link href="/lib/twitter-bootstrap/css/bootstrap.min.css" rel="stylesheet" />
</head>
<body>
    <div id="target" class="m-3">Loading JavaScript client...</div>
    <script type="module" src="/js/client.js"></script>
</body>
</html>
```

Testing the Authentication API

Restart ASP.NET Core. Open a new command prompt and run the command shown in Listing 12-19 in the wwwroot folder to start new web server. This command relies on Node.js, which you installed in Chapter 2. If you have not installed Node.js, then you do so now.

Listing 12-19. Starting a Web Server in the wwwroot Folder

```
npx http-server -p 5100 -c-1
```

This command downloads and executes the JavaScript `http-server` package, which is a light-weight HTTP server. The arguments tell the server to listen for requests on port 5100 and to disable caching, which ensures that any changes you make to the JavaScript client will take effect the next time the browser is reloaded.

Open a new browser tab using the Guest feature so that any existing cookies won't be used. Request `http://localhost:5100`, which will send a request to the new server for the contents of the `index.html` file. The JavaScript client won't be able to populate the table with data because the ASP.NET Core API controller will return a 401 response, indicating that the request has not been authorized. Click the Sign In button, and the client will sign in and receive an ASP.NET Core cookie in the response. The request for the product data is sent again, this time with the new cookie, and the table is populated, as shown in Figure 12-4. Click the button again to sign out, and you will see another 401 error.

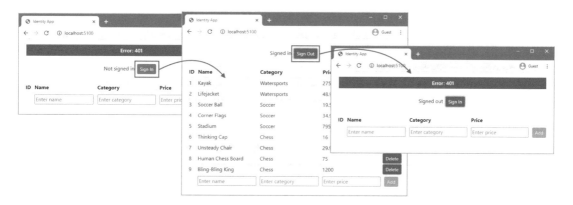

Figure 12-4. *Signing in and out with the API*

Using Bearer Tokens

You cannot rely on cookies if your API supports clients that are not browsers. Bearer tokens are strings that are provided to the client during the sign-in process and then included as a header in subsequent requests. This is essentially the same mechanism as for cookies, but the client takes responsibility for receiving the token and including it in future requests instead of relying on the browser to do the work.

When a client authenticates with the API, the response they receive will include the existing `success` property, plus a `token` that includes the value that will be included in future requests, like this:

```
...
{
  "success": true,
  "token": "eyJhbGciOiJIUzI1NiIsInR5cCI6IkpXVCJ9"
}
...
```

The token value is included in using the Authorization HTTP header in this format:

```
...
Authorization: Bearer eyJhbGciOiJIUzI1NiIsInR5cCI6IkpXVCJ9
...
```

I have shortened the token to make the formatting obvious, and real tokens are much longer. Tokens are not provided when authentication fails, in which case the response will contain just the success property, like this:

```
...
{
  "success": false
}
...
```

Configuring ASP.NET Core for JWT Bearer Tokens

Microsoft provides support for dealing with a specific type of bearer token: the JSON Web Token (JWT). This type of token is specified by RFC 7519 and is used to securely describe a set of claims. The details of JWT are not important for this chapter, where the token is simply given to the client during sign-in and included in subsequent requests. Use a PowerShell command to run the command shown in Listing 12-20 in the IdentityApp folder to install the Microsoft package that supports JWT bearer tokens.

Listing 12-20. Installing a Package

```
dotnet add package Microsoft.AspNetCore.Authentication.JwtBearer --version 5.0.0
```

Add the configuration settings shown in Listing 12-21 to the appsettings.json file. These are the settings that will be used to generate and validate bearer tokens.

Listing 12-21. Adding Configuration Settings in the appsettings.json File

```
{
  "Logging": {
    "LogLevel": {
      "Default": "Information",
      "Microsoft": "Warning",
      "Microsoft.Hosting.Lifetime": "Information"
    }
  },
  "AllowedHosts": "*",
  "ConnectionStrings": {
    "AppDataConnection": "Server=(localdb)\\MSSQLLocalDB;Database=IdentityAppData;Multiple
    ActiveResultSets=true",
    "IdentityConnection": "Server=(localdb)\\MSSQLLocalDB;Database=IdentityAppUserData;
    MultipleActiveResultSets=true"
  },
  "BearerTokens": {
    "ExpiryMins": "60",
```

```
    "Key": "mySuperSecretKey"
  }
}
```

The ExpiryMins property defines the period before tokens will expire. The Key property defines the key that is used to sign and validate tokens.

Listing 12-22 shows the changes to the Startup class that configure the application to support authentication with bearer tokens.

Listing 12-22. Enabling Token Authentication in the Startup.cs File in the IdentityApp Folder

```
using Microsoft.AspNetCore.Builder;
using Microsoft.AspNetCore.Hosting;
using Microsoft.AspNetCore.Http;
using Microsoft.Extensions.DependencyInjection;
using Microsoft.Extensions.Hosting;
using Microsoft.Extensions.Configuration;
using Microsoft.EntityFrameworkCore;
using IdentityApp.Models;
using Microsoft.AspNetCore.Identity;
using Microsoft.AspNetCore.Identity.EntityFrameworkCore;
using Microsoft.AspNetCore.Identity.UI.Services;
using IdentityApp.Services;
using Microsoft.AspNetCore.Authentication.JwtBearer;
using Microsoft.IdentityModel.Tokens;
using System.Text;

namespace IdentityApp {

    public class Startup {

        public Startup(IConfiguration config) => Configuration = config;

        private IConfiguration Configuration { get; set; }

        public void ConfigureServices(IServiceCollection services) {

            // ...statements omitted for brevity...

            services.AddAuthentication()
                .AddFacebook(opts => {
                    opts.AppId = Configuration["Facebook:AppId"];
                    opts.AppSecret = Configuration["Facebook:AppSecret"];
                })
                .AddGoogle(opts => {
                    opts.ClientId = Configuration["Google:ClientId"];
                    opts.ClientSecret = Configuration["Google:ClientSecret"];
                })
                .AddTwitter(opts => {
                    opts.ConsumerKey = Configuration["Twitter:ApiKey"];
                    opts.ConsumerSecret = Configuration["Twitter:ApiSecret"];
                    opts.RetrieveUserDetails = true;
```

343

```
        }).AddJwtBearer(JwtBearerDefaults.AuthenticationScheme, opts => {
            opts.TokenValidationParameters.ValidateAudience = false;
            opts.TokenValidationParameters.ValidateIssuer = false;
            opts.TokenValidationParameters.IssuerSigningKey
                = new SymmetricSecurityKey(Encoding.UTF8.GetBytes(
                    Configuration["BearerTokens:Key"]));
        });

        // ...statements omitted for brevity...
    }

    public void Configure(IApplicationBuilder app, IWebHostEnvironment env) {

        // ...statements omitted for brevity...
    }
    }
}
```

The AddJwtBearer extension method adds an authentication handler that will use JWT tokens and use them to authenticate requests. JWT tokens are intended to securely describe claims between two parties, and there are lots of features to support that goal, both in terms of the data that a token contains and how that data is validated. When using JWT tokens to authenticate clients for an ASP.NET Core API controller, the role of the token is much simpler because the JavaScript client doesn't process the contents of the token and just treats it as an opaque block of data that is included in HTTP requests to identify the client to ASP.NET Core.

This means that I need only the most basic token features. I use the options pattern to set the ValidateAudience and ValidateIssuer properties to false, which reduces the amount of data I have to put into the token later. What is important is the ability to validate the cryptographic signature that tokens include, so I read the secret key from the configuration service and apply it using the options pattern.

```
...
opts.TokenValidationParameters.IssuerSigningKey = new SymmetricSecurityKey(
    Encoding.UTF8.GetBytes(Configuration["BearerTokens:Key"]));
...
```

Updating the API Authentication Controller

The authentication handler set up by the AddJwtBearer method will validate tokens, but the application is responsible for generating them. Listing 12-23 revises the controller that signs API clients into the application so that tokens are used instead of cookies.

Listing 12-23. Using Tokens in the ApiAuthController.cs File in the Controllers Folder

```
using Microsoft.AspNetCore.Identity;
using Microsoft.AspNetCore.Mvc;
using System.ComponentModel.DataAnnotations;
using System.Threading.Tasks;
using SignInResult = Microsoft.AspNetCore.Identity.SignInResult;
using Microsoft.Extensions.Configuration;
using System.IdentityModel.Tokens.Jwt;
using Microsoft.IdentityModel.Tokens;
using System.Linq;
```

```
using System;
using System.Text;

namespace IdentityApp.Controllers {

    [ApiController]
    [Route("/api/auth")]
    public class ApiAuthController: ControllerBase {
        private SignInManager<IdentityUser> SignInManager;
        private UserManager<IdentityUser> UserManager;
        private IConfiguration Configuration;

        public ApiAuthController(SignInManager<IdentityUser> signMgr,
                UserManager<IdentityUser> usrMgr,
                IConfiguration config) {
            SignInManager = signMgr;
            UserManager = usrMgr;
            Configuration = config;
        }

        [HttpPost("signin")]
        public async Task<object> ApiSignIn(
                [FromBody] SignInCredentials creds) {
            IdentityUser user = await UserManager.FindByEmailAsync(creds.Email);
            SignInResult result = await SignInManager.CheckPasswordSignInAsync(user,
                creds.Password, true);
            if (result.Succeeded) {
                SecurityTokenDescriptor descriptor = new SecurityTokenDescriptor {
                    Subject = (await SignInManager.CreateUserPrincipalAsync(user))
                        .Identities.First(),
                    Expires = DateTime.Now.AddMinutes(int.Parse(
                        Configuration["BearerTokens:ExpiryMins"])),
                    SigningCredentials = new SigningCredentials(
                        new SymmetricSecurityKey(Encoding.UTF8.GetBytes(
                            Configuration["BearerTokens:Key"])),
                            SecurityAlgorithms.HmacSha256Signature)
                };
                JwtSecurityTokenHandler handler = new JwtSecurityTokenHandler();
                SecurityToken secToken = new JwtSecurityTokenHandler()
                    .CreateToken(descriptor);
                return new { success = true, token = handler.WriteToken(secToken)};
            }
            return new { success = false };
        }

        //[HttpPost("signout")]
        //public async Task<IActionResult> ApiSignOut() {
        //    await SignInManager.SignOutAsync();
        //    return Ok();
        //}
    }
```

```
    public class SignInCredentials {
        [Required]
        public string Email { get; set; }
        [Required]
        public string Password { get; set; }
    }
}
```

The sign-in process has two key steps. The first step is to validate the password provided by the user. To do this without signing the user into the application, the sign-in manager's CheckPasswordSignInAsync method is used. This method operates on IdentityUser objects, which are obtained from the store from the user manager.

```
...
IdentityUser user = await UserManager.FindByEmailAsync(creds.Email);
SignInResult result = await SignInManager.CheckPasswordSignInAsync(user,
    creds.Password, true);
...
```

If the correct password has been provided, a token is created and sent back in the response. A SecurityTokenDescriptor object is created with the properties described in Table 12-5.

Table 12-5. *The SecurityTokenDescriptor Properties Used to Generate a Token*

Name	Description
Subject	This property is assigned the ClaimsIdentity object whose claims will be included in the token.
Expires	This property is used to specify the DateTime that determines when the token expires. The token won't be validated if a client presents it after this point.
SigningCredentials	This property is used to specify the algorithm and the secret key that will be used to sign the token.

The SecurityTokenDescriptor object is used to create a token using the CreateToken method defined by the JwtSecurityTokenHandler class, which is written as a string using the WriteToken method and sent in the response. Notice that I have commented out the ApiSignOut method. There is no sign-out process when using tokens, and the client simply discards the token if it is no longer required.

For quick reference, Table 12-6 describes the sign-in manager methods used to support bearer token authentication.

Table 12-6. *The SignInManager<IdentityUser> Methods to Support Bearer Tokens*

Name	Description
CheckPasswordSignInAsync(user, password, lockout)	This method checks a password for an IdentityUser object without signing the user into the application. The lockout argument specifies whether an incorrect password will count toward a lockout. Lockouts are described in Chapter 9.
CreateUserPrincipalAsync(user)	This method creates a ClaimsPrincipal object from an IdentityUser object, which is used as the data for the bearer token.

Specifying Token Authentication in the API Controller

The final server-side change is to specify that requests for the API controller should be authenticated using the token handler, as shown in Listing 12-24.

Listing 12-24. Specifying Token Authentication in the ValuesController.cs File in the Controllers Folder

```
using IdentityApp.Models;
using Microsoft.AspNetCore.Mvc;
using System.Collections.Generic;
using System.ComponentModel.DataAnnotations;
using System.Threading.Tasks;
using Microsoft.AspNetCore.Authorization;
using Microsoft.AspNetCore.Authentication.JwtBearer;

namespace IdentityApp.Controllers {

    [Authorize(AuthenticationSchemes = JwtBearerDefaults.AuthenticationScheme)]
    [ApiController]
    [Route("/api/data")]
    public class ValuesController : ControllerBase {

        // ...statements omitted for brevity...
    }

    public class ProductBindingTarget {
        [Required]
        public string Name { get; set; }

        [Required]
        public decimal Price { get; set; }

        [Required]
        public string Category { get; set; }
    }

}
```

The `AuthenticationSchemes` argument to the `Authorize` attribute is used to specify the same name that was used to set up the handler in the `Startup` class.

Updating the JavaScript Client

Now that the server-side pieces are in place, I can update the JavaScript client to receive and use bearer tokens, as shown in Listing 12-25.

Listing 12-25. Using Tokens in the network.js File in the wwwroot/js Folder

```
const baseUrl = "https://localhost:44350/api/data";
const authUrl = "https://localhost:44350/api/auth";

const baseRequestConfig = {
```

```javascript
        credentials: "include"
}

export const signIn = async function (email, password, callback, errorHandler) {
    const response = await fetch(`${authUrl}/signin`, {
        ...baseRequestConfig,
        method: "POST",
        body: JSON.stringify({ email, password }),
        headers: {
            "Content-Type": "application/json"
        }
    });

    if (response.ok) {
        let responseData = await response.json();
        if (responseData.success) {
            baseRequestConfig.headers = {
                "Authorization": `Bearer ${responseData.token}`
            }
        }
        processResponse(response, async () =>
            callback(responseData, errorHandler));
        return;
    }
    processResponse({ ok: false, status: "Auth Failed" }, async () =>
        callback(responseData), errorHandler);
}

export const signOut = async function (callback) {
    //const response = await fetch(`${authUrl}/signout`, {
    //    ...baseRequestConfig,
    //    method: "POST"
    //});
    baseRequestConfig.headers = {};
    processResponse({ ok: true }, callback, callback);
}

export const loadData = async function (callback, errorHandler) {
    const response = await fetch(baseUrl, {
        ...baseRequestConfig,
        redirect: "manual"
    });
    processResponse(response, async () =>
        callback(await response.json()), errorHandler);
}

export const createProduct = async function (product, callback, errorHandler) {
    const response = await fetch(baseUrl, {
        ...baseRequestConfig,
        method: "POST",
        body: JSON.stringify(product),
```

```
        headers: {
            ...baseRequestConfig.headers,
            "Content-Type": "application/json"
        }
    });
    processResponse(response, callback, errorHandler);
}

export const deleteProduct = async function (id, callback, errorHandler) {
    const response = await fetch(`${baseUrl}/${id}`, {
        ...baseRequestConfig,
        method: "DELETE"
    });
    processResponse(response, callback, errorHandler);
}

function processResponse(response, callback, errorHandler) {
    if (response.ok) {
        callback();
    } else {
        errorHandler(response.status);
    }
}
```

The signIn function processes successful responses to get the token, which is added as a header to the object used to configure the requests. The signOut function has been updated to remove the header from the configuration object, which discards the token when the user wants to sign out. An adjustment is required to the createProduct function so that the header required to set the content type of the request is added to the headers defined by the base configuration object.

Testing Token Authentication

Restart ASP.NET Core and restart the HTTP server using the command shown in Listing 12-19. Once both servers have started, use your browser's guest mode to request http://localhost:5100, which will ensure that ASP.NET Core authentication cookies from earlier examples are not used in the authentication process. Even though the mechanism used to authenticate the JavaScript client has changed, the user experience remains the same. The initial request fails because it doesn't include a token. Clicking the Sign In button sends a request to obtain a token, which is used to make another request for the data. Clicking the Sign Out button discards the token, causing the data request to fail, as shown in Figure 12-5.

Figure 12-5. *Authenticating using a bearer token*

Summary

In this chapter, I explained how to authenticate API clients. I explained how to take advantage of the standard ASP.NET Core authentication cookie for quick and easy API authentication. Not all projects can use this approach, so I also explained how to obtain a cookie directly and how to use bearer tokens, which are useful for clients that don't support cookies. In the next part of this book, I revisit the features provided by the Identity API and explain how they work in detail.

PART II

■ ■ ■

Understanding ASP.NET Core Identity

CHAPTER 13

Creating the Example Project

In Part 1, I focused on explaining how to use Identity. In this part of the book, I explain how Identity works, revisiting the major features and describing what happens behind the scenes. I create custom user role stores, use custom user and role classes, and implement many of the interfaces that ASP.NET Core Identity uses.

In this chapter, I create a simple example project that is used in the chapters that follow. I use this project to explain how ASP.NET Core approaches authentication and authorization and how Identity builds on those features.

Creating the Project

Open a new PowerShell command prompt from the Windows Start menu and run the commands shown in Listing 13-1.

Tip You can download the example project for this chapter—and for all the other chapters in this book—from https://github.com/Apress/pro-asp.net-core-identity. See Chapter 1 for how to get help if you have problems running the examples.

Listing 13-1. Creating the Project

```
dotnet new globaljson --sdk-version 5.0.100 --output ExampleApp
dotnet new web --no-https --output ExampleApp --framework net5.0
dotnet new sln -o ExampleApp

dotnet sln ExampleApp add ExampleApp
```

Open the project for editing and make the changes shown in Listing 13-2 to the launchSettings.json file in the Properties folder to set the port that will be used to handle HTTP and requests.

Listing 13-2. Configuring HTTP Ports in the launchSettings.json File in the Properties Folder

```
{
  "iisSettings": {
    "windowsAuthentication": false,
    "anonymousAuthentication": true,
    "iisExpress": {
      "applicationUrl": "http://localhost:5000",
      "sslPort": 0
    }
```

```
    },
    "profiles": {
      "IIS Express": {
        "commandName": "IISExpress",
        "launchBrowser": true,
        "environmentVariables": {
          "ASPNETCORE_ENVIRONMENT": "Development"
        }
      },
      "IdentityApp": {
        "commandName": "Project",
        "dotnetRunMessages": "true",
        "launchBrowser": true,
        "applicationUrl": "http://localhost:5000",
        "environmentVariables": {
          "ASPNETCORE_ENVIRONMENT": "Development"
        }
      }
    }
}
```

Installing the Bootstrap CSS Framework

Use a command prompt to run the commands shown in Listing 13-3 in the ExampleApp folder to initialize the Library Manager tool and install the Bootstrap CSS package, which I use to style HTML content.

Listing 13-3. Installing the Client-Side CSS Package

```
dotnet tool uninstall --global Microsoft.Web.LibraryManager.Cli
dotnet tool install --global Microsoft.Web.LibraryManager.Cli --version 2.1.113
libman init -p cdnjs
libman install twitter-bootstrap@4.5.0 -d wwwroot/lib/twitter-bootstrap
```

Configuring Razor Pages

Create the ExampleApp/Pages folder and add to it a Razor View Imports file named _ViewImports.cshtml with the contents shown in Listing 13-4.

Listing 13-4. The Contents of the _ViewImports.cshtml File in the Pages Folder

```
@namespace ExampleApp.Pages
@addTagHelper *, Microsoft.AspNetCore.Mvc.TagHelpers
@using Microsoft.AspNetCore.Mvc.RazorPages
```

Add a Razor View Start file named _ViewStart.cshtml to the Pages folder with the content shown in Listing 13-5.

Listing 13-5. The Contents of the _ViewStart.cshtml File in the ExampleApp/Pages Folder

```
@{
    Layout = "_Layout";
}
```

Create the Pages/Shared folder and add to it a Razor Layout named _Layout.cshtml with the contents shown in Listing 13-6.

Listing 13-6. The Contents of the _Layout.cshtml File in the Pages/Shared Folder

```
<!DOCTYPE html>

<html>
<head>
    <meta name="viewport" content="width=device-width" />
    <title>ExampleApp</title>
    <link href="/lib/twitter-bootstrap/css/bootstrap.min.css" rel="stylesheet" />
</head>
<body>
    <div>
        @RenderBody()
    </div>
</body>
</html>
```

Add a Razor Page named Test.cshtml to the Pages folder with the content shown in Listing 13-7.

Listing 13-7. The Contents of the Test.cshtml File in the Pages Folder

```
@page

<h4 class="bg-primary m-2 p-2 text-white text-center">
    Example App Razor Page
</h4>
```

This Razor Page will be used to ensure that the project is correctly configured and that the HTML content is styled using the Bootstrap CSS framework.

Configuring the MVC Framework

I use Razor Pages when I need something simple and self-contained. For more complex features, I prefer to use the MVC Framework. Create the ExampleApp/Controllers folder and add to it a class file named HomeController.cs with the code shown in Listing 13-8.

Listing 13-8. The Contents of the HomeController.cs File in the Controllers Folder

```
using Microsoft.AspNetCore.Mvc;

namespace ExampleApp.Controllers {

    public class HomeController: Controller {
```

```
        public IActionResult Test() => View();
    }
}
```

The Home controller defines an action named Test that renders its default view. Create the ExampleApp/ Views folder and add to it a Razor View Imports file named _ViewImports.cshtml with the contents shown in Listing 13-9.

Listing 13-9. The Contents of the _ViewImports.cshtml File in the Views Folder

```
@addTagHelper *, Microsoft.AspNetCore.Mvc.TagHelpers
```

Add a Razor View Start file named _ViewStart.cshtml to the Views folder with the content shown in Listing 13-10.

Listing 13-10. The Contents of the _ViewStart.cshtml File in the Views Folder

```
@{
    Layout = "_Layout";
}
```

Create the Views/Home folder and add to it a Razor View (using the Razor View – Empty template in Visual Studio) named Test.cshtml with the content shown in Listing 13-11.

Listing 13-11. The Contents of the Test.cshtml File in the Views/Home Folder

```
@model string

<h4 class="bg-primary m-2 p-2 text-white text-center">
    @(Model ?? "Example App Controller")
</h4>
```

Configuring the Application

The final step is to configure ASP.NET Core to enable Razor Pages, the MVC Framework, and the features that support them. Replace the contents of the Startup.cs file with the code shown in Listing 13-12.

Listing 13-12. Configuring the Application in the Startup.cs File in the ExampleApp Folder

```
using Microsoft.AspNetCore.Builder;
using Microsoft.AspNetCore.Hosting;
using Microsoft.AspNetCore.Http;
using Microsoft.Extensions.DependencyInjection;

namespace ExampleApp {
    public class Startup {

        public void ConfigureServices(IServiceCollection services) {
            services.AddRazorPages();
            services.AddControllersWithViews();
        }
```

```
public void Configure(IApplicationBuilder app, IWebHostEnvironment env) {
    app.UseDeveloperExceptionPage();
    app.UseStaticFiles();
    app.UseRouting();

    app.UseEndpoints(endpoints => {
        endpoints.MapGet("/", async context => {
            await context.Response.WriteAsync("Hello World!");
        });
        endpoints.MapRazorPages();
        endpoints.MapDefaultControllerRoute();
    });
}
}
}
```

This configuration enables Razor Pages and the MVC Framework and adds support for serving static files, which is required for the CSS stylesheet added to the project in Listing 13-12 and used in the layouts for HTML content.

Testing the Application

Run the command shown in Listing 13-13 in the ExampleApp folder to start ASP.NET Core and wait for HTTP requests.

Listing 13-13. Starting the Application

```
dotnet run
```

Open a new browser window and request http://localhost:5000; you will see the response shown in Figure 13-1, which uses the placeholder code added to projects when they are created using the command in Listing 13-1.

Figure 13-1. *The default application response*

Next, request http://localhost:5000/test and http://localhost:5000/home/test, which will produce the responses shown in Figure 13-2, confirming that Razor Pages and the MVC Framework are working.

Figure 13-2. *Responses from Razor Pages and the MVC Framework*

Summary

In this chapter, I created the example project that I use throughout this part of the book. In the next chapter, I explain how the ASP.NET Core platform approaches request authentication.

CHAPTER 14

■ ■ ■

Working with ASP.NET Core

The examples in this chapter show the same simple authentication and authorization policy implemented in different ways. This may seem repetitive, but I start with a completely custom solution and finish with one that is expressed in just a few code statements, with each iteration using less custom code and more of the built-in features that ASP.NET Core provides.

In this part of the book, I reintroduce terms and concepts that are also described in Part 1 so that you can more easily find the information you need if you have to refer to a chapter in the future.

The objective of this chapter is to show you how requests flow through ASP.NET Core, which provides an important foundation for understanding how Identity works, as described in later chapters. Table 14-1 puts the creation of custom authorization and authentication in context.

Table 14-1. Putting Custom Authorization and Authentication in Context

Question	Answer
What is it?	Custom authentication and authorization work directly with the request pipeline to inspect and evaluate requests.
Why is it useful?	The request pipeline is at the heart of ASP.NET Core, and its features provide the foundation for ASP.NET Core Identity.
How is it used?	Middleware is added to the pipeline that can inspect and modify requests and generate responses. You can write custom middleware for every aspect of an application's operation, but Microsoft provides built-in features, which means this is not required for most projects.
Are there any pitfalls or limitations?	There is no real advantage in writing custom code, other than to understand how ASP.NET Core functions.
Are there any alternatives?	Custom authentication and authorization should not be used in real projects because Microsoft provides ready-to-use alternatives.

© Adam Freeman 2021
A. Freeman, *Pro ASP.NET Core Identity*, https://doi.org/10.1007/978-1-4842-6858-2_14

Table 14-2 summarizes the chapter.

Table 14-2.. *Chapter Summary*

Problem	Solution	Listing
Handle requests in ASP.NET Core	Add a middleware component to the request pipeline.	1–2
Authenticate a request	Create a ClaimsPrincipal object that describes the user's identity.	4–6
Supplement the information known about a user	Add a middleware component that expresses the supplemental information as claims.	7–9
Determine if a request should be granted access to the resource it targets	Assess the claims associated with the request to see if they meet the expected user characteristics.	10–11
Remove the need for the credentials to be required for every request	Create a middleware component that creates a token—such as a cookie—that can be presented in subsequent requests.	12–14, 18–27
Define authorization policies in endpoints	Use the Authorize attribute and create an implementation of the IAuthorizationHandler interface.	15–17

Preparing for This Chapter

This chapter uses the ExampleApp project created in Chapter 13. Most of the features I describe in this chapter are provided by the ASP.NET Core platform and not Razor Pages or the MVC Framework. To maintain focus, I disable all but the essential features and reintroduce them later.

■ **Tip** You can download the example project for this chapter—and for all the other chapters in this book—from https://github.com/Apress/pro-asp.net-core-identity. See Chapter 1 for how to get help if you have problems running the examples.

Add a class file named SecretEndpoint.cs to the ExampleApp folder and add the code shown in Listing 14-1.

Listing 14-1. The Contents of the SecretEndpoint.cs File in the ExampleApp Folder

```
using Microsoft.AspNetCore.Http;
using System.Threading.Tasks;

namespace ExampleApp {

    public class SecretEndpoint {

        public static async Task Endpoint(HttpContext context) {
            await context.Response.WriteAsync("This is the secret message");
        }
    }
}
```

Replace the contents of the Startup.cs file with the code shown in Listing 14-2, which enables only the most basic ASP.NET Core features.

Listing 14-2. Configuring the Application in the Startup.cs File in the ExampleApp Folder

```
using Microsoft.AspNetCore.Builder;
using Microsoft.AspNetCore.Hosting;
using Microsoft.AspNetCore.Http;
using Microsoft.Extensions.DependencyInjection;

namespace ExampleApp {
    public class Startup {

        public void ConfigureServices(IServiceCollection services) {
        }

        public void Configure(IApplicationBuilder app, IWebHostEnvironment env) {

            app.UseRouting();

            app.UseEndpoints(endpoints => {
                endpoints.MapGet("/", async context => {
                    await context.Response.WriteAsync("Hello World!");
                });
                endpoints.MapGet("/secret", SecretEndpoint.Endpoint)
                    .WithDisplayName("secret");
            });
        }
    }
}
```

Use the command prompt to run the command shown in Listing 14-3, which will compile and start the project.

Listing 14-3. Running the Example Project

```
dotnet run
```

Once the ASP.NET Core HTTP server has started, open a new browser window and request http://localhost:5000 and http://localhost:5000/secret. You will see the responses shown in Figure 14-1.

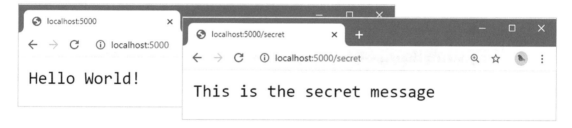

Figure 14-1. Running the example project

Understanding the ASP.NET Core Request Flow

The ASP.NET Core platform creates three objects when it receives an HTTP request: an HttpRequest object that describes the request, an HttpResponse object that describes the response that will be returned to the client, and an HttpContext object that provides access to ASP.NET Core features.

To process the request, ASP.NET Core passes the HttpContext, HttpRequest, and HttpResponse objects to its *middleware components*. Middleware components use the objects to inspect or modify the request and contribute to the response. The middleware components are arranged in a sequence, known as the *request pipeline*, and the ASP.NET Core objects are passed to the ASP.NET Core objects in order. Once the request gets to the last component in the pipeline, the objects are passed back along the line until they return to the start, at which point ASP.NET Core uses the HttpResponse object to send the response to the client, as shown in Figure 14-2.

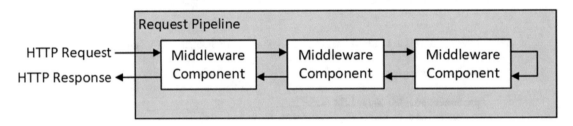

Figure 14-2. *ASP.NET Core request handling*

Understanding the Endpoint Routing Middleware

Middleware components can be as simple as a single function or as complex as a complete framework. The changes to the Startup class in Listing 14-2 defines a pipeline with two related middleware components.

```
using Microsoft.AspNetCore.Builder;
using Microsoft.AspNetCore.Hosting;
using Microsoft.AspNetCore.Http;
using Microsoft.Extensions.DependencyInjection;

namespace ExampleApp {
    public class Startup {

        public void ConfigureServices(IServiceCollection services) {
        }

        public void Configure(IApplicationBuilder app, IWebHostEnvironment env) {

            app.UseRouting();

            app.UseEndpoints(endpoints => {
                endpoints.MapGet("/", async context => {
                    await context.Response.WriteAsync("Hello World!");
                });
```

```
            endpoints.MapGet("/secret", SecretEndpoint.Endpoint)
                .WithDisplayName("secret");
        });
    }
  }
}
```

The highlighted statements enable *endpoint routing*, which matches requests to *endpoints*, which are functions or classes that generate responses for specific URLs. The UseRouting method sets up a middleware component that inspects the HTTP request and attempts to match its URL using one of the endpoints specified by the UseEndpoints method, which uses the selected endpoint to produce a response.

■ **Note**   When I added an endpoint in Listing 14-2, I used the WithDisplayName method, which is a useful feature that makes it easier to identify the endpoint that has been selected to produce a response.

There are two endpoints in the example application. The default endpoint responds to requests for the / URL with a Hello, World message and was added to the project when it was created. The other endpoint also responds with a text message.

```
...
app.UseEndpoints(endpoints => {
    endpoints.MapGet("/", async context => {
        await context.Response.WriteAsync("Hello World!");
    });
    endpoints.MapGet("/secret", SecretEndpoint.Endpoint)
        .WithDisplayName("secret");
});
...
```

In later examples, I replace the default endpoint with more complex ASP.NET Core features, but simple text responses are enough for now. The use of endpoint routing produces a request pipeline with three distinct phases, as shown in Figure 14-3.

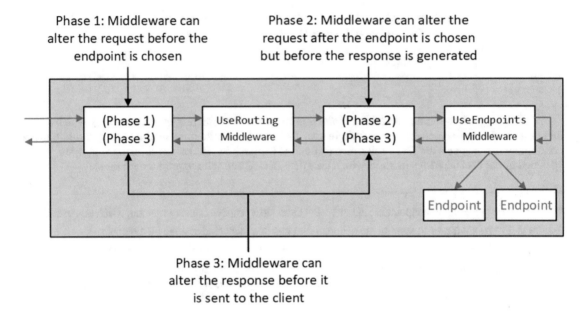

Figure 14-3. *The effect of endpoint routing on the request pipeline*

Because HTTP requests are passed along the pipeline in both directions, middleware can work alongside the endpoint routing system and provides opportunities for adding authentication and authorization to ASP.NET Core applications, as you will see shortly.

An important aspect of the ASP.NET Core request flow is that middleware components can short-circuit the pipeline and generate a response without passing on the request to the remaining components, as shown in Figure 14-4.

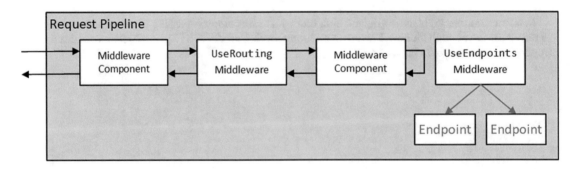

Figure 14-4. *Short-circuiting the request pipeline*

Authenticating and Authorizing Request Flow

There is a natural fit in the request flow for authentication and authorization. Providing credentials to an application can be a complex process. In most web applications, credentials are offered once and result in a token, often an HTTP cookie, that can be presented in subsequent requests. This is known as *signing in*, and invalidating the token is known as *signing out*.

Once the user is signed in, the client includes the token in requests, which allows the user to be identified as the source of the request without presenting credentials again, which is known as *authenticating the request*. Request authentication is performed as early as possible in the request pipeline, in Phase 1, so that subsequent middleware components can use or add to the information the request contains about the user.

Once request authentication has established the identity of the user, authentication middleware can be used in Phase 2 to control access to the endpoint that has been selected to produce a request. The authentication middleware has three possible responses:

1. If the user is allowed access, then do nothing, and the request will continue along the pipeline to the endpoint, which will produce a response.

2. If the request is not authenticated, short-circuit the pipeline with an HTTP 401 status code, which challenges the user to provide credentials. This is known as a *challenge* response.

3. If the request is authenticated but the user is not allowed access, short-circuit the pipeline with an HTTP 403 status code. This is known as a *forbidden* response.

Figure 14-5 shows the authentication and authorization middleware and endpoints in the request pipeline.

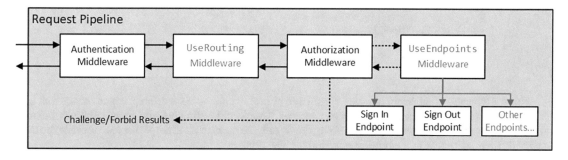

Figure 14-5. *Authentication and authorization in the request pipeline*

In many applications, the challenge and forbid responses are not just HTTP status codes but redirections to a web page that allows authentication or displays a meaningful error message. I start with status code responses and introduce HTML responses later in this chapter.

Understanding Claims

The middleware responsible for authenticating requests needs to describe a user so the authorization middleware can decide whether to send a challenge or forbidden response. ASP.NET Core provides a set of standard classes that are not specific to a single approach to authentication and that are used to consistently describe a user throughout an application.

These classes use *claims-based authentication*, which can be confusing at first because it is designed to be open and flexible and, as a result, can feel vague and ill-defined. A user is represented by a ClaimsPrincipal object. Each user can have multiple identities, which are represented by ClaimsIdentity objects. An identity contains one or more pieces of information about the user, each of which is represented by a Claim.

Create a ExampleApp/Custom folder, add to it a class file named CustomAuthentication.cs, and use it to define the middleware component shown in Listing 14-4.

Listing 14-4. The Contents of the CustomAuthentication.cs File in the Custom Folder

```
using Microsoft.AspNetCore.Http;
using System.Security.Claims;
using System.Threading.Tasks;

namespace ExampleApp.Custom {

    public class CustomAuthentication {
        private RequestDelegate next;

        public CustomAuthentication(RequestDelegate requestDelegate)
                => next = requestDelegate;

        public async Task Invoke(HttpContext context) {
            string user = context.Request.Query["user"];
            if (user != null) {
                Claim claim = new Claim(ClaimTypes.Name, user);
                ClaimsIdentity ident = new ClaimsIdentity("QueryStringValue");
                ident.AddClaim(claim);
                context.User = new ClaimsPrincipal(ident);
            }
            await next(context);
        }
    }
}
```

This middleware component handles sign-in and authentication as a single step, which means that the user needs to present their credentials for every request. This would normally be an unreasonable burden on the user, but this component does something that is only sensible in an example project: it trusts the user to provide their username in the request query string, like this:

```
...
string user = context.Request.Query["user"];
...
```

If the request contains the query string value, it is used to authenticate the request.

■ **Caution**   It should be obvious that this is not a suitable way to identify users in real projects. This part of the book is about explaining the features ASP.NET Core provides. See Part 1 for real workflows that are project-ready.

Several objects are required to authenticate the request. Claims are used to describe every piece of available information about a user, including the user's name. To that end, a Claim object is created.

```
...
Claim claim = new Claim(ClaimTypes.Name, user);
...
```

Claim objects are created with a type and a value. The ClaimTypes class provides a series of constant string values that are used to specify the claim type, which denotes the type of information the claim represents. In this case, the claim contains the username, so I have used the ClaimTypes.Name property as the type. There lots of claim types available—and you can easily create your own—but Table 14-3 lists some commonly used ClaimTypes properties.

Table 14-3. *Commonly Used Claim Types*

Name	Description
Name	This claim type denotes the user's name and is typically used for the user account name.
Role	This claim types denotes a role, which is often used for access control.
Email	This claim types denotes an email address.
GivenName	This claim type denotes the user's given name.
Surname	This claim type denotes the user's surname.

The next step is to create an identity for the user, like this:

```
...
ClaimsIdentity ident = new ClaimsIdentity("QueryStringValue");
ident.AddClaim(claim);
...
```

Individual claims are grouped together in an identity. There are no definitive rules about what an identity represents. That means there can be one identity for all a user's claims or, perhaps, multiple identities to represent how a user is known to multiple back-end systems, depending on what makes the most sense for an application.

■ **Tip** A sensible approach for most web applications is to start with a single identity and use it to group together all the user's claims. You can always add identities if need be, but that won't be required for most projects.

The ClaimsIdentity constructor accepts a string that denotes the authentication type, which I have set to QueryStringValue for this example. There is only one Claim object for the user, which I associate with the identity using the AddClaim method.

The final step is to create a ClaimsPrincipal object using the identity as an argument and assign the ClaimsPrincipal to the User property of the HttpContext object, like this:

```
...
context.User = new ClaimsPrincipal(ident);
...
```

When the middleware component in Listing 14-5 processes a request, it will check for the query string value and, if it is present, authenticate the request by creating a ClaimsPrincipal object that is passed along the request pipeline with the HttpContext object so that details of the user's claims can be processed by other middleware components.

To demonstrate how claims are handled, add a class file named ClaimsReporter.cs to the ExampleApp/ Custom folder and use it to define the middleware component shown in Listing 14-5, which writes out the claims associated with a request.

Listing 14-5. The Contents of the ClaimsReporter.cs File in the Custom Folder

```
using Microsoft.AspNetCore.Http;
using System;
using System.IO;
using System.Linq;
using System.Security.Claims;
using System.Threading.Tasks;

namespace ExampleApp.Custom {
    public class ClaimsReporter {
        private RequestDelegate next;

        public ClaimsReporter(RequestDelegate requestDelegate)
                => next = requestDelegate;

        public async Task Invoke(HttpContext context) {

            ClaimsPrincipal p = context.User;

            Console.WriteLine($"User: {p.Identity.Name}");
            Console.WriteLine($"Authenticated: {p.Identity.IsAuthenticated}");
            Console.WriteLine("Authentication Type "
                + p.Identity.AuthenticationType);

            Console.WriteLine($"Identities: {p.Identities.Count()}");
            foreach (ClaimsIdentity ident in p.Identities) {
                Console.WriteLine($"Auth type: {ident.AuthenticationType},"
                    + $" {ident.Claims.Count()} claims");
                foreach (Claim claim in ident.Claims) {
                    Console.WriteLine($"Type: {GetName(claim.Type)}, "
                        +$"Value: {claim.Value}, Issuer: {claim.Issuer}");
                }
            }
            await next(context);
        }

        private string GetName(string claimType) =>
            Path.GetFileName(new Uri(claimType).LocalPath);
    }
}
```

The code in Listing 14-5 looks more complex than it is because there are several template strings. When the middleware component receives the request, it uses the HttpContext.User property to get the ClaimsPrincipal object and writes out details to the console. The ClaimsPrincipal object defines an Identity property that returns the first identity associated with the user. The Identity property returns an object that implements the IIdentity interface, which provides basic information about the identity using the properties described in Table 14-4.

Table 14-4. *The IIdentity Properties*

Name	Description
Name	Returns the value of the identity's name claim
IsAuthenticated	Returns true if the identity has been authenticated
AuthenticationType	Returns the string that identities the source of the identity and its claims

I use the IIdentity properties to display a summary of the first identity.

```
...
Console.WriteLine($"User: {p.Identity.Name}");
Console.WriteLine($"Authenticated: {p.Identity.IsAuthenticated}");
Console.WriteLine("Authentication Type " + p.Identity.AuthenticationType);
...
```

The ClaimsPrincipal class also provides access to all the identities associated with the user and the complete set of claims, and it provides some convenience members that make access control easier, as I demonstrate later in this chapter.

```
...
Console.WriteLine($"Identities: {p.Identities.Count()}");
foreach (ClaimsIdentity ident in p.Identities) {
    Console.WriteLine($"Auth type: {ident.AuthenticationType},"
        + $" {ident.Claims.Count()} claims");
    foreach (Claim claim in ident.Claims) {
        Console.WriteLine($"Type: {GetName(claim.Type)}, "
            +$"Value: {claim.Value}, Issuer: {claim.Issuer}");
    }
}
...
```

Listing 14-6 adds both new middleware components to the request pipeline.

Listing 14-6. Adding Middleware Components in the Startup.cs File in the ExampleApp Folder

```
using Microsoft.AspNetCore.Builder;
using Microsoft.AspNetCore.Hosting;
using Microsoft.AspNetCore.Http;
using Microsoft.Extensions.DependencyInjection;
using ExampleApp.Custom;

namespace ExampleApp {
    public class Startup {

        public void ConfigureServices(IServiceCollection services) {
        }
```

```
public void Configure(IApplicationBuilder app, IWebHostEnvironment env) {

    app.UseMiddleware<CustomAuthentication>();

    app.UseRouting();

    app.UseMiddleware<ClaimsReporter>();

    app.UseEndpoints(endpoints => {
        endpoints.MapGet("/", async context => {
            await context.Response.WriteAsync("Hello World!");
        });
        endpoints.MapGet("/secret", SecretEndpoint.Endpoint)
            .WithDisplayName("secret");
    });
}
}
}
```

Restart ASP.NET Core and request http://localhost:5000/?user=Alice, and you will see the following messages displayed at the command prompt:

```
...
User: Alice
Authenticated: True
Authentication Type QueryStringValue
Identities: 1
Auth type: QueryStringValue, 1 claims
Type: name, Value: Alice, Issuer: LOCAL AUTHORITY
...
```

The properties provided by the IIdentity interface are mapped onto claims so that the IIdentity. Name property locates the claim I created in Listing 14-6, for example. By default, the source of each claim is LOCAL AUTHORITY, indicating that the data originated within the application. You will see examples of claims from other sources when I show you how to authenticate using third-party services in Chapter 23.

UNDERSTANDING CLAIM TYPE URLS

The values of the ClaimTypes properties used to create claims are URLs so that the value of the ClaimTypes.Name property, for example, is this URL:

http://schemas.xmlsoap.org/ws/2005/05/identity/claims/name

Unfortunately, this URL doesn't work, and it is difficult to get definitive descriptions of claim types and how they should be used. Consequently, claims are used inconsistently by applications, and custom claims are created freely. This can be a problem if you are trying to write code that is agnostic about the authentication systems it supports but isn't a problem in most web application projects where the development team can tailor the application to the specific claims in use.

To display the claim type in Listing 14-6, I used the .NET `Uri` and `Path` classes to process the URL and just write out the last segment of the URL path, like this:

```
...
private string GetName(string claimType) =>
            Path.GetFileName(new Uri(claimType).LocalPath);
...
```

In real projects, you will usually look for claims using the `ClaimTypes` property names, which is more convenient than dealing with the cumbersome URLs, as demonstrated in Part 1.

The `IIdentity.IsAuthenticated` property returns true if the `ClaimsIdentity` has been created with an authentication type constructor argument, like this:

```
...
ClaimsIdentity ident = new ClaimsIdentity("QueryStringValue");
...
```

It is important not to assume that a request has been authenticated just because the `HttpContext.User` property returns an object. ASP.NET Core creates a `ClaimsPrincipal` object with a `ClaimsIdentity` for all `HttpContext` objects by default, although no claims are created and no authentication type is specified, so that the `IsAuthenticated` property returns `false`.

You can see details of the default `ClaimsPrincipal` object by requesting `http://localhost:5000`, which will produce the following console output:

```
...
User:
Authenticated: False
Authentication Type
Identities: 1
Auth type: , 0 claims
...
```

This response denotes a request that has not been authenticated and for which no user information is available.

Adding Claims to a Request

Some applications have access to additional information about users that can be expressed as claims so it can be used by other middleware components. This additional information can be added to the `ClaimsPrincipal` associated with a request, either as claims added to an existing identity or as an additional identity.

Add a class file to the `ExampleApp` folder named `UsersAndClaims.cs` and add the code shown in Listing 14-7.

Listing 14-7. The Contents of the UsersAndClaims.cs File in the ExampleApp Folder

```
using System;
using System.Collections.Generic;
using System.Linq;
using System.Security.Claims;
```

```
namespace ExampleApp {
    public static class UsersAndClaims {

        public static Dictionary<string, IEnumerable<string>> UserData
            = new Dictionary<string, IEnumerable<string>> {
                { "Alice", new [] { "User", "Administrator" } },
                { "Bob", new [] { "User" } },
                { "Charlie", new [] { "User"} }
            };

        public static string[] Users => UserData.Keys.ToArray();

        public static Dictionary<string, IEnumerable<Claim>> Claims =>
            UserData.ToDictionary(kvp => kvp.Key,
                kvp => kvp.Value.Select(role => new Claim(ClaimTypes.Role, role)),
                StringComparer.InvariantCultureIgnoreCase);
    }
}
```

Next, add a class file named RoleMemberships.cs to the ExampleApp/Custom folder and use it to define the middleware component shown in Listing 14-8.

Listing 14-8. The Contents of the RoleMemberships.cs File in the Custom Folder

```
using Microsoft.AspNetCore.Http;
using System.Security.Claims;
using System.Security.Principal;
using System.Threading.Tasks;

namespace ExampleApp.Custom {

    public class RoleMemberships {
        private RequestDelegate next;

        public RoleMemberships(RequestDelegate requestDelegate)
                => next = requestDelegate;

        public async Task Invoke(HttpContext context) {
            IIdentity mainIdent = context.User.Identity;
            if (mainIdent.IsAuthenticated
                    && UsersAndClaims.Claims.ContainsKey(mainIdent.Name)) {
                ClaimsIdentity ident = new ClaimsIdentity("Roles");
                ident.AddClaim(new Claim(ClaimTypes.Name, mainIdent.Name));
                ident.AddClaims(UsersAndClaims.Claims[mainIdent.Name]);
                context.User.AddIdentity(ident);
            }
            await next(context);
        }
    }
}
```

This middleware component uses the map of usernames to roles defined in Listing 14-7. When an authenticated request is received for a user in the map, a new identity is created with role claims, denoting that the user has been granted a specific role. Listing 14-9 adds the new middleware component to the request pipeline.

Listing 14-9. Adding a Middleware Component in the Startup.cs File in the ExampleApp Folder

```
using Microsoft.AspNetCore.Builder;
using Microsoft.AspNetCore.Hosting;
using Microsoft.AspNetCore.Http;
using Microsoft.Extensions.DependencyInjection;
using ExampleApp.Custom;

namespace ExampleApp {
    public class Startup {

        public void ConfigureServices(IServiceCollection services) {
        }

        public void Configure(IApplicationBuilder app, IWebHostEnvironment env) {

            app.UseMiddleware<CustomAuthentication>();
            app.UseMiddleware<RoleMemberships>();
            app.UseRouting();

            app.UseMiddleware<ClaimsReporter>();

            app.UseEndpoints(endpoints => {
                endpoints.MapGet("/", async context => {
                    await context.Response.WriteAsync("Hello World!");
                });
                endpoints.MapGet("/secret", SecretEndpoint.Endpoint)
                    .WithDisplayName("secret");
            });
        }
    }
}
```

Restart ASP.NET Core and request `http://localhost:5000/?user=Alice`. The messages written to the console show two identities and a total of four claims.

```
...
User: Alice
Authenticated: True
Authentication Type QueryStringValue
Identities: 2
Auth type: QueryStringValue, 1 claims
Type: name, Value: Alice, Issuer: LOCAL AUTHORITY
Auth type: Roles, 3 claims
Type: name, Value: Alice, Issuer: LOCAL AUTHORITY
Type: role, Value: User, Issuer: LOCAL AUTHORITY
Type: role, Value: Administrator, Issuer: LOCAL AUTHORITY
...
```

Assessing Claims

The term *claim* reflects the fact that ASP.NET Core doesn't validate the data associated with a user and just passes it along the request pipeline. It is the responsibility of other middleware components to assess claims and decide if they should be trusted. Using query string authentication performed in the example application is dangerously insecure, for example, because it relies on users to honestly identify themselves and so claims arising from that source—and claims that are created based on the original claims—should be treated with suspicion.

Initially, however, I am going to continue as though that were not the case and assume that those claims are trustworthy and can be used for access control, just to demonstrate how claims can be used. Add a class file named CustomAuthorization.cs to the ExampleApp/Custom folder and use it to define the middleware component shown in Listing 14-10.

Listing 14-10. The Contents of the CustomAuthorization.cs File in the Custom Folder

```
using Microsoft.AspNetCore.Http;
using System.Threading.Tasks;

namespace ExampleApp.Custom {

    public class CustomAuthorization {
        private RequestDelegate next;

        public CustomAuthorization(RequestDelegate requestDelegate)
                => next = requestDelegate;

        public async Task Invoke(HttpContext context) {
            if (context.GetEndpoint()?.DisplayName == "secret") {
                if (context.User.Identity.IsAuthenticated) {
                    if (context.User.IsInRole("Administrator")) {
                        await next(context);
                    } else {
                        Forbid(context);
                    }
                } else {
                    Challenge(context);
                }
            } else {
                await next(context);
            }
        }

        public void Challenge(HttpContext context)
                => context.Response.StatusCode = StatusCodes.Status401Unauthorized;

        public void Forbid(HttpContext context)
                => context.Response.StatusCode = StatusCodes.Status403Forbidden;
    }
}
```

There are four possible outcomes when this middleware component processes a request. If the request isn't for the protected endpoint, then it is forwarded along the pipeline because there no authorization is required.

```
...
if (context.GetEndpoint()?.DisplayName == "secret") {
...
```

I use the null conditional operator (the ? character), also known as the *safe navigation operator*, to inspect the DisplayName property of the object returned by the GetEndpoint method, which returns the string assigned to the endpoint using the WithDisplayName method I used in Listing 14-11. No authorization is required if there is no endpoint or the endpoint's display name isn't secret and the request can be passed on.

If there is an endpoint and it has the right name, then I can check to see if the request has been authenticated.

```
...
if (context.User.Identity.IsAuthenticated) {
...
```

I am not checking the source of the authentication in this example. This is a commonly used approach in web applications that use ASP.NET Core Identity and where there is a single trustworthy source of authentication.

If the request has been authenticated, I check to see there is a claim for the Administrator role.

```
...
if (context.User.IsInRole("Administrator")) {
...
```

The IsInRole method is one of several useful methods defined by the ClaimsPrincipal class that work on all claims, regardless of which identity they are associated with, as described in Table 14-5.

Table 14-5. Useful ClaimsPrincipal Methods

Name	Description
FindAll(type)	This method locates all claims with the specified type. There is a version of this method that accepts a predicate function to select claims.
FindFirst(type)	This method locates the first claim with the specified type. There is a version of this method that accepts a predicate function to select a claim.
HasClaim(type, value)	This method returns true if there is a claim with the specified type and value. There is a version of this method that accepts a predicate function to check claims.
IsInRole(role)	This method returns true if there is a claim for the specified role. Identities can be configured with different claim types for roles, but the default type is ClaimTypes.Role.

If there is an Administrator role claim present, then the request is forwarded along the pipeline so that the protected endpoint can generate a response.

The remaining outcomes short-circuit the request pipeline and denote an authorization failure. A *challenge response* is sent when the request has not been authenticated.

```
...
public void Challenge(HttpContext context)
        => context.Response.StatusCode = StatusCodes.Status401Unauthorized;
...
```

A *forbid response* is sent when the request is authenticated but there is no Administrator role claim.

```
...
public void Forbid(HttpContext context)
    => context.Response.StatusCode = StatusCodes.Status403Forbidden;
...
```

The separate Challenge and Forbid methods will help make later examples clearer as I improve the way that the example application deals with authentication and authorization.

UNDERSTANDING THE 401 AND 403 HTTP STATUS CODES

The way I have used the 401 and 403 status codes matches the built-in features that ASP.NET Core provides, which you will see in later examples. Not all frameworks and applications use these status codes in the same way, and you will often find the 401 HTTP status code is used both for challenge and forbidden responses.

When sending a 401 response, the HTTP specification requires the use of the WWW-Authenticate header, which tells clients how they should authenticate users. I did not set this header, partly for simplicity and partly because the application does not authenticate users in a standard way.

Listing 14-11 adds the authorization middleware to the request pipeline.

Listing 14-11. Adding Middleware in the Startup.cs File in the ExampleApp Folder

```
using Microsoft.AspNetCore.Builder;
using Microsoft.AspNetCore.Hosting;
using Microsoft.AspNetCore.Http;
using Microsoft.Extensions.DependencyInjection;
using ExampleApp.Custom;

namespace ExampleApp {
    public class Startup {

        public void ConfigureServices(IServiceCollection services) {
        }

        public void Configure(IApplicationBuilder app, IWebHostEnvironment env) {

            app.UseMiddleware<CustomAuthentication>();
            app.UseMiddleware<RoleMemberships>();
            app.UseRouting();
```

```
app.UseMiddleware<ClaimsReporter>();
app.UseMiddleware<CustomAuthorization>();

app.UseEndpoints(endpoints => {
    endpoints.MapGet("/", async context => {
        await context.Response.WriteAsync("Hello World!");
    });
    endpoints.MapGet("/secret", SecretEndpoint.Endpoint)
        .WithDisplayName("secret");
});
        }
    }
}
```

Restart ASP.NET Core and request http://localhost:5000/secret?user=alice. The custom middleware components will authenticate the request and add an Administrator role claim, which will allow the request to be authorized.

Request http://localhost:5000/secret?user=bob, and you will receive a forbidden response because the request is authenticated but doesn't have the required role claim. Request http://localhost:5000/secret, and you will receive the challenge response because the request is not authenticated. Figure 14-6 shows all three responses.

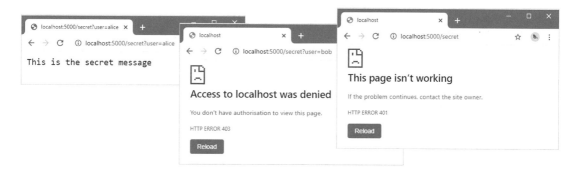

Figure 14-6. *Using custom middleware*

Improving the Authentication and Authorization

The example application has working authentication and authorization, but it is awkward to use. In the sections that follow, I improve the implementation and take advantage of more of the features that ASP.NET Core provides.

Signing In and Out of the Application

Even in my rudimentary system, providing credentials through the query string for every request is awkward. In most projects, there is an endpoint that allows the user to sign in to the application and receive a token in return. This token, which is often an HTTP cookie, is included in subsequent HTTP requests and used to authenticate requests. Another endpoint allows the user to sign out by invalidating the token so that it cannot be used again.

To allow users to sign in and out of the example application, add a class named
CustomSignInAndSignOut.cs to the ExampleApp/Custom folder and add the code shown in Listing 14-12.

Listing 14-12. The Contents of the CustomSignInandSignOut.cs File in the Custom Folder

```
using Microsoft.AspNetCore.Http;
using System.Threading.Tasks;

namespace ExampleApp.Custom {
    public class CustomSignInAndSignOut {

        public static async Task SignIn(HttpContext context) {
            string user = context.Request.Query["user"];
            if (user != null) {
                context.Response.Cookies.Append("authUser", user);
                await context.Response
                    .WriteAsync($"Authenticated user: {user}");
            } else {
                context.Response.StatusCode = StatusCodes.Status401Unauthorized;
            }
        }

        public static async Task SignOut(HttpContext context) {
            context.Response.Cookies.Delete("authUser");
            await context.Response.WriteAsync("Signed out");
        }
    }
}
```

The SignIn method will be an endpoint that gets the username from the query string and adds a cookie
to the response containing the name, which the client will then include in subsequent requests. This is no
more secure than earlier examples because it still trusts the user to honestly identify themselves, but it is
more convenient and easier to use.

The SignOut method in Listing 14-12 will also be used as an endpoint. This method deletes the cookie
so that subsequent requests cannot be authenticated. Listing 14-13 registers the SignIn and SignOut
methods as endpoints in the request pipeline.

Listing 14-13. Adding Endpoints in the Startup.cs File in the ExampleApp Folder

```
using Microsoft.AspNetCore.Builder;
using Microsoft.AspNetCore.Hosting;
using Microsoft.AspNetCore.Http;
using Microsoft.Extensions.DependencyInjection;
using ExampleApp.Custom;

namespace ExampleApp {
    public class Startup {

        public void ConfigureServices(IServiceCollection services) {
        }
```

```
        public void Configure(IApplicationBuilder app, IWebHostEnvironment env) {

            app.UseMiddleware<CustomAuthentication>();
            app.UseMiddleware<RoleMemberships>();
            app.UseRouting();

            app.UseMiddleware<ClaimsReporter>();
            app.UseMiddleware<CustomAuthorization>();

            app.UseEndpoints(endpoints => {
                endpoints.MapGet("/", async context => {
                    await context.Response.WriteAsync("Hello World!");
                });
                endpoints.MapGet("/secret", SecretEndpoint.Endpoint)
                    .WithDisplayName("secret");
                endpoints.Map("/signin", CustomSignInAndSignOut.SignIn);
                endpoints.Map("/signout", CustomSignInAndSignOut.SignOut);
            });
        }
    }
}
```

Listing 14-14 shows the changes to the custom authentication code to use cookies, rather than the query string, to authenticate requests.

Listing 14-14. Using Cookies for Authentication in the CustomAuthentication.cs File in the Custom Folder

```
using Microsoft.AspNetCore.Http;
using System.Security.Claims;
using System.Threading.Tasks;

namespace ExampleApp.Custom {

    public class CustomAuthentication {
        private RequestDelegate next;

        public CustomAuthentication(RequestDelegate requestDelegate)
                => next = requestDelegate;

        public async Task Invoke(HttpContext context) {
            //string user = context.Request.Query["user"];
            string user = context.Request.Cookies["authUser"];
            if (user != null) {
                Claim claim = new Claim(ClaimTypes.Name, user);
                ClaimsIdentity ident = new ClaimsIdentity("QueryStringValue");
                ident.AddClaim(claim);
                context.User = new ClaimsPrincipal(ident);
            }
            await next(context);
        }
    }
}
```

Restart ASP.NET Core, and request `http://localhost:5000/signin?user=alice` to sign in as Alice. Once you are signed in, request `http://localhost:5000/secret`, and your request will be authenticated and authorized, as shown in Figure 14-7.

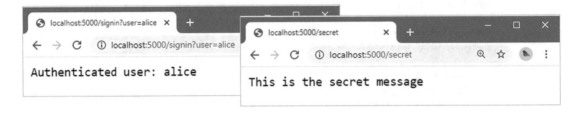

Figure 14-7. *Signing in to the application*

Next, request `http://localhost:5000/signin?user=bob` and then `http://localhost:5000/secret`, which will produce a forbidden result because the request won't have the required role claim. Finally, request `http://localhost:5000/signout` and request `http://localhost:5000/secret`, which will produce the challenge result because the request won't contain the cookie required for authentication. Figure 14-8 shows the forbidden and challenge responses. You will be able to see details of the identities and claims associated with all these requests in the messages displayed at the command prompt.

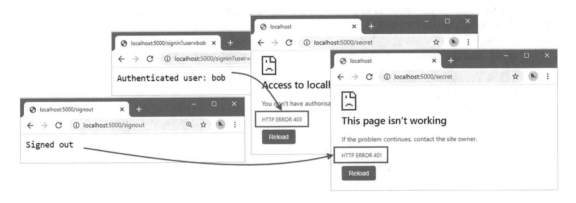

Figure 14-8. *Forbidden and challenge responses*

Defining Authorization Policy in the Endpoint

The examples so far in this chapter have taken advantage of the ASP.NET Core pipeline to authenticate and authorize requests using middleware. This allowed me to describe the different components in detail, but it led me to hard-code my authorization policy into a middleware component, which is not a flexible approach for real projects.

ASP.NET Core provides built-in middleware that allows authorization policies to be defined by applying attributes to endpoints. In Listing 14-15, I applied an attribute to the protected endpoint to describe its access control restrictions.

Listing 14-15. Applying an Attribute in the SecretEndpoint.cs File in the ExampleApp Folder

```
using Microsoft.AspNetCore.Http;
using System.Threading.Tasks;

using Microsoft.AspNetCore.Authorization;

namespace ExampleApp {

    public class SecretEndpoint {

        [Authorize(Roles = "Administrator")]
        public static async Task Endpoint(HttpContext context) {
            await context.Response.WriteAsync("This is the secret message");
        }
    }
}
```

You will be familiar with the Authorize attribute if you have applied access control to Razor Pages or MVC Framework action methods. The Authorize attribute can be applied directly to endpoints, as I have done here, and the Roles argument specifies the role claims required for authorization. I describe other features provided by the Authorize attribute in Chapter 15.

Implementing the Authentication Handler Interface

ASP.NET Core supports a set of interfaces that work with the features provided by the built-in middleware components. In this section, I am going to implement the IAuthorizationHandler interface, which allows me to add a custom authentication scheme that will work with the Authorize attribute I applied in Listing 14-15. Add a class called AuthHandler.cs to the ExampleApp/Custom folder and use it to define the class shown in Listing 14-16.

Listing 14-16. The Contents of the AuthHandler.cs File in the Custom Folder

```
using Microsoft.AspNetCore.Authentication;
using Microsoft.AspNetCore.Http;
using System.Security.Claims;
using System.Threading.Tasks;

namespace ExampleApp.Custom {
    public class AuthHandler : IAuthenticationHandler {
        private HttpContext context;
        private AuthenticationScheme scheme;

        public Task InitializeAsync(AuthenticationScheme authScheme,
                HttpContext httpContext) {
            context = httpContext;
            scheme = authScheme;
            return Task.CompletedTask;
        }
```

```
    public Task<AuthenticateResult> AuthenticateAsync() {
        AuthenticateResult result;
        string user = context.Request.Cookies["authUser"];
        if (user != null) {
            Claim claim = new Claim(ClaimTypes.Name, user);
            ClaimsIdentity ident = new ClaimsIdentity(scheme.Name);
            ident.AddClaim(claim);
            result = AuthenticateResult.Success(
                new AuthenticationTicket(new ClaimsPrincipal(ident),
                    scheme.Name));
        } else {
            result = AuthenticateResult.NoResult();
        }
        return Task.FromResult(result);
    }

    public Task ChallengeAsync(AuthenticationProperties properties) {
        context.Response.StatusCode = StatusCodes.Status401Unauthorized;
        return Task.CompletedTask;
    }

    public Task ForbidAsync(AuthenticationProperties properties) {
        context.Response.StatusCode = StatusCodes.Status403Forbidden;
        return Task.CompletedTask;
    }
  }
}
```

The InitializeAsync method is called to prepare the handler to authenticate a request, providing it with the name of the authentication scheme and the HttpContext object that provides access to the request and response objects. The scheme can be used by classes that provide multiple authentication techniques but is used just to get the name given to the authentication handler when authorization is configured, as demonstrated shortly.

The AuthenticateAsync method is called to authenticate a request, which it does by returning an AuthenticateResult object. The AuthenticateResult class defines static methods that produce objects to represent different authentication outcomes, as described in Table 14-6.

■ **Note** The methods defined by the IAuthenticationHandler interface are asynchronous. I don't need to perform asynchronous operations for the simple authentication in Listing 14-16, which is why the method results are produced with either Task.FromResult or Task.CompletedTask.

Table 14-6. *The Static Methods Defined by the AuthenticateResult Class*

Name	Description
Success(ticket)	This method creates a result indicating that authentication succeeded.
Fail(message)	This method creates a result indicating that authentication failed.
NoResult()	This method creates a result indicating no authentication was performed for this request. For the example application, this means that a request did not contain a cookie named authUser.

The argument to the Success method is an AuthenticationTicket object that describes the authenticated user and the name of the authentication scheme that was used:

```
...
result = AuthenticateResult.Success(new AuthenticationTicket(
    new ClaimsPrincipal(ident), scheme.Name));
...
```

Notice that no code in Listing 14-16 compares the user's claims with the policy defined with the Authorize attribute. When authorization fails, the built-in ASP.NET Core middleware will automatically invoke the ChallengeAsync or ForbidAsync method.

Configuring the Request Pipeline

In Listing 14-17, I have changed the configuration of the request pipeline to remove the custom authentication and authorization middleware I created earlier and to enable the built-in middleware that ASP.NET Core provides.

Listing 14-17. Configuring the Pipeline in the Startup.cs File in the ExampleApp Folder

```
using Microsoft.AspNetCore.Builder;
using Microsoft.AspNetCore.Hosting;
using Microsoft.AspNetCore.Http;
using Microsoft.Extensions.DependencyInjection;
using ExampleApp.Custom;

namespace ExampleApp {
    public class Startup {

        public void ConfigureServices(IServiceCollection services) {
            services.AddAuthentication(opts => {
                opts.AddScheme<AuthHandler>("qsv", "QueryStringValue");
                opts.DefaultScheme = "qsv";
            });
            services.AddAuthorization();
        }
```

```
    public void Configure(IApplicationBuilder app, IWebHostEnvironment env) {

        //app.UseMiddleware<CustomAuthentication>();
        app.UseAuthentication();
        app.UseMiddleware<RoleMemberships>();
        app.UseRouting();

        app.UseMiddleware<ClaimsReporter>();
        //app.UseMiddleware<CustomAuthorization>();
        app.UseAuthorization();

        app.UseEndpoints(endpoints => {
            endpoints.MapGet("/", async context => {
                await context.Response.WriteAsync("Hello World!");
            });
            endpoints.MapGet("/secret", SecretEndpoint.Endpoint)
                .WithDisplayName("secret");
            endpoints.Map("/signin", CustomSignInAndSignOut.SignIn);
            endpoints.Map("/signout", CustomSignInAndSignOut.SignOut);

        });
    }
  }
}
```

Two sets of services are enabled in the ConfigureServices method using the AddAuthentication and AddAuthorization methods. The AddAuthentication method uses the options pattern to register the implementation of the IAuthenticationHandler interface and use it as the default.

```
...
services.AddAuthentication(opts => {
    opts.AddScheme<AuthHandler>("qsv", "QueryStringValue");
    opts.DefaultScheme = "qsv";
});
...
```

The AddScheme method defines a generic type parameter that specifies the IAuthenticationHandler implementation class and regular arguments that specify a name for the authentication scheme and a display name for the scheme, which I have set to qsv and QueryStringValue. (Names for authentication schemes are more important when you are using more than one in the same application.) The DefaultScheme property is used to configure the default authentication scheme, and I have specified the name given to the scheme when it was registered with the AddScheme method.

In addition to the services, two method calls are required to configure the built-in middleware. The UseAuthentication method authenticates requests using the scheme configured in the ConfigureServices method, and the UseAuthorization method enforces access control using the Authorize attribute.

Restart ASP.NET Core, request http://localhost:5000/signin?user=alice, and then request http://localhost:5000/secret to test the new code. There is no visual change, as Figure 14-9 shows, but the authorization is now expressed using the standard attribute and applied using the built-in middleware.

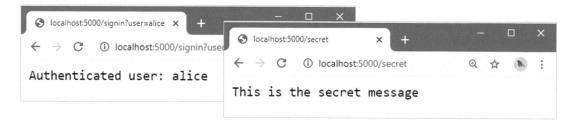

Figure 14-9. *Using the built-in middleware*

There is no change in the objects used to represent the user and their claims. This means that I can leave my RoleMemberships middleware in the pipeline to supply the application with role claims. The ClaimsReporter middleware is also still in the pipeline and will produce the following output when requesting the protected endpoint after signing in as Alice:

```
User: alice
Authenticated: True
Authentication Type qsv
Identities: 2
Auth type: qsv, 1 claims
Type: name, Value: alice, Issuer: LOCAL AUTHORITY
Auth type: Roles, 3 claims
Type: name, Value: alice, Issuer: LOCAL AUTHORITY
Type: role, Value: User, Issuer: LOCAL AUTHORITY
Type: role, Value: Administrator, Issuer: LOCAL AUTHORITY
```

Moving the Sign-In and Sign-Out Code

One drawback of my original approach is that the endpoints that deal with user requests to sign in and out are part of the authentication implementation, which makes it difficult to use a different authentication scheme. To address this problem, the ASP.NET Core authentication middleware supports the IAuthenticationSignInHandler interface, which extends the IAuthenticationHandler interface with methods for signing users into the application. Listing 14-18 updates the handler to implement the new interface and consolidate all the authentication code into a single class.

Listing 14-18. Consolidating Code in the AuthHandler.cs File in the Custom Folder

```
using Microsoft.AspNetCore.Authentication;
using Microsoft.AspNetCore.Http;
using System.Security.Claims;
using System.Threading.Tasks;

namespace ExampleApp.Custom {
    public class AuthHandler : IAuthenticationSignInHandler {
        private HttpContext context;
        private AuthenticationScheme scheme;
```

```
    public Task InitializeAsync(AuthenticationScheme authScheme,
            HttpContext httpContext) {
        context = httpContext;
        scheme = authScheme;
        return Task.CompletedTask;
    }

    // ...other methods omitted for brevity...

    public Task SignInAsync(ClaimsPrincipal user,
            AuthenticationProperties properties) {
        context.Response.Cookies.Append("authUser", user.Identity.Name);
        return Task.CompletedTask;
    }

    public Task SignOutAsync(AuthenticationProperties properties) {
        context.Response.Cookies.Delete("authUser");
        return Task.CompletedTask;
    }
  }
}
```

The SignInAsync and SignOutAsync methods add and remove the cookie that the AuthenticateAsync method uses to authenticate requests. Consolidating the authentication code means that the endpoints no longer work directly with the cookie and can ask ASP.NET Core to sign the user in or out using extension methods for the HttpContext class, as shown in Listing 14-19.

Listing 14-19. Signing In and Out in the CustomSignInAndSignOut.cs File in the Custom Folder

```
using Microsoft.AspNetCore.Authentication;
using Microsoft.AspNetCore.Http;
using System.Threading.Tasks;
using System.Security.Claims;

namespace ExampleApp.Custom {
    public class CustomSignInAndSignOut {

        public static async Task SignIn(HttpContext context) {
            string user = context.Request.Query["user"];
            if (user != null) {
                Claim claim = new Claim(ClaimTypes.Name, user);
                ClaimsIdentity ident = new ClaimsIdentity("qsv");
                ident.AddClaim(claim);
                await context.SignInAsync(new ClaimsPrincipal(ident));
                await context.Response
                    .WriteAsync($"Authenticated user: {user}");
            } else {
                await context.ChallengeAsync();
            }
        }
```

```
public static async Task SignOut(HttpContext context) {
    await context.SignOutAsync();
    await context.Response.WriteAsync("Signed out");
    }
  }
}
```

ASP.NET Core provides a set of extension methods that provide indirect access to the signing and authentication features, as described in Table 14-7.

Table 14-7. *HttpContext Extension Methods for Accessing the Authentication Handler*

Name	Description
AuthenticateAsync() AuthenticateAsync(scheme)	This method authenticates a request. The default scheme will be used if no argument is provided.
SignInAsync(principal) SignInAsync(principal, scheme)	This method signs a user into the application. The default scheme is used if one is not specified.
SignOutAsync() SignOutAsync(scheme)	This method signs a user out of the application. The default scheme is used if one is not specified.
ChallengeAsync() ChallengeAsync(scheme)	This method sends a challenge response. The default scheme is used if one is not specified.
ForbidAsync()ForbidAsync(scheme)	This method sends a forbidden response. The default scheme is used if one is not specified.

These methods use the authentication handlers set up in the Startup class without needing to know which handler will be used, allowing code to be written without dependencies on specific IAuthenticationHandler implementations. Using these methods means that the code in Listing 14-19 is responsible for processing the user's credentials—which is just a query string value in this example—without needing to worry about the token that will be used to authenticate subsequent requests.

Restart ASP.NET Core, request http://localhost:5000/signin?user=alice, and then request http://localhost:5000/secret to test the new code. There is no visual change, and you will see the results shown in Figure 14-9. However, the code that signs Alice into the application no longer deals directly with the cookie that is used to authenticate the request for the protected endpoint. The effect is that validation of the user's credentials has been separated from the scheme that creates the cookie and uses it to validate requests, as shown in Figure 14-10.

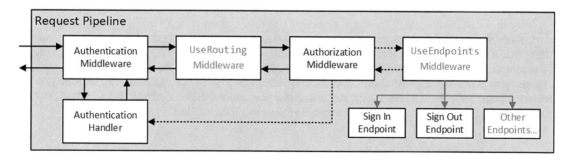

Figure 14-10. *Separating signing in from authentication*

Using HTML Responses

All the responses so far in this chapter have been plain text or just HTTP status codes, which has helped focus on the authentication and authorization processes but isn't what most web applications require. The next improvement to my example is to add an HTML response and provide a more user-friendly mechanism for signing in to and out of the application.

I am going to use Razor Pages for the HTML endpoints, although MVC controllers and views would work equally as well. Add a Razor Page named SignIn.cshtml to the Pages folder with the content shown in Listing 14-20.

Listing 14-20. The Contents of the SignIn.cshtml File in the Pages Folder

```
@page "{code:int?}"
@model ExampleApp.Pages.SignInModel
@using Microsoft.AspNetCore.Http

@if (Model.Code == StatusCodes.Status401Unauthorized) {
    <h3 class="bg-warning text-white text-center p-2">
        401 - Challenge Response
    </h3>
} else if (Model.Code == StatusCodes.Status403Forbidden) {
    <h3 class="bg-danger text-white text-center p-2">
        403 - Forbidden Response
    </h3>
}
<h4 class="bg-info text-white m-2 p-2">
    Current User: @Model.Username
</h4>

<div class="m-2">
    <form method="post">
        <div class="form-group">
            <label>User</label>
            <select class="form-control"
                    asp-for="Username" asp-items="@Model.Users">
            </select>
        </div>
        <button class="btn btn-info" type="submit">Sign In</button>
    </form>
</div>
```

This Razor Page will serve as the sign-in page as well as the challenge and forbidden responses. The user will be able to pick from a list of identities and sign in, which is a more convenient approach than the query strings used in earlier examples. (It is no more secure, however, but I'll show you how to deal with real credentials in later chapters, when I describe the sign-in features provided by ASP.NET Core Identity.) To define the page model for the Razor Page, add the code shown in Listing 14-21 to the SignIn.cshtml.cs file in the Pages folder. You will have to create this file if you are using Visual Studio Code.

Listing 14-21. The Contents of the SignIn.cshtml.cs File in the Pages Folder

```
using Microsoft.AspNetCore.Authentication;
using Microsoft.AspNetCore.Http;
using Microsoft.AspNetCore.Mvc;
using Microsoft.AspNetCore.Mvc.RazorPages;
using Microsoft.AspNetCore.Mvc.Rendering;
using System.Security.Claims;
using System.Threading.Tasks;

namespace ExampleApp.Pages {
    public class SignInModel : PageModel {

        public SelectList Users => new SelectList(UsersAndClaims.Users,
            User.Identity.Name);

        public string Username { get; set; }

        public int? Code { get; set; }

        public void OnGet(int? code) {
            Code = code;
            Username = User.Identity.Name ?? "(No Signed In User)";
        }

        public async Task<ActionResult> OnPost(string username) {
            Claim claim = new Claim(ClaimTypes.Name, username);
            ClaimsIdentity ident = new ClaimsIdentity("simpleform");
            ident.AddClaim(claim);
            await HttpContext.SignInAsync(new ClaimsPrincipal(ident));
            return Redirect("/signin");
        }
    }
}
```

To let users sign out of the application, add a Razor Page named `SignOut.cshtml` to the Pages folder with the content shown in Listing 14-22.

Listing 14-22. The Contents of the SignOut.cshtml File in the Pages Folder

```
@page
@model ExampleApp.Pages.SignOutModel

<h4 class="bg-info text-white m-2 p-2">
    Current User: @Model.Username
</h4>
<div class="m-2">
    <form method="post" >
        <button class="btn btn-info" type="submit">Sign Out</button>
    </form>
</div>
```

When the user submits the form, they will be signed out of the application, which will remove the cookie used for request authentication. To define the page model for the Razor Page, add the code shown in Listing 14-23 to the SignOut.cshtml.cs file in the Pages folder. You will have to create this file if you are using Visual Studio Code.

Listing 14-23. The Contents of the SignOut.cshtml.cs File in the Pages Folder

```
using Microsoft.AspNetCore.Authentication;
using Microsoft.AspNetCore.Mvc;
using Microsoft.AspNetCore.Mvc.RazorPages;
using System.Threading.Tasks;

namespace ExampleApp.Pages {
    public class SignOutModel : PageModel {
        public string Username { get; set; }

        public void OnGet() {
            Username = User.Identity.Name ?? "(No Signed In User)";
        }

        public async Task<ActionResult> OnPost() {
            await HttpContext.SignOutAsync();
            return RedirectToPage("SignIn");
        }
    }
}
```

When the page receives an HTTP POST request, the user is signed out through the SignoutAsync extension method, and the browser is redirected to the SignIn page.

In Listing 14-24, I have updated the authentication handler to redirect the user to the SignIn page instead of sending HTTP status codes for the challenge and forbidden responses.

Listing 14-24. Changing Responses in the AuthHandler.cs File in the Custom Folder

```
using Microsoft.AspNetCore.Authentication;
using Microsoft.AspNetCore.Http;
using System.Security.Claims;
using System.Threading.Tasks;

namespace ExampleApp.Custom {
    public class AuthHandler : IAuthenticationSignInHandler {
        private HttpContext context;
        private AuthenticationScheme scheme;

        // ...other methods omitted for brevity...

        public Task ChallengeAsync(AuthenticationProperties properties) {
            //context.Response.StatusCode = StatusCodes.Status401Unauthorized;
            context.Response.Redirect("/signin/401");
            return Task.CompletedTask;
        }
```

```
        public Task ForbidAsync(AuthenticationProperties properties) {
            //context.Response.StatusCode = StatusCodes.Status403Forbidden;
            context.Response.Redirect("/signin/403");
            return Task.CompletedTask;
        }

        // ...other methods omitted for brevity...
    }
}
```

In Listing 14-25, I have enabled the services and middleware required for Razor Pages and serve the static CSS file from the Bootstrap package.

Listing 14-25. Configuring Razor Pages in the Startup.cs File in the ExampleApp Folder

```
using Microsoft.AspNetCore.Builder;
using Microsoft.AspNetCore.Hosting;
using Microsoft.AspNetCore.Http;
using Microsoft.Extensions.DependencyInjection;
using ExampleApp.Custom;

namespace ExampleApp {
    public class Startup {

        public void ConfigureServices(IServiceCollection services) {
            services.AddAuthentication(opts => {
                opts.AddScheme<AuthHandler>("qsv", "QueryStringValue");
                opts.DefaultScheme = "qsv";
            });
            services.AddAuthorization();
            services.AddRazorPages();
        }

        public void Configure(IApplicationBuilder app, IWebHostEnvironment env) {

            app.UseStaticFiles();
            //app.UseMiddleware<CustomAuthentication>();
            app.UseAuthentication();
            app.UseMiddleware<RoleMemberships>();
            app.UseRouting();

            app.UseMiddleware<ClaimsReporter>();
            //app.UseMiddleware<CustomAuthorization>();
            app.UseAuthorization();

            app.UseEndpoints(endpoints => {
                endpoints.MapGet("/", async context => {
                    await context.Response.WriteAsync("Hello World!");
                });
```

```
            endpoints.MapGet("/secret", SecretEndpoint.Endpoint)
                .WithDisplayName("secret");
            //endpoints.Map("/signin", CustomSignInAndSignOut.SignIn);
            //endpoints.Map("/signout", CustomSignInAndSignOut.SignOut);
            endpoints.MapRazorPages();
        });
    }
  }
}
```

Restart ASP.NET Core, request http://localhost:5000/signin, and sign in as Alice. (You may find that you are already authenticated with a cookie from an earlier example, but this will be replaced as soon as you sign in again.)

Request http://localhost:5000/secret, and you will be granted access to the protected endpoint. Repeat the process as Bob or without signing into the application, and the browser will be redirected to the SignIn page, as shown in Figure 14-11.

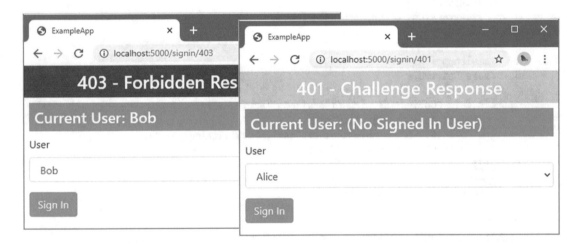

Figure 14-11. *Generating HTML responses*

Using the Built-In Cookie Authentication Handler

Creating a custom authentication handler is useful for this chapter, but a key goal with dealing with access control is to write as little custom code as possible. One consequence of implementing the IAuthenticationSignInHandler interface is that the code that validates user credentials is completely separate from the code that signs users into the application and authenticates requests. And so, to finish this chapter, I am going to replace my custom cookie-based authentication handler with the one that Microsoft provides with ASP.NET Core. Not only has the Microsoft handler been thoroughly tested, but it also manages cookies better and is more flexible and configurable. In Listing 14-26, I have changed the configuration of the application's services to use the built-in cookie authentication handler.

Listing 14-26. Using a Built-In Authentication Handler in the Startup.cs File in the ExampleApp Folder

```
using Microsoft.AspNetCore.Builder;
using Microsoft.AspNetCore.Hosting;
using Microsoft.AspNetCore.Http;
using Microsoft.Extensions.DependencyInjection;
using ExampleApp.Custom;
using Microsoft.AspNetCore.Authentication.Cookies;

namespace ExampleApp {
    public class Startup {

        public void ConfigureServices(IServiceCollection services) {
            services.AddAuthentication(opts => {
                opts.DefaultScheme
                    = CookieAuthenticationDefaults.AuthenticationScheme;
            }).AddCookie(opts => {
                opts.LoginPath = "/signin";
                opts.AccessDeniedPath = "/signin/403";
            });
            services.AddAuthorization();
            services.AddRazorPages();
        }

        public void Configure(IApplicationBuilder app, IWebHostEnvironment env) {
            // ...statements omitted for brevity...
        }
    }
}
```

I have set the DefaultScheme option to the AuthenticationScheme constant defined by the CookieAuthenticationDefaults class, which provides the name of the cookie handler. The AddCookie extension method sets up the built-in cookie authentication handler, which is configured using the options pattern, which is applied to the CookieAuthenticationOptions class.

■ **Note** One key benefit of using the built-in cookie authentication handler is that it serializes a user's claims into the encrypted cookie used for authentication or, if one is available, stores the claims in the ASP.NET Core session data store. Examples in later chapters, such as Chapter 20, use multiple instances of the cookie authentication handler to store cookies for different aspects of complex sign-in and authentication scenarios.

The CookieAuthenticationOptions class defines properties for managing the authentication cookie, the most useful of which are described in Table 14-8.

Table 14-8. *Useful CookieAuthenticationOptions Properties*

Name	Description
AccessDeniedPath	This property defines the URL path the client will be directed to for the forbid response. The default value is /Account/AccessDenied.
LoginPath	This property defines the URL path the client will be directed to for the challenge response. The default value is /Account/Login.
ReturnUrlParameter	This property defines the name of the query string parameter that will be used to store the path requested before a challenge response and can be used to redirect the client after a successful sign-in. The default value is returnUrl.
ExpireTimeSpan	This property defines the lifespan of the authentication cookie. The default value is 14 days.
SlidingExpiration	This property is used to control whether the authentication cookie is automatically reissued with a new expiry date. The default value is true.

For this chapter, I have set LoginPath and AccessDeniedPath to URLs that will be handled by the SignIn Razor Page.

Although I have not set the ReturnUrlParameter option in Listing 14-26, I can use the feature to make the login process smoother, as shown in Listing 14-27.

Listing 14-27. Supporting the Return URL in the SignIn.cshtml.cs File in the Pages Folder

```
using Microsoft.AspNetCore.Authentication;
using Microsoft.AspNetCore.Http;
using Microsoft.AspNetCore.Mvc;
using Microsoft.AspNetCore.Mvc.RazorPages;
using Microsoft.AspNetCore.Mvc.Rendering;
using System.Security.Claims;
using System.Threading.Tasks;

namespace ExampleApp.Pages {
    public class SignInModel : PageModel {

        public SelectList Users => new SelectList(UsersAndClaims.Users,
            User.Identity.Name);

        public string Username { get; set; }

        public int? Code { get; set; }

        public void OnGet(int? code) {
            Code = code;
            Username = User.Identity.Name ?? "(No Signed In User)";
        }

        public async Task<ActionResult> OnPost(string username,
                [FromQuery]string returnUrl) {
            Claim claim = new Claim(ClaimTypes.Name, username);
            ClaimsIdentity ident = new ClaimsIdentity("simpleform");
            ident.AddClaim(claim);
```

```
        await HttpContext.SignInAsync(new ClaimsPrincipal(ident));
        return Redirect(returnUrl ?? "/signin");
    }
  }
}
```

The new parameter for the POST handler method will receive the URL that the client requested before a challenge response is issued. To see the effect of the changes to the application, restart ASP.NET Core, request the http://localhost:5000/signout page, and click the Sign Out button to make sure no user is signed in.

Next, request http://localhost:5000/secret. You will be redirected to the SignIn Razor Page, but the URL will include a returnUrl query string parameter that contains the URL you requested. Authenticate as Alice, and you will be automatically redirected to the protected endpoint, as shown in Figure 14-12.

Figure 14-12. *Using the ASP.NET Core cookie authentication handler*

Summary

In this chapter, I explained the way that ASP.NET Core handles HTTP requests through its pipeline and how middleware components can provide authentication and authorization. I explained the different request flows, including the challenge and forbidden responses, and explained how signing into an application can generate a token that is used to authenticate subsequent requests. Once I established the basic features, I gradually refined my authentication and authorization process using built-in ASP.NET Core features, until only the code required to validate user credentials remained. In the next chapter, I explain how requests are authorized.

CHAPTER 15

Authorizing Requests

In the previous chapter, I focused on the ASP.NET Core request pipeline and the middleware components that authenticate requests and authorize access to endpoints. In this chapter, I dig deeper into the authorization features, explaining the different ways that access can be restricted. These are, once again, features that are provided by ASP.NET Core, and I describe them without using ASP.NET Core Identity. Table 15-1 puts the ASP.NET Core authorization features in context.

Table 15-1. *Putting Request Authorization in Context*

Question	Answer
What is it?	Request authorization is the process of restricting access to endpoints so they can only be accessed by selected users.
Why is it useful?	Request authorization is the complement to authorization and acts as the gatekeeper to the resources managed by the application.
How is it used?	Access control policies are defined and applied to endpoints. When a request is processed, the policy is evaluated to determine if the user associated with the request is entitled to access the endpoint.
Are there any pitfalls or limitations?	Policies are most effective when they are simple and easy to understand. The more complex a policy becomes, the more likely it is to allow unintended access.
Are there any alternatives?	Request authorization is a fundamental feature and is required in any application that contains any endpoint that should not be available to all users.

Table 15-2 summarizes the chapter.

© Adam Freeman 2021
A. Freeman, *Pro ASP.NET Core Identity*, https://doi.org/10.1007/978-1-4842-6858-2_15

Table 15-2. *Chapter Summary*

Problem	Solution	Listing
Define and enforce a custom authorization requirement	Implement the `IAuthorizationRequirement` and `IAuthorizationHandler` interfaces.	8, 9
Apply an authorization policy	Use the `AuthorizationOptions` options pattern to specify a policy described with the `AuthorizationPolicy` class.	10, 11
Use a built-in requirement	Use one of the built-in requirement classes.	12
Combine requirements	Arrange individual requirements in an array.	13
Restrict access to specified authentication schemes	Specify the schemes when creating the policy.	14, 15
Apply policies to endpoints	Use the `Authorize` attribute.	16, 18–22
Specify the default policy	Assign a policy to the `DefaultPolicy` configuration option.	17
Restrict access with multiple policies	Specify multiple policies when applying the `Authorize` attribute.	23
Create exceptions to policies	Use the `AllowAnonymous` attribute.	24
Apply policies to Razor Pages	Use page conventions.	25, 26
Apply policies to controllers	Use filters and the application model.	27–29

Preparing for This Chapter

This chapter uses the `ExampleApp` project created in Chapter 14. The sections that follow describe the preparations required for this chapter.

■ **Tip**   You can download the example project for this chapter—and for all the other chapters in this book—from `https://github.com/Apress/pro-asp.net-core-identity`. See Chapter 1 for how to get help if you have problems running the examples.

Creating an Authorization Reporter

The ASP.NET Core authorization features are easier to understand if you can see their effects without having to repeatedly sign in and make requests as individual users. In this chapter, I replace the standard ASP.NET Core authorization middleware with a component that tests the authorization policy for the target endpoint using the users and claims defined in the `UsersAndClaims` class.

In Listing 15-1, I have added a convenience method to the `UsersAndClaims` class that will produce a sequence of `ClaimsPrincipal` objects and defined an array of authentication scheme names.

Listing 15-1. Adding a Method in the UsersAndClaims.cs File in the ExampleApp Folder

```
using System;
using System.Collections.Generic;
using System.Linq;
using System.Security.Claims;
```

```
namespace ExampleApp {
    public static class UsersAndClaims {
        public static string[] Schemes = new string[] { "TestScheme" };

        public static Dictionary<string, IEnumerable<string>> UserData
            = new Dictionary<string, IEnumerable<string>> {
                { "Alice", new [] { "User", "Administrator" } },
                { "Bob", new [] { "User" } },
                { "Charlie", new [] { "User"} }
            };

        public static string[] Users => UserData.Keys.ToArray();

        public static Dictionary<string, IEnumerable<Claim>> Claims =>
            UserData.ToDictionary(kvp => kvp.Key,
                kvp => kvp.Value.Select(role => new Claim(ClaimTypes.Role, role)),
                StringComparer.InvariantCultureIgnoreCase);

        public static IEnumerable<ClaimsPrincipal> GetUsers() {
            foreach (string scheme in Schemes) {
                foreach (var kvp in Claims) {
                    ClaimsIdentity ident = new ClaimsIdentity(scheme);
                    ident.AddClaim(new Claim(ClaimTypes.Name, kvp.Key));
                    ident.AddClaims(kvp.Value);
                    yield return new ClaimsPrincipal(ident);
                }
            }
        }
    }
}
```

Add a class file named AuthorizationReporter.cs to the ExampleApp/Custom folder and use it to define the middleware component shown in Listing 15-2.

Listing 15-2. The Contents of the AuthorizationReporter.cs File in the Custom Folder

```
using Microsoft.AspNetCore.Authorization;
using Microsoft.AspNetCore.Http;
using System;
using System.Collections.Generic;
using System.Linq;
using System.Security.Claims;
using System.Threading.Tasks;

namespace ExampleApp.Custom {
    public class AuthorizationReporter {
        private string[] schemes = new string[] { "TestScheme" };
        private RequestDelegate next;
        private IAuthorizationPolicyProvider policyProvider;
        private IAuthorizationService authorizationService;
```

```
    public AuthorizationReporter(RequestDelegate requestDelegate,
            IAuthorizationPolicyProvider provider,
            IAuthorizationService service) {
        next = requestDelegate;
        policyProvider = provider;
        authorizationService = service;
    }

    public async Task Invoke(HttpContext context) {
        Endpoint ep = context.GetEndpoint();
        if (ep != null) {
            Dictionary<(string, string), bool> results
                = new Dictionary<(string, string), bool>();
            bool allowAnon = ep.Metadata.GetMetadata<IAllowAnonymous>() != null;
            IEnumerable<IAuthorizeData> authData =
                ep?.Metadata.GetOrderedMetadata<IAuthorizeData>()
                    ?? Array.Empty<IAuthorizeData>();
            AuthorizationPolicy policy = await
                AuthorizationPolicy.CombineAsync(policyProvider, authData);
            foreach (ClaimsPrincipal cp in GetUsers()) {
                results[(cp.Identity.Name ?? "(No User)",
                    cp.Identity.AuthenticationType)] =
                        allowAnon || policy == null
                            || await AuthorizeUser(cp, policy);
            }
            context.Items["authReport"] = results;
            await ep.RequestDelegate(context);
        } else {
            await next(context);
        }
    }

    private IEnumerable<ClaimsPrincipal> GetUsers() =>
        UsersAndClaims.GetUsers()
            .Concat(new[] { new ClaimsPrincipal(new ClaimsIdentity()) });

    private async Task<bool> AuthorizeUser(ClaimsPrincipal cp,
            AuthorizationPolicy policy) {
        return UserSchemeMatchesPolicySchemes(cp, policy)
            && (await authorizationService.AuthorizeAsync(cp, policy)).Succeeded;
    }

    private bool UserSchemeMatchesPolicySchemes(ClaimsPrincipal cp,
            AuthorizationPolicy policy) {
        return policy.AuthenticationSchemes?.Count() == 0 ||
            cp.Identities.Select(id => id.AuthenticationType)
                .Any(auth => policy.AuthenticationSchemes
                    .Any(scheme => scheme == auth));
    }
}
}
```

This component uses features that you are unlikely to need in real projects, but that are interesting anyway and help explain the authorization process. The authorization requirements for an endpoint are available through the HttpContext.GetEndpoint().Metadata property and are expressed using the IAuthorizeData interface. To get an endpoint's requirements, I use the GetOrderedMetadata<IAuthorizeData> method, like this:

```
...
ep?.Metadata.GetOrderedMetadata<IAuthorizeData>() ?? Array.Empty<IAuthorizeData>();
...
```

You will see where the IAuthorizeData objects are created later in this chapter, but for now, it is enough to know that each one represents a requirement that must be met before a request is authorized.

The collection of individual IAuthorizeData objects is converted into a combined authorization policy for the endpoint using the static AuthorizationPolicy.CombineAsync method, using the IAuthorizationPolicyProvider service on which the middleware component declares a constructor dependency.

```
...
AuthorizationPolicy policy = await
    AuthorizationPolicy.CombineAsync(policyProvider, authData);
...
```

The authorization policy can be tested using the IAuthorizationService service, like this:

```
...
await authorizationService.AuthorizeAsync(cp, policy);
...
```

The arguments to the AuthorizeAsync method are the ClaimsPrincipal that requires authorization and the AuthorizationPolicy object produced from the endpoint's middleware. After evaluating the authorization policy, the endpoint is invoked to produce a response.

```
...
await ep.RequestDelegate(context);
...
```

This means that the endpoint will receive the request even if no users would have normally been authorized and also means that the request will be passed directly to the endpoint, skipping over any other middleware in the request pipeline. For these reasons, you should only use the code in Listing 15-2 to understand how authorization works and not deploy it in real projects.

■ **Tip** The code in Listing 15-2 is based on the way that the built-in ASP.NET Core middleware authorizes requests. ASP.NET Core and ASP.NET Core Identity are open source, and exploring the source code is a good way of understanding how features are implemented.

Creating the Report View

To create a partial view that will display the authorization results, add a Razor View named
_AuthorizationReport.cshtml to the ExampleApp/Pages/Shared folder with the content shown in
Listing 15-3. (If you are using Visual Studio, create the file using the Razor View – Empty item template.)

Listing 15-3. The Contents of the _AuthorizationReport.cshtml File in the Pages/Shared Folder

```
@{
    var data = Context.Items["authReport"] as Dictionary<(string, string), bool>
        ?? new Dictionary<(string, string), bool>();
}

<div class="m-2 p-2 border bg-light">
    <h5 class="text-center">Authorization Summary</h5>
    <table class="table table-sm table-bordered table-striped">
        <thead><tr><th>User</th><th>Scheme</th><th>Result</th></tr></thead>
        <tbody>
            @if (data.Count() == 0) {
                <tr><td colspan="3" class="text-center">No Data</td></tr>
            }
            @foreach (var result in data) {
                <tr>
                    <td>@result.Key.Item1</td>
                    <td>@result.Key.Item2</td>
                    <td class="text-white @(result.Value
                            ? "bg-success" : "bg-danger")">
                        @(result.Value ? "Access Granted" : "Access Denied")
                    </td>
                </tr>
            }
        </tbody>
    </table>
</div>
```

The partial view retrieves the authorization data from the HttpContext object and uses it to display a
table containing the results of the tests performed by the middleware component.

Add the element shown in Listing 15-4 to the _Layout.cshtml File in the Pages/Shared folder to include
the partial view.

Listing 15-4. Including a Partial View in the _Layout.cshtml File in the Pages/Shared Folder

```
<!DOCTYPE html>

<html>
<head>
    <meta name="viewport" content="width=device-width" />
    <title>ExampleApp</title>
    <link href="/lib/twitter-bootstrap/css/bootstrap.min.css" rel="stylesheet" />
</head>
```

```
<body>
    <div>
        @RenderBody()
    </div>
    <partial name="_AuthorizationReport" />
</body>
</html>
```

Creating an Endpoint

I need an HTML endpoint so that I can include the partial view in the response that it generates. Add a Razor Page named Secret.cshtml to the Pages folder with the content shown in Listing 15-5.

Listing 15-5. The Contents of the Secret.cshtml File in the Pages Folder

```
@page

<h4 class="bg-info text-center text-white m-2 p-2">
    This is the secret message
</h4>
```

The Razor Page displays a simple HTML message, echoing the endpoint used in Chapter 14.

Configuring the Request Pipeline

In Listing 15-6, I have added the new middleware to the request pipeline, using it to replace the built-authorization in middleware that ASP.NET Core provides. I also enabled the MVC Framework and removed the text-only endpoint used in Chapter 14 so that the /secret URL will be handled by the Razor Page created in Listing 15-5.

Listing 15-6. Configuring the Application in the Startup.cs File in the ExampleApp Folder

```
using Microsoft.AspNetCore.Builder;
using Microsoft.AspNetCore.Hosting;
using Microsoft.AspNetCore.Http;
using Microsoft.Extensions.DependencyInjection;
using ExampleApp.Custom;
using Microsoft.AspNetCore.Authentication.Cookies;

namespace ExampleApp {
    public class Startup {

        public void ConfigureServices(IServiceCollection services) {
            services.AddAuthentication(opts => {
                opts.DefaultScheme
                    = CookieAuthenticationDefaults.AuthenticationScheme;
            }).AddCookie(opts => {
                opts.LoginPath = "/signin";
                opts.AccessDeniedPath = "/signin/403";
            });
```

```
        services.AddAuthorization();
        services.AddRazorPages();
        services.AddControllersWithViews();
    }

    public void Configure(IApplicationBuilder app, IWebHostEnvironment env) {

        app.UseStaticFiles();
        app.UseAuthentication();
        //app.UseMiddleware<RoleMemberships>();
        app.UseRouting();

        //app.UseMiddleware<ClaimsReporter>();
        //app.UseAuthorization();
        app.UseMiddleware<AuthorizationReporter>();

        app.UseEndpoints(endpoints => {
            endpoints.MapGet("/", async context => {
                await context.Response.WriteAsync("Hello World!");
            });
            //endpoints.MapGet("/secret", SecretEndpoint.Endpoint)
            //    .WithDisplayName("secret");
            endpoints.MapRazorPages();
            endpoints.MapDefaultControllerRoute();
        });
    }
}
}
```

Use a command prompt to run the command shown in Listing 15-7 in the ExampleApp folder.

Listing 15-7. Starting the Example Application

```
dotnet run
```

Once ASP.NET Core has started, use a browser to request http://localhost:5000/secret and http://localhost:5000/home/test, and you will receive the responses shown in Figure 15-1.

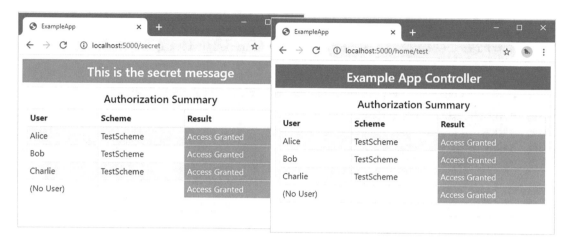

Figure 15-1. *Running the example application*

No authorization policy has been specified for the Razor Page or the Test action method, so the summary shows that all users and unauthenticated requests will be granted access.

Understanding Policies and Requirements

The key building blocks for ASP.NET Core authorization are *policies*, which consist of individual *requirements*. For a request to be authorized, it must meet all the requirements in the policy for the target endpoint. In this section, I create and apply a custom requirement and show you how it is applied before describing the built-in requirements that ASP.NET Core provides.

Defining the Custom Requirement and Handler

Requirements are expressed using classes that implement the IAuthorizationRequirement interface. The IAuthorizationRequirement interface defines no members and is implemented to describe the constraints for a specific requirement. To demonstrate, add a class file named CustomRequirement.cs to the Custom folder and use it to define the class shown in Listing 15-8.

Listing 15-8. The Contents of the CustomRequirement.cs File in the Custom Folder

```
using Microsoft.AspNetCore.Authorization;

namespace ExampleApp.Custom {

    public class CustomRequirement: IAuthorizationRequirement {

        public string Name { get; set; }

    }
}
```

This class implements the IAuthorizationRequirement interface and defines a Name property that will allow a username to be specified. To enforce the requirement, an implementation of the IAuthorizationHandler interface is required. Add a class file named CustomRequirementsHandler.cs to the Custom folder and add the code shown in Listing 15-9.

Listing 15-9. The Contents of the CustomRequirementsHandler.cs File in the Custom Folder

```
using Microsoft.AspNetCore.Authorization;
using System;
using System.Linq;
using System.Threading.Tasks;

namespace ExampleApp.Custom {
    public class CustomRequirementHandler : IAuthorizationHandler {

        public Task HandleAsync(AuthorizationHandlerContext context) {
            foreach (CustomRequirement req in
                context.PendingRequirements.OfType<CustomRequirement>().ToList()) {
                if (context.User.Identities.Any(ident => string.Equals(ident.Name,
                        req.Name, StringComparison.OrdinalIgnoreCase))) {
                    context.Succeed(req);
                }
            }
            return Task.CompletedTask;
        }
    }
}
```

The IAuthorizationHandler interface defines the HandleAsync method, which accepts an AuthorizationHandlerContext context object. AuthorizationHandlerContext defines the members described in Table 15-3.

Table 15-3. The Members Defined by the AuthorizationHandlerContext Class

Name	Description
User	This property returns the ClaimsPrincipal object for the request that requires authorization.
Resource	This property returns the target of the request, which will be an endpoint for the examples in this chapter.
Requirements	This property returns a sequence of all the requirements for the resource/endpoint.
PendingRequirements	This property returns a sequence of the requirements that have not been marked as satisfied.
Succeed(requirement)	This method tells ASP.NET Core that the specified requirement has been satisfied.
Fail()	This method tells ASP.NET Core that a requirement has not been satisfied.

The idea is that an authorization handler will process one or more of the requirements in the policy and, assuming the requirement is satisfied, mark them as succeeded. A request will be authorized if all the requirements succeed. Authorization fails if any handler calls the Fail method. Authorization will also fail if there are outstanding requirements for which a handler has not invoked the Succeed method.

The custom handler in Listing 15-9 gets the list of pending requirements and filters them for the CustomRequirement type like this:

```
...
foreach (CustomRequirement req in
    context.PendingRequirements.OfType<CustomRequirement>().ToList()) {
...
```

The OfType<T> method is a LINQ extension method, and I use the ToList method to force evaluation of the LINQ query because calling the Succeed method will alter the PendingRequirements sequence, which causes an error if the sequence is used directly in a foreach loop. For each CustomRequirement object, I can read the value of the Name property and compare it to the names contained in the user's identities, calling the Succeed method if there is a match.

```
...
if (context.User.Identities.Any(ident =>
    string.Compare(ident.Name, req.Name, true) == 0)) {
        context.Succeed(req);
}
...
```

Creating and Applying the Policy

The next step is to use the custom requirement to create an authorization policy. Add a class named AuthorizationPolicies.cs to the Custom folder with the code shown in Listing 15-10.

Listing 15-10. The Contents of the AuthorizationPolicies.cs File in the Custom Folder

```
using Microsoft.AspNetCore.Authorization;
using System.Linq;

namespace ExampleApp.Custom {

    public static class AuthorizationPolicies {

        public static void AddPolicies(AuthorizationOptions opts) {
            opts.FallbackPolicy = new AuthorizationPolicy(
                new[] {
                    new CustomRequirement() { Name = "Bob" }
                }, Enumerable.Empty<string>());
        }
    }
}
```

Policies are created using the AuthorizationPolicy class, whose constructor accepts a sequence of requirements and a sequence of authentication scheme names. The policy will grant access when all the requirements are satisfied for users who have been authenticated using one of the specified schemes, which I describe later in this chapter. For the moment, I have used an empty array, which will not restrict the policy.

The AuthorizationOptions class is used to configure ASP.NET Core authorization and defines the members described in Table 15-4.

Table 15-4. *AuthorizationOptions Members*

Name	Description
DefaultPolicy	This property defines the policy that will be applied by default when authorization is required but no policy has been selected, such as when the Authorize attribute is applied with no arguments. Any authorized user will be granted access unless a new default policy is defined, as described later in this chapter.
FallbackPolicy	This property defines the policy that is applied when no other policy has been defined. There is no fallback policy by default, which means that all requests will be authorized when there is no explicitly defined policy.
InvokeHandlersAfterFailure	This property determines whether a single failed requirement prevents subsequent requirements from being evaluated. The default value is true, which means that all requirements are evaluated. A false value means that a failure short-circuits the requirement process.
AddPolicy(name, policy) AddPolicy(name, builder)	This method adds a new policy, either using an AuthorizationPolicy object or using a builder function.
GetPolicy(name)	This method retrieves a policy using its name.

For this example, I have assigned my policy to the FallbackPolicy property, which means that it will be used to authorize requests for which no explicit authorization has been defined and which sets a baseline for the minimum authorization required for all requests the application receives. The final step is to apply the policy and register the custom requirements handler as a service, as shown in Listing 15-11.

Listing 15-11. Setting up the Policy in the Startup.cs File in the ExampleApp Folder

```
using Microsoft.AspNetCore.Builder;
using Microsoft.AspNetCore.Hosting;
using Microsoft.AspNetCore.Http;
using Microsoft.Extensions.DependencyInjection;
using ExampleApp.Custom;
using Microsoft.AspNetCore.Authentication.Cookies;
using Microsoft.AspNetCore.Authorization;

namespace ExampleApp {
    public class Startup {

        public void ConfigureServices(IServiceCollection services) {

            services.AddTransient<IAuthorizationHandler, CustomRequirementHandler>();
```

```
        services.AddAuthentication(opts => {
            opts.DefaultScheme
                = CookieAuthenticationDefaults.AuthenticationScheme;
        }).AddCookie(opts => {
            opts.LoginPath = "/signin";
            opts.AccessDeniedPath = "/signin/403";
        });
        services.AddAuthorization(opts => {
            AuthorizationPolicies.AddPolicies(opts);
        });
        services.AddRazorPages();
        services.AddControllersWithViews();
    }

    public void Configure(IApplicationBuilder app, IWebHostEnvironment env) {

        app.UseStaticFiles();
        app.UseAuthentication();
        app.UseRouting();
        app.UseMiddleware<AuthorizationReporter>();

        app.UseEndpoints(endpoints => {
            endpoints.MapGet("/", async context => {
                await context.Response.WriteAsync("Hello World!");
            });
            endpoints.MapRazorPages();
            endpoints.MapDefaultControllerRoute();
        });
    }
}
}
```

Restart ASP.NET Core and request http://localhost:5000/secret. No specific authorization policy has been specified for the Secret Razor Page, so the fallback policy is applied, producing the result shown in Figure 15-2. The results show that the custom policy authorizes only authenticated requests for the username Bob.

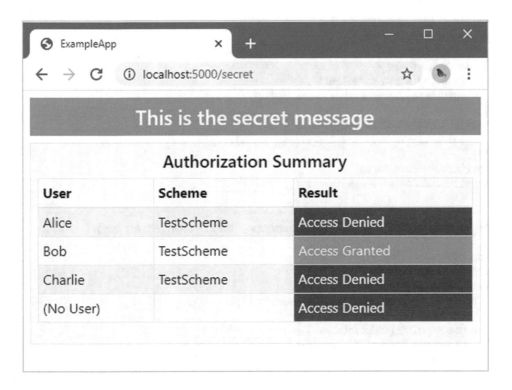

Figure 15-2. *Using an authorization policy*

Using the Built-In Requirements

There are a set of useful built-in requirements and handlers for the most common authorization requirements, as described in Table 15-5, and they can be used instead of custom classes.

Table 15-5. *Useful Built-In Authorization Requirement Classes*

Name	Description
NameAuthorizationRequirement	This requirement is for a case-sensitive name match.
RolesAuthorizationRequirement	This requirement is for a role.
ClaimsAuthorizationRequirement	This requirement is for a claim type and a range of acceptable values.
AssertionRequirement	This requirement evaluates a function using an AuthorizationHandlerContext object and is satisfied if the result is true.
DenyAnonymousAuthorization	This requirement is satisfied by any authenticated user.

Simple policies can be expressed using the name and role requirements. In Listing 15-12, I have replaced my custom requirement with the built-in equivalent.

Listing 15-12. Using a Built-In Requirement in the AuthorizationPolicies.cs in the Custom Folder

```
using Microsoft.AspNetCore.Authorization;
using System.Linq;
using Microsoft.AspNetCore.Authorization.Infrastructure;

namespace ExampleApp.Custom {

    public static class AuthorizationPolicies {

        public static void AddPolicies(AuthorizationOptions opts) {
            opts.FallbackPolicy = new AuthorizationPolicy(
                new IAuthorizationRequirement[] {
                    new NameAuthorizationRequirement("Bob"),
                }, Enumerable.Empty<string>());
        }
    }
}
```

This requirement has the same effect as my custom equivalent, albeit the name comparison is case-sensitive. Restart ASP.NET Core and request http://localhost:5000/secret, and you will see the response shown in Figure 15-2.

Combining Requirements

A policy will grant access only if all its requirements are satisfied, which means that complex policies can be built up using combinations of simple requirements, as shown in Listing 15-13.

Listing 15-13. Combining Requirements in the AuthorizationPolicies.cs File in the Custom Folder

```
using Microsoft.AspNetCore.Authorization;
using System.Linq;
using Microsoft.AspNetCore.Authorization.Infrastructure;

namespace ExampleApp.Custom {

    public static class AuthorizationPolicies {

        public static void AddPolicies(AuthorizationOptions opts) {
            opts.FallbackPolicy = new AuthorizationPolicy(
                new IAuthorizationRequirement[] {
                    new RolesAuthorizationRequirement(
                        new [] { "User", "Administrator" }),
                    new AssertionRequirement(context =>
                        !string.Equals(context.User.Identity.Name, "Bob"))
                }, Enumerable.Empty<string>());
        }
    }
}
```

This policy contains two requirements. The roles requirement will be met by users who are assigned the User or Administrator roles. The assertion requirement is met by any user whose name is not Bob. Restart ASP.NET Core and request http://localhost:500/secret, and you will see that access is granted to both Alice and Charlie, but not to Bob or unauthenticated requests, as shown in Figure 15-3.

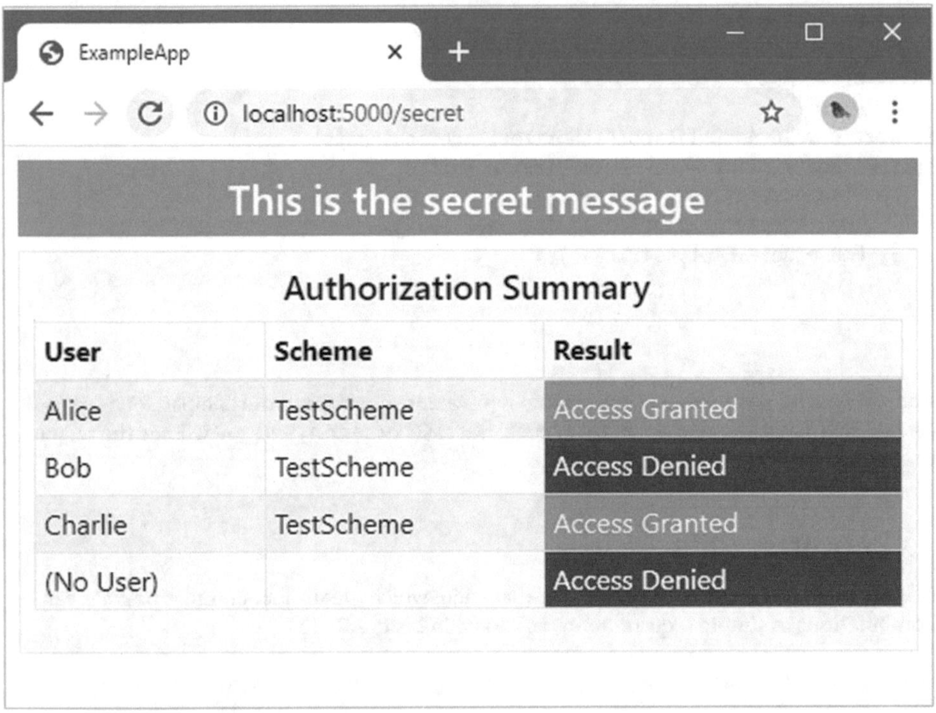

Figure 15-3. *Combining requirements in an authorization policy*

Restricting Access to a Specific Authorization Scheme

The two arguments used to create an AuthorizationPolicy object are a sequence of requirements and a sequence of authentication schemes. I used an empty array in earlier examples, which doesn't restrict the schemes that will be used, but this is a helpful feature in applications that support multiple authentication schemes and need to restrict access to users authenticated with a subset of them. In Listing 15-14, I added a new scheme that will be used by the custom authorization testing middleware.

Listing 15-14. Adding a Scheme in the UsersAndClaims.cs File in the ExampleApp Folder

```
using System;
using System.Collections.Generic;
using System.Linq;
using System.Security.Claims;

namespace ExampleApp {
    public static class UsersAndClaims {
        public static string[] Schemes
            = new string[] { "TestScheme", "OtherScheme" };
```

```
        public static Dictionary<string, IEnumerable<string>> UserData
            = new Dictionary<string, IEnumerable<string>> {
                { "Alice", new [] { "User", "Administrator" } },
                { "Bob", new [] { "User" } },
                { "Charlie", new [] { "User"} }
            };

        public static string[] Users => UserData.Keys.ToArray();

        public static Dictionary<string, IEnumerable<Claim>> Claims =>
            UserData.ToDictionary(kvp => kvp.Key,
                kvp => kvp.Value.Select(role => new Claim(ClaimTypes.Role, role)),
                StringComparer.InvariantCultureIgnoreCase);

        public static IEnumerable<ClaimsPrincipal> GetUsers() {
            foreach (string scheme in Schemes) {
                foreach (var kvp in Claims) {
                    ClaimsIdentity ident = new ClaimsIdentity(scheme);
                    ident.AddClaim(new Claim(ClaimTypes.Name, kvp.Key));
                    ident.AddClaims(kvp.Value);
                    yield return new ClaimsPrincipal(ident);
                }
            }
        }
    }
}
```

In Listing 15-15, I have changed the authorization policy to specify a scheme.

Listing 15-15. Specifying a Scheme in the AuthorizationPolicies.cs File in the Custom Folder

```
using Microsoft.AspNetCore.Authorization;
using System.Linq;
using Microsoft.AspNetCore.Authorization.Infrastructure;

namespace ExampleApp.Custom {

    public static class AuthorizationPolicies {

        public static void AddPolicies(AuthorizationOptions opts) {
            opts.FallbackPolicy = new AuthorizationPolicy(
                new IAuthorizationRequirement[] {
                    new RolesAuthorizationRequirement(
                        new [] { "User", "Administrator" }),
                    new AssertionRequirement(context =>
                        !string.Equals(context.User.Identity.Name, "Bob"))
                }, new string[] { "TestScheme" });
        }
    }
}
```

413

The effect is that the policy requires all its requirements to be met and for the request to have been authenticated using the TestScheme scheme. Restart ASP.NET Core and request http://localhost:5000/secret, and you will see that authorization fails for the ClaimsPrincipal objects whose authentication scheme is OtherScheme, even when their claims meet all the policy requirements, as shown in Figure 15-4. Alice and Charlie are authorized when they have been authenticated by TestScheme but not when they have been authenticated by OtherScheme.

■ **Note** In a real application, the built-in authorization middleware will trigger the standard authorization request flow described in Chapter 14. If the user has been authenticated using one of the policy's schemes, then a forbidden response is sent; otherwise, the challenge response is sent.

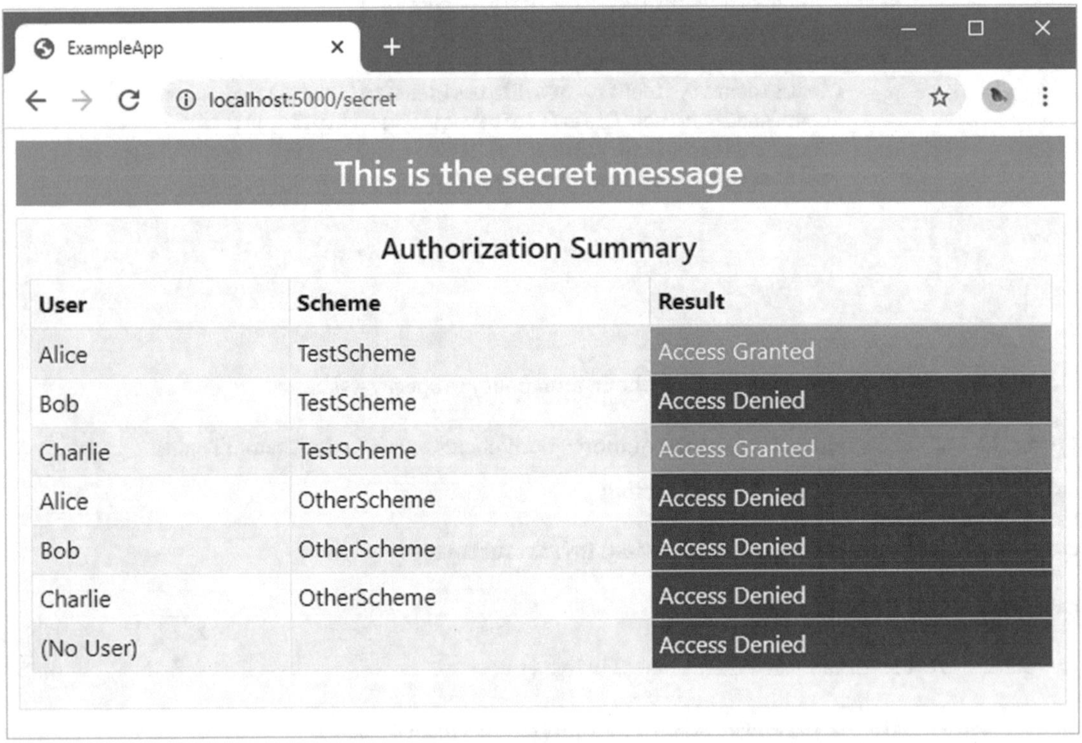

User	Scheme	Result
Alice	TestScheme	Access Granted
Bob	TestScheme	Access Denied
Charlie	TestScheme	Access Granted
Alice	OtherScheme	Access Denied
Bob	OtherScheme	Access Denied
Charlie	OtherScheme	Access Denied
(No User)		Access Denied

Figure 15-4. Specifying an authentication scheme

Targeting Authorization Policies

Changing the fallback policy makes it easy to see how the authorization building blocks fit together, but it has limited use in real projects where targeted access controls are required.

The next step up in authorization granularity is to use the default authorization policy, which is applied where access control is applied without using a specific policy. In Listing 15-16, I have applied the Authorize attribute to the Secret Razor Page, which tells ASP.NET Core that access controls are required.

Listing 15-16. Applying an Attribute in the Secret.cshtml File in the Pages Folder

@page

@using Microsoft.AspNetCore.Authorization

@attribute [Authorize]

```
<h4 class="bg-info text-center text-white m-2 p-2">
    This is the secret message
</h4>
```

The Authorize attribute denotes that authorization is required. I explain how to configure the Authorize attribute shortly, but when it is applied without arguments, ASP.NET Core uses the default authorization policy, which applied the DenyAnonymousAuthorization requirement described in Table 15-5. To see the effect of the default policy, restart ASP.NET Core and request http://localhost:5000/secret, and you will see that all authenticated users are authorized. The fallback policy is still used when there is no other policy available, which you can see by requesting http://localhost:5000/home/test. This request targets the Test action on the Home controller, which has not been decorated with the attribute. Figure 15-5 shows both responses.

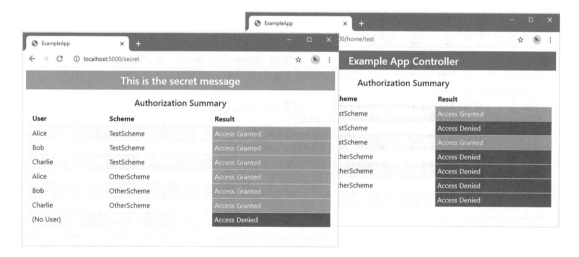

Figure 15-5. *The default authorization policy*

Behind the scenes, the Authorize attribute implements the IAuthorizeData interface, which is used by the ASP.NET Core authorization middleware to discover the authorization requirements for an endpoint. I used the same approach for the custom middleware in Listing 15-2.

```
...
IEnumerable<IAuthorizeData> authData =
    ep?.Metadata.GetOrderedMetadata<IAuthorizeData>()
        ?? Array.Empty<IAuthorizeData>();
AuthorizationPolicy policy = await
    AuthorizationPolicy.CombineAsync(policyProvider, authData);
...
```

This is the link between the Authorize attribute you may have already used in projects and the authorization flow described in this chapter.

Changing the Default Authorization Policy

The default policy can be changed by assigning a policy to the AuthorizationOptions.DefaultPolicy, allowing different behavior to be defined for the Authorize attribute, as shown in Listing 15-17.

Listing 15-17. Changing the Default Policy in the AuthorizationPolicies.cs File in the Custom Folder

```
using Microsoft.AspNetCore.Authorization;
using System.Linq;
using Microsoft.AspNetCore.Authorization.Infrastructure;

namespace ExampleApp.Custom {

    public static class AuthorizationPolicies {

        public static void AddPolicies(AuthorizationOptions opts) {
            opts.FallbackPolicy = new AuthorizationPolicy(
                new IAuthorizationRequirement[] {
                    new RolesAuthorizationRequirement(
                        new [] { "User", "Administrator" }),
                    new AssertionRequirement(context =>
                        !string.Equals(context.User.Identity.Name, "Bob"))
                }, new string[] { "TestScheme" });

            opts.DefaultPolicy = new AuthorizationPolicy(
                new IAuthorizationRequirement[] {
                    new RolesAuthorizationRequirement(
                        new string[] { "Administrator"})
                }, Enumerable.Empty<string>());
        }
    }
}
```

The new policy requires the Administrator role without restriction on the scheme used to authenticate the user. Restart ASP.NET Core and request http://localhost:5000/secret to see the effect of the new default policy, which is shown in Figure 15-6.

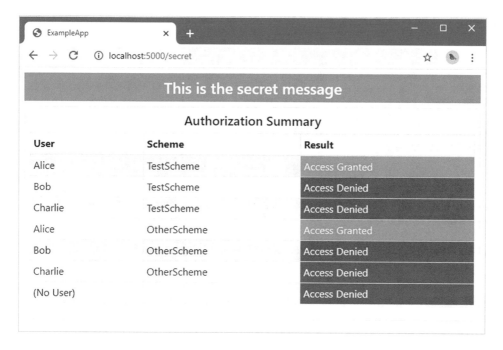

Figure 15-6. *Changing the default authorization policy*

Configuring Targeted Authorization Polices

The policy applied by the `Authorize` attribute can be selected using the properties described in Table 15-6.

Table 15-6. *The Authorize Attribute Properties*

Name	Description
AuthenticationSchemes	This property is used to specify a comma-separated list of allowed authentication schemes.
Policy	This property is used to specify a policy by name.
Roles	This property is used to specify a comma-separated list of allowed roles.

Direct support is provided for role-based authorization, which is the most commonly used approach. Roles that should be granted access are specified as a comma-separated list in a string, as shown in Listing 15-18.

■ **Caution** Role names are not validated because ASP.NET Core doesn't know what role claims are going to be created in advance. If you misspell a role name, you will find that you don't get the authorization policy you expected.

417

Listing 15-18. Specifying Roles in the Secret.cshtml File in the Pages Folder

```
@page

@using Microsoft.AspNetCore.Authorization

@attribute [Authorize(Roles = "Administrator, User")]

<h4 class="bg-info text-center text-white m-2 p-2">
    This is the secret message
</h4>
```

A user who has a role claim for any of the roles specified by the Authorize attribute will be granted access. If you want to restrict access to users who have claims for all roles in a list, then multiple attributes can be used, as shown in Listing 15-19.

Listing 15-19. Using Multiple Attributes in the Secret.cshtml File in the Pages Folder

```
@page

@using Microsoft.AspNetCore.Authorization

@attribute [Authorize(Roles = "Administrator")]
@attribute [Authorize(Roles = "User")]

<h4 class="bg-info text-center text-white m-2 p-2">
    This is the secret message
</h4>
```

When the policy is created, it will contain a role requirement for each of the Authorize attributes, which means that only users who have both Administrator and User role claims will be granted access. Figure 15-7 shows the results of Listing 15-18 and Listing 15-19.

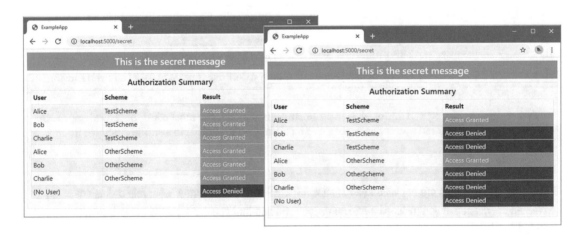

Figure 15-7. *Using the Authorize attribute to specify roles*

Using Named Policies

The Authorize attribute's Roles property is useful but makes it hard to change policies because every instance of the attribute has to be located so that new roles can be specified. The attribute's Policy attribute is more flexible because the authorization policy can be defined once and applied consistently throughout the application. When a change is required, the policy can be modified without needing to change the attributes. Listing 15-20 shows how a new policy is defined.

Listing 15-20. Defining a Policy in the AuthorizationPolicies.cs File in the Custom Folder

```
using Microsoft.AspNetCore.Authorization;
using System.Linq;
using Microsoft.AspNetCore.Authorization.Infrastructure;

namespace ExampleApp.Custom {

    public static class AuthorizationPolicies {

        public static void AddPolicies(AuthorizationOptions opts) {
            opts.FallbackPolicy = new AuthorizationPolicy(
                new IAuthorizationRequirement[] {
                    new RolesAuthorizationRequirement(
                        new [] { "User", "Administrator" }),
                    new AssertionRequirement(context =>
                        !string.Equals(context.User.Identity.Name, "Bob"))
                }, new string[] { "TestScheme" });

            opts.DefaultPolicy = new AuthorizationPolicy(
                new IAuthorizationRequirement[] {
                    new RolesAuthorizationRequirement(
                        new string[] { "Administrator"})
                }, Enumerable.Empty<string>());

            opts.AddPolicy("UsersExceptBob", new AuthorizationPolicy(
                new IAuthorizationRequirement[] {
                    new RolesAuthorizationRequirement(new[] { "User" }),
                    new AssertionRequirement(context =>
                        !string.Equals(context.User.Identity.Name, "Bob"))
                }, Enumerable.Empty<string>()));
        }
    }
}
```

The AuthorizationOptions class provides the AddPolicy method, which accepts a name and an AuthorizationPolicy object. In this case, the name is UsersExceptBob, and the policy has a role requirement for User role and an assertion requirement that the username isn't Bob. In Listing 15-21, I have changed the Authorize attribute applied to the Secret Razor Page to use the Policy property.

Listing 15-21. Specifying a Property in the Secret.cshtml File in the Pages Folder

```
@page

@using Microsoft.AspNetCore.Authorization

@attribute [Authorize(Policy = "UsersExceptBob")]

<h4 class="bg-info text-center text-white m-2 p-2">
    This is the secret message
</h4>
```

Only a single policy can be specified, and, unlike the `Roles` property, the `Policy` property cannot be used with a comma-separated list. Restart ASP.NET Core and request `http://localhost:5000/secret` to see the effect of the new policy, as shown in Figure 15-8.

■ **Tip** The `AuthenticationSchemes` property on the `Authorize` attribute is used to specify one or more authentication schemes. These are added to the list defined by the policy, broadening the range of schemes that will be granted access.

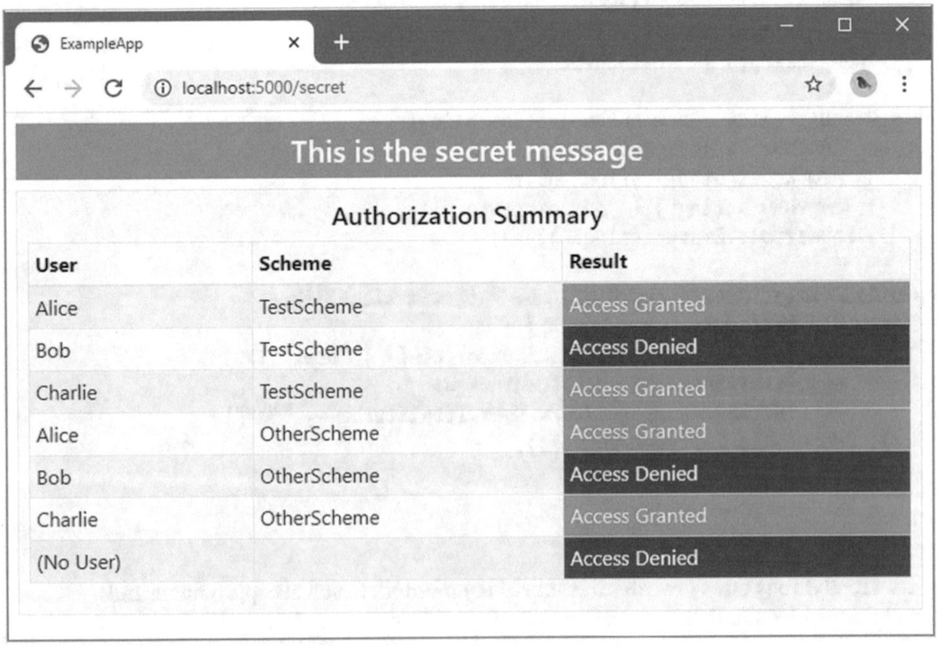

Figure 15-8. Using a named authorization policy

Creating Named Policies Using the Policy Builder

ASP.NET Core provides a more elegant way to create named policies, which allows requirements to be expressed using methods defined by the `AuthorizationPolicyBuilder` class, described in Table 15-7.

Table 15-7. *The AuthorizationPolicyBuilder Methods*

Name	Description
`AddAuthenticationSchemes(schemes)`	This method adds one or more authentication schemes to the set of schemes that will be accepted by the policy.
`RequireAssertion(func)`	This method adds an `AssertionRequirement` to the policy.
`RequireAuthenticatedUser()`	This method adds a `DenyAnonymousAuthorizationRequirement` to the policy, requiring requests to be authenticated.
`RequireClaim(type)`	This method adds a `ClaimsAuthorizationRequirement` to the policy, requiring a specific type of claim with any value.
`RequireClaim(type, values)`	This method adds a `ClaimsAuthorizationRequirement` to the policy, requiring a specific type of claim with one or more acceptable values.
`RequireRole(roles)`	This method adds a `RolesAuthorizationRequirement` to the policy.
`RequireUserName(name)`	This method adds a `NameAuthorizationRequirement` to the policy.
`AddRequirements(reqs)`	This method adds one or more `IAuthorizationRequirement` objects to the policy, which is useful for adding custom requirements.

The methods described in Table 15-7 all return a `AuthorizationPolicyBuilder` object, which allows calls to be chained together to create a policy, as shown in Listing 15-22.

Listing 15-22. Building an Authorization Policy in the AuthorizationPolicies.cs File in the Custom Folder

```
using Microsoft.AspNetCore.Authorization;
using System.Linq;
using Microsoft.AspNetCore.Authorization.Infrastructure;

namespace ExampleApp.Custom {

    public static class AuthorizationPolicies {

        public static void AddPolicies(AuthorizationOptions opts) {
            opts.FallbackPolicy = new AuthorizationPolicy(
                new IAuthorizationRequirement[] {
                    new RolesAuthorizationRequirement(
                        new [] { "User", "Administrator" }),
                    new AssertionRequirement(context =>
                        !string.Equals(context.User.Identity.Name, "Bob"))
                }, new string[] { "TestScheme" });

            opts.DefaultPolicy = new AuthorizationPolicy(
                new IAuthorizationRequirement[] {
                    new RolesAuthorizationRequirement(
                        new string[] { "Administrator"})
                }, Enumerable.Empty<string>());
```

```
                opts.AddPolicy("UsersExceptBob", builder => builder.RequireRole("User")
                    .AddRequirements(new AssertionRequirement(context =>
                        !string.Equals(context.User.Identity.Name, "Bob")))
                    .AddAuthenticationSchemes("OtherScheme"));
        }
    }
}
```

This policy has the same effect as the one defined in Listing 15-20 but has been created using the methods described in Table 15-7.   .

Combining Policies to Narrow Authorization

The Authorize attribute can be applied multiple times to set a wide authorization policy for an endpoint and narrow it for specific actions or handlers, as shown in Listing 15-23.

Listing 15-23. Applying the Attribute in the HomeController.cs File in the Controllers Folder

```
using Microsoft.AspNetCore.Authorization;
using Microsoft.AspNetCore.Mvc;

namespace ExampleApp.Controllers {

    [Authorize]
    public class HomeController: Controller {

        public IActionResult Test() => View();

        [Authorize(Roles = "User", AuthenticationSchemes = "OtherScheme")]
        public IActionResult Protected() => View("Test", "Protected Action");
    }
}
```

The Authorize attribute applied to the HomeController class applies the default policy to all the actions defined by the controller. I modified the default policy earlier, which means that access to the actions will only be granted to users with an Administrator role claim. This is the policy that will be applied to the Test action, but the Protected action has another Authorize attribute, which further narrows the policy by requiring the User role and the OtherScheme authentication scheme. To see the two policies that are created, restart ASP.NET Core and request http://localhost:5000/home/test and http://localhost:5000/home/protected. Access to the Test action is granted to Alice, regardless of how she is authenticated. Access to the Protected action is only granted to Alice when she is authenticated by the OtherScheme authentication scheme. Figure 15-9 shows both results.

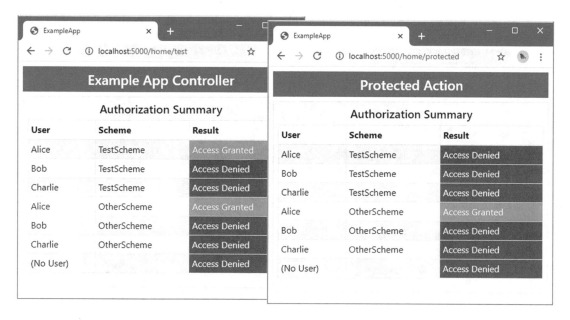

Figure 15-9. *Narrowing an authorization policy*

Creating Policy Exceptions

The AllowAnonymous attribute creates an exception to authorization policies to allow unauthenticated access. This is useful when the default or fallback policy would otherwise be applied or when the Authorize attribute has been used on a controller or Razor Page and you need to create an exception for a single action or handler method. In Listing 15-24, I have added an action method to the Home controller, to which the attribute is applied.

Listing 15-24. Adding an Action in the HomeController.cs File in the Controllers Folder

```
using Microsoft.AspNetCore.Authorization;
using Microsoft.AspNetCore.Mvc;

namespace ExampleApp.Controllers {

    [Authorize]
    public class HomeController: Controller {

        public IActionResult Test() => View();

        [Authorize(Roles = "User", AuthenticationSchemes = "OtherScheme")]
        public IActionResult Protected() => View("Test", "Protected Action");

        [AllowAnonymous]
        public IActionResult Public() => View("Test", "Unauthenticated Action");
    }
}
```

423

The AllowAnonymous attribute is given special treatment by the built-in authorization middleware and short-circuits the normal policy evaluation process to grant access to all requests, regardless of whether they are authenticated. Restart ASP.NET Core, and request http://localhost:5000/home/public to see the effect, which is shown in Figure 15-10.

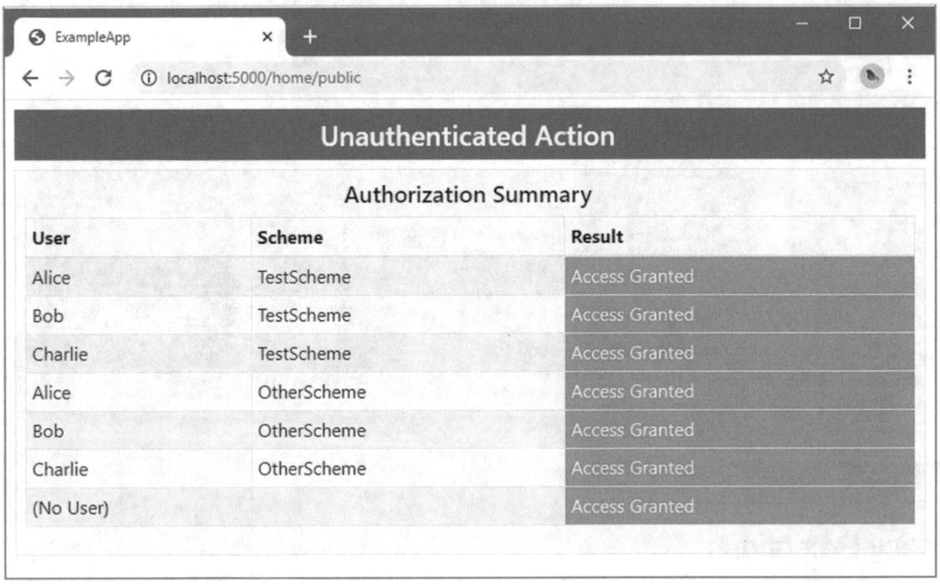

Figure 15-10. *Allowing anonymous access*

PERFORMING AUTHORIZATION IN PAGES AND VIEWS

You can use authorization in views to alter the HTML content for different groups of users. This requires using dependency injection to receive an IAuthorizationService service and using the AuthorizeAsync method in the view to apply an authorization policy, like this:

```
@page
@using Microsoft.AspNetCore.Authorization
@inject IAuthorizationService AuthorizationService

<div>This is content for all users</div>

@if ((await AuthorizationService.AuthorizeAsync(User,
        "UsersExceptBob")).Succeeded) {
    <div>This is the protected content</div>
}
```

I found this technique awkward to use, and it is easy to misapply policies. But, if you do use this feature, then you must ensure that any action methods or handlers that are targeted by the protected content have the same level of authorization to prevent unauthorized users from crafting HTTP requests to perform restricted operations.

Applying Policies Using Razor Page Conventions

If you are using Razor Pages, you can apply authorization policies using the options pattern when configuring services in the Startup class. In Listing 15-25, I have defined a new policy that denies access to users who have an Administrator role claim.

Listing 15-25. Defining a Policy in the AuthorizationPolicies.cs File in the Custom Folder

```
using Microsoft.AspNetCore.Authorization;
using System.Linq;
using Microsoft.AspNetCore.Authorization.Infrastructure;

namespace ExampleApp.Custom {

    public static class AuthorizationPolicies {

        public static void AddPolicies(AuthorizationOptions opts) {

            opts.FallbackPolicy = new AuthorizationPolicy(
                new IAuthorizationRequirement[] {
                    new RolesAuthorizationRequirement(
                        new [] { "User", "Administrator" }),
                    new AssertionRequirement(context =>
                        !string.Equals(context.User.Identity.Name, "Bob"))
                }, new string[] { "TestScheme" });

            opts.DefaultPolicy = new AuthorizationPolicy(
                new IAuthorizationRequirement[] {
                    new RolesAuthorizationRequirement(
                        new string[] { "Administrator"})
                }, Enumerable.Empty<string>());

            opts.AddPolicy("UsersExceptBob", builder => builder.RequireRole("User")
                .AddRequirements(new AssertionRequirement(context =>
                    !string.Equals(context.User.Identity.Name, "Bob")))
                .AddAuthenticationSchemes("OtherScheme"));

            opts.AddPolicy("NotAdmins", builder =>
                builder.AddRequirements(new AssertionRequirement(context =>
                    !context.User.IsInRole("Administrator"))));
        }
    }
}
```

In Listing 15-26, I have used the Razor Pages conventions feature to apply the new policy to the Secret Razor Page.

Listing 15-26. Applying a Policy in the Startup.cs File in the ExampleApp Folder

```
...
public void ConfigureServices(IServiceCollection services) {

    services.AddTransient<IAuthorizationHandler, CustomRequirementHandler>();

    services.AddAuthentication(opts => {
        opts.DefaultScheme
            = CookieAuthenticationDefaults.AuthenticationScheme;
    }).AddCookie(opts => {
        opts.LoginPath = "/signin";
        opts.AccessDeniedPath = "/signin/403";
    });
    services.AddAuthorization(opts => {
        AuthorizationPolicies.AddPolicies(opts);
    });
    services.AddRazorPages(opts => {
        opts.Conventions.AuthorizePage("/Secret", "NotAdmins");
    });
    services.AddControllersWithViews();
}
...
```

The RazorPagesOptions class is used to configure Razor Pages and its Conventions property returns a PageConventionCollection object for which authorization extension methods are available, as described in Table 15-8.

Table 15-8. *The Razor Pages Authorization Extension Methods*

Name	Description
AuthorizePage(page, policy)	This method applies an authorization policy to a specific page.
AuthorizePage(page)	This method applies the default policy to a specific page.
AuthorizeFolder(name, policy)	This method applies an authorization policy to all the pages in a single folder.
AuthorizeFolder(name)	This method applies the default policy to all the pages in a single folder.
AllowAnonymousToPage(page)	This method grants anonymous access to a specific page.
AllowAnonymousToFolder(name)	This method grants anonymous access to all the pages in a single folder.

In Listing 15-26, I used the AuthorizePage method to apply the NotAdmins policy to the Secret Razor Page. To see the effect, restart ASP.NET Core and request http://localhost:5000/secret. The response, shown in Figure 15-11, shows that the NotAdmins policy is combined with the policy UsersExceptBob policy applied to the page by the Authorize attribute, with the result that only Charlie can access the Razor Page and only when authenticated using OtherScheme.

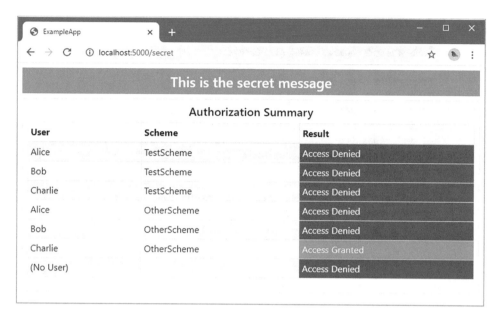

Figure 15-11. *Using an authorization convention*

Applying Policies Using MVC Framework Filters

The MVC Framework doesn't provide equivalent methods to those shown in Table 15-8, and the main alternative is to use a global filter to apply an authorization policy. The drawback with this approach is that the policy is applied to all requests that are processed by an MVC action method. However, with a little effort, it is possible to be more selective by taking advantage of the *application model* features provided to customize the core behavior of the MVC Framework, which is similar to the approach taken by the Razor Pages methods used in the previous section. In preparation for using the application model, I have disabled the customization of the default authorization policy, as shown in Listing 15-27, which will make it easier to see the effect of the new code in this section.

Listing 15-27. Disabling the Custom Default Policy in the AuthorizationPolicies.cs File in the Custom Folder

```
using Microsoft.AspNetCore.Authorization;
using System.Linq;
using Microsoft.AspNetCore.Authorization.Infrastructure;

namespace ExampleApp.Custom {

    public static class AuthorizationPolicies {

        public static void AddPolicies(AuthorizationOptions opts) {
            opts.FallbackPolicy = new AuthorizationPolicy(
                new IAuthorizationRequirement[] {
                    new RolesAuthorizationRequirement(
                        new [] { "User", "Administrator" }),
                    new AssertionRequirement(context =>
                        !string.Equals(context.User.Identity.Name, "Bob"))
                }, new string[] { "TestScheme" });
```

```
        //opts.DefaultPolicy = new AuthorizationPolicy(
        //    new IAuthorizationRequirement[] {
        //        new RolesAuthorizationRequirement(
        //            new string[] { "Administrator"})
        //    }, Enumerable.Empty<string>());

        opts.AddPolicy("UsersExceptBob", builder => builder.RequireRole("User")
            .AddRequirements(new AssertionRequirement(context =>
                !string.Equals(context.User.Identity.Name, "Bob")))
            .AddAuthenticationSchemes("OtherScheme"));

        opts.AddPolicy("NotAdmins", builder =>
            builder.AddRequirements(new AssertionRequirement(context =>
                !context.User.IsInRole("Administrator"))));
    }
  }
}
```

To create the code that will apply the authorization policy, add a class file named AuthorizationPolicyConvention.cs to the ExampleApp/Custom folder with the code shown in Listing 15-28.

Listing 15-28. The Contents of the AuthorizationPolicyConvention.cs File in the Custom Folder

```
using Microsoft.AspNetCore.Authorization;
using Microsoft.AspNetCore.Mvc.ApplicationModels;

namespace ExampleApp.Custom {

    public class AuthorizationPolicyConvention : IActionModelConvention {
        private string controllerName;
        private string actionName;
        private IAuthorizeData attr = new AuthData();

        public AuthorizationPolicyConvention(string controller,
                string action = null, string policy = null,
                string roles = null, string schemes = null) {
            controllerName = controller;
            actionName = action;
            attr.Policy = policy;
            attr.Roles = roles;
            attr.AuthenticationSchemes = schemes;
        }

        public void Apply(ActionModel action) {
            if (controllerName == action.Controller.ControllerName
                    && (actionName == null || actionName == action.ActionName)) {
                foreach (var s in action.Selectors) {
                    s.EndpointMetadata.Add(attr);
                }
            }
        }
    }
}
```

```
    class AuthData : IAuthorizeData {
        public string AuthenticationSchemes { get; set; }
        public string Policy { get; set; }
        public string Roles { get; set; }
    }
}
```

This class implements the `IActionModelConvention` interface, which is the part of the application model feature that allows action methods to be altered. The constructor accepts a controller name and, optionally, the action to which the policy should be applied. There are optional parameters for the authorization policy, the set of acceptable roles, and the acceptable authentication schemes. If no roles or policies are provided, then the default policy will be used. If no action method is specified, then the policy will be applied to all the actions defined by the controller.

During startup, `AuthorizationPolicyConvention` will receive details of all the action methods in the application and will add an object that implements the `IAuthorizeData` interface to the action's endpoint metadata. This is the interface that is implemented by the `Authorize` attribute and that the authorization middleware (and the custom replacement created earlier) looks for to build an authorization policy.

In Listing 15-29, I have used the new class to add policies to the action methods defined by the Home controller.

Listing 15-29. Applying an Authorization Policy in the Startup.cs File in the ExampleApp Folder

```
...
public void ConfigureServices(IServiceCollection services) {

    services.AddTransient<IAuthorizationHandler, CustomRequirementHandler>();

    services.AddAuthentication(opts => {
        opts.DefaultScheme
            = CookieAuthenticationDefaults.AuthenticationScheme;
    }).AddCookie(opts => {
        opts.LoginPath = "/signin";
        opts.AccessDeniedPath = "/signin/403";
    });
    services.AddAuthorization(opts => {
        AuthorizationPolicies.AddPolicies(opts);
    });
    services.AddRazorPages(opts => {
        opts.Conventions.AuthorizePage("/Secret", "NotAdmins");
    });
    services.AddControllersWithViews(opts => {
        opts.Conventions.Add(new AuthorizationPolicyConvention("Home",
            policy: "NotAdmins"));
        opts.Conventions.Add(new AuthorizationPolicyConvention("Home",
            action: "Protected", policy: "UsersExceptBob"));
    });
}
...
```

The conventions apply the NotAdmins policy to all the Home controller's actions and apply the UsersExceptBob policy to just the Protected action. Restart ASP.NET Core and request http://localhost:5000/home/protected to see the effect of the new policies, shown in Figure 15-12, which are applied in combination with the Authorize attributes applied directly to the controller class.

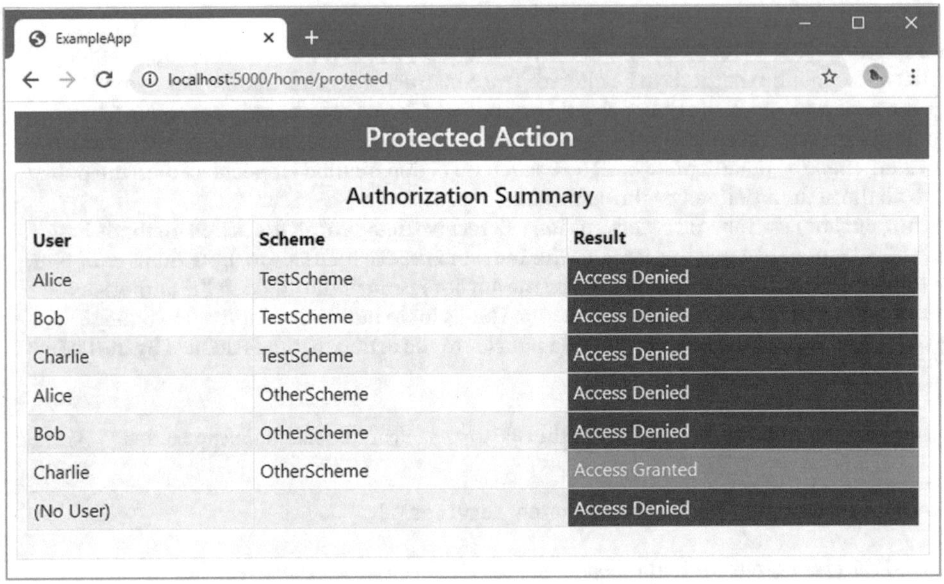

Figure 15-12. *Applying authorization policies using the application model*

Summary

In this chapter, I explained how ASP.NET Core authorizes requests using policies. Authorization policies are a key building block on which Identity relies, even though few applications need to work with them directly. In the next chapter, I introduce Identity to the example project and create a custom user store.

CHAPTER 16

■ ■ ■

Creating a User Store

In this chapter, I add Identity to the example project and create a custom user store. In Part 1, I used the default user store that Microsoft provides, which uses Entity Framework Core to store user data in a relational database, and this is the store you should use in real projects.

The user store I create in this chapter stores its data in memory, which makes it easy to explain how user stores work without getting bogged down in how to serialize and persist the data. Table 16-1 puts the user store in context.

Table 16-1. *Putting the User Store in Context*

Question	Answer
What is it?	The user store is the data repository for Identity data.
Why is it useful?	The user store maintains the data that Identity manages. Without a user store, none of the features that Identity provides would be possible.
How is it used?	The user store is registered as a service and consumed by Identity through the ASP.NET Core dependency injection feature.
Are there any pitfalls or limitations?	The main issue with custom user stores is ensuring that each optional interface is implemented without impacting any of the others. As you will see in later examples, some features are closely related, and care must be taken to ensure consistent results.
Are there any alternatives?	A user store is required to use Identity, but you do not have to create a custom implementation.

Table 16-2 summarizes the chapter.

© Adam Freeman 2021
A. Freeman, *Pro ASP.NET Core Identity*, https://doi.org/10.1007/978-1-4842-6858-2_16

Table 16-2. *Chapter Summary*

Problem	Solution	Listing
Define a custom user class	Create a class that has a unique key property and can store regular and normalized versions of a name. Define additional properties to support the optional features implemented by the user store.	7–8, 24, 31
Define a custom user store	Create an implementation of the IUserStore<T> interface. Additional features can be supported by implementing optional interfaces. Register the store as a service.	11, 14, 22, 25–27
Define a custom normalizer	Create an implementation of the ILookupNormalizer interface. Register the normalizer as a service.	12–14
Access the user store	Use the members of the UserManager<T> class.	15–21, 23, 28–30
Validate user data before it is added to the store	Create an implementation of the IUserValidator<T> method and register it as a service.	35, 26

Preparing for This Chapter

This chapter uses the ExampleApp project from Chapter 15. To prepare for this chapter, replace the Startup class with the code shown in Listing 16-1, which removes the custom authorization middleware used in the previous chapter and replaces it with the built-in authorization. I have also enabled the custom RoleMemberships middleware component as a source of user claims and removed the application model conventions for Razor Pages and the MVC Framework. The MapFallbackToPage method is used to select the Secret Razor Page for requests that are not matched by another endpoint.

■ **Tip** You can download the example project for this chapter—and for all the other chapters in this book—from https://github.com/Apress/pro-asp.net-core-identity. See Chapter 1 for how to get help if you have problems running the examples.

Listing 16-1. The Contents of the Startup.cs File in the ExampleApp Folder

```
using Microsoft.AspNetCore.Builder;
using Microsoft.AspNetCore.Hosting;
using Microsoft.AspNetCore.Http;
using Microsoft.Extensions.DependencyInjection;
using ExampleApp.Custom;
using Microsoft.AspNetCore.Authentication.Cookies;
using Microsoft.AspNetCore.Authorization;

namespace ExampleApp {
    public class Startup {

        public void ConfigureServices(IServiceCollection services) {

            services.AddTransient<IAuthorizationHandler,
                CustomRequirementHandler>();
```

```
            services.AddAuthentication(opts => {
                opts.DefaultScheme
                    = CookieAuthenticationDefaults.AuthenticationScheme;
            }).AddCookie(opts => {
                opts.LoginPath = "/signin";
                opts.AccessDeniedPath = "/signin/403";
            });
            services.AddAuthorization(opts => {
                AuthorizationPolicies.AddPolicies(opts);
            });
            services.AddRazorPages();
            services.AddControllersWithViews();
        }

        public void Configure(IApplicationBuilder app, IWebHostEnvironment env) {

            app.UseStaticFiles();
            app.UseAuthentication();
            app.UseRouting();
            //app.UseMiddleware<AuthorizationReporter>();
            app.UseMiddleware<RoleMemberships>();
            app.UseAuthorization();

            app.UseEndpoints(endpoints => {
                //endpoints.MapGet("/", async context => {
                //    await context.Response.WriteAsync("Hello World!");
                //});
                endpoints.MapRazorPages();
                endpoints.MapDefaultControllerRoute();
                endpoints.MapFallbackToPage("/Secret");
            });
        }
    }
}
```

Disable the custom fallback authorization policy and remove the reference to the OtherScheme from the UsersExceptBob policy, as shown in Listing 16-2.

Listing 16-2. Altering Authorization Policies in the AuthorizationPolicies.cs File in the Custom Folder

```
using Microsoft.AspNetCore.Authorization;
using System.Linq;
using Microsoft.AspNetCore.Authorization.Infrastructure;

namespace ExampleApp.Custom {

    public static class AuthorizationPolicies {

        public static void AddPolicies(AuthorizationOptions opts) {
            //opts.FallbackPolicy = new AuthorizationPolicy(
            //    new IAuthorizationRequirement[] {
            //        new RolesAuthorizationRequirement(
```

```
//                new [] { "User", "Administrator" }),
//           new AssertionRequirement(context =>
//               !string.Equals(context.User.Identity.Name, "Bob"))
//      }, new string[] { "TestScheme" });

opts.AddPolicy("UsersExceptBob", builder =>
        builder.RequireRole("User")
    .AddRequirements(new AssertionRequirement(context =>
        !string.Equals(context.User.Identity.Name, "Bob"))));
    //.AddAuthenticationSchemes("OtherScheme"));

opts.AddPolicy("NotAdmins", builder =>
        builder.AddRequirements(new AssertionRequirement(context =>
            !context.User.IsInRole("Administrator"))));
        }
    }
}
```

Remove the Authorize attribute from the Protected action of the Home controller, as shown in Listing 16-3.

Listing 16-3. Removing an Attribute in the HomeController.cs File in the Controllers Folder

```
using Microsoft.AspNetCore.Authorization;
using Microsoft.AspNetCore.Mvc;

namespace ExampleApp.Controllers {

    [Authorize]
    public class HomeController : Controller {

        public IActionResult Test() => View();

        //[Authorize(Roles = "User", AuthenticationSchemes = "OtherScheme")]
        public IActionResult Protected() => View("Test", "Protected Action");

        [AllowAnonymous]
        public IActionResult Public() => View("Test", "Unauthenticated Action");
    }
}
```

Finally, disable the partial view that displays the authorization results used in Chapter 15, as shown in Listing 16-4.

Listing 16-4. Removing the Partial View in the _Layout.cshtml File in the Pages/Shared Folder

```
<!DOCTYPE html>

<html>
<head>
    <meta name="viewport" content="width=device-width" />
    <title>ExampleApp</title>
```

```
    <link href="/lib/twitter-bootstrap/css/bootstrap.min.css" rel="stylesheet" />
</head>
<body>
    <div>
        @RenderBody()
    </div>
    @*<partial name="_AuthorizationReport" />*@
</body>
</html>
```

The effect of these changes is to restore the built-in authorization features so that users can be signed in at the /signin URL using the Cookie authentication scheme. The custom RoleMemberships middleware component provides a source of user claims that are used by the authorization policies. Run the command shown in Listing 16-5 in the ExampleApp folder to start ASP.NET Core.

Listing 16-5. Starting ASP.NET Core

```
dotnet run
```

Request http://localhost:5000/signin, select Alice from the list, and click the Sign In button. Request http://localhost:5000/secret, and the request will be authenticated using a cookie and granted access to the Secret Razor Page, as shown in Figure 16-1.

Figure 16-1. *Running the example application*

Installing ASP.NET Core Identity

Use a command prompt to run the command shown in Listing 16-6 in the ExampleApp folder to add the core Identity package to the project.

435

Listing 16-6. Adding the Core Identity Package to the Project

```
dotnet add package Microsoft.Extensions.Identity.Core --version 5.0.0
```

Creating an Identity User Store

In earlier chapters, I hard-coded the list of users into the application, which can get you started but quickly becomes difficult to manage and requires a new release every time a user is added or removed. A user store provides a consistent way to manage user data.

Creating the User Class

The first step in creating a user store is to define the user class, instances of which will be used to represent users in the application. No specific base class is required, but the instances of the class must be distinguishable from one another and must be able to store basic information about the user. To define the user class for this chapter, create the ExampleApp/Identity folder and add to it a class file named AppUser.cs with the code shown in Listing 16-7.

Listing 16-7. The Contents of the AppUser.cs File in the Identity Folder

```
using System;

namespace ExampleApp.Identity {
    public class AppUser {

        public string Id { get; set; } = Guid.NewGuid().ToString();

        public string UserName { get; set; }

        public string NormalizedUserName { get; set; }
    }
}
```

The Id property will be assigned a unique identifier representing a user and defaults to a GUID value. The UserName property will store the user's account name in the application. The NormalizedUserName contains a normalized representation of the UserName value, which I explain in the next section. This is a minimal user class to which I will add properties as the user store develops.

I need to be able to easily copy values from one AppUser object to another. This will make it easier to implement the store in the way that Identity expects so that changes to an instance of the user class will be discarded if they are not explicitly saved to the user store. Add a class file named StoreClassExtentions.cs to the Identity folder and use it to define the extension methods shown in Listing 16-8.

Listing 16-8. The Contents of the StoreClassExtentions.cs File in the Identity Folder

```
using System;
using System.Collections;
using System.Collections.Generic;
```

```
namespace ExampleApp.Identity {

    public static class StoreClassExtentions {

        public static T UpdateFrom<T>(this T target, T source) {
            UpdateFrom(target, source, out bool discardValue);
            return target;
        }

        public static T UpdateFrom<T>(this T target, T source, out bool changes) {
            object value;
            int changeCount = 0;
            Type classType = typeof(T);
            foreach (var prop in classType.GetProperties()) {
                if (prop.PropertyType.IsGenericType &&
                    prop.PropertyType.GetGenericTypeDefinition()
                        .Equals(typeof(IList<>))) {
                    Type listType = typeof(List<>).MakeGenericType(prop.PropertyType
                        .GetGenericArguments()[0]);
                    IList sourceList = prop.GetValue(source) as IList;
                    if (sourceList != null) {
                        prop.SetValue(target, Activator.CreateInstance(listType,
                            sourceList));
                    }
                } else {
                    if ((value = prop.GetValue(source)) != null
                            && !value.Equals(prop.GetValue(target))) {
                        classType.GetProperty(prop.Name).SetValue(target, value);
                        changeCount++;
                    }
                }
            }
            changes = changeCount > 0;
            return target;
        }

        public static T Clone<T>(this T original) =>
            Activator.CreateInstance<T>().UpdateFrom(original);
    }
}
```

I have defined methods with generic type parameters so that I can use the same code to handle different classes used by Identity. The UpdateFrom method will copy the value of any non-null property from one object to another, while the Clone method will create a copy of an object. The code in Listing 16-8 is written to support the examples in this part of the book and isn't required when using the standard approach of storing Identity data using Entity Framework Core.

Creating the User Store

The key interface to implement is IUserStore<T>, where T is the user class. This interface defines the core features of a user store using the methods described in Table 16-3. All the methods defined by the interface receive a CancellationToken parameter, which is used to receive notifications that an asynchronous operation should be canceled, and which is shown as the token parameter in the table.

Table 16-3. *IUserStore<T> Methods*

Name	Description
CreateAsync(user, token)	This method creates the specified user in the store.
DeleteAsync(user, token)	This method removes the specified user in the store.
UpdateAsync(user, token)	This method updates the specified user in the store.
FindByIdAsync(id, token)	This method retrieves the user with the specified ID from the store.
FindByNameAsync(name, token)	This method retrieves the user with the specified normalized username.
GetUserIdAsync(user, name)	This method returns the ID from the specified user object.
GetUserNameAsync(name, token)	This method returns the username from the specified user object.
SetUserNameAsync(user, name, token)	This method sets the username for the specified user.
GetNormalizedUserNameAsync(user, token)	This method gets the normalized username for the specified user.
SetNormalizedUserNameAsync(user, name, token)	This method sets the normalized username for the specified user.
Dispose()	This method is inherited from the IDisposable interface and is called to release unmanaged resources before the store object is destroyed.

The methods defined by the IUserStore<T> interface fall into three groups: core storage (creating/deleting/updating users), querying (locating users by name and ID), and handling names (getting and setting natural and normalized usernames). In the sections that follow, I create a user store by focusing on each group of methods in turn and using the C# partial class feature to build up the functionality in multiple class files.

Implementing the Data Storage Methods

I am going to create a memory-based user store for simplicity. The drawback of this approach, of course, is that changes to the user store will be lost when ASP.NET Core is restarted, but it is enough to get started.

Create the ExampleApp/Identity/Store folder and add to it a class file named UserStoreCore.cs, with the code shown in Listing 16-9.

■ **Note** Your code editor may warn you that the `AppUserStore` class doesn't implement all the methods required by the `IUserStore<AppUser>` interface. The code in Listing 16-9 defines a partial class, which means the class members are defined in multiple class files. I will implement the missing methods in the sections that follow.

Listing 16-9. The Contents of the UserStoreCore.cs File in the Identity/Store Folder

```
using Microsoft.AspNetCore.Identity;
using System.Collections.Concurrent;
using System.Threading;
using System.Threading.Tasks;

namespace ExampleApp.Identity.Store {

    public partial class UserStore : IUserStore<AppUser> {
        private ConcurrentDictionary<string, AppUser> users
            = new ConcurrentDictionary<string, AppUser>();

        public Task<IdentityResult> CreateAsync(AppUser user,
                CancellationToken token) {
            if (!users.ContainsKey(user.Id) && users.TryAdd(user.Id, user)) {
                return Task.FromResult(IdentityResult.Success);
            }
            return Task.FromResult(Error);
        }

        public Task<IdentityResult> DeleteAsync(AppUser user,
                CancellationToken token) {
            if (users.ContainsKey(user.Id)
                    && users.TryRemove(user.Id, out user)) {
                return Task.FromResult(IdentityResult.Success);
            }
            return Task.FromResult(Error);
        }

        public Task<IdentityResult> UpdateAsync(AppUser user,
                CancellationToken token) {
            if (users.ContainsKey(user.Id)) {
                users[user.Id].UpdateFrom(user);
                return Task.FromResult(IdentityResult.Success);
            }
            return Task.FromResult(Error);
        }

        public void Dispose() {
            // do nothing
        }
```

```
        private IdentityResult Error => IdentityResult.Failed(new IdentityError {
            Code = "StorageFailure",
            Description = "User Store Error"
        });
    }
}
```

The data structure for the user data is a concurrent dictionary, with each AppUser object stored using its Id value as the key. Implementing the CreateAsync, DeleteAsync, and UpdateAsync methods means managing the data in the dictionary and producing IdentityResult objects to report on the outcome. Successful operations are reported using the IdentityResult.Success property.

```
...
return Task.FromResult(IdentityResult.Success);
...
```

Failed operations are reported using the IdentityResult.Failed method, which accepts one or more IdentityError objects that describe the problem.

```
...
private IdentityResult Error => IdentityResult.Failed(new IdentityError {
    Code = "StorageFailure", Description = "User Store Error"});
...
```

The IdentityError class defines Code and Description properties that are used to describe an error condition. A real user store would be descriptive about the problems it encounters, but for my simple implementation, I produce a general error to indicate a problem.

Implementing the Search Methods

The next group of methods allows the user store to be searched. Add a class file named UserStoreQuery.cs to the ExampleApp/Identity/Store folder and use it to define the partial class shown in Listing 16-10.

Listing 16-10. The Contents of the UserStoreQuery.cs File in the Identity/Store Folder

```
using System.Linq;
using System.Threading;
using System.Threading.Tasks;

namespace ExampleApp.Identity.Store {

    public partial class UserStore {

        public Task<AppUser> FindByIdAsync(string userId,
                CancellationToken token) =>
            Task.FromResult(users.ContainsKey(userId)
                ? users[userId].Clone() : null);

        public Task<AppUser> FindByNameAsync(string normalizedUserName,
                CancellationToken token) =>
```

```
        Task.FromResult(users.Values.FirstOrDefault(user =>
            user.NormalizedUserName == normalizedUserName)?.Clone());
    }
}
```

These methods retrieve AppUser objects from the dictionary. In the case of the FindByIdAsync method, the AppUser objects are stored using Id values as keys, which makes the query simple. The FindByNameAsync requires more work because the query is performed using the NormalizedUserName property, which is not a key. For this method, I use the LINQ FirstOrDefault method to locate a matching object.

In both cases, the Clone extension method defined in Listing 16-8 is used to create copies of the AppUser objects retrieved from the store. This means that any changes made to the AppUser objects are not added to the store until the UpdateAsync method is called.

Implementing the ID and Name Methods

The next set of methods is used to get user IDs and get and set usernames. Add a class file named UserStoreNames.cs to the ExampleApp/Identity/Store folder and use it to define the partial class shown in Listing 16-11.

Listing 16-11. The Contents of the UserStoreNames.cs File in the Identity/Store Folder

```
using System.Threading;
using System.Threading.Tasks;

namespace ExampleApp.Identity.Store {

    public partial class UserStore {

        public Task<string> GetNormalizedUserNameAsync(AppUser user,
            CancellationToken token)
                => Task.FromResult(user.NormalizedUserName);

        public Task<string> GetUserIdAsync(AppUser user,
            CancellationToken token)
                => Task.FromResult(user.Id);

        public Task<string> GetUserNameAsync(AppUser user,
            CancellationToken token)
                => Task.FromResult(user.UserName);

        public Task SetNormalizedUserNameAsync(AppUser user,
            string normalizedName, CancellationToken token)
                => Task.FromResult(user.NormalizedUserName = normalizedName);

        public Task SetUserNameAsync(AppUser user, string userName,
            CancellationToken token)
                => Task.FromResult(user.UserName = userName);
    }
}
```

These methods are easy to implement and are mapped directly onto the properties of the AppUser class.

Creating the Normalizer and Seeding the User Store

Normalization of a name is the process of transforming it so queries will match in all the forms in which the name can be expressed. Without normalization, a name such as Alice will be treated differently from alice, ALICE, and AliCE. This can be a problem for data stores, where a query for alice won't match the stored value Alice, for example.

Rather than write complex query matchers, normalization transforms names so the same value is produced regardless of variations in how the name is expressed. For usernames, conventional normalization means converting all the letters to uppercase or lowercase so that all forms of Alice are expressed as alice. ASP.NET Core Identity normalization is done through the ILookupNormalizer interface, which defines the methods described in Table 16-4.

***Table 16-4.** The Methods Defined by the ILookupNormalizer Method*

Name	Description
NormalizeName(name)	This method is responsible for normalizing usernames.
NormalizeEmail(email)	This method is responsible for normalizing email addresses.

Creating a custom normalizer isn't required to create a custom user store, but I want to demonstrate the key ASP.NET Core Identity building blocks. Add a class named Normalizer.cs to the ExampleApp/Identity/Store folder and use it to define the class shown in Listing 16-12.

***Listing 16-12.** The Contents of the Normalizer.cs File in the Identity/Store Folder*

```
using Microsoft.AspNetCore.Identity;

namespace ExampleApp.Identity.Store {

    public class Normalizer : ILookupNormalizer {

        public string NormalizeName(string name)
            => name.Normalize().ToLowerInvariant();

        public string NormalizeEmail(string email)
            => email.Normalize().ToLowerInvariant();
    }
}
```

It doesn't matter how values are normalized if the process is consistent, and all the ways that a name can be expressed are addressed. It is also a good idea to take advantage of the .NET Unicode normalization feature, which ensures that complex characters are handled consistently. In Listing 16-12, I call the string Normalize method and transform the result to lowercase.

To complete the user store, add a class file named UserStore.cs to the ExampleApp/Identity/Store folder and use it to define the partial class shown in Listing 16-13.

Listing 16-13. The Contents of the UserStore.cs File in the Identity/Store Folder

```
using Microsoft.AspNetCore.Identity;

namespace ExampleApp.Identity.Store {

    public partial class UserStore {

        public ILookupNormalizer Normalizer { get; set; }

        public UserStore(ILookupNormalizer normalizer) {
            Normalizer = normalizer;
            SeedStore();
        }

        private void SeedStore() {

            int idCounter = 0;

            foreach (string name in UsersAndClaims.Users) {
                AppUser user = new AppUser {
                    Id = (++idCounter).ToString(),
                    UserName = name,
                    NormalizedUserName = Normalizer.NormalizeName(name)
                };
                users.TryAdd(user.Id, user);
            }
        }
    }
}
```

This code adds a constructor that accepts a ILookupNormalizer parameter. ASP.NET Core Identity finds the functionality it requires using ASP.NET Core services. The user store will be set up as a service, and when the ASP.NET Core dependency injection feature instantiates the UserStore class, it will instantiate the ILookupNormalizer service to provide the constructor argument.

The constructor assigns the normalizer to a property and calls the SeedStore method, which populates the user store with AppUser objects based on the usernames defined in the UsersAndClaims class.

Configuring Identity and the Custom Services

The application must be configured to set up the custom user store and ASP.NET Core Identity, as shown in Listing 16-14.

Listing 16-14. Configuring the Application in the Startup.cs File in the ExampleApp Folder

```
using Microsoft.AspNetCore.Builder;
using Microsoft.AspNetCore.Hosting;
using Microsoft.AspNetCore.Http;
using Microsoft.Extensions.DependencyInjection;
using ExampleApp.Custom;
using Microsoft.AspNetCore.Authentication.Cookies;
```

```
using Microsoft.AspNetCore.Authorization;
using Microsoft.AspNetCore.Identity;
using ExampleApp.Identity;
using ExampleApp.Identity.Store;

namespace ExampleApp {
    public class Startup {

        public void ConfigureServices(IServiceCollection services) {

            //services.AddTransient<IAuthorizationHandler,
            //    CustomRequirementHandler>();

            services.AddSingleton<ILookupNormalizer, Normalizer>();
            services.AddSingleton<IUserStore<AppUser>, UserStore>();

            services.AddIdentityCore<AppUser>();

            services.AddAuthentication(opts => {
                opts.DefaultScheme
                    = CookieAuthenticationDefaults.AuthenticationScheme;
            }).AddCookie(opts => {
                opts.LoginPath = "/signin";
                opts.AccessDeniedPath = "/signin/403";
            });
            services.AddAuthorization(opts => {
                AuthorizationPolicies.AddPolicies(opts);
            });
            services.AddRazorPages();
            services.AddControllersWithViews();
        }

        public void Configure(IApplicationBuilder app, IWebHostEnvironment env) {

            app.UseStaticFiles();
            app.UseAuthentication();
            app.UseRouting();
            app.UseMiddleware<RoleMemberships>();
            app.UseAuthorization();

            app.UseEndpoints(endpoints => {
                endpoints.MapRazorPages();
                endpoints.MapDefaultControllerRoute();
                endpoints.MapFallbackToPage("/Secret");
            });
        }
    }
}
```

The custom implementations of the Identity interfaces are registered as services using the AddSingleton method, and Identity is added to the application with the AddIdentityCore<T> method, where T is the user class. Identity will use its default implementation for any service that has not already been registered, which means you can be selective about the customization you make.

■ **Note** The AddIdentityCore<T> method is useful when you want greater control over the Identity services and features that are enabled, but the methods used in Part 1 are more suitable for most projects.

Accessing the User Store

Applications don't interface with the user store directly. Instead, Identity provides the UserManager<T> class, where T is the user class. The UserManager<T> class defines a lot of members, and Table 16-5 describes those that relate to the user store. I will describe additional members as I start using other Identity features.

Table 16-5. *Selected UserManager<T> Members*

Name	Description
FindByIdAsync(id)	This method locates an AppUser object user by ID by calling the store's FindByIdAsync method.
FindByNameAsync(username)	This method locates an AppUser object user by username. The username argument is normalized and passed to the store's FindByNameAsync method.
CreateAsync(user)	This method adds the specified AppUser object to the store. The security stamp is set, the user is subjected to validation, and the normalized name and email properties are updated, after which the user object is passed to the store's CreateAsync method. (Storing email addresses is described in the "Adding Optional Store Features" section, and validating a user is described in the "Validating User Data" section.)
UpdateAsync(user)	This method applies the user store's update sequence, described in the following sidebar, committing any changes that have been made.
DeleteAsync(user)	This method removes an AppUser object from the store by passing the user object to the store's DeleteAsync method.
GetUserIdAsync(user)	This method gets the ID for the user object by calling the store's GetUserIdAsync method.
GetUserNameAsync(user)	This method gets the name for the user object by calling the store's GetUserNameAsync method.
SetUserNameAsync(user, name)	This method sets the name for the user object by calling the store's SetUserNameAsync method, after which the security stamp is updated and the user manager's update sequence is performed. The update sequence is described in the following sidebar.

The most important UserManager<T> methods are CreateAsync and UpdateAsync. These methods validate the user object (as described in the "Validating User Data" section), ensure that normalized properties are updated consistently, and create new security stamps (which I describe in Chapter 17).

The UserManager<T> methods that update individual properties are optional, and you can choose to use them or work directly with the properties defined by the user class. The advantage of the UserManager<T> methods is they often perform useful additional work that I describe as I introduce each set of methods.

Setting properties directly works well with the ASP.NET Core model binding feature, making it easy to work with HTML forms, even though this means you must take care to explicitly perform the additional work that UserManager<T> does automatically. You must also remember to call the UpdateAsync method to apply changes to the user store.

In most cases, I work directly with user class properties in this part of the book because of the close fit with model binding, which suits the style of the examples. You don't have to follow this approach in your own projects, and I include details of the work performed by each UserManager<T> method I describe.

UNDERSTANDING THE USER MANAGER UPDATE SEQUENCE

As I introduce the features provided by the UserManager<T>, many of the descriptions of the methods will refer to the user manager update sequence. The UserManager<T> class defines a protected method that is called by many other methods to update data in the store. This method goes through a sequence of steps to prepare a user object. This sequence depends on features that I introduce in later chapters, but for now, it is enough to have a rough sense of the process.

This update sequence performs validation (described in the "Validating User Data" section) and updates the normalized name and email properties (I describe storing email addresses in the "Adding Support for Storing Email Addresses" section) before passing the object to the user store's UpdateAsync method.

Working with User Store Data

To prepare for working with the UserManager<T> class, add the expressions shown in Listing 16-15 to the _ViewImports.cshtml file in the Pages folder.

Listing 16-15. Adding Expressions in the _ViewImports.cshtml File in the Pages Folder

```
@namespace ExampleApp.Pages
@addTagHelper *, Microsoft.AspNetCore.Mvc.TagHelpers
@using Microsoft.AspNetCore.Mvc.RazorPages
@using Microsoft.AspNetCore.Identity
@using System.Security.Claims
@using ExampleApp.Identity
```

Defining these namespaces in a view imports file means that I don't have to import them in each of the Razor Pages that uses Identity features.

Next, create the Pages/Store folder and add to it a Razor Page named Users.cshtml with the content shown in Listing 16-16.

Listing 16-16. The Contents of the Users.cshtml File in the Pages/Store Folder

```
@page "/users/{searchname?}"
@model ExampleApp.Pages.Store.FindUserModel

<div class="m-2">
    <form method="get" class="mb-2" action="/users">
        <div class="container-fluid">
            <div class="row">
                <div class="col-9">
                    <input name="searchname" class="w-100" value="@Model.Searchname"
                        placeholder="Enter Username or ID" />
                </div>
                <div class="col-auto">
                    <button type="submit"
                        class="btn btn-primary btn-sm">Find</button>
                    <a class="btn btn-secondary btn-sm" href="/users">Clear</a>
                </div>
            </div>
        </div>
    </form>
    @if (Model.Users?.Count() > 0) {
        <table class="table table-sm table-striped table-bordered">
            <thead>
                <tr><th>Username</th><th>Normalized</th><th/></tr>
            </thead>
            <tbody>
                @foreach (AppUser user in Model.Users) {
                    <tr>
                        <td>@user.UserName</td>
                        <td>@user.NormalizedUserName</td>
                        <td>
                            <form asp-page-handler="delete" method="post">
                                <partial name="_UserTableRow" model="@user.Id" />
                                <input type="hidden" name="id" value="@user.Id" />
                                <button type="submit" class="btn btn-sm btn-danger">
                                    Delete
                                </button>
                            </form>
                        </td>
                    </tr>
                }
            </tbody>
        </table>
    } else if (!string.IsNullOrEmpty(Model.Searchname)) {
        <h6>No match</h6>
    }
    <a asp-page="edituser" class="btn btn-primary">Create</a>
</div>
```

The Razor Page presents an input element that will allow the user to enter a search term and a table that will display details of the users returned by the search. Each row in the table will display a summary of the user and a series of buttons that will be used to manage the data in the store.

To create the page model, the Users.cshtml.cs class file to define the page model class shown in Listing 16-17. If you created the Users.cshtml file using the Visual Studio Razor Page template, the class file will already have been created. If you are using Visual Studio Code, add a file named Users.cshtml.cs to the ExampleApp/Pages/Store folder.

Listing 16-17. The Contents of the Users.cshtml.cs File in the Pages/Store Folder

```
using ExampleApp.Identity;
using Microsoft.AspNetCore.Identity;
using Microsoft.AspNetCore.Mvc;
using Microsoft.AspNetCore.Mvc.RazorPages;
using System.Collections.Generic;
using System.Linq;
using System.Threading.Tasks;

namespace ExampleApp.Pages.Store {

    public class FindUserModel : PageModel {

        public FindUserModel(UserManager<AppUser> userMgr) {
            UserManager = userMgr;
        }

        public UserManager<AppUser> UserManager { get; set; }

        public IEnumerable<AppUser> Users { get; set; }
            = Enumerable.Empty<AppUser>();

        [BindProperty(SupportsGet = true)]
        public string Searchname { get; set; }

        public async Task OnGet() {
            if (Searchname != null) {
                AppUser nameUser = await UserManager.FindByNameAsync(Searchname);
                if (nameUser != null) {
                    Users = Users.Append(nameUser);
                }
                AppUser idUser = await UserManager.FindByIdAsync(Searchname);
                if (idUser!= null) {
                    Users = Users.Append(idUser);
                }
            }
        }

        public async Task<IActionResult> OnPostDelete(string id) {
            AppUser user = await UserManager.FindByIdAsync(id);
            if (user != null) {
                await UserManager.DeleteAsync(user);
            }
```

```
            return RedirectToPage();
        }
    }
}
```

The page model class for this Razor Page declares a dependency on the UserManager<AppUser> service, through which it searches the store for users, either by name or by ID. The POST handler method receives an ID value and uses it to delete a user by calling the UserManager<T>.DeleteAsync method.

To create the partial view that will display the buttons that will lead to other management features, add a Razor View named _UserTableRow.cshtml to the Pages/Store folder with the content shown in Listing 16-18.

Listing 16-18. The Contents of the _UserTableRow.cshtml File in the Pages/Store Folder

```
@model string

<a asp-page="edituser" asp-route-id="@Model" class="btn btn-sm btn-secondary">
    Edit
</a>
```

When the user clicks the Edit button, the browser is redirected to a Razor Page named EditUser, with a route variable named id that provides the ID of the selected user. Add a Razor Page named EditUser.cshtml to the Pages/Store folder with the content shown in Listing 16-19.

Listing 16-19. The Contents of the EditUser.cshtml File in the Pages/Store Folder

```
@page "/users/edit/{id?}"
@model ExampleApp.Pages.Store.UsersModel

<div asp-validation-summary="All" class="text-danger m-2"></div>

<div class="m-2">
    <form method="post">
        <input type="hidden" name="id" value="@Model.AppUserObject.Id" />
        <table class="table table-sm table-striped">
            <tbody>
                <partial name="_EditUserBasic" model="@Model.AppUserObject" />
            </tbody>
        </table>
        <div>
            <button type="submit" class="btn btn-primary">Save</button>
            <a asp-page="users" class="btn btn-secondary">Cancel</a>
        </div>
    </form>
</div>
```

The Razor Page displays a table that allows user object properties to be displayed and edited, along with a Save button that will apply changes in the user store and a Cancel button that will return to the Users Razor Page. I am going to build up the editing support gradually as I introduce Identity features, and each feature will have its own partial view that adds rows to the table.

Use the EditUser.cshtml.cs file to define the page model class shown in Listing 16-20. You will have to create this file if you are using Visual Studio Code.

Listing 16-20. The Contents of the EditUser.cshtml.cs File in the Pages/Store Folder

```
using ExampleApp.Identity;
using Microsoft.AspNetCore.Identity;
using Microsoft.AspNetCore.Mvc;
using Microsoft.AspNetCore.Mvc.RazorPages;
using System.Threading.Tasks;

namespace ExampleApp.Pages.Store {

    public class UsersModel : PageModel {

        public UsersModel(UserManager<AppUser> userMgr) => UserManager = userMgr;

        public UserManager<AppUser> UserManager { get; set; }

        public AppUser AppUserObject { get; set; } = new AppUser();

        public async Task OnGetAsync(string id) {
            if (id != null) {
                AppUserObject = await UserManager.FindByIdAsync(id) ?? new AppUser();
            }
        }

        public async Task<IActionResult> OnPost(AppUser user) {
            IdentityResult result;
            AppUser storeUser = await UserManager.FindByIdAsync(user.Id);
            if (storeUser == null) {
                result = await UserManager.CreateAsync(user);
            } else {
                storeUser.UpdateFrom(user);
                result = await UserManager.UpdateAsync(storeUser);
            }
            if (result.Succeeded) {
                return RedirectToPage("users", new { searchname = user.Id });
            } else {
                foreach (IdentityError err in result.Errors) {
                    ModelState.AddModelError("", err.Description ?? "Error");
                }
                AppUserObject = user;
                return Page();
            }
        }
    }
}
```

The GET page handler receives an ID value, which is used to locate the user object. The POST handler method relies on the ASP.NET Core model binder to create an AppUser object from the HTTP request. If there isn't an object in the store with the ID received in the request, the object is stored with the CreateAsync method. If there is an existing object, then I copy the property values from the AppUser object created by the model binder to the object retrieved from the user store and then use the UpdateAsync method to store the changes.

```
...
storeUser.UpdateFrom(user);
result = await UserManager.UpdateAsync(storeUser);
...
```

This approach allows me to deal with HTTP requests that provide values for only some of the properties defined by the user class. Without this step, I would overwrite the data in the store with null or default values for those properties for which no value is available in the HTTP request.

The EditUser Razor Page relies on a partial view to display the individual fields for editing, which will make it easier for me to add features later. Add a Razor View named _EditUserBasic.cshtml to the Pages/Store folder, with the content shown in Listing 16-21.

Listing 16-21. The Contents of the _EditUserBasic.cshtml File in the Pages/Store Folder

```
@model AppUser
<tr>
    <td>ID</td>
    <td>@Model.Id</td>
</tr>
<tr>
    <td>Username</td>
    <td>
        <input class="w-00" asp-for="UserName" />
    </td>
</tr>
<tr>
    <td>Normalized UserName</td>
    <td>
        @(Model.NormalizedUserName ?? "(Not Set)")
        <input type="hidden" asp-for="NormalizedUserName" />
    </td>
</tr>
```

Restart ASP.NET Core, request http://localhost:5000/users, enter 1 into the text field and click the Find button. Click the Edit button, change the username to AliceSmith, and click the Save button. The updated summary shows that the new username has been stored, as shown in Figure 16-2.

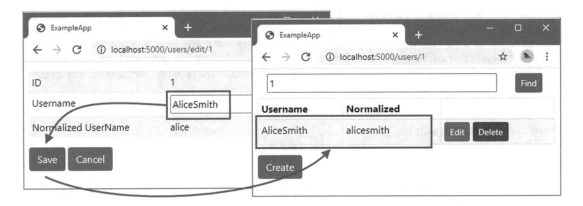

Figure 16-2. *Accessing user data*

The results of operations on the store are described using IdentityResult objects, which I described earlier in the chapter. When an operation fails, I add details of the problem to the model state so that I can use the ASP.NET Core data validation features to present errors to the user. You can see how this works later in the chapter.

Notice that the normalized username is updated when you change the UserName property. This is part of the process performed by the CreateAsync and UpdateAsync methods described in Table 16-3.

Adding Optional Store Features

The user store works, but it doesn't contain enough data to be useful. Identity uses a series of optional interfaces that stores implement to declare they can store additional data types. Table 16-6 describes the most important interfaces. (There are additional interfaces that support signing in and authentication, which I describe in later chapters.)

Table 16-6. *Optional User Store Interfaces*

Name	Description
IQueryableUserStore<T>	This interface is implemented by user stores that allow users to be queried using LINQ. I implement this interface in the "Querying the User Store" section.
IUserEmailStore<T>	This interface is implemented by user stores that can manage email addresses. I implement this interface later in this section.
IUserPhoneNumberStore<T>	This interface is implemented by user stores that can manage phone numbers and addresses. I implement this interface later in this section.
IUserPasswordStore<T>	This interface is implemented by user stores that can manage passwords. I use this interface in Chapter 18.
IUserClaimStore<T>	This interface is implemented by user stores that can manage claims. I use this interface in Chapter 17.
IUserRoleStore<T>	This interface is implemented by user stores that can manage roles. I use this interface in Chapter 17.

Adding Support for Querying the User Store

The Razor Page created in the previous section lets you look up a user by name or ID but requires an exact match. A more flexible approach is to allow the user data to be queried with LINQ and user stores that can be queried implement the IQueryableUserStore<T> interface, which defines the property described in Table 16-7.

Table 16-7. *The IQueryableUserStore<T> Interface*

Name	Description
Users	This property returns an IQueryable<T> object, where T is the store's user class.

The approach I have taken for the custom user store in this chapter makes it easy to add new features by adding another partial class. To add support for querying user data, add a class file named UserStoreQueryable.cs to the Identity/Store folder, with the code shown in Listing 16-22.

Listing 16-22. The Contents of the UserStoreQueryable.cs File in the Identity/Store Folder

```
using Microsoft.AspNetCore.Identity;
using System.Linq;

namespace ExampleApp.Identity.Store {

    public partial class UserStore : IQueryableUserStore<AppUser> {

        public IQueryable<AppUser> Users => users.Values
            .Select(user => user.Clone()).AsQueryable<AppUser>();
    }
}
```

To implement the interface, I use the AsQueryable<T> extension method, which LINQ provides for converting IEnumerable<T> objects into IQueryable<T> objects so they can be used in LINQ queries. The LINQ Select method is used to duplicate the AppUser objects so that changes are not added to the store until an explicit update is performed.

Querying the User Store

The UserManager<T> class defines two properties that are used to access the functionality provided through the IQueryableStore<T> interface, as described in Table 16-8.

Table 16-8. *The UserManager<T> Properties for Queryable User Stores*

Name	Description
SupportsQueryableUsers	This property returns true if the user store implements the IQueryableUserStore<T> interface.
Users	This property returns an IQueryable<T> object, where T is the store's user class.

In Listing 16-23, I have updated the GET handler in the Users Razor Page model class to use the properties in Table 16-8.

Listing 16-23. Querying Users in the Users.cshtml.cs File in the Pages/Store Folder

```
...
public async Task OnGet() {
    if (UserManager.SupportsQueryableUsers) {
        string normalizedName =
            UserManager.NormalizeName(Searchname ?? string.Empty);
        Users = string.IsNullOrEmpty(Searchname)
            ? UserManager.Users.OrderBy(u => u.UserName)
            : UserManager.Users.Where(user => user.Id == Searchname ||
                user.NormalizedUserName.Contains(normalizedName))
                .OrderBy(u => u.UserName);
    } else if (Searchname != null) {
        AppUser nameUser = await UserManager.FindByNameAsync(Searchname);
        if (nameUser != null) {
            Users = Users.Append(nameUser);
        }
        AppUser idUser = await UserManager.FindByIdAsync(Searchname);
        if (idUser!= null) {
            Users = Users.Append(idUser);
        }
    }
}
...
```

It is important to check the value of the SupportsQueryableUsers property before performing a query because reading the Users property will cause an exception if the store doesn't implement the IQueryableStore<T> interface.

In the listing, I use the UserManager<T>.Users property with the LINQ Where method to find AppUser object's whose NormalizedUserName property contains the search term entered into the text field or whose Id property matches the search term exactly. All users are shown if there is no search term specified.

I normalized the search term to perform the LINQ query, which I can do using the normalization methods provided by the UserManager<T> class, described in Table 16-9. These are convenience methods so that components don't have to declare dependencies directly on the ILookupNormalizer service.

Table 16-9. UserManager<T> Normalization Convenience Methods

Name	Description
NormalizeName(name)	This method invokes the NormalizeName method on the ILookupNormalizer service.
NormalizeEmail(email)	This method invokes the NormalizeEmail method on the ILookupNormalizer service.

To perform a query on the user store, restart ASP.NET Core, and request http://localhost:5000/users. Enter a into the text field and click the Find button. Two matches will be displayed, as shown in Figure 16-3.

***Figure 16-3.** Querying the user store*

Adding Support for Storing Email Addresses and Phone Numbers

Most applications store email addresses and phone numbers, either to identify users or to communicate with them. User stores that can manage email addresses implement the IUserEmailStore<T> interface, where T is the user class. The IUserEmailStore<T> interface defines the methods shown in Table 16-10. (As with other user store interfaces, all of the methods shown in the table define a token parameter through which a CancellationToken object is provided, allowing notifications to be received when asynchronous operations are canceled.)

***Table 16-10.** The IUserEmailStore<T> Methods*

Name	Description
FindByEmailAsync(email, token)	This method returns the user class instance that has the specified normalized email address.
GetEmailAsync(user, token)	This method returns the email address of the specified user object.
SetEmailAsync(user, email, token)	This method sets the email address for the specified user object.
GetNormalizedEmailAsync(user, token)	This method returns the normalized email address of the specified user object.
SetNormalizedEmailAsync(user, email, token)	This method sets the normalized email address for the specified user object.
GetEmailConfirmedAsync(user, token)	This method gets the value of the property used to indicate whether the email address has been confirmed, which I demonstrate in Chapter 17.
SetEmailConfirmedAsync(user, confirmed, token)	This method sets the value of the property used to indicate whether the email address has been confirmed, which I demonstrate in Chapter 17.

User stores that can store phone numbers implement the IUserPhoneNumberStore<T> interface, which defines the methods described in Table 16-11.

Table 16-11. *The IUserPhoneNumberStore<T> Methods*

Name	Description
SetPhoneNumberAsync(user, phone, token)	This method sets the telephone number for the specified user.
GetPhoneNumberAsync(user, token)	This method sets the telephone number for the specified user.
GetPhoneNumberConfirmedAsync(user, token)	This method gets the value of the property used to indicate whether the phone number has been confirmed, which I demonstrate in Chapter 17.
SetPhoneNumberConfirmedAsync(user, token)	This method sets the value of the property used to indicate whether the phone number has been confirmed, which I demonstrate in Chapter 17.

The first step is to add properties to the user class to store the email and phone data, as shown in Listing 16-24.

Listing 16-24. Adding Properties to the User Class in the AppUser.cs File in the Identity Folder

```
using System;

namespace ExampleApp.Identity {
    public class AppUser {

        public string Id { get; set; } = Guid.NewGuid().ToString();

        public string UserName { get; set; }

        public string NormalizedUserName { get; set; }

        public string EmailAddress { get; set; }
        public string NormalizedEmailAddress { get; set; }
        public bool EmailAddressConfirmed { get; set; }

        public string PhoneNumber { get; set; }
        public bool PhoneNumberConfirmed { get; set; }
    }
}
```

As with the username, Identity stores regular and normalized versions of the email address, so I have added two properties to the user class for these values. I have also added properties for confirming the user's email address and phone number, which I describe in Chapter 17.

Next, add a class file named UserStoreEmail.cs to the Identity/Store method and use it to define the partial class shown in Listing 16-25, which extends the user store class to support the IUserEmailStore<T> interface.

Listing 16-25. The Contents of the UserStoreEmail.cs File in the Identity/Store Folder

```
using Microsoft.AspNetCore.Identity;
using System.Linq;
using System.Threading;
using System.Threading.Tasks;

namespace ExampleApp.Identity.Store {

    public partial class UserStore : IUserEmailStore<AppUser> {

        public Task<AppUser> FindByEmailAsync(string normalizedEmail,
                CancellationToken token) =>
            Task.FromResult(Users.FirstOrDefault(user =>
                user.NormalizedEmailAddress == normalizedEmail));

        public Task<string> GetEmailAsync(AppUser user,
                CancellationToken token) =>
            Task.FromResult(user.EmailAddress);

        public Task SetEmailAsync(AppUser user, string email,
                CancellationToken token) {
            user.EmailAddress = email;
            return Task.CompletedTask;
        }

        public Task<string> GetNormalizedEmailAsync(AppUser user,
                CancellationToken token) =>
            Task.FromResult(user.NormalizedEmailAddress);

        public Task SetNormalizedEmailAsync(AppUser user, string normalizedEmail,
                CancellationToken token) {
            user.NormalizedEmailAddress = normalizedEmail;
            return Task.CompletedTask;
        }

        public Task<bool> GetEmailConfirmedAsync(AppUser user,
                CancellationToken token) =>
            Task.FromResult(user.EmailAddressConfirmed);

        public Task SetEmailConfirmedAsync(AppUser user, bool confirmed,
                CancellationToken token) {
            user.EmailAddressConfirmed = confirmed;
            return Task.CompletedTask;
        }
    }
}
```

Adding support for optional interfaces is simple once you have the core features in place. The FindByEmailAsync method is implemented using a LINQ query against the Users property defined by the IQueryableUserStore<T> interface. The GetEmailAsync, SetEmailAsync, GetNormalizedEmailAsync, and SetNormalizedEmailAsync methods rely on the properties added to the user class in Listing 16-25. Chapter 17 describes the GetEmailConfirmedAsync and SetEmailConfirmedAsync methods.

Next, add a class file named UserStorePhone.cs to the Identity/Store folder and use it to define the partial class shown in Listing 16-26, which extends the user store to implement the IUserPhoneNumberStore<T> interface.

Listing 16-26. The Contents of the UserStorePhone.cs File in the Identity/Store Folder

```
using Microsoft.AspNetCore.Identity;
using System.Threading;
using System.Threading.Tasks;

namespace ExampleApp.Identity.Store {
    public partial class UserStore : IUserPhoneNumberStore<AppUser> {
        public Task<string> GetPhoneNumberAsync(AppUser user,
            CancellationToken token) => Task.FromResult(user.PhoneNumber);

        public Task SetPhoneNumberAsync(AppUser user, string phoneNumber,
                CancellationToken token) {
            user.PhoneNumber = phoneNumber;
            return Task.CompletedTask;
        }

        public Task<bool> GetPhoneNumberConfirmedAsync(AppUser user,
            CancellationToken token) => Task.FromResult(user.PhoneNumberConfirmed);

        public Task SetPhoneNumberConfirmedAsync(AppUser user, bool confirmed,
                CancellationToken token) {
            user.PhoneNumberConfirmed = confirmed;
            return Task.CompletedTask;
        }
    }
}
```

To seed the user store with email addresses and phone numbers, add the statements shown in Listing 16-27 to the UserStore.cs file in the Identity/Store folder.

Listing 16-27. Adding Seed Data in the UserStore.cs File in the Identity/Store Folder

```
using Microsoft.AspNetCore.Identity;

namespace ExampleApp.Identity.Store {

    public partial class UserStore {

        public ILookupNormalizer Normalizer { get; set; }
```

```
public UserStore(ILookupNormalizer normalizer) {
    Normalizer = normalizer;
    SeedStore();
}

private void SeedStore() {

    int idCounter = 0;

    string EmailFromName(string name) => $"{name.ToLower()}@example.com";

    foreach (string name in UsersAndClaims.Users) {
        AppUser user = new AppUser {
            Id = (++idCounter).ToString(),
            UserName = name,
            NormalizedUserName = Normalizer.NormalizeName(name),
            EmailAddress = EmailFromName(name),
            NormalizedEmailAddress =
                Normalizer.NormalizeEmail(EmailFromName(name)),
            EmailAddressConfirmed = true,
            PhoneNumber = "123-4567",
            PhoneNumberConfirmed = true
        };
        users.TryAdd(user.Id, user);
    }
}
```

The changes in the listing generate email addresses in the example.com domain for each user and assign every user the same phone number. The email addresses are normalized using the NormalizeEmail method described in Table 16-4.

Using Email Addresses and Phone Numbers

The UserManager<T> class defines the members shown in Table 16-12 for dealing with email addresses.

Table 16-12. *The UserManager<T> Members for Email Addresses*

Name	Description
SupportsUserEmail	This property returns true if the store implements the IUserEmailStore<T> interface.
FindByEmailAsync(email)	This method locates a user by email address. The email address is normalized before it is passed to the store's FindByEmailAsync method.
GetEmailAsync(user)	This method returns the email address for the specified instance of the user class.
SetEmailAsync(user, email)	This method sets the email address for the specified instance of the user class. The email address is passed to the store's SetEmailAsync method, and the SetEmailConfirmedAsync method is called to set the confirmed state to false, after which the security stamp is updated and the user store's update sequence is applied. Chapter 17 describes security stamps.

To allow the email address to be edited, add a Razor View named _EditUserEmail.cshtml to the Pages/ Store folder with the content shown in Listing 16-28.

Listing 16-28. The Contents of the _EditUserEmail.cshtml File in the Pages/Store Folder

```
@model AppUser
@inject UserManager<AppUser> UserManager

@if (UserManager.SupportsUserEmail) {
    <tr>
        <td>Email</td>
        <td>
            <input class="w-00" asp-for="EmailAddress" />
        </td>
    </tr>
    <tr>
        <td>Normalized Email</td>
        <td>
            @(Model.NormalizedEmailAddress?? "(Not Set)")
            <input type="hidden" asp-for="NormalizedEmailAddress" />
            <input type="hidden" asp-for="EmailAddressConfirmed" />
        </td>
    </tr>
}
```

There is also a set of members for managing phone numbers, as described in Table 16-13.

Table 16-13. *The UserManager<T> Members for Phone Numbers*

Name	Description
SupportsUserPhoneNumber	This property returns true if the store implements the IUserPhoneNumberStore<T> interface.
GetPhoneNumberAsync(user)	This method gets the phone number for the specified user by calling the store's GetPhoneNumberAsync method.
SetPhoneNumberAsync(user, number)	This method sets the phone number for the user by calling the store's SetPhoneNumberAsync method. The store's SetPhoneNumberConfirmedAsync method is called to set the confirmed state to false, the security stamp is updated (as explained in Chapter 17), the user is subject to validation (as described in the "Validating User Data" section), and the user manager's update sequence is applied.

To allow the phone number to be set, create a Razor View named _EditUserPhone.cshtml in the Pages/Store folder with the content shown in Listing 16-29.

Listing 16-29. The Contents of the _EditUserPhone.cshtml File in the Pages/Store Folder

```
@model AppUser
@inject UserManager<AppUser> UserManager

@if (UserManager.SupportsUserPhoneNumber) {
    <tr>
        <td>Phone</td>
        <td>
            <input class="w-00" asp-for="PhoneNumber" />
            <input type="hidden" asp-for="PhoneNumberConfirmed" />
        </td>
    </tr>
}
```

Add the elements shown in Listing 16-30 to the EditUser.cshtml file in the Pages/Store folder to incorporate the new views into the application.

Listing 16-30. Adding Partial Views in the EditUser.cshtml File in the Pages/Store Folder

```
@page "/users/edit/{id?}"
@model ExampleApp.Pages.Store.UsersModel

<div asp-validation-summary="All" class="text-danger m-2"></div>

<div class="m-2">
    <form method="post">
        <input type="hidden" name="id" value="@Model.AppUserObject.Id" />
        <table class="table table-sm table-striped">
            <tbody>
                <partial name="_EditUserBasic" model="@Model.AppUserObject" />
                <partial name="_EditUserEmail" model="@Model.AppUserObject" />
                <partial name="_EditUserPhone" model="@Model.AppUserObject" />
            </tbody>
        </table>
        <div>
            <button type="submit" class="btn btn-primary">Save</button>
            <a asp-page="users" class="btn btn-secondary">Cancel</a>
        </div>
    </form>
</div>
```

Restart ASP.NET Core, request http://localhost:5000/users, and click the Edit button for one of the users to see the additional properties added for email addresses and phone numbers, as shown in Figure 16-4.

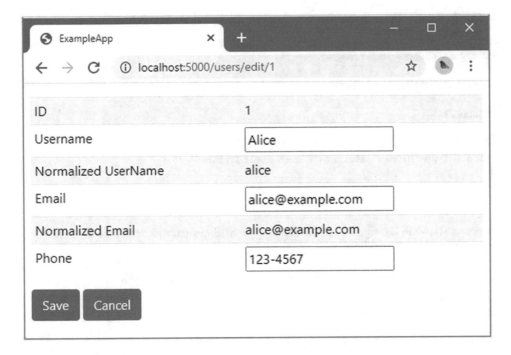

Figure 16-4. *Adding support for storing email addresses and phone numbers*

Adding Custom User Class Properties

User stores can define additional properties that are specific to an application. This is a feature that pre-dates the use of claims and isn't needed because any piece of data about the user can be represented with a claim. But it is still supported, so Listing 16-31 adds new properties to the AppUser class. (I explain how to manage claims in the user store in Chapter 17.)

■ **Note** Custom user class properties are not as useful as they appear because they are not added to the data provider to ASP.NET Core when a user signs in unless you also create a custom translation class, as demonstrated in Chapter 18. My advice is to store all additional data as claims, which is simpler and will automatically be presented to ASP.NET Core.

Listing 16-31. Adding Custom Properties in the AppUser.cs File in the Identity Folder

```
using System;

namespace ExampleApp.Identity {
    public class AppUser {

        public string Id { get; set; } = Guid.NewGuid().ToString();

        public string UserName { get; set; }
```

```
        public string NormalizedUserName { get; set; }

        public string EmailAddress { get; set; }
        public string NormalizedEmailAddress { get; set; }
        public bool EmailAddressConfirmed { get; set; }

        public string PhoneNumber { get; set; }
        public bool PhoneNumberConfirmed { get; set; }

        public string FavoriteFood { get; set; }
        public string Hobby { get; set; }
    }
}
```

The FavoriteFood and Hobby properties are string properties. Add a Razor View named
_EditUserCustom.cshtml to the Pages/Store folder and use it to define the partial view shown in
Listing 16-32, which contains elements required to edit the properties added to the user class in Listing 31.

Listing 16-32. The Contents of the _EditUserCustom.cshtml File in the Pages/Store Folder

```
@model AppUser

<tr>
    <td>Favorite Food</td>
    <td><input class="w-100" asp-for="FavoriteFood" /></td>
</tr>
<tr>
    <td>Hobby</td>
    <td><input class="w-100" asp-for="Hobby" /></td>
</tr>
```

Add the element shown in Listing 16-33 to the EditUser.cshtml file in the Pages/Store folder to
incorporate the partial view into the application.

Listing 16-33. Adding an Element in the EditUser.cshtml File in the Pages/Store Folder

```
@page "/users/edit/{id?}"
@model ExampleApp.Pages.Store.UsersModel

<div asp-validation-summary="All" class="text-danger m-2"></div>

<div class="m-2">
    <form method="post">
        <input type="hidden" name="id" value="@Model.AppUserObject.Id" />
        <table class="table table-sm table-striped">
            <tbody>
                <partial name="_EditUserBasic" model="@Model.AppUserObject" />
                <partial name="_EditUserEmail" model="@Model.AppUserObject" />
                <partial name="_EditUserPhone" model="@Model.AppUserObject" />
                <partial name="_EditUserCustom" model="@Model.AppUserObject" />
            </tbody>
        </table>
```

```
        <div>
            <button type="submit" class="btn btn-primary">Save</button>
            <a asp-page="users" class="btn btn-secondary">Cancel</a>
        </div>
    </form>
</div>
```

To seed the user store with values for the new properties, add the statements shown in Listing 16-34 to the UserStore.cs file in the Identity/Store folder.

Listing 16-34. Seeding the Store in the UserStore.cs File in the Identity/Store Folder

```
using Microsoft.AspNetCore.Identity;
using System.Collections.Generic;

namespace ExampleApp.Identity.Store {

    public partial class UserStore {

        public ILookupNormalizer Normalizer { get; set; }

        public UserStore(ILookupNormalizer normalizer) {
            Normalizer = normalizer;
            SeedStore();
        }

        private void SeedStore() {

            var customData = new Dictionary<string, (string food, string hobby)> {
                { "Alice", ("Pizza", "Running") },
                { "Bob", ("Ice Cream", "Cinema") },
                { "Charlie", ("Burgers", "Cooking") }
            };

            int idCounter = 0;

            string EmailFromName(string name) => $"{name.ToLower()}@example.com";

            foreach (string name in UsersAndClaims.Users) {
                AppUser user = new AppUser {
                    Id = (++idCounter).ToString(),
                    UserName = name,
                    NormalizedUserName = Normalizer.NormalizeName(name),
                    EmailAddress = EmailFromName(name),
                    NormalizedEmailAddress =
                        Normalizer.NormalizeEmail(EmailFromName(name)),
                    EmailAddressConfirmed = true,
                    PhoneNumber = "123-4567",
                    PhoneNumberConfirmed = true,
                    FavoriteFood = customData[name].food,
                    Hobby = customData[name].hobby
                };
```

```
            users.TryAdd(user.Id, user);
        }
    }
}
}
```

Restart ASP.NET Core, request `http://localhost:5000/users`, and click one of the Edit buttons. You will see the custom properties, populated with the seed data, as shown in Figure 16-5.

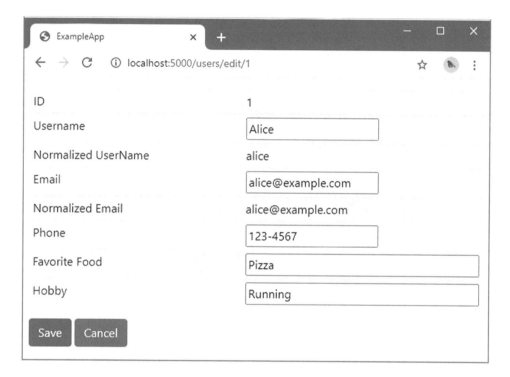

Figure 16-5. *Adding custom properties to the user class*

Validating User Data

Before they pass user objects to the store, the CreateAsync and UpdateAsync methods validate the user object. To see an example of validation, request `http://localhost:5000/users`, click the Edit button for Bob, and enter Charlie into the UserName field. Click Save, and you will see the response shown in Figure 16-6.

Figure 16-6. *A validation response for user data*

Validation constraints are expressed using the IUserValidator<T> interface, where T is the user class. The UserManager<T> class uses dependency injection to receive the set of IUserValidator<T> services that have been registered and validate user objects using the method described in Table 16-14.

Table 16-14. *The IUserValidator<T> Method*

Name	Description
ValidateAsync(manager, user)	This method validates the specified user object and can access the user store through the UserManager<T> parameter. The validation result is expressed with an IdentityResult object.

The default implementation of the IUserValidator<T> interface checks that usernames and email addresses are unique and contain only permitted characters. It is this validator that produced the error message shown in Figure 16-6.

CONFIGURING THE DEFAULT USER VALIDATOR

The default validator can be configured using the options pattern in the Startup class. Two configuration options are available, accessed through the IdentityOptions.User property, like this:

```
...
services.AddIdentityCore<AppUser>(opts => {
    opts.User.AllowedUserNameCharacters = "abcdefghijklmnopqrstuvwxyz";
    opts.User.RequireUniqueEmail = true;
});
...
```

The AllowedUserNameCharacters property specifies the set of characters that usernames can contain. The default value allows uppercase and lowercase characters, numbers, and some symbols. The RequireUniqueEmail property specifies whether email addresses must be unique and defaults to false.

To create a custom validator, add a class file named `EmailValidator.cs` to the `ExampleApp/Identity` folder with the code shown in Listing 16-35.

Listing 16-35. The Contents of the EmailValidator.cs File in the Identity Folder

```
using Microsoft.AspNetCore.Identity;
using System.Linq;
using System.Threading.Tasks;

namespace ExampleApp.Identity {
    public class EmailValidator : IUserValidator<AppUser> {
        private static string[] AllowedDomains = new[] { "example.com", "acme.com" };
        private static IdentityError err
            = new IdentityError { Description = "Email address domain not allowed" };

        public EmailValidator(ILookupNormalizer normalizer) {
            Normalizer = normalizer;
        }

        private ILookupNormalizer Normalizer { get; set; }

        public Task<IdentityResult> ValidateAsync(UserManager<AppUser> manager,
                AppUser user) {
            string normalizedEmail = Normalizer.NormalizeEmail(user.EmailAddress);
            if (AllowedDomains.Any(domain =>
                    normalizedEmail.EndsWith($"@{domain}"))) {
                return Task.FromResult(IdentityResult.Success);
            }
            return Task.FromResult(IdentityResult.Failed(err));
        }
    }
}
```

Care must be taken when registering custom validators. Identity will only add the default validator if there are no existing `IUserValidator<T>` services before the `AddIdentityCore` method is called. This means you should register custom services before the `AddIdentityCore` method if you want to replace the default validator and after the `AddIdentityCore` method if you want to retain the default validator. I want to supplement the default validation, so I registered my custom class after setting up Identity, as shown in Listing 16-36.

Listing 16-36. Registering a User Validator in the Startup.cs File in the ExampleApp Folder

```
...
public void ConfigureServices(IServiceCollection services) {
    services.AddSingleton<ILookupNormalizer, Normalizer>();
    services.AddSingleton<IUserStore<AppUser>, UserStore>();

    services.AddIdentityCore<AppUser>();

    services.AddSingleton<IUserValidator<AppUser>, EmailValidator>();
```

```
    services.AddAuthentication(opts => {
        opts.DefaultScheme
            = CookieAuthenticationDefaults.AuthenticationScheme;
    }).AddCookie(opts => {
        opts.LoginPath = "/signin";
        opts.AccessDeniedPath = "/signin/403";
    });
    services.AddAuthorization(opts => {
        AuthorizationPolicies.AddPolicies(opts);
    });
    services.AddRazorPages();
    services.AddControllersWithViews();
}
...
```

To see the effect of the new validator, restart ASP.NET Core, request `http://localhost:5000/users`, and click the Edit button for the Alice user. Change the Email field to alice@mycompany.com and click the Save button. The new validator class will produce the error shown in Figure 16-7.

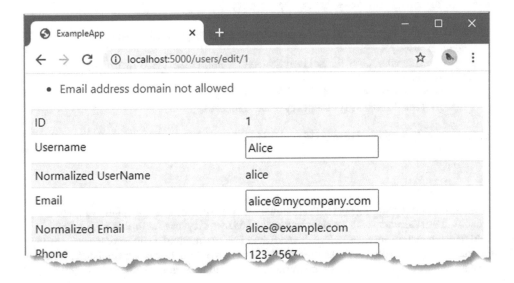

Figure 16-7. *A custom user validator*

Summary

In this chapter, I described the interfaces that are implemented by user store. I created a custom user store that supports core features, as well as support for LINQ queries, email addresses and phone numbers, and custom user class properties. I also explained how user data can be validated before it is added to the store. In the next chapter, I add support for claims, roles, and user confirmations.

CHAPTER 17

■ ■ ■

Claims, Roles, and Confirmations

In this chapter, I continue to add features to the store and build administration tools that use those features through the UserManager<T> class. I start by adding support for storing and managing claims and then use these features to add support for roles, which are given special status in ASP.NET Core and ASP.NET Core Identity because they are so widely used. I also show you how to generate and validate confirmation tokens, which are used to ensure that a user can access the email address or phone number they provide. Table 17-1 puts these features in context.

Table 17-1. *Putting Claims, Roles, and Confirmations in Context*

Question	Answer
What are they?	Roles restrict access to protected resources. Claims store additional data about a user, including roles. Confirmations are tokens sent to the user, which they present back to the application to prove their identity.
Why are they useful?	Roles are widely used to define authorization policies. Claims can also be used for authorization and can be used to store any data about the user. Confirmations ensure the user can be reached through the email address or phone number in the user store.
How are they used?	For roles and claims, the store implements optional interfaces. Confirmations require custom workflows that generate and validate change tokens.
Are there any pitfalls or limitations?	Care must be taken to deal with the normalization of role names, as explained in the "Understanding the Role Normalization Pitfall" section.
Are there any alternatives?	These are optional features and are not required if you do not require role-based access control, need to store additional data, or need to check the user's email address and phone number.

Table 17-2 summarizes the chapter.

© Adam Freeman 2021
A. Freeman, *Pro ASP.NET Core Identity*, https://doi.org/10.1007/978-1-4842-6858-2_17

Table 17-2. Chapter Summary

Problem	Solution	Listing
Support claims in the user store	Implement the IUserClaimStore<T> interface.	2–8
Support roles in the user store	Implement the IUserRoleStore<T> interface.	9–12
Avoid role name normalization issues	Store roles as claims.	13
Support confirmations in the store	Implement the IUserSecurityStampStore<T>, create token generators, and send the tokens the user using the contact details they provide.	14–30

Preparing for This Chapter

This chapter uses the ExampleApp project from Chapter 16. No changes are required to prepare for this chapter. Open a new command prompt, navigate to the ExampleApp folder, and run the command shown in Listing 17-1 to start ASP.NET Core.

■ **Tip** You can download the example project for this chapter—and for all the other chapters in this book—from https://github.com/Apress/pro-asp.net-core-identity. See Chapter 1 for how to get help if you have problems running the examples.

Listing 17-1. Running the Example Application

```
dotnet run
```

Open a new browser window and request http://localhost:5000/users. You will be presented with the user data shown in Figure 17-1. The data is stored only in memory, and changes will be lost when ASP.NET Core is stopped.

Figure 17-1. *Running the example application*

Storing Claims in the User Store

Now that I have the basic features in place, I can start to add features to the store, starting with support for storing a user's claims. Stores that can manage claims implement the IUserClaimStore<T> interface, where <T> is the user class. Table 17-3 describes the methods defined by the IUserClaimStore<T> interface. As with earlier store interfaces, these asynchronous methods define a CancellationToken parameter that is used to receive notifications when an operation is cancelled and is given the name token in the table.

Table 17-3. *The IUserClaimStore<T> Methods*

Name	Description
GetClaimsAsync(user, token)	This method returns an IList<Claim> that contains all the user's claims.
AddClaimsAsync(user, claims, token)	This method adds one or more claims to the user object, which is received as an IEnumerable<Claim>.
RemoveClaimsAsync(user, claims, token)	This method removes one or more claims to the user object, which is received as an IEnumerable<Claim>.
ReplaceClaimAsync(user, oldClaim, newClaim, token)	This method replaces one claim with another. The claims do not have to be of the same type.
GetUsersForClaimAsync(claim, token)	This method returns an IList<T> object, where T is the user class that contains all the users with a specific claim.

To prepare for storing claims, Listing 17-2 extends the user class to support claims.

Listing 17-2. Adding Claims in the AppUser.cs File in the Identity Folder

```
using System;
using System.Collections.Generic;
using System.Security.Claims;

namespace ExampleApp.Identity {
    public class AppUser {

        public string Id { get; set; } = Guid.NewGuid().ToString();

        public string UserName { get; set; }

        public string NormalizedUserName { get; set; }

        public string EmailAddress { get; set; }
        public string NormalizedEmailAddress { get; set; }
        public bool EmailAddressConfirmed { get; set; }

        public string PhoneNumber { get; set; }
        public bool PhoneNumberConfirmed { get; set; }

        public string FavoriteFood { get; set; }
        public string Hobby { get; set; }

        public IList<Claim> Claims { get; set; }
    }
}
```

To extend the example user store to support claims, add a class file named UserStoreClaims.cs to the ExampleApp/Identity/Store folder and use it to define the partial class shown in Listing 17-3.

Listing 17-3. The Contents of the UserStoreClaims.cs File in the Identity/Store Folder

```
using Microsoft.AspNetCore.Identity;
using Microsoft.VisualBasic;
using System;
using System.Collections.Generic;
using System.Linq;
using System.Security.Claims;
using System.Threading;
using System.Threading.Tasks;

namespace ExampleApp.Identity.Store {
    public partial class UserStore : IUserClaimStore<AppUser>,
            IEqualityComparer<Claim> {

        public Task AddClaimsAsync(AppUser user, IEnumerable<Claim> claims,
                CancellationToken token) {
            if (user.Claims == null) {
                user.Claims = new List<Claim>();
            }
```

```
            foreach (Claim claim in claims) {
                user.Claims.Add(claim);
            }
            return Task.CompletedTask;
        }

        public Task<IList<Claim>> GetClaimsAsync(AppUser user,
                CancellationToken token) => Task.FromResult(user.Claims);

        public Task RemoveClaimsAsync(AppUser user, IEnumerable<Claim> claims,
                CancellationToken token) {
            foreach (Claim c in user.Claims.Intersect(claims, this).ToList()) {
                user.Claims.Remove(c);
            }
            return Task.CompletedTask;
        }

        public async Task ReplaceClaimAsync(AppUser user, Claim oldclaim,
                Claim newClaim, CancellationToken token) {
            await RemoveClaimsAsync(user, new[] { oldclaim }, token);
            user.Claims.Add(newClaim);
        }

        public Task<IList<AppUser>> GetUsersForClaimAsync(Claim claim,
                CancellationToken token) =>
            Task.FromResult(
                Users.Where(u => u.Claims.Any(c => Equals(c, claim)))
                    .ToList() as IList<AppUser>);

        public bool Equals(Claim first, Claim second) =>
            first.Type == second.Type && string.Equals(first.Value, second.Value,
                    StringComparison.OrdinalIgnoreCase);

        public int GetHashCode(Claim claim) =>
            claim.Type.GetHashCode() + claim.Value.GetHashCode();
    }
}
```

Identity doesn't enforce restrictions on how a store manages claims, but it is important to understand that the same claim can appear more than once. In Listing 17-3, I have used a dictionary to keep track of objects, using the AppUser.Id property as the key to store collections of Claim objects.

To seed the store with claims, add the statements shown in Listing 17-4 to the UserStore.cs file, which contains the constructor and seed data for the user store class.

Listing 17-4. Seeding Claims in the UserStore.cs File in the Identity/Store Folder

```
using Microsoft.AspNetCore.Identity;
using System.Collections.Generic;
using System.Linq;
using System.Security.Claims;
```

```
namespace ExampleApp.Identity.Store {

    public partial class UserStore {

        public ILookupNormalizer Normalizer { get; set; }

        public UserStore(ILookupNormalizer normalizer) {
            Normalizer = normalizer;
            SeedStore();
        }

        private void SeedStore() {

            var customData = new Dictionary<string, (string food, string hobby)> {
                { "Alice", ("Pizza", "Running") },
                { "Bob", ("Ice Cream", "Cinema") },
                { "Charlie", ("Burgers", "Cooking") }
            };

            int idCounter = 0;

            string EmailFromName(string name) => $"{name.ToLower()}@example.com";

            foreach (string name in UsersAndClaims.Users) {
                AppUser user = new AppUser {
                    Id = (++idCounter).ToString(),
                    UserName = name,
                    NormalizedUserName = Normalizer.NormalizeName(name),
                    EmailAddress = EmailFromName(name),
                    NormalizedEmailAddress =
                        Normalizer.NormalizeEmail(EmailFromName(name)),
                    EmailAddressConfirmed = true,
                    PhoneNumber = "123-4567",
                    PhoneNumberConfirmed = true,
                    FavoriteFood = customData[name].food,
                    Hobby = customData[name].hobby
                };
                user.Claims =  UsersAndClaims.UserData[user.UserName]
                    .Select(role => new Claim(ClaimTypes.Role, role)).ToList();
                users.TryAdd(user.Id, user);
            }
        }
    }
}
```

The new code populates the store with Role claims using seed data defined in the UsersAndClaims class.

CHAPTER 17 ■ CLAIMS, ROLES, AND CONFIRMATIONS

Managing Claims in the User Store

The UserManager<T> class provides a set of methods that provide access to claims when the user store class implements the IUserClaimStore<T> interface, as described in Table 17-4, along with a property that allows support for claims to be checked.

Table 17-4. *The UserManager<T> Members for Claims*

Name	Description
SupportsUserClaim	This property returns true if the user store implements the IUserClaimStore<T> interface.
GetClaimsAsync(user)	This method returns the list of claims for the specified user by calling the store's GetClaimsAsync method.
GetUsersForClaimAsync(claim)	This method returns the list of users that have the specified claim by calling the store's GetUsersForClaimAsync method.
AddClaimsAsync(user, claims)	This method adds multiple claims to the specified user and commits the change to the store by calling the store's AddClaimsAsync method, after which the user manager's update sequence is performed.
AddClaimAsync(user, claim)	This convenience method creates an array containing the single claim and passes it to the AddClaimsAsync method.
ReplaceClaimAsync(user, oldClaim, newClaim)	This method replaces a claim for the specified user by calling the store's ReplaceClaimAsync method, after which the user manager's update sequence is performed.
RemoveClaimsAsync(user, claims)	This method removes multiple claims from the specified user and commits the change to the store by calling the store's RemoveClaimsAsync method, after which the user manager's update sequence is performed.
RemoveClaimAsync(user, claim)	This convenience method creates an array containing the claim and calls the RemoveClaimsAsync method.

To manage claims, add a Razor View named _ClaimsRow.cshtml to the Pages/Store folder and use it to define the partial view shown in Listing 17-5. If you are using Visual Studio, you can create this file using the Razor View – Empty item template.

Listing 17-5. The Contents of the _ClaimsRow.cshtml File in the Pages/Store Folder

```
@model (string id, Claim claim, bool newClaim)

@{ string hash = Model.claim.GetHashCode().ToString(); }

<td>
    <form method="post" id="@hash">
        <input type="hidden" name="id" value="@Model.id" />
        <input type="hidden" name="oldtype" value="@Model.claim.Type" />
        <input type="hidden" name="oldValue" value="@Model.claim.Value" />
    </form>
```

```
        <select name="type" asp-for="claim.Type" form="@hash">
            <option value="@ClaimTypes.Role">ROLE</option>
            <option value="@ClaimTypes.GivenName">GIVENNAME</option>
            <option value="@ClaimTypes.Surname">SURNAME</option>
        </select>
</td>
<td>
        <input class="w-100" name="value" value="@Model.claim.Value" form="@hash" />
</td>
<td>
        <button asp-page-handler="@(Model.newClaim ? "add" : "edit")"
            form="@hash" type="submit" class="btn btn-sm btn-info">
                @(Model.newClaim ? "Add" : "Save")
        </button>
        @if (!Model.newClaim) {
            <button asp-page-handler="delete" form="@hash" type="submit"
                class="btn btn-sm btn-danger">Delete</button>
        }
</td>
```

This partial view produces a set of table cells that contain a select element and a text field for a claim. The select element allows the type of a claim to be selected, and the text field allows the value to be edited. There are buttons in each row to save changes or delete the claim. Claims can have any string value as their type, but to keep the example simple, the partial view only supports the Role, GivenName, and Surname claim types, using values from the ClaimTypes class.

Add a Razor Page named Claims.cshtml to the Pages/Store folder with the contents shown in Listing 17-6.

Listing 17-6. The Contents of the Claims.cshtml File in the Pages/Store Folder

```
@page "/users/claims/{id?}"
@model ExampleApp.Pages.Store.ClaimsModel

@{
    Claim newClaim = new Claim(string.Empty, string.Empty);
}

<h4 class="bg-primary text-white text-center p-2">Claims</h4>

<div class="m-2">
    <table class="table table-sm table-striped">
        <thead><tr><th>Type</th><th>Value</th><th/></tr></thead>
        <tbody>
            @foreach (Claim claim in Model.Claims) {
                <tr>
                    <partial name="_ClaimsRow"
                        model="@((Model.AppUserObject.Id, claim, false))" />
                </tr>
            }
```

```
            <tr>
                <partial name="_ClaimsRow"
                    model="@((Model.AppUserObject.Id, newClaim, true))" />
            </tr>
        </tbody>
    </table>
    <div>
        <a asp-page="users" class="btn btn-secondary">Back</a>
    </div>
</div>
```

The Razor Page uses the _ClaimsRow partial view to display a user's claims. To define the page model, add the code shown in Listing 17-7 to the Claims.cshtml.cs file. (You will have to create this file if you are using Visual Studio Code.)

Listing 17-7. The Contents of the Claims.cshtml.cs File in the Pages/Store Folder

```
using System;
using System.Collections.Generic;
using System.Linq;
using System.Security.Claims;
using System.Threading.Tasks;
using Microsoft.AspNetCore.Identity;
using Microsoft.AspNetCore.Mvc;
using Microsoft.AspNetCore.Mvc.RazorPages;
using ExampleApp.Identity;

namespace ExampleApp.Pages.Store {

    public class ClaimsModel : PageModel {

        public ClaimsModel(UserManager<AppUser> userMgr) => UserManager = userMgr;

        public UserManager<AppUser> UserManager { get; set; }

        public AppUser AppUserObject { get; set; } = new AppUser();

        public IList<Claim> Claims { get; set; } = new List<Claim>();

        public string GetName(string claimType) =>
            (Uri.IsWellFormedUriString(claimType, UriKind.Absolute)
                ? System.IO.Path.GetFileName(new Uri(claimType).LocalPath)
                : claimType).ToUpper();

        public async Task OnGetAsync(string id) {
            if (id != null) {
                AppUserObject = await UserManager.FindByIdAsync(id) ?? new AppUser();
                Claims = (await UserManager.GetClaimsAsync(AppUserObject))
                    .OrderBy(c => c.Type).ThenBy(c => c.Value).ToList();
            }
        }
    }
```

```
        public async Task<IActionResult> OnPostAdd(string id, string type,
                string value) {
            AppUser user = await UserManager.FindByIdAsync(id);
            await UserManager.AddClaimAsync(user, new Claim(type, value));
            return RedirectToPage();
        }

        public async Task<IActionResult> OnPostEdit(string id, string oldType,
                string type, string oldValue, string value) {
            AppUser user = await UserManager.FindByIdAsync(id);
            if (user != null) {
                await UserManager.ReplaceClaimAsync(user,
                    new Claim(oldType, oldValue), new Claim(type, value));
            }
            return RedirectToPage();
        }

        public async Task<IActionResult> OnPostDelete(string id, string type,
                string value) {
            AppUser user = await UserManager.FindByIdAsync(id);
            await UserManager.RemoveClaimAsync(user, new Claim(type, value));
            return RedirectToPage();
        }
    }
}
```

The page model provides its view with claims data obtained through the UserManager<T > class, using the methods described in Table 17-3. Changes to a user's claims are also performed using the UserManager<T> class, allowing claims to be created, edited, and deleted.

To integrate the claims feature into the rest of the application, add the expressions shown in Listing 17-8 to the _UserTableRow.cshtml file in the Pages/Store folder.

Listing 17-8. Adding a Button in the _UserTableRow.cshtml File in the Pages/Store Folder

```
@model string
@inject UserManager<AppUser> UserManager

<a asp-page="edituser" asp-route-id="@Model" class="btn btn-sm btn-secondary">
    Edit
</a>
@if (UserManager.SupportsUserClaim) {
    <a asp-page="claims" asp-route-id="@Model" class="btn btn-sm btn-info">
        Claims
    </a>
}
```

An if expression determines whether the user store supports claims, and a button that navigates to the Claims Razor Page is displayed if it does. Restart ASP.NET Core and request http://localhost:5000/users. Click the Claims button for Alice, and you will see the set of claims stored for that user, as shown in Figure 17-2. You can use the form to add claims or change claim types and values. Claims can be removed by clicking the Delete button.

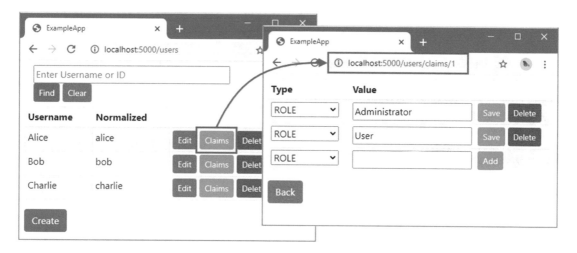

Figure 17-2. *Managing claims through the UserManager<T> class*

Storing Roles in the User Store

Even though roles can be expressed as claims, support for roles predates the adoption of claims, and roles remain the most common way to manage authorization. User stores that can manage roles implement the IUserRoleStore<T> interface, where T is the user class. The IUserRoleStore<T> interface defines the methods described in Table 17-5. As with user store interfaces, the methods in Table 17-5 define a CancellationToken parameter that is used to receive notifications when an asynchronous operation is canceled.

■ **Caution** The way that Identity manages roles presents a trap for the unwary, as explained in the "Understanding the Role Normalization Pitfall" section later in this chapter.

Table 17-5. *The IUserRoleStore<T> Methods*

Name	Description
GetUsersInRoleAsync(role, token)	This method returns a list of user objects representing the users who have been assigned to the specified role.
GetRolesAsync(user, token)	This method returns a list of the role names for the specified user.
IsInRoleAsync(user, roleName, token)	This method returns true if the specified user is a member of the specified role.
AddToRoleAsync(user, roleName, token)	This method adds the specified user to a role.
RemoveFromRoleAsync(user, roleName, token)	This method removes the specified user from a role.

To extend the user store to manage role data, add a class file named UserStoreRoles.cs to the Identity/Store folder and use it to define the partial class shown in Listing 17-9.

Listing 17-9. The Contents of the UserStoreRoles.cs File in the Identity/Store Folder

```
using Microsoft.AspNetCore.Identity;
using System.Collections.Generic;
using System.Linq;
using System.Security.Claims;
using System.Threading;
using System.Threading.Tasks;

namespace ExampleApp.Identity.Store {
    public partial class UserStore : IUserRoleStore<AppUser> {

        public Task<IList<AppUser>> GetUsersInRoleAsync(string roleName,
                CancellationToken token)
            => GetUsersForClaimAsync(new Claim(ClaimTypes.Role, roleName), token);

        public async Task<IList<string>> GetRolesAsync(AppUser user,
                CancellationToken token)
            => (await GetClaimsAsync(user, token))
                .Where(claim => claim.Type == ClaimTypes.Role)
                .Distinct().Select(claim => Normalizer.NormalizeName(claim.Value))
                .ToList();

        public async Task<bool> IsInRoleAsync(AppUser user, string
                normalizedRoleName, CancellationToken token)
            => (await GetRolesAsync(user, token)).Any(role =>
                    Normalizer.NormalizeName(role) == normalizedRoleName);

        public Task AddToRoleAsync(AppUser user, string roleName,
                CancellationToken token)
            => AddClaimsAsync(user, GetClaim(roleName), token);

        public async Task RemoveFromRoleAsync(AppUser user,
                string normalizedRoleName, CancellationToken token) {
            IEnumerable<Claim> claimsToDelete = (await GetClaimsAsync(user, token))
                .Where(claim => claim.Type == ClaimTypes.Role
                    && Normalizer.NormalizeName(claim.Value) == normalizedRoleName);
            await RemoveClaimsAsync(user, claimsToDelete, token);
        }

        private IEnumerable<Claim> GetClaim(string role) =>
            new[] { new Claim(ClaimTypes.Role, role) };
    }
}
```

ASP.NET Core Identity doesn't dictate how a user store manages roles. Since I already have support for managing claims and roles can easily be expressed as claims, I have implemented the IUserRoleStore<T> interface by storing claims with the Role type. The only complication is that the methods that the UserManager<T> class provides for managing roles, which are described in Table 17-6 in the next section, normalize the names of roles for consistency. This is a sensible policy but means additional work is required in Listing 17-9 to ensure that role names are mapped onto claims properly. (No seed data is required for this example because the store is already seeded with role claims.)

Managing Roles in the User Store

The UserManager<T> class provides a set of methods that provide access to roles when the user store class implements the IUserRoleStore<T> interface, as described in Table 17-6, along with a property that allows support for roles to be checked.

Table 17-6. *The UserManager<T> Members for Roles*

Name	Description
SupportsUserRole	This property returns true when the user store implements the IUserRoleStore<T> interface.
AddToRoleAsync(user, role)	This method adds the user to a role. The role name is normalized, and the store's IsInRoleAsync is used to determine if the user is already in the role, in which case an exception is thrown. Otherwise, the store's AddToRoleAsync method is used to add the user to the role, after which the user manager's update sequence is performed.
AddToRolesAsync(user, roles)	This convenience method adds the user to multiple roles using the same approach as the AddToRoleAsync method. The update sequence is performed once the user has been added to all of the roles.
RemoveFromRoleAsync(user, role)	This method removes a user from a role. The role is normalized, and the store's IsInRoleAsync method is used to make sure the user is a member of the role before the store's RemoveFromRoleAsync is called, followed by the user manager's update sequence.
RemoveFromRolesAsync(user, roles)	This convenience method removes the user from multiple roles using the same approach as the RemoveFromRoleAsync method. The user manager's update sequence is performed once the user has been removed from all of the roles.
GetRolesAsync(user)	This method returns the user's roles, expressed as a list that is obtained from the user store's GetRolesAsync method.
IsInRoleAsync(user, role)	This method returns true if the user has the specified role. The role is normalized before being passed to the user store's IsInRoleAsync method.
GetUsersInRoleAsync(role)	This method returns a list of users who have the specified role. The role is normalized before being passed to the user store's GetUsersInRoleAsync method.

To manage a user's roles, add a Razor Page named UserRoles.cshtml to the Pages/Store folder, with the content shown in Listing 17-10.

Listing 17-10. *The Contents of the UserRoles.cshtml File in the Pages/Store Folder*

```
@page "/users/roles/{id?}"
@model ExampleApp.Pages.Store.UserRolesModel

<h4 class="bg-primary text-white text-center p-2">Roles</h4>
<div class="m-2">
    <table class="table table-sm table-striped">
        <thead><tr><th>Role</th><th/></tr></thead>
        <tbody>
            @foreach (string role in Model.Roles) {
                <tr>
                    <td>@role</td>
                    <td>
                        <form method="post">
                            <input type="hidden" name="id" value="@Model.Id" />
                            <input type="hidden" name="role" value="@role" />
                            <button type="submit" class="btn btn-sm btn-danger"
                                    asp-page-handler="delete">
                                Delete
                            </button>
                        </form>
                    </td>
                </tr>
            }
            <tr>
                <td>
                    <form method="post" id="newRole">
                        <input type="hidden" name="id" value="@Model.Id" />
                        <input class="w-100" name="newRole" placeholder="Add Role" />
                    </form>
                </td>
                <td>
                    <button type="submit" class="btn btn-sm btn-primary"
                            asp-page-handler="add" form="newRole">
                        Add
                    </button>
                </td>
            </tr>
        </tbody>
    </table>
    <div>
        <a asp-page="users" class="btn btn-secondary">Back</a>
    </div>
</div>
```

The Razor Page presents a table containing the roles to which the user has been assigned, along with a Delete button that will remove the user from the role. There is a row in the table that allows the user to be added to new roles.

Add the code shown in Listing 17-11 to the UserRoles.cshtml.cs file to define the page model class. (You will have to create this file if you are using Visual Studio Code.)

Listing 17-11. The Contents of the UserRoles.cshtml.cs File in the Pages/Store Folder

```csharp
using ExampleApp.Identity;
using Microsoft.AspNetCore.Identity;
using Microsoft.AspNetCore.Mvc;
using Microsoft.AspNetCore.Mvc.RazorPages;
using System.Collections.Generic;
using System.Linq;
using System.Threading.Tasks;

namespace ExampleApp.Pages.Store {

    public class UserRolesModel : PageModel {

        public UserRolesModel(UserManager<AppUser> userManager)
            => UserManager = userManager;

        public UserManager<AppUser> UserManager { get; set; }

        public IEnumerable<string> Roles { get; set; } = Enumerable.Empty<string>();

        [BindProperty(SupportsGet = true)]
        public string Id { get; set; }

        public async void OnGet() {
            AppUser user = await GetUser();
            if (user != null) {
                Roles = await UserManager.GetRolesAsync(user);
            }
        }

        public async Task<IActionResult> OnPostAdd(string newRole) {
            await UserManager.AddToRoleAsync(await GetUser(), newRole);
            return RedirectToPage();
        }

        public async Task<IActionResult> OnPostDelete(string role) {
            await UserManager.RemoveFromRoleAsync(await GetUser(), role);
            return RedirectToPage();
        }

        private Task<AppUser> GetUser() => Id == null
            ? null : UserManager.FindByIdAsync(Id);
    }
}
```

The page model class uses the method defined by the UserManager<T> class to find AppUser objects and manages role assignments using the methods described in Table 17-6. The GET handler method gets the current role assignments for the user; the POST handler methods add and delete role memberships.

In Listing 17-12, I have added a button to the _UserTableRow.cshtml partial view that navigates to the UserRoles Razor Page if the user store supports role data.

Listing 17-12. Adding a Button in the _UserTableRow.cshtml File in the Pages/Store Folder

```
@model string
@inject UserManager<AppUser> UserManager

<a asp-page="edituser" asp-route-id="@Model" class="btn btn-sm btn-secondary">
    Edit
</a>
@if (UserManager.SupportsUserClaim) {
    <a asp-page="claims" asp-route-id="@Model" class="btn btn-sm btn-info">
        Claims
    </a>
}

@if (UserManager.SupportsUserRole) {
    <a asp-page="userroles" asp-route-id="@Model" class="btn btn-sm btn-info">
        Roles
    </a>
}
```

Restart ASP.NET Core, request http://localhost:5000/users, and click the Roles button for one of the users. The roles displayed will correspond to the user's role claims, although the names will be normalized, as shown in Figure 17-3. Bear in mind that the roles stored in the database won't be used for authorization until Chapter 18.

Figure 17-3. *Managing roles*

Understanding the Role Normalization Pitfall

There is a mismatch between the way that ASP.NET Core assesses roles and the way roles are stored by Identity. When a user is assigned to a role using the methods described in Table 17-6, the name of the role is normalized before it is added to the store.

When ASP.NET Core assesses role requirements specified through the Authorize attribute, it uses the ClaimsPrincipal.IsInRole, which performs a case-sensitive search for matching role claims. This can often fail to match roles whose names have been normalized in the store. You can see the effect of the normalization in Figure 17-3. Even though Alice has role claims for the User and Administrator roles, they are displayed as user and administrator.

There are three ways of avoiding this problem. The first is to express role requirements to match the normalized roles names in the store. This is a simple fix, but it only works when you can be confident that the normalizer won't change. This means that roles should be specified in uppercase (e.g., ADMINISTRATOR) when the default Identity normalizer is used and lowercase (e.g., administrator) for the normalizer I created in Chapter 16.

The second approach is to use the normalized role name assigned to a user object as a key to locate the non-normalized name in another data store. This is the approach that the Entity Framework Core user store uses and is the reason that a role store was required to use roles in Part 1, even though I didn't need any of the direct features that the role store provided (and which are described in Chapter 19).

The remaining approach is to manage roles as claims directly, avoiding the normalization performed by the UserManager<T> methods. None of these approaches is ideal, but I prefer to store roles as claims because it means that a future change to the normalizer doesn't break role-based authorization. In Chapter 19, I create a custom role store and demonstrate how it can be used to create a master list of roles.

In Listing 17-13, I have modified the UserRoles page model class to obtain roles as claims.

Listing 17-13. Using Claims in the UserRoles.cshtml.cs File in the Pages/Store Folder

```
using ExampleApp.Identity;
using Microsoft.AspNetCore.Identity;
using Microsoft.AspNetCore.Mvc;
using Microsoft.AspNetCore.Mvc.RazorPages;
using System.Collections.Generic;
using System.Linq;
using System.Threading.Tasks;
using System.Security.Claims;

namespace ExampleApp.Pages.Store {

    public class UserRolesModel : PageModel {

        public UserRolesModel(UserManager<AppUser> userManager)
            => UserManager = userManager;

        public UserManager<AppUser> UserManager { get; set; }

        public IEnumerable<string> Roles { get; set; } = Enumerable.Empty<string>();

        [BindProperty(SupportsGet = true)]
        public string Id { get; set; }

        public async void OnGet() {
            AppUser user = await GetUser();
            if (user != null) {
                //Roles = await UserManager.GetRolesAsync(user);
                Roles = (await UserManager.GetClaimsAsync(user))?
                    .Where(c => c.Type == ClaimTypes.Role).Select(c => c.Value);
            }
        }
    }
```

```
public async Task<IActionResult> OnPostAdd(string newRole) {
    //await UserManager.AddToRoleAsync(await GetUser(), newRole);
    await UserManager.AddClaimAsync(await GetUser(),
        new Claim(ClaimTypes.Role, newRole));
    return RedirectToPage();
}

public async Task<IActionResult> OnPostDelete(string role) {
    await UserManager.RemoveFromRoleAsync(await GetUser(), role);
    return RedirectToPage();
}

private Task<AppUser> GetUser() => Id == null
    ? null : UserManager.FindByIdAsync(Id);
}
}
```

Getting the user's roles and adding a new role are performed using the methods that manage claims. I don't need to change the code that removes a role because that operation can be done using the normalized role name without causing any problems. Restart ASP.NET Core and view the roles for Alice; you will see that the role names are now mixed case, as shown in Figure 17-4.

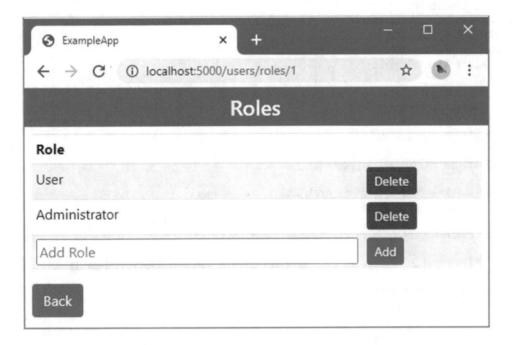

Figure 17-4. *Avoiding the role normalization pitfall*

Confirming User Contact Data

Confirmation is the process of verifying that the contact data in the store for a user is correct. A user can enter a valid phone number or email address, but it is important to confirm they can receive calls or emails before using those values, especially when they are used to sign into the application or as part of a password recovery process.

Understanding the Confirmation Process

The confirmation process is performed by generating a token and sending it to the user through the communications channel being confirmed. This means, for example, that the token is emailed to confirm an email address and sent as an SMS text message to a phone number.

The user then provides the token to the application to demonstrate they control the email address or phone number. In the case of emails, this typically involves clicking a link that includes the token, as shown in Figure 17-5. In the case of SMS messages, the user typically enters the token into an HTML form.

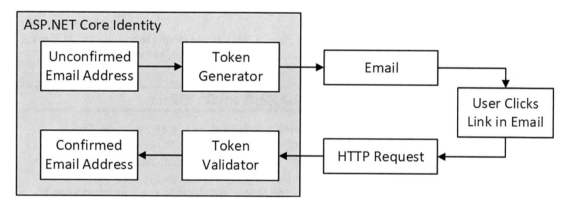

Figure 17-5. *The confirmation sequence*

Creating the Email and SMS Service Providers

The confirmation process requires the ability to send confirmation emails or texts to users, which requires the use of a third-party service or, in a corporate setting, central servers.

For this book, I am going to only simulate the process of sending emails and SMS messages. The process of configuring communications providers is a topic in its own right and beyond the scope of this book. Create the ExampleApp/Services folder and add to it a class file named EmailService.cs with the code shown in Listing 17-14.

Listing 17-14. The Contents of the EmailService.cs File in the Services Folder

```
using ExampleApp.Identity;
using System;

namespace ExampleApp.Services {
```

```
public interface IEmailSender {

    public void SendMessage(AppUser user, string subject, params string[] body);
}

public class ConsoleEmailSender : IEmailSender {

    public void SendMessage(AppUser user, string subject, params string[] body) {
        Console.WriteLine("--- Email Starts ---");
        Console.WriteLine($"To: {user.EmailAddress}");
        Console.WriteLine($"Subject: {subject}");
        foreach (string str in body) {
            Console.WriteLine(str);
        }
        Console.WriteLine("--- Email Ends ---");
    }
}
}
```

The IEmailSender interface defines an abstract interface for sending emails, and ConsoleEmailSender implements the interface and simulates sending an email by writing messages to the console.

USING EMAIL AND SMS PROVIDERS

My advice is to use commercial email and SMS services rather than try to set up your own. Getting messaging working properly can be difficult, and it is easy to misconfigure the services so that your users receive too many or too few messages. If you don't know where to start, then try Twilio (https://www.twilio.com) or Amazon's Simple Notification Service (https://aws.amazon.com/sns). Twilio is the provider that Microsoft partners with for Azure, and Amazon Web Services needs no introduction. I have no relationship with either service, but both provide a C# API and offer a range of pricing options, including free tiers. If you dislike SendGrid or Amazon Web Services, there are many alternatives from which to choose.

Next, add a class file named SMSService.cs to the ExampleApp/Services folder with the code shown in Listing 17-15.

Listing 17-15. The Contents of the SMSService.cs File in the Services Folder

```
using ExampleApp.Identity;
using System;

namespace ExampleApp.Services {

    public interface ISMSSender {

        public void SendMessage(AppUser user, params string[] body);
    }
```

```
public class ConsoleSMSSender : ISMSSender {

    public void SendMessage(AppUser user, params string[] body) {
        Console.WriteLine("--- SMS Starts ---");
        Console.WriteLine($"To: {user.PhoneNumber}");
        foreach (string str in body) {
            Console.WriteLine(str);
        }
        Console.WriteLine("--- SMS Ends ---");
    }
}
}
```

The ISMSSender interface defines an abstract interface for sending SMS messages, and ConsoleSMSSender implements the interface and simulates sending an SMS by writing messages to the console. Listing 17-16 registers the email and SMS classes as services so they can be consumed through dependency injection.

Listing 17-16. Registering Services in the Startup.cs File in the ExampleApp Folder

```
using Microsoft.AspNetCore.Builder;
using Microsoft.AspNetCore.Hosting;
using Microsoft.AspNetCore.Http;
using Microsoft.Extensions.DependencyInjection;
using ExampleApp.Custom;
using Microsoft.AspNetCore.Authentication.Cookies;
using Microsoft.AspNetCore.Authorization;
using Microsoft.AspNetCore.Identity;
using ExampleApp.Identity;
using ExampleApp.Identity.Store;
using ExampleApp.Services;

namespace ExampleApp {
    public class Startup {

        public void ConfigureServices(IServiceCollection services) {
            services.AddSingleton<ILookupNormalizer, Normalizer>();
            services.AddSingleton<IUserStore<AppUser>, UserStore>();
            services.AddSingleton<IEmailSender, ConsoleEmailSender>();
            services.AddSingleton<ISMSSender, ConsoleSMSSender>();
            services.AddIdentityCore<AppUser>();

            services.AddSingleton<IUserValidator<AppUser>, EmailValidator>();

            services.AddAuthentication(opts => {
                opts.DefaultScheme
                    = CookieAuthenticationDefaults.AuthenticationScheme;
            }).AddCookie(opts => {
                opts.LoginPath = "/signin";
                opts.AccessDeniedPath = "/signin/403";
            });
```

```
        services.AddAuthorization(opts => {
            AuthorizationPolicies.AddPolicies(opts);
        });
        services.AddRazorPages();
        services.AddControllersWithViews();
    }

    public void Configure(IApplicationBuilder app, IWebHostEnvironment env) {

        app.UseStaticFiles();
        app.UseAuthentication();
        app.UseRouting();
        //app.UseMiddleware<RoleMemberships>();
        app.UseAuthorization();

        app.UseEndpoints(endpoints => {
            endpoints.MapRazorPages();
            endpoints.MapDefaultControllerRoute();
            endpoints.MapFallbackToPage("/Secret");
        });
    }
}
}
```

Storing Security Stamps in the User Store

The next step is to implement the optional interface for the user store that adds support for managing security stamps. A security stamp is a token that is updated every time a change is made to a user, which prevents confirmation tokens from being validated if there have been subsequent changes to the user's details. This avoids the situation where a user receives a confirmation token, changes their email address again, and only then validates the token, with the result that the user's ability to receive emails at the new address isn't properly validated. Security stamps are strings, and Listing 17-17 updates the user class to add a property for a stamp.

Listing 17-17. Adding a Property in the AppUser.cs File in the Identity Folder

```
using System;
using System.Collections.Generic;
using System.Security.Claims;

namespace ExampleApp.Identity {
    public class AppUser {

        public string Id { get; set; } = Guid.NewGuid().ToString();

        public string UserName { get; set; }

        public string NormalizedUserName { get; set; }

        public string EmailAddress { get; set; }
        public string NormalizedEmailAddress { get; set; }
```

```
        public bool EmailAddressConfirmed { get; set; }

        public string PhoneNumber { get; set; }
        public bool PhoneNumberConfirmed { get; set; }

        public string FavoriteFood { get; set; }
        public string Hobby { get; set; }

        public IList<Claim> Claims { get; set; }

        public string SecurityStamp { get; set; }
    }
}
```

User stores that can manage security stamps implement the IUserSecurityStampStore<T> interface, which defines the methods described in Table 17-7. As with earlier examples, the type T is the user class, and the token parameter is a CancellationToken object that is used when asynchronous tasks are cancelled.

Table 17-7. *The IUserSecurityStampStore<T> Methods*

Name	Description
SetSecurityStampAsync(user, stamp, token)	This method sets a new security stamp for the specified user.
GetSecurityStampAsync(user, token)	This method retrieves the specified user's security stamp.

To extend the example user store to implement the interface, add a class file named UserStoreSecurityStamps.cs to the Identity/Store folder and use it to define the partial class shown in Listing 17-18.

Listing 17-18. The Contents of the UserStoreSecurityStamps.cs File in the Identity/Store Folder

```
using Microsoft.AspNetCore.Identity;
using System.Threading;
using System.Threading.Tasks;

namespace ExampleApp.Identity.Store {
    public partial class UserStore : IUserSecurityStampStore<AppUser> {

        public Task<string> GetSecurityStampAsync(AppUser user,
                CancellationToken token) =>
            Task.FromResult(user.SecurityStamp);

        public Task SetSecurityStampAsync(AppUser user, string stamp,
                CancellationToken token) {
            user.SecurityStamp = stamp;
            return Task.CompletedTask;
        }
    }
}
```

The interface implementation is simple and has only to read and write the SecurityStamp property defined in Listing 17-17.

Updating the Security Stamp

The security stamp for a user object can be accessed directly through the property added in Listing 17-17 or through the UserManager<T> members described in Table 17-8.

Table 17-8. *The UserManager<T> Members for Security Stamps*

Name	Description
SupportsUserSecurityStamp	This property returns true if the user store implements the IUserSecurityStampStore<T> interface.
GetSecurityStampAsync(user)	This method returns the current security stamp for the specified user by calling the user store's GetSecurityStampAsync method.
UpdateSecurityStampAsync(user)	This method updates the security stamp for the specified user. The stamp is generated by the UserManager<T> class using random data passed to the user store's SetSecurityStampAsync method, after which the user manager's update sequence is performed.

Add a Razor View named _EditUserSecurityStamp.cshtml to the Pages/Store folder with the content shown in Listing 17-19.

Listing 17-19. The Contents of the _EditUserSecurityStamp.cshtml File in the Pages/Store Folder

```
@model AppUser
@inject UserManager<AppUser> UserManager

@if (UserManager.SupportsUserSecurityStamp) {
    <tr>
        <td>Security Stamp</td>
        <td>@Model.SecurityStamp</td>
    </tr>
}
```

Add the element shown in Listing 17-20 to incorporate the new partial view into the application.

Listing 17-20. Displaying the Security Stamp in the EditUser.cshtml File in the Pages/Store Folder

```
@page "/users/edit/{id?}"
@model ExampleApp.Pages.Store.UsersModel

<div asp-validation-summary="All" class="text-danger m-2"></div>

<div class="m-2">
    <form method="post">
        <input type="hidden" name="id" value="@Model.AppUserObject.Id" />
        <table class="table table-sm table-striped">
```

```
            <tbody>
                <partial name="_EditUserBasic" model="@Model.AppUserObject" />
                <partial name="_EditUserEmail" model="@Model.AppUserObject" />
                <partial name="_EditUserPhone" model="@Model.AppUserObject" />
                <partial name="_EditUserCustom" model="@Model.AppUserObject" />
                <partial name="_EditUserSecurityStamp"
                    model="@Model.AppUserObject" />
            </tbody>
        </table>
        <div>
            <button type="submit" class="btn btn-primary">Save</button>
            <a asp-page="users" class="btn btn-secondary">Cancel</a>
        </div>
    </form>
</div>
```

The current stamp is displayed when the user store supports security stamps. The UserManager<T>
methods that set property values automatically update the security stamp, but I have to perform this task
directly since I am setting user object properties directly, as shown in Listing 17-21.

Listing 17-21. Updating the Security Stamp in the EditUser.cshtml.cs File in the Pages/Identity Folder

```
...
public async Task<IActionResult> OnPost(AppUser user) {
    IdentityResult result;
    AppUser storeUser = await UserManager.FindByIdAsync(user.Id);
    if (storeUser == null) {
        result = await UserManager.CreateAsync(user);
    } else {
        storeUser.UpdateFrom(user, out bool changed);
        if (changed && UserManager.SupportsUserSecurityStamp) {
            await UserManager.UpdateSecurityStampAsync(storeUser);
        }
        result = await UserManager.UpdateAsync(storeUser);
    }
    if (result.Succeeded) {
        return RedirectToPage("users", new { searchname = user.Id });
    } else {
        foreach (IdentityError err in result.Errors) {
            ModelState.AddModelError("", err.Description ?? "Error");
        }
        AppUserObject = user;
        return Page();
    }
}
...
```

The CreateAsync method automatically generates a security stamp, which is why I only update the
stamp explicitly when I use the UpdateAsync method and when one or more properties are changed. In
Listing 17-22, I have updated the code that seeds the user store to include security stamps in the initial data.

Listing 17-22. Seeding with Security Stamps in the UserStore.cs File in the Identity/Store Folder

```
...
foreach (string name in UsersAndClaims.Users) {
    AppUser user = new AppUser {
        Id = (++idCounter).ToString(),
        UserName = name,
        NormalizedUserName = Normalizer.NormalizeName(name),
        EmailAddress = EmailFromName(name),
        NormalizedEmailAddress =
            Normalizer.NormalizeEmail(EmailFromName(name)),
        EmailAddressConfirmed = true,
        PhoneNumber = "123-4567",
        PhoneNumberConfirmed = true,
        FavoriteFood = customData[name].food,
        Hobby = customData[name].hobby,
        SecurityStamp = "InitialStamp"
    };
    users.TryAdd(user.Id, user);
...
```

Users that are created through the UserManager<T> class will have security stamps generated automatically, but this additional step is required for seed users to prevent exceptions when the security stamp is changed.

To make sure that security stamps are working, restart ASP.NET Core, request http://localhost:5000/users/edit/1, and enter a new value into the Hobby field. Click the Save button and then click the Edit button for the Alice user, and you will see the new security stamp, as shown in Figure 17-6. A new security stamp is generated each time you make a change.

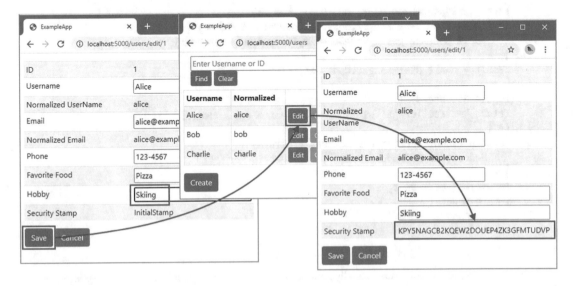

Figure 17-6. *Updating a security stamp*

Creating a Confirmation Token Generator

The security token that is sent to the user is produced by a *token generator*. Identity provides a set of default token generators, but creating a custom generator helps demonstrate how the process works. Token generators implement the IUserTwoFactorTokenProvider<T> interface, where T is the user class. The interface defines the methods described in Table 17-9.

Table 17-9. The IUserTwoFactorTokenProvider<T> Methods

Name	Description
CanGenerateTwoFactorTokenAsync(manager, token)	This method returns true if the generator can produce a token for the specified UserManager<T> and user object.
GenerateAsync(purpose, manager, user)	This method generates a string confirmation token for the specified purpose for a given user and user manager.
ValidateAsync(purpose, token, manager, user)	This method validates a token that has been generated for the specified person, user, and user manager. The method returns true if the token is valid and false otherwise.

There are no restrictions on how tokens should be generated and validated, but tokens should be simple, easy to process, and not easily altered (so that a token for one user cannot be edited to become a token to confirm details from another user, for example).

The default Identity token generator creates *time-based one-time passwords* (TOTPs), which are often used as part of a two-factor sign-in process, as described in Chapters 20 and 21.

For this chapter, I am going to take a simpler approach that will let me explain the process of confirming user details without the complexity of generating secure tokens. As with many of the examples in this part of the book, you should not use this approach in real projects and should instead rely on the tokens generators that Identity provides. To create the custom token generator, add a class file named SimpleTokenGenerator. cs to the ExampleApp/Identity folder and use it to define the class shown in Listing 17-23.

Listing 17-23. The Contents of the SimpleTokenGenerator.cs File in the Identity Folder

```
using Microsoft.AspNetCore.Identity;
using System;
using System.Security.Cryptography;
using System.Text;
using System.Threading.Tasks;

namespace ExampleApp.Identity {
    public abstract class SimpleTokenGenerator :
            IUserTwoFactorTokenProvider<AppUser> {

        protected virtual int CodeLength { get; } = 6;

        public virtual Task<bool> CanGenerateTwoFactorTokenAsync(
            UserManager<AppUser> manager, AppUser user) =>
                Task.FromResult(manager.SupportsUserSecurityStamp);

        public virtual Task<string> GenerateAsync(string purpose,
                UserManager<AppUser> manager, AppUser user)
            => Task.FromResult(GenerateCode(purpose, user));
```

495

```
    public virtual Task<bool> ValidateAsync(string purpose, string token,
        UserManager<AppUser> manager, AppUser user)
    => Task.FromResult(GenerateCode(purpose, user).Equals(token));

    protected virtual string GenerateCode(string purpose, AppUser user) {
        HMACSHA1 hashAlgorithm =
            new HMACSHA1(Encoding.UTF8.GetBytes(user.SecurityStamp));
        byte[] hashCode = hashAlgorithm.ComputeHash(
            Encoding.UTF8.GetBytes(GetData(purpose, user)));
        return BitConverter.ToString(hashCode[^CodeLength..]).Replace("-", "");
    }

    protected virtual string GetData(string purpose, AppUser user)
        => $"{purpose}{user.SecurityStamp}";
}

public class EmailConfirmationTokenGenerator : SimpleTokenGenerator {

    protected override int CodeLength => 12;

    public async override Task<bool> CanGenerateTwoFactorTokenAsync(
            UserManager<AppUser> manager, AppUser user) {
        return await base.CanGenerateTwoFactorTokenAsync(manager, user)
            && !string.IsNullOrEmpty(user.EmailAddress)
            && !user.EmailAddressConfirmed;
    }
}

public class PhoneConfirmationTokenGenerator : SimpleTokenGenerator {

    protected override int CodeLength => 3;

    public async override Task<bool> CanGenerateTwoFactorTokenAsync(
            UserManager<AppUser> manager, AppUser user) {
        return await base.CanGenerateTwoFactorTokenAsync(manager, user)
            && !string.IsNullOrEmpty(user.PhoneNumber)
            && !user.PhoneNumberConfirmed;
    }
}
}
```

I have defined a base class that is used as the base for classes that generate tokens suitable for inclusion conforming email addresses and phone numbers. The tokens are generated as hash codes of strings that include the purpose of the token, the address of number being confirmed, and the user's current security stamp.

```
...
protected virtual string GetData(string purpose, AppUser user)
    => $"{purpose}{user.SecurityStamp}";
...
```

The inclusion of the purpose ensures that a token is valid for only one type of confirmation. The inclusion of the security stamp ensures that tokens are invalidated when a change is made to the user object, ensuring that the token can be used only until a change is made in the user store.

The email and SMS confirmation tokens are different lengths. This is not a requirement, but users who receive tokens over SMS will often have to type them into an HTML form, and it is important to make that process easy. Listing 17-24 registers the token generators with ASP.NET Core Identity.

Listing 17-24. Registering a Token Generator in the Startup.cs File in the ExampleApp Folder

```
...
public void ConfigureServices(IServiceCollection services) {
    services.AddSingleton<ILookupNormalizer, Normalizer>();
    services.AddSingleton<IUserStore<AppUser>, UserStore>();
    services.AddSingleton<IEmailSender, ConsoleEmailSender>();
    services.AddSingleton<ISMSSender, ConsoleSMSSender>();

    services.AddIdentityCore<AppUser>(opts => {
        opts.Tokens.EmailConfirmationTokenProvider = "SimpleEmail";
        opts.Tokens.ChangeEmailTokenProvider = "SimpleEmail";
    })
    .AddTokenProvider<EmailConfirmationTokenGenerator>("SimpleEmail")
    .AddTokenProvider<PhoneConfirmationTokenGenerator>(
        TokenOptions.DefaultPhoneProvider);

    services.AddSingleton<IUserValidator<AppUser>, EmailValidator>();

    services.AddAuthentication(opts => {
        opts.DefaultScheme
            = CookieAuthenticationDefaults.AuthenticationScheme;
    }).AddCookie(opts => {
        opts.LoginPath = "/signin";
        opts.AccessDeniedPath = "/signin/403";
    });
    services.AddAuthorization(opts => {
        AuthorizationPolicies.AddPolicies(opts);
    });
    services.AddRazorPages();
    services.AddControllersWithViews();
}
...
```

The AddTokenProvider extension method is used to register a token generator, along with a name by which it will be known. The options pattern is used to select a token generator for a particular purpose. The IdentityOptions.Tokens property returns a TokenOptions object, which defines the properties shown in Table 17-10 for specifying token generators.

Table 17-10. *The TokenOptions Properties for Confirmation Token Generators*

Name	Description
DefaultProvider	This property specifies the name of the token generator that will be used by default. It is set to Default.
DefaultEmailProvider	This property specifies the name of the token generator used for email confirmations. It is set to Email.
DefaultPhoneProvider	This property specifies the name of the token generator used for phone confirmations. It is set to Phone.
ChangeEmailTokenProvider	This property specifies the token generator used for email changes. It uses DefaultProvider by default. (See the explanation after the table for more information about this property.)
EmailConfirmationTokenProvider	This property specifies the token generator used for email changes. It uses DefaultProvider by default. (See the explanation after the table for more information about this property.)
ChangePhoneNumberTokenProvider	This property specifies the token generator used for phone number changes. It uses DefaultPhoneProvider by default.
PasswordResetTokenProvider	This property specifies the token generator for confirming password changes.

When registering a token generator, you use the AddTokenProvider method to register the class with a name. The idea is that you can use TokenOptions.DefaultPhoneProvider, for example, and your generator will be used as the default generator for phone number confirmations, like this:

```
...
.AddTokenProvider<PhoneConfirmationTokenGenerator>(
    TokenOptions.DefaultPhoneProvider);
...
```

Unfortunately, the TokenOptions class uses the DefaultProvider property as the value for the ChangeEmailTokenProvider and EmailConfirmationTokenProvider configuration options. This means you must use a custom name for your token generator and perform the additional step of setting the ChangeEmailTokenProvider and EmailConfirmationTokenProvider options, like this:

```
...
services.AddIdentityCore<AppUser>(opts => {
    opts.Tokens.EmailConfirmationTokenProvider = "SimpleEmail";
    opts.Tokens.ChangeEmailTokenProvider = "SimpleEmail";
})
...
```

There are two configuration properties for email token generators, and it is a good idea to set both. I explain when each generator property is used in the next section.

Creating the Confirmation Workflow

The UserManager<T> class provides methods for generating and validating confirmation tokens, as described in Table 17-11.

Table 17-11. *The UserManager<T> Methods for Generating and Validating Tokens*

Name	Description
GenerateUserTokenAsync(user, provider, purpose)	This method uses the named provider to generate a token for the specified user and purpose.
VerifyUserTokenAsync(user, provider, purpose, token)	This method returns true if the named token generator validates the token for the specified user and purpose.

These methods are useful when you are working directly with the properties defined by the user class. The UserManager<T> class also provides convenience methods that simplify the confirmation process, as described in Table 17-12.

Table 17-12. *The UserManager<T> Email Confirmation Convenience Methods*

Name	Description
GenerateEmailConfirmationTokenAsync(user)	This method generates a token for the specified user with the EmailConfirmationTokenProvider token generator, using the email address currently in the user store.
ConfirmEmailAsync(user, token)	This method validates a token for the specified user using the EmailConfirmationTokenProvider generator. If the token is valid, the email confirmation property is set to true. The user's email property is not changed.
GenerateChangeEmailTokenAsync(user, email)	This method generates a token for the specified user with the ChangeEmailTokenProvider token generator. The user store is not modified.
ChangeEmailAsync(user, email, token)	This method validates a token for the specified user using the ChangeEmailTokenProvider generator. If the token is valid, the email address is updated, the email confirmation property is set to true, the security stamp is updated, and the user manager's update sequence is performed.

The GenerateEmailConfirmationTokenAsync and ConfirmEmailAsync methods are used to confirm the email address that is already in the store, which can be useful if you have a self-service registration process and you want to confirm the user's details when a new account is created. The GenerateChangeEmailTokenAsync and ChangeEmailAsync methods are used to confirm new email addresses so that the user store isn't updated until the email address has been confirmed. Note that each pair of methods uses a distinct combination of token generator and token purpose, which means that ChangeEmailAsync method can't be used to validate tokens generated by the GenerateEmailConfirmationTokenAsync method. Table 17-13 describes the set of UserManager<T> methods for confirming phone numbers.

Table 17-13. *The UserManager<T> Phone Confirmation Convenience Methods*

Name	Description
GenerateChangePhoneNumberToken Async(user, phone)	This method generates a token for the specified user with the ChangePhoneNumberTokenProvider token generator, using the specified phone number.
VerifyChangePhoneNumberToken Async(user, token, phone)	This method returns true if the specified token is valid for the specified phone number.
ChangePhoneNumberAsync(user, phone, token)	This convenience method validates a token for the specified user. If the token is valid, the phone number is updated, and the phone confirmation property is set to true, after which the security stamp is updated, and the user manager's update sequence is performed.

To support email and phone confirmations in the example application, add a Razor Page named EmailPhoneChange.cshtml to the Pages/Store folder with the content shown in Listing 17-25.

Listing 17-25. The Contents of the EmailPhoneChange.cshtml File in the Pages/Store Folder

```
@page "/change/{id}/{dataType}"
@model ExampleApp.Pages.Store.EmailPhoneChangeModel

<h4 class="bg-primary text-white text-center p-2">Change</h4>

<div class="m-2">
    <form method="post">
        <div class="form-group">
            <label>
                @Model.LabelText
            </label>
            <input class="form-control" name="dataValue"
                value="@Model.CurrentValue" />
        </div>
        <button type="submit" class="btn btn-primary">Change</button>
        <a href="@($"/users/edit/{Model.AppUser.Id}")" class="btn btn-secondary">
            Cancel
        </a>
    </form>
</div>
```

The Razor Page presents a simple HTML form that allows a new value to be entered for either the email address or the phone number, which is determine from the URL. To provide the data for the form and to generate the confirmation tokens, add the code shown in Listing 17-26 to the page model class. (You will have to create this file if you are using Visual Studio Code.)

Listing 17-26. The Contents of the EmailPhoneChange.cshtml.cs File in the Pages/Store Folder

```
using ExampleApp.Identity;
using ExampleApp.Services;
using Microsoft.AspNetCore.Identity;
using Microsoft.AspNetCore.Mvc;
```

```
using Microsoft.AspNetCore.Mvc.RazorPages;
using System.Threading.Tasks;

namespace ExampleApp.Pages.Store {

    public class EmailPhoneChangeModel : PageModel {

        public EmailPhoneChangeModel(UserManager<AppUser> manager,
                IEmailSender email, ISMSSender sms) {
            UserManager = manager;
            EmailSender = email;
            SMSSender = sms;
        }

        public UserManager<AppUser> UserManager { get; set; }
        public IEmailSender EmailSender { get; set; }
        public ISMSSender SMSSender { get; set; }

        [BindProperty(SupportsGet = true)]
        public string DataType { get; set; }

        public bool IsEmail => DataType.Equals("email");

        public AppUser AppUser { get; set; }

        public string LabelText => DataType ==
            "email" ? "Email Address" : "Phone Number";

        public string CurrentValue => IsEmail
            ? AppUser.EmailAddress : AppUser.PhoneNumber;

        public async Task OnGetAsync(string id, string data) {
            AppUser = await UserManager.FindByIdAsync(id);
        }

        public async Task<IActionResult> OnPost(string id, string dataValue) {
            AppUser = await UserManager.FindByIdAsync(id);
            if (IsEmail) {
                string token = await UserManager
                    .GenerateChangeEmailTokenAsync(AppUser, dataValue);
                EmailSender.SendMessage(AppUser, "Confirm Email",
                    "Please click the link to confirm your email address:",
                  $"http://localhost:5000/validate/{id}/email/{dataValue}:{token}");
            } else {
                string token = await UserManager
                    .GenerateChangePhoneNumberTokenAsync(AppUser, dataValue);
                SMSSender.SendMessage(AppUser,
                    $"Your confirmation token is {token}");
            }
```

```
            return RedirectToPage("EmailPhoneConfirmation",
                new { id = id, dataType = DataType, dataValue = dataValue });
        }
    }
}
```

The GET page handler method locates the user whose data is being modified so that the current values can be displayed in the HTML form. The POST page handler method generates confirmation tokens and generates either an email or SMS message that provides the user with the token, after which a redirection is performed.

To provide the confirmation step, add a Razor Page named EmailPhoneConfirmation.cshtml to the Pages/Store folder with the content shown in Listing 17-27.

Listing 17-27. The Contents of the EmailPhoneConfirmation.cshtml File in the Pages/Store Folder

```
@page "/validate/{id}/{dataType}/{dataValue?}"
@model ExampleApp.Pages.Store.EmailPhoneConfirmationModel

<div asp-validation-summary="All" class="text-danger m-2"></div>

<h4 class="bg-primary text-white text-center p-2">Confirmation</h4>

<div class="m-2">
    <form method="post">
        <input type="hidden" name="id" value="@Model.AppUser.Id" />
        <input type="hidden" name="dataValue" value="@Model.DataValue" />
        <div class="form-group">
            <label>
                Enter Confirmation Token
            </label>
            <input class="form-control" name="token" />
        </div>
        <button type="submit" class="btn btn-primary">Confirm</button>
        <a href="@($"/users/edit/{Model.AppUser.Id}")" class="btn btn-secondary">
            Cancel
        </a>
    </form>
</div>
```

The page displays an input element into which the user can enter a confirmation code. To complete the confirmation process, add the code shown in Listing 17-28 to the page model class. (You will have to create this file if you are using Visual Studio Code.)

Listing 17-28. The Contents of the EmailPhoneConfirmation.cshtml.cs File in the Pages/Store Folder

```
using ExampleApp.Identity;
using Microsoft.AspNetCore.Identity;
using Microsoft.AspNetCore.Mvc;
using Microsoft.AspNetCore.Mvc.RazorPages;
using System.Threading.Tasks;
```

```
namespace ExampleApp.Pages.Store {

    public class EmailPhoneConfirmationModel : PageModel {

        public EmailPhoneConfirmationModel(UserManager<AppUser> manager)
            => UserManager = manager;

        public UserManager<AppUser> UserManager { get; set; }

        [BindProperty(SupportsGet = true)]
        public string DataType { get; set; }

        [BindProperty(SupportsGet = true)]
        public string DataValue { get; set; }

        public bool IsEmail => DataType.Equals("email");

        public AppUser AppUser { get; set; }

        public async Task<IActionResult> OnGetAsync(string id) {
            AppUser = await UserManager.FindByIdAsync(id);
            if (DataValue != null && DataValue.Contains(':')) {
                string[] values = DataValue.Split(":");
                return await Validate(values[0], values[1]);
            }
            return Page();
        }

        public async Task<IActionResult> OnPostAsync(string id,
                string token, string dataValue) {
            AppUser = await UserManager.FindByIdAsync(id);
            return await Validate(dataValue, token);
        }

        private async Task<IActionResult> Validate(string value, string token) {
            IdentityResult result;
            if (IsEmail) {
                result = await UserManager.ChangeEmailAsync(AppUser, value, token);
            } else {
                result = await UserManager.ChangePhoneNumberAsync(AppUser, value,
                    token);
            }
            if (result.Succeeded) {
                return Redirect($"/users/edit/{AppUser.Id}");
            } else {
                foreach (IdentityError err in result.Errors) {
                    ModelState.AddModelError(string.Empty, err.Description);
                }
                return Page();
            }
        }
    }
}
```

The page model class will validate tokens that are received through the HTML form and received through the URL, which will allow users to click the links in the emails they receive.

The final step is to add buttons that will allow the user's email address and phone numbers to be changed. For email, make the changes shown in Listing 17-29 to the _EditUserEmail partial view.

Listing 17-29. Confirming Email Changes in the _EditUserEmail.cshtml File in the Pages/Store Folder

```
@model AppUser
@inject UserManager<AppUser> UserManager

@if (UserManager.SupportsUserEmail) {
    <tr>
        <td>Email</td>
        <td>
            @if (await UserManager.FindByIdAsync(Model.Id) == null) {
                <input class="w-00" asp-for="EmailAddress" />
            } else {
                @Model.EmailAddress
                <a asp-page="EmailPhoneChange" asp-route-id="@Model.Id"
                    asp-route-datatype="email"
                    class="btn btn-sm btn-secondary align-top">Change</a>
            }
        </td>
    </tr>
    <tr>
        <td>Normalized Email</td>
        <td>
            @(Model.NormalizedEmailAddress?? "(Not Set)")
            <input type="hidden" asp-for="NormalizedEmailAddress" />
            <input type="hidden" asp-for="EmailAddressConfirmed" />
        </td>
    </tr>
}
```

For phone numbers, make the changes shown in Listing 17-30 to the _EditUserPhone partial view.

Listing 17-30. Confirming Phone Changes in the _EditUserPhone.cshtml File in the Pages/Store Folder

```
@model AppUser
@inject UserManager<AppUser> UserManager

@if (UserManager.SupportsUserPhoneNumber) {
    <tr>
        <td>Phone</td>
        <td>
            @if (await UserManager.FindByIdAsync(Model.Id) == null) {
                <input class="w-00" asp-for="PhoneNumber" />
            } else {
                @Model.PhoneNumber
                <a asp-page="EmailPhoneChange" asp-route-id="@Model.Id"
                    asp-route-datatype="phone"
                    class="btn btn-sm btn-secondary align-top">Change</a>
```

```
        }
        <input type="hidden" asp-for="PhoneNumberConfirmed" />
    </td>
</tr>
}
```

Restart ASP.NET Core, and request `http://localhost:5000/users`. Click the Edit button for the Alice user and click the Change button to edit the email address. If you look at the output produced by ASP.NET Core, you will see a simulated email message like this:

```
--- Email Starts ---
To: alice@example.com
Subject: Confirm Email
Please click the link to confirm your email address:
http://localhost:5000/validate/1/email/alicesmith@example.com:CAD4E404EED9129055BF41D4
--- Email Ends ---
```

You will see the same confirmation code as shown earlier because the security stamp is set to a fixed value when the user store is seeded. Subsequent changes will produce different codes because the stamp will change randomly. You can navigate to the URL shown in the email or enter the validation code directly (the code follows the : character in the path and is `CAD4E404EED9129055BF41D4` in this example). Once the change has been confirmed, the updated email address is displayed, as shown in Figure 17-7.

Figure 17-7. *Changing an email address*

Click the Change button next to the user's phone number, enter a new number and click the Change button. A simulated SMS message will be displayed in the console output, like this:

```
--- SMS Starts ---
To: 123-4567
Your confirmation token is B1278F
--- SMS Ends ---
```

Copy the code displayed in your message—which will be different from the one shown earlier—into the text field and click the Confirm button. The confirmation token will be validated, and the modified user data will be displayed, as shown in Figure 17-8.

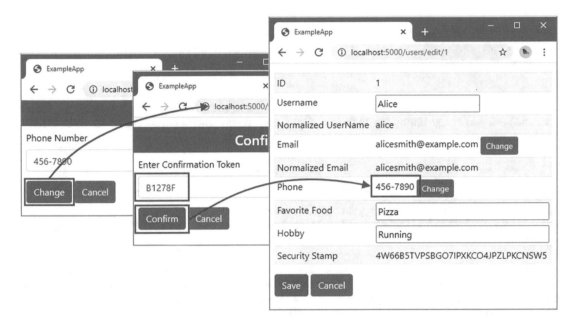

Figure 17-8. *Changing a phone number*

The validation features still applied to the data but not until after a confirmation token has been validated. You can see this by attempting to make a change to an email address outside of the example.com domain, which is the restriction imposed by the custom validator defined in Chapter 16. When you enter the confirmation code (or navigate to the URL given in the email), you will see a validation error, as shown in Figure 17-9, and the email address will not be updated.

Figure 17-9. *A validation error when changing an email address*

You will also receive a validation error if you enter a different token from the one specified in the message, change the URL to specify a different email address, or alter the user object so that it contains a different security stamp. All of these actions will cause the verification process to fail because the token received from the user won't match the one generated by the application during the validation process.

Summary

In this chapter, I extended the user store to support roles and claims and set up the confirmation process for email addresses and phone numbers. In the next chapter, I extend the user store to support passwords so that users can sign into the application.

CHAPTER 18

■ ■ ■

Signing In with Identity

In this chapter, I extend the user store to support passwords and create the services that support user sign-ins. I explain how passwords are stored, how they are validated, and how the entire process can be customized. Table 18-1 puts the features described in this chapter in context.

Table 18-1. *Putting Signing In in Context*

Question	Answer
What is it?	Signing in is the process by which the user identifies themselves to the application. Passwords are the conventional means with which users sign in and that prove their identity because they are the only person who knows the password.
Why is it useful?	Signing in generates a token, usually a cookie, that is included in subsequent requests so that the user can interact with the application without needing to provide further proof of their identity.
How is it used?	The user store is extended to store passwords, and a service is defined that hashes passwords so they can be stored securely. As part of the sign-in process, the data in the user store is transformed into a series of claims that are provided to ASP.NET Core through a `ClaimsPrincipal` object.
Are there any pitfalls or limitations?	Users tend to pick poor passwords and will subvert onerous password policies. Applications that manage sensitive data or operations should combine passwords with additional forms of identification, as described in Chapters 20 and 21.
Are there any alternatives?	Identity can be configured to support external authentication where responsibility for identifying users is delegated to a third party. See Chapters 22 and 23.

Table 18-2 summarizes the chapter.

© Adam Freeman 2021
A. Freeman, *Pro ASP.NET Core Identity*, https://doi.org/10.1007/978-1-4842-6858-2_18

Table 18-2. *Chapter Summary*

Problem	Solution	Listing
Provide ASP.NET Core with the data in the user store when a user signs in	Create an implementation of the `IUserClaims PrincipalFactory<T>` interface.	2
Sign users into an application	Use the `SignInManager<T>` class.	3–4, 10, 11
Stwore passwords in the user store	Implement the `IUserPasswordStore<T>` interface.	5, 7–9
Change or recovery passwords	Use the methods provided by the `UserManager<T>` class.	12–19,23–25
Restrict the passwords that a user can choose	Create an implementation of the `IPasswordValidator<T>` interface.	20–22

Preparing for This Chapter

This chapter uses the `ExampleApp` project from Chapter 17. No changes are required to prepare for this chapter. Open a new command prompt, navigate to the `ExampleApp` folder, and run the command shown in Listing 18-1 to start ASP.NET Core.

■ **Tip** You can download the example project for this chapter—and for all the other chapters in this book—from `https://github.com/Apress/pro-asp.net-core-identity`. See Chapter 1 for how to get help if you have problems running the examples.

Listing 18-1. Running the Example Application

```
dotnet run
```

Open a new browser window and request `http://localhost:5000/users`. You will be presented with the user data shown in Figure 18-1. The data is stored only in memory, and changes will be lost when ASP. NET Core is stopped.

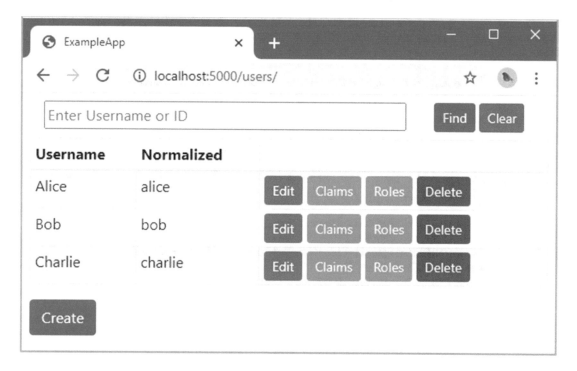

Figure 18-1. *Running the example application*

Signing Users In

The user store has taken shape, along with the tools that use it through the UserManager<T> class. In this section, I am going to demonstrate how Identity is used to sign users into the application and, once signed in, how requests are authenticated.

Creating the Claims Principal Factory

The AppUser user class is currently unrelated to the ClaimsPrincipal objects that represented users in earlier chapters. To bridge between these two ways of representing users, Identity uses the IUserClaimsPrincipal Factory<T> interface, where T is the user class, which defines the single method described in Table 18-3.

Table 18-3. *The IUserClaimsPrincipalFactory<T> Method*

Name	Description
CreateAsync(user)	This method creates a ClaimsPrincipal object that represents the specified user.

The flexibility that is available in the implementation of the user store is possible because of this interface, which connects the bespoke user class and its many features with the classes that ASP.NET Core uses for signing in, authentication, and authorization. Identity includes a default implementation of this interface, which creates a ClaimsPrincipal object using the UserManager<T> methods.

To create an implementation of the IUserClaimsPrincipalFactory<T> interface that is tailored to the AppUser class, add a class file named AppUserClaimsPrincipalFactory.cs to the ExampleApp/Identity folder and use it to define the class shown in Listing 18-2.

Listing 18-2. The Contents of the AppUserClaimsPrincipalFactory.cs File in the Identity Folder

```
using Microsoft.AspNetCore.Identity;
using System.Security.Claims;
using System.Threading.Tasks;

namespace ExampleApp.Identity {
    public class AppUserClaimsPrincipalFactory :
        IUserClaimsPrincipalFactory<AppUser> {

        public Task<ClaimsPrincipal> CreateAsync(AppUser user) {
            ClaimsIdentity identity
                = new ClaimsIdentity(IdentityConstants.ApplicationScheme);
            identity.AddClaims(new [] {
                new Claim(ClaimTypes.NameIdentifier, user.Id),
                new Claim(ClaimTypes.Name, user.UserName),
                new Claim(ClaimTypes.Email, user.EmailAddress)
            });
            if (!string.IsNullOrEmpty(user.Hobby)) {
                identity.AddClaim(new Claim("Hobby", user.Hobby));
            }
            if (!string.IsNullOrEmpty(user.FavoriteFood)) {
                identity.AddClaim(new Claim("FavoriteFood", user.FavoriteFood));
            }
            if (user.Claims != null) {
                identity.AddClaims(user.Claims);
            }
            return Task.FromResult(new ClaimsPrincipal(identity));
        }
    }
}
```

The class creates a ClaimsIdentity object that is populated with claims from the AppUser Id, UserName, EmailAddress, Hobby, and FavoriteFood properties, as well as any additional Claim objects that have been stored for the user.

■ **Tip** Notice that I have used the IdentityConstants.ApplicationScheme value when creating the ClaimsIdentity object in Listing 18-2. This scheme name indicates that a user has been authenticated by Identity and is expected by some Identity features. I describe additional IdentityConstants values in later chapters.

GETTING USER OBJECTS FROM CLAIMSPRINCIPAL OBJECTS

The `UserManager<T>` class defines the `GetUserAsync` method, which accepts a `ClaimsPrincipal` object and returns the associated user object. It does this by using the value of the `NameIdentifier` claim as the argument to the `FindByIdAsync` method, querying the user store. The method returns `null` if the `ClaimsPrincipal` object doesn't have a `NameIdentifier` claim or if the user store doesn't contain a user object for the claim value.

Signing Users In

Identity provides the `SignInManager<T>` class to handle signing users into an application. Table 18-4 describes the basic methods provided by the `SignInManager<T>` class that are used to sign users in and out. I describe further methods as I explain more advanced features.

Table 18-4. *The Basic SignInManager<T> Methods*

Name	Description
`SignInAsync(user, persistent)`	This method signs the specified user into the application. The persistent argument specifies whether the authentication cookie will persist after the browser has closed.
`SignInWithClaimsAsync(user, persistent, claims)`	This method signs the user into the application and adds the specified claims to the principal identity.
`SignOutAsync()`	This method signs out the user.

In Listing 18-3, I have updated the page model for the SignIn Razor Page to use the `UserManager<T>` and `SignInManager<T>` classes.

Listing 18-3. Using Identity in the SignIn.cshtml.cs File in the Pages Folder

```
using Microsoft.AspNetCore.Authentication;
using Microsoft.AspNetCore.Http;
using Microsoft.AspNetCore.Mvc;
using Microsoft.AspNetCore.Mvc.RazorPages;
using Microsoft.AspNetCore.Mvc.Rendering;
using System.Security.Claims;
using System.Threading.Tasks;
using Microsoft.AspNetCore.Identity;
using System.Linq;
using ExampleApp.Identity;

namespace ExampleApp.Pages {
    public class SignInModel : PageModel {

        public SignInModel(UserManager<AppUser> userManager,
                SignInManager<AppUser> signInManager) {
```

```
            UserManager = userManager;
            SignInManager = signInManager;
        }

        public UserManager<AppUser> UserManager { get; set; }
        public SignInManager<AppUser> SignInManager { get; set; }

        public SelectList Users => new SelectList(
            UserManager.Users.OrderBy(u => u.EmailAddress),
                "EmailAddress", "EmailAddress");

        public string Username { get; set; }

        public int? Code { get; set; }

        public void OnGet(int? code) {
            Code = code;
            Username = User.Identity.Name ?? "(No Signed In User)";
        }

        public async Task<ActionResult> OnPost(string username,
                [FromQuery]string returnUrl) {
            //Claim claim = new Claim(ClaimTypes.Name, username);
            //ClaimsIdentity ident = new ClaimsIdentity("simpleform");
            //ident.AddClaim(claim);
            //await HttpContext.SignInAsync(new ClaimsPrincipal(ident));
            AppUser user = await UserManager.FindByEmailAsync(username);
            await SignInManager.SignInAsync(user, false);
            return Redirect(returnUrl ?? "/signin");
        }
    }
}
```

Identity is designed to integrate easily into ASP.NET Core. I have added a constructor to receive UserManager<T> and SignInManager<T> objects through dependency injection. This allows me to present a list of users, which I have listed using their email address, just to demonstrate that the data is coming from the store. Once a user has been selected, I get an AppUser object through the UserManager<T>. FindByEmailAsync method and sign that user into the application using the SignInManager<T>. SignInAsync method.

Configuring the Application

The final step is to register the claims principal factory class so that it will be used by Identity and set up the SignInManager<T> service, as shown in Listing 18-4.

Listing 18-4. Configuring the Application in the Startup.cs File in the ExampleApp Folder

```
using Microsoft.AspNetCore.Builder;
using Microsoft.AspNetCore.Hosting;
using Microsoft.AspNetCore.Http;
using Microsoft.Extensions.DependencyInjection;
```

```
using ExampleApp.Custom;
using Microsoft.AspNetCore.Authentication.Cookies;
using Microsoft.AspNetCore.Authorization;
using Microsoft.AspNetCore.Identity;
using ExampleApp.Identity;
using ExampleApp.Identity.Store;
using ExampleApp.Services;

namespace ExampleApp {
    public class Startup {

        public void ConfigureServices(IServiceCollection services) {
            services.AddSingleton<ILookupNormalizer, Normalizer>();
            services.AddSingleton<IUserStore<AppUser>, UserStore>();
            services.AddSingleton<IEmailSender, ConsoleEmailSender>();
            services.AddSingleton<ISMSSender, ConsoleSMSSender>();
            services.AddSingleton<IUserClaimsPrincipalFactory<AppUser>,
                AppUserClaimsPrincipalFactory>();

            services.AddIdentityCore<AppUser>(opts => {
                opts.Tokens.EmailConfirmationTokenProvider = "SimpleEmail";
                opts.Tokens.ChangeEmailTokenProvider = "SimpleEmail";
            })
            .AddTokenProvider<EmailConfirmationTokenGenerator>("SimpleEmail")
            .AddTokenProvider<PhoneConfirmationTokenGenerator>
                (TokenOptions.DefaultPhoneProvider)
            .AddSignInManager();

            services.AddSingleton<IUserValidator<AppUser>, EmailValidator>();

            services.AddAuthentication(opts => {
                opts.DefaultScheme = IdentityConstants.ApplicationScheme;
            }).AddCookie(IdentityConstants.ApplicationScheme, opts => {
                opts.LoginPath = "/signin";
                opts.AccessDeniedPath = "/signin/403";
            });
            services.AddAuthorization(opts => {
                AuthorizationPolicies.AddPolicies(opts);
            });
            services.AddRazorPages();
            services.AddControllersWithViews();
        }

        public void Configure(IApplicationBuilder app, IWebHostEnvironment env) {

            app.UseStaticFiles();
            app.UseAuthentication();
            app.UseRouting();
            //app.UseMiddleware<RoleMemberships>();
            app.UseAuthorization();
```

```
app.UseEndpoints(endpoints => {
    endpoints.MapRazorPages();
    endpoints.MapDefaultControllerRoute();
    endpoints.MapFallbackToPage("/Secret");
});
        }
    }
}
```

I used the AddSingleton method to register the AppUserClaimsPrincipalFactory class as the implementation to be used for the IUserClaimsPrincipalFactory<AppUser> interface.

The AddSignInManager method is added to the chain of methods used to set up Identity and sets up the SignInManager<T> service. The other changes alter the name of the authentication scheme, reflecting the use of Identity to sign users into the application and authenticate requests.

I have also commented out the statement that applies the custom role middleware so that the only source of claims and roles is the user store.

Restart ASP.NET Core and request http://localhost:5000/signin. Choose alice@example. com from the drop-down list and click the Sign In button to sign into the application. Request http://localhost:5000/secret, and the authorization policy applied to the Secret Razor Page will be evaluated using the claims generated from the AppUser object by the factory class. Alice's claims meet the policy and access is granted, as shown in Figure 18-2.

■ **Tip** If signing in has no effect, you may find that you are already authenticated using a cookie from a previous chapter. If that's the case, request http://localhost:5000/signout and click the Sign Out button. This will clear the existing cookie and allow you to sign in again using Identity. If that doesn't work, clear your browser history and try again.

Figure 18-2. *Using Identity to sign in to the application*

Repeat the process and select bob@example.com to sign in as Bob. Request http://localhost:5000/ secret; access will be denied because Bob's claims do not meet the policy requirements, as shown in Figure 18-3.

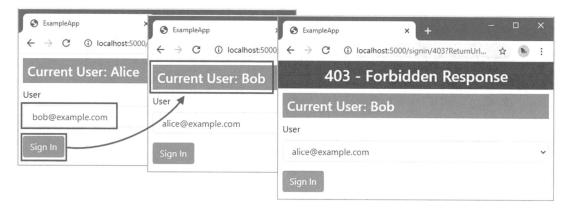

Figure 18-3. *Enforcing authorization policies in the example application*

Signing In Users with Passwords

Trusting users to pick their account from a drop-down list has been useful, but it is time to introduce passwords. In the sections that follow, I explain how Identity stores and uses passwords and how they are used in the sign-in process.

Updating the User Class

Passwords are not stored directly. Instead, a hash code is created from a user's password and stored as a proxy for the password itself. When the user presents a password during sign-in, a hash code is created from the candidate password and compared to the hash code in the user store. If the user has supplied the right password, the two hash codes will be the same. In Listing 18-5, I have added a property to the AppUser class for a user's password.

Listing 18-5. Adding a Property in the AppUser.cs File in the Identity Folder

```
using System;
using System.Collections.Generic;
using System.Security.Claims;

namespace ExampleApp.Identity {
    public class AppUser {

        public string Id { get; set; } = Guid.NewGuid().ToString();

        public string UserName { get; set; }

        public string NormalizedUserName { get; set; }

        public string EmailAddress { get; set; }
        public string NormalizedEmailAddress { get; set; }
        public bool EmailAddressConfirmed { get; set; }
```

```
        public string PhoneNumber { get; set; }
        public bool PhoneNumberConfirmed { get; set; }

        public string FavoriteFood { get; set; }
        public string Hobby { get; set; }

        public IList<Claim> Claims { get; set; }

        public string SecurityStamp { get; set; }
        public string PasswordHash { get; set; }
    }
}
```

There are more complex options for signing in, which I describe in later examples, but for now, a simple string password is a good place to start.

Creating the Password Hasher

Identity relies on implementations of the IPasswordHasher<T> interface to generate hash codes from passwords, where <T> is the user class. The interface defines the methods shown in Table 18-5.

Table 18-5. *The IPasswordHasher<T> Methods*

Name	Description
HashPassword(user, password)	This method returns a hashed representation of a password for the specified user.
VerifyHashedPassword(user, storedHash, password)	This method verifies that a password provided by the specified user matches the supplied hashed representation. The result is expressed using a value from the PasswordVerificationResult enum: Failed, Success, or SuccessRehashNeeded. (This last value is used to indicate that the algorithm used by the application has changed and the password hash code should be updated.)

To create a custom implementation of the interface, add a class file named SimplePasswordHasher.cs to the ExampleApp/Identity folder and use it to define the class shown in Listing 18-6.

Listing 18-6. The Contents of the SimplePasswordHasher.cs File in the Identity Folder

```
using Microsoft.AspNetCore.Identity;
using System;
using System.Security.Cryptography;
using System.Text;

namespace ExampleApp.Identity {
    public class SimplePasswordHasher : IPasswordHasher<AppUser> {

        public SimplePasswordHasher(ILookupNormalizer normalizer)
            => Normalizer = normalizer;

        private ILookupNormalizer Normalizer { get; set; }
```

```
        public string HashPassword(AppUser user, string password) {
            HMACSHA256 hashAlgorithm =
                new HMACSHA256(Encoding.UTF8.GetBytes(user.Id));
            return BitConverter.ToString(hashAlgorithm.ComputeHash(
                    Encoding.UTF8.GetBytes(password)));
        }

        public PasswordVerificationResult VerifyHashedPassword(AppUser user,
            string storedHash, string password)
                => HashPassword(user, password).Equals(storedHash)
                    ? PasswordVerificationResult.Success
                    : PasswordVerificationResult.Failed;
    }
}
```

The built-in password hasher that Identity provides generates robust hashes from passwords, using a good cryptographic algorithm that is applied carefully and thoroughly. To demonstrate, I have adopted an approach that is simpler and should not be used in real projects. The SimplePasswordHasher class represents passwords by simply combining using the HMACSHA256 hashing algorithm with the user's ID as the key. Listing 18-7 registers the SimplePasswordHasher class, so it will be used to resolve dependencies on the IPasswordHasher<AppUser> interface.

Listing 18-7. Registering a Service in the Startup.cs File in the ExampleApp Folder

```
...
public void ConfigureServices(IServiceCollection services) {
    services.AddSingleton<ILookupNormalizer, Normalizer>();
    services.AddSingleton<IUserStore<AppUser>, UserStore>();
    services.AddSingleton<IEmailSender, ConsoleEmailSender>();
    services.AddSingleton<ISMSSender, ConsoleSMSSender>();
    services.AddSingleton<IUserClaimsPrincipalFactory<AppUser>,
        AppUserClaimsPrincipalFactory>();
    services.AddSingleton<IPasswordHasher<AppUser>, SimplePasswordHasher>();

    services.AddIdentityCore<AppUser>(opts => {
        opts.Tokens.EmailConfirmationTokenProvider = "SimpleEmail";
        opts.Tokens.ChangeEmailTokenProvider = "SimpleEmail";
    })
    .AddTokenProvider<EmailConfirmationTokenGenerator>("SimpleEmail")
    .AddTokenProvider<PhoneConfirmationTokenGenerator>
        (TokenOptions.DefaultPhoneProvider)
    .AddSignInManager();

    services.AddSingleton<IUserValidator<AppUser>, EmailValidator>();

    services.AddAuthentication(opts => {
        opts.DefaultScheme = IdentityConstants.ApplicationScheme;
    }).AddCookie(IdentityConstants.ApplicationScheme, opts => {
        opts.LoginPath = "/signin";
        opts.AccessDeniedPath = "/signin/403";
    });
```

```
    services.AddAuthorization(opts => {
        AuthorizationPolicies.AddPolicies(opts);
    });
    services.AddRazorPages();
    services.AddControllersWithViews();
}
...
```

Storing Password Hashes in the User Store

When an application manages its own passwords, it needs a user store that implements the
IUserPasswordStore<T> interface, where T is the user class. This interface defines the methods described in
Table 18-6. All these methods define the token parameter that receives a CancellationToken object used to
receive notifications when asynchronous operations are canceled.

Table 18-6. *The IUserPasswordStore<T> Methods*

Name	Description
HasPasswordAsync(user, token)	This method returns true if the specified user has a password.
GetPasswordHashAsync(user, token)	This method returns the stored password data for the specified user.
SetPasswordHashAsync(user, passwordHash, token)	This method stores a new password hash for the specified user.

To add support for storing passwords, add a class file named UserStorePasswords.cs to the Identity/
Store folder and use it to define the partial class shown in Listing 18-8.

Listing 18-8. The Contents of the UserStorePasswords.cs File in the Identity/Store Folder

```
using Microsoft.AspNetCore.Identity;
using System.Threading;
using System.Threading.Tasks;

namespace ExampleApp.Identity.Store {

    public partial class UserStore : IUserPasswordStore<AppUser> {

        public Task<string> GetPasswordHashAsync(AppUser user,
            CancellationToken token) => Task.FromResult(user.PasswordHash);

        public Task<bool> HasPasswordAsync(AppUser user, CancellationToken token)
            => Task.FromResult(!string.IsNullOrEmpty(user.PasswordHash));

        public Task SetPasswordHashAsync(AppUser user, string passwordHash,
                CancellationToken token) {
            user.PasswordHash = passwordHash;
            return Task.CompletedTask;
        }
    }
}
```

The new statements shown in Listing 18-9 add passwords to the seed data in the user store. Since passwords are stored as hashes, I declared a dependency on the password hasher, which I use to generate the stored values.

Listing 18-9. Adding Passwords in the UserStore.cs File in the Identity/Store Folder

```
using Microsoft.AspNetCore.Identity;
using System.Collections.Generic;
using System.Linq;
using System.Security.Claims;

namespace ExampleApp.Identity.Store {

    public partial class UserStore {

        public ILookupNormalizer Normalizer { get; set; }

        public IPasswordHasher<AppUser> PasswordHasher { get; set; }

        public UserStore(ILookupNormalizer normalizer,
                IPasswordHasher<AppUser> passwordHasher) {
            Normalizer = normalizer;
            PasswordHasher = passwordHasher;
            SeedStore();
        }

        private void SeedStore() {

            var customData = new Dictionary<string, (string food, string hobby)> {
                { "Alice", ("Pizza", "Running") },
                { "Bob", ("Ice Cream", "Cinema") },
                { "Charlie", ("Burgers", "Cooking") }
            };

            int idCounter = 0;

            string EmailFromName(string name) => $"{name.ToLower()}@example.com";

            foreach (string name in UsersAndClaims.Users) {
                AppUser user = new AppUser {
                    Id = (++idCounter).ToString(),
                    UserName = name,
                    NormalizedUserName = Normalizer.NormalizeName(name),
                    EmailAddress = EmailFromName(name),
                    NormalizedEmailAddress =
                        Normalizer.NormalizeEmail(EmailFromName(name)),
                    EmailAddressConfirmed = true,
                    PhoneNumber = "123-4567",
                    PhoneNumberConfirmed = true,
                    FavoriteFood = customData[name].food,
                    Hobby = customData[name].hobby,
                    SecurityStamp = "InitialStamp"
                };
```

```
        user.Claims = UsersAndClaims.UserData[user.UserName]
            .Select(role => new Claim(ClaimTypes.Role, role)).ToList();
        user.PasswordHash = PasswordHasher.HashPassword(user, "MySecret1$");
        users.TryAdd(user.Id, user);
        }
    }
  }
}
```

For simplicity, I have set all the users' passwords to the same value: MySecret1$. I show you how to create a password change workflow in the "Changing and Recovering Passwords" section.

Signing In to the Application with Passwords

The SignInManager<T> class defines methods that accept a password when signing a user in, as described in Table 18-7.

Table 18-7. *The SignInManager<T> Methods for Signing In with Passwords*

Name	Description
PasswordSignInAsync(user, password, persistent, lockout)	This method signs in the user with the specified password. The persistent argument specifies whether the cookie remains valid when the browser is restarted, and the lockout argument specifies whether failed logins lock out the user, as explained in Chapter 20.
PasswordSignInAsync(username, password, persistent, lockout)	This is a convenience method that retrieves the user objects from the store using the specified username and attempts to sign in with a password.

The result produced by the methods in Table 18-7 is an instance of the SignInResult class, which defines the properties described in Table 18-8.

Table 18-8. *SignInResult Properties*

Name	Description
Succeeded	This property returns true if the user was successfully signed into the application and false otherwise.
IsLockedOut	This property returns true if the sign in attempt was unsuccessful because the user is locked out. I explain lockouts in Chapter 20.
IsNotAllowed	This property returns true if the user is not allowed to sign into the application, which I explain in Chapter 20.
RequiresTwoFactor	This property returns true if the user is required to provide additional credentials, which I explain in Chapter 20.

The most important SignInResult property is Suceeded, which returns true or false to indicate the outcome of the sign-in attempt. The other properties are used to provide additional detail about why an attempt was refused, all of which rely on features that are described in other chapters.

In Listing 18-10, I have updated the SignIn Razor Page to prompt for a password that is used to sign the user into the application.

Listing 18-10. Using a Password in the SignIn.cshtml File in the Pages Folder

```
@page "{code:int?}"
@model ExampleApp.Pages.SignInModel
@using Microsoft.AspNetCore.Http

@if (Model.Code == StatusCodes.Status401Unauthorized) {
    <h3 class="bg-warning text-white text-center p-2">
        401 - Challenge Response
    </h3>
} else if (Model.Code == StatusCodes.Status403Forbidden) {
    <h3 class="bg-danger text-white text-center p-2">
        403 - Forbidden Response
    </h3>
}
<h4 class="bg-info text-white m-2 p-2">
    Current User: @Model.Username
</h4>

<div class="m-2">
    <form method="post">
        <div class="form-group">
            <label>User</label>
            <select class="form-control"
                    asp-for="Username" asp-items="@Model.Users">
            </select>
        </div>
        <div class="form-group">
            <label>Password</label>
            <input class="form-control" type="password" name="password" />
        </div>
        <button class="btn btn-info" type="submit">Sign In</button>
    </form>
</div>
```

The user is presented with an input element into which a password is entered. To process the password, I made the changes shown in Listing 18-11 to the page model class.

Listing 18-11. Using Passwords in the SignIn.cshtml.cs File in the Pages Folder

```
using Microsoft.AspNetCore.Authentication;
using Microsoft.AspNetCore.Http;
using Microsoft.AspNetCore.Mvc;
using Microsoft.AspNetCore.Mvc.RazorPages;
using Microsoft.AspNetCore.Mvc.Rendering;
using System.Security.Claims;
using System.Threading.Tasks;
using Microsoft.AspNetCore.Identity;
using System.Linq;
```

```
using ExampleApp.Identity;
using SignInResult = Microsoft.AspNetCore.Identity.SignInResult;

namespace ExampleApp.Pages {
    public class SignInModel : PageModel {

        public SignInModel(UserManager<AppUser> userManager,
        SignInManager<AppUser> signInManager) {
            UserManager = userManager;
            SignInManager = signInManager;
        }

        public UserManager<AppUser> UserManager { get; set; }
        public SignInManager<AppUser> SignInManager { get; set; }

        public SelectList Users => new SelectList(
            UserManager.Users.OrderBy(u => u.EmailAddress),
                "EmailAddress", "NormalizedEmailAddress");

        public string Username { get; set; }

        public int? Code { get; set; }

        public void OnGet(int? code) {
            Code = code;
            Username = User.Identity.Name ?? "(No Signed In User)";
        }

        public async Task<ActionResult> OnPost(string username,
                string password, [FromQuery]string returnUrl) {
            SignInResult result = SignInResult.Failed;
            AppUser user = await UserManager.FindByEmailAsync(username);
            if (user != null && !string.IsNullOrEmpty(password)) {
                result = await SignInManager.PasswordSignInAsync(user, password,
                    false, true);
            }
            if (!result.Succeeded) {
                Code = StatusCodes.Status401Unauthorized;
                return Page();
            }
            return Redirect(returnUrl ?? "/signin");
        }
    }
}
```

This value is used as an argument to the PasswordSignInAsync method to sign the user into the application:

```
...
result = await SignInManager.PasswordSignInAsync(user, password, false, true);
...
```

In addition to the user and password, the arguments passed to the `PasswordSignInAsync` method tell Identity that the cookie used to authenticate requests should not persist when the browser is closed and that repeated failed attempts should result in an account lockout, which I implement in Chapter 20.

I use the existing features of the Razor Page to display an error message when the user doesn't supply a password or when the password doesn't match the one in the user store.

There are two classes named `SignInResult` in the packages used in ASP.NET Core, and the C# compiler cannot tell which one is required, which is why I have used this `using` statement:

```
...
using SignInResult = Microsoft.AspNetCore.Identity.SignInResult;
...
```

This tells the compiler that the Identity class named `SignInResult` should be used, resolving the ambiguity so I can use the `SignInResult` type in the code without qualifying It with a namespace.

Restart ASP.NET Core and request `http://localhost:5000/signin`. Select `alice@example.com` from the list and enter MySecret1$ into the password field. Click Sign In; the password will be validated, and Alice will be signed into the application, as shown in Figure 18-4. You will see the 401 – Challenge response if you omit the password or enter a different password, which is also shown in Figure 18-4.

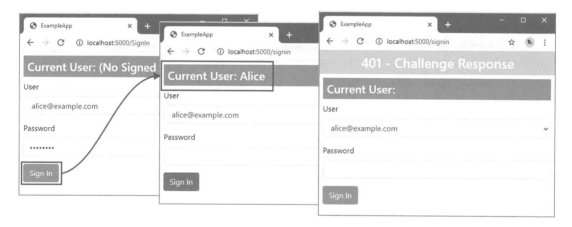

Figure 18-4. *Signing into the application with a password*

Managing Passwords

Passwords require several management workflows. The `UserManager<T>` class defines members that support the management of passwords, which I introduce in the sections that follow.

Changing and Recovering Passwords

The fundamental task for passwords is to allow a new one to be selected. This can be an intended change, where the existing password is known but a new one is required, or unintended, where the existing password has been forgotten and a new one must be defined so the user can sign in to the application. The `UserManager<T>` class defines the methods shown in Table 18-9 for changing passwords.

Table 18-9. *The UserManager<T> Methods for Changing Passwords*

Name	Description
HasPasswordAsync(user)	This method returns true if the user has a password, using the user store's HasPasswordAsync method.
AddPasswordAsync(user, password)	This method adds a password to the store for the specified user. The password is validated (described following the table) and hashed before it is passed to the user store's SetPasswordHashAsync method, a new security stamp is generated, and the user manager's update sequence is performed. An exception will be thrown if the user store's GetPasswordHashAsync method returns anything other than null.
RemovePasswordAsync(user)	This method sets the password for the specified user to null in the user store, generates a new security stamp, and performs the user manager's update sequence.
ChangePasswordAsync(user, oldPassword, newPassword)	This method performs a password change for the specified user. The old password is checked, and the new password is validated (described after the table) and hashed before being passed to the user store's SetPasswordHashAsync method. A new security stamp is generated, and the user manager's update sequence is performed.
GeneratePasswordResetToken Async(user)	This method generates a token that can be used to confirm a password reset.
ResetPasswordAsync(user, token, newPassword)	This method checks a password reset token and, if it is valid, stores the specified password for the user. The password hashed and passed to the user store's SetPasswordHashAsync method, a new security stamp is generated, and the user manager's update sequence is performed.

To allow a password to be changed, add a Razor Page named PasswordChange.cshtml to the Pages/Store folder with the content shown in Listing 18-12.

Listing 18-12. The Contents of the PasswordChange.cshtml File in the Pages/Store Folder

```
@page "/password/change/{success:bool?}"
@model ExampleApp.Pages.Store.PasswordChangeModel

<h4 class="bg-primary text-white text-center p-2">Change Password</h4>

<div asp-validation-summary="All" class="text-danger m-2"></div>

@if (Model.Success) {
    <h5 class="bg-success text-white text-center p-2">Password Changed</h5>
}

<div class="m-2">
    <form method="post">
        <table class="table table-sm table-striped">
            <tbody>
                <tr><th>Your Username</th>
                    <td>@HttpContext.User.Identity.Name</td></tr>
```

```
                <tr>
                    <th>Existing Password</th>
                    <td><input class="w-100" type="password" name="oldPassword" />
                    </td>
                </tr>
                <tr>
                    <th>New Password</th>
                    <td><input class="w-100" type="password" name="newPassword" />
                    </td>
                </tr>
            </tbody>
        </table>
        <div class="text-center">
            <button class="btn btn-primary">Change</button>
            <a class="btn btn-secondary" asp-page="/SignIn">Back</a>
        </div>
    </form>
</div>
```

The Razor Page presents the user with input elements for the existing and new passwords. Use the
PasswordChange.cshtml.cs file to define the page model class shown in Listing 18-13. (You will need to
create this file if you are using Visual Studio Code.)

Listing 18-13. The Contents of the PasswordChange.cshtml.cs File in the Pages/Store Folder

```
using System.Threading.Tasks;
using ExampleApp.Identity;
using Microsoft.AspNetCore.Identity;
using Microsoft.AspNetCore.Mvc;
using Microsoft.AspNetCore.Mvc.RazorPages;

namespace ExampleApp.Pages.Store {
    public class PasswordChangeModel : PageModel {

        public PasswordChangeModel(UserManager<AppUser> manager) =>
            UserManager = manager;

        public UserManager<AppUser> UserManager { get; set; }

        [BindProperty(SupportsGet = true)]
        public bool Success { get; set; } = false;

        public async Task<IActionResult> OnPost(string oldPassword,
                string newPassword) {
            string username = HttpContext.User.Identity.Name;
            if (username != null) {
                AppUser user = await UserManager.FindByNameAsync(username);
                if (user != null && !string.IsNullOrEmpty(oldPassword)
                        && !string.IsNullOrEmpty(newPassword)) {
                    IdentityResult result = await UserManager.ChangePasswordAsync(
                        user, oldPassword, newPassword);
```

```
                if (result.Succeeded) {
                    Success = true;
                } else {
                    foreach (IdentityError err in result.Errors) {
                        ModelState.AddModelError("", err.Description);
                    }
                }
            }
        }
        return Page();
    }
  }
}
```

In this example, I rely on the ASP.NET Core `HttpContext.User` property to provide me with details of the signed-in user, which I can then use to get the `AppUser` object that represents the user from the store. I call the `ChangePasswordAsync` method to change the password using the values provided by the user. The result of the `ChangePasswordAsync` method is an `IdentityResult` object that indicates whether the operation was successful and provides error details if it was not. If there are errors, I add them to the ASP. NET Core model state so they can be displayed to the user.

Resetting Passwords

The process for changing a password is simple because we can be confident that only the user knows their existing password, which is the same standard of security the application requires for signing in.

Performing a password reset is more complex because the user has forgotten or lost the password. Instead, a confirmation step is required, which generates a token and is sent to the user outside of the application, most often as a link sent by email or a code sent by SMS. The user clicks the link or enters the code into an HTML form and selects a new password.

I do not cover the selection and configuration of email and SMS services in this book, so I will simulate sending the confirmation token by writing messages to the console.

I can use the token generator used earlier to confirm phone number address changes. Listing 18-14 registers the token generator so it will be used for password resets.

Listing 18-14. Registering a Token Generator in the Startup.cs File in the ExampleApp Folder

```
...
services.AddIdentityCore<AppUser>(opts => {
    opts.Tokens.EmailConfirmationTokenProvider = "SimpleEmail";
    opts.Tokens.ChangeEmailTokenProvider = "SimpleEmail";
    opts.Tokens.PasswordResetTokenProvider = TokenOptions.DefaultPhoneProvider;
})
.AddTokenProvider<EmailConfirmationTokenGenerator>("SimpleEmail")
.AddTokenProvider<PhoneConfirmationTokenGenerator>(TokenOptions.DefaultPhoneProvider)
.AddSignInManager();
...
```

The options pattern is used to set the `IdentityOptions.Tokens.PasswordResetTokenProvider` property, whose value specifies the name of the password reset token generator. Next, add a Razor Page named `PasswordReset.cshtml` to the Pages/Store folder with the content shown in Listing 18-15.

Listing 18-15. The Contents of the PasswordReset.cshtml File in the Pages/Store Folder

```
@page "/password/reset"
@model ExampleApp.Pages.Store.PasswordResetModel

<h4 class="bg-primary text-white text-center p-2">Password Reset</h4>

<div class="m-2">
    <form method="post">
        <div class="form-group">
            <label>Email Address</label>
            <input class="form-control" name="email"  />
        </div>
        <button class="btn btn-primary mt-2" type="submit">Reset Password</button>
    </form>
</div>
```

The Razor Page displays a simple form that allows the user to enter their email address. To implement the page model class, add the code shown in Listing 18-16 to the PasswordReset.cshtml.cs file in the Pages/Store folder. (You will have to create this file if you are using Visual Studio Code.)

Listing 18-16. The Contents of the PasswordReset.cshtml.cs File in the Pages/Store Folder

```
using ExampleApp.Identity;
using ExampleApp.Services;
using Microsoft.AspNetCore.Identity;
using Microsoft.AspNetCore.Mvc;
using Microsoft.AspNetCore.Mvc.RazorPages;
using System.Threading.Tasks;

namespace ExampleApp.Pages.Store {

    public class PasswordResetModel : PageModel {

        public PasswordResetModel(UserManager<AppUser> manager,
                ISMSSender sender) {
            UserManager = manager;
            SMSSender = sender;
        }

        public UserManager<AppUser> UserManager { get; set; }
        public ISMSSender SMSSender { get; set; }

        public async Task<IActionResult> OnPost(string email) {
            AppUser user  = await UserManager.FindByEmailAsync(email);
            if (user != null) {
                string token =
                    await UserManager.GeneratePasswordResetTokenAsync(user);
                SMSSender.SendMessage(user, $"Your password reset token is {token}");
            }
```

```
            return RedirectToPage("PasswordResetConfirm", new { email = email });
        }
    }
}
```

The handler method queries the user store for the AppUser object and uses the GeneratePasswordResetTokenAsync method to produce a token, which is sent to the user via (simulated) SMS, after which the client is redirected.

To allow the user to provide a new password and the confirmation token, add a Razor Page named PasswordResetConfirm.cshtml to the Pages/Store folder with the content shown in Listing 18-17.

Listing 18-17. The Contents of the PasswordResetConfirm.cshtml File in the Pages/Store Folder

```
@page "/password/reset/{email}"
@model ExampleApp.Pages.Store.PasswordResetConfirmModel

<h4 class="bg-primary text-white text-center p-2">Password Reset</h4>

<div asp-validation-summary="All" class="text-danger m-2"></div>

@if (Model.Changed) {
    <h5 class="bg-success text-white text-center p-2">Password Changed</h5>
    <div class="text-center">
        <a href="/signin" class="btn btn-primary m-2">OK</a>
    </div>
} else {
    <div class="m-2">
        <form method="post">
            <div class="form-group">
                <label>Email Address</label>
                <input class="form-control" name="email" value="@Model.Email" />
            </div>
            <div class="form-group">
                <label>New Password</label>
                <input class="form-control" name="password" type="password" />
            </div>
            <div class="form-group">
                <label>Confirmation Token</label>
                <input class="form-control" name="token"  />
            </div>
            <button class="btn btn-primary mt-2" type="submit">
                Reset Password
            </button>
        </form>
    </div>
}
```

The view section of the page displays either a form that allows the password and code to be entered or a summary that confirms the password has been changed. To define the page model class, add the code shown in Listing 18-18 to the PasswordResetConfirm.cshtml.cs file in the Pages/Store folder. (You will have to create this file if you are using Visual Studio Code.)

Listing 18-18. The Contents of the PasswordResetConfirm.cshtml.cs File in the Pages/Store Folder

```
using System;
using System.Collections.Generic;
using System.Linq;
using System.Threading.Tasks;
using ExampleApp.Identity;
using Microsoft.AspNetCore.Identity;
using Microsoft.AspNetCore.Mvc;
using Microsoft.AspNetCore.Mvc.RazorPages;

namespace ExampleApp.Pages.Store {

    public class PasswordResetConfirmModel : PageModel {

        public PasswordResetConfirmModel(UserManager<AppUser> manager)
            => UserManager = manager;

        public UserManager<AppUser> UserManager { get; set; }

        [BindProperty(SupportsGet = true)]
        public string Email { get; set; }

        [BindProperty(SupportsGet = true)]
        public bool Changed { get; set; } = false;

        public async Task<IActionResult> OnPostAsync(string password, string token) {
            AppUser user = await UserManager.FindByEmailAsync(Email);
            if (user != null) {
                IdentityResult result = await UserManager.ResetPasswordAsync(user,
                    token, password);
                if (result.Succeeded) {
                    return RedirectToPage(new { Changed = true });
                } else {
                    foreach (IdentityError err in result.Errors) {
                        ModelState.AddModelError("", err.Description);
                    }
                }
            } else {
                ModelState.AddModelError("", "Password Change Error");
            }
            return Page();
        }
    }
}
```

The page handler method uses the ResetPasswordAsync method to change the password and adds an error to the model state if the password change fails or if the email address provided by the user can't be located in the user store.

Integrating the Password Features

To integrate password changes with the rest of the application, add the elements shown in Listing 18-19 to the SignIn Razor Page.

Listing 18-19. Integrating Password Features in the SignIn.cshtml File in the Pages Folder

```
@page "{code:int?}"
@model ExampleApp.Pages.SignInModel
@using Microsoft.AspNetCore.Http

@if (Model.Code == StatusCodes.Status401Unauthorized) {
    <h3 class="bg-warning text-white text-center p-2">
        401 - Challenge Response
    </h3>
} else if (Model.Code == StatusCodes.Status403Forbidden) {
    <h3 class="bg-danger text-white text-center p-2">
        403 - Forbidden Response
    </h3>
}
<h4 class="bg-info text-white m-2 p-2">
    Current User: @Model.Username
</h4>

<div class="m-2">
    <form method="post">
        <div class="form-group">
            <label>User</label>
            <select class="form-control"
                    asp-for="Username" asp-items="@Model.Users">
            </select>
        </div>
        <div class="form-group">
            <label>Password</label>
            <input class="form-control" type="password" name="password" />
        </div>
        <button class="btn btn-info" type="submit">Sign In</button>
        @if (User.Identity.IsAuthenticated) {
            <a asp-page="/Store/PasswordChange" class="btn btn-secondary"
                asp-route-id="@Model.User?
                        .FindFirst(ClaimTypes.NameIdentifier)?.Value">
                Change Password
            </a>
        } else {
            <a class="btn btn-secondary" href="/password/reset">Reset Password</a>
        }
    </form>
</div>
```

The button the user sees depends on whether the user has signed in. If they are signed in, then the application assumes they know their password and can perform a password change without requiring confirmation. If there is no signed-in user, then the user is presented with a button to perform a password reset. Restart ASP.NET Core and request http://localhost:5000/signin.

Sign in as alice@example.com with the password MySecret1$. Once you are signed in, you will see the Change Password button, which will lead you to the password change feature for the signed-in user, as shown in Figure 18-5.

Enter MySecret1$ into the Existing Password field and MySecret2$ into the New Password field. Click Change and the user's password will be updated.

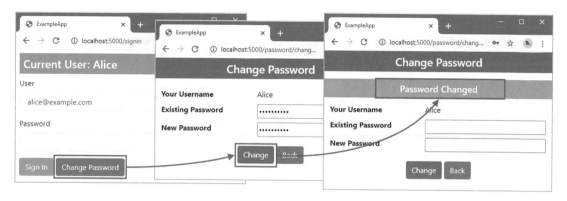

Figure 18-5. *Performing a password change*

To test the password reset feature, request http://localhost:5000/signout and sign the existing user out of the application. Next, request http://localhost:5000/signin and click the Reset Password button. Enter bob@example.com into the text field and click the Reset Password button. The display will change to prompt you for a new password and to render the validation code, as shown in Figure 18-6.

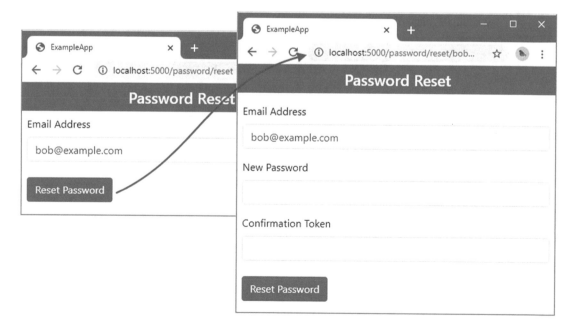

Figure 18-6. *Performing a password reset*

Examine the console output from ASP.NET Core, and you will see a simulated SMS message like this one:

```
--- SMS Starts ---
To: 123-4567
Your password reset token is C91430
--- SMS Ends ---
```

Enter MySecret2$ into the New Password field, enter C91430 into the Confirmation Token field, and click the Reset Password button. The password will be reset, as shown in Figure 18-7. You can now sign into the application using the new password.

■ **Note** The confirmation code is C91430 because the seed data uses a fixed value for the security stamp when it adds users to the store. Subsequent changes generate different security stamps and, as a consequence, different confirmation tokens.

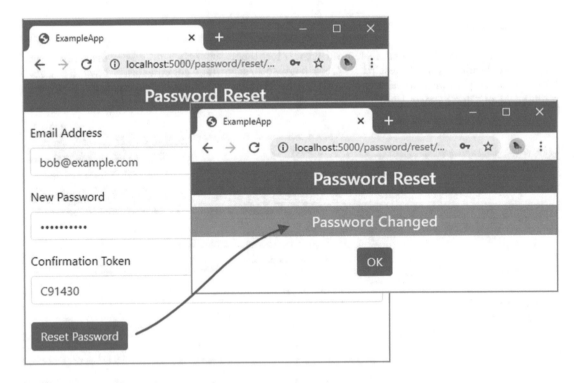

Figure 18-7. *Completing the password reset*

Validating Passwords

I was specific about the passwords used to test new features because Identity applies a password validation policy by default. Attempt a password change or reset using mysecret as the new password, for example, and you will see a series of error messages, as shown in Figure 18-8.

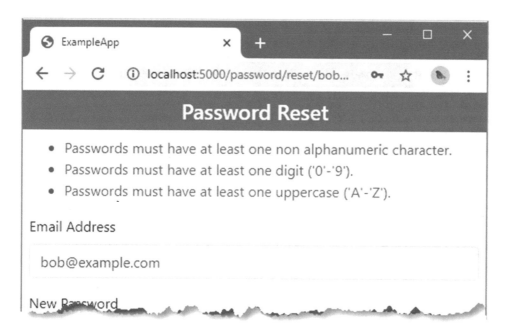

Figure 18-8. *Identity password validation*

The validation policy is configured using the options pattern. The IdentityOptions.Password property returns an instance of the PasswordOptions class, which defines the properties described in Table 18-10.

Table 18-10. *The PasswordOptions Properties*

Name	Description
RequiredLength	This property specifies the minimum length for a password. The default value is 6.
RequiredUniqueChars	This property specifies the minimum number of unique characters in a password. The default value is 1.
RequireNonAlphanumeric	This property specifies whether passwords must contain a nonalphanumeric character, such as a punctuation mark. The default value is true.
RequireLowercase	This property specifies whether passwords must contain at least one lowercase character. The default value is true.
RequireUppercase	This property specifies whether passwords must contain at least one uppercase character. The default value is true.
RequireDigit	This property specifies whether passwords must contain at least one numeric digit. The default value is true.

535

The combined effect of the default values is that passwords must contain at least six characters, which must be a mix of uppercase and lowercase, numbers, and punctuation. Listing 18-20 uses the options pattern to change the password validation policy.

Listing 18-20. Changing the Password Validation Policy in the Startup.cs File in the ExampleApp Folder

```
...
services.AddIdentityCore<AppUser>(opts => {
    opts.Tokens.EmailConfirmationTokenProvider = "SimpleEmail";
    opts.Tokens.ChangeEmailTokenProvider = "SimpleEmail";
    opts.Tokens.PasswordResetTokenProvider = TokenOptions.DefaultPhoneProvider;
    opts.Password.RequireNonAlphanumeric = false;
    opts.Password.RequireLowercase = false;
    opts.Password.RequireUppercase = false;
    opts.Password.RequireDigit = false;
    opts.Password.RequiredLength = 8;
})
.AddTokenProvider<EmailConfirmationTokenGenerator>("SimpleEmail")
.AddTokenProvider<PhoneConfirmationTokenGenerator>(TokenOptions.DefaultPhoneProvider)
.AddSignInManager();
...
```

In this listing, I have disabled the requirements for mixing types of character and increased the minimum length requirement.

CHOOSING A SENSIBLE PASSWORD VALIDATION POLICY

Most password validation policies are intended to force the user to pick strong passwords but rarely work as intended. The only effect of restrictive password validation is an increase in the effort users will apply to bypass them.

The best practice has changed in recent years to focus on enforcing only a minimum length for passwords (usually eight characters), which should be supplemented by two-factor authentication (which I describe in Chapter 20) and features such as account lockout (also described in Chapter 20) and blocking commonly weak passwords (demonstrated in the next section).

There are some good sources for describing modern password restrictions, including Microsoft (https://docs.microsoft.com/en-us/microsoft-365/admin/misc/password-policy-recommendations) and NIST (https://pages.nist.gov/800-63-3/sp800-63b.html) and Wikipedia (https://en.wikipedia.org/wiki/Password_policy).

Adding Custom Password Validation

The UserManager<T> class performs password validation by using dependency injection to receive the set of services for the IPasswordValidator<T> interface, which defines the method described in Table 18-11. Each registered IPasswordValidator<T> implementation is asked to validate passwords before they are hashed and stored.

Table 18-11. *The IPasswordValidator<T> Method*

Name	Description
ValidateAsync(manager, user, password	This method validates a password for the specified user, with access to the user store provided through the specified UserManager<T>. The result is an IdentityResult object.

To implement a custom password validator, I am going to perform two checks. The first check is to block the 20 most common passwords. There are many lists of common passwords available, and I have chosen 20 as a manageable number for this example.

The second check is to exclude passwords that have been exposed publicly using the excellent api. pwnedpasswords.com web service provided by haveibeenpwned.com, which is documented at https:// haveibeenpwned.com/API/v3#PwnedPasswords. The web service accepts the first five characters from a SHA1 hash generated from a password and returns a list of all the matching hashes from the extensive database of publicly exposed passwords. This allows clients to check passwords without sending the complete hash code, and if the hash of the password to validate appears in the response from the web service, it will not pass validation. The web service helpful includes the number of times a password has been exposed.

■ **Note** The point of this example is to demonstrate the use of a remote web service for password validation, which can be useful because the data sets for bad passwords are too large and too volatile to include directly in projects. But that's not to say that you should use this specific web service or that you should automatically invalidate any password that has been compromised. The more passwords you exclude, the more frustrated your users will become when they choose a password.

Add a class named PasswordValidator.cs to the ExampleApp/Identity folder and use it to define the class shown in Listing 18-21.

Listing 18-21. The Contents of the PasswordValidator.cs File in the Identity Folder

```
using Microsoft.AspNetCore.Identity;
using System;
using System.Linq;
using System.Net.Http;
using System.Threading.Tasks;
using System.Security.Cryptography;
using System.Text;
using System.Collections.Generic;

namespace ExampleApp.Identity {
    public class PasswordValidator : IPasswordValidator<AppUser> {
        // set this field to false to disable the web service check
        private const bool remoteCheck = true;

        public async Task<IdentityResult> ValidateAsync(UserManager<AppUser> manager,
                AppUser user, string password) {
            IEnumerable<IdentityError> errors = CheckTop20(password);
```

```
        if (remoteCheck) {
            errors = errors.Concat(await CheckHaveIBeenPwned(password));
        }
        return errors.Count() == 0
            ? IdentityResult.Success : IdentityResult.Failed(errors.ToArray());
    }

    private async Task<IEnumerable<IdentityError>> CheckHaveIBeenPwned(
            string password) {
        string hash = BitConverter.ToString(SHA1.Create()
            .ComputeHash(Encoding.UTF8.GetBytes(password)))
            .Replace("-", string.Empty);
        string firstSection = hash[0..5];
        string secondSection = hash[5..];
        HttpResponseMessage response = await new HttpClient()
            .GetAsync($"https://api.pwnedpasswords.com/range/{firstSection}");
        string matchingHashes = await response.Content.ReadAsStringAsync();
        string[] matches = matchingHashes.Split("\n",
            StringSplitOptions.RemoveEmptyEntries);
        string match = matches.FirstOrDefault(match =>
            match.StartsWith(secondSection,
                StringComparison.CurrentCultureIgnoreCase));
        if (match == null) {
            return Enumerable.Empty<IdentityError>();
        } else {
            long count = long.Parse(match.Split(":")[1]);
            return new[] {new IdentityError {
                Description = $"Password has been compromised {count:NO} times"
            }};
        }
    }

    private IEnumerable<IdentityError> CheckTop20(string password) {
        if (commonPasswords.Any(commonPassword =>
            string.Equals(commonPassword, password,
                StringComparison.CurrentCultureIgnoreCase))) {
            return new [] {
                new IdentityError {
                    Description = "The top 20 passwords cannot be used"
                }
            };
        }
        return Enumerable.Empty<IdentityError>();
    }

    private static string[] commonPasswords = new[] {
        "123456", "123456789", "qwerty", "password", "1111111", "12345678",
        "abc123", "1234567", "password1", "12345", "1234567890", "123123",
        "000000", "Iloveyou", "1234", "1q2w3e4r5t", "Qwertyuiop", "123",
        "Monkey", "Dragon"};
    }
}
```

The validator checks to see if the password selected by the user is on a statically defined list of passwords and sends a request to the web service. The result of both checks is combined into an IdentityResult, which Identity will send back to the Razor Page that has requested a password change. Listing 18-22 registers the validator as a service. As with the user validator I defined in Chapter 16, the service is defined after the AddIdentityCore method is called so that the new validator supplements the built-in one. If I had defined the service before the AddIdentityCore method, then the new validator would replace the built-in one.

■ **Note**   Readers who are following the examples offline can set the remoteCheck field defined in Listing 18-21 to false. This will disable the web service check but still invalidate passwords from the statically defined top 20 list.

Listing 18-22. Defining a Service in the Startup.cs File in the ExampleApp Folder

```
...
public void ConfigureServices(IServiceCollection services) {
    services.AddSingleton<ILookupNormalizer, Normalizer>();
    services.AddSingleton<IUserStore<AppUser>, UserStore>();
    services.AddSingleton<IEmailSender, ConsoleEmailSender>();
    services.AddSingleton<ISMSSender, ConsoleSMSSender>();
    services.AddSingleton<IUserClaimsPrincipalFactory<AppUser>,
        AppUserClaimsPrincipalFactory>();
    services.AddSingleton<IPasswordHasher<AppUser>, SimplePasswordHasher>();

    services.AddIdentityCore<AppUser>(opts => {
        opts.Tokens.EmailConfirmationTokenProvider = "SimpleEmail";
        opts.Tokens.ChangeEmailTokenProvider = "SimpleEmail";
        opts.Tokens.PasswordResetTokenProvider = TokenOptions.DefaultPhoneProvider;

        opts.Password.RequireNonAlphanumeric = false;
        opts.Password.RequireLowercase = false;
        opts.Password.RequireUppercase = false;
        opts.Password.RequireDigit = false;
        opts.Password.RequiredLength = 8;
    })
    .AddTokenProvider<EmailConfirmationTokenGenerator>("SimpleEmail")
    .AddTokenProvider<PhoneConfirmationTokenGenerator>
        (TokenOptions.DefaultPhoneProvider)
    .AddSignInManager();

    services.AddSingleton<IUserValidator<AppUser>, EmailValidator>();
    services.AddSingleton<IPasswordValidator<AppUser>, PasswordValidator>();

    services.AddAuthentication(opts => {
        opts.DefaultScheme
            = IdentityConstants.ApplicationScheme;
```

```
}).AddCookie(IdentityConstants.ApplicationScheme, opts => {
    opts.LoginPath = "/signin";
    opts.AccessDeniedPath = "/signin/403";
});
services.AddAuthorization(opts => {
    AuthorizationPolicies.AddPolicies(opts);
});
services.AddRazorPages();
services.AddControllersWithViews();
}
...
```

Restart ASP.NET Core request http://localhost:5000/signin and click the Reset Password or Change Password button, depending on whether a user is signed into the application. Try changing the password to qwerty, and you will see validation errors from both the built-in and custom password validators, as shown in Figure 18-9.

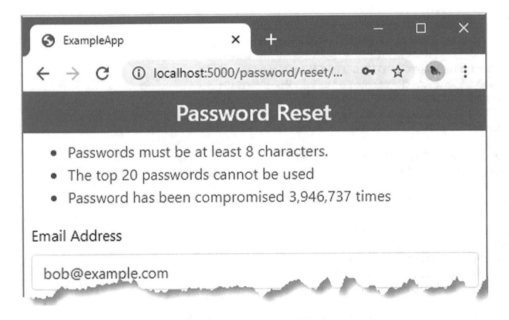

Figure 18-9. *Validating passwords*

Setting Passwords Administratively

The UserManager<T> class defines a convenience method for creating users and assigning an initial password, as shown in Table 18-12 for future quick reference.

Table 18-12. *The UserManager<T> Method for Creating Users with Passwords*

Name	Description
CreateAsync(user, password)	This method validates the password, creates a new password hash, and calls the user's store SetPasswordHashAsync method. A new security stamp is generated, and the user manager's CreateAsync method is called.

Administrative password resets require a different approach because the administrator doesn't know the user's password and there is no method for changing a password without either the existing password or a confirmation code. I find the most reliable way to let an administrator change a password is to remove the existing password and add a new one.

To add support for setting passwords, add a Razor View named _EditUserPassword.cshtml to the Pages/Store folder with the content shown in Listing 18-23.

Listing 18-23. The Contents of the _EditUserPassword.cshtml File in the Pages/Store Folder

```
@model AppUser
@inject UserManager<AppUser> UserManager

@if (UserManager.SupportsUserPassword) {
    <tr>
        <td>New Password</td>
        <td>
            <input class="w-00" name="newPassword" />
        </td>
    </tr>
}
```

The view renders an input element whose name doesn't correspond to any of the properties defined by the AppUser class, which will allow me to handle password changes without the model binding process trying to assign a raw password string when a hashed password is required.

Add the element shown in Listing 18-24 to the EditUser.cshtml file to incorporate the new partial view into the application.

Listing 18-24. Incorporating a Partial View in the EditUser.cshtml File in the Pages/Store Folder

```
@page "/users/edit/{id?}"
@model ExampleApp.Pages.Store.UsersModel

<div asp-validation-summary="All" class="text-danger m-2"></div>

<div class="m-2">
    <form method="post">
        <input type="hidden" name="id" value="@Model.AppUserObject.Id" />
        <table class="table table-sm table-striped">
            <tbody>
                <partial name="_EditUserBasic" model="@Model.AppUserObject" />
                <partial name="_EditUserEmail" model="@Model.AppUserObject" />
                <partial name="_EditUserPhone" model="@Model.AppUserObject" />
                <partial name="_EditUserCustom" model="@Model.AppUserObject" />
                <partial name="_EditUserPassword" model="@Model.AppUserObject" />
```

```
                <partial name="_EditUserSecurityStamp"
                        model="@Model.AppUserObject" />
            </tbody>
        </table>
        <div>
            <button type="submit" class="btn btn-primary">Save</button>
            <a asp-page="users" class="btn btn-secondary">Cancel</a>
        </div>
    </form>
</div>
```

In Listing 18-25, I have updated the `EditUser` page model class to change passwords.

Listing 18-25. Changing Passwords in the EditUser.cshtml.cs File in the Pages/Store Folder

```
using ExampleApp.Identity;
using Microsoft.AspNetCore.Identity;
using Microsoft.AspNetCore.Mvc;
using Microsoft.AspNetCore.Mvc.RazorPages;
using System.Threading.Tasks;

namespace ExampleApp.Pages.Store {

    public class UsersModel : PageModel {

        public UsersModel(UserManager<AppUser> userMgr) => UserManager = userMgr;

        public UserManager<AppUser> UserManager { get; set; }

        public AppUser AppUserObject { get; set; } = new AppUser();

        public async Task OnGetAsync(string id) {
            if (id != null) {
                AppUserObject = await UserManager.FindByIdAsync(id) ?? new AppUser();
            }
        }

        public async Task<IActionResult> OnPost(AppUser user, string newPassword) {
            IdentityResult result = IdentityResult.Success;
            AppUser storeUser = await UserManager.FindByIdAsync(user.Id);
            if (storeUser == null) {
                if (string.IsNullOrEmpty(newPassword)) {
                    ModelState.AddModelError("", "Password Required");
                    return Page();
                }
                result = await UserManager.CreateAsync(user, newPassword);
            } else {
                storeUser.UpdateFrom(user, out bool changed);
                if (newPassword != null) {
                    if (await UserManager.HasPasswordAsync(storeUser)) {
                        await UserManager.RemovePasswordAsync(storeUser);
                    }
```

```
                    result = await UserManager.AddPasswordAsync(storeUser,
                        newPassword);
                }
                if (changed && UserManager.SupportsUserSecurityStamp) {
                    await UserManager.UpdateSecurityStampAsync(storeUser);
                }
                if (result != null && result.Succeeded) {
                    result = await UserManager.UpdateAsync(storeUser);
                }
            }
            if (result.Succeeded) {
                return RedirectToPage("users", new { searchname = user.Id });
            } else {
                foreach (IdentityError err in result.Errors) {
                    ModelState.AddModelError("", err.Description ?? "Error");
                }
                AppUserObject = user;
                return Page();
            }
        }
    }
}
```

Restart ASP.NET Core, request http://localhost:5000/users, and click the Edit button for one of the users. You will see the new text field, which can be used to select a new password, as shown in Figure 18-10.

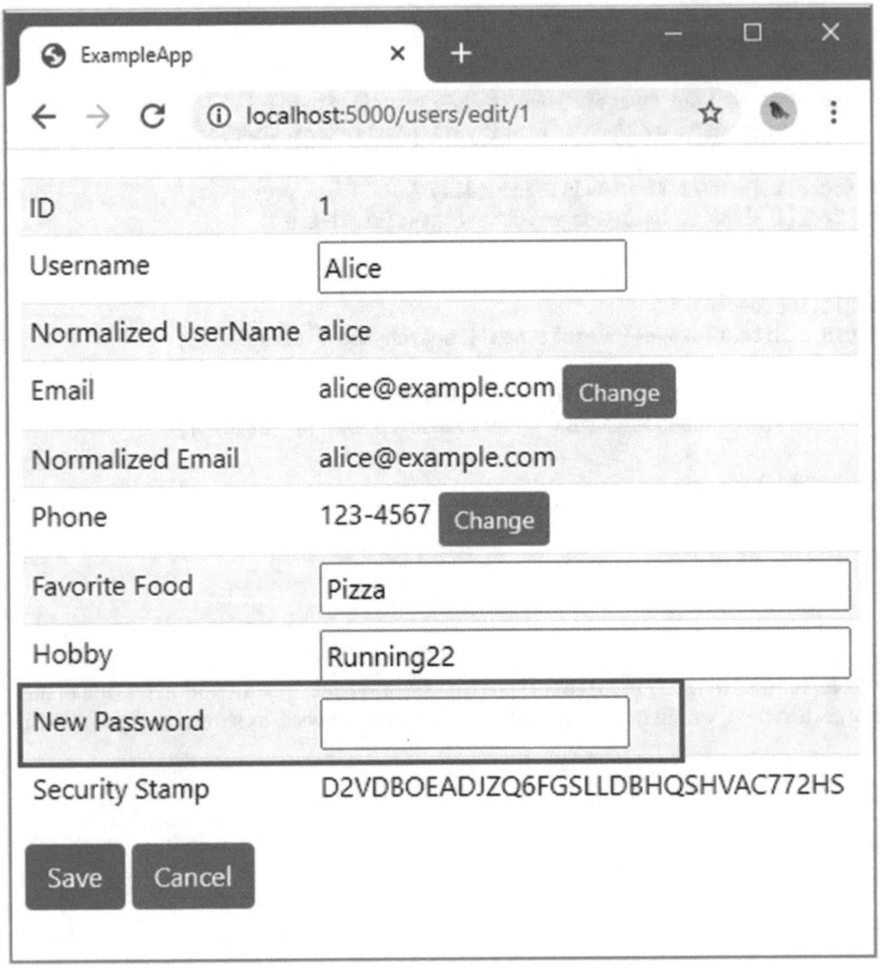

Figure 18-10. *Changing a password*

Summary

In this chapter, I extended the user store so that it can manage passwords and created the workflows for signing the user into the application, changing passwords, and recovering passwords. I also explained how passwords are validated and demonstrated custom password validation. In the next chapter, I create a role store.

CHAPTER 19

■ ■ ■

Creating a Role Store

In this chapter, I create and use a role store. As earlier chapters have shown, Identity doesn't need a role store to use roles, and the use of a role store is entirely optional and the features that are provided are not needed in most projects. That said, a role store can be a useful way to ensure that roles are used consistently. Table 19-1 puts role stores in context.

Table 19-1. *Putting Roles Stores in Context*

Question	Answer
What is it?	The role store allows additional data to be associated with roles.
Why is it useful?	The role store has some useful validation features and can be used to store additional claims, which are added to the ClaimsPrincipal objects created when a user signs in.
How is it used?	A role class and an implementation of the IRoleStore<T> interface are created.
Are there any pitfalls or limitations?	Most projects do not need the features that the role store provides, which is not widely understood.
Are there any alternatives?	The role store is an optional feature and is not required to use roles in ASP.NET Core Identity.

Table 19-2 summarizes the chapter.

Table 19-2. *Chapter Summary*

Problem	Solution	Listing
Create a role store	Define a role class and create an implementation of the IRoleStore<T> interface. Register the implementation as a service for dependency injection.	2–5, 7,8
Support LINQ queries in a custom role store	Implement the IQueryableRoleStore<T> interface.	6
Manage the roles in the role store	Use the RoleManager<T> class.	9, 10, 20–23
Validate roles before they are added to the role store	Create an implementation of the IRoleValidator<T> interface.	11, 12
Enforce role consistency	Use the role store as the master list of permissible role memberships	13, 14
Store claims with roles	Implement the IRoleClaimStore<T> interface.	15–19

Preparing for This Chapter

This chapter uses the ExampleApp project from Chapter 18. No changes are required to prepare for this chapter. Open a new command prompt, navigate to the ExampleApp folder, and run the command shown in Listing 19-1 to start ASP.NET Core.

■ **Tip** You can download the example project for this chapter—and for all the other chapters in this book—from https://github.com/Apress/pro-asp.net-core-identity. See Chapter 1 for how to get help if you have problems running the examples.

Listing 19-1. Running the Example Application

```
dotnet run
```

Open a new browser window and request http://localhost:5000/users. You will be presented with the user data shown in Figure 19-1. The data is stored only in memory, and changes will be lost when ASP.NET Core is stopped.

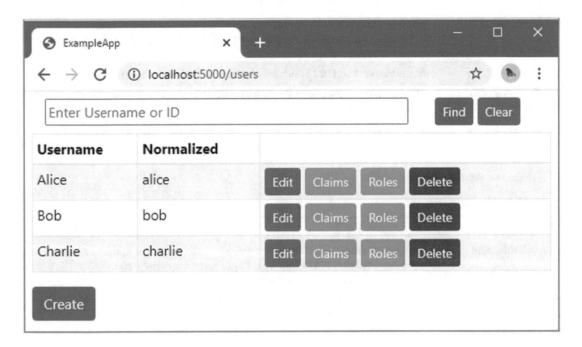

Figure 19-1. Running the example application

Creating a Custom Role Store

At the moment, roles are represented in the user store as claims. If an authorization policy requires role membership, access will be granted to users who have a Role claim with the required role name. This approach is suitable for most web applications, which typically rely on a small number of roles, but there are some limitations.

The first limitation is that a role doesn't exist until the first time a user is granted a Role claim with a specific value. So, for example, there is no Manager role known to the application until the first time a Role claim with a value of Manager is created for a user. This can lead to quirks in the application because it is difficult to determine if a specific role exists but there are no users assigned to it or if that role doesn't exist at all. All the application can do is query the claims in the user store.

The second limitation is that it is difficult to enforce consistency, which means that typos can cause unexpected application behaviors. It is easy to mistype role names so that some users are assigned to the Administrator role (singular) while others are assigned to the Administrators role (plural). Users will either be denied access to features to which they are entitled or, worse, be granted access to features from which they should be excluded.

To help manage complex sets of roles, Identity supports a *role store*, which is used to define and manage the roles an application requires. In the sections that follow, I create a role store for the example application and demonstrate its use.

Creating the Role Class

The starting point is to define a class that will be instantiated to represent roles. This class, known as the *role class*, plays the same role as the user class does in the user store. Add a class file named AppRole.cs to the ExampleApp/Identity folder and use it to define the class shown in Listing 19-2.

Listing 19-2. The Contents of the AppRole.cs File in the Identity Folder

```
using System;

namespace ExampleApp.Identity {

    public class AppRole {

        public string Id { get; set; } = Guid.NewGuid().ToString();

        public string Name { get; set; }

        public string NormalizedName { get; set; }
    }
}
```

There are no restrictions on how the role class is defined, and I started with a minimum setup of an Id property that will uniquely identify a role, a Name property that will be displayed to users, and a NormalizedName, which will be used to store a normalized representation of the Name value and will help ensure that comparisons using names are consistent.

Creating the Role Store

Role stores are defined by the IRoleStore<T> interface, where T is the role class. I am going to follow the same approach I took for the user store and build up the role store gradually using partial classes, each of which implements a group of related methods from the IRoleStore<T> interface. Table 19-3 describes the methods defined by the IRoleStore<T> interface. The token parameter defined by the methods in Table 19-3 is a CancellationToken object that is used to receive notifications when an asynchronous task is canceled.

Table 19-3. *The IRoleStore<T> Methods*

Name	Description
CreateAsync(role, token)	This method adds the specified role to the store.
UpdateAsync(role, token)	This method updates the specified role in the store, committing any pending changes persistently.
DeleteAsync(role, token)	This method removes the specified role object from the role store.
GetRoleIdAsync(role, token)	This method gets the ID of the specified role object.
GetRoleNameAsync(role, token)	This method gets the name of the specified role object.
SetRoleNameAsync(role, name, token)	This method sets the name of the specified role object.
GetNormalizedRoleNameAsync(role, token)	This method gets the normalized name of the specified role object.
SetNormalizedRoleNameAsync(role, name, token)	This method sets the normalized name of the specified role object.
FindByIdAsync(id, token)	This method retrieves the role object with the specified ID from the store.
FindByNameAsync(name, token)	This method retrieves the role object with the specified normalized name from the store.
Dispose()	This method is inherited from the IDisposable interface and is called to release unmanaged resources before the store object is destroyed.

All the methods described in Table 19-3 return an IdentityResult object that indicates the outcome of the operation and provides details of any problems that occur.

Implementing the Data Storage Methods

The data storage methods defined by the IRoleStore<T> interface address managing the collection of roles managed by the store. Add a class file named RoleStoreCore.cs to the Identity/Store folder and use it to define the partial class shown in Listing 19-3. (Your code editor will indicate an error for this class until all the partial classes in this part of the chapter have been created.)

Listing 19-3. The Contents of the RoleStoreCore.cs File in the Identity/Store Folder

```
using Microsoft.AspNetCore.Identity;
using System.Collections.Concurrent;
using System.Threading;
using System.Threading.Tasks;

namespace ExampleApp.Identity.Store {
    public partial class RoleStore: IRoleStore<AppRole> {
        private ConcurrentDictionary<string, AppRole> roles
            = new ConcurrentDictionary<string, AppRole>();

        public Task<IdentityResult> CreateAsync(AppRole role,
                CancellationToken token) {
            if (!roles.ContainsKey(role.Id) && roles.TryAdd(role.Id, role)) {
                return Task.FromResult(IdentityResult.Success);
            }
            return Task.FromResult(Error);
        }

        public Task<IdentityResult> DeleteAsync(AppRole role,
                CancellationToken token) {
            if (roles.ContainsKey(role.Id) && roles.TryRemove(role.Id, out role)) {
                return Task.FromResult(IdentityResult.Success);
            }
            return Task.FromResult(Error);
        }

        public Task<IdentityResult> UpdateAsync(AppRole role,
                CancellationToken token) {
            if (roles.ContainsKey(role.Id)) {
                roles[role.Id].UpdateFrom(role);
                return Task.FromResult(IdentityResult.Success);
            }
            return Task.FromResult(Error);
        }

        public void Dispose() {
            // do nothing
        }

        private IdentityResult Error => IdentityResult.Failed(new IdentityError {
            Code = "StorageFailure",
            Description = "Role Store Error"
        });
    }
}
```

I have followed the same approach for storing roles as I did for user objects in Chapter 16. The data will be stored in memory using a ConcurrentDictionary object, with the AppRole.Id property used as the key. Restarting ASP.NET Core will reset the role store, and any changes are lost.

Implementing the Name Methods

The next set of methods is responsible for providing Identity with access to the basic information about the role, which is done by mapping the methods onto the properties defined by the role object. Add a class file named RoleStoreNames.cs to the ExampleApp/Identity/Store folder and use it to define the partial class shown in Listing 19-4.

Listing 19-4. The Contents of the RoleStoreNames.cs File in the Identity/Store Folder

```
using System.Threading;
using System.Threading.Tasks;

namespace ExampleApp.Identity.Store {

    public partial class RoleStore {

        public Task<string> GetRoleIdAsync(AppRole role, CancellationToken token)
            => Task.FromResult(role.Id);

        public Task<string> GetRoleNameAsync(AppRole role, CancellationToken token)
            => Task.FromResult(role.Name);

        public Task SetRoleNameAsync(AppRole role, string roleName,
                CancellationToken token) {
            role.Name = roleName;
            return Task.CompletedTask;
        }

        public Task<string> GetNormalizedRoleNameAsync(AppRole role,
            CancellationToken token) => Task.FromResult(role.NormalizedName);

        public Task SetNormalizedRoleNameAsync(AppRole role, string normalizedName,
                CancellationToken token) {
            role.NormalizedName = normalizedName;
            return Task.CompletedTask;
        }
    }
}
```

Implementing the Search Methods

The next set of methods allow role objects to be located by ID or name. Add a class file named RoleStoreQuery.cs to the ExampleApp/Identity/Store folder and use it to define the partial class shown in Listing 19-5.

Listing 19-5. The Contents of the RoleStoreQuery.cs File in the Identity/Store Folder

```
using System.Linq;
using System.Threading;
using System.Threading.Tasks;
```

```
namespace ExampleApp.Identity.Store {

    public partial class RoleStore {

        public Task<AppRole> FindByIdAsync(string id, CancellationToken token)
            => Task.FromResult(roles.ContainsKey(id) ? roles[id].Clone() : null);

        public Task<AppRole> FindByNameAsync(string name, CancellationToken token)
            => Task.FromResult(roles.Values.FirstOrDefault(r => r.NormalizedName ==
                    name)?.Clone());
    }
}
```

Notice that these methods use the Clone extension method defined in Listing 19-5 to create objects that can be modified by the application and then committed to the store. This is an important measure that prevents changes that the user abandons from being stored.

Making the Store Queryable

Role stores can implement the optional IQueryableRoleStore<T> interface, where T is the role class, to create a role store that can be queried easily with LINQ. The IQueryableRoleStore<T> defines the property described in Table 19-4.

Table 19-4. *The IQueryableRoleStore<T> Interface*

Name	Description
Roles	This property returns an IQueryable<T> object, where T is the role class.

To implement the optional interface, make the changes shown in Listing 19-6 to the partial class defined in the RoleStoreQuery.cs file.

Listing 19-6. Implementing an Interface in the RoleStoreQuery.cs File in the Identity/Store Folder

```
using System.Linq;
using System.Threading;
using System.Threading.Tasks;
using Microsoft.AspNetCore.Identity;

namespace ExampleApp.Identity.Store {

    public partial class RoleStore: IQueryableRoleStore<AppRole> {

        public Task<AppRole> FindByIdAsync(string id, CancellationToken token)
            => Task.FromResult(roles.ContainsKey(id) ? roles[id].Clone() : null);

        public Task<AppRole> FindByNameAsync(string name, CancellationToken token)
            => Task.FromResult(roles.Values.FirstOrDefault(r => r.NormalizedName ==
                    name)?.Clone());
```

```
    public IQueryable<AppRole> Roles =>
        roles.Values.Select(role => role.Clone()).AsQueryable<AppRole>();
    }
}
```

Once again, it is important to return objects that can be modified outside of the store, such that changes are stored only when the UpdateAsync method is called.

Seeding the Role Store and Configuring the Application

Now I have implemented the IRoleStore<T> and IQueryableRoleStore<T> interfaces, I can finish the store by adding some seed data. Add a class file named RoleStore.cs to the ExampleApp/Identity/Store folder and use it to define the partial class shown in Listing 19-7.

Listing 19-7. The Contents of the RoleStore.cs File in the Identity/Store Folder

```
using Microsoft.AspNetCore.Identity;
using System.Collections.Generic;

namespace ExampleApp.Identity.Store {

    public partial class RoleStore {

        public ILookupNormalizer Normalizer { get; set; }

        public RoleStore(ILookupNormalizer normalizer) {
            Normalizer = normalizer;
            SeedStore();
        }

        private void SeedStore() {

            var roleData = new List<string> {
                "Administrator", "User", "Sales", "Support"
            };

            int idCounter = 0;

            foreach (string roleName in roleData) {
                AppRole role = new AppRole {
                    Id = (++idCounter).ToString(),
                    Name = roleName,
                    NormalizedName = Normalizer.NormalizeName(roleName)
                };
                roles.TryAdd(role.Id, role);
            }
        }
    }
}
```

The code in Listing 19-7 seeds the role store with four roles. Role names are normalized using an implementation of the ILookupNormalizer interface, which I introduced in Chapter 16.

Listing 19-8 configures the application to use the role store.

Listing 19-8. Using a Role Store in the Startup.cs File in the ExampleApp Folder

```
using Microsoft.AspNetCore.Builder;
using Microsoft.AspNetCore.Hosting;
using Microsoft.AspNetCore.Http;
using Microsoft.Extensions.DependencyInjection;
using ExampleApp.Custom;
using Microsoft.AspNetCore.Authentication.Cookies;
using Microsoft.AspNetCore.Authorization;
using Microsoft.AspNetCore.Identity;
using ExampleApp.Identity;
using ExampleApp.Identity.Store;
using ExampleApp.Services;

namespace ExampleApp {
    public class Startup {

        public void ConfigureServices(IServiceCollection services) {
            services.AddSingleton<ILookupNormalizer, Normalizer>();
            services.AddSingleton<IUserStore<AppUser>, UserStore>();
            services.AddSingleton<IEmailSender, ConsoleEmailSender>();
            services.AddSingleton<ISMSSender, ConsoleSMSSender>();
            //services.AddSingleton<IUserClaimsPrincipalFactory<AppUser>,
            //    AppUserClaimsPrincipalFactory>();
            services.AddSingleton<IPasswordHasher<AppUser>, SimplePasswordHasher>();
            services.AddSingleton<IRoleStore<AppRole>, RoleStore>();

            services.AddIdentityCore<AppUser>(opts => {
                opts.Tokens.EmailConfirmationTokenProvider = "SimpleEmail";
                opts.Tokens.ChangeEmailTokenProvider = "SimpleEmail";
                opts.Tokens.PasswordResetTokenProvider =
                    TokenOptions.DefaultPhoneProvider;

                opts.Password.RequireNonAlphanumeric = false;
                opts.Password.RequireLowercase = false;
                opts.Password.RequireUppercase = false;
                opts.Password.RequireDigit = false;
                opts.Password.RequiredLength = 8;

            })
            .AddTokenProvider<EmailConfirmationTokenGenerator>("SimpleEmail")
            .AddTokenProvider<PhoneConfirmationTokenGenerator>
                (TokenOptions.DefaultPhoneProvider)
            .AddSignInManager()
            .AddRoles<AppRole>();
```

```
            services.AddSingleton<IUserValidator<AppUser>, EmailValidator>();
            services.AddSingleton<IPasswordValidator<AppUser>, PasswordValidator>();
            services.AddSingleton<IUserClaimsPrincipalFactory<AppUser>,
                AppUserClaimsPrincipalFactory>();

            services.AddAuthentication(opts => {
                opts.DefaultScheme = IdentityConstants.ApplicationScheme;
            }).AddCookie(IdentityConstants.ApplicationScheme, opts => {
                opts.LoginPath = "/signin";
                opts.AccessDeniedPath = "/signin/403";
            });
            services.AddAuthorization(opts => {
                AuthorizationPolicies.AddPolicies(opts);
            });
            services.AddRazorPages();
            services.AddControllersWithViews();
        }

        public void Configure(IApplicationBuilder app, IWebHostEnvironment env) {

            app.UseStaticFiles();
            app.UseAuthentication();
            app.UseRouting();
            app.UseAuthorization();

            app.UseEndpoints(endpoints => {
                endpoints.MapRazorPages();
                endpoints.MapDefaultControllerRoute();
                endpoints.MapFallbackToPage("/Secret");
            });
        }
    }
}
```

The AddSingleton method is used to define a service so that the RoleStore class is used to resolve dependencies on the IRoleStore<AppRole> interface.

The AddRoles<T> method is used to specify the class that will represent roles, which is AppUser in this case. This is a convenience method that registers a service for the RoleManager<T> class (described in the next section) and sets up the default role validator service (described in the "Validating Roles" section).

I have moved the statement that sets up the custom claims principal factory service. The AddRoles method sets up a default factory service, even if one is already registered, which is the opposite behavior of most Identity methods. I have moved the statement that registers the AppUserClaimsPrincipalFactory class as the factory service so that it replaces the service created by the AddRoles method.

■ **Note** Identity provides an AddRoleStore<T> extension method that can be used to specify the role store class. Care must be taken when using this method because it creates a scoped service, which means that a new instance of the role store class will be created for every HTTP request. A scoped service is useful when storing data with Entity Framework Core, but for this chapter, I need to explicitly define the service with the AddSingleton method so that all requests share a single instance of the RoleStore class.

Managing Roles

Roles are managed through the RoleManager<T> class, where T is the role class. Table 19-5 describes the basic members defined by the RoleManager<T> class. There are additional members, which I describe later in the chapter.

Table 19-5. *The Basic RoleManager<T> Members*

Name	Description
SupportsQueryableRoles	This property returns true if the role store implements the IQueryableRoleStore<T> interface.
Roles	This property returns an IQueryable<T> object when the role store implements the IQueryableRoleStore<T> interface. An exception will be thrown if this property is read and the user store doesn't implement the interface.
CreateAsync(role)	This method adds the specified role object to the store. The role is subjected to validation (described in the "Validating Roles" section), and the normalized name is set before being passed to the role store's CreateAsync method.
UpdateAsync(role)	This method updates the specified role in the store, persisting any changes that have been made. The role is subjected to validation (described in the "Validating Roles" section), and the normalized name is set before being passed to the role store's UpdateAsync method.
DeleteAsync(role)	This method removes the specified role from the store by calling the role store's DeleteAsync method.
RoleExistsAsync(name)	This method returns true if the role store contains a role with the specified name, which is normalized before being passed to the role store.
FindByIdAsync(id)	This method returns the role with the specified ID, or null if there is no such role.
FindByNameAsync(name)	This method returns the role with the specified name or null if there is no such role. The role name is normalized before it is passed to the role store's FindByNameAsync method.

To manage the roles in the store, add a Razor Page named Roles.cshtml to the Pages/Store folder with the content shown in Listing 19-9.

Listing 19-9. *The Contents of the Roles.cshtml File in the Pages/Store Folder*

```
@page "/roles"
@model ExampleApp.Pages.Store.RolesModel

<h4 class="bg-secondary text-white text-center p-2">Roles</h4>

<div asp-validation-summary="All" class="text-danger m-2"></div>

<table class="table table-striped table-sm">
    <thead><tr><th>Name</th><th># Users in Role</th><th/></tr></thead>
```

```html
<tbody>
    @foreach (AppRole role in Model.Roles) {
        <tr>
            <td class="pl-2">
                <input name="name" form="@role.Id" value="@role.Name" />
            </td>
            <td>@((await Model.GetUsersInRole(role)).Count())</td>
            <td class="text-right pr-2">
                <form method="post" id="@role.Id">
                    <input type="hidden" name="id" value="@role.Id" />
                    <button type="submit" class="btn btn-danger btn-sm"
                        asp-page-handler="delete">Delete</button>
                    <button type="submit" class="btn btn-info btn-sm"
                        asp-page-handler="save">Save</button>
                </form>
            </td>
        </tr>
    }
    <tr>
        <td>
            <input name="name" form="newRole" placeholder="Enter Role Name" />
        </td>
        <td></td>
        <td class="text-right pr-2">
            <form method="post" id="newRole">
                <button type="submit" class="btn btn-info btn-sm"
                        asp-page-handler="create">
                    Create
                </button>
            </form>
        </td>
    </tr>
</tbody>
</table>
```

The page displays the roles known to the application in a table, allowing the name to be edited or the role to be deleted. There is also a table row that allows a new role to be created.

Add the code shown in Listing 19-10 to the Roles.cshtml.cs file to define the page model. You will have to create this file if you are using Visual Studio Code.

Listing 19-10. The Contents of the Roles.cshtml.cs File in the Pages/Store Folder

```csharp
using ExampleApp.Identity;
using Microsoft.AspNetCore.Identity;
using Microsoft.AspNetCore.Mvc;
using Microsoft.AspNetCore.Mvc.RazorPages;
using System.Collections.Generic;
using System.Linq;
using System.Threading.Tasks;
```

```
namespace ExampleApp.Pages.Store {

    public class RolesModel : PageModel {

        public RolesModel(UserManager<AppUser> userManager,
                RoleManager<AppRole> roleManager) {
            UserManager = userManager;
            RoleManager = roleManager;
        }

        public UserManager<AppUser> UserManager { get; set; }
        public RoleManager<AppRole> RoleManager { get; set; }

        public IEnumerable<AppRole> Roles => RoleManager.Roles.OrderBy(r => r.Name);

        public async Task<IList<AppUser>> GetUsersInRole(AppRole role) =>
            await UserManager.GetUsersInRoleAsync(role.Name);

        public async Task<IActionResult> OnPostDelete(string id) {
            AppRole role = await RoleManager.FindByIdAsync(id);
            if (role != null) {
                IdentityResult result = await RoleManager.DeleteAsync(role);
                if (!result.Succeeded) {
                    return ProcessErrors(result.Errors);
                }
            }
            return RedirectToPage();
        }

        public async Task<IActionResult> OnPostSave(AppRole editedRole) {
            IdentityResult result = await RoleManager.UpdateAsync(editedRole);
            if (!result.Succeeded) {
                return ProcessErrors(result.Errors);
            }

            return RedirectToPage();
        }

        public async Task<IActionResult> OnPostCreate(AppRole newRole) {
            IdentityResult result = await RoleManager.CreateAsync(newRole);
            if (!result.Succeeded) {
                return ProcessErrors(result.Errors);
            }
            return RedirectToPage();
        }

        private IActionResult ProcessErrors(IEnumerable<IdentityError> errors) {
            foreach (IdentityError err in errors) {
                ModelState.AddModelError("", err.Description);
            }
```

```
            return Page();
        }
    }
}
```

Restart ASP.NET Core and request `http://localhost:5000/roles`, and you will see the list of roles from the role store, as shown in Figure 19-2. You can change the name of a role, delete a role, and create a new role.

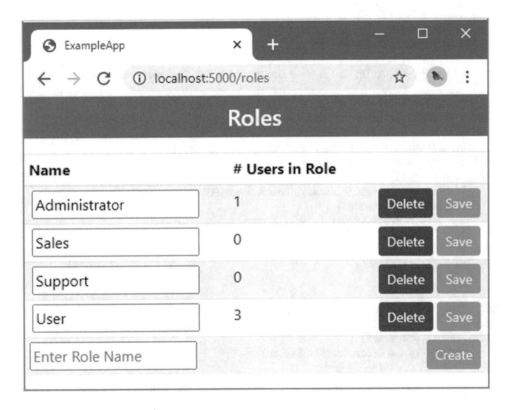

Figure 19-2. *Managing roles*

It is important to understand that the authoritative repository for role memberships is the user store, not the role store. This can seem counterintuitive, but, as you will see in later examples, the role store exists to supplement the features provided by the user store and not to replace them.

So, for example, I had to use the `UserManager<T>` class in Listing 19-10 to determine how many users have been assigned to each role stored in the role store. The roles in the role store may not be the complete set of roles used by the application, which you can see by changing the name of the User role and then changing it back, which produces the sequence shown in Figure 19-3.

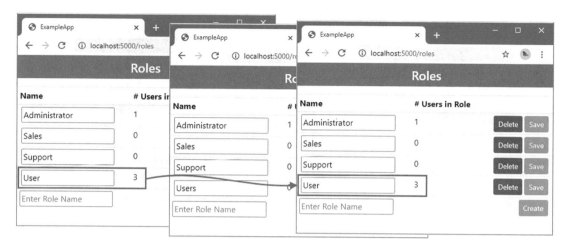

Figure 19-3. Understanding the relationship between the user and role stores

When you rename the role, there is no longer a User role in the role store, but that doesn't stop users from being assigned to that role because that data is in the user store.

Validating Roles

The RoleManager<T> class's CreateAsync and UpdateAsync methods perform a validation check before passing the role onto the role store. Role validation is performed by services that implement the IRoleValidator<T> interface, where T is the role class. The validation interface defines the method described in Table 19-6.

Table 19-6. The Method Defined by the IRoleValidator<T> Interface

Name	Description
ValidateAsync(manager, role)	This method is called to validate the specified role on behalf of the specified role manager. The method returns an IdentityResult object, which indicates whether validation was successful and provides details of the validation errors if it was not.

Identity provides a built-in role validator that ensures that role names are not empty strings and role names are unique within the role store. Validation errors are expressed using IdentityResult objects that are returned by the CreateAsync and UpdateAsync methods when roles fail validation. You can see the errors reported by the built-in validator by requesting http://localhost:5000/roles and clicking the Create button without entering text into the adjacent text field, as shown in Figure 19-4. Enter the name of an existing role, such as **User**, and click the Create button to see the error reported when a role name is already in use, also shown in Figure 19-4.

Figure 19-4. *The built-in Identity role validation*

Creating a Custom Role Validator

To create a custom validator, add a class file named RoleValidator.cs to the ExampleApp/Identity folder and use it to define the class shown in Listing 19-11.

Listing 19-11. The Contents of the RoleValidator.cs File in the Identity Folder

```
using Microsoft.AspNetCore.Identity;
using System.Threading.Tasks;

namespace ExampleApp.Identity {
    public class RoleValidator : IRoleValidator<AppRole> {

        private static IdentityError error = new IdentityError {
            Description = "Names cannot be plural/singular of existing roles"
        };

        public async Task<IdentityResult> ValidateAsync(RoleManager<AppRole> manager,
                AppRole role) {
            if (await manager.FindByNameAsync(role.Name.EndsWith("s")
                ? role.Name[0..^1] : role.Name + "s") == null) {
                return IdentityResult.Success;
            }
            return IdentityResult.Failed(error);
        }
    }
}
```

The validator prevents role names that simply add or omit the letter s from the name of an existing role. I find that I start out defining roles with singular names (administrator, user, etc.) and then accidentally switch to plurals (administrators, users, and so on). The validator checks for this mistake but still allows roles whose names end with an *s*, such as Sales, to be created, just as long as there isn't already a Sale role in the store.

In Listing 19-12, I have registered the validator as an implementation of the IRoleValidator<AppRole> interface. I have done this after the AddIdentityCore method is called so that the new validator is used in addition to the built-in Identity role validator. If I had registered the service before the AddIdentityCore method, the custom validator would have replaced the built-in one.

Listing 19-12. Registering the Validator in the Startup.cs File in the ExampleApp Folder

```
...
public void ConfigureServices(IServiceCollection services) {
    services.AddSingleton<ILookupNormalizer, Normalizer>();
    services.AddSingleton<IUserStore<AppUser>, UserStore>();
    services.AddSingleton<IEmailSender, ConsoleEmailSender>();
    services.AddSingleton<ISMSSender, ConsoleSMSSender>();
    //services.AddSingleton<IUserClaimsPrincipalFactory<AppUser>,
    //    AppUserClaimsPrincipalFactory>();
    services.AddSingleton<IPasswordHasher<AppUser>, SimplePasswordHasher>();
    services.AddSingleton<IRoleStore<AppRole>, RoleStore>();

    services.AddIdentityCore<AppUser>(opts => {
        opts.Tokens.EmailConfirmationTokenProvider = "SimpleEmail";
        opts.Tokens.ChangeEmailTokenProvider = "SimpleEmail";
        opts.Tokens.PasswordResetTokenProvider =
            TokenOptions.DefaultPhoneProvider;

        opts.Password.RequireNonAlphanumeric = false;
        opts.Password.RequireLowercase = false;
        opts.Password.RequireUppercase = false;
        opts.Password.RequireDigit = false;
        opts.Password.RequiredLength = 8;

    })
    .AddTokenProvider<EmailConfirmationTokenGenerator>("SimpleEmail")
    .AddTokenProvider<PhoneConfirmationTokenGenerator>
        (TokenOptions.DefaultPhoneProvider)
    .AddSignInManager()
    .AddRoles<AppRole>();

    services.AddSingleton<IUserValidator<AppUser>, EmailValidator>();
    services.AddSingleton<IPasswordValidator<AppUser>, PasswordValidator>();
    services.AddSingleton<IUserClaimsPrincipalFactory<AppUser>,
        AppUserClaimsPrincipalFactory>();
    services.AddSingleton<IRoleValidator<AppRole>, RoleValidator>();

    services.AddAuthentication(opts => {
        opts.DefaultScheme = IdentityConstants.ApplicationScheme;
    }).AddCookie(IdentityConstants.ApplicationScheme, opts => {
        opts.LoginPath = "/signin";
        opts.AccessDeniedPath = "/signin/403";
    });
    services.AddAuthorization(opts => {
        AuthorizationPolicies.AddPolicies(opts);
    });
```

```
    services.AddRazorPages();
    services.AddControllersWithViews();
}
...
```

Restart ASP.NET Core and request http://localhost:5000/roles. Try to create a role named Users, and you will see the error message displayed in Figure 19-5 because there is already a role in the store named User.

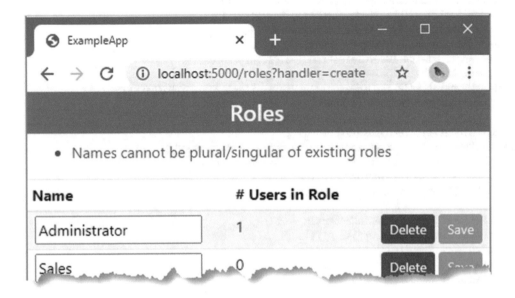

Figure 19-5. *Validating roles*

Enforcing Role Consistency

One reason to create a role store is to enforce consistency, ensuring that a typo doesn't assign a user to the wrong role. Identity doesn't provide built-in support for restricting roles to names that exist in the role store, but it is a simple process to implement manually. The first step is to restrict the roles to which users can be assigned, as shown in Listing 19-13.

Listing 19-13. Using the Role Store in the UserRoles.cshtml.cs File in the Pages/Store Folder

```
using ExampleApp.Identity;
using Microsoft.AspNetCore.Identity;
using Microsoft.AspNetCore.Mvc;
using Microsoft.AspNetCore.Mvc.RazorPages;
using System.Collections.Generic;
using System.Linq;
using System.Threading.Tasks;
using System.Security.Claims;
using Microsoft.AspNetCore.Mvc.Rendering;
```

```
namespace ExampleApp.Pages.Store {

    public class UserRolesModel : PageModel {

        public UserRolesModel(UserManager<AppUser> userManager,
                RoleManager<AppRole> roleManager) {
            UserManager = userManager;
            RoleManager = roleManager;
        }

        public UserManager<AppUser> UserManager { get; set; }
        public RoleManager<AppRole> RoleManager { get; set; }

        public IEnumerable<string> Roles { get; set; } = Enumerable.Empty<string>();
        public SelectList AvailableRoles { get; set; }

        [BindProperty(SupportsGet = true)]
        public string Id { get; set; }

        public async void OnGet() {
            AppUser user = await GetUser();
            if (user != null) {
                Roles = (await UserManager.GetClaimsAsync(user))
                    .Where(c => c.Type == ClaimTypes.Role).Select(c => c.Value);
                AvailableRoles = new SelectList(RoleManager.Roles
                    .OrderBy(r => r.Name)
                    .Select(r => r.Name).Except(Roles));
            }
        }

        public async Task<IActionResult> OnPostAdd(string newRole) {
            await UserManager.AddClaimAsync(await GetUser(),
                new Claim(ClaimTypes.Role, newRole));
            return RedirectToPage();
        }

        public async Task<IActionResult> OnPostDelete(string role) {
            await UserManager.RemoveFromRoleAsync(await GetUser(), role);
            return RedirectToPage();
        }

        private Task<AppUser> GetUser() => Id == null
            ? null : UserManager.FindByIdAsync(Id);
    }
}
```

The changes add a page model property named AvailableRoles, which provides a sequence of roles to which the user has not been assigned. Role membership is case-insensitive, but the UserManager<T> normalizes role names before they are added to the user store, so I have to compare the Name properties of the AppRole objects in the role store to populate the AvailableRoles property. Listing 19-14 uses a select element to constrain the roles that can be chosen.

■ **Note** I have used the Name, rather than the NormalizedName, properties in Listing 19-13 because of the way I worked around the normalized role name issue described in Chapter 17. If you decide to use normalized role names, then the NormalizedName property should be used to enforce role consistency.

Listing 19-14. Constraining Role Selection in the UserRoles.cshtml File in the Pages/Store Folder

```
@page "/users/roles/{id?}"
@model ExampleApp.Pages.Store.UserRolesModel

<h4 class="bg-primary text-white text-center p-2">Roles</h4>
<div class="m-2">
    <table class="table table-sm table-striped">
        <thead><tr><th>Role</th><th/></tr></thead>
        <tbody>
            @foreach (string role in Model.Roles) {
                <tr>
                    <td>@role</td>
                    <td>
                        <form method="post">
                            <input type="hidden" name="id" value="@Model.Id" />
                            <input type="hidden" name="role" value="@role" />
                            <button type="submit" class="btn btn-sm btn-danger"
                                    asp-page-handler="delete">
                                Delete
                            </button>
                        </form>
                    </td>
                </tr>
            }
            <tr>
                <td>
                    <form method="post" id="newRole">
                        <input type="hidden" name="id" value="@Model.Id" />
                        <select asp-items="@Model.AvailableRoles"
                            name="newRole" class="w-100">
                        </select>
                    </form>
                </td>
                <td>
                    <button type="submit" class="btn btn-sm btn-primary"
                            asp-page-handler="add" form="newRole">
                        Add
                    </button>
                </td>
            </tr>
        </tbody>
    </table>
```

```
<div>
    <a asp-page="users" class="btn btn-secondary">Back</a>
</div>
</div>
```

Restart ASP.NET Core, request http://localhost:5000/users, and click the Roles button for Alice. The select element only allows the user to be assigned to roles that are in the store, as shown in Figure 19-6.

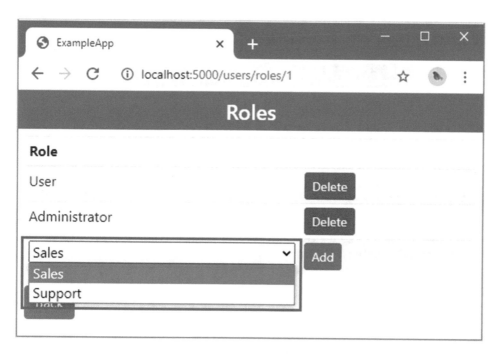

Figure 19-6. *Constraining role assignment*

Storing Claims with Roles

Roles can be assigned claims so that assigning a user to a role in the store gives the user the claims associated with that role. This is a useful way of managing complex sets of claims consistently and means that you don't have to manually add large sets of claims to individual users. In the sections that follow, I show you how to extend the role store to handle claims and explain how these claims are used.

Extending the Role Class

The first step is to add a property to the role class that will represent the claims associated with a role, as shown in Listing 19-15.

Listing 19-15. Adding a Property in the AppRole.cs File in the Identity Folder

```
using System;
using System.Collections.Generic;
using System.Security.Claims;

namespace ExampleApp.Identity {

    public class AppRole {

        public string Id { get; set; } = Guid.NewGuid().ToString();

        public string Name { get; set; }

        public string NormalizedName { get; set; }

        public IList<Claim> Claims { get; set; }
    }
}
```

Extending the Role Store

The IRoleClaimStore<T> interface is implemented by role stores that can manage claims, where T is the role class. The interface defines the methods described in Table 19-7. (The methods described in the table define a CancellationToken parameter. Unlike other interfaces, this parameter is optional.)

Table 19-7. *The IRoleClaimStore<T> Methods*

Name	Description
GetClaimsAsync(role)	This method returns the claims associated with the specified role.
AddClaimAsync(role. claim)	This method adds a claim to the specified role.
RemoveClaimAsync(role, claim)	This method removes a claim from the specified role.

To add claims support to the role store, add a class file named RoleStoreClaims.cs to the ExampleApp/Identity/Store folder and use it to define the partial class shown in Listing 19-16.

Listing 19-16. The Contents of the RoleStoreClaims.cs File in the Identity/Store Folder

```
using Microsoft.AspNetCore.Identity;
using System.Collections.Generic;
using System.Linq;
using System.Security.Claims;
using System.Threading;
using System.Threading.Tasks;
```

```
namespace ExampleApp.Identity.Store {
    public partial class RoleStore : IRoleClaimStore<AppRole> {

        public Task AddClaimAsync(AppRole role, Claim claim,
                CancellationToken token = default) {
            role.Claims.Add(claim);
            return Task.CompletedTask;
        }

        public Task<IList<Claim>> GetClaimsAsync(AppRole role,
                CancellationToken token = default) =>
            Task.FromResult(role.Claims ?? new List<Claim>());

        public Task RemoveClaimAsync(AppRole role, Claim claim,
                CancellationToken token = default) {
            role.Claims = role.Claims.Where(c => !(string.Equals(c.Type, claim.Type)
                && string.Equals(c.Value, claim.Value))).ToList<Claim>();
            return Task.CompletedTask;
        }
    }
}
```

The implementation of the interface uses the `Claims` property added to the `AppRole` class in Listing 19-16.

Extending the Claims Principal Factory

The claims associated with a role are processed by the claims principal factory. As I explained in Chapter 15, this is the connection point between Identity and the authorization features of ASP.NET Core. In Listing 19-17, I have updated the custom claims principal factory I created in Chapter 18 to get the roles to which the user has been assigned from the user store, retrieve the corresponding role from the role store, and process the role's claims.

Listing 19-17. Processing Role Claims in the AppUserClaimsPrincipalFactory.cs File in the Identity Folder

```
using Microsoft.AspNetCore.Builder;
using Microsoft.AspNetCore.Identity;
using System.Security.Claims;
using System.Threading.Tasks;

namespace ExampleApp.Identity {
    public class AppUserClaimsPrincipalFactory :
            IUserClaimsPrincipalFactory<AppUser> {

        public AppUserClaimsPrincipalFactory(UserManager<AppUser> userManager,
                RoleManager<AppRole> roleManager) {
            UserManager = userManager;
            RoleManager = roleManager;
        }

        public UserManager<AppUser> UserManager { get; set; }
        public RoleManager<AppRole> RoleManager { get; set; }
```

```
public async Task<ClaimsPrincipal> CreateAsync(AppUser user) {
    ClaimsIdentity identity
        = new ClaimsIdentity(IdentityConstants.ApplicationScheme);
    identity.AddClaims(new[] {
        new Claim(ClaimTypes.NameIdentifier, user.Id),
        new Claim(ClaimTypes.Name, user.UserName),
        new Claim(ClaimTypes.Email, user.EmailAddress)
    });
    if (!string.IsNullOrEmpty(user.Hobby)) {
        identity.AddClaim(new Claim("Hobby", user.Hobby));
    }
    if (!string.IsNullOrEmpty(user.FavoriteFood)) {
        identity.AddClaim(new Claim("FavoriteFood", user.FavoriteFood));
    }
    if (user.Claims != null) {
        identity.AddClaims(user.Claims);
    }

    if (UserManager.SupportsUserRole && RoleManager.SupportsRoleClaims) {
        foreach (string roleName in await UserManager.GetRolesAsync(user)) {
            AppRole role = await RoleManager.FindByNameAsync(roleName);
            if (role != null && role.Claims != null) {
                identity.AddClaims(role.Claims);
            }
        }
    }
    return new ClaimsPrincipal(identity);
    }
  }
}
```

The factory class was set up using the AddSingleton method in Listing 19-17, which was fine because the class didn't contain any features that prevented a single instance from processing concurrent requests. The changes in Listing 19-17 included dependencies on the UserManager<T> and RoleManager<T> services, both of which have a scope lifecycle. Since a singleton service cannot declare a dependency on a scoped service, I have to change the lifecycle of the factory class, as shown in Listing 19-18.

Listing 19-18. Changing a Service Lifecycle in the Startup.cs File in the ExampleApp Folder

```
...
services.AddSingleton<IUserValidator<AppUser>, EmailValidator>();
services.AddSingleton<IPasswordValidator<AppUser>, PasswordValidator>();
services.AddScoped<IUserClaimsPrincipalFactory<AppUser>,
    AppUserClaimsPrincipalFactory>();
services.AddSingleton<IRoleValidator<AppRole>, RoleValidator>();
...
```

Without this change, an exception will be thrown when ASP.NET Core starts because the dependency injection system won't be able to resolve the dependencies declared by the factory class.

Seeding the Role Store with Claims

To seed the store with claims, add the statements shown in Listing 19-19 to the RoleStore.cs file in the Identity/Store folder.

Listing 19-19. Seeding Claims in the RoleStore.cs File in the Identity/Store Folder

```
using Microsoft.AspNetCore.Identity;
using System.Collections.Generic;
using System.Security.Claims;
using System.Linq;

namespace ExampleApp.Identity.Store {

    public partial class RoleStore {

        public ILookupNormalizer Normalizer { get; set; }

        public RoleStore(ILookupNormalizer normalizer) {
            Normalizer = normalizer;
            SeedStore();
        }

        private void SeedStore() {

            var roleData = new List<string> {
                "Administrator", "User", "Sales", "Support"
            };

            var claims = new Dictionary<string, IEnumerable<Claim>> {
                { "Administrator", new [] { new Claim("AccessUserData", "true"),
                    new Claim(ClaimTypes.Role, "Support") } },
                { "Support", new [] { new Claim(ClaimTypes.Role, "User" )} }
            };

            int idCounter = 0;

            foreach (string roleName in roleData) {
                AppRole role = new AppRole {
                    Id = (++idCounter).ToString(),
                    Name = roleName,
                    NormalizedName = Normalizer.NormalizeName(roleName)
                };
                if (claims.ContainsKey(roleName)) {
                    role.Claims = claims[roleName].ToList<Claim>();
                }
                roles.TryAdd(role.Id, role);
            }
        }
    }
}
```

569

The changes create additional claims so that membership of the Administrator role, for example, will lead to an additional role claim for the Support role and an AccessUserData claim whose value is true (there is no meaning attributed to the AccessUserData claim, which I have created just to show that claims other than roles can be made).

Managing Claims

The RoleManager<T> class defines the members shown in Table 19-8 for managing the claims associated with a role.

Table 19-8. *The RoleManager<T> Members for Managing Claims*

Name	Description
SupportsRoleClaims	This property returns true if the role store implements the IRoleClaimStore<T> interface.
GetClaimsAsync(role)	This method returns the claims associated with the specified role by calling the store's GetClaimsAsync method.
AddClaimAsync(role, claim)	This method adds a claim to the specified role by calling the store's AddClaimAsync method. The role is subjected to validation, and the normalized name is set before being passed to the role store's UpdateAsync method.
RemoveClaimAsync(role, claim)	This method removes a claim from the specified role by calling the store's RemoveClaimAsync method. The role is subjected to validation, and the normalized name is set before being passed to the role store's UpdateAsync method.

To manage the claims associated with a role, add a Razor Page named RoleClaims.cshtml to the Pages/Store folder with the content shown in Listing 19-20.

Listing 19-20. The Contents of the RoleClaims.cshtml File in the Pages/Store Folder

```
@page "/roles/claims/{id?}"
@model ExampleApp.Pages.Store.RoleClaimsModel

@{ Claim newClaim = new Claim(string.Empty, string.Empty); }

<h4 class="bg-primary text-white text-center p-2">@Model.Role.Name Claims</h4>

<div class="m-2">
    <table class="table table-sm table-striped">
        <thead><tr><th>Type</th><th>Value</th><th/></tr></thead>
        <tbody>
            @foreach (Claim claim in Model.Claims) {
                <tr>
                    <partial name="_ClaimsRow"
                        model="@((Model.Role.Id, claim, false))" />
                </tr>
            }
```

```
            <tr>
                <partial name="_ClaimsRow"
                    model="@((Model.Role.Id, newClaim, true))" />
            </tr>
        </tbody>
    </table>
    <div>
        <a asp-page="roles" class="btn btn-secondary">Back</a>
    </div>
</div>
```

The view part of the Razor Page displays a sequence of claims provided by the page model class, using the _ClaimsRow.cshtml partial view. To create the page model that will provide the claims, add the code shown in Listing 19-21 to the RoleClaims.cshtml.cs file. (You will have to create this file if you are using Visual Studio Code.)

Listing 19-21. The Contents of the RoleClaims.cshtml.cs File in the Pages/Store Folder

```
using ExampleApp.Identity;
using Microsoft.AspNetCore.Identity;
using Microsoft.AspNetCore.Mvc;
using Microsoft.AspNetCore.Mvc.RazorPages;
using System.Collections.Generic;
using System.Linq;
using System.Security.Claims;
using System.Threading.Tasks;

namespace ExampleApp.Pages.Store {

    public class RoleClaimsModel : PageModel {

        public RoleClaimsModel(RoleManager<AppRole> roleManager)
            => RoleManager = roleManager;

        public RoleManager<AppRole> RoleManager { get; set; }

        public AppRole Role { get; set; }

        public IEnumerable<Claim> Claims => Role.Claims ?? new List<Claim>();

        public async Task OnGet(string id) {
            Role = await RoleManager.FindByIdAsync(id);
        }

        public async Task<IActionResult> OnPostAdd(string id, string type,
                string value) {
            Role = await RoleManager.FindByIdAsync(id);
            await RoleManager.AddClaimAsync(Role, new Claim(type, value));
            return RedirectToPage();
        }
```

```
        public async Task<IActionResult> OnPostEdit(string id, string type,
                string value, string oldType, string oldValue) {
            Role = await RoleManager.FindByIdAsync(id);
            await RoleManager.RemoveClaimAsync(Role, new Claim(oldType, oldValue));
            await RoleManager.AddClaimAsync(Role, new Claim(type, value));
            return RedirectToPage();
        }

        public async Task<IActionResult> OnPostDelete(string id, string type,
                string value) {
            Role = await RoleManager.FindByIdAsync(id);
            await RoleManager.RemoveClaimAsync(Role, new Claim(type, value));
            return RedirectToPage();
        }
    }
}
```

The page model class defines handler methods that add, edit, and delete claims, using the methods provided by the role manager class described in Table 19-8. To integrate the claim feature into the rest of the application, add the elements shown in Listing 19-22 to the Roles.cshtml file.

Listing 19-22. Integrating Claims into the Roles.cshtml File in the Pages/Store Folder

```
@page "/roles"
@model ExampleApp.Pages.Store.RolesModel

<h4 class="bg-secondary text-white text-center p-2">Roles</h4>

<div asp-validation-summary="All" class="text-danger m-2"></div>

<table class="table table-striped table-sm">
    <thead>
        <tr><th>Name</th><th># Users in Role</th><th># Claims</th><th/></tr>
    </thead>
    <tbody>
        @foreach (AppRole role in Model.Roles) {
            <tr>
                <td class="pl-2">
                    <input name="name" form="@role.Id" value="@role.Name" />
                </td>
                <td>@((await Model.GetUsersInRole(role)).Count())</td>
                <td>@(role.Claims?.Count() ?? 0)
                    <a asp-page="RoleClaims" class="btn btn-secondary btn-sm ml-2"
                        asp-route-id="@role.Id">Edit</a>
                </td>
                <td class="text-right pr-2">
                    <form method="post" id="@role.Id">
                        <input type="hidden" name="id" value="@role.Id" />
                        <button type="submit" class="btn btn-danger btn-sm"
                            asp-page-handler="delete">Delete</button>
```

```
                        <button type="submit" class="btn btn-info btn-sm"
                            asp-page-handler="save">Save</button>

                    </form>
                </td>
            </tr>
        }
        <tr>
            <td>
                <input name="name" form="newRole" placeholder="Enter Role Name" />
            </td>
            <td></td>
            <td></td>
            <td class="text-right pr-2">
                <form method="post" id="newRole">
                    <button type="submit" class="btn btn-info btn-sm"
                        asp-page-handler="create">
                        Create
                    </button>
                </form>
            </td>
        </tr>
    </tbody>
</table>
```

The number of claims for each role is displayed, along with an anchor element that navigates to the RoleClaims Razor Page.

Displaying Claims

To see the way that claims are assigned to the user, add a Razor Page named LiveClaims.cshtml to the Pages folder with the content shown in Listing 19-23.

Listing 19-23. The Contents of the LiveClaims.cshtml File in the Pages Folder

```
@page
@using System.Security.Claims
@using ExampleApp.Identity
@using Microsoft.AspNetCore.Identity
@inject UserManager<AppUser> UserManager

@{

    string GetName(string claimType) =>
            (Uri.IsWellFormedUriString(claimType, UriKind.Absolute)
                ? System.IO.Path.GetFileName(new Uri(claimType).LocalPath)
                : claimType);
}

<h4 class="bg-secondary text-white text-center p-2">
    Live Claims for @(User.Identity.Name ?? "No User")
</h4>
```

```
<table class="table table-sm table-striped table-bordered">
    <thead><tr><th>Type</th><th>Value</th></tr></thead>
    <tbody>
        @foreach (Claim claim in User.Claims) {
            <tr><td>@GetName(claim.Type)</td><td>@claim.Value</td></tr>
        }
    </tbody>
</table>
```

Restart ASP.NET Core, request `http://localhost:5000/signout`, and click the Sign Out button. Select alice@example.com from the list, enter **MySecret1$** into the password field, and click the Sign In button. Navigate to `http://localhost:5000/liveclaims`, and you will see the claims that have been created for the user, as shown in Figure 19-7.

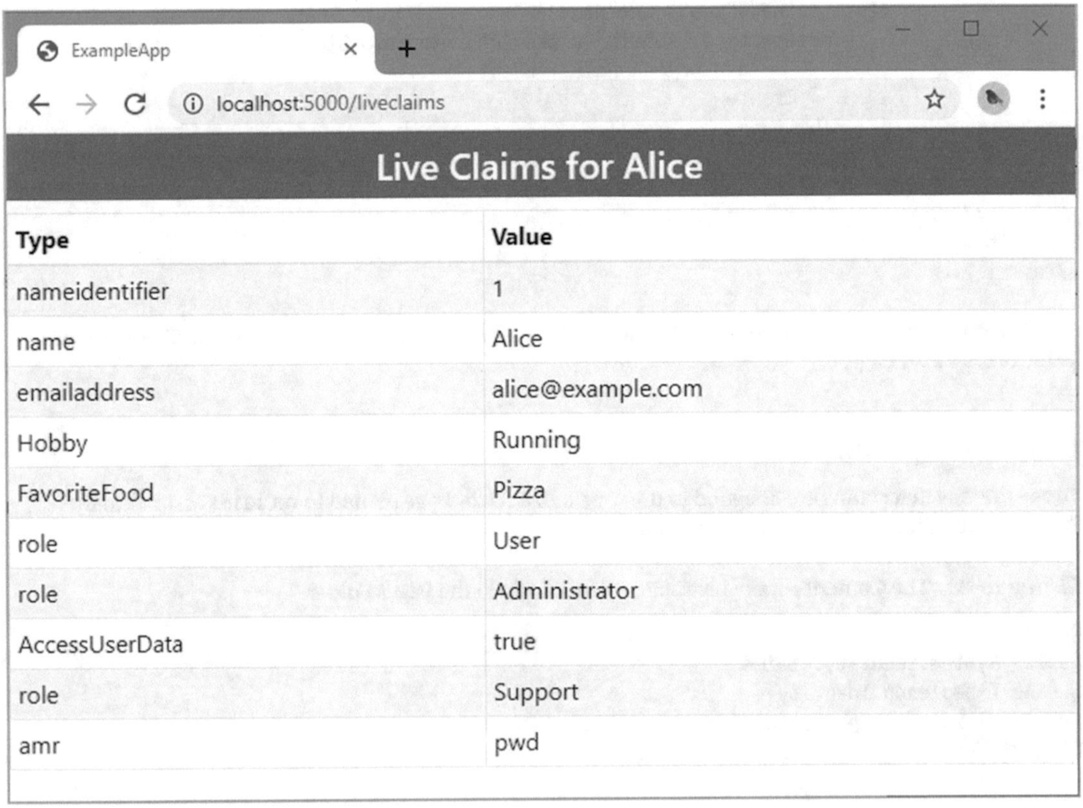

Figure 19-7. *Claims derived from roles*

As the figure shows, the set of claims created by the factory incorporates the additional role and the `AccessUserData` claims defined in the seed data.

■ **Note** One of the claims shown in Figure 19-7 has the type `amr` and the value `pwd`. This claim is created by the `SignInManager<T>` class, as I explain in Chapter 20.

574

It is important to remember that the claims principal factory is used only when a user signs in, which means that changes made to the claims in the role store do not take effect immediately. Request `http://localhost:5000/roles`, click the Edit button for the `Administrator` role, and create a Manager role claim, as shown in Figure 19-8.

Figure 19-8. *Adding a claim to a role*

Navigate to `http://localhost:5000/liveclaims`, and you will see the list of claims for Alice does not include the new role. Sign out of the application, sign in again, and request `http://localhost:5000/liveclaims`. During the signing-in process, the claims principal factory creates a new `ClaimsPrincipal` object containing the new role claim, as shown in Figure 19-9.

role	User
role	Administrator
AccessUserData	true
role	Support
role	Manager
amr	pwd

Figure 19-9. *The effect of signing in on claims*

Summary

In this chapter, I created a role store. I described the features that role stores provides. I demonstrated how to validate roles, how to use the role store to ensure consistency in role assignments, and how to store claims. In the next chapter, I describe how lockouts and two-factor authentication are implemented.

CHAPTER 20

■ ■ ■

Lockouts and Two-Factor Sign-Ins

In this chapter, I describe how account lockouts are supported and explain the mechanisms behind two-factor authentication. Table 20-1 puts these features into context.

Table 20-1. Putting Lockouts and Two-Factor Sign-Ins in Context

Question	Answer
What are they?	Lockouts prevent a user from signing in after a specified number of failed attempts. Two-factor sign-ins require the user to provide additional credentials during the sign-in process.
Why are they useful?	Both features are intended to improve security. Lockouts prevent attackers from repeatedly trying to guess passwords. Two-factor authentication requires attackers to have access to the user's additional credentials.
How are they used?	Both features are implemented using optional user store interfaces.
Are there any pitfalls or limitations?	Users can find both features frustrating, and it is important to make the workflows as clear and as easy to use as possible.
Are there any alternatives?	The best alternative is to use external authentication, where the process of identifying users is delegated to a third party. See Chapter 22 for details.

Table 20-2 summarizes the chapter.

Table 20-2. Chapter Summary

Problem	Solution	Listing
Support account lockouts	Implement the `IUserLockoutStore<T>` interface and use the user manager methods for management.	2–5, 7, 8
Configure lockouts	Use the options pattern.	6
Restrict access to confirmed accounts	Create an implementation of the `IUserConfirmation<T>` interface.	9–12
Support two-factor authentication	Implement the `IUserTwoFactorStore<T>` interface and use the methods defined by the sign-in manager to sign users in.	13–29

Preparing for This Chapter

This chapter uses the ExampleApp project from Chapter 19. No changes are required to prepare for this chapter. Open a new command prompt, navigate to the ExampleApp folder, and run the command shown in Listing 20-1 to start ASP.NET Core.

■ **Tip** You can download the example project for this chapter—and for all the other chapters in this book—from https://github.com/Apress/pro-asp.net-core-identity. See Chapter 1 for how to get help if you have problems running the examples.

Listing 20-1. Running the Example Application

```
dotnet run
```

Open a new browser window and request http://localhost:5000/users. You will be presented with the user data shown in Figure 20-1. The data is stored only in memory, and changes will be lost when ASP.NET Core is stopped.

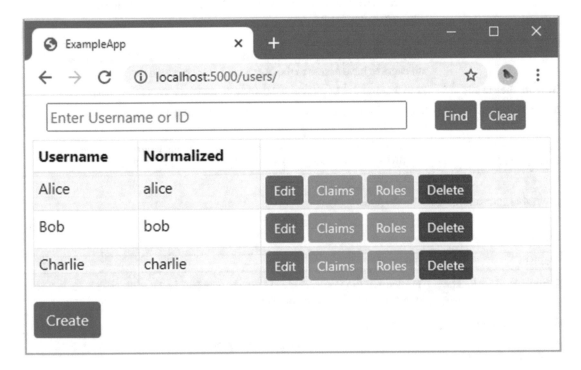

Figure 20-1. *Running the example application*

Enabling Lockouts

When account lockouts are used, Identity keeps track of how many failed attempts to sign in are made. If there are too many failed attempts in a short period, the account will be locked out, meaning that the user won't be signed in even if the correct password is provided. Lockouts are a useful feature for preventing attackers from repeatedly trying to guess a user's passwords, although care must be taken because lockouts can also be frustrating to legitimate users who can't remember their password. (It is for this reason that lockouts should be used with a relaxed password validation policy, as explained in Chapter 19.)

Extending the User Class

The first step is to extend the user class to add properties for keeping track of whether a user account supports lockouts and the current lockout status, as shown in Listing 20-2.

Listing 20-2. Adding Properties in the AppUser.cs File in the Identity Folder

```
using System;
using System.Collections.Generic;
using System.Security.Claims;

namespace ExampleApp.Identity {
    public class AppUser {

        public string Id { get; set; } = Guid.NewGuid().ToString();

        public string UserName { get; set; }

        public string NormalizedUserName { get; set; }

        public string EmailAddress { get; set; }
        public string NormalizedEmailAddress { get; set; }
        public bool EmailAddressConfirmed { get; set; }

        public string PhoneNumber { get; set; }
        public bool PhoneNumberConfirmed { get; set; }

        public string FavoriteFood { get; set; }
        public string Hobby { get; set; }

        public IList<Claim> Claims { get; set; }

        public string SecurityStamp { get; set; }
        public string PasswordHash { get; set; }

        public bool CanUserBeLockedout { get; set; } = true;
        public int FailedSignInCount { get; set; }
        public DateTimeOffset? LockoutEnd { get; set; }
    }
}
```

CanUserBeLockedout will be used to determine if a specific user can be locked out. The FailedSignInCount property will record how many failed sign-in attempts have been made. The LockoutEnd property will keep track of when a lockout will end and returns null when the user is not locked out.

Enabling Lockouts in the User Store

The next step is to extend the user store so that it implements the IUserLockoutStore<T> interface, where T is the user class. This interface defines the methods described in Table 20-3, which are used to keep track of failed sign-in attempts and whether an account is locked. As with the methods defined by other user store interfaces, the token parameter in Table 20-3 is a CancellationToken object that is used to receive notifications when an asynchronous operation is canceled.

Table 20-3. *The IUserLockoutStore<T> Methods*

Name	Description
GetLockoutEnabledAsync(user, token)	This method is used to determine if the specifier user is subject to lockouts.
SetLockoutEnabledAsync(user, enabled, token)	This method sets whether the specified user is subject to lockouts.
IncrementAccessFailedCountAsync(user, token)	This method increments the number of failed sign-in attempts for the specified user.
GetAccessFailedCountAsync(user, token)	This method returns the number of failed sign-in attempts for the specified user.
ResetAccessFailedCountAsync(user, token)	This method resets the number of failed sign-in attempts for the specified user.
SetLockoutEndDateAsync(user, end, token)	This method sets the end of the lockout period for the specified user, expressed as a DateTimeOffset value.
GetLockoutEndDateAsync(user, token)	This method gets the end of the lockout period for the specified user, expressed as a DateTimeOffset value.

The user store only has to keep track of the lockout data and is not responsible for interpreting the data or enforcing lockouts. Add a class file named UserStoreLockouts.cs to the ExmapleApp/Identity/Store folder and use it to define the partial class shown in Listing 20-3.

Listing 20-3. The Contents of the UserStoreLockouts.cs File in the Identity/Store Folder

```
using Microsoft.AspNetCore.Identity;
using System;
using System.Threading;
using System.Threading.Tasks;

namespace ExampleApp.Identity.Store {
    public partial class UserStore : IUserLockoutStore<AppUser> {
```

```
    public Task SetLockoutEnabledAsync(AppUser user, bool enabled,
            CancellationToken token) {
        user.CanUserBeLockedout = enabled;
        return Task.CompletedTask;
    }

    public Task<bool> GetLockoutEnabledAsync(AppUser user,
        CancellationToken token) => Task.FromResult(user.CanUserBeLockedout);

    public Task<int> GetAccessFailedCountAsync(AppUser user,
        CancellationToken token) => Task.FromResult(user.FailedSignInCount);

    public Task<int> IncrementAccessFailedCountAsync(AppUser user,
        CancellationToken token) => Task.FromResult( ++user.FailedSignInCount);

    public Task ResetAccessFailedCountAsync(AppUser user,
        CancellationToken token) {
            user.FailedSignInCount = 0;
            return Task.CompletedTask;
    }

    public Task SetLockoutEndDateAsync(AppUser user, DateTimeOffset? lockoutEnd,
            CancellationToken token) {
        user.LockoutEnd = lockoutEnd;
        return Task.CompletedTask;
    }

    public Task<DateTimeOffset?> GetLockoutEndDateAsync(AppUser user,
        CancellationToken token) => Task.FromResult(user.LockoutEnd);
    }
}
```

The interface implementation follows the pattern shown in earlier chapters and maps the methods described in Table 20-3 onto the properties added to the AppUser class.

Managing Account Lockouts

It is important to provide the means to end lockouts that have been triggered by accident. Applications that use lockouts but are deployed without manual overrides typically run into problems when a VIP user, such as the company CEO, locks themselves out of the application. Such users do not appreciate an explanation of your security policy and do not expect to wait until the lockout ends naturally. The UserManager<T> class provides a set of members for working with lockouts, as described in Table 20-4.

Table 20-4. *The UserManager<T> Members for Lockouts*

Name	Description
SupportsUserLockout	This property returns true if the user store implements the IUserLockoutStore<T> interface.
IsLockedOutAsync(user)	This method returns true if the specified user is locked out, which it does by calling the store's GetLockoutEnabledAsync method to see if the user is subject to lockouts and then the store's GetLockoutEndDateAsync method to see if there is a lockout in place.
SetLockoutEnabledAsync (user, enabled)	This method calls the store's SetLockoutEnabledAsync method for the specified user and then performs user validation, updates the normalized username and email address, and then applies the user manager's update sequence.
GetLockoutEnabledAsync(user)	This method calls the store's GetLockoutEnabledAsync method for the specified user.
GetLockoutEndDateAsync(user)	This method calls the store's GetLockoutEndDateAsync method for the specified user.
SetLockoutEndDateAsync(user, end)	This method calls the store's SetLockoutEndDateAsync method for the specified user and then performs user validation, updates the normalized username and email address, and applies the user manager's update sequence.
AccessFailedAsync(user)	This method increments the failed sign-in counter for the specified user by calling the store's IncrementAccessFailedCountAsync method. If the number of failed attempts exceeds the configuration setting (described in the next section), the store's SetLockoutEndDateAsync method is called to lock the account, after which user validation is performed and the user manager's update sequence is applied. The number of failed attempts is reset when the account is locked.
GetAccessFailedCountAsync(user)	This method returns the number of failed attempts for the specified user by calling the user store's GetAccessFailedCountAsync method.
ResetAccessFailedCountAsync(user)	This method calls the store's ResetAccessFailedCountAsync method, performs user validation, and then applies the user manager's update sequence.

For the most part, the methods in Table 20-4 map directly onto the methods implemented by the user store. The exception is the AccessFailedAsync method, which increments the failed sign-in counter until it reaches a configured limit, after which the account is put into lockout.

Add a Razor Page named UserLockouts.cshtml to the ExampleApp/Pages/Store folder, with the contents shown in Listing 20-4.

Listing 20-4. The Contents of the UserLockouts.cshtml File in the Pages/Store Folder

```
@page "/users/lockout"
@model ExampleApp.Pages.Store.UserLockoutsModel

<h4 class="bg-primary text-white text-center p-2">User Lockouts</h4>
```

```
<div class="m-2">
    <table class="table table-sm table-striped">
        <thead><tr><th>Username</th><th>Lockout</th><th/></tr></thead>
        <tbody>
            @foreach (AppUser user in Model.Users) {
                <tr>
                    <td>@user.UserName</td>
                    <td>@(await Model.GetLockoutStatus(user))</td>
                    <td>
                        <form method="post">
                            <input type="hidden" name="id" value="@user.Id" />
                            @if (await Model.UserManager.IsLockedOutAsync(user)) {
                                <button class="btn btn-sm btn-secondary"
                                        type="submit">
                                    Unlock
                                </button>
                            } else {
                                <span class="mx-1">
                                    <input type="number" name="mins" value="10" />
                                    mins
                                </span>
                                <button class="btn btn-sm btn-danger" type="submit">
                                    Lock
                                </button>
                            }
                        </form>
                    </td>
                </tr>
            }
        </tbody>
    </table>
</div>
```

The content presents a list of users, with buttons that lock and unlock accounts. To define the page model, add the code shown in Listing 20-5 to the UserLockouts.cshtml.cs file. (You will have to create this file if you are using Visual Studio Code.)

Listing 20-5. The Contents of the UserLockouts.cshtml.cs File in the Pages/Store Folder

```
using ExampleApp.Identity;
using Microsoft.AspNetCore.Identity;
using Microsoft.AspNetCore.Mvc;
using Microsoft.AspNetCore.Mvc.RazorPages;
using System;
using System.Collections.Generic;
using System.Linq;
using System.Threading.Tasks;

namespace ExampleApp.Pages.Store {

    public class UserLockoutsModel : PageModel {
```

```
public UserLockoutsModel(UserManager<AppUser> manager)
    => UserManager = manager;

public UserManager<AppUser> UserManager { get; set; }

public IEnumerable<AppUser> Users => UserManager.Users
    .OrderByDescending(u => UserManager.IsLockedOutAsync(u).Result)
    .ThenBy(u => u.UserName);

public async Task<string> GetLockoutStatus(AppUser user) {
    if (await UserManager.IsLockedOutAsync(user)) {
        TimeSpan remaining = (await UserManager.GetLockoutEndDateAsync(user))
            .GetValueOrDefault().Subtract(DateTimeOffset.Now);
        return $"Locked Out ({ remaining.Minutes } mins "
            + $"{ remaining.Seconds} secs remaining)";
    }
    return "(No Lockout)";
}

public async Task<IActionResult> OnPost(string id, int mins) {
    await UserManager.SetLockoutEndDateAsync((await
        UserManager.FindByIdAsync(id)), DateTimeOffset.Now.AddMinutes(mins));
    return RedirectToPage();
}
    }
}
```

The page model class performs a LINQ query to provide the view with users sorted by their lockout status and defines a POST handler method that locks or unlocks accounts by calling the SetLockoutEndDateAsync method. When an account is unlocked, the end of the lockout period is set to the current time. When an account is locked, the end of the lockout period is set to the number of minutes into the future specified in the HTTP request.

Configuring Lockouts

The options pattern is used to configure the lockout feature. The IdentityOptions class that is used to configure Identity defines a Lockout property that returns a LockoutOptions object. The LockoutOptions class defines the properties described in Table 20-5.

Table 20-5. *The LockoutOptions Properties*

Name	Description
AllowedForNewUsers	This property specifies whether newly created user accounts will be subject to lockouts. The default value is true.
MaxFailedAccessAttempts	This property specifies how many failed attempts are allowed before a lockout. The default value is 5.
DefaultLockoutTimeSpan	This property specifies the default lockout duration, expressed as a TimeSpan. The default value is 5 minutes.

In Listing 20-6, I have used the options pattern to reduce the number of failed sign-in attempts that trigger a lockout.

Listing 20-6. Configuring Lockouts in the Startup.cs File in the ExampleApp Folder

```
...
services.AddIdentityCore<AppUser>(opts => {
    opts.Tokens.EmailConfirmationTokenProvider = "SimpleEmail";
    opts.Tokens.ChangeEmailTokenProvider = "SimpleEmail";
    opts.Tokens.PasswordResetTokenProvider =
        TokenOptions.DefaultPhoneProvider;

    opts.Password.RequireNonAlphanumeric = false;
    opts.Password.RequireLowercase = false;
    opts.Password.RequireUppercase = false;
    opts.Password.RequireDigit = false;
    opts.Password.RequiredLength = 8;
    opts.Lockout.MaxFailedAccessAttempts = 3;
})
.AddTokenProvider<EmailConfirmationTokenGenerator>("SimpleEmail")
.AddTokenProvider<PhoneConfirmationTokenGenerator>
    (TokenOptions.DefaultPhoneProvider)
.AddSignInManager()
.AddRoles<AppRole>();
...
```

Displaying a Lockout Notification

The final step is to make it obvious to the user when a lockout has been applied to their account. Not all applications provide this notification, but it offers the advantage of making it obvious to the user that further attempts to enter the password won't succeed. In Listing 20-7, I have modified the page model class for the SignIn Razor Page so that its view includes an error message, through which I provide details of lockouts.

Listing 20-7. Providing Lockout Details in the SignIn.cshtml.cs File in the Pages Folder

```
using Microsoft.AspNetCore.Authentication;
using Microsoft.AspNetCore.Http;
using Microsoft.AspNetCore.Mvc;
using Microsoft.AspNetCore.Mvc.RazorPages;
using Microsoft.AspNetCore.Mvc.Rendering;
using System.Security.Claims;
using System.Threading.Tasks;
using Microsoft.AspNetCore.Identity;
using System.Linq;
using ExampleApp.Identity;
using SignInResult = Microsoft.AspNetCore.Identity.SignInResult;
using System;

namespace ExampleApp.Pages {
    public class SignInModel : PageModel {
```

```
public SignInModel(UserManager<AppUser> userManager,
SignInManager<AppUser> signInManager) {
    UserManager = userManager;
    SignInManager = signInManager;
}

public UserManager<AppUser> UserManager { get; set; }
public SignInManager<AppUser> SignInManager { get; set; }

public SelectList Users => new SelectList(
    UserManager.Users.OrderBy(u => u.EmailAddress),
        "EmailAddress", "NormalizedEmailAddress");

public string Username { get; set; }

public int? Code { get; set; }

public string Message { get; set; }

public void OnGet(int? code) {
    if (code == StatusCodes.Status401Unauthorized) {
        Message = "401 - Challenge Response";
    } else if (code == StatusCodes.Status403Forbidden) {
        Message = "403 - Forbidden Response";
    }
    Username = User.Identity.Name ?? "(No Signed In User)";
}

public async Task<ActionResult> OnPost(string username,
        string password, [FromQuery] string returnUrl) {
    SignInResult result = SignInResult.Failed;
    AppUser user = await UserManager.FindByEmailAsync(username);
    if (user != null && !string.IsNullOrEmpty(password)) {
        result = await SignInManager.PasswordSignInAsync(user, password,
            false, true);
    }
    if (!result.Succeeded) {
        if (result.IsLockedOut) {
            TimeSpan remaining = (await UserManager
                .GetLockoutEndDateAsync(user))
                .GetValueOrDefault().Subtract(DateTimeOffset.Now);
            Message = $"Locked Out for {remaining.Minutes} mins and"
                + $" {remaining.Seconds} secs";
        } else {
            Message = "Access Denied";
        }
        return Page();
    }
    return Redirect(returnUrl ?? "/signin");
}
}
}
}
```

If the result from the SignInManager<T>.PasswordSignInAsync method reports that the user is locked out, then I get the end time and work out how many minutes and seconds remain. In Listing 20-8, I have updated the view part of the Razor Page to display the Message property defined in Listing 20-7, instead of using the Code property to create its message strings.

Listing 20-8. Updating the View in the SignIn.cshtml File in the Pages/Store Folder

```
@page "{code:int?}"
@model ExampleApp.Pages.SignInModel
@using Microsoft.AspNetCore.Http

@if (!string.IsNullOrEmpty(Model.Message)) {
    <h3 class="bg-danger text-white text-center p-2">
        @Model.Message
    </h3>
}

<h4 class="bg-info text-white m-2 p-2">
    Current User: @Model.Username
</h4>

<div class="m-2">
    <form method="post">
        <div class="form-group">
            <label>User</label>
            <select class="form-control"
                    asp-for="Username" asp-items="@Model.Users">
            </select>
        </div>
        <div class="form-group">
            <label>Password</label>
            <input class="form-control" type="password" name="password" />
        </div>
        <button class="btn btn-info" type="submit">Sign In</button>
        @if (User.Identity.IsAuthenticated) {
            <a asp-page="/Store/PasswordChange" class="btn btn-secondary"
                asp-route-id="@Model.User?
                        .FindFirst(ClaimTypes.NameIdentifier)?.Value">
                Change Password
            </a>
        } else {
            <a class="btn btn-secondary" href="/password/reset">
                Reset Password
            </a>
        }
    </form>
</div>
```

Restart ASP.NET Core and request http://localhost:5000/signin. Repeatedly enter an incorrect password and click the Sign In button. An "access denied" message is displayed for the first two failed attempts. After the third failed attempt, the account will be locked, and the remaining time displayed, as shown in Figure 20-2.

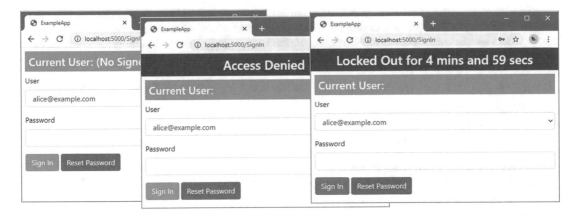

Figure 20-2. *Displaying lockouts to the user*

Restricting Signing In to Confirmed Accounts

The SignInManager<T> class performs a pre-signing check to make sure that accounts are not blocked. In addition to lockouts, accounts that have not been confirmed, or whose email or phone number has not been confirmed, can be blocked. This feature is enabled using the options pattern, where the IdentityOptions. SignIn property returns an instance of the SignInOptions class, which defines the properties described in Table 20-6.

Table 20-6. *SignInOptions Properties*

Name	Description
RequireConfirmedEmail	When this property is true, only accounts with confirmed email addresses can sign in. The email address confirmation is determined by calling the UserManager<T>.IsEmailConfirmedAsync method. The default value is false.
RequireConfirmedPhoneNumber	When this property is true, only accounts with confirmed phone numbers can sign in. I have not demonstrated support for phone numbers, but the process is similar to email address confirmation. The phone number confirmation is determined by calling the UserManager<T>.IsPhoneNumberConfirmedAsync method. The default value is false.
RequireConfirmedAccount	When this property is true, only confirmed accounts can sign in. Confirmation status is determined using the IUserConfirmation<T> interface, described after the table. The default implementation of this interface checks that the user's email address is confirmed, which means that this setting is the same as the RequireConfirmedEmail setting unless a custom implementation of the interface is used. The default value is false.

The most interesting of the properties described in Table 20-6 is RequireConfirmedAccount, which allows custom confirmation criteria to be defined through the IUserConfirmation<T> interface, which defines the method described in Table 20-7.

Table 20-7. *The IUserConfirmation<T> Method*

Name	Description
IsConfirmedAsync(userManager, user)	This method returns a bool indicating whether the specified user is confirmed.

T is the user class, and the IsConfirmedAsync method receives a UserManager<T> object and the user object to validate. Any confirmation criteria can be used in a custom implementation of the IUserConfirmation<T> interface.

Add a class file named UserConfirmation.cs to the ExampleApp/Identity folder with the contents shown in Listing 20-9.

Listing 20-9. The Contents of the UserConfirmation.cs File in the Identity Folder

```
using Microsoft.AspNetCore.Identity;
using System.Linq;
using System.Threading.Tasks;

namespace ExampleApp.Identity {
    public class UserConfirmation : IUserConfirmation<AppUser> {

        public async Task<bool> IsConfirmedAsync(UserManager<AppUser> manager,
                AppUser user) =>
            await manager.IsInRoleAsync(user, "Administrator")
                || (await manager.GetClaimsAsync(user))
                    .Any(claim => claim.Type == "UserConfirmed"
                        && string.Compare(claim.Value, "true", true) == 0);
    }
}
```

The IsConfirmedAsync method allows users to sign in if they have been assigned the Administrator role or have a UserConfirmed claim whose value is true. In Listing 20-10, I have extended the set of claims that can be assigned to a user to include UserConfirmed claims.

Listing 20-10. Adding a Claim Type in the _ClaimsRow.cshtml File in the Pages/Store Folder

```
@model (string id, Claim claim, bool newClaim)

@{ string hash = Model.claim.GetHashCode().ToString(); }

<td>
    <form method="post" id="@hash">
        <input type="hidden" name="id" value="@Model.id" />
        <input type="hidden" name="oldtype" value="@Model.claim.Type" />
        <input type="hidden" name="oldValue" value="@Model.claim.Value" />
    </form>
    <select name="type" asp-for="claim.Type" form="@hash">
        <option value="@ClaimTypes.Role">ROLE</option>
        <option value="@ClaimTypes.GivenName">GIVENNAME</option>
```

```
            <option value="@ClaimTypes.Surname">SURNAME</option>
            <option value="UserConfirmed">UserConfirmed</option>
        </select>
</td>
<td>
    <input class="w-100" name="value" value="@Model.claim.Value" form="@hash" />
</td>
<td>
    <button asp-page-handler="@(Model.newClaim ? "add" : "edit")"
        form="@hash" type="submit" class="btn btn-sm btn-info">
            @(Model.newClaim ? "Add" : "Save")
    </button>
    @if (!Model.newClaim) {
        <button asp-page-handler="delete" form="@hash" type="submit"
            class="btn btn-sm btn-danger">Delete</button>
    }
</td>
```

In Listing 20-11, I have updated the page model class for the SignIn Razor Page to check the
SignInResult.IsNotAllowed property in the result produced by the SignInManager, which will be true
when the user doesn't meet the confirmation criteria specified by the properties in Table 20-7.

Listing 20-11. Displaying a Message in the SignIn.cshtml.cs File in the Pages Folder

```
...
public async Task<ActionResult> OnPost(string username,
        string password, [FromQuery] string returnUrl) {
    SignInResult result = SignInResult.Failed;
    AppUser user = await UserManager.FindByEmailAsync(username);
    if (user != null && !string.IsNullOrEmpty(password)) {
        result = await SignInManager.PasswordSignInAsync(user, password,
            false, true);
    }
    if (!result.Succeeded) {
        if (result.IsLockedOut) {
            TimeSpan remaining = (await UserManager
                .GetLockoutEndDateAsync(user))
                .GetValueOrDefault().Subtract(DateTimeOffset.Now);
            Message = $"Locked Out for {remaining.Minutes} mins and"
                + $" {remaining.Seconds} secs";
        } else if (result.IsNotAllowed) {
            Message = "Sign In Not Allowed";
        } else {
            Message = "Access Denied";
        }
        return Page();
    }
    return Redirect(returnUrl ?? "/signin");
}
...
```

The final step is to register the UserConfirmation class as a service and enable its use through the options pattern, as shown in Listing 20-12.

Listing 20-12. Configuring the Application in the Startup.cs File in the ExampleApp Folder

```
...
public void ConfigureServices(IServiceCollection services) {
    services.AddSingleton<ILookupNormalizer, Normalizer>();
    services.AddSingleton<IUserStore<AppUser>, UserStore>();
    services.AddSingleton<IEmailSender, ConsoleEmailSender>();
    services.AddSingleton<ISMSSender, ConsoleSMSSender>();
    //services.AddSingleton<IUserClaimsPrincipalFactory<AppUser>,
    //    AppUserClaimsPrincipalFactory>();
    services.AddSingleton<IPasswordHasher<AppUser>, SimplePasswordHasher>();
    services.AddSingleton<IRoleStore<AppRole>, RoleStore>();
    services.AddSingleton<IUserConfirmation<AppUser>, UserConfirmation>();

    services.AddIdentityCore<AppUser>(opts => {
        opts.Tokens.EmailConfirmationTokenProvider = "SimpleEmail";
        opts.Tokens.ChangeEmailTokenProvider = "SimpleEmail";
        opts.Tokens.PasswordResetTokenProvider =
            TokenOptions.DefaultPhoneProvider;

        opts.Password.RequireNonAlphanumeric = false;
        opts.Password.RequireLowercase = false;
        opts.Password.RequireUppercase = false;
        opts.Password.RequireDigit = false;
        opts.Password.RequiredLength = 8;
        opts.Lockout.MaxFailedAccessAttempts = 3;
        opts.SignIn.RequireConfirmedAccount = true;
    })
    .AddTokenProvider<EmailConfirmationTokenGenerator>("SimpleEmail")
    .AddTokenProvider<PhoneConfirmationTokenGenerator>
        (TokenOptions.DefaultPhoneProvider)
    .AddSignInManager()
    .AddRoles<AppRole>();

    services.AddSingleton<IUserValidator<AppUser>, EmailValidator>();
    services.AddSingleton<IPasswordValidator<AppUser>, PasswordValidator>();
    services.AddScoped<IUserClaimsPrincipalFactory<AppUser>,
        AppUserClaimsPrincipalFactory>();
    services.AddSingleton<IRoleValidator<AppRole>, RoleValidator>();

    services.AddAuthentication(opts => {
        opts.DefaultScheme = IdentityConstants.ApplicationScheme;
    }).AddCookie(IdentityConstants.ApplicationScheme, opts => {
        opts.LoginPath = "/signin";
        opts.AccessDeniedPath = "/signin/403";
    });
    services.AddAuthorization(opts => {
        AuthorizationPolicies.AddPolicies(opts);
    });
```

```
    services.AddRazorPages();
    services.AddControllersWithViews();
}
...
```

Restart ASP.NET Core and request http://localhost:5000/signin. Sign into the application as bob@example.com with the password MySecret1$, and you will see the error message shown in Figure 20-3, which is shown because Bob has not been assigned the Administrator role and does not have the UserConfirmed claim.

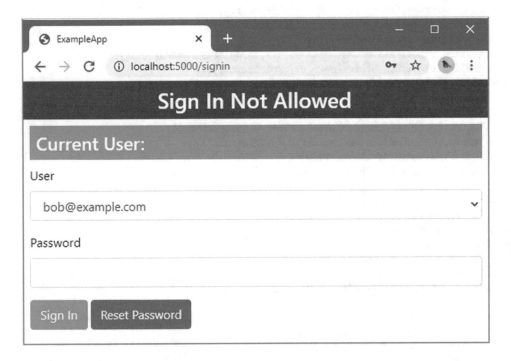

Figure 20-3. Preventing signing in with a custom confirmation requirement

Navigate to http://localhost:5000/users, click the Claims button for Bob, and add a UserConfirmed claim with a value of true. Return to http://localhost:5000/signin and repeat the sign-in process for Bob. Now that the user has been given the claim, the custom confirmation requirement will be satisfied, and sign-in will be permitted, as shown in Figure 20-4.

Figure 20-4. *Meeting the custom confirmation requirement*

Using Two-Factor Authentication

Two-factor authentication, often referred to as *2FA*, requires the user to provide two forms of evidence, known as *factors*, to prove their identity to the application when signing in. To make it more difficult to impersonate the user, the factors are generally chosen from different categories in the following list:

- *Something the user knows*: This is generally a password.

- *Something the user has:* This can be a security token, a specific device, a swipe card, or a security key.

- *Something inherent to the user:* This is typically addressed using a physical characteristic, such as a fingerprint or iris scan, or facial renunciation.

There is wide scope for each category. An inherent characteristic could be the user's location, for example, although this can be difficult to establish.

The most common combination is something the user knows and something the user has, and this is generally implemented as a password and a specific device. In this chapter, I show you how to use confirmation codes as the second factor, which relies on the user having a specific phone number to receive the codes via SMS. In Chapter 21, I show you how to use an authenticator application, which is a more sophisticated alternative.

MULTIFACTOR VS. TWO-FACTOR AUTHENTICATION

Recently, the term *two-factor* has been replaced by *multifactor*, which is intended to indicate that some situations may require more than two factors to provide an acceptable level of protection.

This is well-intentioned, but each additional requirement you add makes it more difficult for legitimate users to sign in and adds to the application's support and administration overhead.

My advice is to start with two factors and get the behaviors established with your users before attempting to ratchet up the security with additional factors. And, as I have already noted, the harder you make it to use an application, the more effort your users will make to subvert your security policies. There are no benefits to three or more factors if you don't have the willing cooperation of your users.

Updating the User Class

Identity allows two-factor authentication to be configured for individual users. To keep track of two-factor authentication, add the property shown in Listing 20-13 to the AppUser class.

Listing 20-13. Adding a Property in the AppUser.cs File in the Identity Folder

```
using System;
using System.Collections.Generic;
using System.Security.Claims;

namespace ExampleApp.Identity {
    public class AppUser {

        public string Id { get; set; } = Guid.NewGuid().ToString();

        public string UserName { get; set; }

        public string NormalizedUserName { get; set; }

        public string EmailAddress { get; set; }
        public string NormalizedEmailAddress { get; set; }
        public bool EmailAddressConfirmed { get; set; }

        public string PhoneNumber { get; set; }
        public bool PhoneNumberConfirmed { get; set; }

        public string FavoriteFood { get; set; }
        public string Hobby { get; set; }

        public IList<Claim> Claims { get; set; }

        public string SecurityStamp { get; set; }
        public string PasswordHash { get; set; }

        public bool CanUserBeLockedout { get; set; } = true;
        public int FailedSignInCount { get; set; }
        public DateTimeOffset? LockoutEnd { get; set; }

        public bool TwoFactorEnabled { get; set; }
    }
}
```

In Listing 20-14, I have updated the seed data added to the store to set the two-factor property for the example users.

Listing 20-14. Updating the Seed Data in the UserStore.cs File in the Identity/Store Folder

```
...
private void SeedStore() {

    var customData = new Dictionary<string, (string food, string hobby)> {
        { "Alice", ("Pizza", "Running") },
        { "Bob", ("Ice Cream", "Cinema") },
        { "Charlie", ("Burgers", "Cooking") }
    };
    var twoFactorUsers = new[] { "Alice", "Charlie" };
    int idCounter = 0;

    string EmailFromName(string name) => $"{name.ToLower()}@example.com";

    foreach (string name in UsersAndClaims.Users) {
        AppUser user = new AppUser {
            Id = (++idCounter).ToString(),
            UserName = name,
            NormalizedUserName = Normalizer.NormalizeName(name),
            EmailAddress = EmailFromName(name),
            NormalizedEmailAddress =
                Normalizer.NormalizeEmail(EmailFromName(name)),
            EmailAddressConfirmed = true,
            PhoneNumber = "123-4567",
            PhoneNumberConfirmed = true,
            FavoriteFood = customData[name].food,
            Hobby = customData[name].hobby,
            SecurityStamp = "InitialStamp",
            TwoFactorEnabled = twoFactorUsers.Any(tfName => tfName == name)
        };
        user.Claims =  UsersAndClaims.UserData[user.UserName]
            .Select(role => new Claim(ClaimTypes.Role, role)).ToList();
        user.PasswordHash = PasswordHasher.HashPassword(user, "MySecret1$");
        users.TryAdd(user.Id, user);
    }
}
...
```

The changes enable two-factor authentication for Alice and Charlie.

Extending the User Store to Support Two-Factor Authentication

The next step is to extend the user store to implement the IUserTwoFactorStore<T> interface, which is used to keep track of which users are required to use two-factor authentication and which defines the methods described in Table 20-8. As with all the other user store interfaces I have described, these methods define a CancellationToken parameter named token that is used to receive a notification when an asynchronous task is canceled.

Table 20-8. *The IUserTwoFactorStore<T> Methods*

Name	Description
GetTwoFactorEnabledAsync(user, token)	This method returns true if the specified user should use two-factor authentication.
SetTwoFactorEnabledAsync(user, enabled, token)	This method sets the two-factor authentication requirement for the specified user.

Add a class file named UserStoreTwoFactor.cs to the ExampleApp/Identity/Store folder and use it to define the partial class shown in Listing 20-15.

Listing 20-15. The Contents of the UserStoreTwoFactor.cs File in the Identity/Store Folder

```
using Microsoft.AspNetCore.Identity;
using System.Threading;
using System.Threading.Tasks;

namespace ExampleApp.Identity.Store {
    public partial class UserStore : IUserTwoFactorStore<AppUser> {

        public Task<bool> GetTwoFactorEnabledAsync(AppUser user,
            CancellationToken token) => Task.FromResult(user.TwoFactorEnabled);

        public Task SetTwoFactorEnabledAsync(AppUser user, bool enabled,
                CancellationToken token) {
            user.TwoFactorEnabled = enabled;
            return Task.CompletedTask;
        }
    }
}
```

The implementation of the interface maps the methods described in Table 20-8 into the property added to the AppUser class in the previous section.

USING SMS FOR TWO-FACTOR AUTHENTICATION

There are differing opinions about the use of SMS for two-factor authentication. Without a doubt, SMS is susceptible to a range of attacks, and there have been documented examples of phones being cloned or transferred so that confirmation codes can be intercepted.

On the other hand, SMS is cheap, effective, and almost universally available. Smartphone authenticators (described in Chapter 21) or hardware security tokens may be more secure, but not all users have smartphones, and not all projects can supply users with tokens.

There were headlines in 2016 when a draft document from the National Institute of Standards and Technology (NIST) deprecated the use of SMS for two-factor authentication, and this has led some to believe that SMS should no longer be used. However, in the final release of that document, SMS was not deprecated, but attention was drawn to the risks inherent in SMS, such as SIM changes and phone number porting. (See https://pages.nist.gov/800-63-3 for details.)

You should perform risk assessments for your projects, but my advice is not to dismiss SMS unless you have a well-understood security requirement and have tight control over the devices your users carry and the apps they can install.

Managing Two-Factor Authentication

The UserManager<T> method provides a set of members for managing the two-factor authentication settings in the user store, as described in Table 20-9.

Table 20-9. *The UserManager<T> members for Managing Two-Factor Authentication*

Name	Description
SupportsUserTwoFactor	This property returns true if the user store implements the IUserTwoFactorStore<T> interface, where T is the user class.
GetTwoFactorEnabledAsync(user)	This method calls the user store's GetTwoFactorEnabledAsync method to get the two-factor setting for the specified user.
SetTwoFactorEnabledAsync(user, enabled)	This method sets the two-factor setting for the specified user by calling the user store's SetTwoFactorEnabledAsync method, after which the security stamp is updated, and the user manager's update sequence is performed.
GenerateTwoFactorTokenAsync(user, provider)	This method generates a security token that the user will provide to identify themselves in the final step of the process described in the next section.

The UserManager<T> class provides only basic features because the important two-factor features are handled by the SignInManager<T> class, which I describe shortly. To manage the two-factor authentication settings, add a Razor View named _EditUserTwoFactor.cshtml to the ExampleApp/Pages/Store folder with the content shown in Listing 20-16.

Listing 20-16. The Contents of the _EditUserTwoFactor.cshtml File in the Pages/Store Folder

```
@model AppUser
@inject UserManager<AppUser> UserManager

@if (UserManager.SupportsUserTwoFactor) {
    <tr>
        <td>Two-Factor</td>
        <td><input asp-for="TwoFactorEnabled"/></td>
    </tr>
}
```

Following the pattern used throughout this part of the book, I am working directly with the properties defined by the AppUser class and not the methods described in Table 20-9, although I use the SupportsUserTwoFactor property to confirm that the user store supports two-factor settings. Add the element shown in Listing 20-17 to the EditUser.cshtml file to incorporate the new view into the application.

Listing 20-17. Adding a Partial View in the EditUser.cshtml File in the Pages/Store Folder

```
@page "/users/edit/{id?}"
@model ExampleApp.Pages.Store.UsersModel

<div asp-validation-summary="All" class="text-danger m-2"></div>

<div class="m-2">
    <form method="post">
        <input type="hidden" name="id" value="@Model.AppUserObject.Id" />
        <table class="table table-sm table-striped">
            <tbody>
                <partial name="_EditUserBasic" model="@Model.AppUserObject" />
                <partial name="_EditUserEmail" model="@Model.AppUserObject" />
                <partial name="_EditUserPhone" model="@Model.AppUserObject" />
                <partial name="_EditUserCustom" model="@Model.AppUserObject" />
                <partial name="_EditUserPassword" model="@Model.AppUserObject" />
                <partial name="_EditUserTwoFactor" model="@Model.AppUserObject" />
                <partial name="_EditUserSecurityStamp"
                        model="@Model.AppUserObject" />
            </tbody>
        </table>
        <div>
            <button type="submit" class="btn btn-primary">Save</button>
            <a asp-page="users" class="btn btn-secondary">Cancel</a>
        </div>
    </form>
</div>
```

Restart ASP.NET Core, request `http://localhost:5000/users`, and click the Edit button for one of the users. You will see a checkbox that allows the two-factor authentication option to be changed, as shown in Figure 20-5.

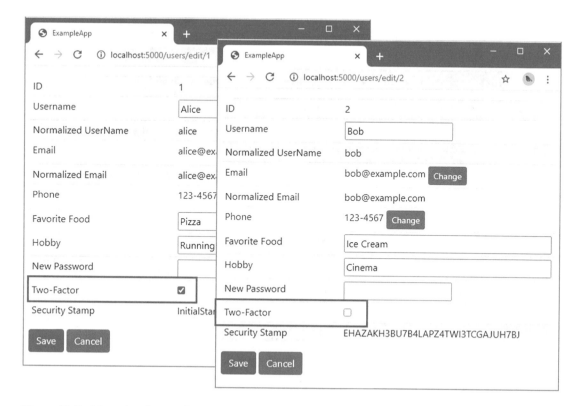

Figure 20-5. *Managing the two-factor authentication setting*

Signing In with Two Factors

Now that the foundation is in place, it is time to change the sign-in process to support two-factor authentication for those users who require it. It is helpful to focus on the process before diving into the way it is implemented. There are three steps.

1. The first step is a normal password sign-in. The user provides their account name and their password to the application, which are validated against the data in the user store. The user is signed into the application if they don't require two-factor authentication, and the process ends. The process also ends if the user has provided the wrong password. If the user has provided the correct password and requires two-factor authentication, a cookie identifying the user is added to the response, and the client is sent a redirection to the URL for the next step of the process.

2. The request the client sends to the next URL contains the cookie, which is extracted from the request and used to identify the user. This cookie is only used for two-factor sign-ins and doesn't allow the user to sign in to the application yet. A confirmation code is sent to the user using the contact information in the user store associated with the user identified by the cookie created in the previous step. The client is sent a redirection to the URL for the next step in the process.

3. The client is prompted for the security code they have been sent, and the user account is once again identified by the cookie that was created in the first step. If the code is valid, the user is signed into the application. A cookie is added to the response that will authenticate subsequent requests and grant the user access to the application, completing the sign-in process. If the code is invalid, the application can elect to prompt the user again or terminate the process.

The part of the process that causes confusion is the cookie, which is used to identify the user but doesn't grant them access to the application. This cookie is created using the standard Identity authentication features but uses a different cookie name and contains only enough (encrypted) data to identify the user without including any additional information about the user account and its roles and claims. Table 20-10 describes the methods that the SignInManager<T> class provides for the two-factor sign in process.

Table 20-10. *The SignInManager<T> Methods for Two-Factor Sign-In*

Name	Description
PasswordSignInAsync(user, password, persist, lockout)	This is the standard password sign-in method, which returns a SignInResult object that indicates whether two-factor authentication is required and adds the cookie to the response.
GetTwoFactorAuthenticationUserAsync()	This method retrieves user information from the cookie created by the first phase of the two-factor sign-in process.
TwoFactorSignInAsync(provider, code persistent, remember)	This method validates a code for the specified user and signs the user into the application if it is valid. The persistent argument determines if the authentication cookie will persist when the browser is closed, and the remember argument determines whether a cookie is created that will bypass the sign-in process, as described in the next section.

ASP.NET Core Identity supports an optional feature that adds a cookie to the response once a user has completed two-factor authentication and that bypasses the two-factor requirement the next time the user signs in from the same client. When this feature is used, the user is signed into the application with just a regular password sign-in.

This is a useful feature for making two-factor signing in more palatable to users because they only have to provide the second factor when the cookie expires or if they sign in from a different client. Creating the cookie to remember clients is controlled by the remember argument passed to the TwoFactorSignInAsync method described in Table 20-10 and can also be managed through the SignInManager<T> methods described in Table 20-11.

Table 20-11. *The SignInManager<T> Methods for Remembering Two-Factor Clients*

Name	Description
RememberTwoFactorClient Async(user)	This method adds a cookie to the response to indicate that the user has completed a two-factor sign-in. This method is called automatically when the remember argument to the TwoFactorSignInAsync method is true.
IsTwoFactorClientRemembered Async(user)	This method inspects the request to see if it contains a cookie that indicates the current user has previously completed a two-factor sign in and should be allowed to bypass the second factor.
ForgetTwoFactorClientAsync (user)	This method deletes the cookie that remembers the client.

Creating the Two-Factor Token Generator

The first step is to create the generator for the tokens that will be given to the user in step 2 of the sign-in process, which is done with an implementation of the IUserTwoFactorTokenProvider<T> interface. For this chapter, I am going to build on the SimpleTokenGenerator class. Add a class file named TwoFactorSignInTokenGenerator.cs to the ExampleApp/Identity folder and use it to define the class shown in Listing 20-18.

Listing 20-18. The Contents of the TwoFactorSignInTokenGenerator.cs File in the Identity Folder

```
using Microsoft.AspNetCore.Identity;
using System.Threading.Tasks;

namespace ExampleApp.Identity {

    public class TwoFactorSignInTokenGenerator : SimpleTokenGenerator {

        protected override int CodeLength => 3;

        public override Task<bool> CanGenerateTwoFactorTokenAsync(
                UserManager<AppUser> manager, AppUser user) {
            return Task.FromResult(user.TwoFactorEnabled);
        }
    }
}
```

The key difference from the token generators from earlier examples is the implementation of the CanGenerateTwoFactorTokenAsync method, which tells Identity that tokens are available for any user whose TwoFactorEnabled property is true.

Configuring the Token Generator and Cookie Authentication Handler

The ASP.NET Core cookie authentication handler can be used to create the cookies required by the two-factor sign-in process. Listing 20-19 shows the configuration changes required in the ConfigureServices method of the Startup class to set up the sign-in cookies and register the two-factor token generator.

Listing 20-19. Configuring the Application in the Startup.cs File in the ExampleApp Folder

```
...
public void ConfigureServices(IServiceCollection services) {
    services.AddSingleton<ILookupNormalizer, Normalizer>();
    services.AddSingleton<IUserStore<AppUser>, UserStore>();
    services.AddSingleton<IEmailSender, ConsoleEmailSender>();
    services.AddSingleton<ISMSSender, ConsoleSMSSender>();
    //services.AddSingleton<IUserClaimsPrincipalFactory<AppUser>,
    //    AppUserClaimsPrincipalFactory>();
    services.AddSingleton<IPasswordHasher<AppUser>, SimplePasswordHasher>();
    services.AddSingleton<IRoleStore<AppRole>, RoleStore>();
    services.AddSingleton<IUserConfirmation<AppUser>, UserConfirmation>();

    services.AddIdentityCore<AppUser>(opts => {
        opts.Tokens.EmailConfirmationTokenProvider = "SimpleEmail";
        opts.Tokens.ChangeEmailTokenProvider = "SimpleEmail";
        opts.Tokens.PasswordResetTokenProvider =
            TokenOptions.DefaultPhoneProvider;

        opts.Password.RequireNonAlphanumeric = false;
        opts.Password.RequireLowercase = false;
        opts.Password.RequireUppercase = false;
        opts.Password.RequireDigit = false;
        opts.Password.RequiredLength = 8;
        opts.Lockout.MaxFailedAccessAttempts = 3;
        opts.SignIn.RequireConfirmedAccount = true;
    })
    .AddTokenProvider<EmailConfirmationTokenGenerator>("SimpleEmail")
    .AddTokenProvider<PhoneConfirmationTokenGenerator>
        (TokenOptions.DefaultPhoneProvider)
    .AddTokenProvider<TwoFactorSignInTokenGenerator>
        (IdentityConstants.TwoFactorUserIdScheme)
    .AddSignInManager()
    .AddRoles<AppRole>();

    services.AddSingleton<IUserValidator<AppUser>, EmailValidator>();
    services.AddSingleton<IPasswordValidator<AppUser>, PasswordValidator>();
    services.AddScoped<IUserClaimsPrincipalFactory<AppUser>,
        AppUserClaimsPrincipalFactory>();
    services.AddSingleton<IRoleValidator<AppRole>, RoleValidator>();

    services.AddAuthentication(opts => {
        opts.DefaultScheme = IdentityConstants.ApplicationScheme;
    }).AddCookie(IdentityConstants.ApplicationScheme, opts => {
        opts.LoginPath = "/signin";
        opts.AccessDeniedPath = "/signin/403";
    })
    .AddCookie(IdentityConstants.TwoFactorUserIdScheme)
    .AddCookie(IdentityConstants.TwoFactorRememberMeScheme);
```

```
    services.AddAuthorization(opts => {
        AuthorizationPolicies.AddPolicies(opts);
    });
    services.AddRazorPages();
    services.AddControllersWithViews();
}
...
```

The `IdentityConstants` class defines two properties that are used as authentication scheme names. The `TwoFactorUserIdScheme` property identifies the scheme used for the cookie sent to the client after a successful password login in stage 1 of the two-factor process. The `TwoFactorRememberMeScheme` property specifies the scheme used for the cookie that remembers clients after a successful two-factor login. Authentication handlers are required for schemes, even if the application doesn't remember clients.

Changing the Password Sign-In Process

To support two-factor sign-ins, I need to check the `SignInResult` object produced by the `SignInManager<T>.PasswordSignInAsync` to see if the `RequiresTwoFactor` property is true. If it is, then I need to redirect the browser to the URL that handles the second factor. Listing 20-20 shows the changes to the POST handler method for the `SignIn` Razor Page.

Listing 20-20. Supporting Two-Factors in the SignIn.cshtml.cs File in the Pages Folder

```
...
public async Task<ActionResult> OnPost(string username,
        string password, [FromQuery] string returnUrl) {
    SignInResult result = SignInResult.Failed;
    AppUser user = await UserManager.FindByEmailAsync(username);
    if (user != null && !string.IsNullOrEmpty(password)) {
        result = await SignInManager.PasswordSignInAsync(user, password,
            false, true);
    }
    if (!result.Succeeded) {
        if (result.IsLockedOut) {
            TimeSpan remaining = (await UserManager
                .GetLockoutEndDateAsync(user))
                .GetValueOrDefault().Subtract(DateTimeOffset.Now);
            Message = $"Locked Out for {remaining.Minutes} mins and"
                + $" {remaining.Seconds} secs";
        } else if (result.RequiresTwoFactor) {
            return RedirectToPage("/SignInTwoFactor", new { returnUrl = returnUrl });
        } else if (result.IsNotAllowed) {
            Message = "Sign In Not Allowed";
        } else {
            Message = "Access Denied";
        }
        return Page();
    }
    return Redirect(returnUrl ?? "/signin");
}
...
```

It is important to perform the redirection only when the RequiresTwoFactor property is true and not to do so automatically when the user has the two-factor requirement enabled. This is because a failed password sign doesn't progress to the next stage and because the feature that remembers successful two-factor sign-ins may allow the user to sign in with just a password.

Supporting the Second Factor

Add a Razor Page named SignInTwoFactor.cshtml to the ExampleApp/Pages folder with the content shown in Listing 20-21.

Listing 20-21. The Contents of the SignInTwoFactor.cshtml File in the Pages Folder

```
@page
@model ExampleApp.Pages.SignInTwoFactorModel

<h4 class="bg-info text-white m-2 p-2">Two Factor Sign In</h4>

<div asp-validation-summary="All" class="text-danger m-2"></div>

<span class="m-2"> We have sent a security code to your phone. </span>
<a asp-page="/SignInTwoFactor" class="btn btn-sm btn-secondary">Resend Code</a>

<div class="m-2">
    <form method="post">
        <div class="form-group">
            <label>Enter security Code:</label>
            <input class="form-control" name="smscode"/>
        </div>
        <div class="form-check">
            <input class="form-check-input" type="checkbox" name="rememberMe" />
            <label class="form-check-label">Remember Me</label>
        </div>
        <div class="mt-2">
            <button class="btn btn-info" type="submit"
                    disabled="@(!ModelState.IsValid)">Sign In</button>
            <a asp-page="/Signin" class="btn btn-secondary">Cancel</a >
        </div>
    </form>
</div>
```

The user is presented with an input element that allows a code to be entered, and buttons to sign in, cancel, or send a new code. To define the page model for the Razor Page, add the code shown in Listing 20-22 to the SignInTwoFactor.cshtml.cs file in the Pages folder. (You will have to create this file if you are using Visual Studio Code.)

Listing 20-22. The Contents of the SignInTwoFactor.cshtml.cs File in the Pages Folder

```
using ExampleApp.Identity;
using ExampleApp.Services;
using Microsoft.AspNetCore.Identity;
using Microsoft.AspNetCore.Mvc;
using Microsoft.AspNetCore.Mvc.RazorPages;
```

```csharp
using System.Threading.Tasks;
using SignInResult = Microsoft.AspNetCore.Identity.SignInResult;

namespace ExampleApp.Pages {

    public class SignInTwoFactorModel : PageModel {

        public SignInTwoFactorModel(UserManager<AppUser> userManager,
                    SignInManager<AppUser> signInManager,
                    ISMSSender sender) {
            UserManager = userManager;
            SignInManager = signInManager;
            SMSSender = sender;
        }

        public UserManager<AppUser> UserManager { get; set; }
        public SignInManager<AppUser> SignInManager { get; set; }
        public ISMSSender SMSSender { get; set; }

        public async Task OnGet() {
            AppUser user = await SignInManager.GetTwoFactorAuthenticationUserAsync();
            if (user != null) {
                await UserManager.UpdateSecurityStampAsync(user);
                string token = await UserManager.GenerateTwoFactorTokenAsync(user,
                    IdentityConstants.TwoFactorUserIdScheme);
                SMSSender.SendMessage(user, $"Your security code is {token}");
            }
        }

        public async Task<IActionResult> OnPost(string smscode, string rememberMe,
                [FromQuery] string returnUrl) {
            AppUser user = await SignInManager.GetTwoFactorAuthenticationUserAsync();
            if (user != null) {
                SignInResult result = await SignInManager.TwoFactorSignInAsync(
                    IdentityConstants.TwoFactorUserIdScheme, smscode, true,
                        !string.IsNullOrEmpty(rememberMe));
                if (result.Succeeded) {
                    return Redirect(returnUrl ?? "/");
                } else if (result.IsLockedOut) {
                    ModelState.AddModelError("", "Locked out");
                } else if (result.IsNotAllowed) {
                    ModelState.AddModelError("", "Not allowed");
                } else {
                    ModelState.AddModelError("", "Authentication failed");
                }
            }
            return Page();
        }
    }
}
```

The GET handler method uses the GetTwoFactorAuthenticationUserAsync method to retrieve details of the user who is signing in. It is important to remember that the user isn't signed into the application until they have completed the entire process and that only this method should be used to get the user's details. Once the user details have been obtained, the user's security token is updated to invalidate any previous tokens, and the GenerateTwoFactorTokenAsync method is used to generate a token that is sent to the user through the ISMSSender service, which simulates sending SMS messages by writing console messages.

The POST handler method receives the security code, the user's choice for remembering the client, and, optionally, the URL to return to once sign-in is complete. The GetTwoFactorAuthenticationUserAsync method is used to get the user's details again, and the TwoFactorSignInAsync method is used to validate the token and complete the sign-in process.

Forgetting the Client

The final step is to give the user the option to forget the client when they log out, ensuring that the full two-factor sign-in process is required when they next log in. Add the elements shown in Listing 20-23 to the SignOut Razor Page.

Listing 20-23. Adding Elements in the SignOut.cshtml File in the Pages Folder

```
@page
@model ExampleApp.Pages.SignOutModel

<h4 class="bg-info text-white m-2 p-2">
    Current User: @Model.Username
</h4>
<div class="m-2">
    <form method="post" >
        <div class="form-check m-2">
            <input class="form-check-input" type="checkbox" name="forgetMe" />
            <label class="form-check-label">Forget Me</label>
        </div>
        <button class="btn btn-info" type="submit">Sign Out</button>
    </form>
</div>
```

The changes in Listing 20-24 update the page model class so that the POST handler method receives the value from the checkbox and forgets the client.

Listing 20-24. Forgetting the Client in the SignOut.cshtml.cs File in the Pages Folder

```
using Microsoft.AspNetCore.Authentication;
using Microsoft.AspNetCore.Mvc;
using Microsoft.AspNetCore.Mvc.RazorPages;
using System.Threading.Tasks;
using Microsoft.AspNetCore.Identity;
using ExampleApp.Identity;

namespace ExampleApp.Pages {
    public class SignOutModel : PageModel {
        public string Username { get; set; }
```

```
    public SignOutModel(SignInManager<AppUser> manager)
        => SignInManager = manager;

    public SignInManager<AppUser> SignInManager { get; set; }

    public void OnGet() {
        Username = User.Identity.Name ?? "(No Signed In User)";
    }

    public async Task<ActionResult> OnPost(string forgetMe) {
        if (!string.IsNullOrEmpty(forgetMe)) {
            await SignInManager.ForgetTwoFactorClientAsync();
        }
        await HttpContext.SignOutAsync();
        return RedirectToPage("SignIn");
    }
    }
}
```

The ForgetTwoFactorClientAsync method is used to delete the cookie that allows the user to bypass part of the two-factor process.

Testing Two-Factor Sign-In

Restart ASP.NET Core, request http://localhost:5000/signout, and click the Sign Out button to delete any existing cookies created by earlier examples. Next, request http://localhost:5000/secret, which will produce a challenge response and begin the two-factor process. Select alice@example.com with the select element, enter MySecret1$ into the password field, and click the Sign In button. The password will be validated, and you will be prompted to enter the security code. Look at the console output, and you will see a message like this:

```
--- SMS Starts ---
To: 123-4567
Your security code is A06E9C
--- SMS Ends ---
```

Enter the security code shown in your message, which will be different from the one shown here, select the Remember Me option, and click the Sign In button. The sign-in process is complete, and you will be redirected to the /secret URL, as shown in Figure 20-6.

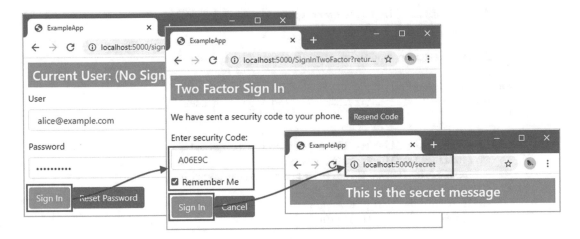

Figure 20-6. *The two-factor sign-in process*

To test the feature that remembers the client, request http://localhost:5000/signout, and click the Sign Out button without enabling the checkbox. Request http://localhost:5000/secret, select alice@ example.com when presented with the challenge response, and enter MySecret1$ into the password field. Click Sign In, and you will be redirected to the /secret URL without being prompted for a security code, as shown in Figure 20-7.

Figure 20-7. *The sign-in process with a remembered client*

If you check the option to forget the client, you will be prompted for the security code again.

Restricting the Scope of Remembered Clients

Remembering clients is a useful feature for making signing in easier for users, but you may want to force a complete two-factor sign in for especially sensitive operations. The `SignInManager<T>` class adds a claim to the `ClaimsPrincipal` object that represents the user, making it possible to determine whether a remembered client allowed the user to skip part of the two-factor process. In Listing 20-25, I have defined an authorization policy that checks for the claim added by the `SignInManager<T>` class when the full two-factor sign-in process has been performed.

Listing 20-25. Creating an Authorization Policy in the Startup.cs File in the ExampleApp Folder

```
...
services.AddAuthorization(opts => {
    AuthorizationPolicies.AddPolicies(opts);
    opts.AddPolicy("Full2FARequired", builder => {
        builder.RequireClaim("amr", "mfa");
    });
});
...
```

The policy requires a claim whose type is `amr` with the value `mfa`. The term AMR refers to Authentication Method Reference, which is specified by RFC8176, which standardizes claims that describe authentication methods. (See `https://tools.ietf.org/html/rfc8176` for details.) The `mfa` value indicates the user has signed in using multifactor authentication. The user will still have an `amr` claim even if they have bypassed the second factor or are configured for single-factor sign-ins, but the claim value will be `pwd`, indicating password-based authentication.

Defining an Authorization Failed Landing Page

The standard authorization features cannot be used in this situation because the user is signed in as far as Identity is concerned, which means that failing to meet the authorization requirement defined in Listing 20-25 will result in a forbidden response, instead of a challenge response that will allow the user to go through the full two-factor process. Instead, I need a landing page that will explain to the user that a full login is required and sign them out so they can sign in again without the client being remembered. Add a Razor Page named `Full2FARequired.cshtml` to the `ExampleApp/Pages` folder with the content shown in Listing 20-26.

Listing 20-26. The Contents of the Full2FARequired.cshtml File in the Pages Folder

```
@page
@model ExampleApp.Pages.Full2FARequiredModel

<h4 class="bg-primary text-white text-center p-2">Two-Factor Sign In Required</h4>

<form method="post">
    <div class="m-2">
        The full two-factor sign in process is required. Click the
        OK button to sign out of the application so you can sign in
        using with a password and a security code.
    </div>
    <button class="btn btn-primary mx-2" type="submit">OK</button>
</form>
```

The page displays an explanatory message and a button the user will click to sign out of the application and forget the client. To define the page model class, add the code shown in Listing 20-27 to the Full2FARequired.cshtml.cs file in the Pages folder. (You will have to create this file if you are using Visual Studio Code.)

Listing 20-27. The Contents of the Full2FARequired.cshtml.cs File in the Pages Folder

```
using ExampleApp.Identity;
using Microsoft.AspNetCore.Authentication;
using Microsoft.AspNetCore.Identity;
using Microsoft.AspNetCore.Mvc;
using Microsoft.AspNetCore.Mvc.RazorPages;
using System.Threading.Tasks;

namespace ExampleApp.Pages {

    public class Full2FARequiredModel : PageModel {

        public Full2FARequiredModel(UserManager<AppUser> userManager,
                SignInManager<AppUser> signInManager) {
            UserManager = userManager;
            SignInManager = signInManager;
        }

        public UserManager<AppUser> UserManager { get; set; }
        public SignInManager<AppUser> SignInManager { get; set; }

        public async Task<IActionResult> OnPostAsync(string returnUrl) {
            AppUser user = await UserManager.GetUserAsync(HttpContext.User);
            if (await SignInManager.IsTwoFactorClientRememberedAsync(user)) {
                await SignInManager.ForgetTwoFactorClientAsync();
            }
            await HttpContext.SignOutAsync();
            return Redirect($"/signin?returnUrl={returnUrl}");
        }
    }
}
```

The POST handler method uses the methods provided by the SignInManager<T> class to forget the client and then signs the user out through the HttpContext.SignOutAsync method.

■ **Caution** Do not use the SignInManager<T>.SignOutAsync method to sign out of the application because it will throw an exception, reporting there is no handler for the external scheme.

Creating the Page and Action Filters

The standard authorization features are not useful in this situation, and I need to create a page filter to apply the policy in Razor Pages and an action filter to apply the policy in controllers. There is enough common code in page and action filters to allow a single class to be used for both. Add a class file named Full2FARequiredFilterAttribute.cs to the Examples/Identity folder and use it to define the code shown in Listing 20-28.

Listing 20-28. The Contents of the Full2FARequiredFilterAttribute.cs File in the Identity Folder

```
using Microsoft.AspNetCore.Authorization;
using Microsoft.AspNetCore.Http;
using Microsoft.AspNetCore.Mvc;
using Microsoft.AspNetCore.Mvc.Filters;
using Microsoft.Extensions.DependencyInjection;
using System;
using System.Threading.Tasks;

namespace ExampleApp.Identity {

    public class Full2FARequiredFilterAttribute : Attribute,
            IAsyncPageFilter, IAsyncActionFilter {

        public async Task OnActionExecutionAsync(ActionExecutingContext context,
                ActionExecutionDelegate next) {
            IActionResult result = await ApplyPolicy(context.HttpContext);
            if (result != null) {
                context.Result = result;
            } else {
                await next.Invoke();
            }
        }

        public async Task OnPageHandlerExecutionAsync(PageHandlerExecutingContext
                context, PageHandlerExecutionDelegate next) {
            IActionResult result = await ApplyPolicy(context.HttpContext);
            if (result != null) {
                context.Result = result;
            } else {
                await next.Invoke();
            }
        }

        public async Task<IActionResult> ApplyPolicy(HttpContext context) {
            IAuthorizationService authService =
                context.RequestServices.GetService<IAuthorizationService>();
            if (!(await authService.AuthorizeAsync(context.User,
                "Full2FARequired")).Succeeded) {
                return new RedirectToPageResult("/Full2FARequired",
                    new { returnUrl = Path(context) });
            }
            return null;
        }

        public Task OnPageHandlerSelectionAsync(PageHandlerSelectedContext context) {
            return Task.CompletedTask;
        }
```

```
        private string Path(HttpContext context) =>
            $"{context.Request.Path}{context.Request.QueryString}";
    }
}
```

The filter uses the IAuthorizationService service to enforce the Full2FARequired policy and creates a redirection to the landing page if the policy requirements are not met.

Applying the Filter to a Page

To create a resource that will require a full two-factor sign-in, add a Razor Page named VerySecret.cshtml in the ExampleApp/Pages folder with the content shown in Listing 20-29.

Listing 20-29. The Contents of the VerySecret.cshtml File in the Pages Folder

```
@page
@using Microsoft.AspNetCore.Authorization
@using ExampleApp.Identity
@attribute [Authorize]
@attribute [Full2FARequiredFilter]

<h4 class="bg-info text-center text-white m-2 p-2">
    This is the VERY secret message
</h4>
```

The application of the Authorize attribute ensures that users that are not signed in are presented with the standard challenge response. The Full2FARequiredFilter deals with two-factor users who bypassed the second factor because their client was remembered by the application.

Testing the Full Two-Factor Requirement

The process for testing the full two-factor requirement is complex and requires multiple steps, each of which must be followed exactly. The goal is to have logged in with two factors and have the application remember the client, sign out, log back in without needing to provide the second factor, and then request the VerySecret page. Here are the steps required to perform the test:

1. Restart ASP.NET Core.

2. Request http://localhost:5000/signout, select the Forget Me option, and click the Sign Out button.

3. Request http://localhost:5000/verysecret. You will receive the standard challenge response.

4. Select alice@example.com using the element, enter MySecret1$ into the password field, and click the Sign In button.

5. Enter the security code that is written to the console into the Enter Security Code text field displayed by the browser. Check the Remember Me option and click the Sign In button.

   This is not the end of the test process, but, at this point, you are authenticated using both factors and will see the content produced by the VerySecret Razor Page, as shown in Figure 20-8.

Figure 20-8. *The first part of the test process*

6. Request `http://localhost:5000/signout`, ensure the Forget Me option is unchecked, and click the Sign Out button. You will be redirected to the `SignIn` Razor Page.

7. Select alice@example.com using the element, enter MySecret1$ into the password field, and click the Sign In button. You will be authenticated without providing a second factor because your client has been remembered.

8. Request `http://localhost:5000/verysecret`. Instead of seeing the requested page, you will be redirected to the landing page. Click OK, go through the two-factor sign in process, and, once authenticated, you will see the protected content, as shown in Figure 20-9.

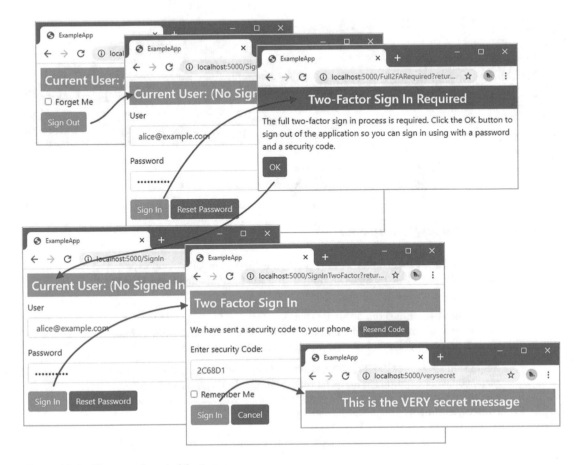

Figure 20-9. *The second part of the test process*

The test process is complex, but the overall result is that the VerySecret Razor Page can be accessed only by users who have signed in by providing two factors.

Summary

In this chapter, I explained how lockouts are implemented and showed you how to restrict access to accounts that have been confirmed. I also demonstrated the features that Identity uses to support two-factor authentication, for which I generated simulated SMS messages. In the next chapter, I continue on the theme of two-factor authentication and describe how authenticators and recovery codes are implemented.

CHAPTER 21

■ ■ ■

Authenticators and Recovery Codes

In this chapter, I describe how ASP.NET Core Identity supports authenticators for two-factor authentication and how to provide users with recovery codes for emergency access when their second factor isn't available. Table 21-1 puts these features in context.

Table 21-1. *Putting Authenticators and Recovery Codes in Context*

Question	Answer
What are they?	Authenticators are apps that are configured with a secret key, after which they generate codes that can be used as part of a two-factor authentication process. Recovery codes are single-use codes that can be used as second factors, typically when an authenticator app has been lost.
Why are they useful?	Authenticators offer a more secure sign-in process than SMS. Recovery codes are useful because they allow users to sign in even when their second factor is unavailable.
How are they used?	Authenticators are set up with an initial key generated using Identity. During sign-in, the current code displayed by the authenticator is provided by the user and validated by Identity using the key. Recovery codes are entered as part of the sign-in process.
Are there any pitfalls or limitations?	Authenticators are typically smartphone apps, which not all users have access to. Recovery codes require users to prepare in advance, remember the codes when they need them, and generate new codes when they run out.
Are there any alternatives?	Alternative second factors can be used. Authentication can be delegated to third parties using the external authentication feature described in Chapter 22. Recovery codes are optional but should be used whenever two-factor authentication is enabled.

© Adam Freeman 2021
A. Freeman, *Pro ASP.NET Core Identity*, https://doi.org/10.1007/978-1-4842-6858-2_21

Table 21-2 summarizes the chapter.

Table 21-2. *Chapter Summary*

Problem	Solution	Listing
Support authenticators in two-factor sign-ins	Extend the user store by implementing the `IUserAuthenticatorKeyStore<T>` interface and manage the keys with the user manager methods.	3–8
Sign in users with an authenticator	Use the `TwoFactorAuthenticatorSignInAsync` method provided by the sign-in manager class.	9–12
Support recovery codes in two-factor sign-ins	Extend the user store by implementing the `IUserTwoFactorRecovery CodeStore<T>` interface and manage the codes with the user manager methods.	13–18
Sign in users with a recovery code	Use the `TwoFactorRecoveryCodeSignInAsync` method provided by the sign-in manager class.	19–21

Preparing for This Chapter

This chapter uses the ExampleApp project from Chapter 20. To prepare for this chapter, disable the custom user confirmation service, as shown in Listing 21-1.

Listing 21-1. Disabling a Service in the Startup.cs File in the ExampleApp Folder

```
...
public void ConfigureServices(IServiceCollection services) {
    services.AddSingleton<ILookupNormalizer, Normalizer>();
    services.AddSingleton<IUserStore<AppUser>, UserStore>();
    services.AddSingleton<IEmailSender, ConsoleEmailSender>();
    services.AddSingleton<ISMSSender, ConsoleSMSSender>();
    //services.AddSingleton<IUserClaimsPrincipalFactory<AppUser>,
    //    AppUserClaimsPrincipalFactory>();
    services.AddSingleton<IPasswordHasher<AppUser>, SimplePasswordHasher>();
    services.AddSingleton<IRoleStore<AppRole>, RoleStore>();
    //services.AddSingleton<IUserConfirmation<AppUser>, UserConfirmation>();
...
```

Open a new command prompt, navigate to the ExampleApp folder, and run the command shown in Listing 21-2 to start ASP.NET Core.

■ **Tip** You can download the example project for this chapter—and for all the other chapters in this book—from `https://github.com/Apress/pro-asp.net-core-identity`. See Chapter 1 for how to get help if you have problems running the examples.

Listing 21-2. Running the Example Application

```
dotnet run
```

Open a new browser window and request `http://localhost:5000/users`. You will be presented with the user data shown in Figure 21-1. The data is stored only in memory, and changes will be lost when ASP. NET Core is stopped.

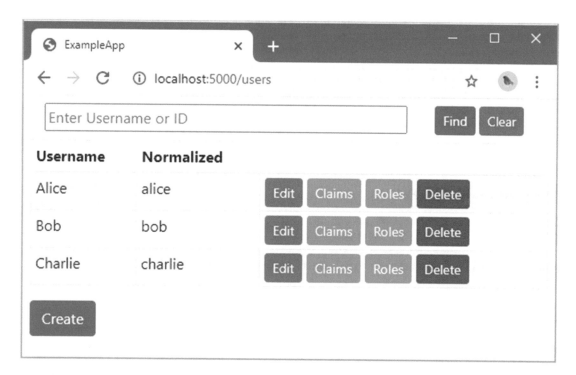

Figure 21-1. *Running the example application*

Using an Authenticator

One of the drawbacks of using SMS for two-factor authentication is that the user must have cell coverage to receive the security codes. One way to solve this problem is to use an *authenticator*, which is an app specifically intended to generate security codes while offline.

Authenticators have a setup phase and a code generation phase. During the setup phase, the ASP. NET Core Identity creates a key, also called a *seed*, which is shared with the authenticator app and stored securely. The key can be shared by copying and pasting a string of characters or, if the authenticator is a smartphone app, scanning a QR code.

During the code generation phase, the authenticator and Identity both use the same algorithm to generate a code using the shared key plus a modifier (also known as a *moving factor*) that ensures keys are different and cannot be intercepted and reused by an attacker. The authenticator displays the code to the user, which presents it to the application just as they would a code received via SMS. The user is signed in if the code generated by the authenticator matches the one generated by Identity.

To generate the same code, the authenticator and Identity need to use the same key and modifier. The key is shared when the authenticator is set up, but the modifier must be different for each sign-in. There are two standard ways to select a modifier: using a counter or using the current time. Codes that are generated using a counter are called *HMAC-based one-time passwords* (HOTPs), and codes generated using the time are called *time-based one-time passwords* (TOTPs). The challenge is that the authenticator and the application must be able to select the same modifier without being able to communicate.

When a counter is used, the authenticator and Identity both keep track of a counter. The authenticator increments the counter when the user presses a button and Identity increments the counter when the user is signed in. The two counters can drift apart if the user presses the button but doesn't use the code, so Identity must check a range of possible counter values during validation. A manual resynchronization process is required if the authenticator counter is incremented outside of the range that Identity checks.

The time-based approach works out how many intervals of a fixed duration have occurred since a specific time. The authenticator and Identity will produce the same modifier if they count the number of three-minute intervals that have occurred since the January 1, 1970, UTC, for example, just as long as the clocks they use are roughly synchronized. The clocks don't have to be completely synchronized—being accurate within a single time interval is close enough. The user won't be able to sign in if the clocks are further adrift because the authenticator and Identity will use different modifiers to produce the security codes.

TOTPs are more widely used because they are simpler to validate and don't require a resynchronization process. I generate TOTPs in the examples in this chapter.

Extending the User Class

The first step toward supporting authenticators is to extend the user class to keep track of the key. Add the properties shown in Listing 21-3 to the AppUser class.

Listing 21-3. Adding Properties in the AppUser.cs File in the Identity Folder

```
using System;
using System.Collections.Generic;
using System.Security.Claims;

namespace ExampleApp.Identity {
    public class AppUser {

        public string Id { get; set; } = Guid.NewGuid().ToString();

        public string UserName { get; set; }

        public string NormalizedUserName { get; set; }

        public string EmailAddress { get; set; }
        public string NormalizedEmailAddress { get; set; }
        public bool EmailAddressConfirmed { get; set; }

        public string PhoneNumber { get; set; }
        public bool PhoneNumberConfirmed { get; set; }

        public string FavoriteFood { get; set; }
        public string Hobby { get; set; }

        public IList<Claim> Claims { get; set; }
```

```
        public string SecurityStamp { get; set; }
        public string PasswordHash { get; set; }

        public bool CanUserBeLockedout { get; set; } = true;
        public int FailedSignInCount { get; set; }
        public DateTimeOffset? LockoutEnd { get; set; }

        public bool TwoFactorEnabled { get; set; }
        public bool AuthenticatorEnabled { get; set; }
        public string AuthenticatorKey { get; set; }
    }
}
```

The new properties will be used to denote the user has an authenticator and to store the shared key that will be used to generate security codes. Each user has a key, and changing the key will prevent the user from signing in until the key has been shared with the authenticator.

Storing Authenticator Keys in the User Store

The IUserAuthenticatorKeyStore<T> interface is implemented by user stores that can manage authenticator keys. The interface defines the methods described in Table 21-3. As with the other user store interfaces described in this part of the book, the methods in Table 21-3 define a CancellationToken parameter named token, which is used to receive notifications when a task is canceled.

Table 21-3. *The IUserAuthenticatorKeyStore<T> Methods*

Name	Description
SetAuthenticatorKeyAsync(user, key, token)	This method sets the authenticator key for the specified user.
GetAuthenticatorKeyAsync(user, token)	This method gets the authenticator key for the specified user.

To add support for authenticator keys to the user store, add a class file named UserStoreAuthenticatorKeys.cs to the Identity/Store folder and use it to define the partial class shown in Listing 21-4.

Listing 21-4. The Contents of the UserStoreAuthenticatorKeys.cs File in the Identity/Store Folder

```
using Microsoft.AspNetCore.Identity;
using System.Threading;
using System.Threading.Tasks;

namespace ExampleApp.Identity.Store {
    public partial class UserStore : IUserAuthenticatorKeyStore<AppUser> {

        public Task<string> GetAuthenticatorKeyAsync(AppUser user,
                CancellationToken cancellationToken)
            => Task.FromResult(user.AuthenticatorKey);
```

```
        public Task SetAuthenticatorKeyAsync(AppUser user, string key,
                CancellationToken cancellationToken) {
            user.AuthenticatorKey = key;
            return Task.CompletedTask;
        }
    }
}
```

The implementation of the interface maps the methods onto the AppUser properties. The user store isn't responsible for generating the keys or tokens.

Managing Authenticator Keys

Authenticators require a setup phase so that the key can be shared. The UserManager<T> class provides the members described in Table 21-4 for working with authenticators.

Table 21-4. *The UserManager<T> Members for Authenticators*

Name	Description
SupportsUserAuthenticatorKey	This property returns true if the store implements the IUserAuthenticatorKeyStore<T> interface.
GetAuthenticatorKeyAsync(user)	This method gets the user's authenticator key by calling the store method with the same name.
GenerateNewAuthenticatorKey()	This method generates a new key.
ResetAuthenticatorKeyAsync(user)	This method resets the authenticator key for the specified user. The GenerateNewAuthenticatorKey method is used to generate a new key, which is assigned to the user by calling the store's SetAuthenticatorKeyAsync method. A new security stamp is generated, and the user manager's update sequence is performed to save the changes.

During the setup phase, the authenticator must be given the key generated by the application. This can be done by having the user copying and pasting the key string, but QR codes provide an elegant alternative for authenticators running on smartphones. ASP.NET Core Identity doesn't include the ability to generate QR codes directly, but Microsoft suggests the use of the QRCode.js JavaScript package. Run the command shown in Listing 21-5 in the ExampleApp folder to add the QRCode.js package to the project.

Listing 21-5. Adding a JavaScript Package

```
libman install qrcodejs@1.0.0 -d wwwroot/lib/qrcode
```

To generate a key and display it to the user, add a Razor Page named AuthenticatorSetup.cshtml to the Pages folder with the contents shown in Listing 21-6.

Listing 21-6. The Contents of the AuthenticatorSetup.cshtml File in the Pages Folder

```
@page "{id}"
@model ExampleApp.Pages.AuthenticatorSetupModel

<h4 class="bg-primary text-white text-center p-2">Authenticator Key</h4>

<div class="m-2">
    <table class="table table-sm table-bordered">
        <tbody>
            <tr>
                <th>User</th>
                <td>@Model.AppUser.UserName</td>
                @if (Model.AuthenticatorUrl != null) {
                    <td rowspan="3">
                        <div id="qrcode"></div>
                        <script type="text/javascript"
                            src="~/lib/qrcode/qrcode.min.js"></script>
                        <script type="text/javascript">
                            new QRCode(document.getElementById("qrcode"), {
                                text: "@Model.AuthenticatorUrl",
                                width: 150,
                                height: 150
                            });
                        </script>
                    </td>
                }
            </tr>
            <tr>
                <th>Authenticator Key</th>
                <td>@(Model.AppUser.AuthenticatorKey ?? "(No Key)")</td>
            </tr>
            <tr>
                <th>Authenticator Enabled</th>
                <td>
                    <span class="font-weight-bold
                        @(Model.AppUser.AuthenticatorEnabled
                            ? "text-success": "text-danger")">
                        @Model.AppUser.AuthenticatorEnabled
                    </span>
                </td>
            </tr>
        </tbody>
    </table>
</div>

<form method="post" class="m-1">
    <input type="hidden" name="Id" value="@Model.Id" />
    <div class="mt-2">
        <button class="btn btn-primary m-1" asp-route-task="enable">
            Enable Authenticator
        </button>
```

```
        <button class="btn btn-secondary m-1" asp-route-task="disable">
            Disable Authenticator
        </button>
        <button class="btn btn-info m-1">Generate New Key</button>
        <a href="/users" class="btn btn-secondary">Back</a>
    </div>
</form>
```

The page displays the current key for a user and whether the use of the authenticator is enabled. There are buttons that toggle the user of authenticators and generate new keys. A QR code is displayed using a page model property named AuthenticatorUrl.

To define the page model class, add the code shown in Listing 21-7 to the AuthenticatorSetup. cshtml.cs file. (You will have to create this file if you are using Visual Studio Code.)

Listing 21-7. The Contents of the AuthenticatorSetup.cshtml.cs File in the Pages Folder

```
using ExampleApp.Identity;
using Microsoft.AspNetCore.Identity;
using Microsoft.AspNetCore.Mvc;
using Microsoft.AspNetCore.Mvc.RazorPages;
using System.Threading.Tasks;

namespace ExampleApp.Pages {

    public class AuthenticatorSetupModel : PageModel {

        public AuthenticatorSetupModel(UserManager<AppUser> userManager) =>
            UserManager = userManager;

        public UserManager<AppUser> UserManager { get; set; }

        [BindProperty(SupportsGet = true)]
        public string Id { get; set; }

        public AppUser AppUser { get; set; }

        public string AuthenticatorUrl { get; set; }

        public async Task OnGetAsync() {
            AppUser = await UserManager.FindByIdAsync(Id);
            if (AppUser != null) {
                if (AppUser.AuthenticatorKey != null) {
                    AuthenticatorUrl =
                        $"otpauth://totp/ExampleApp:{AppUser.EmailAddress}"
                        + $"?secret={AppUser.AuthenticatorKey}";
                }
            }
        }

        public async Task<IActionResult> OnPostAsync(string task) {
            AppUser = await UserManager.FindByIdAsync(Id);
```

```
        if (AppUser != null) {
            switch (task) {
                case "enable":
                    AppUser.AuthenticatorEnabled = true;
                    AppUser.TwoFactorEnabled = true;
                    break;
                case "disable":
                    AppUser.AuthenticatorEnabled = false;
                    AppUser.TwoFactorEnabled = false;
                    break;
                default:
                    await UserManager.ResetAuthenticatorKeyAsync(AppUser);
                    break;
            }
            await UserManager.UpdateAsync(AppUser);
        }
        return RedirectToPage();
    }
  }
}
```

The GET handler method uses the UserManager<T>.GetUserAsync to get the AppUser object that represents the signed-in user and reads the value of the AuthenticatorKey and AuthenticatorEnabled properties. The POST handler method sets the AuthenticatorEnabled property and, if required, uses the UserManager<T>.ResetAuthenticatorKeyAsync method to generate a new key.

Authenticators that can scan a QR code expect to receive a URL in the format otpauth://totp/<label>?secret=<key>, where <label> identifies the user account and where <key> is the secret key.

■ **Tip** See https://github.com/google/google-authenticator/wiki/Key-Uri-Format for full details of the URL format used for authenticator QR codes.

To incorporate the new Razor Page into the application, add the element shown in Listing 21-8 to the _UserTableRow partial view.

Listing 21-8. Adding a Feature in the _UserTableRow.cshtml File in the Pages/Store Folder

```
@model string
@inject UserManager<AppUser> UserManager

<a asp-page="edituser" asp-route-id="@Model" class="btn btn-sm btn-secondary">
    Edit
</a>
@if (UserManager.SupportsUserClaim) {
    <a asp-page="claims" asp-route-id="@Model" class="btn btn-sm btn-info">
        Claims
    </a>
}
```

```
@if (UserManager.SupportsUserRole) {
    <a asp-page="userroles" asp-route-id="@Model" class="btn btn-sm btn-info">
        Roles
    </a>
}
@if (UserManager.SupportsUserAuthenticatorKey) {
    <a asp-page="/authenticatorsetup" asp-route-id="@Model"
        class="btn btn-sm btn-success">
        Authenticator
    </a>
}
```

Enabling Authenticators in Two-Factor Sign-Ins

The authenticator will replace the security code sent via SMS in the two-factor sign-in process. The SignInManager<T> class provides the method described in Table 21-5 that supports working with authenticators.

Table 21-5. *The SignInManager<T> Method for Authenticators*

Name	Description
TwoFactorAuthenticatorSignIn Async(code, persistent, remember)	This method works the same way as the TwoFactorSignInAsync method, except the code is validated by the authenticator token provider.

In Listing 21-9, I updated the SignInTwoFactor page to determine if the user is set up for an authenticator and, if so, display an appropriate message.

Listing 21-9. Supporting Authenticators in the SignInTwoFactor.cshtml File in the Pages Folder

```
@page
@model ExampleApp.Pages.SignInTwoFactorModel

<h4 class="bg-info text-white m-2 p-2">Two Factor Sign In</h4>

<div asp-validation-summary="All" class="text-danger m-2"></div>

@if (Model.AuthenticatorEnabled) {
    <span class="m-2"> Enter the code displayed by your authenticator. </span>
} else {
    <span class="m-2"> We have sent a security code to your phone. </span>
    <a asp-page="/SignInTwoFactor" class="btn btn-sm btn-secondary">Resend Code</a>
}

<div class="m-2">
    <form method="post">
        <div class="form-group">
```

```
            <label>Enter security Code:</label>
            <input class="form-control" name="code"/>
        </div>
        <div class="form-check">
            <input class="form-check-input" type="checkbox" name="rememberMe" />
            <label class="form-check-label">Remember Me</label>
        </div>
        <div class="mt-2">
            <button class="btn btn-info" type="submit"
                    disabled="@(!ModelState.IsValid)">Sign In</button>
            <a asp-page="/Signin" class="btn btn-secondary">Cancel</a >
        </div>
    </form>
</div>
```

In Listing 21-10, I have updated the page model class to support the changes in the view and to validate authenticator security codes.

Listing 21-10. Supporting Authenticators in the SignInTwoFactor.cshtml.cs File in the Pages Folder

```
using ExampleApp.Identity;
using ExampleApp.Services;
using Microsoft.AspNetCore.Identity;
using Microsoft.AspNetCore.Mvc;
using Microsoft.AspNetCore.Mvc.RazorPages;
using System.Threading.Tasks;
using SignInResult = Microsoft.AspNetCore.Identity.SignInResult;

namespace ExampleApp.Pages {

    public class SignInTwoFactorModel : PageModel {

        public SignInTwoFactorModel(UserManager<AppUser> userManager,
                    SignInManager<AppUser> signInManager,
                    ISMSSender sender) {
            UserManager = userManager;
            SignInManager = signInManager;
            SMSSender = sender;
        }

        public UserManager<AppUser> UserManager { get; set; }
        public SignInManager<AppUser> SignInManager { get; set; }
        public ISMSSender SMSSender { get; set; }

        public bool AuthenticatorEnabled { get; set; }

        public async Task OnGet() {
            AppUser user = await SignInManager.GetTwoFactorAuthenticationUserAsync();
            if (user != null) {
                AuthenticatorEnabled = user.AuthenticatorEnabled;
                if (!AuthenticatorEnabled) {
                    await UserManager.UpdateSecurityStampAsync(user);
                    string token = await UserManager.GenerateTwoFactorTokenAsync(
```

```
                user, IdentityConstants.TwoFactorUserIdScheme);
            SMSSender.SendMessage(user, $"Your security code is {token}");
        }
    }
}

public async Task<IActionResult> OnPost(string code, string rememberMe,
        [FromQuery] string returnUrl) {
    AppUser user = await SignInManager.GetTwoFactorAuthenticationUserAsync();
    if (user != null && !string.IsNullOrEmpty(code)) {
        SignInResult result = SignInResult.Failed;
        AuthenticatorEnabled = user.AuthenticatorEnabled;
        bool rememberClient = !string.IsNullOrEmpty(rememberMe);
        if (AuthenticatorEnabled) {
            string authCode = code.Replace(" ", string.Empty);
            result = await SignInManager.TwoFactorAuthenticatorSignInAsync(
                authCode, false, rememberClient);
        } else {
            result = await SignInManager.TwoFactorSignInAsync(
                IdentityConstants.TwoFactorUserIdScheme, code,
                true, rememberClient);
        }
        if (result.Succeeded) {
            return Redirect(returnUrl ?? "/");
        } else if (result.IsLockedOut) {
            ModelState.AddModelError("", "Locked out");
        } else if (result.IsNotAllowed) {
            ModelState.AddModelError("", "Not allowed");
        } else {
            ModelState.AddModelError("", "Authentication failed");
        }
    }
    return Page();
}
    }
}
```

Some authenticators display security codes as groups of three digits, which means users will often enter codes with spaces. To prevent errors, I remove any spaces from the code the user provides and use the SignInManager<T>.TwoFactorAuthenticatorSignInAsync method to sign the user into the application.

Configuring the Application

The token generator used for authenticators is set using the TokenOptions.DefaultAuthenticatorProvider property, as shown in Listing 21-11.

Listing 21-11. Configuring the Application in the Startup.cs File in the ExampleApp Folder

```
...
services.AddIdentityCore<AppUser>(opts => {
    opts.Tokens.EmailConfirmationTokenProvider = "SimpleEmail";
    opts.Tokens.ChangeEmailTokenProvider = "SimpleEmail";
    opts.Tokens.PasswordResetTokenProvider =
        TokenOptions.DefaultPhoneProvider;

    opts.Password.RequireNonAlphanumeric = false;
    opts.Password.RequireLowercase = false;
    opts.Password.RequireUppercase = false;
    opts.Password.RequireDigit = false;
    opts.Password.RequiredLength = 8;
    opts.Lockout.MaxFailedAccessAttempts = 3;
    opts.SignIn.RequireConfirmedAccount = true;
})
.AddTokenProvider<EmailConfirmationTokenGenerator>("SimpleEmail")
.AddTokenProvider<PhoneConfirmationTokenGenerator>
    (TokenOptions.DefaultPhoneProvider)
.AddTokenProvider<TwoFactorSignInTokenGenerator>
    (IdentityConstants.TwoFactorUserIdScheme)
.AddTokenProvider<AuthenticatorTokenProvider<AppUser>>
    (TokenOptions.DefaultAuthenticatorProvider)
.AddSignInManager()
.AddRoles<AppRole>();
...
```

Authenticators work because the application and the app are using the same algorithm and key to generate security codes, which means I can't create a custom token generator unless I also create a custom authenticator app. Fortunately, Identity provides the AuthenticatorTokenProvider<T> class, which generates TOTP tokens for T, the user class. In Listing 21-11, I used the AddTokenProvider method to register AuthenticatorTokenProvider<AppUser> as the token provider for authenticators.

Creating the Seed Data

The final step is to add some seed data to make the authenticator support easier to test, as shown in Listing 21-12.

Listing 21-12. Adding Seed Data in the UserStore.cs File in the Identity/Store Folder

```
using Microsoft.AspNetCore.Identity;
using System.Collections.Generic;
using System.Linq;
using System.Security.Claims;

namespace ExampleApp.Identity.Store {

    public partial class UserStore {

        public ILookupNormalizer Normalizer { get; set; }
```

```csharp
public IPasswordHasher<AppUser> PasswordHasher { get; set; }

public UserStore(ILookupNormalizer normalizer,
        IPasswordHasher<AppUser> passwordHasher) {
    Normalizer = normalizer;
    PasswordHasher = passwordHasher;
    SeedStore();
}

private void SeedStore() {

    var customData = new Dictionary<string, (string food, string hobby)> {
        { "Alice", ("Pizza", "Running") },
        { "Bob", ("Ice Cream", "Cinema") },
        { "Charlie", ("Burgers", "Cooking") }
    };
    var twoFactorUsers = new[] { "Alice", "Charlie" };
    var authenticatorKeys = new Dictionary<string, string> {
        {"Alice", "A4GG2BNKJNKKFOKGZRGBVUYIAJCUHEW7" }
    };
    int idCounter = 0;

    string EmailFromName(string name) => $"{name.ToLower()}@example.com";

    foreach (string name in UsersAndClaims.Users) {
        AppUser user = new AppUser {
            Id = (++idCounter).ToString(),
            UserName = name,
            NormalizedUserName = Normalizer.NormalizeName(name),
            EmailAddress = EmailFromName(name),
            NormalizedEmailAddress =
                Normalizer.NormalizeEmail(EmailFromName(name)),
            EmailAddressConfirmed = true,
            PhoneNumber = "123-4567",
            PhoneNumberConfirmed = true,
            FavoriteFood = customData[name].food,
            Hobby = customData[name].hobby,
            SecurityStamp = "InitialStamp",
            TwoFactorEnabled = twoFactorUsers.Any(tfName => tfName == name)
        };
        user.Claims =  UsersAndClaims.UserData[user.UserName]
            .Select(role => new Claim(ClaimTypes.Role, role)).ToList();
        user.PasswordHash = PasswordHasher.HashPassword(user, "MySecret1$");
        if (authenticatorKeys.ContainsKey(name)) {
            user.AuthenticatorKey = authenticatorKeys[name];
            user.AuthenticatorEnabled = true;
        }
        users.TryAdd(user.Id, user);
    }
}
}
}
```

The changes in Listing 21-12 set an authenticator key for Alice but not the other users.

Setting Up an Authenticator

You can set up an authenticator on behalf of a user and email them the key if they have a confirmed email address. Or you can choose to let the user set up the authenticator on their own, either during self-service account creation or after they have signed into the application.

Restart ASP.NET Core, request `http://localhost:5000/users`, and click the Authenticator button for the Alice user. You will see the authenticator configuration for Alice, which shows her secret key as a string and a QR code, as shown in Figure 21-2.

Figure 21-2. *Enabling the authenticator*

CHOOSING AN AUTHENTICATOR APP

It doesn't matter which authenticator app you use, just as long as it can generate standard TOTP codes. The main choices are the smartphone authenticator apps from Google or Microsoft (available for free in the app stores for iOS and Android). I like Authy (authy.com), which is produced by Twilio and has desktop versions alongside the usual smartphone apps. I used the Windows version of Authy for the screenshots in this chapter because the smartphone apps do not allow screenshots to be taken (to stop other apps from obtaining security codes). If you don't want to install an app, you can use the JavaScript-based authenticator available at `https://totp.danhersam.com`, which will generate TOTP codes for a specified key.

This is the key I added to the seed data in Listing 21-12. Using your authenticator app, set up a new account, which can be done by copying the key as a string or scanning the QR code. Follow your app's process for completing the process, which may ask you to select a nickname, choose an icon, and so on. Figure 21-3 shows the process using the Windows version of the Authy app. At the end of the process, your authenticator will start showing you security codes, which change every 30 seconds.

Figure 21-3. *Setting up the authenticator*

Using an Authenticator to Sign In

To test signing in with an authenticator, request `http://localhost:5000/signout`, ensure the Forget Me option is checked, and click the Sign Out button.

Next, request `http://localhost:5000/signin`, select `alice@example.com` from the list, enter MySecret1$ as the password, and click the Sign In button. Enter the code currently displayed by your authenticator app into the text field and click the Sign In button. You will be signed into the application if the code you entered matches the code generated by Identity, as shown in Figure 21-4.

***Figure 21-4.** Signing in with an authenticator*

Using Recovery Codes

Recovery codes are used to sign in when the user is unable to receive security codes or access their authenticator app. Ahead of time, the user is given a set of codes that can be redeemed during sign-in. Each recovery code can be redeemed once to sign in, after which it is invalid. In the sections that follow, I explain how ASP.NET Core Identity supports recovery codes and demonstrate their use.

Storing Recovery Codes

User stores that can manage recovery codes implement the IUserTwoFactorRecoveryCodeStore<T> interface, where T is the user class. The interface defines the methods described in Table 21-6. As with earlier user store interfaces, these methods define a CancellationToken parameter named token that is used to receive notifications when an asynchronous task is canceled.

***Table 21-6.** The IUserTwoFactorRecoveryCodeStore<T> Methods*

Name	Description
ReplaceCodesAsync(user, codes, token)	This method replaces the existing set of recovery codes with a new set, expressed as an IEnumerable<string> object.
RedeemCodeAsync(user, code, token)	This method redeems a code for the specified user. The method returns true if the code is value and false otherwise. The code must be invalidated after it is redeemed.
CountCodesAsync(user, token)	This method returns the number of valid recovery codes available for the user.

To get started, I added a class file named RecoveryCode.cs to the ExampleApp/Identity/Store folder and used it to define the class shown in Listing 21-13, which will represent a single recovery code.

Listing 21-13. The Contents of the RecoveryCode.cs File in the Identity/Store Folder

```
namespace ExampleApp.Identity.Store {

    public class RecoveryCode {

        public string Code { get; set; }
        public bool Redeemed { get; set; }
    }
}
```

To extend the user store, add a class file named UserStoreRecoveryCodes.cs to the ExampleApp/
Identity/Store folder and use it to define the partial class shown in Listing 21-14.

Listing 21-14. The Contents of the UserStoreRecoveryCodes.cs File in the Identity/Store Folder

```
using Microsoft.AspNetCore.Identity;
using System;
using System.Collections.Generic;
using System.Linq;
using System.Threading;
using System.Threading.Tasks;

namespace ExampleApp.Identity.Store {

    public interface IReadableUserTwoFactorRecoveryCodeStore
            : IUserTwoFactorRecoveryCodeStore<AppUser> {
        Task<IEnumerable<RecoveryCode>> GetCodesAsync(AppUser user);
    }

    public partial class UserStore : IReadableUserTwoFactorRecoveryCodeStore {
        private IDictionary<string, IEnumerable<RecoveryCode>> recoveryCodes
            = new Dictionary<string, IEnumerable<RecoveryCode>>();

        public async Task<int> CountCodesAsync(AppUser user, CancellationToken token)
            => (await GetCodesAsync(user)).Where(code => !code.Redeemed).Count();

        public Task<IEnumerable<RecoveryCode>> GetCodesAsync(AppUser user) =>
            Task.FromResult(recoveryCodes.ContainsKey(user.Id)
                ? recoveryCodes[user.Id] : Enumerable.Empty<RecoveryCode>());

        public async Task<bool> RedeemCodeAsync(AppUser user, string code,
                CancellationToken token) {
            RecoveryCode rc = (await GetCodesAsync(user))
                .FirstOrDefault(rc => rc.Code == code && !rc.Redeemed);
            if (rc != null) {
                rc.Redeemed = true;
                return true;
            }
            return false;
        }
}
```

```
        public Task ReplaceCodesAsync(AppUser user, IEnumerable<string>
                recoveryCodes, CancellationToken token) {
            this.recoveryCodes[user.Id] = recoveryCodes
                .Select(rc => new RecoveryCode { Code = rc, Redeemed = false });
            return Task.CompletedTask;
        }
    }
}
```

The interface provided by Identity doesn't provide a means to read the user's recovery codes once they have been stored. I find that users are more likely to use recovery codes if they can inspect the codes and see which ones have already been redeemed, so I defined the IReadableUserTwoFactorRecoveryCodeStore interface, which extends IUserTwoFactorRecoveryCodeStore<AppUser> by adding a method that allows the codes associated with the user to be retrieved.

Seeding the Data Store

Recovery codes can be any string that is known only by the application and the user. In Listing 21-15, I have added a set of codes to the seed data added to the store when it is created, which will make it easier to demonstrate the recovery code feature.

Listing 21-15. Adding Recovery Codes in the UserStore.cs File in the Identity/Store Folder

```
using Microsoft.AspNetCore.Identity;
using System.Collections.Generic;
using System.Linq;
using System.Security.Claims;

namespace ExampleApp.Identity.Store {

    public partial class UserStore {

        public ILookupNormalizer Normalizer { get; set; }

        public IPasswordHasher<AppUser> PasswordHasher { get; set; }

        public UserStore(ILookupNormalizer normalizer,
                IPasswordHasher<AppUser> passwordHasher) {
            Normalizer = normalizer;
            PasswordHasher = passwordHasher;
            SeedStore();
        }

        private void SeedStore() {

            var customData = new Dictionary<string, (string food, string hobby)> {
                { "Alice", ("Pizza", "Running") },
                { "Bob", ("Ice Cream", "Cinema") },
                { "Charlie", ("Burgers", "Cooking") }
            };
            var twoFactorUsers = new[] { "Alice", "Charlie" };
```

```
        var authenticatorKeys = new Dictionary<string, string> {
            {"Alice", "A4GG2BNKJNKKFOKGZRGBVUYIAJCUHEW7" }
        };
        var codes = new[] { "abcd1234", "abcd5678" };
        int idCounter = 0;

        string EmailFromName(string name) => $"{name.ToLower()}@example.com";

        foreach (string name in UsersAndClaims.Users) {
            AppUser user = new AppUser {
                Id = (++idCounter).ToString(),
                UserName = name,
                NormalizedUserName = Normalizer.NormalizeName(name),
                EmailAddress = EmailFromName(name),
                NormalizedEmailAddress =
                    Normalizer.NormalizeEmail(EmailFromName(name)),
                EmailAddressConfirmed = true,
                PhoneNumber = "123-4567",
                PhoneNumberConfirmed = true,
                FavoriteFood = customData[name].food,
                Hobby = customData[name].hobby,
                SecurityStamp = "InitialStamp",
                TwoFactorEnabled = twoFactorUsers.Any(tfName => tfName == name)
            };
            user.Claims =  UsersAndClaims.UserData[user.UserName]
                .Select(role => new Claim(ClaimTypes.Role, role)).ToList();
            user.PasswordHash = PasswordHasher.HashPassword(user, "MySecret1$");
            if (authenticatorKeys.ContainsKey(name)) {
                user.AuthenticatorKey = authenticatorKeys[name];
                user.AuthenticatorEnabled = true;
            }
            users.TryAdd(user.Id, user);
            recoveryCodes.Add(user.Id, codes.Select(c =>
                new RecoveryCode() { Code = c }).ToArray());
        }
    }
  }
}
```

Recovery codes should be random, which they are when creating using the methods provided by the UserManager<T> class, which I describe in the next section. For ease of testing, however, I have defined two codes that are assigned to allow any user to sign in.

Managing Recovery Codes

The UserManager<T> class provides the methods described in Table 21-7 for managing recovery codes.

Table 21-7. *The UserManager<T> Methods for Recovery Codes*

Name	Description
GenerateNewTwoFactor RecoveryCodesAsync (user, number)	This method generates the specified number of recovery codes for a user. The news codes are passed to the store's ReplaceCodesAsync method, after which the user manager's update sequence is performed. Fewer codes may be generated than the number specified.
RedeemTwoFactorRecovery CodeAsync(user, code)	This method redeems a recovery code for the specified user by calling the store's RedeemCodeAsync method. If the code is valid, the user manager's update sequence is performed. The result of this method is an IdentiyResult, which is used to indicate whether the code was successfully redeemed.
CountRecoveryCodes Async(user)	This method returns the number of unredeemed codes available for the specified user.

Add a Razor Page named RecoveryCodes.cshtml to the Pages/Store folder with the content shown in Listing 21-16.

Listing 21-16. The Contents of the RecoveryCodes.cshtml File in the Pages/Store Folder

```
@page "{id}"
@model ExampleApp.Pages.Store.RecoveryCodesModel

<h4 class="bg-primary text-white text-center p-2">Recovery Codes</h4>

<h6 class="text-center">There are @Model.RemainingCodes codes remaining</h6>

<div class="mx-5">
    <table class="table table-sm table-striped table-bordered">
        <tbody>
            @for (int row = 0; row < Model.Codes.Length; row += 2) {
                <tr>
                    @for (int index = row; index < row + 2; index++) {
                        var rc = Model.Codes[index];
                        <td class="text-d">
                            @if (rc.Redeemed) {
                                <del>@rc.Code</del>
                            } else {
                                @rc.Code
                            }
                        </td>
                    }
                </tr>
            }
        </tbody>
    </table>
</div>
<div class="m-2 text-center">
    <form method="post">
```

```
        <input type="hidden" name="id" value="@Model.AppUser.Id" />
        <button class="btn btn-primary">Generate New Codes</button>
        <a href="@($"/users/edit/{Model.AppUser.Id}")" class="btn btn-secondary">
            Cancel
        </a>
    </form>
</div>
```

The view part of the page displays the recovery codes for a user, whose ID is received through the routing system. All of the user's codes are displayed, but those that are redeemed are struck through. Add the code shown in Listing 21-17 to the RecoveryCodes.cshtml.cs file to define the page model class. (You will have to create this file if you are using Visual Studio Code.)

Listing 21-17. The Contents of the RecoveryCodes.cshtml.cs File in the Pages/Store Folder

```
using ExampleApp.Identity;
using ExampleApp.Identity.Store;
using Microsoft.AspNetCore.Identity;
using Microsoft.AspNetCore.Mvc;
using Microsoft.AspNetCore.Mvc.RazorPages;
using System.Collections.Generic;
using System.Linq;
using System.Threading.Tasks;

namespace ExampleApp.Pages.Store {

    public class RecoveryCodesModel : PageModel {

        public RecoveryCodesModel(UserManager<AppUser> manager,
                IUserStore<AppUser> store) {
            UserManager = manager;
            UserStore = store;
        }

        public UserManager<AppUser> UserManager { get; set; }
        public IUserStore<AppUser> UserStore { get; set; }

        public AppUser AppUser { get; set; }

        public RecoveryCode[] Codes { get; set; }
        public int RemainingCodes { get; set;}

        public async Task OnGetAsync(string id) {
            AppUser = await UserManager.FindByIdAsync(id);
            if (AppUser != null) {
                Codes = (await GetCodes()).OrderBy(c => c.Code).ToArray();
                RemainingCodes = await UserManager.CountRecoveryCodesAsync(AppUser);
            }
        }
```

```
    public async Task<IActionResult> OnPostAsync(string id) {
        AppUser = await UserManager.FindByIdAsync(id);
        await UserManager.GenerateNewTwoFactorRecoveryCodesAsync(AppUser, 10);
        return RedirectToPage();
    }

    private async Task<IEnumerable<RecoveryCode>> GetCodes() {
        if (UserStore is IReadableUserTwoFactorRecoveryCodeStore) {
            return await (UserStore as
                IReadableUserTwoFactorRecoveryCodeStore).GetCodesAsync(AppUser);
        }
        return Enumerable.Empty<RecoveryCode>();
    }
  }
}
```

To obtain the user's recovery codes, the page model class declares a constructor dependency on
IUserStore<AppUser>, which provides access to the store and which is then cast to an implementation of the
IReadableUserTwoFactorRecoveryCodeStore interface. This allows the GET handler method to populate the
Codes property so its contents can be displayed to the user. The POST handler method is called when a new
set of codes is required and calls the user manager's GenerateNewTwoFactorRecoveryCodesAsync method.

To incorporate the recovery codes into the rest of the application, add the elements shown in
Listing 21-18 to the _EditUserTwoFactor.cshtml file in the Pages/Store folder.

Listing 21-18. Adding Content in the _EditUserTwoFactor.cshtml File in the Pages/Store Folder

```
@model AppUser
@inject UserManager<AppUser> UserManager

@if (UserManager.SupportsUserTwoFactor) {
    <tr>
        <td>Two-Factor</td>
        <td><input asp-for="TwoFactorEnabled"/></td>
    </tr>
}
@if (UserManager.SupportsUserTwoFactorRecoveryCodes) {
    <tr>
        <td>Recovery Codes</td>
        <td>
            @(await UserManager.CountRecoveryCodesAsync(Model)) codes remaining
                <a asp-page="RecoveryCodes" asp-route-id="@Model.Id"
                    class="btn btn-sm btn-secondary align-top">Change</a>
        </td>
    </tr>
}
```

Restart ASP.NET Core, request http://localhost:5000/users, and click the Edit button for Alice.
You will see a row in the table that shows how many codes are available. Click the Change button, and you
will see the user's recovery codes. Click the Generate New Codes button, and a new set of codes will be
produced, as shown in Figure 21-5. The new codes will be lost when ASP.NET Core restarts because the user
store is memory based.

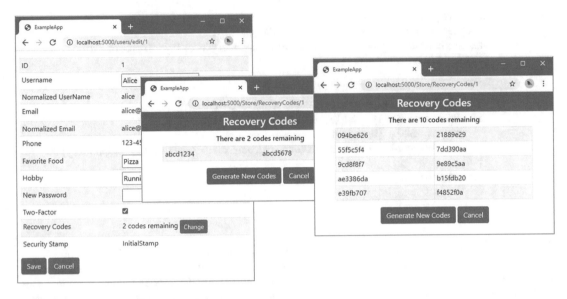

Figure 21-5. *Managing recovery codes*

Using Recovery Codes to Sign In

Recovery codes are redeemed when the user is unable to receive a security code, either through SMS/email or an authenticator. The `SignInManager<T>` class provides the method described in Table 21-8 for signing in with a recovery code.

Table 21-8. *The SignInManager<T> Recovery Code Method*

Name	Description
TwoFactorRecovery CodeSignInAsync(code)	This method completes the two-factor sign-in process using the specified code. The RetrieveTwoFactorInfoAsync method is used to retrieve details of the user signing in, and the user manager's RedeemTwoFactorRecoveryCodeAsync method is used to validate the code. If the code is valid, the user is signed into the application. The option to remember the client is disabled for sign-ins performed with a recovery code.

Add a Razor Page named `SignInRecoveryCode.cshtml` to the `Pages` folder and add the content shown in Listing 21-19.

Listing 21-19. The Contents of the SignInRecoveryCode.cshtml File in the Pages Folder

```
@page
@model ExampleApp.Pages.SignInRecoveryCodeModel

<h4 class="bg-info text-white m-2 p-2">Two Factor Sign In</h4>

<div asp-validation-summary="All" class="text-danger m-2"></div>

<div class="m-2">
```

```
<form method="post">
    <div class="form-group">
        <label>Enter Recovery Code:</label>
        <input class="form-control" name="code"/>
    </div>
    <div class="mt-2">
        <button class="btn btn-info" type="submit">Sign In</button>
        <a asp-page="/Signin" class="btn btn-secondary">Cancel</a>
    </div>
</form>
</div>
```

The view part of the page displays an input element into which the user can enter one of their recovery codes. To define the page model class, add the code shown in Listing 21-20 to the SignInRecoveryCode.cshtml.cs file in the Pages folder. (You will have to create this file if you are using Visual Studio Code.)

Listing 21-20. The Contents of the SignInRecoveryCode.cshtml.cs File in the Pages Folder

```
using ExampleApp.Identity;
using Microsoft.AspNetCore.Identity;
using Microsoft.AspNetCore.Mvc;
using Microsoft.AspNetCore.Mvc.RazorPages;
using System.Threading.Tasks;
using SignInResult = Microsoft.AspNetCore.Identity.SignInResult;

namespace ExampleApp.Pages {

    public class SignInRecoveryCodeModel : PageModel {

        public SignInRecoveryCodeModel(SignInManager<AppUser> manager)
            => SignInManager = manager;

        public SignInManager<AppUser> SignInManager { get; set; }

        public async Task<IActionResult> OnPostAsync (string code,
                string returnUrl) {
            if (string.IsNullOrEmpty(code)) {
                ModelState.AddModelError("", "Code required");
            } else {
                SignInResult result =
                    await SignInManager.TwoFactorRecoveryCodeSignInAsync(code);
                if (result.Succeeded) {
                    return Redirect(returnUrl ?? "/");
                } else {
                    ModelState.AddModelError("", "Sign In Failed");
                }
            }
            return Page();
        }
    }
}
```

The page model class uses the SignInManager<T>.TwoFactorRecoveryCodeSignInAsync method to try to complete the two-factor sign in process using the recovery code provided by the user. A validation error is displayed if the user has not provided a code or the code is invalid.

To allow the user to provide a recovery code, add the element shown in Listing 21-21 to the SignInTwoFactor Razor Page.

Listing 21-21. Adding an Element in the SignInTwoFactor.cshtml File in the Pages Folder

```
@page
@model ExampleApp.Pages.SignInTwoFactorModel

<h4 class="bg-info text-white m-2 p-2">Two Factor Sign In</h4>

<div asp-validation-summary="All" class="text-danger m-2"></div>

@if (Model.AuthenticatorEnabled) {
    <span class="m-2"> Enter the code displayed by your authenticator. </span>
} else {
    <span class="m-2"> We have sent a security code to your phone. </span>
    <a asp-page="/SignInTwoFactor" class="btn btn-sm btn-secondary">Resend Code</a>
}

<div class="m-2">
    <form method="post">
        <div class="form-group">
            <label>Enter security Code:</label>
            <input class="form-control" name="code"/>
        </div>
        <div class="form-check">
            <input class="form-check-input" type="checkbox" name="rememberMe" />
            <label class="form-check-label">Remember Me</label>
            <a asp-page="SigninRecoveryCode" class="btn btn-sm btn-secondary ml-3"
                asp-route-returnurl="@HttpContext.Request.Query["returnUrl"]">
                    Use Recovery Code
            </a>
        </div>
        <div class="mt-2">
            <button class="btn btn-info" type="submit"
                    disabled="@(!ModelState.IsValid)">Sign In</button>
            <a asp-page="/Signin" class="btn btn-secondary">Cancel</a >
        </div>
    </form>
</div>
```

Restart ASP.NET Core, request http://localhost:5000/signout, select the Forget Me option, and click the Sign Out button. This ensures that no user is signed in and the client will not be remembered.

Request http://localhost:5000/secret to trigger the challenge response. Select alice@example.com from the list and enter MySecret1$ into the password field. Click the Sign In button, and you will advance to the second stage of the sign-in process. Click the Use Recovery Code button, enter abcd1234 into the text field, and click the Sign In button. You will be signed into the application and redirected to the /secret URL, as shown in Figure 21-6.

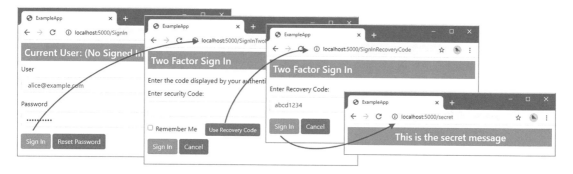

Figure 21-6. *Using a recovery code*

Request `http://localhost:5000/store/recoverycodes/1`, and you will see the recovery codes for the Alice user. The code you used to sign in is shown as redeemed, as shown in Figure 21-7.

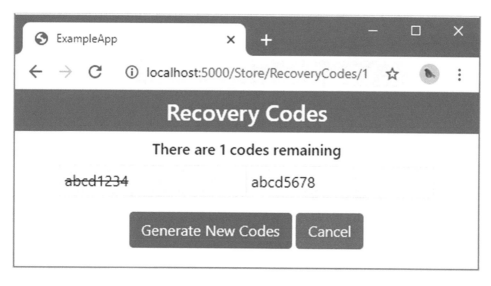

Figure 21-7. *The effect of using a recovery code*

Summary

In this chapter, I described the Identity support for authenticators as part of a two-factor sign-in. Authenticators are set up using a secret key, which is used to generate tokens that the user can present to the application and that can be validated by Identity using the same key. I also described the support for recovery codes, which provide an important means for signing into the application when the second factor in a two-factor process is unavailable. In the next chapter, I describe external authentication, where the user authentication process is handled by a third party.

CHAPTER 22

■ ■ ■

External Authentication, Part 1

In this chapter, I explain how external authentication works. This is a complex process, even by the high standard set by other ASP.NET Core Identity features, and there is a lot of detail to take in. The examples in this chapter use a simulated third-party service, which allows me to explain the interactions in a controlled way. In Chapter 23, I add support for working with real services from Google and Facebook. Table 22-1 puts external authentication in context.

Table 22-1. *Putting External Authentication in Context*

Question	Answer
What is it?	External authentication delegates the process of identifying users to a third-party service, typically provided by a major technology company or social media platform.
Why is it useful?	External authentication allows users to sign in to applications without having to create and remember an additional password. It can also provide access to stronger sign-in security than is supported directly by ASP.NET Core Identity.
How is it used?	The process is complicated, but the user's browser is redirected to the external service, which authenticates the user and communicates the result to the ASP.NET Core application. The result is verified by ASP.NET Core directly with the external service, and the user is signed in.
Are there any pitfalls or limitations?	The main issue is complexity, although this is not as much of an issue if you use the external authentication packages provided by Microsoft, which are described in Part 1.
Are there any alternatives?	External authentication is an optional feature, and projects do not have to use it.

Preparing for This Chapter

This chapter uses the ExampleApp project from Chapter 21. No changes are required for this chapter. Open a new command prompt, navigate to the ExampleApp folder, and run the command shown in Listing 22-1 to start ASP.NET Core.

■ **Tip** You can download the example project for this chapter—and for all the other chapters in this book— from `https://github.com/Apress/pro-asp.net-core-identity`. See Chapter 1 for how to get help if you have problems running the examples.

A. Freeman, *Pro ASP.NET Core Identity*, https://doi.org/10.1007/978-1-4842-6858-2_22

Listing 22-1. Running the Example Application

```
dotnet run
```

Open a new browser window and request `http://localhost:5000/users`. You will be presented with the user data shown in Figure 22-1. The data is stored only in memory and changes will be lost when ASP. NET Core is stopped.

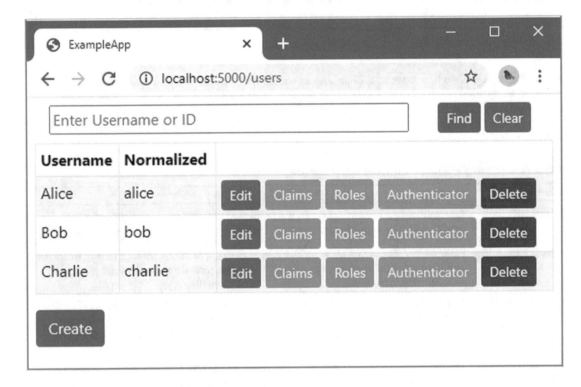

Figure 22-1. *Running the example application*

Preparing for External Authentication

When external authentication is used, the process of obtaining and validating a user's credentials is handled outside of the ASP.NET Core application (hence the term *external*). For corporate applications, this typically means that authentication is delegated to a service that is shared between multiple applications, allowing users to sign into several applications with a single set of credentials. In customer-facing applications, authentication is often handled by social media platforms, such as Google or Facebook, where users are likely to already have accounts set up.

Identity doesn't apply any constraints on how external authentication is performed and relies on an authentication handler to take care of the details. Authentication handlers for external services implement the same IAuthenticationHandler interface I described in Chapter 14. This approach is consistent with the basic Identity features and means that an application can support multiple external services by having an authentication handler for each one. External authentication has three phases, *preparation, authentication,* and *correlation,* which I describe in the following text.

Authentication handlers are part of the ASP.NET Core platform and are not specific to Identity. To help keep the focus on Identity features, I am going to create an authentication handler that returns canned results, without actually performing authentication. In later examples, I replace the canned results, initially to access a test authentication service and then to perform authentication with real social media platforms. Add a class file named ExternalAuthHandler.cs to the ExampleApp/Custom folder and use it to define the class shown in Listing 22-2.

Listing 22-2. The Contents of the ExternalAuthHandler.cs File in the Custom Folder

```
using Microsoft.AspNetCore.Authentication;
using Microsoft.AspNetCore.Http;
using System.Threading.Tasks;

namespace ExampleApp.Custom {
    public class ExternalAuthHandler : IAuthenticationHandler {

        public AuthenticationScheme Scheme { get; set; }
        public HttpContext Context { get; set; }

        public Task InitializeAsync(AuthenticationScheme scheme,
                HttpContext context) {
            Scheme = scheme;
            Context = context;
            return Task.CompletedTask;
        }

        public Task<AuthenticateResult> AuthenticateAsync() {
            return Task.FromResult(AuthenticateResult.NoResult());
        }

        public Task ChallengeAsync(AuthenticationProperties properties) {
            return Task.CompletedTask;
        }

        public Task ForbidAsync(AuthenticationProperties properties) {
            return Task.CompletedTask;
        }
    }
}
```

This is a minimal implementation of the IAuthenticationHandler interface that contains just enough code to compile. I add features to the class as I explain how the external authentication process works in the sections that follow.

Implementing the Selection Phase

The external authentication process presents the user with the option to authenticate using an external service. The SignInManager<T> class provides access to the authentication schemes available for external service through the method described in Table 22-2.

Table 22-2. *The SignInManager<T> Method for External Authentication Schemes*

Name	Description
GetExternalAuthentication SchemesAsync()	This asynchronous method returns a sequence of AuthenticationScheme objects, each of which can be used for external authentication.

There is an oddity in the GetExternalAuthenticationSchemesAsync method, which is that only authentication schemes that have been registered with a DisplayName property are returned. In Listing 22-3, I have created a new scheme, with a DisplayName, that uses the handler created in Listing 22-2.

■ **Tip** The second argument to the AddScheme<T> method is optional and can be omitted if you need to create a scheme that should not be selected by the GetExternalAuthenticationSchemesAsync method.

Listing 22-3. Defining an Authentication Scheme in the Startup.cs File in the ExampleApp Folder

```
...
services.AddAuthentication(opts => {
    opts.DefaultScheme = IdentityConstants.ApplicationScheme;
    opts.AddScheme<ExternalAuthHandler>("demoAuth", "Demo Service");
}).AddCookie(IdentityConstants.ApplicationScheme, opts => {
    opts.LoginPath = "/signin";
    opts.AccessDeniedPath = "/signin/403";
})
.AddCookie(IdentityConstants.TwoFactorUserIdScheme)
.AddCookie(IdentityConstants.TwoFactorRememberMeScheme);
...
```

In Listing 22-4, I have added content to the view section of the SignIn Razor Page that presents the user with a button for each of the external authentication schemes.

Listing 22-4. Offering External Authentication in the SignIn.cshtml File in the Pages Folder

```
@page "{code:int?}"
@model ExampleApp.Pages.SignInModel
@using Microsoft.AspNetCore.Http

@if (!string.IsNullOrEmpty(Model.Message)) {
    <h3 class="bg-danger text-white text-center p-2">@Model.Message</h3>
}

<h4 class="bg-info text-white m-2 p-2">Current User: @Model.Username</h4>

<div class="container-fluid">
    <div class="row">
        <div class="col-6 border p-2 h-100">
            <h4 class="text-center">Local Authentication</h4>
            <form method="post">
                <div class="form-group">
                    <label>User</label>
```

```html
                    <select class="form-control"
                            asp-for="Username" asp-items="@Model.Users">
                    </select>
                </div>
                <div class="form-group">
                    <label>Password</label>
                    <input class="form-control" type="password"
                        name="password" value="MySecret1$" />
                </div>
                <button class="btn btn-info" type="submit">Sign In</button>
                @if (User.Identity.IsAuthenticated) {
                    <a asp-page="/Store/PasswordChange" class="btn btn-secondary"
                        asp-route-id="@Model.User?
                                .FindFirst(ClaimTypes.NameIdentifier)?.Value">
                            Change Password
                    </a>
                } else {
                    <a class="btn btn-secondary" href="/password/reset">
                        Reset Password
                    </a>
                }
            </form>
        </div>
        <div class="col-6 text-center">
            <div class="border p-2 h-100">
                <form method="post">
                    <h4>External Authentication</h4>
                    <div class="mt-4 w-75">
                        @foreach (var scheme in
                                await Model.SignInManager
                                    .GetExternalAuthenticationSchemesAsync()) {
                            <div class="mt-2 text-center">
                                <button class="btn btn-block btn-secondary
                                            m-1 mx-5" type="submit"
                                        asp-page="/externalsignin"
                                        asp-route-returnUrl=
                                            "@Request.Query["returnUrl"]"
                                        asp-route-providername="@scheme.Name">
                                    @scheme.DisplayName
                                </button>
                            </div>
                        }
                    </div>
                </form>
            </div>
        </div>
    </div>
</div>
```

The new layout separates the local authentication options from the buttons that will lead to external authentication, which you can see if you restart ASP.NET Core and request `http://localhost:5000/signin`, as shown in Figure 22-2. Clicking the Demo Service button targets a page that I will create in the next step.

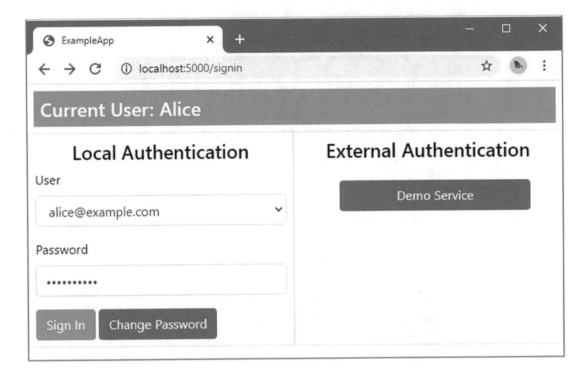

Figure 22-2. *Presenting the user with external authentication options*

Understanding the Preparation Phase

In the preparation phase, the application configures external authentication and starts the authentication process. To configure authentication, an `AuthenticationProperties` object is created, which is used to store state data that will be needed later. Table 22-3 describes the most important properties defined by the `AuthenticationProperties` class.

Table 22-3. *The Most Important AuthenticationProperties Properties*

Name	Description
Items	This property is used to store authentication state data using an `IDictionary<string, string?>` object.
RedirectUri	This property specifies the URL to which the user's browser should be redirected at the end of the authentication phase.

The Items collection property is used by the SignInManager<T> class to store data that it needs once the authentication phase is complete. The RedirectUri specifies the URL to which the authentication handler should redirect the user's browser once they are authenticated and that will be responsible for performing the correlation phase.

The SignInManager<T> class provides the ConfigureExternalAuthenticationProperties method for creating the AuthenticationProperties object, as described in Table 22-4.

Table 22-4. *The SignInManager<T> Method for the Preparation Phase*

Name	Description
ConfigureExternalAuthentication Properties(provider, redirectUrl, userId)	This method creates an AuthenticationProperties object. The provider value is added to the Items collection, and the redirectUrl value is assigned to the RedirectUri property. The optional userId parameter is added to the Items collection as an anti-cross-site request forgery measure and is used when a user is already signed in.

The Razor Page or controller returns a ChallengeResult, which selects the authentication handler and the AuthenticationProperties object created by the ConfigureExternalAuthenticationProperties method. This results in the authentication handler's ChallengeAsync method being called using the AuthenticationProperties object as an argument, ending the preparation phase.

Add a Razor Page named ExternalSignIn.cshtml to the Pages folder with the content shown in Listing 22-5.

Listing 22-5. The Contents of the ExternalSignIn.cshtml File in the Pages Folder

```
@page
@model ExampleApp.Pages.ExternalSignInModel

<h4 class="bg-info text-white text-center p-2">External Authentication</h4>
```

This is just placeholder content for the moment because the view part of the page isn't required until later. For the moment, the focus is on the page model class. Add the code shown in Listing 22-6 to the ExternalSignIn.cshtml.cs file in the Pages folder. (You will have to create this file if you are using Visual Studio Code.)

Listing 22-6. The Contents of the ExternalSignIn.cshtml.cs File in the Pages Folder

```
using ExampleApp.Identity;
using Microsoft.AspNetCore.Authentication;
using Microsoft.AspNetCore.Identity;
using Microsoft.AspNetCore.Mvc;
using Microsoft.AspNetCore.Mvc.RazorPages;

namespace ExampleApp.Pages {

    public class ExternalSignInModel : PageModel {

        public ExternalSignInModel(SignInManager<AppUser> signInManager) {
            SignInManager = signInManager;
        }
```

```
        public SignInManager<AppUser> SignInManager { get; set; }

        public IActionResult OnPost(string providerName,
                string returnUrl = "/") {

            string redirectUrl = Url.Page("./ExternalSignIn",
                pageHandler: "Correlate", values: new { returnUrl });
            AuthenticationProperties properties = SignInManager
              .ConfigureExternalAuthenticationProperties(providerName,
                 redirectUrl);
            return new ChallengeResult(providerName, properties);
        }
    }
}
```

There two levels of redirection to be handled when preparing for external authentication. The standard sign-in process captures the URL that the user requested that led to the challenge response. This value is added as a query string parameter of the URL to which the authentication handler should redirect the browser after the user has been authenticated, like this:

```
...
string redirectUrl = Url.Page("./ExternalSignIn", pageHandler: "Correlate",
    values: new { returnUrl });
...
```

The pageHandler value includes the name of the hander method that will receive the redirected request. I have named the method Correlate in this example, and I will define this method shortly.

Understanding the Authentication Phase

In the authentication phase, the authentication handler is responsible for guiding the user through the process required by the external service. The details of this process are not visible to ASP.NET Core Identity, but most external authentication is done using the OAuth protocol, which I describe later in this chapter. For now, however, I am going to authenticate the user without requiring any credentials to demonstrate the overall process. Add the code shown in Listing 22-7 to the ExternalAuthHandler class.

Listing 22-7. Performing Authentication in the ExternalAuthHandler.cs File in the Custom Folder

```
using Microsoft.AspNetCore.Authentication;
using Microsoft.AspNetCore.Http;
using System.Threading.Tasks;
using System.Security.Claims;
using Microsoft.AspNetCore.Identity;

namespace ExampleApp.Custom {
    public class ExternalAuthHandler : IAuthenticationHandler {

        public AuthenticationScheme Scheme { get; set; }
        public HttpContext Context { get; set; }
```

```
    public Task InitializeAsync(AuthenticationScheme scheme,
            HttpContext context) {
        Scheme = scheme;
        Context = context;
        return Task.CompletedTask;
    }

    public Task<AuthenticateResult> AuthenticateAsync() {
        return Task.FromResult(AuthenticateResult.NoResult());
    }

    public async Task ChallengeAsync(AuthenticationProperties properties) {
        ClaimsIdentity identity = new ClaimsIdentity(Scheme.Name);
        identity.AddClaims(new[] {
            new Claim(ClaimTypes.NameIdentifier, "SomeUniqueID"),
            new Claim(ClaimTypes.Email, "alice@example.com"),
            new Claim(ClaimTypes.Name, "Alice")
        });
        ClaimsPrincipal principal = new ClaimsPrincipal(identity);
        await Context.SignInAsync(IdentityConstants.ExternalScheme,
            principal, properties);
        Context.Response.Redirect(properties.RedirectUri);
    }

    public Task ForbidAsync(AuthenticationProperties properties) {
        return Task.CompletedTask;
    }
  }
}
```

It is the outcome from the ChallengeAsync method that is important, even though the handler isn't really performing authentication. A ClaimsPrincipal object is created, with a ClaimsIdentity that describes the authenticated user from the perspective of the external authentication service. For this test handler, this means there are claims to provide a unique ID, an email address, and a name.

Once the handler has created the ClaimsPrincipal, the HttpContext.SignInAsync method is used to sign in the external user with a special scheme, like this:

```
...
await Context.SignInAsync(IdentityConstants.ExternalScheme,
    principal, properties);
...
```

The IdentityConstants.ExternalScheme is used to sign in the external user to prepare for the next phase in the process. The other arguments to the SignInAsync method are the ClaimsPrincipal object and the AuthenticationProperties object, which ensures that the state data received by the handler is preserved. Once the external user has been signed in, the handler issues a redirection to the URL specified by the AuthenticationProperties parameter's RedirectUri method.

```
...
Context.Response.Redirect(properties.RedirectUri);
...
```

To support the `IdentityConstants.ExternalScheme` scheme, add the statement shown in Listing 22-8 to the `Startup` class.

Listing 22-8. Adding the Cookie Handler in the Startup.cs File in the ExampleApp Folder

```
...
services.AddSingleton<IUserValidator<AppUser>, EmailValidator>();
services.AddSingleton<IPasswordValidator<AppUser>, PasswordValidator>();
services.AddScoped<IUserClaimsPrincipalFactory<AppUser>,
    AppUserClaimsPrincipalFactory>();
services.AddSingleton<IRoleValidator<AppRole>, RoleValidator>();

services.AddAuthentication(opts => {
    opts.DefaultScheme = IdentityConstants.ApplicationScheme;
    opts.AddScheme<ExternalAuthHandler>("demoAuth", "Demo Service");
}).AddCookie(IdentityConstants.ApplicationScheme, opts => {
    opts.LoginPath = "/signin";
    opts.AccessDeniedPath = "/signin/403";
})
.AddCookie(IdentityConstants.TwoFactorUserIdScheme)
.AddCookie(IdentityConstants.TwoFactorRememberMeScheme)
.AddCookie(IdentityConstants.ExternalScheme);
...
```

All external authentication results in a sign-in using `IdentityConstants.ExternalScheme`, regardless of which external service is used. This allows `SignInManager<T>` to get the external user details, as described in the next section.

Understanding the Correlation Phase

The correlation phase determines which Identity user account is associated with the external authentication. So, for example, if Alice authenticates using Google, the correlation process uses the claims that the handler associated with the `ClaimsPrincipal` object to determine that this login is related to the local Alice account.

The way external logins are correlated to local accounts can be adapted to each project and each external authentication service. For the example app, I am going to use a three-stage approach.

1. Check the user store to see if the external login has already been associated with a local account. If it has been, sign the local user into the application.

2. If not, look for a local account with a matching email address. If there is a match, associate the login in the store and sign the user into the application.

3. If there is no matching email address, prompt the user to create a new account.

The external authentication handler defined in Listing 22-8 authenticates only a single user, so I will leave the third part of the process until later in the chapter, where I introduce a wider range of authentication features.

The approach I have outlined relies on the ability to keep track of user logins, which is done by storing `UserLoginInfo` objects in the user store. The `UserLoginInfo` class defines the properties shown in Table 22-5.

Table 22-5. *The UserLoginInfo Properties*

Name	Description
LoginProvider	This is the name of the authentication handler for the external service.
ProviderKey	This is the unique identifier by which the external service recognizes the user.
ProviderDisplayName	This is the name of the external service that will be displayed to the user.

   Identity only needs to keep track of the unique ID by which the user is known to the external service and details of the authentication service (which are generally the same as the authentication handler details).

Extending the User Store

User stores that can store external logins implement the IUserLoginStore<T> interface, which defines the methods described in Table 22-6. (Like the other store interfaces, these methods define a CancellationToken parameter named token.)

Table 22-6. *The IUserLoginStore<T> Methods*

Name	Description
GetLoginsAsync(user, token)	This method returns an IList<UserLoginInfo> containing the external logins for the specified user.
AddLoginAsync(user, login, token)	This method stores a UserLoginInfo for the specified user.
RemoveLoginAsync(user, loginProvider, providerKey)	This method removes the UserLoginInfo with the specified provider and key.
FindByLoginAsync(loginProvider, providerKey)	This method locates the user who has a UserLoginInfo with the specified provider and key.

   To add support for storing login information, add the property shown in Listing 22-9 to the AppUser class.

Listing 22-9. Adding a Property in the AppUser.cs File in the Identity Folder

```
using System;
using System.Collections.Generic;
using System.Security.Claims;
using Microsoft.AspNetCore.Identity;

namespace ExampleApp.Identity {
    public class AppUser {

        public string Id { get; set; } = Guid.NewGuid().ToString();

        public string UserName { get; set; }

        public string NormalizedUserName { get; set; }
```

```
        public string EmailAddress { get; set; }
        public string NormalizedEmailAddress { get; set; }
        public bool EmailAddressConfirmed { get; set; }

        public string PhoneNumber { get; set; }
        public bool PhoneNumberConfirmed { get; set; }

        public string FavoriteFood { get; set; }
        public string Hobby { get; set; }

        public IList<Claim> Claims { get; set; }

        public string SecurityStamp { get; set; }
        public string PasswordHash { get; set; }

        public bool CanUserBeLockedout { get; set; } = true;
        public int FailedSignInCount { get; set; }
        public DateTimeOffset? LockoutEnd { get; set; }

        public bool TwoFactorEnabled { get; set; }
        public bool AuthenticatorEnabled { get; set; }
        public string AuthenticatorKey { get; set; }

        public IList<UserLoginInfo> UserLogins { get; set; }
    }
}
```

To implement the interface in the example store, add a class file named UserStoreLogins.cs to the ExampleApp/Identity/Store folder and use it to define the partial class shown in Listing 22-10.

Listing 22-10. The Contents of the UserStoreLogins.cs File in the Identity/Store Folder

```
using Microsoft.AspNetCore.Identity;
using System.Collections.Generic;
using System.Linq;
using System.Threading;
using System.Threading.Tasks;

namespace ExampleApp.Identity.Store {

    public partial class UserStore : IUserLoginStore<AppUser> {

        public Task<IList<UserLoginInfo>> GetLoginsAsync(AppUser user,
                CancellationToken token)
            => Task.FromResult(user.UserLogins ?? new List<UserLoginInfo>());

        public Task AddLoginAsync(AppUser user, UserLoginInfo login,
                CancellationToken token) {
            if (user.UserLogins == null) {
                user.UserLogins = new List<UserLoginInfo>();
            }
```

```
            user.UserLogins.Add(login);
            return Task.CompletedTask;
        }

        public async Task RemoveLoginAsync(AppUser user, string loginProvider,
                string providerKey, CancellationToken token)
            => user.UserLogins = (await GetLoginsAsync(user, token)).Where(login
                => !login.LoginProvider.Equals(loginProvider)
                    && !login.ProviderKey.Equals(providerKey)).ToList();

        public Task<AppUser> FindByLoginAsync(string loginProvider,
                string providerKey, CancellationToken token) =>
            Task.FromResult(Users.FirstOrDefault(u => u.UserLogins != null &&
                u.UserLogins.Any(login => login.LoginProvider.Equals(loginProvider)
                    && login.ProviderKey.Equals(providerKey))));
    }
}
```

Since the user store in the example application is memory-based, I can keep track of the UserLoginInfo objects using a dictionary, with AppUser objects as keys. The UserManager<T> class defines the methods shown in Table 22-7 for managing the external logins in the user store.

Table 22-7. *The UserManager<T> Methods for Managing External Logins*

Name	Description
FindByLoginAsync(provider, key)	This method calls the user store's FindByLoginAsync method to locate the local user associated with the specified provider and key.
GetLoginsAsync(user)	This method calls the user store's GetLoginsAsync method to return an IList<UserLoginInfo> containing the external logins associated with the specified local user.
AddLoginAsync(user, login)	This method calls the user store's AddLoginAsync method to associate the specified external login with the local user, after which the user manager's update sequence is performed. An exception is thrown if it already contains the specified login (which is determined by calling the FindByLoginAsync method).
RemoveLoginAsync(user, provider, key)	This method calls the store's RemoveLoginAsync method to remove the external login, after which the user's security stamp is updated and the user manager's update sequence is performed.

Correlating and Storing Logins

The SignInManager<T> class defines the methods shown in Table 22-8 for obtaining the ClaimsPrincipal created by the external authentication handler and signing in local users.

Table 22-8. *The SignInManager<T> Methods for Correlating External Logins*

Name	Description
GetExternalLoginInfoAsync()	This method returns an ExternalLoginInfo object for the external login that can be added to the user store. It does this by retrieving the ClaimsPrincipal object created by the external authentication handler. The value of the NameIdentifier claims is used as a unique ID. The provider name is obtained from a property named LoginProvider in the Items collection of the AuthentionProperties object associated with the login. The display name is obtained from the results of the GetExternalAuthenticationSchemesAsync method.
ExternalLoginSignInAsync (provider, key, isPersistent, bypassTwoFactor)	This method uses the FindByLoginAsync method to locate the user with a login that matches the specified provider and key and signs them into the application. The isPersistent argument controls whether the sign-in cookie persists after the browser is closed. The bypassTwoFactor argument determines if the two-factor feature will be bypassed.

The login correlation is performed when the authentication handler redirects the browser following the completion of the authentication phase. The GetExternalLoginInfoAsync method returns an instance of the ExternalLoginInfo class, which is derived from UserLoginInfo and defines the additional properties described in Table 22-9.

Table 22-9. *The ExternalLoginInfo Properties*

Name	Description
Principal	This property returns the ClaimsPrincipal object created by the external authentication handler.
AuthenticationTokens	This property returns a sequence of authentication tokens, which I describe in Chapter 23.
AuthenticationProperties	This property returns the AuthenticationProperties object associated with the external login.

Add the code shown in Listing 22-11 to define the handler methods that deal with the correlation in the example application.

Listing 22-11. Processing the External Login in the ExternalSignIn.cshtml.cs File in the Pages Folder

```
using ExampleApp.Identity;
using Microsoft.AspNetCore.Authentication;
using Microsoft.AspNetCore.Identity;
using Microsoft.AspNetCore.Mvc;
using Microsoft.AspNetCore.Mvc.RazorPages;
using System.Linq;
using System.Security.Claims;
using System.Threading.Tasks;
using SignInResult = Microsoft.AspNetCore.Identity.SignInResult;
```

```
namespace ExampleApp.Pages {

    public class ExternalSignInModel : PageModel {

        public ExternalSignInModel(SignInManager<AppUser> signInManager,
                UserManager<AppUser> userManager) {
            SignInManager = signInManager;
            UserManager = userManager;
        }

        public SignInManager<AppUser> SignInManager { get; set; }
        public UserManager<AppUser> UserManager { get; set; }

        public string ProviderDisplayName { get; set; }

        public IActionResult OnPost(string providerName,
                string returnUrl = "/") {

            string redirectUrl = Url.Page("./ExternalSignIn",
                pageHandler: "Correlate", values: new { returnUrl });
            AuthenticationProperties properties = SignInManager
              .ConfigureExternalAuthenticationProperties(providerName,
                    redirectUrl);
            return new ChallengeResult(providerName, properties);
        }

        public async Task<IActionResult> OnGetCorrelate(string returnUrl) {
            ExternalLoginInfo info = await SignInManager.GetExternalLoginInfoAsync();
            AppUser user = await UserManager.FindByLoginAsync(info.LoginProvider,
                info.ProviderKey);
            if (user == null) {
                string externalEmail =
                    info.Principal.FindFirst(ClaimTypes.Email)?.Value
                        ?? string.Empty;
                user = await UserManager.FindByEmailAsync(externalEmail);
                if (user == null) {
                    return RedirectToPage("/ExternalAccountConfirm",
                        new { returnUrl });
                } else {
                    await UserManager.AddLoginAsync(user, info);
                }
            }
            SignInResult result = await SignInManager.ExternalLoginSignInAsync(
                info.LoginProvider, info.ProviderKey, false, false);
            if (result.Succeeded) {
                return RedirectToPage("ExternalSignIn", "Confirm",
                    new { info.ProviderDisplayName, returnUrl });
            } else if (result.RequiresTwoFactor) {
                string postSignInUrl = this.Url.Page("/ExternalSignIn", "Confirm",
                    new { info.ProviderDisplayName, returnUrl });
                return RedirectToPage("/SignInTwoFactor",
```

```
                    new { returnUrl = postSignInUrl });
            }
            return RedirectToPage(new { error = true, returnUrl });
        }

        public async Task OnGetConfirmAsync() {
            string provider = User.FindFirstValue(ClaimTypes.AuthenticationMethod);
            ProviderDisplayName =
                (await SignInManager.GetExternalAuthenticationSchemesAsync())
                    .FirstOrDefault(s => s.Name == provider)?.DisplayName ?? provider;
        }
    }
}
```

When the OnGetCorrelate method is called, I use the GetExternalLoginInfoAsync method to get the ExternalLoginInfo object that describes the external login. Using the details provided by the ExternalLoginInfo, I query the user store for an existing external login to get the AppUser object that represents the user.

If there is no matching login, I locate an email claim from the external ClaimsPrincipal and use it to query the user store. If there is a matching user, I store the external login for future use.

If I have found a user, either using the login or by email address, I sign them into the application using the SignInManager<T>.ExternalLoginSignInAsync method, like this:

```
...
SignInResult result = await SignInManager.ExternalLoginSignInAsync(
    info.LoginProvider, info.ProviderKey, false, false);
...
```

There is an option to bypass two-factor security when signing in with an external login, but I have chosen to leave two-factor enabled to demonstrate how it works. If the user is signed in without two-factor, I redirect them to the Confirm handler, which uses the view part of the page to display a summary of the external login.

```
...
string postSignInUrl = this.Url.Page("/ExternalSignIn", "Confirm",
    new { info.ProviderDisplayName, returnUrl });
return RedirectToPage("/SignInTwoFactor", new { returnUrl = postSignInUrl });
...
```

To display a summary of the external authentication process, add the content shown in Listing 22-12 to the ExternalSignIn.cshtml file.

Listing 22-12. Displaying a Summary in the ExternalSignIn.cshtml File in the Pages Folder

```
@page
@model ExampleApp.Pages.ExternalSignInModel

<h4 class="bg-info text-white text-center p-2">External Authentication</h4>

@{
    string returnUrl = Request.Query["returnUrl"].Count == 0 ?
        "/" : Request.Query["returnUrl"];
}
```

```
@if (Request.Query["error"].Count() > 0) {
    <h5 class="bg-danger text-white text-center m-2 p-2">
        Something went wrong. You could not be signed into the application.
    </h5>
    <h5 class="text-center m-2 p-2">@Request.Query["error"]</h5>
    <div class="text-center">
        <a class="btn btn-info text-center" href="@returnUrl">OK</a>
    </div>
} else {
    <h5 class="text-center">
        @User.Identity.Name has been authenticated by @Model.ProviderDisplayName
    </h5>

    <div class="text-center">
        <a class="btn btn-info text-center" href="@returnUrl">Continue</a>
    </div>
}
```

I added some basic error handling to the ExternalSignIn page, which I will use once I have added a broader range of external authentication features.

Restart ASP.NET Core, request http://localhost:5000/signout, select the Forget Me option, and click the Sign Out button to sign out of the application. Request http://localhost:5000/secret to trigger the challenge response. Click the Demo Service button to authenticate using the external handler. At present, the handler will immediately authenticate the request for the Alice user and redirect the browser to the ExternalSignIn Razor Page. (I will expand the features of the external handler so that it prompts for a password.) The application uses the email address it receives from the external authentication handler to correlate the sign-in with the local Alice user account. This account is configured for two-factor authentication with an authenticator, and you will be prompted to enter the current authenticator code. Enter the authenticator code (or use a recovery code), and a summary of the external login will be displayed. Click the OK button, and the browser will be redirected to the protected content, as shown in Figure 22-3.

Figure 22-3. *The external authentication workflow*

Understanding the OAuth Authentication Process

Identity places no restrictions on how external authentication is performed, but most services use the OAuth protocol. In the sections that follow, I explain each step in the OAuth authentication process and implement. In the sections that follow, I explain the authentication sequence and the data that is exchanged at each stage. Each authentication service is slightly different, but you can expect to encounter most of the details I describe in any service that uses OAuth, although you should also expect some variations for each provider, as I demonstrate in Chapter 23 when I add support for real services.

■ **Tip** You don't need to know the OAuth specification to follow the examples in this chapter, but you can dig into the details at `https://oauth.net` if you are interested.

Preparing for External Authentication

Before deployment, the application is registered with the authentication service. Registration requirements differ, but the result is two pieces of data used in the authentication process: the client ID and the client secret.

I demonstrate how these data items are used in detail in the sections that follow, but the client ID can be shared publicly and is just used to identify which application authentication requests are for. The client secret, as the name suggests, should not be shared publicly and is sent only in requests to the authentication service. Table 22-10 describes these data items for quick reference.

Table 22-10. *The Data Items Created During Application Registration*

Name	Description
Client ID	The client ID is included in requests to let the authentication service know which application wants to authenticate a user. This allows the authentication service to present the user with details about the application so they can make an informed choice about whether to provide access to their data.
Client secret	The client secret is included in requests to prove to the authentication service that they originate from the application. This relies on the secret being kept confidential, which means it should not be shared with users and should not be included in public source code repositories.

Preparing the Simulated External Authentication Controller

For simplicity, I am going to use a controller in the existing ExampleApp project to represent the external authentication service. This will allow me to demonstrate the use of HTTP requests in the external authentication process without needing to create and run a separate server. Add a class file named `DemoExternalAuthController.cs` to the `ExampleApp/Controllers` folder and add the code shown in Listing 22-13.

Listing 22-13. The Contents of the DemoExternalAuthController.cs File in the Controllers Folder

```
using Microsoft.AspNetCore.Mvc;
using System.Collections.Generic;

namespace ExampleApp.Controllers {
```

```
class UserRecord {
    public string Id { get; set; }
    public string Name { get; set; }
    public string EmailAddress { get; set; }
    public string Password { get; set; }
    public string Code { get; set; }
    public string Token { get; set; }
}

public class DemoExternalAuthController : Controller {
    private static string expectedID = "MyClientID";
    private static string expectedSecret = "MyClientSecret";
    private static List<UserRecord> users  = new List<UserRecord> {
        new UserRecord() {
            Id = "1", Name = "Alice", EmailAddress = "alice@example.com",
            Password = "myexternalpassword"
        },
         new UserRecord {
            Id = "2", Name = "Dora", EmailAddress = "dora@example.com",
            Password = "myexternalpassword"
        }
    };
}
}
```

The controller defines fields that specify the expected values for the client ID and client secret. In a real external service, each application that has been registered will have an ID and secret, but I need only one set of values to demonstrate the authentication sequence in the example application. The controller in Listing 22-13 also defines some basic user data that will be used in the authentication process.

Preparing the Authentication Handler

Make the change shown in Listing 22-14 to the ExternalAuthHandler class to prepare for authentication using the controller created in the previous section.

Listing 22-14. Preparing the Handler in the ExternalAuthHandler.cs File in the Custom Folder

```
using Microsoft.AspNetCore.Authentication;
using Microsoft.AspNetCore.Http;
using System.Threading.Tasks;
using System.Security.Claims;
using Microsoft.AspNetCore.Identity;
using Microsoft.Extensions.Options;

namespace ExampleApp.Custom {

    public class ExternalAuthOptions {
        public string ClientId { get; set; } = "MyClientID";
        public string ClientSecret { get; set; } = "MyClientSecret";
    }
```

```
    public class ExternalAuthHandler : IAuthenticationHandler {

        public ExternalAuthHandler(IOptions<ExternalAuthOptions> options) {
            Options = options.Value;
        }

        public AuthenticationScheme Scheme { get; set; }
        public HttpContext Context { get; set; }

        public ExternalAuthOptions Options { get; set; }

        public Task InitializeAsync(AuthenticationScheme scheme,
                HttpContext context) {
            Scheme = scheme;
            Context = context;
            return Task.CompletedTask;
        }

        public Task<AuthenticateResult> AuthenticateAsync() {
            return Task.FromResult(AuthenticateResult.NoResult());
        }

        public async Task ChallengeAsync(AuthenticationProperties properties) {

            // TODO - authentication implementation
        }

        public Task ForbidAsync(AuthenticationProperties properties) {
            return Task.CompletedTask;
        }
    }
}
```

I have removed the test code I used earlier in the chapter and added support for receiving configuration settings using the options pattern on the ExternalAuthOptions class. Add the statement shown in Listing 22-15 to the Startup class to apply the options pattern, which allows easy configuration changes.

Listing 22-15. Applying the Options Pattern in the Startup.cs File in the ExampleApp Folder

```
...
public void ConfigureServices(IServiceCollection services) {
    services.AddSingleton<ILookupNormalizer, Normalizer>();
    services.AddSingleton<IUserStore<AppUser>, UserStore>();
    services.AddSingleton<IEmailSender, ConsoleEmailSender>();
    services.AddSingleton<ISMSSender, ConsoleSMSSender>();
    services.AddSingleton<IPasswordHasher<AppUser>, SimplePasswordHasher>();
    services.AddSingleton<IRoleStore<AppRole>, RoleStore>();

    services.AddOptions<ExternalAuthOptions>();

    services.AddIdentityCore<AppUser>(opts => {
        opts.Tokens.EmailConfirmationTokenProvider = "SimpleEmail";
```

```
    opts.Tokens.ChangeEmailTokenProvider = "SimpleEmail";
    opts.Tokens.PasswordResetTokenProvider =
        TokenOptions.DefaultPhoneProvider;
...
```

Step 1: Redirecting to the Authentication Service URL

The process starts when the user clicks the button to start the authentication process. The request causes
ASP.NET Core to ask the authentication handler class to produce a challenge response. The handler
responds by redirecting the user's browser to a URL provided by the authentication service, as shown in
Figure 22-4.

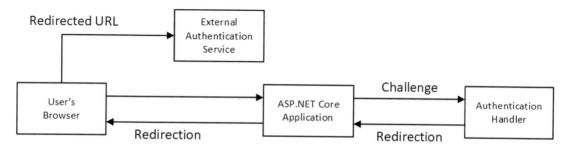

Figure 22-4. *Redirecting the user's browser to the external authentication service*

The handler uses the query string of the redirection URL to convey information to the authentication
service via the user's browser: the client ID, the return URL, the scope, and an optional piece of state data.
As an example, the query string of the URL to which the browser is redirected has this structure, where real
values are substituted for the placeholder that I have denoted with the < and > characters:

```
?client_id=<Client ID>&redirect_uri=<Return URL>&scope=<Scope>&state=<State Data>
```

As explained in the previous section, the client ID is created when the application is registered with the
authentication service and identifies the requests that are from a specific application. This value is sent using
the client_id parameter.

The return URL tells the authentication service where to redirect the client once the user has been
authenticated, which I describe in the next section. The return URL is sent using the redirect_uri
parameter.

The scope describes the data that the application requires for the user. The most popular authentication
services are provided by companies like Google and Facebook, whose services combine basic authentication
and access to more complex APIs so that applications can get user data, such as messages and calendar
appointments. Applications include a scope string in the redirection URL to specify the access they require,
which allows the authentication service to ask the user if they consent to access. The scope is sent using
the scope query string parameter. Each authentication service defines scopes, and some services require
applications to declare the scope they require during registration.

Finally, state data is included in the URL so that the application can keep track of the authentication
process. Not all applications need state data because they can keep track of which user the authentication
relates to by adding cookies to the responses sent to the user's browser, but the OAuth specification
recommends that a value should still be included in the request as protection against cross-site request
forgery (CSRF) attacks. The state data is sent using the state query string parameter.

Table 22-11 summarizes the query string parameters the application includes in the redirection URL for quick reference.

Table 22-11. *The Query String Parameters Included in the Redirection URL*

Name	Description
client_id	This parameter sends the client ID, which identifies the application to the authentication service, as described in the previous section.
redirect_uri	This parameter sends the URL to which the authentication service should redirect the user's browser once authentication is complete.
scope	This parameter sends the scope, which specifies the data and services that the application requires.
state	This parameter sends a state data value, which is used by the application to correlate related requests and to protect against cross-site forgery attacks.
response_type	This parameter specifies the type of response and must be set to code.

Updating the External Authentication Controller

In Listing 22-16, I have added an action method that simulates an external service. This action will be the target of the redirection.

Listing 22-16. Adding an Action in the DemoExternalAuthController.cs File in the Controllers Folder

```
using Microsoft.AspNetCore.Mvc;
using System.Collections.Generic;

namespace ExampleApp.Controllers {

    class UserRecord {
        public string Id { get; set; }
        public string Name { get; set; }
        public string EmailAddress { get; set; }
        public string Password { get; set; }
        public string Code { get; set; }
        public string Token { get; set; }
    }

    public class ExternalAuthInfo {
        public string client_id { get; set; }
        public string client_secret { get; set; }
        public string redirect_uri { get; set; }
        public string scope { get; set; }
        public string state { get; set; }
        public string response_type { get; set; }
        public string grant_type { get; set; }
        public string code { get; set; }
    }
```

```
public class DemoExternalAuthController : Controller {
    private static string expectedID = "MyClientID";
    private static string expectedSecret = "MyClientSecret";
    private static List<UserRecord> users  = new List<UserRecord> {
        new UserRecord() {
            Id = "1", Name = "Alice", EmailAddress = "alice@example.com",
            Password = "myexternalpassword"
        },
         new UserRecord {
            Id = "2", Name = "Dora", EmailAddress = "dora@example.com",
            Password = "myexternalpassword"
        }
    };

    public IActionResult Authenticate([FromQuery] ExternalAuthInfo info)
     => expectedID == info.client_id ? View((info, string.Empty))
            : View((info, "Unknown Client"));
}
}
```

I have defined a class named ExternalAuthInfo to make it easier to send and receive the data that the authentication process requires. The new action method, named Authenticate, renders a view to prompt the user for their credentials. The same view is used to display an error message if the request doesn't contain the expected client ID. Notice that any errors are this stage are displayed to the user and are not communicated to the application.

■ **Note** Most authentication services require redirect_uri URL to be registered in advance and will display an error if a different value is received in the request.

To define the view used by the Authenticate action, create the Views/DemoExternalAuth folder and add to it a Razor View named Authenticate.cshtml with the content shown in Listing 22-17.

Listing 22-17. The Contents of the Authenticate.cshtml File in the Views/DemoExternalAuth Folder

```
@model (ExampleApp.Controllers.ExternalAuthInfo info, string error)

@{
    IEnumerable<(string, string)> KeyValuePairs =
        typeof(ExampleApp.Controllers.ExternalAuthInfo).GetProperties()
            .Select(pi => (pi.Name, pi.GetValue(Model.info)?.ToString()));
}

<div class="bg-dark text-white p-2">
    <h4 class="text-center">Demo External Authentication Service</h4>
    <div class="bg-light text-dark m-4 p-5 border">

        @if (!string.IsNullOrEmpty(Model.error)) {
            <div class="h3 bg-danger text-white text-center m-2 p-2">
```

```
                    <div>Something Went Wrong</div>
                    <div class="h5">(@Model.error)</div>
                </div>
            } else {
                <div asp-validation-summary="All" class="text-danger m-2"></div>
                <form method="post" asp-action="Authenticate">
                    @foreach (var tuple in KeyValuePairs) {
                        if (!string.IsNullOrEmpty(tuple.Item2)) {
                            <input type="hidden" name="@tuple.Item1"
                                value="@tuple.Item2" />
                        }
                    }
                    <div class="p-2">
                        <div class="form-group">
                            <label>Email</label>
                            <input name="email" class="form-control" />
                        </div>
                        <div class="form-group">
                            <label>Password</label>
                            <input name="password" type="password"
                                class="form-control" />
                        </div>
                        <button type="submit" class="btn btn-sm btn-dark">
                            Authenticate & Return
                        </button>
                    </div>
                </form>
            }
        </div>
    </div>
</div>
```

This view simulates the response from the external authentication service and contains a form that submits the user's credentials, along with hidden input elements that contain the values provided by the application in the redirection request.

Updating the Authentication Handler

In Listing 22-18, I have revised the authentication handler so that it sends the redirection when asked to issue a challenge response.

■ **Note**   I am writing the authentication handler using protected virtual methods so that I can easily create subclasses to work with real authentication services in Chapter 23.

Listing 22-18. Performing the Redirection in the ExternalAuthHanlder.cs File in the Custom Folder

```
using Microsoft.AspNetCore.Authentication;
using Microsoft.AspNetCore.Http;
using System.Threading.Tasks;
using System.Security.Claims;
```

```csharp
using Microsoft.AspNetCore.Identity;
using Microsoft.Extensions.Options;
using System.Collections.Generic;
using Microsoft.AspNetCore.DataProtection;

namespace ExampleApp.Custom {

    public class ExternalAuthOptions {
        public string ClientId { get; set; } = "MyClientID";
        public string ClientSecret { get; set; } = "MyClientSecret";

        public virtual string RedirectRoot { get; set; } = "http://localhost:5000";
        public virtual string RedirectPath { get; set; } = "/signin-external";
        public virtual string Scope { get; set; } = "openid email profile";
        public virtual string StateHashSecret { get; set; } = "mysecret";

        public virtual string AuthenticationUrl { get; set; }
            = "http://localhost:5000/DemoExternalAuth/authenticate";
    }

    public class ExternalAuthHandler : IAuthenticationHandler {

        public ExternalAuthHandler(IOptions<ExternalAuthOptions> options,
                IDataProtectionProvider dp) {
            Options = options.Value;
            DataProtectionProvider = dp;
        }

        public AuthenticationScheme Scheme { get; set; }
        public HttpContext Context { get; set; }
        public ExternalAuthOptions Options { get; set; }
        public IDataProtectionProvider DataProtectionProvider { get; set; }
        public PropertiesDataFormat PropertiesFormatter { get; set; }

        public Task InitializeAsync(AuthenticationScheme scheme,
                HttpContext context) {
            Scheme = scheme;
            Context = context;
            PropertiesFormatter = new PropertiesDataFormat(DataProtectionProvider
                .CreateProtector(typeof(ExternalAuthOptions).FullName));
            return Task.CompletedTask;
        }

        public Task<AuthenticateResult> AuthenticateAsync() {
            return Task.FromResult(AuthenticateResult.NoResult());
        }

        public async Task ChallengeAsync(AuthenticationProperties properties) {
            Context.Response.Redirect(await GetAuthenticationUrl(properties));
        }
```

```
protected virtual Task<string>
        GetAuthenticationUrl(AuthenticationProperties properties) {
    Dictionary<string, string> qs = new Dictionary<string, string>();
    qs.Add("client_id", Options.ClientId);
    qs.Add("redirect_uri", Options.RedirectRoot + Options.RedirectPath);
    qs.Add("scope", Options.Scope);
    qs.Add("response_type", "code");
    qs.Add("state", PropertiesFormatter.Protect(properties));
    return Task.FromResult(Options.AuthenticationUrl
        + QueryString.Create(qs));
}

public Task ForbidAsync(AuthenticationProperties properties) {
    return Task.CompletedTask;
}
    }
}
```

The ChallengeAsync method now sends a redirection to the URL that will authenticate the user. To do this, I have defined additional configuration options. The RedirectUri option is used to specify the URL to which the authentication service will redirect the browser after authentication. For the example application, this will be http://localhost:5000/signin-external, and I explain how to handle requests sent to that URL in Step 3.

The Scope option uses a typical scope, although real services differ in the scope they expect, and the values are usually determined when registering an application for authentication. The value I used is the same as the one used by the Google authentication handler that Microsoft provides and that I demonstrated in Chapter 23.

The state value uses the ASP.NET Core data protection feature to securely include a serialized representation of the AuthenticationProperties object in the redirection URL. This data will be returned to the authentication handler later in the authentication process.

You can test the redirection by restart ASP.NET Core, requesting http://localhost:5000/signin, and clicking the Demo Service button. The response will redirect your browser to the (simulated) external authentication service, as shown in Figure 22-5.

Figure 22-5. *Testing the redirection step*

As part of the authentication process, the user will be asked to approve the application's access to their data. This can be done as simply as including a description of the application when the user is prompted for their credentials or as a separate prompt that requires explicit confirmation.

Step 2: Authenticating the User

The ASP.NET Core Identity application doesn't participate in the external authentication process, which is conducted privately between the user and the authentication service, as shown in Figure 22-6.

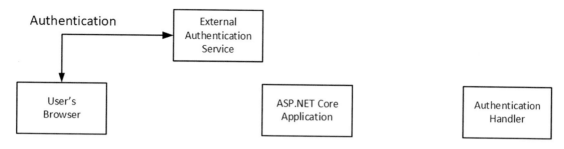

Figure 22-6. *Authenticating with the external service*

In Listing 22-19, I have added an action method to receive the credentials provided by the user and validate them.

Listing 22-19. Authenticating the User in the DemoExternalAuthController.cs File in the Controllers Folder

```
using Microsoft.AspNetCore.Mvc;
using System.Collections.Generic;
using System.Linq;

namespace ExampleApp.Controllers {

    class UserRecord {
        public string Id { get; set; }
        public string Name { get; set; }
        public string EmailAddress { get; set; }
        public string Password { get; set; }
        public string Code { get; set; }
        public string Token { get; set; }
    }

    public class ExternalAuthInfo {
        public string client_id { get; set; }
        public string client_secret { get; set; }
        public string redirect_uri { get; set; }
        public string scope { get; set; }
        public string state { get; set; }
        public string response_type { get; set; }
        public string grant_type { get; set; }
        public string code { get; set; }
    }

    public class DemoExternalAuthController : Controller {
        private static string expectedID = "MyClientID";
        private static string expectedSecret = "MyClientSecret";
        private static List<UserRecord> users = new List<UserRecord> {
            new UserRecord() {
                Id = "1", Name = "Alice", EmailAddress = "alice@example.com",
                Password = "myexternalpassword"
            },
             new UserRecord {
                Id = "2", Name = "Dora", EmailAddress = "dora@example.com",
                Password = "myexternalpassword"
            }
        };

        public IActionResult Authenticate([FromQuery] ExternalAuthInfo info)
         => expectedID == info.client_id ? View((info, string.Empty))
                : View((info, "Unknown Client"));
```

```
[HttpPost]
public IActionResult Authenticate(ExternalAuthInfo info, string email,
        string password) {
    if (string.IsNullOrEmpty(email) || string.IsNullOrEmpty(password)) {
        ModelState.AddModelError("", "Email and password required");
    } else {
        UserRecord user = users.FirstOrDefault(u =>
            u.EmailAddress.Equals(email) && u.Password.Equals(password));
        if (user != null) {
            // user has been successfully authenticated
        } else {
            ModelState.AddModelError("", "Email or password incorrect");
        }
    }
    return View((info, ""));
}
```

One benefit of using an external authentication service is that it allows applications to take advantage of security factors that are not directly supported by ASP.NET Core Identity. For example, Google and Facebook both offer external authentication services that support FIDO2, which relies on a hardware authenticator device that is accessed through a browser API (and which is described in detail at https://fidoalliance. org/fido2). Identity doesn't support FIDO2 directly but can benefit from its use by using Google or Facebook as an external authentication service.

For this example, the controller that simulates the external service has a static set of email addresses and passwords, which are used to check the credentials received by the action method. The new action method uses the ASP.NET Core model state feature to display an error if the credentials cannot be validated.

Step 3: Receiving the Authorization Code

When the user grants access to the data the application requires, the external authentication service replies with a redirection to the return URL from step 1, as shown in Figure 22-7.

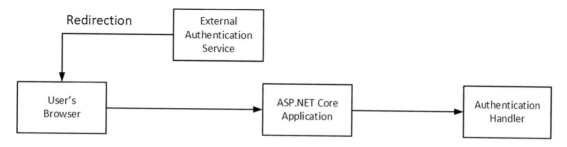

Figure 22-7. *Receiving the authorization code*

The authentication service uses the query string of the redirect URI to send data to the application via the user's browser: a scope, an authorization code, and a state data value if one was used in step 1. The authorization code tells the application that the user has been authenticated and has granted access to the data specified by the scope.

Note that the data itself is not included in the request—that happens in a later step. Table 22-12 summarizes the query string parameters the application includes in the redirection URL for quick reference.

Updating the External Authentication Controller

In Listing 22-20, I have added the redirection to the action method that authenticates the user. The query string for the redirection contains the data values described in Table 22-12.

Table 22-12. *The Query String Parameters Included in the Redirection URL*

Name	Description
code	This code is exchanged in the next step for an access token.
state	This is the same value used in step 1 and can be used by applications to correlate requests to determine which user the redirection relates to and to protect against cross-site request forgery attacks.

Listing 22-20. Redirecting in the DemoExternalAuthController.cs File in the Controllers Folder

```
using Microsoft.AspNetCore.Mvc;
using System.Collections.Generic;
using System.Linq;

namespace ExampleApp.Controllers {

    class UserRecord {
        public string Id { get; set; }
        public string Name { get; set; }
        public string EmailAddress { get; set; }
        public string Password { get; set; }
        public string Code { get; set; }
        public string Token { get; set; }
    }

    public class ExternalAuthInfo {
        public string client_id { get; set; }
        public string client_secret { get; set; }
        public string redirect_uri { get; set; }
        public string scope { get; set; }
        public string state { get; set; }
        public string response_type { get; set; }
        public string grant_type { get; set; }
        public string code { get; set; }
    }

    public class DemoExternalAuthController : Controller {
        private static string expectedID = "MyClientID";
        private static string expectedSecret = "MyClientSecret";
        private static List<UserRecord> users = new List<UserRecord> {
        new UserRecord() {
```

```
            Id = "1", Name = "Alice", EmailAddress = "alice@example.com",
            Password = "myexternalpassword", Code = "12345"
        },
        new UserRecord {
            Id = "2", Name = "Dora", EmailAddress = "dora@example.com",
            Password = "myexternalpassword", Code = "56789"
        }
    };

    public IActionResult Authenticate([FromQuery] ExternalAuthInfo info)
        => expectedID == info.client_id ? View((info, string.Empty))
            : View((info, "Unknown Client"));


    [HttpPost]
    public IActionResult Authenticate(ExternalAuthInfo info, string email,
            string password) {
        if (string.IsNullOrEmpty(email) || string.IsNullOrEmpty(password)) {
            ModelState.AddModelError("", "Email and password required");
        } else {
            UserRecord user = users.FirstOrDefault(u =>
                u.EmailAddress.Equals(email) && u.Password.Equals(password));
            if (user != null) {
                return Redirect(info.redirect_uri
                    + $"?code={user.Code}&scope={info.scope}"
                    + $"&state={info.state}");
            } else {
                ModelState.AddModelError("", "Email or password incorrect");
            }
        }
        return View((info, ""));
    }
}

}
```

The URL to which the browser is redirected is determined using the redirect_uri, scope, and state values provided by the authentication handler in step 1. The query string also includes a code value, which I have defined statically for each user. In a real authentication service, the code values are generated dynamically.

Updating the Authentication Handler

The authentication handler needs to be able to receive the redirected request. ASP.NET Core defines the IAuthenticationRequestHandler interface, which is derived from the IAuthenticationHandler interface, and defines the additional method described in Table 22-13.

Table 22-13. *The IAuthenticationRequestHandler Method*

Name	Description
HandleRequestAsync()	This method is called for every request, allowing the authentication handler to intercept requests. The method returns a bool value, which indicates whether the processing of this request should stop. A result of true prevents the request from being passed along the request pipeline.

The HandleRequestAsync method is called automatically by the ASP.NET Core authentication middleware and allows authentication handlers to intercept requests without the need to create custom middleware classes or endpoints. In Listing 22-21, I have revised the example authentication handler to implement the IAuthenticationRequestHandler interface to receive the authorization code from the authentication service.

Listing 22-21. Receiving the Code in the ExternalAuthHandler.cs File in the Custom Folder

```
...
public class ExternalAuthHandler : IAuthenticationRequestHandler {

    public ExternalAuthHandler(IOptions<ExternalAuthOptions> options,
            IDataProtectionProvider dp) {
        Options = options.Value;
        DataProtectionProvider = dp;
    }

    // ...statements omitted for brevity...

    public Task ForbidAsync(AuthenticationProperties properties) {
        return Task.CompletedTask;
    }

    public virtual async Task<bool> HandleRequestAsync() {
        if (Context.Request.Path.Equals(Options.RedirectPath)) {
            string authCode = await GetAuthenticationCode();
            return true;
        }
        return false;
    }

    protected virtual Task<string> GetAuthenticationCode() {
        return Task.FromResult(Context.Request.Query["code"].ToString());
    }
}
...
```

The implementation of the HandleRequestAsync method checks to see if the URL for the request matches the one specified by the RedirectUri configuration option. If it does match, then the authentication code is extracted from the request by the GetAuthenticationCode method. If the request doesn't match, it is passed along the pipeline as normal.

■ **Caution**   Multiple instances of the authentication handler will be created and used to handle the different steps in the authentication sequence. Do not rely on storing data in instance variables or properties because those values will not be available to the object created to deal with the next step in the sequence.

Step 4: Exchanging the Authorization Code for an Access Token

So far, the application and the authentication service have communicated indirectly, passing data by redirecting the user's browser. In this step, the application contacts the authentication service directly to exchange the authorization code for an access token, which is used in the next step to get the user's data. Figure 22-8 shows the code-for-token exchange.

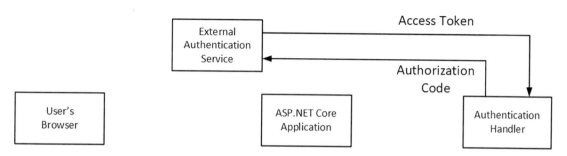

Figure 22-8. *Exchanging an authorization code for an access token*

In general, this step is performed with an HTTP POST request, where the authorization code is included in the request body. Table 22-14 describes the data values commonly included in the request.

Table 22-14. *The Data Values Sent in the Code Exchange Request*

Name	Description
code	This property is used to send the authorization code received in the previous step.
redirect_uri	This property is used to send the same URL that was used in step 1.
client_id	This property is used to send the client ID, created when the application was registered with the authentication service.
client_secret	This property is used to send the client secret, created when the application was registered with the authentication service. Some services require the application to authenticate itself differently.
state	This parameter sends a state data value, which is used by the application to correlate related requests and to protect against cross-site forgery attacks.
grant_type	This property must be set to authorization_code.

In the response to the HTTP request, the authentication sends a JSON document that contains an access token, along with additional data. Table 22-15 describes the JSON properties that will be sent.

Table 22-15. *The JSON Document Properties Received in the Code Exchange*

Name	Description
access_token	This property provides the access token, which is used in the next step.
expires_in	This property specifies the lifespan of the token in seconds. The token must be used within this period.
scope	This property specifies the scope that the token provides access to. This may not be the same scope that was requested in step 1.
token_type	This property specifies the token type. The most common value is Bearer, which means that the token should be included as a header in requests for data.
state	This property contains the state value included in the request.

The authentication service can also send the application an error, indicating that something went wrong in the exchange process. Errors are described using a JSON document with the properties described in Table 22-16.

Table 22-16. *The Error JSON Document Properties*

Name	Description
error	All error responses contain this property, which contains an error code describing the problem.
state	This property contains the state value included in the request if one was specified.
error_description	This property provides a human-readable description of the error. This property is optional.
error_uri	This property provides a URL for a human-readable web page that contains a description of the error. This property is optional.

■ **Note** There are other points in the process where the specification allows the authentication service to send an error to the application, but these are not always used consistently, and some are optional. The token exchange is the step where errors are most likely to be reported because it is the first time that the application and the authentication service communicate directly.

The important property is error, which identifies the error that has occurred. The OAuth specification defines a set of values for the error property, such as invalid_request, which is used when the request is missing required data, or access_denied, when the user doesn't grant the application access to their data.

I am not going to handle all of the errors that are described in the specification because, from the perspective of the ASP.NET Core application, I only care about the outcome of the process. It can be helpful to examine error types to identify the cause of persistent problems and configuration issues, but otherwise, I just need to display a "something went wrong" message when an error occurs.

Updating the External Authentication Controller

In Listing 22-22, I have added tokens to each user record and defined an action method that simulates the code-for-token exchange process.

Listing 22-22. Adding an Action in the DemoExternalAuthController.cs File in the Controllers Folder

```
...
public class DemoExternalAuthController : Controller {
    private static string expectedID = "MyClientID";
    private static string expectedSecret = "MyClientSecret";

    private static List<UserRecord> users  = new List<UserRecord> {
        new UserRecord() {
            Id = "1", Name = "Alice", EmailAddress = "alice@example.com",
            Password = "myexternalpassword", Code = "12345", Token = "token1"
        },
        new UserRecord {
            Id = "2", Name = "Dora", EmailAddress = "dora@example.com",
            Password = "myexternalpassword", Code = "56789", Token = "token2"
        }
    };

    public IActionResult Authenticate([FromQuery] ExternalAuthInfo info)
        => expectedID == info.client_id ? View((info, string.Empty))
                : View((info, "Unknown Client"));

    [HttpPost]
    public IActionResult Authenticate(ExternalAuthInfo info, string email,
            string password) {
        if (string.IsNullOrEmpty(email) || string.IsNullOrEmpty(password)) {
            ModelState.AddModelError("", "Email and password required");
        } else {
            UserRecord user = users.FirstOrDefault(u =>
                u.EmailAddress.Equals(email) && u.Password.Equals(password));
            if (user != null) {
                return Redirect(info.redirect_uri
                    + $"?code={user.Code}&scope={info.scope}"
                    + $"&state={info.state}");
            } else {
                ModelState.AddModelError("", "Email or password incorrect");
            }
        }
        return View((info, ""));
    }

    [HttpPost]
    public IActionResult Exchange([FromBody] ExternalAuthInfo info) {
        UserRecord user = users.FirstOrDefault(user => user.Code.Equals(info.code));
        if (user == null || info.client_id != expectedID
                || info.client_secret != expectedSecret) {
            return Json(new { error = "unauthorized_client" });
```

```
        } else {
            return Json(new {
                access_token = user.Token,
                expires_in = 3600,
                scope = "openid+email+profile",
                token_type = "Bearer",
                info.state
            });
        }
    }
}
...
```

The action method locates the user with the specified code and returns the user's token. In a real authentication service, the tokens are generated dynamically, which means you cannot rely on always receiving the same token for a given user.

Updating the Authentication Handler

In Listing 22-23, I have added support for obtaining a token to the authentication handler, targeting the action method defined in the previous section.

Listing 22-23. Obtaining a Token in the ExternalAuthHandler.cs File in the Custom Folder

```
using Microsoft.AspNetCore.Authentication;
using Microsoft.AspNetCore.Http;
using System.Threading.Tasks;
using System.Security.Claims;
using Microsoft.AspNetCore.Identity;
using Microsoft.Extensions.Options;
using System.Collections.Generic;
using Microsoft.AspNetCore.DataProtection;
using System.Net.Http;
using System.Net.Http.Json;
using System.Text.Json;
using Microsoft.Extensions.Logging;

namespace ExampleApp.Custom {

    public class ExternalAuthOptions {
        public string ClientId { get; set; } = "MyClientID";
        public string ClientSecret { get; set; } = "MyClientSecret";

        public virtual string RedirectRoot { get; set; } = "http://localhost:5000";
        public virtual string RedirectPath { get; set; } = "/signin-external";
        public virtual string Scope { get; set; } = "openid email profile";
        public virtual string StateHashSecret { get; set; } = "mysecret";

        public virtual string AuthenticationUrl { get; set; }
            = "http://localhost:5000/DemoExternalAuth/authenticate";
        public virtual string ExchangeUrl { get; set; }
```

```
        = "http://localhost:5000/DemoExternalAuth/exchange";
    public virtual string ErrorUrlTemplate { get; set; }
        = "/externalsignin?error={0}";
}

public class ExternalAuthHandler : IAuthenticationRequestHandler {

    public ExternalAuthHandler(IOptions<ExternalAuthOptions> options,
            IDataProtectionProvider dp, ILogger<ExternalAuthHandler> logger) {
        Options = options.Value;
        DataProtectionProvider = dp;
        Logger = logger;
    }

    public AuthenticationScheme Scheme { get; set; }
    public HttpContext Context { get; set; }
    public ExternalAuthOptions Options { get; set; }
    public IDataProtectionProvider DataProtectionProvider { get; set; }
    public PropertiesDataFormat PropertiesFormatter { get; set; }
    public ILogger<ExternalAuthHandler> Logger { get; set; }
    public string ErrorMessage { get; set; }

    public Task InitializeAsync(AuthenticationScheme scheme,
            HttpContext context) {
        Scheme = scheme;
        Context = context;
        PropertiesFormatter = new PropertiesDataFormat(DataProtectionProvider
            .CreateProtector(typeof(ExternalAuthOptions).FullName));
        return Task.CompletedTask;
    }

    public Task<AuthenticateResult> AuthenticateAsync() {
        return Task.FromResult(AuthenticateResult.NoResult());
    }

    public async Task ChallengeAsync(AuthenticationProperties properties) {
        Context.Response.Redirect(await GetAuthenticationUrl(properties));
    }

    protected virtual Task<string>
            GetAuthenticationUrl(AuthenticationProperties properties) {
        Dictionary<string, string> qs = new Dictionary<string, string>();
        qs.Add("client_id", Options.ClientId);
        qs.Add("redirect_uri", Options.RedirectRoot + Options.RedirectPath);
        qs.Add("scope", Options.Scope);
        qs.Add("response_type", "code");
        qs.Add("state", PropertiesFormatter.Protect(properties));
        return Task.FromResult(Options.AuthenticationUrl
            + QueryString.Create(qs));
    }
```

```
public Task ForbidAsync(AuthenticationProperties properties) {
    return Task.CompletedTask;
}

public virtual async Task<bool> HandleRequestAsync() {
    if (Context.Request.Path.Equals(Options.RedirectPath)) {
        string authCode = await GetAuthenticationCode();
        (string token, string state) = await GetAccessToken(authCode);
        if (!string.IsNullOrEmpty(token)) {
            // todo - process token
        }
        Context.Response.Redirect(string.Format(Options.ErrorUrlTemplate,
            ErrorMessage));
        return true;
    }
    return false;
}

protected virtual Task<string> GetAuthenticationCode() {
    return Task.FromResult(Context.Request.Query["code"].ToString());
}

protected virtual async Task<(string code, string state)>
        GetAccessToken(string code) {
    string state = Context.Request.Query["state"];
    HttpClient httpClient = new HttpClient();
    httpClient.DefaultRequestHeaders.Add("Accept", "application/json");
    HttpResponseMessage response = await httpClient
        .PostAsJsonAsync(Options.ExchangeUrl,
            new {
                code,
                redirect_uri = Options.RedirectRoot + Options.RedirectPath,
                client_id = Options.ClientId,
                client_secret = Options.ClientSecret,
                state,
                grant_type = "authorization_code",
            });
    string jsonData = await response.Content.ReadAsStringAsync();
    JsonDocument jsonDoc = JsonDocument.Parse(jsonData);
    string error = jsonDoc.RootElement.GetString("error");
    if (error != null) {
        ErrorMessage = "Access Token Error";
        Logger.LogError(ErrorMessage);
        Logger.LogError(jsonData);
    }
    string token = jsonDoc.RootElement.GetString("access_token");
    string jsonState = jsonDoc.RootElement.GetString("state") ?? state;
    return error == null ? (token, state) : (null, null);
}

    }
}
```

The new method sends an HTTP POST request with the data values described in Table 22-16 and parses the JSON response using the built-in .NET Core JSON support. For simplicity, I have used a tuple as the result from the method, which allows me to return an error, the access code, and the state data returned by the authentication service. If the server has sent an error, the HandleRequestAsync method redirects the browser to the URL specified by the ErrorUrl configuration option. I'll create a Razor Page that displays an error message to the user later. I also log the error, including the JSON response. This is useful when adding support for new authentication services, which can be a trial-and-error process.

Step 5: Requesting User Data from the Authentication Service

The next step is to request the user's data from the authentication service. This is typically done as an HTTP GET request with the access token included as an Authorization header, as shown in Figure 22-9. No other information needs to be included in the request because the authentication service can use the tokens it issues to determine which user and application a token relates to.

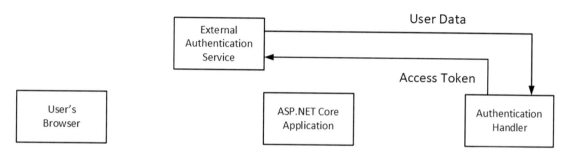

Figure 22-9. *Requesting user data*

The authentication service responds with JSON data that describes the user. As an example, here is a typical data response from the Google authentication service:

```
...
{
  "id": "102888805263382592",
  "email": "adam@adam-freeman.com",
  "verified_email": true,
  "name": "Adam Freeman",
  "given_name": "Adam",
  "family_name": "Freeman",
  "picture": "https://lh6.googleusercontent.com/s96-c/photo.jpg",
  "locale": "en"
}
...
```

The data that the application receives depends on the authentication service and the scope that has been requested. The data that the example controller produces is simpler but will be sufficient for this chapter.

Updating the External Authentication Controller

In Listing 22-24, I have added an action method named data that receives an access token and returns the data for a user.

Listing 22-24. Providing User Data in the DemoExternalAuthController.cs File in the Controllers Folder

```
...
public class DemoExternalAuthController : Controller {
    private static string expectedID = "MyClientID";
    private static string expectedSecret = "MyClientSecret";

    // ...statements and methods omitted for brevity...

    [HttpGet]
    public IActionResult Data([FromHeader] string authorization) {
        string token = authorization?[7..];
        UserRecord user = users.FirstOrDefault(user => user.Token.Equals(token));
        if (user != null) {
            return Json(new { user.Id, user.EmailAddress, user.Name });
        } else {
            return Json(new { error = "invalid_token" });
        }
    }
}
...
```

The access token will be obtained from the Authorization header, which is formatted so that it starts with Bearer, followed by a space, followed by the access token. The action method extracts the token from the header, locates the corresponding user data, and returns a JSON document that has id, emailAddress and name properties. (The case of the property names will be transformed automatically so that EmailAddress becomes emailAddress in the JSON document, for example.)

Updating the Authentication Handler

In the authentication handler, an HTTP GET request with an Authorization header is sent to the user, and a JSON document is returned. A set of Claim objects is created to represent the user data provided by the authentication service, and these objects are used to create a ClaimsPrincipal object that is signed into the application using the HttpContext.SignInAsync method, as shown in Listing 22-25.

Listing 22-25. Getting User Data in the ExternalAuthHandler.cs File in the Custom Folder

```
using Microsoft.AspNetCore.Authentication;
using Microsoft.AspNetCore.Http;
using System.Threading.Tasks;
using System.Security.Claims;
using Microsoft.AspNetCore.Tdentity;
using Microsoft.Extensions.Options;
using System.Collections.Generic;
using Microsoft.AspNetCore.DataProtection;
using System.Net.Http;
using System.Net.Http.Json;
```

```
using System.Text.Json;
using Microsoft.Extensions.Logging;
using System.Net.Http.Headers;

namespace ExampleApp.Custom {

    public class ExternalAuthOptions {
        public string ClientId { get; set; } = "MyClientID";
        public string ClientSecret { get; set; } = "MyClientSecret";

        public virtual string RedirectRoot { get; set; } = "http://localhost:5000";
        public virtual string RedirectPath { get; set; } = "/signin-external";
        public virtual string Scope { get; set; } = "openid email profile";
        public virtual string StateHashSecret { get; set; } = "mysecret";

        public virtual string AuthenticationUrl { get; set; }
            = "http://localhost:5000/DemoExternalAuth/authenticate";
        public virtual string ExchangeUrl { get; set; }
            = "http://localhost:5000/DemoExternalAuth/exchange";
        public virtual string ErrorUrlTemplate { get; set; }
            = "/externalsignin?error={0}";
        public virtual string DataUrl { get; set; }
            = "http://localhost:5000/DemoExternalAuth/data";
    }

    public class ExternalAuthHandler : IAuthenticationRequestHandler {

        // ...methods omitted for brevity...

        public virtual async Task<bool> HandleRequestAsync() {
            if (Context.Request.Path.Equals(Options.RedirectPath)) {
                string authCode = await GetAuthenticationCode();
                (string token, string state) = await GetAccessToken(authCode);
                if (!string.IsNullOrEmpty(token)) {
                    IEnumerable<Claim> claims = await GetUserData(token);
                    if (claims != null) {
                        ClaimsIdentity identity = new ClaimsIdentity(Scheme.Name);
                        identity.AddClaims(claims);
                        ClaimsPrincipal claimsPrincipal
                            = new ClaimsPrincipal(identity);
                        AuthenticationProperties props
                            = PropertiesFormatter.Unprotect(state);
                        await Context.SignInAsync(IdentityConstants.ExternalScheme,
                            claimsPrincipal, props);
                        Context.Response.Redirect(props.RedirectUri);
                        return true;
                    }
                }
                Context.Response.Redirect(string.Format(Options.ErrorUrlTemplate,
                    ErrorMessage));
                return true;
```

```
        }
        return false;
    }

    // ...methods omitted for brevity...

    protected virtual async Task<IEnumerable<Claim>>
      GetUserData(string accessToken) {
        HttpRequestMessage msg = new HttpRequestMessage(HttpMethod.Get,
            Options.DataUrl);
        msg.Headers.Authorization = new AuthenticationHeaderValue("Bearer",
            accessToken);
        HttpResponseMessage response = await new HttpClient().SendAsync(msg);
        string jsonData = await response.Content.ReadAsStringAsync();
        JsonDocument jsonDoc = JsonDocument.Parse(jsonData);

        var error = jsonDoc.RootElement.GetString("error");
        if (error != null) {
            ErrorMessage = "User Data Error";
            Logger.LogError(ErrorMessage);
            Logger.LogError(jsonData);
            return null;
        } else {
            return GetClaims(jsonDoc);
        }
    }

    protected virtual IEnumerable<Claim> GetClaims(JsonDocument jsonDoc) {
        List<Claim> claims = new List<Claim>();
        claims.Add(new Claim(ClaimTypes.NameIdentifier,
            jsonDoc.RootElement.GetString("id")));
        claims.Add(new Claim(ClaimTypes.Name,
            jsonDoc.RootElement.GetString("name")));
        claims.Add(new Claim(ClaimTypes.Email,
            jsonDoc.RootElement.GetString("emailAddress")));
        return claims;
    }
  }
}
```

Throughout the authentication process, I have been using the AuthenticationProperties object received by the ChallengeAsync method as the state data in the redirections and requests to the authentication service. This has allowed me to preserve the data provided by the SignInManager<T> class at the start of the process so that I can use it when creating the ClaimsPrincipal object. First, I unprotected the serialized data, like this:

```
...
AuthenticationProperties props = PropertiesFormatter.Unprotect(state);
...
```

The Unprotect method re-creates the AuthenticationProperties object, which the authentication server returns without modification. I then use this object when signing in the ClaimsPrincipal object, like this:

```
...
await Context.SignInAsync(IdentityConstants.ExternalScheme, claimsPrincipal, props);
...
```

This is important because the AuthenticationProperties object contains data values that the SignInManager<T>.GetExternalLoginInfoAsync method looks for. The external sign-in won't be detected if you don't preserve and use this data when signing in.

Completing the External Authentication Process

The authentication handler is complete, and all that remains is to add the Razor Page that will create an Identity user when the correlation process fails. I prepared for this step in the "Understanding the Correlation Phase" section earlier in the chapter, but I couldn't easily add the feature because the authentication handler always authenticated requests with the same user ID. Now that I have built a simulated external authentication service, I can go back and finish up. Add a Razor Page named ExternalAccountConfirm.cshtml to the Pages folder with the contents shown in Listing 22-26. The name of this page was specified by the code in Listing 22-11.

Listing 22-26. The Contents of the ExternalAccountConfirm.cshtml File in the Pages Folder

```
@page
@model ExampleApp.Pages.ExternalAccountConfirmModel

<h4 class="bg-info text-white text-center p-2">Create Account</h4>

<div asp-validation-summary="All" class="text-danger m-2"></div>

<form method="post" class="m-2">
    <input type="hidden" asp-for="@Model.ReturnUrl" />
    <div class="form-group">
        <label>Name</label>
        <input class="form-control" name="username"
               value="@Model.AppUser.UserName" />
    </div>
    <div class="form-group">
        <label>Email Address</label>
        <input readonly class="form-control"
               asp-for="@Model.AppUser.EmailAddress" />
    </div>
    <div class="form-group">
        <label>Authentication Scheme</label>
        <input readonly class="form-control"
               asp-for="@Model.ProviderDisplayName" />
    </div>
    <button class="btn btn-info" type="submit">
        Create Account
    </button>
    <a href="/signin" class="btn btn-secondary">Cancel</a>
</form>
```

In a real application, this page can be used to gather the data the application requires that is not provided by the authentication service, but, for this example, I present read-only fields for the user's email address and authentication scheme and allow only the username to be edited.

To implement the page model class, add the code shown in Listing 22-27 to the ExternalAccountConfirm.cshtml.cs file in the Pages folder. You will have to create this file if you are using Visual Studio Code.

Listing 22-27. The Contents of the ExternalAccountConfirm.cshtml.cs File in the Pages Folder

```
using ExampleApp.Identity;
using Microsoft.AspNetCore.Identity;
using Microsoft.AspNetCore.Mvc;
using Microsoft.AspNetCore.Mvc.RazorPages;
using System.Security.Claims;
using System.Threading.Tasks;

namespace ExampleApp.Pages {

    public class ExternalAccountConfirmModel : PageModel {

        public ExternalAccountConfirmModel(UserManager<AppUser> userManager,
                SignInManager<AppUser> signInManager) {
            UserManager = userManager;
            SignInManager = signInManager;
        }

        public UserManager<AppUser> UserManager { get; set; }
        public SignInManager<AppUser> SignInManager { get; set; }

        public AppUser AppUser { get; set; } = new AppUser();

        public string ProviderDisplayName { get; set; }

        [BindProperty(SupportsGet = true)]
        public string ReturnUrl { get; set; }

        public async Task<IActionResult> OnGetAsync() {
            ExternalLoginInfo info = await SignInManager.GetExternalLoginInfoAsync();
            if (info == null) {
                return Redirect(ReturnUrl);
            } else {
                ClaimsPrincipal external = info.Principal;
                AppUser.EmailAddress = external.FindFirstValue(ClaimTypes.Email);
                AppUser.UserName = external.FindFirstValue(ClaimTypes.Name);
                ProviderDisplayName = info.ProviderDisplayName;
                return Page();
            }
        }
    }
```

```
public async Task<IActionResult> OnPostAsync(string username) {
    ExternalLoginInfo info = await SignInManager.GetExternalLoginInfoAsync();

    if (info != null) {
        ClaimsPrincipal external = info.Principal;
        AppUser.UserName = username;
        AppUser.EmailAddress = external.FindFirstValue(ClaimTypes.Email);
        AppUser.EmailAddressConfirmed = true;
        IdentityResult result = await UserManager.CreateAsync(AppUser);
        if (result.Succeeded) {
            await UserManager.AddClaimAsync(AppUser,
                new Claim(ClaimTypes.Role, "User"));
            await UserManager.AddLoginAsync(AppUser, info);
            await SignInManager.ExternalLoginSignInAsync(info.LoginProvider,
                info.ProviderKey, false);
            return Redirect(ReturnUrl);
        } else {
            foreach (IdentityError err in result.Errors) {
                ModelState.AddModelError(string.Empty, err.Description);
            }
        }
    } else {
        ModelState.AddModelError(string.Empty, "No external login found");
    }
    return Page();
}
```

The GET handler method uses the `SignInManager<T>.GetExternalLoginInfoAsync` method to get the external sign-in created by the authentication handler. The claims created by the handler are used to set values for the `AppUser` properties, which are displayed to the user.

The POST handler method also creates an `AppUser` object from the external sign-in, with the addition of the value provided by the user for the `UserName` property. The `UserManager<T>` class is used to add the `AppUser` object to the store, add a claim for the `User` role, and store the external login details. The user is then signed into the application with the `SignInManager.ExternalLoginSignInAsync` method.

The validation performed by the `UserManager<T>` class is still applied when creating user objects based on external logins. For the example application, this means that the username must be unique, the email address must be in the `example.com` domain, and the email address must be confirmed before the user is signed in. I trust that the email address has been confirmed by the authentication service, so I set the `EmailAddressConfirmed` property to `true` before storing the `AppUser` object. If your application is unable to trust the authentication service's confirmation process, then you will need to extend the process of creating an account to send the user a confirmation code.

To test the login for an existing user, restart ASP.NET Core and request `http://localhost:5000/signout`. Check the Forget Me option and click the Sign Out button to sign out of the application. Next, request `http://localhost:5000/secret`, which will trigger the challenge response and offer the choice of a local or external login. Click Demo Service, and the browser will be redirected to the simulated authentication service. Enter alice@example.com into the Email field, enter myexternalpassword into the Password field, and click the Authenticate & Return button. You will be redirected to the application and prompted for an authenticator code because the user Alice is set up for two-factor authentication. Click the Sign In button, and you will see the external authentication summary. Click the Continue button, and you will be redirected to the /secret URL. Figure 22-10 shows the key parts of the sequence.

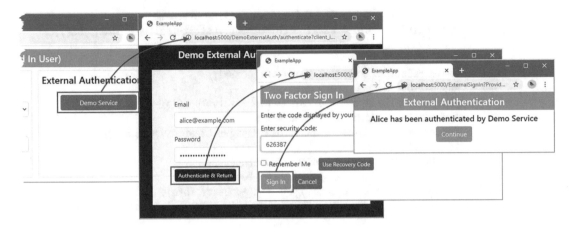

Figure 22-10. *External authentication*

Repeat the process and sign in as dora@example.com with the password myexternalpassword to see the process when there is no local account, as shown in Figure 22-11.

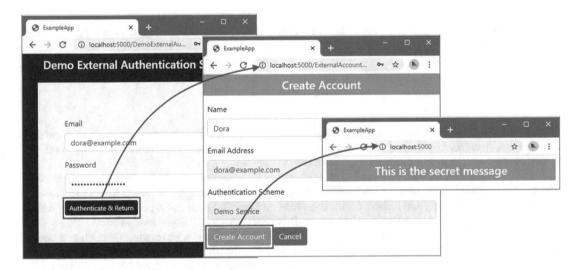

Figure 22-11. *External authentication without a local account*

Summary

In this chapter, I explained the process by which external services can be used to authenticate users on behalf of an ASP.NET Core application, using data stored by ASP.NET Core Identity. The process is complex, but the results can be worthwhile because it allows users to use their accounts on large-scale platforms, often taking advantage of security options that are not directly supported by Identity. In the next chapter, I replace the simulated external service with real ones.

CHAPTER 23

External Authentication, Part 2

In this chapter, I complete my description of the Identity features by showing you how to store authentication tokens received from external services and by adding support for authentication with the real services provided by Google and Facebook.

Preparing for This Chapter

This chapter uses the ExampleApp project from Chapter 22. To prepare for this chapter, comment out the statement in the Startup class that registers the custom user validation class, as shown in Listing 23-1. The validator restricts email addresses to specific domains, which won't work when using creating accounts from real authentication services.

Listing 23-1. Disabling the User Validation Class in the Startup.cs File in the ExampleApp Folder

```
...
services.AddIdentityCore<AppUser>(opts => {
    opts.Tokens.EmailConfirmationTokenProvider = "SimpleEmail";
    opts.Tokens.ChangeEmailTokenProvider = "SimpleEmail";
    opts.Tokens.PasswordResetTokenProvider =
        TokenOptions.DefaultPhoneProvider;

    opts.Password.RequireNonAlphanumeric = false;
    opts.Password.RequireLowercase = false;
    opts.Password.RequireUppercase = false;
    opts.Password.RequireDigit = false;
    opts.Password.RequiredLength = 8;
    opts.Lockout.MaxFailedAccessAttempts = 3;
    opts.SignIn.RequireConfirmedAccount = true;
})
.AddTokenProvider<EmailConfirmationTokenGenerator>("SimpleEmail")
.AddTokenProvider<PhoneConfirmationTokenGenerator>
    (TokenOptions.DefaultPhoneProvider)
.AddTokenProvider<TwoFactorSignInTokenGenerator>
    (IdentityConstants.TwoFactorUserIdScheme)
.AddTokenProvider<AuthenticatorTokenProvider<AppUser>>
    (TokenOptions.DefaultAuthenticatorProvider)
.AddSignInManager()
.AddRoles<AppRole>();
```

© Adam Freeman 2021
A. Freeman, *Pro ASP.NET Core Identity*, https://doi.org/10.1007/978-1-4842-6858-2_23

```
//services.AddSingleton<IUserValidator<AppUser>, EmailValidator>();
services.AddSingleton<IPasswordValidator<AppUser>, PasswordValidator>();
services.AddScoped<IUserClaimsPrincipalFactory<AppUser>,
    AppUserClaimsPrincipalFactory>();
services.AddSingleton<IRoleValidator<AppRole>, RoleValidator>();
...
```

Open a new command prompt, navigate to the ExampleApp folder, and run the command shown in Listing 23-2 to start ASP.NET Core.

■ **Tip** You can download the example project for this chapter—and for all the other chapters in this book— from https://github.com/Apress/pro-asp.net-core-identity. See Chapter 1 for how to get help if you have problems running the examples.

Listing 23-2. Running the Example Application

```
dotnet run
```

Open a new browser window, request http://localhost:5000/signout, and click the Sign Out button to remove any authentication cookies created in previous chapters. Next, request http://localhost:5000/secret, which will produce the response shown in Figure 23-1, which allows sign-in using local credentials or with an external service.

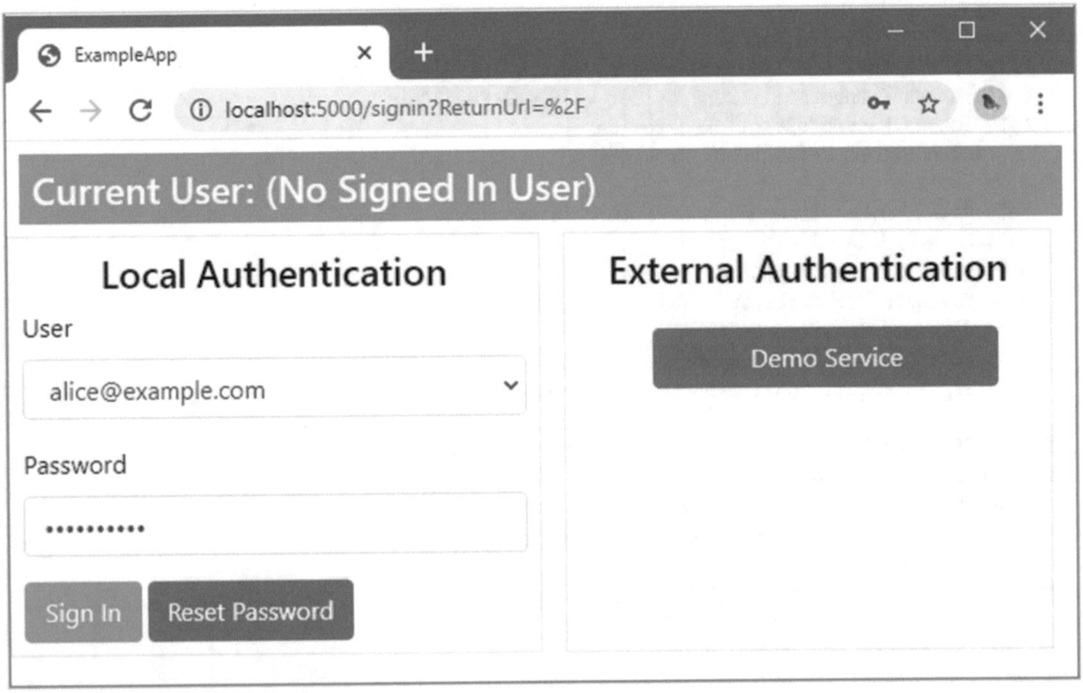

Figure 23-1. *Running the example application*

Storing Authentication Tokens

Some external authentication services provide tokens that can be used to access additional APIs. As a general rule, the set of required APIs is included in the scope requested by the application so that the user can be prompted to grant appropriate access when they are authenticated. The access token that is used to get user data during the authentication process can then be used to access the other APIs.

There is a clash of terminology between the *access tokens* produced by the OAuth authentication process and the *authentication tokens* supported by Identity. This has arisen because Identity is providing a general feature that can be used to store tokens produced by any authentication process, even though OAuth has emerged as the de facto standard.

UNDERSTANDING THE COST OF ADDITIONAL APIS

The major authentication services produce tokens that can be used widely. Google, in particular, has a wide range of APIs that provide access to just about every service it offers, including access to email, calendar, and search data.

But the cost of using these APIs can be high. Not only do some providers charge for each access to the APIs, but there is often a paid-for validation service during which the service provider assesses the application to ensure that user data is handled appropriately. This can be expensive—at the time of writing, the Google validation process can cost between $15,000 and $75,000 and requires a significant amount of work.

For this reason, I create a simulated API in this chapter to demonstrate how tokens are stored and used. I do not demonstrate the use of Google or Facebook APIs, even though I create authentication handlers for these services.

Creating the Simulated External API Controller

To simulate an API that uses access tokens for validation, add a class file named DemoExternalApiController.cs to the Controllers folder and use it to define the controller shown in Listing 23-3.

Listing 23-3. The Contents of the DemoExternalApiController.cs File in the Controllers Folder

```
using Microsoft.AspNetCore.Mvc;
using System.Collections.Generic;

namespace ExampleApp.Controllers {

    [ApiController]
    [Route("api/[controller]")]
    public class DemoExternalApiController: Controller {

        private Dictionary<string, string> data
            = new Dictionary<string, string> {
                { "token1", "This is Alice's external data" },
                { "token2", "This is Dora's external data" },
            };
```

```
        [HttpGet]
        public IActionResult GetData([FromHeader] string authorization) {
            if (!string.IsNullOrEmpty(authorization)) {
                string token = authorization?[7..];
                if (!string.IsNullOrEmpty(token) && data.ContainsKey(token)) {
                    return Json(new { data = data[token] });
                }
            }
            return NotFound();
        }
    }
}
```

The controller defines a single action that provides a JSON object based on the token included in the Authorization request header. This is a simple example, but it provides enough functionality to demonstrate the use of an access token.

Extending the User Class

To prepare for storing access tokens, add the property to the AppUser class, as shown in Listing 23-4.

Listing 23-4. Adding a Property in the AppUser.cs File in the Identity Folder

```
using System;
using System.Collections.Generic;
using System.Security.Claims;
using Microsoft.AspNetCore.Identity;
using Microsoft.AspNetCore.Authentication;

namespace ExampleApp.Identity {
    public class AppUser {

        public string Id { get; set; } = Guid.NewGuid().ToString();

        public string UserName { get; set; }

        public string NormalizedUserName { get; set; }

        public string EmailAddress { get; set; }
        public string NormalizedEmailAddress { get; set; }
        public bool EmailAddressConfirmed { get; set; }

        public string PhoneNumber { get; set; }
        public bool PhoneNumberConfirmed { get; set; }

        public string FavoriteFood { get; set; }
        public string Hobby { get; set; }

        public IList<Claim> Claims { get; set; }
```

```
        public string SecurityStamp { get; set; }
        public string PasswordHash { get; set; }

        public bool CanUserBeLockedout { get; set; } = true;
        public int FailedSignInCount { get; set; }
        public DateTimeOffset? LockoutEnd { get; set; }

        public bool TwoFactorEnabled { get; set; }
        public bool AuthenticatorEnabled { get; set; }
        public string AuthenticatorKey { get; set; }

        public IList<UserLoginInfo> UserLogins { get; set; }
        public IList<(string provider, AuthenticationToken token)>
            AuthTokens { get; set; }
    }
}
```

Identity provides the AuthenticationToken class, which defines Name and Value properties. To store tokens, I need to be able to keep track of the source of each token, so I have used a list of (string, AuthenticationToken) tuples for simplicity.

Extending the User Store

The IUserAuthenticationTokenStore<T> interface is implemented by user stores that can manage access tokens, where T is the user class. The interface defines the methods shown in Table 23-1. These methods define a CancellationToken parameter named canceltoken that is used to receive a notification when an asynchronous task is canceled.

Table 23-1. *The IUserAuthenticationTokenStore<T> Methods*

Name	Description
GetTokenAsync(user, provider, name, cancelToken)	This method returns the token granted to a user with the specified name generated by the specified provider.
SetTokenAsync(user, provider, name, cancelToken)	This method stores a token for the user, with the specified provider and name.
RemoveTokenAsync(user, provider, name, cancelToken)	This method removes the token with the specified provider and name for the specified user.

Add a class file named UserStoreAuthenticationTokens.cs to the Identity/Store folder and use it to define the partial class shown in Listing 23-5.

Listing 23-5. The Contents of the UserStoreAuthenticationTokens.cs File in the Identity/Store Folder

```
using Microsoft.AspNetCore.Authentication;
using Microsoft.AspNetCore.Identity;
using System.Collections.Generic;
using System.Linq;
```

```
using System.Threading;
using System.Threading.Tasks;

namespace ExampleApp.Identity.Store {
    public partial class UserStore : IUserAuthenticationTokenStore<AppUser> {

        public Task<string> GetTokenAsync(AppUser user, string loginProvider,
                string name, CancellationToken cancelToken) {
            return Task.FromResult(user.AuthTokens?
                .FirstOrDefault(t => t.provider == loginProvider
                    && t.token.Name == name).token.Value);
        }

        public Task RemoveTokenAsync(AppUser user, string loginProvider,
                string name, CancellationToken cancelToken) {
            if (user.AuthTokens!= null) {
                user.AuthTokens= user.AuthTokens.Where(t =>
                    t.provider != loginProvider
                        && t.token.Name != name).ToList();
            }
            return Task.CompletedTask;
        }

        public Task SetTokenAsync(AppUser user, string loginProvider,
             string name, string value, CancellationToken cancelToken) {
            if (user.AuthTokens== null) {
                user.AuthTokens= new List<(string, AuthenticationToken)>();
            }
            user.AuthTokens.Add((loginProvider, new AuthenticationToken {
                Name = name, Value = value }));
            return Task.CompletedTask;
        }
    }
}
```

The implementation of the interface uses the property defined in Listing 23-4 to store access tokens as tuples.

Managing Authentication Tokens

The UserManager<T> class provides the members described in Table 23-2 for managing authentication tokens in the user store.

Table 23-2. *The UserManager<T> Members for Managing Authentication Tokens*

Name	Description
SupportsUserAuthenticationTokens	This property returns true if the user store implements the IUserAuthenticationTokenStore<T> interface.
GetAuthenticationTokenAsync (user, provider, name)	This method retrieves a token by calling the user store's GetTokenAsync method.
SetAuthenticationTokenAsync (user, provider, name)	This method stores a token by calling the user store's SetTokenAsync method, after which the update sequence is performed.
RemoveAuthenticationTokenAsync (user, provider, name)	This method removes a token by calling the user store's RemoveTokenAsync method, after which the update sequence is applied.

The SignInManager<T> class also defines a method that is useful for managing authentication tokens, as described in Table 23-3.

Table 23-3. *The SignInManager<T> Method for Managing Authentication Tokens*

Name	Description
UpdateExternalAuthentication TokensAsync(login)	This method stores the access tokens in the specific ExternalLoginInfo object and stores them using the user manager's SetAuthenticationTokenAsync method.

Storing External Authentication Access Tokens

The UpdateExternalAuthenticationTokensAsync method provided by the SignInManager<T> class populates the user store with the authentication tokens found in the ExternalLoginInfo. AuthenticationTokens property. In Listing 23-6, I have updated the external authentication handler to store the tokens it receives.

Listing 23-6. Storing Tokens in the ExternalAuthHandler.cs File in the Custom Folder

```
...
public virtual async Task<bool> HandleRequestAsync() {
    if (Context.Request.Path.Equals(Options.RedirectPath)) {
        string authCode = await GetAuthenticationCode();
        (string token, string state) = await GetAccessToken(authCode);
        if (!string.IsNullOrEmpty(token)) {
            IEnumerable<Claim> claims = await GetUserData(token);
            if (claims != null) {
                ClaimsIdentity identity = new ClaimsIdentity(Scheme.Name);
                identity.AddClaims(claims);
                ClaimsPrincipal claimsPrincipal
                    = new ClaimsPrincipal(identity);
                AuthenticationProperties props =
                    PropertiesFormatter.Unprotect(state);
```

```
            props.StoreTokens(new[] { new AuthenticationToken {
                Name = "access_token", Value = token } });
            await Context.SignInAsync(IdentityConstants.ExternalScheme,
                claimsPrincipal, props);
            Context.Response.Redirect(props.RedirectUri);
            return true;
        }
    }
    Context.Response.Redirect(string.Format(Options.ErrorUrlTemplate,
        ErrorMessage));
    return true;
    }
    return false;
}
...
```

The new statement in Listing 23-6 adds the access token obtained from the OAuth authentication process to the AuthenticationProperties object using the StoreTokens extension method. This is one of the extension methods available for managing tokens, as described in Table 23-4.

Table 23-4. *Useful AuthenticationProperties Token Extension Methods*

Name	Description
GetTokens()	This method returns the authentication tokens that have been stored in the AuthenticationProperties object.
GetTokenValue(name)	This method returns the value of the token with the specified name, or null if there is no such token.
StoreTokens(tokens)	This method stores tokens expressed as an IEnumerable<AuthenticationToken> sequence.
UpdateTokenValue(name, value)	This method updates the value for a specific token.

The authentication handler adds the tokens to the AuthenticationProperties object, which is then available to the SignInManager<T> service when a user has been signed in. In Listing 23-7, I use the SignInManager<T>.UpdateExternalAuthenticationTokensAsync method to retrieve the tokens and add them to the user store.

Listing 23-7. Storing Authentication Tokens in the ExternalSignIn.cshtml.cs File in the Pages Folder

```
...
public async Task<IActionResult> OnGetCorrelate(string returnUrl) {
    ExternalLoginInfo info = await SignInManager.GetExternalLoginInfoAsync();

    AppUser user = await UserManager.FindByLoginAsync(info.LoginProvider,
        info.ProviderKey);
    if (user == null) {
        string externalEmail =
            info.Principal.FindFirst(ClaimTypes.Email)?.Value ?? string.Empty;
        user = await UserManager.FindByEmailAsync(externalEmail);
```

```
        if (user == null) {
            return RedirectToPage("/ExternalAccountConfirm",
                new { returnUrl });
        } else {
            UserLoginInfo firstLogin = user?.UserLogins?.FirstOrDefault();
            if (firstLogin != null && firstLogin.LoginProvider
                    != info.LoginProvider) {
                return RedirectToPage(new {
                    error =
                    $"{firstLogin.ProviderDisplayName} Authentication Expected"
                });
            } else {
                await UserManager.AddLoginAsync(user, info);
            }
        }
    }
    SignInResult result = await SignInManager.ExternalLoginSignInAsync(
            info.LoginProvider, info.ProviderKey, false, false);
    await SignInManager.UpdateExternalAuthenticationTokensAsync(info);
    if (result.Succeeded) {
        return RedirectToPage("ExternalSignIn", "Confirm",
            new { info.ProviderDisplayName, returnUrl });
    } else if (result.RequiresTwoFactor) {
        string postSignInUrl = this.Url.Page("/ExternalSignIn", "Confirm",
            new { info.ProviderDisplayName, returnUrl });
        return RedirectToPage("/SignInTwoFactor",
            new { returnUrl = postSignInUrl });
    }
    return RedirectToPage(new { error = true, returnUrl });
}
...
```

I also need to perform the same task when creating an account following an external login, as shown in Listing 23-8.

Listing 23-8. Storing Tokens in the ExternalAccountConfirm.cshtml.cs File in the Pages Folder

```
...
public async Task<IActionResult> OnPostAsync(string username) {
    ExternalLoginInfo info = await SignInManager.GetExternalLoginInfoAsync();

    if (info != null) {
        ClaimsPrincipal external = info.Principal;
        AppUser.UserName = username;
        AppUser.EmailAddress = external.FindFirstValue(ClaimTypes.Email);
        AppUser.EmailAddressConfirmed = true;
        IdentityResult result = await UserManager.CreateAsync(AppUser);
        if (result.Succeeded) {
            await UserManager.AddClaimAsync(AppUser,
                new Claim(ClaimTypes.Role, "User"));
            await UserManager.AddLoginAsync(AppUser, info);
            await SignInManager.ExternalLoginSignInAsync(info.LoginProvider,
```

```
            info.ProviderKey, false);
        await SignInManager.UpdateExternalAuthenticationTokensAsync(info);
        return Redirect(ReturnUrl);
    } else {
        foreach (IdentityError err in result.Errors) {
            ModelState.AddModelError(string.Empty, err.Description);
        }
    }
} else {
    ModelState.AddModelError(string.Empty, "No external login found");
}
return Page();
}
...
```

The result is that the user store is populated with the authentication tokens provided by the authentication handler.

Using a Stored Authentication Token

The application can access stored tokens through the UserManager<T> class and use them to send requests to APIs that will use them to authenticate requests. Create a Razor Page named ApiData.cshtml in the Pages folder and add the content shown in Listing 23-9.

Listing 23-9. The Contents of the ApiData.cshtml File in the Pages Folder

```
@page
@model ExampleApp.Pages.ApiDataModel
@attribute [Microsoft.AspNetCore.Authorization.Authorize]
<h4 class="bg-info text-center text-white m-2 p-2">Data: @Model.Data</h4>
```

The view part of the page displays the value of a page model property named Data. To implement the page model, add the code shown in Listing 23-10 to the ApiData.cshtml.cs file in the Pages folder. (You will have to create this file if you are using Visual Studio Code.)

Listing 23-10. The Contents of the ApiData.cshtml.cs File in the Pages Folder

```
using ExampleApp.Identity;
using Microsoft.AspNetCore.Authentication;
using Microsoft.AspNetCore.Identity;
using Microsoft.AspNetCore.Mvc.RazorPages;
using System.Net.Http;
using System.Net.Http.Headers;
using System.Text.Json;
using System.Threading.Tasks;

namespace ExampleApp.Pages {

    public class ApiDataModel : PageModel {
```

```
public ApiDataModel(UserManager<AppUser> userManager) {
    UserManager = userManager;
}

public UserManager<AppUser> UserManager { get; set; }

public string Data { get; set; } = "No Data";

public async Task OnGetAsync () {
    AppUser user = await UserManager.GetUserAsync(HttpContext.User);
    if (user != null) {
        string token = await UserManager.GetAuthenticationTokenAsync
            (user, "demoAuth", "access_token");
        if (!string.IsNullOrEmpty(token)) {
            HttpRequestMessage msg = new HttpRequestMessage(
                HttpMethod.Get,
                "http://localhost:5000/api/DemoExternalApi");
            msg.Headers.Authorization = new AuthenticationHeaderValue
                ("Bearer", token);
            HttpResponseMessage resp
                = await new HttpClient().SendAsync(msg);
            JsonDocument doc = JsonDocument.Parse(await
                resp.Content.ReadAsStringAsync());
            Data = doc.RootElement.GetString("data");
        }
    }
}
}
```

The GET handler method retrieves the authorization token produced by the demoAuth scheme and uses it for the Authorization header in a request to the demonstration controller. The response from the controller is parsed into JSON and used to set the value of the Data property that is displayed by the view part of the page.

Restart ASP.NET Core, request http://localhost:5000/signout, and click the Sign Out button to sign out of the application. Request http://localhost:5000/apidata, which will trigger a challenge response. Click the Demo Service button to sign in with the external authentication service and sign in using alice@example.com as the email address and myexternalpassword as the password. Enter the code from your authenticator application, click the Sign In button, and then click the Continue button when the sign-in confirmation page is displayed. Once you have signed into the application, you will be redirected to the /apidata URL, which will use the stored token to get data from the demonstration controller. Figure 23-2 shows the entire sequence.

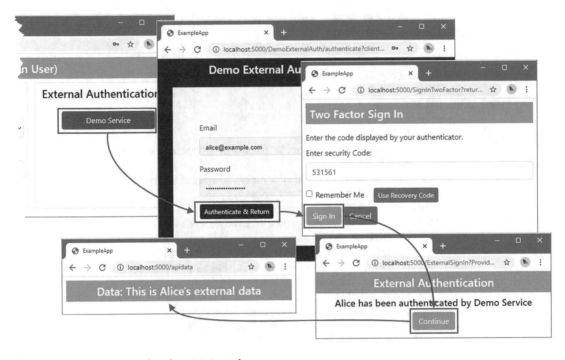

Figure 23-2. *Using a stored authentication token*

Adding Support for Real External Authentication Services

Now that all of the building blocks are in place, I can add support for real external authentication services. In the sections that follow, I extend the external authentication handler created in Chapter 22 to support the OAuth services provided by Google and Facebook, which provide the most popular authentication services.

I have not created an authentication handler for Twitter, which is also widely used for authentication. Twitter does provide an authentication service, but it uses an older version of the OAuth specification, which is more complex than the updated version used by most services. See Chapter 11 for details of how to set up the built-in Twitter authentication handler that Microsoft provides for ASP.NET Core.

Supporting Google Authentication

To register the example application, navigate to `https://console.developers.google.com` and sign in with a Google account. Click the OAuth Consent Screen option and select External for User Type, which will allow any Google account to authenticate for your application.

■ **Tip** You may see a message telling you that no APIs are available to use yet. This is not important when you only need to authenticate users.

Click Create, and you will be presented with a form. Enter **ExampleApp** into the App Name field and enter your email address in the User Support Email and Developer Contact Information sections of the form. The rest of the form can be left empty for the example application.

Click Save and Continue, and you will be presented with the scope selection screen, which is used to specify the scopes that your application requires.

Click the Add or Remove Scopes button, and you will be presented with the list of scopes that your application can request. Select three scopes: openid, auth/userinfo.email, and auth/userinfo.profile. Click the Update button to save your selection.

Click Save and Continue to return to the OAuth consent screen and then click Back to Dashboard. Figure 23-3 shows the sequence for configuring the consent screen.

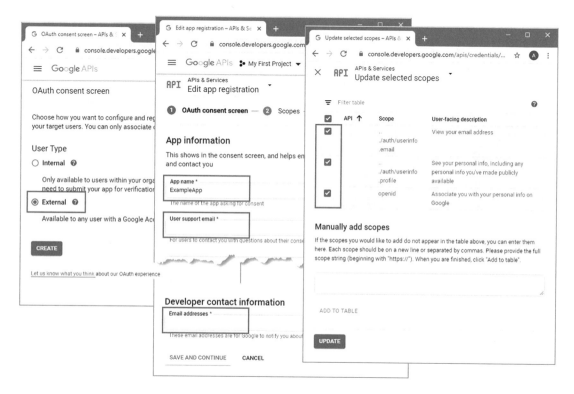

Figure 23-3. *Configuring the Google OAuth consent screen*

■ **Tip** You can find the Google documentation for OAuth at https://developers.google.com/identity/ protocols/oauth2/web-server.

Configuring Application Credentials

The next step is to create credentials for the application. Click the Credentials link, click the Create Credentials button at the top of the page, and select OAuth Client ID from the list of options.

Select Web Application from the Application Type list and enter **ExampleApp** in the Name field. Click Add URL in the Authorized Redirect URIs section and enter **http://localhost:5000/signin-google** into the text field. Click the Create button, and you will be presented with the client ID and client secret for your application, as shown in Figure 23-4 (although I have blurred the details since these are for my account). Make a note of the ID and secret.

UNDERSTANDING THE REDIRECT URL

To configure the example application, I have specified the URL `http://localhost:5000/signin-google`. The redirection URLs are evaluated by the browser, and since the browser and the ASP. NET Core application are running on the same machine, using localhost in the URL means that the redirection performed by the Google service will target the example application.

For real applications, you must use a URL that contains a hostname that can be correctly evaluated by your users' browsers. This can be a corporate hostname for line-of-business applications or a name registered in the global DNS for internet-facing applications. You should not use localhost except during development.

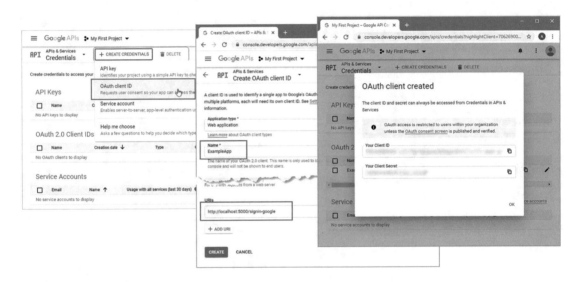

Figure 23-4. Configuring application credentials

Creating the Authentication Handler

The next step is to create an authentication handler that will use the Google OAuth service to authenticate users. Add a class file named `GoogleHandler.cs` to the `Custom` folder with the code shown in Listing 23-11.

Listing 23-11. The Contents of the GoogleHandler.cs File in the Custom Folder

```
using Microsoft.AspNetCore.Authentication;
using Microsoft.AspNetCore.DataProtection;
using Microsoft.AspNetCore.Http;
using Microsoft.Extensions.Logging;
using Microsoft.Extensions.Options;
using System;
using System.Collections.Generic;
using System.Security.Claims;
using System.Text.Json;
```

```
using System.Threading.Tasks;

namespace ExampleApp.Custom {

    public class GoogleOptions : ExternalAuthOptions {
        public override string RedirectPath { get; set; } = "/signin-google";
        public override string AuthenticationUrl =>
            "https://accounts.google.com/o/oauth2/v2/auth";
        public override string ExchangeUrl =>
            "https://www.googleapis.com/oauth2/v4/token";
        public override string DataUrl =>
            "https://www.googleapis.com/oauth2/v2/userinfo";
    }

    public class GoogleHandler : ExternalAuthHandler {

        public GoogleHandler(IOptions<GoogleOptions> options,
            IDataProtectionProvider dp,
            ILogger<GoogleHandler> logger) : base(options, dp, logger) {}

        protected override IEnumerable<Claim> GetClaims(JsonDocument jsonDoc) {
            List<Claim> claims = new List<Claim>();
            claims.Add(new Claim(ClaimTypes.NameIdentifier,
                jsonDoc.RootElement.GetString("id")));
            claims.Add(new Claim(ClaimTypes.Name,
                jsonDoc.RootElement.GetString("name")?.Replace(" ", "_")));
            claims.Add(new Claim(ClaimTypes.Email,
                jsonDoc.RootElement.GetString("email")));
            return claims;
        }

        protected async override Task<string> GetAuthenticationUrl(
                AuthenticationProperties properties) {
            if (CheckCredentials()) {
                return await base.GetAuthenticationUrl(properties);
            } else {
                return string.Format(Options.ErrorUrlTemplate, ErrorMessage);
            }
        }

        private bool CheckCredentials() {
            string secret = Options.ClientSecret;
            string id = Options.ClientId;
            string defaultVal = "ReplaceMe";
            if (string.IsNullOrEmpty(secret) || string.IsNullOrEmpty(id)
                || defaultVal.Equals(secret) || defaultVal.Equals(secret)) {
                    ErrorMessage = "External Authentication Secret or ID Not Set";
                    Logger.LogError("External Authentication Secret or ID Not Set");
                return false;
            }
```

```
        return true;
      }
   }
}
```

The handler is derived from the ExternalAuthHandler class created in Chapter 22. To support the Google service, I have defined a new callback URL and specified the URLs for each part of the process, which I have summarized in Table 23-5.

Table 23-5. *The Google OAuth URLs*

Step	URL
Authentication	`https://accounts.google.com/o/oauth2/v2/auth`
Token Exchange	`https://www.googleapis.com/oauth2/v4/token`
User Data	`https://www.googleapis.com/oauth2/v2/userinfo`

I also have to map a different set of JSON properties to claims when signing a user into the application. Each authentication service returns data in a different format, and I find the easiest approach to writing an authentication handler is to print out the JSON response and pick out the properties I require. For this example, I have used the id, name, and email properties.

Notice that I replace any spaces when I create the Name claim, like this:

```
...
claims.Add(new Claim(ClaimTypes.Name,
    jsonDoc.RootElement.GetString("name")?.Replace(" ", "_")));
...
```

The Google data will contain a name such as Adam Freeman, which won't be accepted as an Identity account name. To avoid a validation error, I replace spaces with underscores (the _ character).

I also defined a method named CheckCredentials in Listing 23-11. You must create your own client ID and client secret and use them to configure the application. The CheckCredentials method is called in the GetAuthenticationUrl method and displays an error if the credentials have not been set.

Configuring the Application

The final step is to register the authentication handler and specify the client ID and secret, as shown in Listing 23-12. Use the ID and secret you created in the previous section instead of the placeholder strings in the listing.

Listing 23-12. Configuring the Application in the Startup.cs File in the ExampleApp Folder

```
...
public void ConfigureServices(IServiceCollection services) {
    services.AddSingleton<ILookupNormalizer, Normalizer>();
    services.AddSingleton<IUserStore<AppUser>, UserStore>();
    services.AddSingleton<IEmailSender, ConsoleEmailSender>();
    services.AddSingleton<ISMSSender, ConsoleSMSSender>();
    services.AddSingleton<IPasswordHasher<AppUser>, SimplePasswordHasher>();
    services.AddSingleton<IRoleStore<AppRole>, RoleStore>();
```

```
services.AddOptions<ExternalAuthOptions>();

services.Configure<GoogleOptions>(opts => {
    opts.ClientId = "ReplaceMe";
    opts.ClientSecret = "ReplaceMe";
});

// ...statements omitted for brevity...

services.AddAuthentication(opts => {
    opts.DefaultScheme = IdentityConstants.ApplicationScheme;
    opts.AddScheme<ExternalAuthHandler>("demoAuth", "Demo Service");
    opts.AddScheme<GoogleHandler>("google", "Google");
}).AddCookie(IdentityConstants.ApplicationScheme, opts => {
    opts.LoginPath = "/signin";
    opts.AccessDeniedPath = "/signin/403";
})
.AddCookie(IdentityConstants.TwoFactorUserIdScheme)
.AddCookie(IdentityConstants.TwoFactorRememberMeScheme)
.AddCookie(IdentityConstants.ExternalScheme);

services.AddAuthorization(opts => {
    AuthorizationPolicies.AddPolicies(opts);
    opts.AddPolicy("Full2FARequired", builder => {
        builder.RequireClaim("amr", "mfa");
    });
});
services.AddRazorPages();
services.AddControllersWithViews();
}
...
```

The Configure method is used to configure the GoogleOptions object that will be provided to the authentication handler through dependency injection. The other change in the listing registers the Google authentication handler with the AddScheme method.

USING SERVICE-SPECIFIC QUERY STRING PARAMETERS

Most services support optional query strings in the authentication redirection URL that control additional features. One useful option for the Google service is login_hint, which can be set to the email address of the user who is to be authenticated. Google will use the email address to simplify the authentication process.

Restart ASP.NET Core and request http://localhost:5000/secret. When challenged, click the Google button, and you will be prompted to sign in with a Google account and grant access to the application, as shown in Figure 23-5.

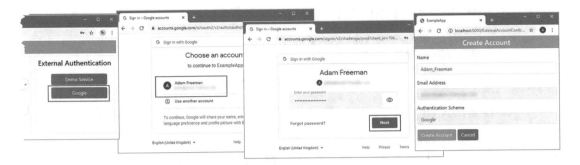

Figure 23-5. *Authenticating users with Google*

Once authenticated, you will be presented with the Create Account screen, which displays the name and email address of the Google account. Click the Create Account button to create a new Identity account and redirection to the protected resource. You can see the account that has been created by requesting `http://localhost:5000/users`, which will display the newly created account alongside those used to seed the user store, as shown in Figure 23-6.

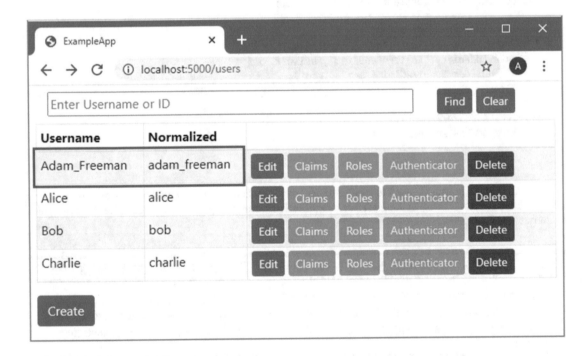

Figure 23-6. *Inspecting the newly created account*

Supporting Facebook Authentication

To register the application with Facebook, go to `https://developers.facebook.com/apps` and sign in with your Facebook account. Click the Create App button, select Build Connected Experiences from the list, and click the Continue button. Enter **ExampleApp** into the App Display Name field and click the Create App button. Figure 23-7 shows this sequence.

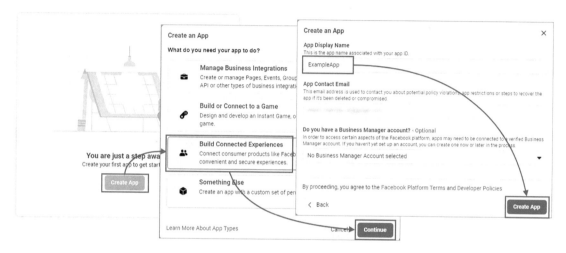

Figure 23-7. *Creating a new application*

Once you have created a Facebook application, you will be returned to the developer dashboard and presented with a list of optional products to use. Locate Facebook Login and click the Setup button. You will see a set of quick-start options, but they can be ignored because the important configuration options are shown under the Facebook Login ➤ Settings section that appears on the left side of the dashboard display, as shown in Figure 23-8.

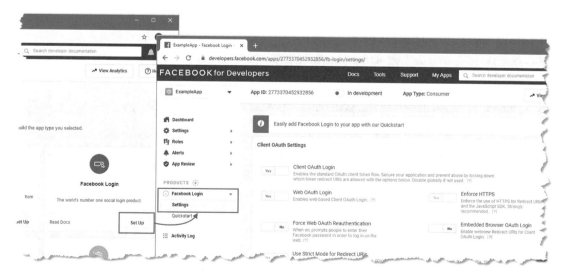

Figure 23-8. *The Facebook Login settings*

No configuration changes are required for the example application because Facebook makes it easy to use OAuth during the development of a project. When you are ready to deploy the application, you will need to return to this page and finalize your configuration, including providing the public-facing redirection URL, which will replace the localhost URL I use in this chapter. Details of the configuration options are included in the Facebook Login documentation, which can be found at `https://developers.facebook.com/docs/ facebook-login`.

Obtaining Application Credentials

Navigate to the Basic section in the Settings area to get the App ID and App Secret values, as shown in Figure 23-9, which are the terms that Facebook uses for the client ID and secret. (The App Secret value is hidden until you click the Show button.) Make a note of these values, which will be required to configure the application.

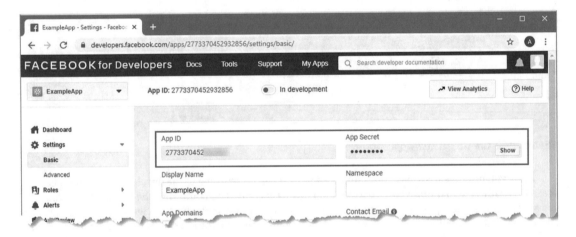

Figure 23-9. *The application credentials for external authentication*

Creating the Authentication Handler

Add a class file named `FacebookHandler.cs` to the `Custom` folder and use it to define the class shown in Listing 23-13.

Listing 23-13. The Contents of the FacebookHandler.cs File in the Custom Folder

```
using Microsoft.AspNetCore.Authentication;
using Microsoft.AspNetCore.DataProtection;
using Microsoft.AspNetCore.Http;
using Microsoft.Extensions.Logging;
using Microsoft.Extensions.Options;
using System;
using System.Collections.Generic;
using System.Security.Claims;
using System.Text.Json;
```

```
namespace ExampleApp.Custom {

    public class FacebookOptions : ExternalAuthOptions {
        public override string RedirectPath { get; set; } = "/signin-facebook";
        public override string Scope { get; set; } = "email";

        public override string AuthenticationUrl =>
            "https://www.facebook.com/v8.0/dialog/oauth";
        public override string ExchangeUrl =>
            "https://graph.facebook.com/v8.0/oauth/access_token";
        public override string DataUrl =>
            "https://graph.facebook.com/v8.0/me?fields=name,email";
    }

    public class FacebookHandler : ExternalAuthHandler {

        public FacebookHandler(IOptions<FacebookOptions> options,
            IDataProtectionProvider dp,
            ILogger<FacebookHandler> logger) : base(options, dp, logger) {

            string secret = Options.ClientSecret;
            if (string.IsNullOrEmpty(secret) || "MyClientSecret"
                    .Equals(secret, StringComparison.OrdinalIgnoreCase)) {
                logger.LogError("External Authentication Secret Not Set");
            }
        }

        protected override IEnumerable<Claim> GetClaims(JsonDocument jsonDoc) {
            List<Claim> claims = new List<Claim>();

            claims.Add(new Claim(ClaimTypes.NameIdentifier,
                jsonDoc.RootElement.GetString("id")));
            claims.Add(new Claim(ClaimTypes.Name,
                jsonDoc.RootElement.GetString("name")?.Replace(" ", "_")));
            claims.Add(new Claim(ClaimTypes.Email,
                jsonDoc.RootElement.GetString("email")));
            return claims;
        }
    }
}
```

The handler is derived from the ExternalAuthHandler class created in Chapter 22. To support the Facebook service, I have defined a new callback URL and specified the URLs for each part of the process, which I have summarized in Table 23-6.

Table 23-6. *The Facebook OAuth URLs*

Step	URL
Authentication	`https://www.facebook.com/v8.0/dialog/oauth`
Token Exchange	`https://graph.facebook.com/v8.0/oauth/access_token`
User Data	`https://graph.facebook.com/v8.0/me`

The Facebook authentication service requires individual data fields to be selected using a `fields` query string parameter, which is why the value for the `DataUrl` configuration options is as follows:

```
...
https://graph.facebook.com/v8.0/me?fields=name,email
...
```

For the example application, I require the `name` and `email` fields. The complete set of fields is described at `https://developers.facebook.com/docs/graph-api/reference/user`.

Configuring the Application

To configure the application, add the statements shown in Listing 23-14 to the `ConfigureServices` method of the `Startup` class, ensuring that you use the client ID and secret that were displayed in the Facebook developer dashboard when you registered the application.

Listing 23-14. Configuring the Application in the Startup.cs File in the ExampleApp Folder

```
...
public void ConfigureServices(IServiceCollection services) {
    services.AddSingleton<ILookupNormalizer, Normalizer>();
    services.AddSingleton<IUserStore<AppUser>, UserStore>();
    services.AddSingleton<IEmailSender, ConsoleEmailSender>();
    services.AddSingleton<ISMSSender, ConsoleSMSSender>();
    services.AddSingleton<IPasswordHasher<AppUser>, SimplePasswordHasher>();
    services.AddSingleton<IRoleStore<AppRole>, RoleStore>();

    services.AddOptions<ExternalAuthOptions>();

    services.Configure<GoogleOptions>(opts => {
        opts.ClientId = "ReplaceMe";
        opts.ClientSecret = "ReplaceMe";
    });

    services.Configure<FacebookOptions>(opts => {
        opts.ClientId = "ReplaceMe";
        opts.ClientSecret = "ReplaceMe";
    });

    // ...statements omitted for brevity...

    services.AddAuthentication(opts => {
        opts.DefaultScheme = IdentityConstants.ApplicationScheme;
        opts.AddScheme<ExternalAuthHandler>("demoAuth", "Demo Service");
```

```
    opts.AddScheme<GoogleHandler>("google", "Google");
    opts.AddScheme<FacebookHandler>("facebook", "Facebook");
}).AddCookie(IdentityConstants.ApplicationScheme, opts => {
    opts.LoginPath = "/signin";
    opts.AccessDeniedPath = "/signin/403";
})
.AddCookie(IdentityConstants.TwoFactorUserIdScheme)
.AddCookie(IdentityConstants.TwoFactorRememberMeScheme)
.AddCookie(IdentityConstants.ExternalScheme);

services.AddAuthorization(opts => {
    AuthorizationPolicies.AddPolicies(opts);
    opts.AddPolicy("Full2FARequired", builder => {
        builder.RequireClaim("amr", "mfa");
    });
});
services.AddRazorPages();
services.AddControllersWithViews();
}
...
```

Restart ASP.NET Core, request `http://localhost:5000/signout`, and click the Sign Out button. This will ensure that the external login performed through the Google service won't be used. Request `http://localhost:5000/secret`, and you will be challenged to sign in. Click the Facebook button, and you will be prompted to sign in with a Facebook account, as shown in Figure 23-10. Once you have signed in, you will be prompted to create an Identity account using the Facebook details, and then you will be redirected to the protected resource.

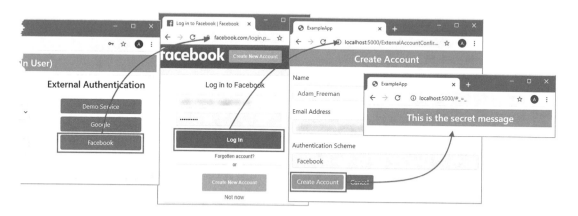

Figure 23-10. *Authenticating users with Facebook*

Simplifying the Sign-In Process

I introduced different methods of signing into the example application gradually so I could explain how important Identity features work. The result, however, is confusing because users can choose a different authentication option each time they sign in, and, worse, users have different sets of options depending on how their account was created.

If a user has an account that has been created with a password, they can choose to sign in with the password or choose any of the external authentication providers, just as long as the email address provided in the external user data matches the email address in the Identity user store. But if a user account is created following external authentication, the user won't have a password in the store and can only log in with an external provider, although they are free to switch between providers.

The overall effect is confusing, not least because all users are presented with the complete set of authentication options, even though they won't all work for every account. I am going to tidy this up by selecting a single authentication scheme for each user.

Updating the Sign-In Page

My policy will be simple: once a user has signed in with an external service, then that will be their only sign-in method. You don't have to follow this policy, but it has the advantage of being simple, consistent, and easy for the user to understand.

In Listing 23-15, I replaced the contents of the view part of the SignIn Razor page to support the new policy.

Listing 23-15. Replacing the Contents of the SignIn.cshtml File in the Pages Folder

```
@page "{code:int?}"
@model ExampleApp.Pages.SignInModel
@using Microsoft.AspNetCore.Http

@if (!string.IsNullOrEmpty(Model.Message)) {
    <h3 class="bg-danger text-white text-center p-2">@Model.Message</h3>
}

<h4 class="bg-info text-white m-2 p-2">Current User: @Model.Username</h4>

<div class="container-fluid">
    <div class="row">
        <div class="col">
            <form method="post">
                <div class="form-group">
                    <label>User</label>
                    <select class="form-control"
                            asp-for="Username" asp-items="@Model.Users">
                    </select>
                </div>
                <button class="btn btn-info" type="submit">Sign In</button>
            </form>
        </div>
    </div>
    <div class="row">
        <div class="col text-center p-2">
            <div class="border p-2">
                <h6>Create a New Account</h6>
                <form method="post">
                    @foreach (var scheme in await Model.SignInManager
                            .GetExternalAuthenticationSchemesAsync()) {
                        <button class="btn btn-secondary m-2" type="submit"
```

```
                        asp-page="/externalsignin"
                        asp-route-returnUrl="@Request.Query["returnUrl"]"
                        asp-route-providername="@scheme.Name">
                            @scheme.DisplayName
                    </button>
                }
            </form>
        </div>
    </div>
</div>
</div>
```

The new layout removes the option to enter a password and groups the external authentication buttons with a "Create a New Account" message. In Listing 23-16, I have updated the SignIn page model class so that the POST handler method locates the user and performs a redirection for either external authentication or password authentication.

Listing 23-16. Redirecting for Authentication in the SignIn.cshtml.cs File in the Pages Folder

```csharp
using Microsoft.AspNetCore.Authentication;
using Microsoft.AspNetCore.Http;
using Microsoft.AspNetCore.Mvc;
using Microsoft.AspNetCore.Mvc.RazorPages;
using Microsoft.AspNetCore.Mvc.Rendering;
using System.Security.Claims;
using System.Threading.Tasks;
using Microsoft.AspNetCore.Identity;
using System.Linq;
using ExampleApp.Identity;
using SignInResult = Microsoft.AspNetCore.Identity.SignInResult;
using System;

namespace ExampleApp.Pages {
    public class SignInModel : PageModel {

        public SignInModel(UserManager<AppUser> userManager,
                SignInManager<AppUser> signInManager) {
            UserManager = userManager;
            SignInManager = signInManager;
        }

        public UserManager<AppUser> UserManager { get; set; }
        public SignInManager<AppUser> SignInManager { get; set; }

        public SelectList Users => new SelectList(
            UserManager.Users.OrderBy(u => u.EmailAddress),
                "EmailAddress", "NormalizedEmailAddress");

        public string Username { get; set; }

        public int? Code { get; set; }
```

```
        public string Message { get; set; }

        public void OnGet(int? code) {
            if (code == StatusCodes.Status401Unauthorized) {
                Message = "401 - Challenge Response";
            } else if (code == StatusCodes.Status403Forbidden) {
                Message = "403 - Forbidden Response";
            }
            Username = User.Identity.Name ?? "(No Signed In User)";
        }

        public async Task<IActionResult> OnPost(string username,
                [FromQuery] string returnUrl) {
            AppUser user = await UserManager.FindByEmailAsync(username);
            UserLoginInfo loginInfo = user?.UserLogins?.FirstOrDefault();
            if (loginInfo != null) {
                return RedirectToPage("/ExternalSignIn", new {
                    returnUrl, providerName = loginInfo.LoginProvider
                });
            }
            return RedirectToPage("SignInPassword", new { username, returnUrl });
        }
    }
}
```

If the user has external logins, then the first one in the store is used for authentication with a redirection to the ExternalSignIn page. If the user does have an external login—or there is no such user in the store—then a redirection to the SignInPassword page is performed, which I create in the next section.

Creating the Password Page

The next step is to create a new Razor Page that will prompt for passwords and validate them. Add a Razor Page named SignInPassword.cshtml to the Pages folder with the content shown in Listing 23-17.

Listing 23-17. The Contents of the SignInPassword.cshtml File in the Pages Folder

```
@page
@model ExampleApp.Pages.SignInPasswordModel

<div asp-validation-summary="All" class="text-danger m-2"></div>

 <form method="post" class="p-2">
    <input type="hidden" name="returnUrl" value="@Model.ReturnUrl" />
    <div class="form-group">
        <label>User</label>
        <input class="form-control" readonly name="username"
            value="@Model.Username" />
    </div>
    <div class="form-group">
        <label>Password</label>
        <input class="form-control" type="password" name="password" />
    </div>
```

```
        <button class="btn btn-info" type="submit">Sign In</button>
        @if (User.Identity.IsAuthenticated) {
            <a asp-page="/Store/PasswordChange" class="btn btn-secondary"
                asp-route-id="@Model.User?
                            .FindFirst(ClaimTypes.NameIdentifier)?.Value">
                    Change Password
            </a>
        } else {
            <a class="btn btn-secondary" href="/password/reset">
                Reset Password
            </a>
        }
</form>
```

To define the page model class, add the code shown in Listing 23-18 to the SignInPassword.cshtml.cs file. (You will have to create this file if you are using Visual Studio Code.)

Listing 23-18. The Contents of the SignInPassword.cshtml File in the Pages Folder

```csharp
using ExampleApp.Identity;
using Microsoft.AspNetCore.Identity;
using Microsoft.AspNetCore.Mvc;
using Microsoft.AspNetCore.Mvc.RazorPages;
using System;
using System.Threading.Tasks;
using SignInResult = Microsoft.AspNetCore.Identity.SignInResult;

namespace ExampleApp.Pages {

    public class SignInPasswordModel : PageModel {

        public SignInPasswordModel(UserManager<AppUser> userManager,
                SignInManager<AppUser> signInManager) {
            UserManager = userManager;
            SignInManager = signInManager;
        }

        public UserManager<AppUser> UserManager { get; set; }
        public SignInManager<AppUser> SignInManager { get; set; }

        public string Username { get; set; }
        public string ReturnUrl { get; set; }

        public void OnGet(string username, string returnUrl) {
            Username = username;
            ReturnUrl = returnUrl;
        }

        public async Task<ActionResult> OnPost(string username,
                string password, string returnUrl) {
            SignInResult result = SignInResult.Failed;
            AppUser user = await UserManager.FindByEmailAsync(username);
```

```
            if (user != null && !string.IsNullOrEmpty(password)) {
                result = await SignInManager.PasswordSignInAsync(user, password,
                    false, true);
            }
            if (!result.Succeeded) {
                if (result.IsLockedOut) {
                    TimeSpan remaining = (await UserManager
                        .GetLockoutEndDateAsync(user))
                        .GetValueOrDefault().Subtract(DateTimeOffset.Now);
                    ModelState.AddModelError("",
                        $"Locked Out for {remaining.Minutes} mins and"
                            + $" {remaining.Seconds} secs");
                } else if (result.RequiresTwoFactor) {
                    return RedirectToPage("/SignInTwoFactor", new { returnUrl });
                } else if (result.IsNotAllowed) {
                    ModelState.AddModelError("", "Sign In Not Allowed");
                } else {
                    ModelState.AddModelError("", "Access Denied");
                }
                Username = username;
                ReturnUrl = returnUrl;
                return Page();
            }
            return Redirect(returnUrl ?? "/signin");
        }
    }
}
```

The page model class for this page reuses code that was previously part of the SignIn page and does not introduce any new features.

Adding a GET Handler Method for External Authentication

In Listing 23-19, I have added a GET handler method to the page model class for the ExternalSignIn Razor Page. This allows me to easily start the external authentication process by sending form data in a POST request or with a redirection, which uses a GET request.

Listing 23-19. Adding a Handler Method in the ExternalSignIn.cshtml.cs File in the Pages Folder

```
using ExampleApp.Identity;
using Microsoft.AspNetCore.Authentication;
using Microsoft.AspNetCore.Identity;
using Microsoft.AspNetCore.Mvc;
using Microsoft.AspNetCore.Mvc.RazorPages;
using System.Linq;
using System.Security.Claims;
using System.Threading.Tasks;
using SignInResult = Microsoft.AspNetCore.Identity.SignInResult;
```

```
namespace ExampleApp.Pages {

    public class ExternalSignInModel : PageModel {

        public ExternalSignInModel(SignInManager<AppUser> signInManager,
                UserManager<AppUser> userManager) {
            SignInManager = signInManager;
            UserManager = userManager;
        }

        public SignInManager<AppUser> SignInManager { get; set; }
        public UserManager<AppUser> UserManager { get; set; }

        public string ProviderDisplayName { get; set; }

        public IActionResult OnGet(string error, string providerName,
                string returnUrl)
            => error == null ? OnPost(providerName, returnUrl) : Page();

        public IActionResult OnPost(string providerName,
                string returnUrl = "/") {
            string redirectUrl = Url.Page("./ExternalSignIn",
                pageHandler: "Correlate", values: new { returnUrl });
            AuthenticationProperties properties = SignInManager
              .ConfigureExternalAuthenticationProperties(providerName,
                    redirectUrl);
            return new ChallengeResult(providerName, properties);
        }

        // ...methods omitted for brevity...
    }
}
```

Care should be taken when using the handler method for one HTTP verb to call a handler for another because odd results can be produced. In this case, however, the POST handler method produces a challenge result that leads to a redirection, which presents no issues.

Restricting Additional External Authentication

The final step in the process is to change the correlation part of the external authentication process so that only one external authentication scheme can be used to sign in, as shown in Listing 23-20.

Listing 23-20. Preventing Additional Sign-Ins in the ExternalSignIn.cshtml.cs File in the Pages Folder

```
...
public async Task<IActionResult> OnGetCorrelate(string returnUrl) {
    ExternalLoginInfo info = await SignInManager.GetExternalLoginInfoAsync();
    AppUser user = await UserManager.FindByLoginAsync(info.LoginProvider,
        info.ProviderKey);
    if (user == null) {
        string externalEmail =
```

```
                info.Principal.FindFirst(ClaimTypes.Email)?.Value
                    ?? string.Empty;
        user = await UserManager.FindByEmailAsync(externalEmail);
        if (user == null) {
            return RedirectToPage("/ExternalAccountConfirm",
                new { returnUrl });
        } else {
            UserLoginInfo firstLogin = user?.UserLogins?.FirstOrDefault();
            if (firstLogin != null
                    && firstLogin.LoginProvider != info.LoginProvider) {
                return RedirectToPage(
                    new {
                        error =
                          $"{firstLogin.ProviderDisplayName} Authentication Expected"
                    });
            } else {
                await UserManager.AddLoginAsync(user, info);
            }
        }
    }
    SignInResult result = await SignInManager.ExternalLoginSignInAsync(
            info.LoginProvider, info.ProviderKey, false, false);
    if (result.Succeeded) {
        return RedirectToPage("ExternalSignIn", "Confirm",
            new { info.ProviderDisplayName, returnUrl });
    } else if (result.RequiresTwoFactor) {
        string postSignInUrl = this.Url.Page("/ExternalSignIn", "Confirm",
            new { info.ProviderDisplayName, returnUrl });
        return RedirectToPage("/SignInTwoFactor",
            new { returnUrl = postSignInUrl });
    }
    return RedirectToPage(new { error = true, returnUrl });
}
...
```

An error message is displayed if the user signs in using the wrong external authentication service. To see the revised sequence, restart ASP.NET Core, request http://localhost:5000/signout, and click the Sign Out button to remove existing authentication cookies.

Request http://localhost:5000/signin and click the Google button. Go through the process of signing in and creating an Identity account. Request http://localhost:5000/signin again, but this time click the Facebook button. Sign in with an account that has the same email address as your Google account, and you will see the error shown in Figure 23-11.

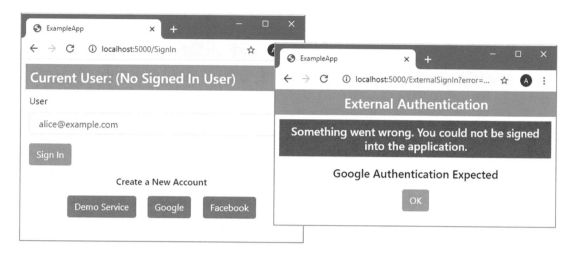

Figure 23-11. *Restricting signing in with external authentication*

Summary

In this chapter, I showed you how to store authentication tokens, which can be used with external services and built on the foundation from Chapter 22 to implement custom authentication support for the services provided by Google and Facebook.

And that's all I have to teach you about ASP.NET Core Identity. I can only hope that you have enjoyed reading this book as much as I enjoyed writing it, and I wish you every success in your ASP.NET Core and ASP.NET Core Identity projects.

Index

■ V, W, X, Y, Z

Printed in the United States
by Baker & Taylor Publisher Services